AMERICA'S GOD

America's God

*From Jonathan Edwards to
Abraham Lincoln*

MARK A. NOLL

UNIVERSITY PRESS

2002

OXFORD
UNIVERSITY PRESS

Oxford   New York
Auckland   Bangkok   Buenos Aires   Cape Town   Chennai
Dar es Salaam   Delhi   Hong Kong   Istanbul   Karachi   Kolkata
Kuala Lumpur   Madrid   Melbourne   Mexico City   Mumbai   Nairobi
São Paulo   Shanghai   Singapore   Taipei   Tokyo   Toronto
and an associated companys in Berlin

Copyright © 2002 by Oxford University Press, Inc.

Published by Oxford University Press, Inc.,
198 Madison Avenue, New York, New York 10016

www.oup.com

Oxford is a registered trademark of Oxford University Press

Library of Congress Cataloging-in-Publication Data
Noll, Mark A., 1946–
America's God : from Jonathan Edwards to Abraham Lincoln / Mark A. Noll.
p.   cm.
Includes bibliographical references and index.
ISBN 0-19-515111-9
1. Theology, Doctrinal—United States—History—18th century.
2. Protestantism—United States—History—18th century.
3. United States—Church history—18th century.   4. Theology, Doctrinal—
United States—History—19th century.   5. Protestantism—United
States—History—19th century.   6. United States—Church history—19th century.   I. Title.
BT30.U6 N65 2002
230'.0973—dc21   2001053114

Material in this book originally appeared in much different form in the following
essays:

"The Bible and Slavery," *Religion and the American Civil War*, ed. Randall
Miller et al. (1998). Used by permission of Oxford University Press, Inc.

"Both Pray to the Same God: The Singularity of Lincoln's Faith in the Era of the
Civil War," *Journal of the Abraham Lincoln Association* 18 (Winter 1997): 1–26.
Used by permission of University of Illinois Press.

"The Rise and Long Life of the Protestant Enlightenment in America,"
*Knowledge and Belief in America: Enlightenment Traditions and Modern
Religious Thought*, ed. William M. Shea and Peter A. Huff. Reprinted with the
permission of Cambridge University Press.

"The American Revolution and Protestant Evangelicalism," *The Journal of
Interdisciplinary History* XXIII (1993): 615–638. Used by permission of the
Massachusetts Institute of Technology and the journal's editors.

9   8   7   6   5   4   3
Printed in the United States of America
on acid-free paper

To

George Marsden

Acknowledgments

Acknowledging colleagues, friends, and family members who help bring a book to completion is an altogether salutary testimony to the networks of human support that make life in general worthwhile. When a book takes as long as this one to get written, the sense of indebtedness for scholarly insight, practical assistance, friendly encouragement, and edifying rebuke—offered almost always in friendship, sometimes in love—is nearly overwhelming. The payment of intellectual debts, mostly to scholars not known to me personally, is reserved for the bibliography; here I am humbled to thank the many people, including some who also appear there, for personal kindnesses extended in connection with this book or its earlier anticipations.

At the beginning, I am pleased to acknowledge the assistance on topics treated in these pages that I received many years ago at Trinity Evangelical Divinity School from David Wells, John Woodbridge, and the late John Gerstner, and then at Vanderbilt University from Douglas Leach, Paul Hardacre, and the late Richard Wolf. Although I was never officially a student of Robert Handy or Eugene Genovese, I am deeply gratified for the friendly guidance they offered on several occasions.

For insights, photocopied sources, leads to books, and a few interpretive challenges, I am most grateful to many scholars whose work intersects with my own, especially Catherine Brekus, Bob Calhoon, Allen Guelzo, and Gregg Roeber; and then also to students who seemed to have moved very quickly from taking to giving instruction on the subjects of this book: Douglas Sweeney, Stephen Graham, Bill DiPuccio, Gary Pranger, Kurt Berends, Peter Wallace, Max Vanderpool, Bryan Bademan, Louise Burton, Stewart Davenport, Heather Curtis, Christian Sawyer, and Beth Anne Johnson. I thank especially Steve Marini for sharing so freely his research on the late eighteenth century, and Jim Turner for doing the same with his space in Flanner

Hall. For most appreciated translation help with French sources, I thank the late Wahneta Mullin, and for the long extract in Italian from the *Civiltà Cattolica*, Maria Walford. It is a pleasure also to thank scholars from outside the United States whose friendship has meant as much personally as their work does academically, including David Bebbington, Richard Carwardine, David Hempton, Deryck Lovegrove, Jim Moore, and John Wolffe from Britain, and Michael Gauvreau, Marguerite Van Die, and Bill Westfall from Canada.

John Wilson and David Livingstone have been faithful comrades in arms on many projects touching the borders of the themes treated in this book.

Peter Wallace, Rachel Maxson, and Jeff Gustafson were outstanding student assistants who know well the parts for which they should be identified as coauthors. Ethan Schrum and Peter Swarr were also a great help.

At Wheaton College, I am thankful for unusually generous provision of the scholar's basic necessities—time, money, space, and library help—to Richard Chase, John Fawcett, Stan Jones, Ward Kriegbaum, Gary Larson, Duane Litfin, David Malone, Paul Snezek, Patricia Ward, and several generations of Inter-Library Loan specialists; for general intellectual stimulation to the whole faculty but especially Lyle Dorsett, Alan Jacobs, Steven Kang, Roger Lundin, Jim Mathisen, Chris Mitchell, Jerry Root, and John Walford; for very particular help on antebellum American religion to Kathryn Long; for endlessly patient assistance to the omnicompetent Carmin Ballou, Jennifer Farmer, Katri Brewer, and especially Beatrice Horne and Anita Dodson; and for years of steady management of the history department to Tom Kay.

Philanthropies are often unsung heroes, so I am pleased to sing the praises of the National Endowment for the Humanities, the Institute for Advanced Christian Studies, and the Pew Evangelical Scholars Program at Notre Dame, whose generous grants bought precious time.

For invitations to try out material reworked for this book, I am grateful to the Woodrow Wilson Center (and Bill Shea); the *Journal of Interdisciplinary History* (and Robert Rotberg with Theodore Rabb); the 1994 Religion and the Civil War conference at Louisville Theological Seminary (and Charles Reagan Wilson with Randall Miller and Skip Stout); the 1994 conference on Jonathan Edwards at Indiana University (and Stephen Stein); the Yale Divinity School (and Skip Stout); the Abraham Lincoln Association (and Thomas Schwartz); the July 1996 Anglo-American Historical Conference (and John Wolffe); Penn State University (and Gregg Roeber); the University of Chicago (and Leon Kass); Gordon College (and Tom Askew); the Library of Congress (and Jim Hutson); Colonial Williamsburg (and John Turner); Northern Illinois University (and Allan Kulikoff); Regent College, Vancouver (and Don Lewis); Bethel College, North Newton, Kansas (and Jim Juhnke with Keith Sprunger); the February 2000 Commonwealth Fund Conference (and Melvyn Stokes); Asbury Theological Seminary (and David Bauer); and the University of Toledo (and Ruth Herndon with Andy Brake).

Several of those already acknowledged have been active participants in programs of Wheaton's Institute for the Study of American Evangelicals. To others who have made that loose network of scholars my ongoing graduate education, I am pleased to thank Randall Balmer, Daniel Bays, Edith Blumhofer, Jim Bratt, Joel Carpenter, Larry Eskridge, Michael Hamilton, Darryl Hart, and Richard Hughes. Nathan Hatch and Skip Stout have opened so many doors for me that I have lost count, but I hope I never lose a sense of gratitude for them and their friendship. About another great friend, it is a source of painful pleasure to record that the last bit of my prose read by the late George Rawlyk was the section on populist theologians from chapter 8 and that he approved.

To four friends and scholars who read major sections of the manuscript as it was taking shape, my gratitude goes beyond words. Daniel Walker Howe, Bruce Kuklick, George Marsden, and Grant Wacker have all written much to guide my own explorations, but nothing could mean more than the kindness they showed in pushing me to rethink conclusions, simplify arguments, tighten logic, and clarify the prose.

It is a privilege to thank my brother, Craig, for fraternal and spiritual support, and also for copyediting this book with such willing skill. At Oxford University Press it has been a great privilege to work again with Cynthia Read, as well as with Theodore Calderara and Jennifer Rozgonyi Kowing.

Families often come last in acknowledgments, but only because they are first in life. Dean and Mary Noll Venables are now professional researchers themselves and know what it is like. David and Bethany Davis Noll may be surprised to find out how often in days gone by religion lay behind technological advances in communication. And while working for many years on many tightly-wound-up people in the past, it has been good to live with a relaxed Robert Noll in the present. For Maggie Noll there are the deepest thanks to be offered as librarian, organizer, and fellow heir, but most of all for herself.

This book took much longer to finish than I had originally hoped. The result from trying to coordinate reading and writing over a long period is, I fear, a volume less tightly argued than it should be. Yet my greatest regret about this lapse of time lies in delaying the recognition conveyed by the dedication to a scholar, teacher, and friend who, more than any other, opened up to me the path of Christian learning and who has been there every step of the way.

Wheaton, Illinois   M. A. N.
October 2001

Contents

Tables

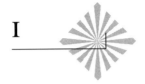

INTRODUCTORY

*Christ took flesh and was made man in a particular time and place,
family, nationality, tradition and customs and sanctified them, while still
being for all men in every time and place. Wherever he is taken by the
people of any day, time and place, he sanctifies that culture—he is living
in it. . . . But to acknowledge this is not to forget that there is another,
and equally important, force at work among us. Not only does God in
His mercy take people as they are: He takes them to transform them into
what He wants them to be.*
                    —Andrew Walls, "Africa and Christian Identity," 1980

I

Introduction

Theology and History

This book is a contextual history of Christian theology. Its pages describe evolutionary changes in Christian doctrine that occurred from the 1730s to the 1860s, a period when theology played an extraordinarily important role in American thought, but the emphasis throughout is on the contexts—ecclesiastical, social, political, intellectual, and commercial—in which those changes took place. Because it features connections between theological development and early American history, the book often asks how religion influenced the early United States. Yet Christian theology, not the United States, is the primary concern.

The book's main narrative describes a shift away from European theological traditions, descended directly from the Protestant Reformation, toward a Protestant evangelical theology decisively shaped by its engagement with Revolutionary and post-Revolutionary America. It is not an exaggeration to claim that this nineteenth-century Protestant evangelicalism differed from the religion of the Protestant Reformation as much as sixteenth-century Reformation Protestantism differed from the Roman Catholic theology from which it emerged.

The changes taking place in American religious thought from the 1730s to the 1860s were part of a general shift within Western religious life. Other English-speaking regions were also experiencing the move from early-modern to modern religion marked by heightened spiritual inwardness, a new confidence in individual action, and various accommodations to the marketplace. Without attempting a full comparative history, this book will nonetheless suggest that the pace and direction of theological change in the United States

3

differed from what occurred in other largely Protestant countries of the North Atlantic region.

Western Protestantism in the eighteenth and early nineteenth centuries was moving from establishment forms of religion, embedded in traditional, organic, premodern political economies, to individualized and affectional forms, adapted to modernizing, rational, and market-oriented societies.[1] Theological manifestations of these changes can be described in several ways. They first reoriented specific beliefs: God was perceived less often as transcendent and self-contained, more often as immanent and relational. Divine revelation was equated more simply with the Bible alone than with Scripture embedded in a self-conscious ecclesiastical tradition. The physical world created by God was more likely to be regarded as understandable, progressing, and malleable than as mysterious, inimical, and fixed. Theological method came to rely less on instinctive deference to inherited confessions and more on self-evident propositions organized by scientific method.[2]

Theological changes of the eighteenth and nineteenth centuries also involved a shift in meaning for key concepts that operated in both religious and political life, for example, "freedom," "justice," "virtue," and "vice." For theology, the process at work was the same as Gordon Wood once described for intellectual developments more generally: "Although words and concepts may remain outwardly the same for centuries, their particular functions and meanings do not and could not remain static—not as long as individuals attempt to use them to explain new social circumstances and make meaningful new social behavior."[3] In America as much was happening in theology from new meanings given to old words as from the introduction of new vocabularies.

The years from 1730 to 1865 witnessed theological debates that were every bit as contentious as those from earlier periods in the Christian West, and the specific theological questions receiving the most concentrated attention were also usually inherited from previous generations: To what extent was human nature incapacitated by sin? How did the fall of Adam and Eve affect later generations? How did God's grace work to rescue sinners? What was the best way to describe the atonement with God won by Christ on the cross? What should believers expect when attempting to live a Christian life? Could there be some kind of Christian perfection before eternity? But these questions were increasingly debated—among elites, among the people at large, and between elites and populists—in forms molded by the times.

Throughout this period, the theological spectrum in America was broadening considerably. Alongside well-publicized discussions at the center of public attention, the spectrum always included convictions going out of favor among the generality as well as beliefs espoused by prophets at the margins. Gender, race, and region contributed to the pluriformity of theology, as did diverse opinions on the wisdom of abandoning European styles of church-state establishment. Even with full attention to internal diversity, however, it is clear that the center of theological gravity was moving away from the norms of the European past toward norms defined by the American present. That movement was more rapid in the North and West than in the South, but in all regions it was more pronounced than in other countries of the North Atlantic region, where varieties of Protestant evangelicalism were also on the rise.

A word, indeed, is necessary about the central place of evangelicalism in this narrative. For the period under consideration the most widely recognized religious voices for the American public were Protestant. From the 1790s and with gathering force in the decades leading to the Civil War, the most prominent Protestant voices were also self-consciously evangelical. If, however, developments affecting evangelical Protestants are central in this study, I do intend to fulfill the promise of the title and direct at least some attention to how American circumstances affected religious reflections among non-Protestant theists, especially Roman Catholics (but also deists and Jews), as well as among Unitarians and high-church Episcopalians who were Protestant but not evangelical. At the center, nonetheless, remains the incredible welter of Protestants who considered themselves evangelical or who have been treated by later historians as if they were. The most serviceable general definition for this modern evangelicalism has been provided by the British historian David W. Bebbington. It stresses four characteristics: biblicism (or reliance on the Bible as ultimate religious authority), conversionism (or an emphasis on the new birth), activisim (or energetic, individualistic engagement in personal and social duties), and crucicentrism (or focus on Christ's redeeming work as the heart of true religion).[4] But as Bebbington and all other students have noted, evangelicals always appeared in countless variations.

That evangelical hodge-podge must begin with the articulate Congregationalists and Presbyterians, who, because they published so much and occupied such elite social positions, have regularly been allowed to stand for the whole of American theology during this period.[5] That hodge-podge also included Methodists, the most numerous religious movement in America from the Revolution to the Civil War, but a tradition whose historiography until recently has been as weak as its life on the ground was strong. It took in Baptists, "Christians," Restorationists, and other sectarians whose theology promoted anti-formalist principles that vigorously contested the hegemonic formalism of Congregationalists and Presbyterians.[6] It included African Americans, who increasingly found a theological voice in antebellum decades. And it also involved intellectually self-conscious communities of European confessional Protestants—Lutherans, German Reformed, Dutch Reformed, and low-church Episcopalians—whose theologians shared a great deal with the formalist evangelicals but who nonetheless retained varying degrees of intellectual independence. Evangelical Protestants figured most prominently in the era's most dramatic theological transformations, but almost every group of American theists was touched by some of the elements defining those transformations.

A Social History of Theology

Pursuing what might be called a social history of ideas makes possible a connected narrative of causes and effects, or at least of plausible relations between circumstances and actions occasioned by those circumstances.[7] Thus, in what follows, social and political events are enlisted to help explain grand shifts in theological conviction. For example, I suggest that a revolution in late-Puritan understanding of the church during the 1740s allowed American patriots several decades later to harness Puritan notions of the covenant to support a largely secular political revolution. I argue that the antitraditional character of the Revolution's political ideology predisposed Christian thinkers of the early nineteenth century to the antitraditional intellectual principles of the Scottish Enlightenment. I try to show why evangelical conceptions of virtue and vice advanced so rapidly in a new republic created by leaders who did not embrace evangelical religion. And I offer an explanation for why in the decades before the Civil War so many evangelical Protestants in the North as well as in the South—but not evangelicals in Canada or the British Isles—were convinced that the Bible sanctioned slavery. Explaining changes of theological conviction by reference to political and intellectual events does not necessarily entail a reduction of religion to more basic secular realities. Rather, attempting to comprehend religion and society in the same narrative allows for a story with flesh and blood instead of a bloodless ballet of abstract dogmas.

A contextual approach to theological history is especially useful for explaining why Christian belief evolved along different lines in the predominantly Protestant United States than it did in Protestant Europe. In this effort, I am following the path of early foreign visitors to the United States, who frequently used social contexts to explain American religion. Most famously, Alexis de Tocqueville drew a telling contrast between the religious situations in France and America by referring to political circumstances: "On my arrival in the United States it was the religious aspect of the country that first struck my eye. As I prolonged my stay, I perceived the great political consequences that flowed from these new facts. Among us, I had seen the spirit of religion and the spirit of freedom almost always move in contrary directions. Here I found them united intimately with one another: they reigned together on the same soil."[8] Yet de Tocqueville was far from the only outsider to describe American religion in terms of American society and vice versa. In 1832 Achille Murat, an exiled Bonapartist, whose religious ideal was a unitary society with an established church, nonetheless could not help but be impressed by "the thousand and one sects which divide the people of the United States. Merely to enumerate them would be impossible, for they change every day, appear, disappear, unite, separate, and evince nothing stable but their instability. . . . Yet, with all this liberty, there is no country in which the people are so religious as in the United States."[9]

At the end of the story told here, the surprisingly vigorous religious vision of Abraham Lincoln's Second Inaugural Address drew immediate reaction from Europeans knowledgeable about circumstances on both sides of the Atlantic. The émigré historian and theologian Philip Schaff, who was visiting his homelands in 1865, told German and Swiss audiences, "I do not believe that any royal, princely, or republican state document of recent times can be compared to this inaugural address for genuine Christian wisdom and gentleness."[10] What Schaff and other foreign observers of the time noted makes for an important interpretive question: Why did Lincoln, though never a church member, use the Bible more freely in this speech and also address questions of theological significance more directly than his near-peers as heads of state in other Protestant lands who were dedicated members of Christian churches like William Gladstone in Britain or Abraham Kuyper in the Netherlands?

Comparisons

A social history of theology also hints at explanations for contrasts with specific European regions. In the early eighteenth century, the dominant Christian theologies in America were quite similar to the dominant theologies prevailing in Scotland, Northern Ireland, the Netherlands, and Switzerland.[11] As in colonial America, theology in these regions was primarily Calvinistic or Reformed or at least overwhelmingly theocentric. Methodologically, it was confessional, biblical, and even scholastic. Internal contentions lay mostly between inherited Reformed confessions and rationalistic anticipations of the Enlightenment. In all of these regions, as throughout the rest of Europe, theology was controlled by a learned elite operating under the protection of an established state church.

The situation in England was different primarily because of continuing reactions to the failed Puritan revolution of the mid-seventeenth century.[12] While a variety of post-Puritan and dissenting Protestant opinions paralleled the main emphases of Reformed Protestantism elsewhere in Europe, English religious thought at the end of the seventeenth century was dominated by a cautious monarchical church more wary of enthusiasm than eager to promote dogmatic particulars. England's dominant Anglican theology linked loyalty to the monarch, belief in God as designer of the universe, and the imperatives of social order. By the early eighteenth century, intellectual reaction to the traumas of a religiously inspired Civil War had pushed theology in a rationalistic, antienthusiastic direction, as much following the anticredal impetus of John Locke's *Reasonableness of Christianity as Delivered in the Scriptures* (1695) as the specific convictions of either Puritans or high Anglicans. If theology in the English colonies was marginally closer to the traditional Reformed theology on the European continent and Britain's Celtic fringe than to contemporary theology in England, those colonies joined Protestant Britain and Europe's Reformed Protestant regions in affirming substantially similar positions.

From the late seventeenth century and with accelerating force throughout the eighteenth, a new set of circumstances appeared in all of these areas.[13] These circumstances included a struggle for the control of religion between aristocratic elites and middle-order Protestants reasserting the priesthood of all believers. It was the era when pietism on the Continent and evangelicalism in Great Britain emerged as powerful movements that (depending on one's perspective) opened a way to inward spiritual renewal or threatened to subvert society. It was also the period when Enlightenment understandings of the individual self, experience, and the burdensome past were taken up by all sorts, including most pietists and evangelicals as well as many confessional Christians.[14]

Yet by the early nineteenth century—and despite a relatively common starting point, common exposure to the new piety, and common appropriations of moderate forms of the Enlightenment—the American theological situation had come to differ markedly from Protestant patterns elsewhere.[15] In Scotland, the long sway of a Moderate party during the eighteenth century gave way in the 1790s to the rise of an evangelical party and a resurgence of confessional Calvinism; the result was to leave Scottish theology in 1840 remarkably similar to its status 150 years before.[16] In Northern Ireland, both traditional Calvinistic and traditional monarchical theologies were stronger in 1840 than they had been in the early eighteenth century.[17] In Holland and Switzerland a series of sharp divides had opened up between defenders of Calvinism and modern substitutes for Calvinism, between traditional biblical emphases and liberal philosophical concerns, and between pietistic theologians of the people and learned neologians at the universities.[18]

By the mid-nineteenth century, theology in England was in some ways drawing closer to theology in America, especially because of the vigorous evangelical movements inside and outside the Church of England that paralleled similar movements in North America. Yet important differences remained, especially because of the strength of the high-church Oxford Movement in England, the rapid advance of utilitarian thought, and the continued influence of Anglicanism as an established church. American theology had not yet witnessed anything like—from opposite ends of the religious spectrum—John Henry Newman's Anglo-Catholicism or John Stuart Mill's secular utilitarianism.[19] Similarly, the central role that the established churches of England and Scotland occupied in defining the morality of British economic life had no parallel in America.[20]

Until 1812 English-speaking Canada appeared ready to follow the United States in theology as in other cultural spheres. But the war beginning that year and an influx of British immigrants over the next two decades combined to promote a Canadian Protestantism distinct from that in the United States. Political and religious loyalty to British Methodists, Anglicans, Presbyterians, and Baptists led to a Canadian Protestant theology that for the rest of the nineteenth century moved away from, rather than in harmony with, the American pattern.[21]

More than at the start of the eighteenth century, in other words, American theology by 1850 was distinct from theology in Protestant Europe. By contrast to Scottish and Northern Irish theologians, most Americans had moved further away from the convictions of confessional Calvinism. And by contrast to the Swiss and the Dutch, Americans, with only a few exceptions, remained more committed to the Bible and the experience of conversion as foundational religious authorities. Furthermore, by contrast to both English and Canadian theologians, Americans were less traditional, less corporate, and less ecclesiastical, but also—in a difference with enduring effect—more effectively attuned to the convictions of the working and middle classes.

At several points in the book, I attempt to sharpen these international comparisons, although the claim will not be made that the history of specifically American events can explain comparative differences completely. General developments in Western intellectual history—especially a growing confidence in human reason (the Enlightenment) and a growing confidence in human sensibility (romanticism)—were at work variously among theologians in America as well as elsewhere. Historical developments in other countries affected local theologies as much as American events shaped American religious thought. Proper qualifications having been made, however, even this crude introduction is enough for stating a thesis: Broad trends in Western culture as a whole can account for some of the important differences between theology in America and theology in Protestant Europe, but they were not as influential as the specific social contexts in which Americans did their work.[22]

The American Synthesis

By the early nineteenth century, a surprising intellectual synthesis, distinctly different from the reigning intellectual constructs in comparable Western societies, had come to prevail throughout the United States. It was a surprise both because little in colonial history before the mid-eighteenth century anticipated its formation and because it came into being only as an indirect result of the American Revolution, the era's greatest intellectual as well as political event. The formation of this synthesis, in turn, explains much about what followed in the history of American thought from the early nineteenth century. Along with more distinctly religious factors, the plausibility, flexibility, and popularity of this synthesis at all social levels was a key to the remarkable Christianization that occurred in the United States, both North and South, during the period 1790–1865. How the creation and outworking of that synthesis imparted a distinctly American cast to theology is the story told by this book.

The synthesis was a compound of evangelical Protestant religion, republican political ideology, and commonsense moral reasoning.[23] Through the time of the Civil War, that synthesis defined the boundaries for a vast quantity of American thought, while also providing an ethical framework, a moral compass, and a vocabulary of suasion for much of the nation's public life. It set, quite naturally, the boundaries within which formal theological effort took place. Since the Civil War, the synthesis has declined in importance for both formal thought and public life, though not without leaving an enduring stamp upon the mental habits of some religious communities and episodic marks upon the public discourse.[24]

The synthesis was most visible in the links constructed between religion and public life. As an instance, the 1833 amendment to the Massachusetts

Constitution that did away with the last church establishment remaining from the colonial period nonetheless paused to affirm that "the public worship of God, and instructions in piety, religion, and morality, promote the happiness and prosperity of a people, and the security of republican government."[25] When these words were written, Alexis de Tocqueville had only just returned to France from his memorable tour of the North American continent, and he was making the same point descriptively rather than prescriptively: "I do not know if all Americans have faith in their religion—for who can read to the bottom of hearts?—but I am sure that they believe it necessary to the maintenance of republican institutions. This opinion does not belong only to one class of citizens or to one party, but to the entire nation; one finds it in all ranks."[26]

The synthesis operated just as manifestly at the intersection of theology and popular philosophy. Contemporaries who differed dramatically in their religious convictions were nonetheless linked tightly to each other by philosophical method. In the early nineteenth century, for example, serious differences divided Harvard's professor of logic and metaphysics, the Unitarian Levi Hedge; Yale's president and modified Calvinist Timothy Dwight; the upstart Restorationist Alexander Campbell, who was exploiting the open American environment to restore the primitive church of the New Testament; and the first professor of theology at Princeton Seminary, the conservative Presbyterian Archibald Alexander. Yet from these contentious corners of America's religious landscape resounded the same devotion to moral philosophical first principles. Dwight, in 1793, for example, set out an American credo that prevailed widely for at least the next two generations:

> The faculties, necessary to form a competent judge of all these facts, are the usual senses of men, and that degree of understanding which we customarily term Common-sense. . . . A plain man, thus qualified, would, as perfectly as Aristotle, or Sir Isaac Newton, know whether Christ lived, preached, wrought miracles, suffered, died, appeared alive after death, and ascended to Heaven. The testimony of the senses, under the direction of Common-sense, is the deciding, and the only testimony, by which the existence of these facts must be determined.[27]

It was the same for Alexander in 1808 when he defended the need for divine revelation by appealing to "self-evident principles to which every rational mind assents as soon as they are proposed . . . truths in morals, in which all men do as certainly agree as in mathematical axioms."[28] For Hedge in 1821 these same principles served as a basis for defending a position on the human will that Alexander would have found abhorrent: "The moral freedom of man is not a question of speculation, to be settled by abstract reasoning. . . . It is a question of fact to be decided by feeling. . . . We believe we are free, because we feel that we are so."[29] Three years later, Campbell demonstrated why the creeds that elitists like Dwight, Alexander, and Hedge defended were so preposterous: "To present . . . a sectarian creed composed, as they are all, of propositions, deduced by logical inferences, and couched in philosophical language, to all those who are fit subjects of salvation of Heaven . . . for their examination or adoption, shocks all common sense."[30] These examples only hint at the weight of custom that by the 1820s had joined Protestant precepts securely to the principles of republican and commonsense reasoning.

This synthesis of religious, political, and philosophical principles was never monolithic in either public or religious spheres.[31] But even if each of its elements was contested, the confluence of the three interpretive systems and the cultural significance of that confluence was unmistakable. For the articulation of Christian theology, this synthesis was profoundly significant. The process by which evangelical Protestantism came to be aligned with republican convictions and commonsense moral reasoning was also the process that gave a distinctively *American* shape to Christian theology by the time of the Civil War.

Elements of the Synthesis

The Protestant evangelicals who came to dominate religious life in the early United States shared an emphasis on conversion, the supreme religious authority of the Bible, and an active life of personal holiness. They were the descendants of Reformed immigrants—English Puritans to New England, Scottish and Scotch-Irish Presbyterians to the middle and southern colonies, and low-church Anglicans to the Chesapeake. But nineteenth-century evangelicals were also the heirs of two full generations of revival, beginning with the Great Awakening of the 1730s and 1740s and continuing through local, episodic awakenings in nearly every region of the colonies-become-states.

By the time these evangelicals came to prominence, most Americans were already committed, as a result of the successful War for Independence, to a republican conception of politics. In this view, the exercise of political power could be sanctified by the virtue of people and magistrates, or turned into tyranny by the vices of rulers and ruled. Like the Protestantism of the early nineteenth century, this republicanism also existed in many varieties, some harking back to the classic tradition of civic humanism, others allied with a more modern liberalism, and still others featuring "Commonwealth," "country," or "Real Whig" elements.[32]

By the late eighteenth century most Americans likewise shared both a mistrust of intellectual authorities inherited from previous generations and a belief that true knowledge arose from the use of one's own senses—whether the external senses for information about nature and society or the moral sense for ethical and aesthetic judgments. Most Americans were thus united in the conviction that people had to think for themselves in order to know science, morality, economics, politics, and especially theology. For some Americans this certainty was rooted in formal study guided by thinkers of the Scottish Enlightenment who developed careful theories concerning "common sense."

For many others, including burgeoning numbers of Methodists and simple "Christians," it was a product of epistemological self-assertion that heeded no creed but the Bible.

For each aspect of the synthesis, as well as for the synthesis itself, variants abounded. Men and women often appropriated it differently.[33] In the South it took longer to convert traditional concepts like "honor" and "virtue" to evangelical norms, but that transformation did take place.[34] The remarkable thing, however, is not that differences existed but that they were confined within a fairly narrow range. The extent of the synthesis is suggested by its power among even Roman Catholics, whose fellow religionists in Europe remained securely opposed to all rapprochement with Protestantism, republicanism, and epistemological self-sufficiency.[35] To sum up a situation that many historians now take for granted: after the 1780s, republicanism (wherever found along a continuum from classical to liberal) had come to prevail in America; very soon thereafter, commonsense principles (whether defined in elite or populist terms) were almost as widely spread; and in the same post-Revolutionary period, Protestant evangelicalism (however divided into contending sects) became the dominant American religion.

The way in which evangelicalism and civic humanism merged during the Revolutionary period to form a Christian republicanism has been the subject of several solid studies in the last quarter century.[36] Although not as much attention has been paid to the marriage of evangelicalism and commonsense moral reasoning, the conjunction of the two is just as well established. As a result of much fine work, therefore, the presence—and, to some extent, the rise—of the synthesis is now thoroughly understood.

What for the most part has not been done is to show how unexpected, in the longer historical view, the emergence of the synthesis was; how much the American intellectual story differed from Protestant developments in parallel societies; how intimately the republican-evangelical-commonsense synthesis was woven into the fabric of American public life through the time of the Civil War; and how powerfully both this intellectual synthesis and Protestant participation in American public life shaped the writing of Christian theology. It is not my argument that the blending of evangelical Protestantism with republicanism and commonsense reasoning explains theological development exhaustively. Other influences did continue to have a powerful effect, including the enduring weight of theological tradition among many Catholics, Lutherans, and high-church Episcopalians, as well as in some of the more evangelical denominations. For almost all religious leaders, the Bible remained an ever-present resource, even when put to unexpectedly innovative uses.[37] Americans in the period 1790–1865 also continued to absorb European influences, especially from England, with the strongest impulses at first from the Wesleys, then from those who founded voluntary organizations to distribute the Bible or attack slavery, then from Samuel Taylor Coleridge's intuitive Anglicanism, and then from the Oxford Movement. By the 1830s currents from Germany and France were also affecting American theology.[38]

It is, however, indicative of the American character of theology between the Revolution and the Civil War that, even with a considerable expansion of creative biblical interpretations, almost all Scripture, whether traditional or newly recorded, was interpreted by hermeneutical canons arising from the same commonsense and republican conventions of thought. In addition, even with important influences from Europe fully acknowledged, there still was less theological borrowing from Britain and the Continent in the period between the Revolution and the Civil War than at any time before or since in American religious history.

Neither is it the contention of this book that Protestant contacts with republican politics and commonsense philosophy were the only relationships that influenced the writing of theology. The expansion of market economies, especially when linked to liberal principles about the rights of individuals, certainly became a theological as well as social factor in this period. Other systems of political thought affected theological reasoning as well, including Lockean liberalism, the traditions of the common law, and historic arguments defining a just war. Granting due weight to these other influences, it was still the case that the most distinctly American features of theology between the Revolution and the Civil War arose from the evangelical Protestant alliance with commonsense reasoning and republican ideology.

The Shape of the Book

In at least five respects, the American confluence of evangelicalism, republicanism, and common sense was an oddity in eighteenth-century Western societies. Sketching these circumstances introduces the main themes of the book.

I. A first curiosity concerns the religious history of the late-colonial period, particularly the Great Awakening and its effects. It is a story of unintended consequences. Leaders of the Awakening—from Jonathan Edwards in Northampton, Massachusetts, Joseph Bellamy in rural Connecticut, Gilbert Tennent in New Brunswick, New Jersey, and Samuel Davies in Virginia, to George Whitefield, who went everywhere—knew what they were after when they enlisted affective rhetoric to preach about intractable human depravity and supernal divine grace. They were trying to reawaken the church for the sake of the church itself, to reassert the sovereignty of God's divine love in conversion, to exalt the substitutionary, penal work of Christ as God's way of reconciliation with sinners, to demonstrate the necessity of conversion as a prerequisite for truly virtuous living, and by these means to check the worldliness promoted by the era's new forms of commerce and entertainment. Yet the pursuit of such goals had ironic consequences. The awakeners preached a higher, more spiritual vision of the church, yet the result was decline in the very notion of church and a transfer of religious commitment from the church to the nation. They focused on God's role in conversion yet brought about an exaltation of human activity in the process of salvation. They preached a traditional doctrine of the atonement yet opened the way toward redefining the work of Christ as an outworking of governmental relationships rather than the assuagement of God's wrath. They rooted true virtue in supernatural conversion yet created conditions for a new concept of virtuous living as in principle available to every person by nature alone. The unintended theological consequences of the Awakening is the story told in chapter 3.

2. The evangelical Protestantism that rose to prominence in the early United States was descended from the colonial Awakenings, the Puritan movement, and the Protestant Reformation. More generally, it was an offshoot of the Western Christian tradition. But the republicanism that American evangelicals embraced so warmly in the second half of the eighteenth century had always been regarded with suspicion in that Western Christian tradition, it was not taken up by the early Protestants, it was only ambiguously related to Puritanism, and it was never promoted directly by the leaders of the Great Awakening. Rather, both contemporary observers in the seventeenth and eighteenth centuries and modern historians have viewed republican political views as much more closely connected with theological heterodoxy than with theological orthodoxy. That history of antagonism between republicanism and classical Christianity works counterintuitively against the later American assumption that there is a natural fit, even a supernaturally ordained harmony, between the Christian God and republican liberty. The singularly American marriage of republicanism with religion is the subject of the fourth and fifth chapters below.

3. It was almost the same for the alliance between evangelicalism and commonsense moral philosophy. The principal Reformers, the main Puritans, and supremely Jonathan Edwards stood unambiguously opposed to key elements of the eighteenth-century's "new moral philosophy"—especially the argument that the ability to make reliable moral judgments existed naturally in the whole human race. By contrast, the main Protestant traditions from early in the sixteenth century through the mid-eighteenth century, and not just the Calvinists, had taught a different doctrine: although God might provide a minimal moral consciousness to all humans by nature, genuine virtue could be practiced only by redeemed sinners who had been acted upon by God's grace in Christ and called into the church. Despite this Protestant heritage, by the early nineteenth century evangelicals had joined other Americans in taking up commonsense principles as their guide for ethics, metaphysics, and even the foundations of theology. How evangelicals made the transition from opposing to accepting the era's "new moral philosophy," how they embraced its conclusions along with an ardent devotion to newfangled scientific methods—and by so doing created the context in which "American theology" was written—is the subject of chapter 6.

4. The ninth and tenth chapters explore another curiosity. By the 1830s and 1840s the synthesis of evangelicalism, republicanism, and common sense had become, not only the most powerful value system *in* the nation, but also the most powerful value system *defining* the nation. Abraham Lincoln's references to Americans as God's "almost chosen people" (1861) and to the Civil War as a contest where "both [sides] read the same Bible, and pray to the

same God" (1865) were among the most memorable of an endless parade of assertions about the Christian character of the United States.[39] The surprising thing about such ascriptions is not that nineteenth-century Americans regarded their nation in messianic terms, since this conceit was rooted in English ideas of national chosenness, Puritan assumptions about covenant with God, and the convictions of a wide range of Revolutionary and post-Revolutionary leaders (deists, the orthodox, sectarians) who believed that God had especially blessed the new United States.[40] The surprising thing was, rather, how evangelical these affirmations of national chosenness became in early United States history. The most important founding fathers were not evangelical. In the period when the colonies broke from Britain, evangelicalism was a marginal and declining influence among the political elites who called national assemblies, provided the most important written justifications for independence, and then drew up the Constitution. As a factor in the early religious makeup of the thirteen new states, evangelical impulses may not have been as weak as historians sometimes picture them,[41] but they were fragmented, indecisive, and inchoate, and they barely existed in most of the southern half of the new country. At the very time, in other words, when the United States came into existence, the evangelicalism that would soon play such a central role in the nation's dominant cultural synthesis, and play that role in the South as well as the North, was weaker than ever before or since. The problem that evangelical weakness in the founding era poses for understanding later American history is the subject of chapter 9. Chapter 10 treats the surge that carried evangelicals from cultural marginality in the Revolutionary years to dominance in the nineteenth century.

5. A last curiosity about the synthesis of evangelical Christianity with republicanism and commonsense moral reasoning is that the United States of America was the only place where it happened. To heighten the singularity of the American experience, chapter 4 expands at length on the English-speaking Protestant regions that by 1800 were either rejecting outright or forcefully suppressing republican convictions. Other chapters in the book pause to note the surprise—sometimes the indignation—of European visitors who found especially remarkable the link between America's evangelical Christianity and its political and intellectual institutions. Near the end of the book there is again brief treatment of theological development in other English-speaking Protestant nations in order to underscore the importance of context for the writing of theology. Those sketches both highlight the effect that American events worked on religious thought in the United States and further illustrate the general embeddedness of all such thought in its particular social settings.

Since this book is a history of theology as well as a history of the contexts in which it was written, we start with a brief summary in chapter 2 of the mostly traditional character of colonial American theology before 1750. At considerably greater length, chapters 7 and 8 survey the main lines of theological development during the Revolutionary period and the last decade of the eighteenth century. One more chapter provides additional scene-setting for explaining the distinctly American shape of theology in the nineteenth century—

chapter 11, which sketches the ideological transformations that allowed American evangelicals to appropriate republican and commonsense principles that most of their Protestant contemporaries in Europe continued to spurn.

Six chapters then follow on the full-blown American theology that emerged after the Revolutionary era. These chapters, which feature Calvinists and Methodists as the era's most influential religious forces, are alert especially to substantive shifts in convictions about basic theological issues, like the nature of sin, human will, the atonement, and true virtue. Where possible, however, these chapters focus most intently on assumptions of "common sense" in the nontechnical usage of the term—described by historian Thomas Haskell as "the comfortable certainties of 'what everybody knows.'"[42] Even more than alterations in doctrinal conviction, changes in these assumptions carry us directly to the places where deep cultural contexts exerted their most significant effects.

The next four chapters attempt a theological history of the Civil War, which was a much more actively religious struggle than the earlier War for Independence. The well-considered judgment of James McPherson is that the "Civil War armies were, arguably, the most religious in American history."[43] Specific details underscore how much America's public religion had changed from the 1770s to the 1860s. Although the most memorable hymns composed to mark the Revolution came from the Trinitarian Congregationalist William Billings, they featured an Old Testament God of Battles riding to the rescue of the American patriots, as in "Chester":

> Let tyrants shake their iron rod
> And slav'ry Clank her galling Chains
> We fear them not we trust in god
> New englands god for ever reigns.[44]

By contrast, although the most enduring hymn of the Civil War was written by a Unitarian, Julia Ward Howe, it nonetheless exalted the saving work of Christ:

> In the beauty of the lilies Christ was born across the sea,
> With a glory in his bosom that transfigures you and me:
> As he died to make men holy, let us die to make men free,
>   while God is marching on.[45]

The book's account of developments between 1776 and 1865 is intended as an explanation for why formal religious thought, at the time of the firing upon Fort Sumter, was both more explicitly Christian and more explicitly American than at the time of the Revolution. Against this background, chapter 21 contrasts the surprisingly profound theological utterances of Abraham Lincoln with the disappointingly predictable statements from the prominent clergy of his day. If a broader contextual narrative is required for understanding this contrast, it is also critical for understanding the special problem of the Bible and slavery. During the generation that culminated in the Civil War, no society on earth was as preoccupied with Scripture as the United States.

And no comparable era in the history of Christianity ever witnessed so vigorous a defense of the simplicity of biblical interpretation. That defense, however, posed a drastic problem, since by 1860 a majority of evangelical Protestants, North as well as South, was concluding that the Bible sanctioned the kind of slavery then prevailing in the Southern states. To this majority it was self-evident from a simple reading of Scripture that slavery enjoyed a divine sanction of some kind, yet at the same time the minority of Americans who held that the Bible forbade slavery also felt their scriptural interpretations were simply self-evident. The great difficulty posed by this standoff was that, short of warfare, no means seemed to exist for adjudicating these self-evident, but conflicting, interpretations of Scripture. Another difficulty was that no body of Protestants elsewhere in the English-speaking world agreed that the Bible sanctioned slavery.

The story of how "simple" readings of the Bible led to such an impasse is far from simple. Chapters 18, 19, and 20 attempt an explanation by showing how thoroughly the American assumptions about interpretation had been shaped by republican, commonsense, and evangelical understandings of the world. This complex story of a hermeneutical conundrum reveals the tragedy, in the strict sense of the word, of the American biblical defense of slavery. Precisely the synthesis of awakened Christianity, republicanism, and common sense that enabled evangelicals to contribute so much to constructing the national culture prevented evangelicals from offering a scriptural Word from God to address the crisis that ripped apart the country that they, as much as any other group, had created.

The book's concluding chapter offers a brief recapitulation and assessment of the terrain it has traversed. It notes that the great military conflicts of the United States' founding century turn out to have marked a beginning as well as an end for the alliance of evangelicalism, republicanism, and common sense. The synthesis was created from the crucible of the Revolution. While the synthesis did not perish in the Civil War, it was greatly diminished because of that conflict; never again would it drive the nation and its thought as it had from the early days of the republic to the stillness at Appomattox.

At the outset I must plead guilty to some slipperiness in using interchangeably the terms "theology," "religious thought," and "writings about God and humanity." While the book covers mostly the discourse of acknowledged theological elites, I am more concerned about relating articulated religious beliefs to their social settings than in worrying about the question of who should be included or excluded. In the early years of the nineteenth century, a self-consciously professional study of theology did emerge from the church- and public-centered practices of earlier centuries. But even as this professional study led to increasingly formal debates among cognoscenti, those debates were never far removed from day-to-day concerns about social well-being and the moral health of the nation. This book could not have been written without the exemplary scholars who have focused with great acumen on the internal, formal development of religious ideas. But its aim is somewhat different.

Religious beliefs as expressed by the small fraction of all Americans who published, and whose works were then discussed, debated, contested, or ridiculed as part of the public record, are the focus here. Historical practice of recent decades has shown how rewarding it is to push beneath such an elite stratum in order to recover the voices of ordinary people. With full knowledge and approval of such work, I have nonetheless chosen to present my title as *America's God* rather than *Elite America's God* because of two historical convictions: that many nonpublishing citizens read, pondered, and considered themselves part of the circles of debate created by the published theology examined in this volume; and that during the years from 1730 to 1865, most residents in the United States, as well as outside, if they thought about "America" at all, did so in terms of the public realm of discourse that is the focus here.

It is appropriate to note also that scriptural quotations are taken from the King James Version, which was the Bible of choice for almost all Americans throughout the decades treated in this book. I have attempted to explain theological and political terms when they first appear, but a glossary has also been provided for the most important of such items.

A final preliminary word is in order to acknowledge that, as with other highly charged subjects, the historical study of theology cannot be carried out with ideological indifference. For that reason it is appropriate to state that I approach the study of (primarily) Christian theology in America as a professing Christian myself. Yet while not wanting to hide this personal stance, my hope for the book is that it might approach the ideal expressed by Caroline Walker Bynum in her remarkable study of the meaning of food for religious women in the Middle Ages. Bynum's *Holy Feast and Holy Fast* is, she wrote, "about then, not about now. . . . My commitment, vision, and method are historical; I intend to reveal the past in its strangeness as well as its familiarity. My point is to argue that women's behavior and women's writing must be understood in the context of social, economic, and ecclesiastical structures, theological and devotional traditions, very different from our own. If readers leave this book simply condemning the past as peculiar, I shall have failed. But I shall have failed just as profoundly if readers draw direct answers to modern problems from the lives I chronicle."[46] In trying to follow Bynum's lead, I want to tell the story of theology between Jonathan Edwards and Abraham Lincoln historically rather than with a theological ax to grind. It is of course impossible to neutralize theological standpoint, but I hope (for reasons that are in the end also theological) that in this book the historian wins out over the theologian.

Theology in Colonial America

For understanding American theology at the time of the Civil War, it is necessary to begin at least a century and a half before. Religious beliefs and theological methods in the American colonies through the first half of the eighteenth century were vastly different from what they became in the next century. Sketching the main theological convictions of the major ecclesiastical traditions as they had developed in colonial America to about 1750 provides a basis for that contrast.[1]

The foundation of American theology was European theology. Until about 1750 the major theological voices of the colonies' major ecclesiastical traditions testified uniformly to the durability of inherited Protestant traditions. Congregational Puritanism provided far and away the most influential formal theology in the colonies, but almost all other varieties were also decisively stamped by their old-world origins. Those theologies were instinctively traditional, habitually deferential to inherited authority, and deliberately suspicious of individual self-assertion. The center of formal religion throughout the colonies remained the being, prerogatives, and actions of God, although this central affirmation was construed in different ways. Some theological traditions stressed God's provision of grace for personal salvation, some God's revealed will as the norm for churches, others God's general will as the foundation for social order, and still others God's appointed ministers as mediators of his guidance for humanity.

Such traditional theology was as fully articulated into its social and political contexts as later "American theology." Christian believers in colonial America, though overwhelmingly Protestant, still assumed that God had structured society like a pyramid and that contentment with one's created place was a godly virtue. The respect owed to pastors was an instance of the deference due to all whom God had placed in their superior stations. The colonists' allegiance to written confessions was connected to the breakup of medieval Catholic authority and the search by Protestants for secure alternatives to the universal ideal of visible church authority. The construction of Puritan and Anglican establishments in the new world reproduced in separate colonial regions notions of godly uniformity that had competed with each other in England from the 1540s to the 1650s. The Puritan understanding of covenant as a theological device was as much a product of late-Tudor, early-Stuart search for intellectual and social order as were parallel understandings of constitution in politics and contracts in commerce. Similarly, Anglican notions of God-ordained social order shared Stuart aspirations for governance by divine right and then Newtonian conceptions of rule-governed cosmic order.[2]

Early theology in America differed from what came later not because it was disentangled from culture while the latter was entangled. The difference, rather, lay in the altered circumstances to which theologians spoke. For intellectual balance of trade, colonial theology enjoyed greater control over its own resources and so functioned as a net exporter of ideas, in contrast to the situation during the nineteenth century, when theology became a net importer of ideas. That kind of conclusion, however, is a judgment about what happened with respect to the circumstances of theology. It takes for granted that the writing of theology is always a contextual enterprise.

For all major colonial traditions, theological legacies from the old world remained definitive.[3] Following the drift of the English state-church after the Restoration of 1660, colonial Anglicans looked for theological guidance less to their confession from the Reformation era (the Thirty-nine Articles) and more to the sense of cosmic divine order that Anglican apologists held their church to embody.[4] This attitude, however, defined the most traditional theological order in North America, or at least the most "un-American," as protests against eighteenth-century attempts to install an Anglican bishop in the colonies would suggest. Colonial Presbyterians, Dutch Reformed, German Reformed, and Lutherans were expressly creedal churches, with confessions from the Reformation continuing to serve as official statements of belief. In the context of European debates with Roman Catholics, an increasing degree of Bible-centered radicalism can be observed in moving from the Lutherans' Augsburg Confession of 1530 to the Heidelberg Catechism of 1563 (primary standard for the German and Dutch Reformed), to the Presbyterians' Westminster Confession and Catechisms of 1646–1648. But in the new world, all of these confessions were roughly equivalent in both the doctrines they affirmed and the conservative stances they took on the promulgation of doctrine. If anything, colonial churches were noteworthy for taking such standards more seriously than did the churches they left behind.

The record of colonial Presbyterianism is particularly instructive at this point. Precisely at a time when English Presbyterians in the eighteenth century were moving away from strict allegiance to the Westminster Confession and a substantial number of Irish Presbyterians were doing so even more rapidly, colonial American Presbyterians concluded after serious debate that the

Westminster standards should remain a nonnegotiable floor of church doctrine.[5] In 1742 even the colonies' noncreedal, antiestablishmentarian Baptists
adopted a confession of faith from the old world, the London Baptist Confession of 1689. This "Philadelphia Confession," as it became known in America,
was a lightly edited version of the Presbyterians' Westminster Confession.
Its straightforward Calvinistic assertions were every bit as traditional on predestination, divine sovereignty, the imputation of Adam's sin, and Christ's
righteousness as those of the Baptists' establishmentarian opponents.[6] For all
these traditions, formal theology remained a task of attaching the present to
the past rather than opening the present to the future.

Colonial Puritanism was in a theological class by itself.[7] The Puritans of
New England possessed the colonies' most articulate and widely published
theologians. They were the one group of colonists who aspired to establish
an entire society on the basis of their theology, and the only ones to have
partially succeeded. By the 1740s Puritan theology was indeed breaking apart
into divergent strands of pietists, rationalists, and conservatives. Yet into that
decade, an identifiably Puritan tradition survived in New England, where
theology retained the major Calvinist emphases as these had been defined in
the founding generation by John Cotton (1584–1652), Thomas Hooker (1586–
1647), and Richard Mather (1596–1669). Significant variations might exist,
but an Augustinian-Calvinist picture of the fallen human condition, of merciful
divine sovereignty in redemption, and of the self-authenticating all-sufficiency
of divine revelation still prevailed. Through the first third of the eighteenth
century, Puritan theologians assumed that there was a given (rather than constructed) character to human nature, the world, and God's ways of reaching
out to the world. They took for granted that the central religious task was to
orient the self to the prerogatives of God as those prerogatives had been revealed in Scripture.[8]

In the first decades of the eighteenth century, these themes were the
leitmotifs of two notable theological landmarks. First was Samuel Willard's
Compleat Body of Divinity (1726), an extensive exposition of the Westminster
Shorter Catechism, 50% longer than Calvin's *Institutes*, which a demanding
public finally succeeded in bringing to print eighteen years after its author's
death. Willard (1640–1707) was a Boston preacher and sometime acting president of Harvard College, whose substantial interest in ethical questions indicated his acquaintance with the new moral philosophers. But in its substance
Willard's theology carried on the emphases of his Puritan predecessors, especially in its depiction of how human nature was morally crippled by sin
and in its account of God's sovereign action in salvation. "Philosophy," he
wrote in the *Compleat Body*, "tells us, that life-actions require life in the agent.
And spiritual actions must derive from a spiritual life; gracious actions must
flow from grace. Call this an habit, or a virtue, or a principle; it must be an
ability to do these things, which it had not naturally, but must be given it."[9]

The second landmark was the remarkable corpus of published theology
from Cotton Mather (1663–1728), a neurotic dynamo who at the height of his
energetic career accounted for a quarter to a third of all religious works pub-

lished annually in the colonies. As the long-time colleague-pastor to his father, Increase, at Boston's Old North Church, Mather shared his age's fascination with the new science, proposed countless reforming schemes, and
cultivated the kind of piety that would later mark evangelical religion. Yet
by insisting on the supremacy of scriptural revelation over all other forms of
knowledge, by defending predestination as a comfortable doctrine for the
spiritually anguished, and by urging cooperation between leaders of church
and state, Mather offered a grand recapitulation of the Puritan theological
enterprise. His words from a 1715 funeral sermon nicely illustrate both the
exuberant orthography he affected and the traditional Puritanism he championed: "The *goodness* of One who is a *Good Man*, begins with a deep Apprehension and Acknowledgment of his *Badness*. . . . 'Tis a *Regeneration* that
makes a Good Man. . . . But having dug this *Low* for the *Foundation*, we must
then see to it that there be the *Rock* in the Foundation. What I mean is, *A Faith*
which brings us into an *Union* with our SAVIOUR. . . . Our Saviour has told us,
Jn. XV 5. *Without me, you can do nothing.*"[10]

The sustained power of such theocentric convictions is suggested by the
fact that Benjamin Colman (1673–1747), the era's most productive preacher-
theologian after Mather, but an individual of very different temperament,
maintained them as well. Colman, who unlike Cotton Mather had lived in
England and enjoyed firsthand contact with fashionable Dissenters of the day,
was the first pastor of Boston's Brattle Street Church, a congregation founded
by the city's educational and mercantile elite for the express purpose of offering a refined refuge from the Mathers' rigorous piety (and from the Mathers).
Colman enjoyed expatiating on the splendors revealed by Newtonian science,
and he displayed a weakness for liturgy that greatly distressed Cotton Mather.
Yet in his picture of human nature turned aside from God because of sin, his
ascription to God of the entire motive power in redemption, his denial of a
universal moral sense, and his reliance upon the Scriptures as the sole source
for the saving knowledge of God, Colman was a thoroughly traditional Puritan. For all his intellectual sophistication, he was the key Boston pastor promoting the early works of Jonathan Edwards. For all his refinement, he was
the one who invited George Whitefield to preach in Boston. Colman's patronage of these younger Calvinists was part of his larger effort to rejuvenate
the Puritan inheritance.[11]

Jonathan Edwards

The work of Jonathan Edwards (1703–1758) attested most fully to the vigor
of the Puritans' inherited Calvinism. Twentieth-century students are partially
correct in drawing attention to the modernity of Edwards's intellectual universe, for he was influenced by the sensationalist epistemology of Locke's
Essay on Human Understanding, he marveled at the lofty regularities portrayed in Newton's science, and he accepted the affectional emphases in the
new moral philosophy of his age. But if he was the colonial American who

most deeply engaged the new era's thought, he was also the colonial American who most thoroughly repudiated it.[12]

Because Edwards cast such a long shadow over the theological history of the next century, it is important to outline the main convictions that shone through a body of work remarkable for its cohesion, its reflection of scriptural study, its alertness to contemporary science, and its skill at restating historic Calvinism in the philosophical vocabulary of the eighteenth century.[13] While studying theology after his graduation from Yale College in 1720, Edwards underwent a conversion during which, as he later put it, "there came into my soul, and was as it were diffused through it, a sense of the glory of the divine being."[14] To communicate this divine glory became the burden of his life as pastor and theologian.

As the minister of the established Congregational Church in Northampton, Massachusetts, Edwards guided intense seasons of revival in 1734–1735 and again in 1740–1742. Yet in 1750 he was dismissed from his pulpit in Northampton when he disrupted long-established community practices by insisting that children make a creditable testimony of saving faith before being admitted as full members. This personal crisis (and also domestic crisis, since Edwards had a large family) became a theological opportunity when he moved to a parish in frontier Stockbridge, Massachusetts. Preaching to a congregation of native Americans and a small colonial church freed time during which the treatises were completed for which he later won theological renown. Edwards died on 22 March 1758, from an inoculation against smallpox, only weeks after beginning his service as president of the College of New Jersey in Princeton.

The unifying center of Edwards's theology was the glory of God depicted as an active, harmonious, ever-unfolding source of absolutely perfect Being marked by supernal beauty and love. The cast of his mind was relentlessly intellectual—"many theorems, that appeared hard and barren to others, were to him pleasant and fruitful fields, where his mind would expatiate with peculiar case, profit and entertainment," was the way his friend and student Samuel Hopkins put it.[15] As a result, his theological convictions were worked out in response to abstruse metaphysical questions as well as in the biblical exposition that was his main business as a preaching minister. As a thinker, Edwards most resembled two other philosophically inclined Christian intellectuals of his era, the French Catholic Nicholas Malebranche (1638–1715) and the Anglican George Berkeley (1685–1753). Although the three did not respond to each others' work, they shared a commitment to philosophical idealism as the necessary counter to what they perceived as the materialist drift of their age.

Edwards's career as a publishing theologian began with his *Narrative of Surprising Conversions*, a work first written as a letter to Benjamin Colman in 1736 to explain the course of revival in Northampton. Soon the rather breathless tone of this work gave way to more discriminating analyses in *Some Thoughts concerning the Present Revival of Religion in New England* (1743) and *A Treatise on the Religious Affections* (1746). These works drew upon

Edwards's experience in the revival to argue that true religion was a matter of the affections, or what might today be called habitual inclinations at the core of a person's being. *Religious Affections* detailed at length the kinds of religious emotions that were largely irrelevant to a determination of true spirituality (e.g., those manifesting a particular intensity). Rather, true spirituality could be shown by twelve "marks" of affectional attachment to God, of which the last and most definite was consistent Christian practice.

The view of salvation that lay behind Edwards's analysis of revival was consistently Calvinistic. He held that the root of human sinfulness was antagonism toward God. Living faith involved much more than facts about God; it required a new "taste" of divine beauty, holiness, and truth. The fullest treatment of this soteriology came in 1754 when he published *A Careful and Strict Inquiry into the Modern Prevailing Notions of That Freedom of Will, Which Is Supposed to Be Essential to Moral Agency, Virtue and Vice, Reward and Punishment, Praise and Blame*. Here Edwards argued that the "will" was not a discrete independent faculty but rather a description of the person acting on his or her choices. To "will" something was to act consistently with one's character and in accord with the strongest motives on and in a person. The minute care with which Edwards attacked the notion of self-determining human faculties and with which he linked volition to character made this work a landmark for theologians in America, Scotland, and Wales for over a century.

A posthumously published treatise, *Original Sin* (1758), expanded on the view of human nature present in *Freedom of the Will*. By suggesting that all humanity took part seminally in Adam's fall, Edwards hoped to show that individuals were both responsible for their own sinfulness and bound by a fallen nature until converted by God's sovereign grace. Edwards's exposition in this work established the terms for discussing fallen human nature that later New Englanders debated with endless variations for a full century, but that Presbyterians could never quite understand.

The burden of Edwards's thought is shown unmistakably by the last book he prepared for publication, *Two Dissertations. (I) Concerning the End for Which* GOD *Created the World. (II) The Nature of True Virtue.* (Edwards died in 1758; it appeared in 1765.) Although this was not the last book Edwards hoped to write, it did provide an unusually fitting capstone to his theological career. Its thesis broadened central themes from his earlier writings on revival and on the controversial doctrines of traditional Calvinism. For ethics it argued again what he had previously asserted for the inner spiritual life in his *Treatise on Religious Affections* and for conversion in his *Freedom of the Will*—no truly good thing, strictly speaking, exists that is not always and everywhere dependent upon God. Edwards's own statements contain the sharpest possible antithesis to what would become American convictions in the generations after his passing. Against the exaltation of human happiness as the central concern of life, he argued in the first dissertation, "All that is ever spoken of in the Scripture as an ultimate end of God's works is included in that one phrase, 'the glory of God.'" Against the construal of virtue as ei-

ther disinterested public service or private female purity, the second dissertation asserted, "'Tis evident that true virtue must chiefly consist in love to
God; the Being of beings, infinitely the greatest and best of beings."[16] Paul
Ramsey, the leading modern authority on Edwards's ethical writings, defined
succinctly the bond between the two dissertations: "The 'end' for which God
created the world must be the 'end' of a truly virtuous and holy life."[17] The
lengths to which Edwards was pushed in his brilliant renovation of Calvinist
theology may have been a sign of that theology's insecurity as much as of its
strength. It is nonetheless important that, in the same years when traffic began
to increase between traditional Reformed theology and the new vocabulary
of republican liberty, New England witnessed its most subtle and most able
restatement of inherited Calvinist convictions.

Presbyterians

Outside of New England, the most articulate theologians were Presbyterians,
the denomination that was spread most widely in the colonies and that most
assiduously promoted the old-world ideal of the learned minister. Some of
the leaders of colonial Presbyterianism came from late-Puritan Yale College,
but most received their education privately from veteran pastors like the renowned William Tennent (1673–1746) of Neshaminy, Pennsylvania, whose
tutelage rivaled the century's colleges in intellectual depth and theological
acumen. The intellectual leaders of colonial Presbyterianism, though approaching the twin ideals from different directions, tried to advance both traditional theology and the era's new evangelical piety. The four most important were Jonathan Dickinson (1688–1747), Gilbert Tennent (1703–1764),
Samuel Finley (1715–1766), and Samuel Davies (1723–1761), who among
themselves accounted for about a third of the nearly 500 works published by
Presbyterians in the colonial era. They were popular not just because of their
own energy but because other Presbyterians read what they wrote.[18]

   The provenance of these four illustrate the regional and ethical mixture
that contributed to the vitality of colonial Presbyterianism. Gilbert Tennent
was born in County Armagh, Ireland, and was trained by his father, William,
who had been educated at Edinburgh and served as a minister of the Church
of Ireland before migrating to America and becoming a Presbyterian.
Dickinson was born in Massachusetts and educated at Yale before taking a
Presbyterian church in Elizabethtown, New Jersey. Davies was the son of
Welsh immigrants to Delaware and gained renown as the founder of
Presbyterianism in Virginia. Finley was born in Ireland, immigrated to Philadelphia, probably studied with William Tennent in Neshaminy, and itinerated for a brief period as a revivalist before settling in Nottingham, Maryland, where he conducted a distinguished classical academy alongside his
church. Tennent, Dickinson, and Finley in 1746 became founding trustees of
the College of New Jersey, while Dickinson, Davies, and Finley later served
as presidents of that mostly Presbyterian enterprise.

The theology promoted by these prominent leaders was more directly pietistic than old-world Presbyterianism, as indicated by the hymns Davies wrote as one of the colonies' first published poets. In this verse he sounded similar themes to what the Presbyterians were proclaiming in their sermons:

> Pardon from an offended God!
> Pardon for sins of deepest dye!
> Pardon bestowed through Jesus' blood!
> Pardon that brings the rebel nigh!
> Who is a pard'ning God like thee?
> Or who has grace so rich and free?[19]

Colonial Presbyterian theology was also sometimes more sectarian than the theology of Scotland's established Kirk. Gilbert Tennent's 1740 sermon "The Danger of an Unconverted Ministry," which he preached at Nottingham, Maryland, a few years before Finley arrived, called upon listeners to leave churches where they considered the pastors to be unredeemed. Tennent later recanted this outburst, but even the tempered revivalism that all four practiced revealed a flexibility toward ecclesiastical order with only a few parallels in the Scottish or Irish homelands.

Along with a measure of innovation, however, colonial Presbyterianism remained solidly committed to the high Calvinism of its Westminster Confession and Catechisms. Transplanted New Englanders like Dickinson chafed under the necessity of subscribing to the confession, but unlike similar resentment in England and Ireland, Dickinson's antisubscriptionist views were fueled by an activistic pietism rather than an incipient rationalism. Colonial Presbyterians did eventually go into schism because of differences over revivalism. But that schism, which lasted from 1741 to 1758, featured a division between those who felt that the Westminster Confession could be maintained alongside an emphasis on revival opposed to those who maintained the conservative belief that Presbyterian confessionalism was damaged by revival. Like the Moderate-Popular conflict in Scotland and the New Light–Old Light conflict in Ireland, the colonies' Old Side–New Side schism revealed contrasting attitudes toward Presbyterian traditions. But unlike the Scottish, and even more unlike the Irish, American Presbyterians remained actively committed to the traditional Calvinism of the Westminster standards. With their New Light Congregationalist associates of New England, the leading Presbyterian New Side ministers were their denomination's chief revivalists as well as their most effective proponents of traditional Reformed theology.[20]

Anglicans

The colonies' foremost Anglicans in the first decades of the eighteenth century were the Virginia commissary James Blair (1656–1743), founding president of the College of William and Mary, and Thomas Bray (1658–1730), a missionary to the colonies with the Society for the Propagation of the Gospel in Foreign Parts, who served briefly in Maryland and then provided support for American causes after returning to England. While Blair and Bray were not Calvinists, these Anglican leaders nonetheless promoted a traditional teaching that exalted divine grace as the key to salvation. Their general point of view—described by historian J. F. Woolverton as "low church obedience to moral law"—identified them as pious Anglican traditionalists rather than early devotees of an Age of Reason.[21]

The colonies' leading Anglican thinker of the eighteenth century, Samuel Johnson, faced as many obstacles in promoting his religion against Puritan theological order as Blair and Bray experienced in their struggle against the forces of Southern social disorder. Johnson (1696–1772) was born in Connecticut, where he enjoyed a Puritan education. He completed his work for a B.A. at the very new Yale College in 1714, two years before Jonathan Edwards entered as a student.[22] Unlike Edwards, who became a champion of this historic Calvinist tradition, Johnson and several other young ministers scandalized all New England in 1722 by joining the Anglican church. As a rector in Stratford, Connecticut, and then as president of New York City's King's College (predecessor of Columbia University), Johnson read widely in the most up-to-date philosophical works of the day and produced a steady stream of sermons, polemical tracts, and philosophical investigations. His *Elementa Philosophica*, published by Benjamin Franklin in 1752, was the colonies' first philosophy textbook. For such efforts, Johnson became the obvious choice to head the Anglicans' new American college. When he arrived in New York to take up that position in 1754, "no other Anglican priest," as a historian of early Columbia puts it, "could touch Johnson's reputation as an intellectual, educator, and religious leader."[23]

Johnson's works are especially important, since his convictions so stoutly opposed both the Puritans' Calvinist past and the contemporary efforts of Jonathan Edwards to renovate traditional Calvinism. Johnson, thus, was an Arminian who consistently defended a freedom for human volition that contradicted Calvinist predestination. In a sermon from 1751, for example, he drew the contradiction sharply: "We are intuitively certain from looking into ourselves, that our soul or spirit is indeed a principle of free activity or has a power given it of God of freely exerting and determining itself."[24]

Yet if Johnson was no Puritan Calvinist, neither did he embrace the era's up-to-date convictions about God and humanity. In fact, he took an intellectual stand against the rising metaphysics of his day that aligned him almost exactly with Edwards. Both, that is, protested against what they perceived as materialism latent in the popular uses of Newton's mechanical view of matter. Where Johnson followed Bishop George Berkeley in holding that the universe was an immaterial reality conceived by the mind of God, Edwards came to nearly the same conclusions through independent theological reasoning. So God-centered was Johnson's universe that many of his theological assertions accorded as well with Edwards's Calvinism as his ontology accorded with Edwards's metaphysics. As an example, the discourse in which Johnson defended free will was entitled "A Sermon on the Entire Dependence of the Creature upon God." Apart from its brief comments on the will, it bears an uncanny resemblance to Edwards's 1731 exposition "God Glorified in the Work of Redemption, by the Greatness of Man's Dependence upon Him, in the Whole of It." In his sermon Johnson could affirm that "it was from the exertion of the Almighty will and power of God, that we at first came into being, and . . . it is from the continued exertion of the same Almighty will and power of God every moment that we continue to exist, to think and act." To understand God and the world aright was to see an important reality—"it is literally true that we have no sufficiency of ourselves, to think or do any thing as of our selves, but that our sufficiency is of God." That reality, in turn, was of "great use . . . to promote in us true humility which is the foundation of every other virtue. How should it beget in us the deepest and most abasing sense of our own impotence and nothingness, that God may be all in all?"[25] Johnson's reference to "virtue" in traditional theological terms, no less than his fixation upon God as the ever-active re-creator of human life, bound his theological concerns much more closely to Edwards than either, as spokesmen for antagonistic churches, could have acknowledged themselves.

That degree of intellectual accord between Johnson and Edwards is especially important for gauging the character of colonial theology at the midpoint of the eighteenth century. Johnson, unlike Edwards, was neither a genius nor a Calvinist. Yet that so much of his theological discourse moved in the same direction as Edwards's, and that these two were widely recognized as the leading lights of the dominant churches in the colonies, says much about the classical character of theology on the eve of the Revolutionary era.

During the first half of the eighteenth century, clergymen throughout the colonies encouraged human striving toward God, but only fringe theologians held that humans assisted in their own salvation. Natural theology (or the effort to reason from contact with the physical world to the character of God) was beginning to assume a new prominence, but it still functioned mostly within a framework constructed by notions of active divine providence. Believers and nonbelievers alike were enjoined to follow God's law, but the leading theologians described law-keeping more as a reflection of divine glory than as a path to human happiness. In New England, all citizens were reminded of their covenant duties, but ideas of covenant were still dominated by conceptions of divine grace. Theologians looked to the inbreaking of the millennium, but as a gift of God's mercy instead of an accomplishment by redeemed humanity.

Sectarians and Awakeners

In the pre-Revolutionary period even the major voices of sectarian movements were overwhelmingly traditional. The New Jersey and Pennsylvania Quaker John Woolman (1720–1772) is a good example of a theologically astute outsider whose views—especially on revelation and personal Christian responsibility—set him apart him from the Protestant mainstream defined by Congregationalists, Anglicans, Presbyterians, and the Continental Reformed churches. Yet before being recorded as a Friends minister in 1748, Woolman underwent a season of conversion marked by at least some of the same experiences that more traditional Protestants expected. This conversion moved him, however, to embrace the Quaker doctrine of the Inner Light of Christ, a teaching far too subjective for leaders of the main colonial denominations. The phrases that Woolman employed to describe this experience were, however, surprisingly similar to words Jonathan Edwards also used for a similar experience at about the same age in his own life. For Woolman it meant being drawn "to love God as an invisible, incomprehensible being" and "to love him in all his manifestations in the visible world."[26] In the 1750s Woolman embarked upon the public activity for which he continues to be admired, particularly his opposition to slavery and his support for the decision by Pennsylvania Quakers to withdraw from the government of Pennsylvania during the French and Indian War in order to preserve the Quaker peace testimony. In these actions Woolman was guided by examples from, as he put it, "faithful Friends in early times." Motivation for this activity rested, in other words, on traditional Quaker theology, and there is no indication that modern notions of "liberty" or of a natural moral sense influenced his convictions in the slightest.[27]

The continuing power of a religion with scant room for the intensely this-worldly preoccupations of republicanism or the optimistic universalism of moral-sense philosophy was demonstrated at midcentury by the convulsive religious excitement of the Great Awakening. This movement was promoted by preachers—Theodorus Frelinghuysen, Gilbert Tennent, and especially George Whitefield—who affirmed a traditional theology. The presence of what Ruth Bloch has called a "vast reservoir of ethnic immigrant Calvinism" aided its rapid spread, and it featured self-conscious efforts to promote what Charles Hambrick-Stowe has styled "traditional themes and old titles."[28] Whatever its long-term consequences, the revival had the immediate effect of drawing Americans *closer* to their Reformed theological partners in Britain. The revival also became the occasion for the century's greatest theologian, Jonathan Edwards, to restate the precepts of Calvinism with rigorous force. To be sure, by 1740 some colonists were questioning Calvinistic certainties, and Protestant theology had certainly moved in the direction of activism, moralism, and even individualism during the its first American century. At the same time, theology in the American colonies remained classically theocentric. The colonies' main theological traditions were Reformed Protestant. Its most visible, influential, well-articulated, and enduring monument was the covenantal Calvinism of Puritan New England.

This theological inheritance did not vanish in the century or more that followed. It did, however, fragment, and its broken pieces were recombined with a whole range of new intellectual associations. The result was an evolution of theology that can be explained, though not exhaustively, by examining the political and intellectual landscapes through which it passed.

A generation ago, Edmund Morgan summarized a significant portion of eighteenth-century intellectual history in a single limpid sentence: "In 1740 America's leading intellectuals were clergymen and thought about theology; in 1790 they were statesmen and thought about politics."[29] The narrative that follows attempts to explain how that transition from 1740 to 1790 occurred. It also hopes to illuminate a story that stretched beyond 1790 to at least 1865, when America's leading statesman could expound a complex, subtle theology while its leading theologians were being consumed by politics.

3

The Long Life and Final Collapse of the Puritan Canopy

The creation of American theology required first the displacement of European theology. The transition that mattered most for the future United States took place in New England, and the event that most clearly symbolized that transition was the dismissal of Jonathan Edwards from his Northampton, Massachusetts, pulpit in 1750. The views of God and humanity that Edwards preached as a leader of the colonial Great Awakening were aimed at the rejuvenation of traditional Protestant piety. Yet Edwards's strongly held opinions on the church had the effect of shaking American theology loose from that kind of piety. From the revivals arose new evangelical churches, activities, instincts, and ways of expounding Christian doctrine. Before that rise could occur, older expectations for church and theology inherited from Europe had to give way. A process that ended with an intimate union between evangelical Protestant religion and Revolutionary politics began with disruption in the historic colonial churches.

One consequence of that disruption was an accelerating pace of exchange between the language of hereditary Protestantism and the languages of civic and intellectual culture that earlier had been antagonistic to orthodox belief. As Protestants began to edge toward republican and commonsense commitments, they moved away from Puritanism as a protective theological canopy. Under that canopy New Englanders had pursued their reflections, not only about God, self, and society, but also about how thinking itself should proceed. The disintegration of Puritanism as a comprehensive life system was the first critical move toward an American theology.

Several plausible explanations have been offered for that disintegration. It appears, alternatively, as the fracture of an integral society torn apart by guilt at the outmigration of land-starved sons,[1] the collapse of clerical hegemony,[2] the incorporation of New England into Britain's burgeoning market economy,[3] or the replacement of local ecclesiastical authority focusing on outward observance with personal religion concentrated on inward piety.[4] For a history of theology, however, it is more appropriate to describe the disintegration of Puritanism as an exchange of integrating concepts. Given up was the covenant, a long-lived and explicitly biblical construct for linking together God, self, church, and society. In its place came a mixed set of modern alternatives that used social or political, but not primarily theological, categories to unify existence. The disintegration of the Puritan theological canopy decisively altered the intellectual balance of trade for theology. Once the Puritan way of holding together God, self, and society fragmented, other means, which were not as tightly rooted in classic Protestantism, took over those integrative functions.

Puritan theology had never been an exclusively religious construct. Contemporary understandings of contract, compact, and corporation—as well as surges of English and Scottish nationalism—had influenced the early Puritans as they constructed their covenant theology from biblical materials.[5] Patterns of reasoning from the new science, especially the empirical ideals of Francis Bacon, affected the Puritans as they traced what the Westminster Confession of 1646 called those "good and necessary consequences" that "may be deduced from Scripture" for the ordering of life.[6] Yet in England for roughly the century before the Restoration of the monarchy in 1660, and in Congregational New England until the early eighteenth century, Puritan thought flowed primarily from theological springs. The disintegration that occurred in America from the 1730s was ironic, since it was caused in part by a revival of the same sort of experiential Calvinism that had first inspired the Puritan vision of a total Christian society.

That disintegration—the ground-clearing phase anticipating a new American era in Protestant theology—is the subject of this chapter. The replacement of the Puritans' integrated covenantal theology by Christian republicanism and Christian common sense preserved many aspects of the Puritan synthesis, and it did not immediately redirect the course of theology in America. By the beginning of the nineteenth century, however, and in conjunction with the social, economic, political, and religious consequences of the Revolution, the exchange of integrating canopies had momentous theological effects.

But why, for a study pointing toward theology in the United States during the nineteenth century, pay so much attention to only one religious tradition, and that from only one American region? The answer is that New England, though representing only a minority of Americans (32% of the population in the thirteen colonies in 1740, only 23% in the sixteen states at 1800), exerted an influence far beyond its size on the intellectual culture of the new United States. Puritanism is the only colonial religious system that modern historians take seriously as a major religious influence on the Revolution.[7] During the War for Independence, a vibrant Christian republicanism from New England, compounded of remnant Puritan messianism and Real Whig political analysis, persuaded other colonists to think that the new nation in its entirety might be specially elect of God like a new ancient Israel. In the generations after independence, New Englanders led the way in writing the history of the new nation. As illustrated most clearly by the influential works of the Boston brahmin George Bancroft, they found the temptation irresistible to write American history as New England's story—cultural *and* religious, moral *and* political—writ large.[8] Historians of Christianity, as illustrated by Robert Baird's pioneering church history *Religion in America* (1843), did the same, despite Baird's own midstate and Presbyterian origins.[9] Well into the new century, the number of religious publications from New England dwarfed the number appearing from other regions of the country.[10] A modern historian of Puritanism, Stephen Foster, has succinctly explained why the Puritan heritage carried such intellectual weight in the new republic. In Foster's account, New Englanders entered the contest over national self-definition with "disciplined intellectual skills and organizational talent." Most important, "in an intensely Protestant country they had inherited what was still the most highly articulated and comprehensive vision." So long as Protestant Christianity remained the default religion for most Americans, whether they practiced it actively or not, New Englanders would be in the lead. They "used the same language as the rest of the country with, in effect, a more complete grammar inherited from a Puritan past."[11] Only the South resisted the culture-defining sway of New England, and that resistance was woven into a culture that gave a distinctive shape to Southern theology throughout the entire antebellum era.

For understanding the history of Christian theology in America, it is necessary to begin before there was an America settled by Europeans. The pre-history of American theology includes a long-standing Western Christian assumption about the unity of all spheres of life under God, a somewhat narrower set of Protestant convictions about how traditional Western Christendom needed to be reformed, and still narrower patterns of belief associated with the Reformed or Calvinistic wing of the Reformation. It was a version of this Reformed Protestantism that the Puritans brought to New England. Given such background, it is possible to understand why the colonial revivals both rejuvenated religion and destroyed an older theological understanding of social integration, and by so doing fostered conditions generally propitious for the migration of political languages into theological speech.

Reformed Theology as a Renewal of Christendom

The importance of Puritanism for American theological history is more easily grasped if it is regarded as an English Protestant extension of Christendom. After the legalization of Christianity in fourth-century Rome, after its promotion by Constantine (ruled 312–337), Theodosius (379–395), and lesser Christian emperors, and especially after the rise of the papacy as a civil force (manifest at least by the pontificate of Leo I in the mid-fifth century), the pattern of Christendom was in place that survived with vigor for at least thirteen centuries. In this pattern, thinking about Christianity and thinking about social and political realities were always overlapping exercises. Europeans (and their colonial offspring) simply took it for granted that Christian truth and truth about the civil order were integrally connected.[12]

Despite what some later interpreters clamed for the major Protestant reformers as nursemaids of liberty, they did not question the necessity of civil and religious integration (and also coercion to enforce religious conformity).[13] In the sixteenth century, only radicals beyond the pale doubted the propriety of Luther's reliance on the prince as "a bishop of necessity" or Calvin's assignment to the magistracy of jurisdiction over the First Table of the Law.[14] Throughout the sixteenth and seventeenth centuries, incipient nationalism, nascent capitalism, and the New Learning challenged the traditional European synthesis of religion and society more directly than did the religious teachings of the major Protestant reformers, but even these modernizing forces did not sunder what Christendom had joined together.

In 1553, a full lifetime before the Puritan separatists stumbled onto Massachusetts's rocky shore at Plymouth, a crucial moment occurred for later theological development in America. In that year the Roman Catholic Mary Tudor succeeded her Protestant younger half brother, Edward VI, as England's monarch. About 300 of the Protestants who in the previous decades had worked to reform the English church went to the stake. Another substantial group embarked for the Continent. For later developments in America, it was critical that these exiles found a refuge on Reformed rather than Lutheran soil.[15]

To that time, the Protestant movement in England had been an eclectic mixture, taking as much from Lutheran as from Reformed influences, but also marked by a full spectrum of indigenous English influences from Wycliffites and Lollards on the left to pious Catholic promoters of the New Learning on the right. When Protestants left England during the reign of Catholic Queen Mary, however, they went to Reformed cities like Strasbourg, Frankfurt, or Calvin's Geneva. Lutheran lands, to which at least some of the refugees may have been drawn, were closed. Following Luther's death in 1546, internal theological strife had badly disrupted his movement. At the same time, the Lutheran princes were suffering serious military reverses in struggles with the Holy Roman Emperor, Charles V, who was also a first cousin of Mary Tudor. Divided politically by doctrinal and personal strife, weakened politically by defeat at the hand of the emperor, Lutheran Europe was hardly in a position to welcome refugees from Britain.

The situation was quite different among the Reformed. Although Calvin had only shortly before won out over his opponents in Geneva, he welcomed the British eagerly. Churches and schools were put at their disposal. The aid he offered scholars seeking to improve upon William Tyndale's earlier translation of the Scriptures led to the immensely influential Geneva Bible. The reception in Strasbourg, Frankfurt, and other cities under Reformed influence was almost as warm.[16] When Mary died in 1558 and was succeeded by her discreetly Protestant half sister, Elizabeth, most of the refugees returned home. As they did so, the "thorough" English Protestants immediately began to agitate for the same sort of reforms they had witnessed on the Continent. Even more, these advanced Protestants promoted a distinctly Reformed understanding of how to renovate (but not replace) the historic unities of Christendom.

What this Reformed cast of mind meant for narrow theological issues did not make much difference. International Protestantism—whether Lutheran, Reformed, or Anglican—hovered around a narrow range of theological opinions. Lutheran-Reformed differences on whether Christ's resurrected body was, strictly speaking, in heaven (Reformed) or everywhere (Lutheran), on whether the *communicatio idiomatum* between Christ's human and divine natures involved extensive exchange (Lutheran) or more modest exchange (Reformed), or on whether the Ten Commandments should be taught first as preparation for grace (Lutheran) or later as gratitude in response to grace (Reformed) were only moderately significant issues. Within both camps a spectrum of opinions existed, and theological differences between major figures during the first generations, as between Luther and Calvin themselves, were never earthshaking.[17]

In the broader application of theology to life, however, Reformed and Lutheran differences were more significant.[18] Lutherans held that God worked in the world through diverse means—through the church and its proclamation of salvation, but also through the structures of state, economy, and family, which God had created as relatively autonomous agents of his authority. The critical matter was that Lutherans saw *two* kingdoms through which God ruled the world. The effect of this two-kingdom theology was to segregate forms of reasoning; adepts in the church concentrated on formal theology, while lay practitioners in the world accepted prudential, practical reasoning as the way to order society.

The Reformed, by contrast, were both more medieval and more modern—more medieval because they insisted that God exercised his sovereignty over the world as an organic unity, more modern because they derived principles for that ordering from Scripture as opposed to tradition. God elected individuals to salvation; he incorporated them into his body, the church; through them he then exercised his providential control over the world as a whole. The Reformed attacked Catholic dogma, but they reasserted a Catholic kind of Christendom by insisting that God's rule should encompass everything.

This Reformed approach had a much greater effect on how theology was applied than on how theology was formulated. By comparison with other Christian traditions, the Reformed invitation to exert oneself in the world for the glory of God was more engaged and less ironic than the Lutheran, less ascetic and altogether more confident about the redeemable goodness of human institutions than the Anabaptists, more democratic and less monastic than the Catholics, and more material and less liturgical than the Orthodox. The Reformed of every rank in society were expected to function as theologians, since social, political, economic, and artistic spheres of life were also God's concern. From this broad mandate came an outpouring of Reformed practical theology. Expressed in their own categories, the Reformed promoted the authority of Scripture over every sphere of life, the God-given dignity of work, the sacredness of all vocations (not just the religious), the possibility that institutions could be sanctified to God, the employment of material means for godly ends, and the use of the mind as a spiritual exercise.

In practical terms, the Reformed commitment to the theological significance of everyday life led to the development of something like Protestant metaphysics, Protestant epistemology, Protestant science, Protestant politics, Protestant social and economic theory, Protestant art, and Protestant poetics.[19] The development of these Reformed spheres of intellectual and cultural activity never occurred without substantial influence from sources not specifically religious. In Switzerland, the southern German regions, Hungary, Holland, and the British Isles, the Reformed perspective could be used to mask economic or political aggression. More commonly, it emerged from a complicated mix of sacred and secular motives.[20] Yet wherever sufficient Reformed strength existed, the assumption also existed that biblical Christianity had something fairly definite to say about everything.

Rarely in the Geneva of John Calvin or Theodore Beza, John Knox's Scotland, or the Huguenot fortresses of southern France did Reformed Protestants pause to contemplate the magnitude of their self-appointed tasks. Rarely did the self-denying principles of their own theology check the hubris of the elect. They did not usually act as if they believed what their own theology said about the huge gap between divine omniscience and human finitude, nor did they seem to really believe their own claim that even believers continued to abuse the gifts of God for idolatrous, selfish ends. Rarely were the Reformed as sharp-eyed to catch their own compromises with worldly reasoning as they were to pounce upon the inconsistencies of Roman Catholics, Lutherans, or rival Reformed communities. But for the sake of theological construction, the Reformed enjoyed the great advantage of believing that all influences shaping thought were themselves theological influences. So long as this conviction remained in place, the Reformed remained in control of their own theology.

When, however, in the inevitable flow of events, the white heat of reforming zeal cooled, or when the reach of the Protestant Internationale exceeded the capacity of Reformed agitators actually to convert their own societies, the Reformed approach generated its own special difficulties. Reformed theologies that shaped culture were singularly susceptible to being shaped by currents within cultures, especially at those moments when the intellectual energy of the wider society began to match the religious energy of the church. The Reformed eagerness to treat culture as a theological construct and to shape culture in accord with theological principle depended on a comprehensive understanding of culture—a steady bifocal gaze at the new birth of persons alongside the kingdom-possibilities of society. The genius of Reformed Protestantism was its ability to keep both possibilities in view. The ever-present threat to Reformed Protestantism was its proximity to the world.

Contrasting attitudes toward the relationship between redeemed selves and the broader society produced contrasting perils. From the one side, some who were nurtured by Reformed faith eventually welcomed the blurring of faith and society and slid easily into an accommodation to the world. Such ones—like John Locke and the Unitarian Presbyterians of late seventeenth-century

England, or Protestant rationalists who emerged in Holland, Switzerland, and France—retained certain aspects of Reformed morals, ethos, or even religion, but only as subordinate matters in larger worldviews constructed in part to defend against Reformed enthusiasm.[21] From the other side, Reformed Protestants who felt the expansion of worldly concerns as a threat instead of an opportunity reacted in the opposite direction and sought the blaze of personal faith, even if it meant burning up the comprehensive social arrangements that early Protestants saw as their reasonable service to God.[22] The movements of pietistic and evangelical revival of the late seventeenth and eighteenth centuries took this latter course.

Either move—toward secularization or revival—imperiled the integral Reformed approach to life in the world. By threatening the integrating framework, both perils also threatened the ability of the Reformed to control their own theology. The secularist move was the more obvious threat, for how could life-transforming doctrine be drawn from Scripture once Scripture was supplanted by other authorities?[23] Yet the pietistic, evangelical move could be almost as destructive. Individuals and communities accustomed to think about the world religiously—who regarded politics, social relationships, economics, and all other spheres of life as religious domains—did not abandon life in the world when they became pietists or evangelicals. Rather, awakened piety could divert attention from larger questions of worldview and then allow secular forces to do their work unimpeded. Within Reformed circles, a revitalization of heart religion rarely closed the borders to the larger world, but such revivals often left those borders unattended.

Incidents in the History of the Puritan Covenant

Whether or not the preceding paragraphs describe a universal religious situation, they do describe the intellectual history of the Puritans. Despite notorious difficulties of definition, it is possible to follow the best recent authors and to characterize Puritanism as a religious movement combining medieval commitments to the unity of society with Reformed Protestant views of personal salvation, that is, Calvin's soteriology with Erasmus's Christendom.[24] These complementary convictions drove the Puritans to push for ecclesiastical reform, what Patrick Collinson has styled the search for "'a further reformation,' the logical completion of reconstituting the national church, which in their view had been arrested halfway."[25] Stephen Foster finds the continuity of Puritanism in a set of attitudes linking God, self, church, and society: "At each point in the movement's history the same central Puritan vision endured: the magistracy guaranteed the social conditions under which the laity, part volunteers and part conscripts, pursued their individual destinies in a collective context interpreted and mediated by the clergy."[26]

This breadth of view explains why Henry Parker could write in 1641 that there were "Puritans in Church policy, Puritans in religion, Puritans in State and Puritans in morality."[27] It also explains why Puritanism could erect a canopy for theology as well as defend a set of specific theological convictions. When efforts to reform England and the English church were checked, some Puritans began to think about the possibility of a gathered church, a communion in which the purity of grace was realized even before the imperfections of English nation and church were burned away.[28] This tendency would inspire Congregationalists in New England and a plethora of Puritan denominations in revolutionary England (1642–1660). But it was never more than a tendency. Except for a very few Separatists, the longing for a pure church never replaced the equally strong drive to reform the entire nation. Nor were Puritan Independents (Congregationalists) ever separatistic in the way that Roman Catholic monks or Anabaptist sectarians were separatistic. The search for gathered or called-out churches sharpened Puritan zeal for comprehensive reform because it existed alongside of, rather than as a replacement for, zeal to reform the nation.

By the early seventeenth century, English Puritans had developed the major themes that came to fruition in New England: the centrality of the new birth, the assumption of a unified society, and the church as the central link between personal religion and national reform. Above all and integrating all was the covenant, a motif at once profoundly biblical and profoundly flexible.[29]

The chief recommendation of the covenantal system was that it explained both divine grace and human obligation by reference to encompassing biblical narratives. From the Old Testament, Puritans drew on God's unconditional choice of Israel and the conditional privileges entailed by obeying God's law. In the New Testament, they found the demonstration of a new promise, or covenant, from God in Christ. As proclaimed in the works of many Puritan divines and as summarized in doctrinal standards like the Westminster Confession, the covenantal system worked powerfully to knit the world together. All people were spiritually incapacitated by the sinfulness of Adam and their own sinful deeds and so could not live up to the original standards of God's righteousness (the covenant of works). But God in mercy sent his Son to pay the moral debt and vicariously to incur God's righteous anger for those who had broken covenant. On the basis of Christ's work, God established a covenant of grace with the elect, setting forth the condition of salvation as faith in Jesus and providing the faith to fulfill that condition. The believer's part of the bargain was to love God and obey his law, a task that by faith in Christ could be approached with hope of success.

As covenant themes developed in early New England, it seemed natural that the first work of faith should be covenanting with God and other believers to form individual churches.[30] The notion of a particular church covenant emerged only slowly from the practice of England's comprehensive national church, and New England Puritans instinctively maintained that national element, even as they created particular churches. The church covenant—mediating between regenerate persons and societies populated with sinners as well as saints—became a focal point for tension in New England. As ways of interpreting particular church covenants changed, so did the implications of church membership.

New England Puritans followed English precedent and consistently viewed their whole society as standing in covenant with God. Since the head (magistracy) and heart (clergy) of society participated together in the covenant of grace, New Englanders did not doubt that the society they constructed was also a sacredly covenanted community. References to Israel, like John Winthrop's justly renowned sermon aboard the *Arbella* in 1630, were never casual: God had called out not only persons but a people with whom he sustained a "more neare bond of mariage . . . wherein he hath taken us to be his after a most strickt and peculiar manner which will make him the more Jealous of our love and obedience soe he tells the people of Israell, you onely have I knowne of all the families of the Earthe therefore will I punishe you for your Transgressions."[31] The history of New England through the mid-eighteenth century unfolded within the framework provided by these covenants. They defined both limits beyond which the society could not stray and the issues that Puritans contested endlessly among themselves.

The covenantal system was critical for early New England theology in two ways. It first provided biblical language for the basic doctrines of the faith. To be lost without God meant condemnation under conditions spelled out in the covenant of works. To be reconciled with God through the work of the Son meant to experience God's loving power of election displayed in the covenant of grace. To be accepted by the community of the faithful was to live in church covenant. To follow God's law was to keep covenant. To support holiness in society was to improve the national covenant. Finally, to participate in ritual church renewals and to hear the festal preaching of the jeremiad that occurred with increasing regularity over the last third of the seventeenth century was to renew the covenant collectively. The Puritans employed a theological vocabulary that extended far beyond the language of covenant, but covenant always remained basic to expressing their faith.

Second, it also provided an expansive vocabulary for embracing large-scale social, political, and even economic realms. Because the sense of social cohesion was expressed in terms of covenant, Puritans always were ready with doctrinal explanations for political and social events. Large-scale tumults (from epidemics or earthquakes to rises in prices, disputes within the colonial assemblies, and conflict with Britain), as well as large-scale blessings (from full harvests to military victory to resolution of disputes with the mother country), took place, respectively, because humans broke covenant or because God was faithful in keeping covenant. With the vocabulary of covenant so prominent in analyzing the ailments and progress of New England, and with the narrowly doctrinal meanings of Puritan theology so tightly secured to covenantal language, the covenantal way of talking about political, social, economic, and intellectual affairs protected the theological dogmas of Puritanism. The reach of covenantal language—from the individual through the church to society as a whole—constituted the Puritan canopy for theology narrowly defined.

The effort to build a commonwealth where all levels of organization were shaped by divine reality—the effort that never could succeed in England—

achieved remarkable success in New England's first century. Improvisational creativity by early leaders established the beachhead. The crucial institutional bond between truly Christian churches and a hopefully Christian commonwealth was provided by constituting the male church members and the voters (freemen) as the same group.[32] Neither the entrance of elected deputies into the legislative and executive realms (1634) nor the formal erection of a bicameral general court (1641) altered the resolve to maintain personal faith and social well-being in tandem. As a later Puritan would phrase it with specific reference to the integrating device: "The Covenant of Grace is cloathed with Church-Covenant in a Political visible Church-way."[33]

Maintaining the covenant-based New England Way required steering around major obstacles. The "erroneous and very dangerous" opinions of Roger Williams struck provokingly at the synthesis—by denying that a supposed national covenant gave magistrates any rights over either conscience or Native Americans—but were effectively excised.[34] The "antinomian" threat was graver from the confident assertion of Anne Hutchinson that law-keeping was secondary for those who were saved by grace. Massachusetts's governors were appalled by even the slightest hint that grace could be defined as opposing the good works necessary for a godly society; they were opposed just as resolutely to the private meetings (or conventicles) that Hutchinson sponsored and that they interpreted as undermining the comprehensive authority of the Puritan churches. Hutchinson's activities were, indeed, heading toward a sectarianism contradicting the comprehensive Puritan vision, yet just as truly they arose from the Puritans' basic understanding of God's relation to the world. As the history of Jonathan Edwards and the Great Awakening would show, Hutchinson's kind of grace-inspired conventicalism, rather than Williams's moral scrupulosity, was always the most volatile threat to the Puritan scheme. Yet Williams and Hutchinson found out what later American dissidents would also discover: to strike at the reigning sacred synthesis anywhere was to call it into question everywhere. Their banishments showed both friends and foes of the New England Way that firm discipline was required to protect the covenant people.

The need to improvise a Half-Way Covenant after only one generation in the new world revealed faults within the New England Way, but also the capacity of Puritan leaders to maintain the tension between, as Robert Pope once wrote, "a moral, covenanted society" (including every citizen) and "truly reformed churches" (made up only of the elect).[35] The questions before specially called synods in 1657 and 1662 had the potential of unraveling the Puritan synthesis: How should baptized adults who did not make a profession of personal regeneration be treated? More important, what about baptism for the children of those in church covenant who had not yet professed regenerating faith? The twin ideals of the great experiment—churches made up of genuine believers and a society subject to the covenant of grace and the law of God—were coming into conflict.

The New Englanders were up to the challenge. In 1662 a synod decreed that the children of church members were always to be "personally under the

Watch, Discipline and Government of that Church." Baptized adults who did not relate a personal experience of salvation could not participate in the Lord's Supper, which was reserved as a sign for those who stood in the covenant of grace. But they could bring their children for baptism, and so continue to participate in ecclesiastical and social covenants.[36] Concern for the comprehensiveness of the Puritan vision prevailed, yet substantial encouragement for personal holiness remained. By preserving the Lord's Supper and admittance as full church members to the professedly regenerated, the new birth remained a crux. By keeping most of the rising generation officially in the church, the sacredness of society survived. A small, adroit adjustment in what it meant to take part in the church covenant preserved the covenantal bonds linking God with individuals, churches, and society. It also preserved the canopy for Puritan theology, which in its major points remained pretty much the same after the Half-Way decision as before.

Reaction to the synod's decision in 1662 presents an instructive contrast to developments eighty years later in the Great Awakening. At both times wholehearted proponents of the covenant of grace protested against anything that might detract from the centrality of personal salvation. In the decades following 1662, that sectarian thrust was contained within the larger Puritan framework. In the 1740s the framework cracked and could not be repaired.

To father Increase (1639–1723) and son Cotton Mather (1663–1728), who were the principal spokesmen for the New England Way during the half century from 1675 to 1725, the Half-Way system, when joined to periodic renewals of the covenant, preserved the integrity of New England—spiritual, civil, ecclesiastical, and covenantal.[37] By contrast, Solomon Stoddard (1643–1729) of Northampton, Massachusetts, in the Connecticut River Valley, weighed the original Half-Way synthesis, despaired of its shortcomings, and proposed radical revisions in order to rescue what in his mind were two separate desiderata: the integrity of the gospel and the divinely ordained prerogatives of a Christian nation.[38]

In the face of a century of English and American efforts that had made churches the practical link in covenantal theory, Stoddard declared in 1700, "The doctrine of the particular churches [founded as covenantal institutions by adherents claiming to stand in the covenant of grace] is wholly unscriptural, [it] is the reason that many among us are shut out of the church, to whom church privileges do belong."[39] Instead of particular church covenants, Stoddard held that a national covenant existed whenever any people subscribed in the aggregate to the Christian religion. Stoddard's ecclesiology and his reinterpretation of the covenant were based on the assumption that New England was a Christian nation, or in his terms, "the Commonwealth of Israel."[40] According to Stoddard, the national covenant allowed, even required, all citizens to partake of the Lord's Supper. The title of his most famous polemic was *The Inexcusableness of Neglecting the Worship of God, under a Pretence of Being in an Unconverted Condition.* It argued that since the Lord's Supper was a seal, not of personal regeneration, but of the truth of God's revelation in Christ and of God's willingness to covenant with Christian nations, it was appropriate that all in such a national covenant take part in it for their own good.[41]

Stoddard's proposals were important because they anticipated later conditions in American theology, especially in his willingness to jettison the cohesion of covenants in order to preserve individual aspects of the Puritan system. Stoddard's proposals kept the language of covenant to describe personal salvation and to show how God cared for nations. But by pulling church order out of the system of interlocking covenants, he moved away from the Puritans' historic integration of theology and society. These moves anticipated the change that came about during the Great Awakening when Stoddard's grandson, Jonathan Edwards, though repudiating the specific innovations of his grandfather, joined Stoddard in greatly de-emphasizing the integrated system of covenants. One can quibble with Patricia Tracy's chronology, but her sense of Stoddard's significance for a much broader history could not be more insightful: "The unquestioned linkage of Calvinist church and intrusive state that was particularly Puritan in America ended with the reign of 'Pope' Stoddard in Northampton."[42]

Observed from the perspective of 1700, Stoddard represented only one more episode in the Puritan effort to seek heart religion and social wholeness together. Observed from the perspective of 1800, however, Stoddard had singled out for special attention the very parts of the Puritan synthesis that would soon fly apart. By abandoning the covenant as a unifying rationale for New England in order to preach the gospel more effectively, Stoddard prepared the way for the all-out evangelism of his grandson, Jonathan Edwards. By continuing to stress the ideal of a unified, Christian commonwealth, he anticipated those who opposed the social divisiveness of Jonathan Edwards's revivalism.

During the late 1760s and early 1770s, New England ministers and a few laymen once again picked up the debate on who, properly speaking, should be the members of a truly Christian church. Joseph Bellamy, a follower of Edwards and a defender of the church as a body of the regenerate, quoted Stoddard in support of his evangelistic efforts. Bellamy's opponents, who argued for unregenerate membership in order to preserve a society in covenant with God, also appealed to Stoddard.[43] Both sides were correct. The difference was that a debate once internalized within a single person later divided the New England clergy in two.

The Great Awakening

Despite Stoddard's influential life and the considerable publicity given to both his revival "harvests" and his ecclesiastical innovations, New England church life followed the path of the founders as defended by the Mathers. Modifications of the original scheme won out over the radical steps that Stoddard urged. These modifications included the Half-Way Covenant, periodic mass renewals of the covenant, Cotton Mather's proposals in his influential *Bonifacius* (1709) for a systematic doing of good, and efforts by ministers to formalize their collective authority in the Massachusetts Proposals (narrowly defeated in 1705) and Connecticut's Saybrook Platform (successfully implemented in 1708). The development of the New England Way in the nearly forty years between the publication of Stoddard's *Doctrine of Instituted Churches* (1700) and Jonathan Edwards's *Faithful Narrative of the Surprising Work of God* (1737) has received little attention.[44] Doctrinal orthodoxy continued to prevail, although somewhat more thinly and less passionately than earlier. Some three-fourths of New England churches continued the Half-Way practice, thus maintaining the great Puritan tradition of integrating self, church, and society in covenant with God.[45] At the end of the seventeenth century, New England's best-known minister after the Mathers, Samuel Willard of Boston, published a series of works that exhibited the continuing force of covenantal thinking:

> (1680) *The Duty of a People That Have Renewed Their Covenant with God. Opened and Urged in a Sermon Preached to the Second Church in Boston in New-England, March 17, 1679–80; after That Church Had Explicitly and Most Solemnly Renewed the Ingagement of Themselves to God, and One to Another.*
>
> (1682) *Covenant-Keeping the Way to Blessedness; or, A Brief Discourse Wherein Is Shown the Connexion Which There Is between the Promise, on God's Part, and Duty on Our Part, in the Covenant of Grace; As It Was Delivered in Several Sermons Preached in Order to Solemn Renewing of Covenant.*
>
> (1690) *The Doctrine of the Covenant of Redemption. Wherein Is Laid the Foundation of All Our Hopes and Happiness.*[46]

The Puritan canopy still prevailed.

After the start of the new century, the contexts for theology in New England were, to be sure, undergoing substantial change. The formulation of dogma could not be insulated from the great changes of the era, which included an increasingly commercial spirit; a gathering consternation over difficulties in finding land within traditional towns for the rising generation and the concomitant spectacle of young people hiving off into unsettled areas; the beginning of politics outside the scope of the churches; a growing longing for English books, fashions, styles, and demeanor; the spiraling prestige of Newtonian science; and a broadening influence for new philosophies from Britain.[47] Yet amid these social and intellectual changes the main representatives of the traditional theology—either in formal discourses or week-by-week sermons—betrayed little interest in refitting dogma to fit the changing times. Rather, they seemed to be expecting that traditional theology would comprehend the world as it changed about them.[48]

It was into such a situation—into a society undergoing significant social and intellectual evolution but, for theological purposes, still securely within the Puritan framework—that the Great Awakening came. Jon Butler is correct to question whether the Awakening should be considered a neatly defined and easily localized event. But if the Awakening is understood as a renewal of pietistic popular Calvinism—anticipated in the mid-1730s by the preaching of Jonathan Edwards and other ministers who sought a renewal of traditional piety, fanned into a Two-Years' Wonder (1740–1742) by George Whitefield, and then continuing in widely scattered local revivals—then the notion of a Great Awakening remains indispensable.[49] In the more general history of American religion, the Awakening marked a transition from clerical to lay religion, from the minister as an inherited authority figure to self-empowered mobilizer, from the definition of Christianity by doctrine to its definition by piety, and from a state church encompassing all of society to a gathered church made up only of the converted.

More specifically for a history of theology, the Awakening was the moment when Puritanism—the colonies' strongest traditional form of Protestant theology, as well as its most consistent effort at comprehensive Christian thinking—gave way as a total intellectual system. In particular, the unifying understanding of the church as a covenantal institution joining covenanted individuals into a covenanted society collapsed into competing ideals of the church. Each of the new competitors broke in some way the integrating force of earlier Puritanism, and none could provide an explicitly religious substitute for the doing of theology. The theological history that followed the Awakening retained many Puritan elements, but it no longer proceeded under the Puritan canopy.

Jonathan Edwards's Ecclesiology as the End of the Puritan Canopy

Much of the book that follows uses Jonathan Edwards—especially what Edwards thought he could take for granted—as a benchmark against which to measure theological change. Here, however, it is important to see how convictions and practices that Edwards himself promoted actually accelerated such changes. The critical matter was not Edwards's theology of God, humanity, or salvation; it was rather what he held about the nature of the church and the relationship of the church to society that created a substantially new context for the writing of theology. The removal of the Puritan theological canopy can be described as an episode in political or intellectual history. It was a time when other ordering concepts, especially notions of republican liberty and universal moral reason, replaced the Puritan understanding of Christendom as the integrating context for theology. But the change was also an episode in church history. Even while external colonial contexts were changing, so also was Puritan theology evolving internally. The decade of the 1740s witnessed the first significant interchanges between historic republican and Christian vocabularies. It also witnessed the publication of Jonathan Edwards's views on the church. For the future history of theology, the latter was as important as the former.

Edwards dealt with the subject of church membership, and also the relationship of church and society, in two works, one written shortly before, and the other shortly after, he was dismissed from his Northampton church in

1750.[50] The dismissal occurred when Edwards abandoned his grandfather Stoddard's practice of open communion and instead began to insist that candidates for church membership (and the privilege of communion) offer a convincing statement of saving faith. The dismissal itself was tangible evidence that incompatible understandings of the covenant could no longer be held together.[51] In his two published works, Edwards's key move was to repudiate a long history of New England thought by shifting emphasis on covenant away from the complex nexus of person, church, and society to a simpler bond between the converted individual and the church.

Edwards's argument hinged upon demonstrating that there was no "visibility" to Christianity apart from actual Christianity, no participation in the institutions of God's gracious covenant without actually partaking of that covenant. As Edwards saw it, a visible saint professes "the religion of Jesus Christ," in which "piety of heart" is "vastly the most important part of that religion, and is in effect all"; a saint professes no "religion and virtue that is the result of common grace . . . but saving grace"; a saint is one in whom the heart, the key to real Christianity, is converted; a saint professes a "saving interest in [Christ] and relation to him"; and a saint is one who knows that "there is only one sort of sincerity which belongs to that covenant [of grace]; and that is a gracious sincerity."[52]

Edwards's technical exercise in definition was also his battle cry: those who were not in his sense visible saints were not saints at all. As he would later argue in *Freedom of the Will* and *Nature of True Virtue*, here he also contended that there was no permanent goodness or morality in a life that was not regenerate.[53] The antithesis was stark: "There are two competitors for the kingdom of this world, *Christ* and *Satan*; the design of a public profession of religion is, to declare on which side men are."[54]

Since there could be no equivocation concerning saintship, there could also be no equivocating about the church.[55] Edwards's great stress on conversion had thrown up a sharp ecclesiastical question—"Whether, according to the rules of Christ, any ought to be admitted to the communion and privileges of members of the visible church of Christ in complete standing, but such as are in profession, and in the eye of the church's Christian judgment, godly or gracious persons?" Edwards's answer was unequivocal: "None ought to be admitted as members of the visible church of Christ but visible and professing saints."[56] Edwards did not assume that hypocrisy would vanish under his plan, but he did maintain that those who hypocritically answered to the name of visible saints brought damnation upon themselves; moreover, they did not destroy the visible holiness of the church so long as their hypocrisy was dealt with when discovered. By contrast, the professedly unregenerate had to be excluded, since, in words that echoed John Winthrop's sermon from 1630, "the bond of Christian brotherly love" demanded that members be actually Christians.[57] In a word, Edwards's ecclesiology reflected his belief that the effects of true grace were tangible, visible, and reliably discernible.

With this conception of the church, Edwards could not countenance his grandfather Stoddard's desire to welcome the professedly unregenerate to the

Lord's Supper. In that rite, as Edwards understood it, Christ's people shared what Christ had actually accomplished for them. Nor should the professedly unregenerate—no matter how they have been deceived into considering themselves Half-Way members or "visible" members by national covenant—expect baptism for their children, since "the baptism of infants is the seal of those promises made to the seed of the righteous." The sacraments, both baptism and the Lord's Supper, were expressly "covenant privileges."[58]

By defining the sacraments in this light, Edwards overturned a century's evolution of covenantal thought. For him, baptism and the Lord's Supper sealed the covenant of grace, strictly defined, not a Half-Way Covenant or a national covenant. Edwards's words repeated Solomon Stoddard's attack on the integration of covenants but switched the categories: "The New Testament informs us but of one covenant God enters into with mankind through Christ, and that is the covenant of grace." This covenant, in which grace is given to the recipient and the recipient pledges to love and obey God, takes place in the heart and is confirmed through the sacraments, which "by their own act publicly confirm and seal this covenant."[59] No basis exists for postulating an "external" as opposed to the "internal" covenant. The notion of an "external" covenant is a fiction that greatly obscured the reality of God's truly gracious dealings with humanity: "The New Testament affords no more foundation for supposing two real and properly distinct covenants of grace, than it does to suppose two sorts of real Christians."[60]

Outraged responses to this reasoning were not surprising. In Northampton and other New England towns, covenant privileges, no matter how modified by traditional Puritan qualifications, had become crucial for family well-being and social wholeness.[61] Opponents of revival did not usually take offense at what Edwards and like-minded ministers preached about sin and salvation, since with only a few exceptions most of these opponents also preached a Calvinism stressing the traditional requirement for repentance and grace. Yet they were deeply offended by the threat that Edwards represented to New England families and society as a whole.

The sense that Edwards was undermining something very important led his Northampton opponents to seek a champion. The champion they found turned out to be Edwards's cousin Solomon Williams (1700–1776) of Lebanon, Connecticut.[62] Williams, as it happens, had supported the revival in its early days. On the visible purity of the church, however, Williams could not follow his learned cousin. Rather in an orgy of his own erudition, Williams's *True State of the Question concerning the Qualifications Necessary to Lawful Communion in the Christian Sacraments* argued that both external and internal covenants were valid, that Edwards confused entering "into Covenant, with keeping Covenant," that the Lord's Supper sealed not the covenant of grace itself but an "engagement to fulfill it," and that the undisputed reality of hypocrisy invalidated Edwards's attempt to segregate the regenerate from the unregenerate.[63]

Behind these essentially theological arguments, however, lay a concern for the traditional New England community. Williams introduced his essay

by taking for granted that Edwards's plan would disrupt society: "I apprehended the reviving that Dispute was needless, and that it would be attended
with unhappy Consequences, especially at a Time so divided, and distracted,
as the present State of the Country is: when *Arminian, Independent, Antinomian* Errors, if not worse, are spreading, and propagated with so much
Diligence, and Zeal." Later Williams tried to tar Edwards with the brush of
"the *Anabaptists*, and *Independents*," accused him of aiding the Church of
England and "the independent Antinomian Separations," and even linked him
with "the Romish priests" who tyrannize their congregations.[64] Williams's
readers in 1751 knew that Arminianism meant the Church of England (and a
few liberal clergymen in Boston). Tutored by the colonists who were beginning to exploit the categories of Real Whig political reasoning, more of their
fellows were coming to think that the Church of England constituted as grave
a threat to the civil and religious liberties of New England as did the Roman
Catholic Church.[65] They knew that Anabaptism meant the kind of civil disorder that had ravaged Münster during the Reformation. And they had to look
no farther than neighboring towns to see Separates and Baptists following
the logic of Edwards's scheme to its apparent conclusions in an antinomian
disregard for the laws of Massachusetts and Connecticut.[66] Edwards may have
scored technical points by his own theological erudition, but the abrogation
of interlocking covenants was too dangerously revolutionary. The gravest
threat posed by Edwards was to society; to contain this threat Williams entered the literary battle.[67]

It is necessary to state matters clearly about Edwards's concern for society. In some respects, Edwards remained a traditional Puritan who believed
that God, self, church, and society were intimately interconnected. Like his
grandfather Stoddard he could speak (at least into the 1740s) of New England
as a people in covenant with God.[68] Yet Edwards also departed from the
Puritan heritage by failing to use the covenant—or any other biblically derived metaphor—as an integrating platform linking God, self, church, and
society. It is not true, as H. Richard Niebuhr and Perry Miller both contended,
that Edwards had no interest in politics. But both Niebuhr and Miller, though
shaky on details, were correct on the main point—Edwards's vision for a
virtuous society sustained no organic theological relationship to his vision
for regenerated hearts and a purified church.[69]

Rather, when Edwards spoke of religion, his vision contracted. Late in his
time at Northampton, he even began to question the time-honored notion,
which he had once preached routinely, that New England was a covenanted
people. Since the New Testament, he wrote in 1749, "informs us but of one
covenant God enters into with mankind through Christ, and that is the covenant of grace," and since the "covenant with the patriarchs contained other
things that were appendages to that everlasting covenant of grace . . . [such
as] those that annexed the blessing to the land of Canaan, and the progeny of
Isaac and Jacob," it was a delusion to think that New England as a whole
enjoyed a special covenant with God. Whatever Edwards had thought earlier, by the late 1740s he held that Israel was a type of spiritual blessings to

come in the gospel, not of other geographic countries or national peoples that would arise under God's special blessing.[70]

Edwards's farewell sermon at Northampton on 1 July 1750 illustrates his single-mindedness in defending the covenant of grace. In this memorable performance he maintained that his entire ministry, including promotion of the ecclesiastical policy for which he was being sacked, was based on "the gospel-covenant." In contrast to Williams who feared for the prosperity of society if Edwards's practice prevailed, Edwards feared for society if erroneous doctrine should take hold.[71] For Edwards, ecclesiastical and social covenants were as the moon in the glance of the midday sun of the covenant of grace.

Of course, as a well-bread scion of the New England Way, Edwards denied vehemently that he was a sectarian, or a "separate," bent on destroying the social order. In prefaces to the *Humble Inquiry* and the farewell sermon, Edwards denounced "unjustifiable *separations . . . censorious outcries* against the standing minister and churches in general . . . [the] assuming, self-confident, contentious, uncharitable *separating spirit*; . . . with [its] many other extravagant and wicked ways."[72] In the heat of the controversy over church membership, however, Edwards's defense of an exalted covenant of grace certainly appeared to be sectarian, and by the standards of New England's Puritan history, it was. As displayed sharply in *Humble Inquiry* and *Misrepresentations Corrected*, the covenant for Edwards no longer served as an all-embracing theological rationale. To make the covenant more powerful for the church, Edwards was willing to relinquish its all-purpose functions for society. It was precisely this move that also spelled the dissolution of Puritan theology as the all-purpose guardian of thought.

Broader Significance

In its wake the Great Awakening left at least five distinct ecclesiastical factions in New England, each of which appropriated a different aspect of the covenant. Separatist and Baptist radicals followed out Edwardsean themes to what they considered logical conclusions and applied the covenant only to themselves and their gathered churches. New Light non-Separates like Edwards maintained formal allegiance to an integrated system of covenants but came to deny that membership in the social covenant conferred ecclesiastical privileges under the covenant of grace. Old Calvinist traditionalists, unwilling to chose between the covenant for individuals and the covenant for New England, defended the standing order as an adequate protection for the health of both religion and society. Rationalistic Congregationalists and latitudinarian Anglicans opted for the social covenant at the expense of the personal covenant of grace and sought to create a haven from the strife generated by revivals. Somewhat later a party of moderate Calvinists self-consciously altered Edwards's views on human nature and divine purpose in order to preserve his goals for evangelism and church renewal.

Significantly, Jonathan Edwards made his most forceful practical arguments about the nature of the covenant at exactly the time when the general
effects of revivalistic Calvinism and the general drift of New England history
were pushing toward new forms of thought. If the covenant was breaking apart
as the prime metaphor for theological integration, it did not mean that New
Englanders abandoned the search for intellectual integration as such. What
surfaced as a replacement for the covenant was a mélange of themes, forged
together by the fervor of the new evangelical piety and the heat of political
conflict. In particular, the revival's shaking effects were the occasion for New
Englanders to seek other means for shoring up the weakened canopy of biblically oriented covenant theology. For many, the answer was some form of
republican political theory, which seemed to be, as elsewhere in the Atlantic
world, in the words of Alasdair MacIntyre, "the project of *restoring* a community of virtue."[73]

The new trope of theological integration has been called "civil millennialism," "the sanctification of American Nationalism," or "Christian republicanism."[74] Whatever it is called, this new integrating construct retained aspects of the Puritan covenant, especially the conviction that God actively
punished evil and directly rewarded piety. But after 1750—in the wake of
increasingly republican perceptions, accelerating participation in the crisis
of empire, and fragmenting force of the Puritan covenant—evil increasingly
came to be styled "vice" and piety "virtue." As these new usages prevailed,
concepts from political ideology and political economy secured a place in the
language of theology, and forces were unleashed that led to the displacement
of clergymen as supreme intellectual authorities. Vestiges of the older Puritan usage continued to bestow a diffuse aura of sacred earnestness on public
spokesmen who could enlist covenantal vocabulary for their own purposes.
With the theological covenant in disarray, however, new languages, defined
by the needs of the mid-eighteenth century instead of the early seventeenth,
were reestablishing the bond between private faith and public life.

Jonathan Edwards's works of 1749 and 1752 appeared in a brief interlude
between the two imperial wars that did give a tremendous impetus to the new
political ideology. For the general public, Edwards's reasoning about the
church was much less urgent than news about the battles and negotiations of
these wars. For what happened after he passed from the scene, ideologically
as well as theologically, Edwards was not responsible. Certainly the power
of his reasoning about the covenantal bond between redeemed individuals
and a purified church cut through a measure of ambiguity that had grown up
around the notion of covenant in New England's history. Certainly as well,
one can imagine a counterfactual history in which New Light churches, taking their cue from Edwards, strictly maintained his covenant of grace and so
stopped speaking of social and political affairs as if they shared in the history
of salvation. If New Light clergy did continue to regard the imperial conflicts
of the eighteenth century as pertaining to the history of salvation and did not
turn aside to the kind of sectarianism adumbrated in Edwards's ecclesiastical
works, it is a function of their histories and not of Edwards's.

Yet what Edwards did in his effort to reattach the converted individual to a purified church was to weaken the covenant as a general canopy for theological reflection. For better and for worse, it meant a great deal that New England never produced in the second half of the eighteenth century a figure such as Edwards had been in the first half of the century—that is, a Christian thinker able to perform the discriminating surgery on republican conceptions of virtue, vice, slavery, tyranny, and liberty that Edwards performed on his era's new affectional ethics and its Newtonian science. Because there never arose an Edwards to take the measure of republican political ideology, the Edwards that did exist—the Edwards who highlighted but also dismembered the Puritan concept of covenant—had the effect in his writing of weakening one era's theological canopy without offering anything to take its place and so opened thought to a subtle, yet powerful, move from theology to politics, and intellectual leadership to a shift from the clergy to men of state.

II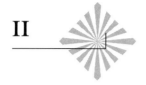

SYNTHESIS

Would the being independent of England make you more free? Far, very far from it. It would hardly be possible for you to steer clear, between anarchy and tyranny. But suppose, after numberless dangers and mischiefs, you should settle into one or more republics: would a republican government give you more liberty, either religious or civil? By no means. No governments under heaven are so despotic as the republican: no subjects are governed in so arbitrary a manner, as those of a commonwealth.
  —John Wesley, *A Calm Address to Our American Colonies*, 1775

Republican forms of government are the best repositories of the Gospel: I therefore suppose they are intended as preludes to a glorious manifestation of its power and influence upon the hearts of men. The language of these free and equal governments seems to be like that of John the Baptist of old, "Prepare ye the way of the Lord—make his paths strait."
  —Benjamin Rush, letter to Elhanan Winchester, 12 November 1791

Republicanism and Religion

The American Exception

During the last decade of the eighteenth century, public life in Great Britain and North America was filled with conflict and foreboding. The progress of the Revolution in France from lofty humanitarianism to armed bloodshed first inspired, then perplexed, and finally terrified large numbers of English-speakers on both sides of the Atlantic. Once again Britain mobilized to wage yet another war in the seemingly endless series of engagements with France that now stretched back far beyond the memory of any living Briton. In Scotland, hints of radicalism were enough to precipitate a full-scale reaction in favor of King George III, Prime Minister Pitt, and the king's Scottish lieutenants. In Ireland, a decade of mounting unrest culminated in 1798 with rebellion and the invasion of a French army. Regular British troops, assisted by loyal Irish yeomanry, savagely put down the rebels and easily overcame the invaders. Yet aftershocks of this failed revolution—including the end of a separate Irish parliament and the eclipse of incipient cooperation between Catholics and Protestants—have long afflicted the island. In the United States, the tempered optimism inspired by the Constitution and the reassuring presence of George Washington as head of the new government did not survive Washington's tenure in office. From the mid-1790s, civil unrest, class warfare, and political strife, all accompanied by rabid attack journalism, disturbed American public life. The United States' international fortunes were also precarious, with the major European powers, including France, its crucial ally in the War for Independence, preying on American ships and menacing the new nation's fragile borders. An even greater fragility marked British settlements in Canada, where a thin population, spread from Louisbourg on Cape

Breton Island to the northern shores of Lake Ontario, looked to a distracted mother country for protection. Canadian leaders faced the immense task of governing a disparate collection of communities: the Quebecois were Catholic and French, while in Nova Scotia and Ontario a motley collection of Loyalists forced out of the United States, other Americans eager for cheap land, and a sprinkling of settlers from Europe competed for existence.[1]

As they had done during periods of public crisis for more than a century, Christian believers in the North Atlantic region were driven by invasion, rebellion, ideological strife, and attendant social disorder to a restatement of social and religious first principles. Much was shared in the pronouncements of ministers, lay believers, and ecclesiastical bodies throughout the English-speaking world during these crises.[2] The region's hereditary Protestantism offered a wide repertoire of standard biblical passages, familiar sermonic conventions, and well-worn jeremiads from earlier times of social unrest. In England, Scotland, Ireland, and the Canadas, as well as in the United States, the faithful gathered at special days of fast and thanksgiving to pray for peace, ministers rang the changes on connections between social well-being and godliness, and congregations were called to repentance. But on one account the statements of American Protestants differed substantially from those made elsewhere in the North Atlantic world. American Christians, despite substantial conflicts among themselves, took for granted a fundamental compatibility between orthodox Protestant religion and republican principles of government. Most English-speaking Protestants outside the United States did not.

Americans have long been accustomed to think of the values of religion and the values of republicanism as supporting each other. The bitterness of the Civil War, for example, was due at least in part to the intensity with which both North and South defended conflicting visions of "Christian liberty." To this day, the Pledge of Allegiance—by conjoining "one nation *under God* with *liberty* and justice for all"—testifies to a resilient intermixture of religious and republican vocabularies. The long American habit of uniting these value systems has dulled awareness of how strikingly original the new nation's "Christian republicanism" actually was. In fact, among a panoply of exceptional things about the American founding, one of the most unusual was the commitment by almost all religious people in the new United States to a distinctly republican vision of public life. This American position was unusual, not only by comparison with English-speaking contemporaries in the late eighteenth century, but also because almost all observers outside the United States assumed that republican thinking contradicted the principles of traditional religion.

For the writing of theology in the American environment, this confluence of republican and Christian allegiances was critical. What the Puritan canopy had once supplied as a boundary for theology, America's republican Christian convictions would provide for later generations. To illustrate the singularity of this context for theological formation, it is useful to cite comments by Dietrich Bonhoeffer after he visited the United States in the 1930s. Bonhoeffer saw everywhere the presence of popular republican assumptions:

"America calls herself the land of the free. Under this term today she understands the right of the individual to independent thought, speech and action. In this context, religious freedom is, for the American, an obvious possession." To Bonhoeffer, it was especially noteworthy that "praise of this freedom may be heard from pulpits everywhere." It was even more noteworthy what he took this freedom to signify: it "means possibility, the possibility of unhindered activity given by the world to the church." For a history of American theology it is important to see why Bonhoeffer thought the Americans he observed at church in New York, New England, and the South were making a mistake. To Bonhoeffer it was not axiomatic that a republican exaltation of freedom merged smoothly with Christianity. Rather, he held that "the freedom of the church is not where it has possibilities, but only where the Gospel really and in its own power makes room for itself on earth, even and precisely when no such possibilities are offered to it. The essential freedom of the church is not a gift of the world to the church, but the freedom of the Word of God itself to gain a hearing." In fact, he even thought that the American fascination with freedom might presage a decline—"a church which is free in this way becomes secularised more quickly than a church which does not possess freedom or possibility." His conclusion was that "freedom as an institutional possession is not an essential mark of the church," since "whether the churches of God are really free can only be decided by the actual preaching of the Word of God."[3] Bonhoeffer's assessment of America arose out of his own involvement in the German church struggle, but it nonetheless remains an important modern reminder of the singularity of America's Christian republicanism. To grasp something of that republicanism will also be to grasp something essential about the Christian theologians who took it up.

The Meaning of Republicanism

The republicanism of the early United States provided a vocabulary for resisting British tyranny, offered a framework for the Constitution, and established norms for public behavior in the new nation. These republican commitments were, however, more a soft-edged series of ideals than a sharply defined set of principles. In the early 1790s Tom Paine complained about this lack of precision: "It has always been the political craft of courtiers and court governments to abuse something which they called republicanism; but what republicanism was, or is, they never attempt to explain."[4] Yet the absence of a settled definition did not stop public figures from trying to impose order on the concept.

Writing in *The Federalist*, for example, Alexander Hamilton held that "the corner stone of republican government" was simply "the prohibition of titles of nobility." Thomas Jefferson provided a more elaborate, but equally concrete, definition: he felt that if Virginia could outlaw entail and primogeniture, end tax support of religion, and provide for a system of universal public education, the result would be "a system by which every fibre would be eradicated of antient or future aristocracy; and a foundation laid for a government truly republican." John Adams reasoned in more abstract terms: The "true and only definition of a republic," he wrote in 1787, was "a government, in which all men, rich and poor, magistrates and subjects, officers and people, masters and servants, the first citizen and the last, are equally subject to the laws." At just about the same time James Madison defined a republic as "a government in which the scheme of representation takes place." For his part, Paine held that republicanism, in contrast to monarchy, which led rulers to use "arbitrary power" in promoting their own interests, was "government established and conducted for the interest of the public, as well individually, as collectively." Paine also concluded that "the government of America, which is wholly on the system of representation, is the only real republic in character and practice that now exists."[5] Such wide variation demands that historians respect the flexibility of the term.

Yet despite a wide range of definitions, American republican language returned consistently to two main themes: fear of abuses from illegitimate power and a nearly messianic belief in the benefits of liberty. It presupposed, in the succinct summary of Blair Worden, that "man is a citizen, not (like Hobbes' man) a subject." Moreover, "his citizenship is dependent on the free exercise of his virtue and of his reason, and upon his participation, as an elector of representatives and as arms-bearer, in the communal affairs of his country."[6] Early American republicanism was a fluid construct because patriots were heirs to several overlapping political traditions, beginning with the civic humanism of Machiavelli and the Renaissance city-states of northern Italy. Especially important from this originating source was the emphasis upon reason as the means for attaining freedom from outside domination and for political participation.[7] To this strand, seventeenth-century English history added the ideology of the "commonwealthmen" who had defended the prerogatives of local communities against both divine-right monarchy and the Puritans' biblical absolutism.[8] The term "republicanism," in the sense of a system at odds with monarchy and the ancient church-state establishment, was a new coinage at the end of the seventeenth century.[9] After the Glorious Revolution of 1688 and the accession of the Hanovers in 1715, republican ideas mostly percolated beneath the surface of respectable society in England, Scotland, and Ireland. The most ardent spokesmen for liberty and those most alert to corruption in high places were known as Real Whigs because they wanted the principles of 1688 carried to what they thought were logical conclusions.[10] These Whigs usually represented "country" interests opposing the venal machinations of the power-engrossing "court."[11] From these civic humanist, commonwealth, and country sources, Britain's Real Whigs supplied a vocabulary that became ubiquitous in the American colonies from the midcentury wars with France through the Revolution, the years of the Confederation, the debate over the Constitution, and into the new nation.

That vocabulary reflected a consistent view of the political world. In this picture, the exercise of government was thought to enhance human flourishing if it could be structured to preserve freedom; but if government arbitrarily abridged liberty, the result could only be individual degradation and national decline. The critical oppositions were virtue against corruption, liberty against slavery. To preserve freedom, especially the freedom to control one's own property, the leaders of state as well as citizens with access to public power had to comport themselves with what Machiavelli styled *virtù*, a term that his early English editors rendered as "public spirit" but that eventually came to be ambiguously translated "virtue."[12] By contrast, if power were allowed to accumulate without check, if competition for power encouraged "factions" to promote their private interests, or if a love of luxury supplanted the exercise of public-spirited service, then corruption followed inevitably. The unchecked progress of vice, in turn, destroyed individuals, society, and states. No one set of concrete political applications flowed from these convictions— early republicans were, for example, usually not in favor of democracy, since they distrusted mob action almost as much as aristocratic decadence. Defenders of republican principles did usually support mixed governments and political systems with self-conscious checks and balances. Moreover, the republican interpretation of history usually held that the "common good" (common weal = commonwealth, the usual English word to translate *res publica*) of "the people" was the main victim of the corrupt engrossment of power. Thus, republicans came to display more willingness to strengthen the democratic part of government than did their contemporaries. By the 1790s most American and the more radical European republicans like Tom Paine held monarchy to be a contradiction of republican values, though many earlier republicans had not carried their principles to that conclusion.[13]

The central republican conviction was belief in the reciprocity of personal morality and social well-being. Changes over time did take place in what personal morality and a healthy society meant, but underneath those changes endured a remarkably fixed alliance between a language of liberty and a language of virtue. Virtue, originally defined as disinterested public service transcending the passions, promoted freedom and social well-being; vice, marked especially by luxury, self-seeking, idleness, and frivolity, promoted tyranny and social decay.

Republicanism versus Religion

These republican themes have been so widely embraced by both religious and nonreligious Americans that it is now difficult to understand why defenders of traditional religion once looked with such suspicion on civic humanist, commonwealth, Real Whig, and country convictions. Yet such suspicion was in fact the norm until the unusual convergence of republicanism and Christianity in the American founding.

Traditional Christian complaints were recited for several centuries as a common litany: Republican instincts prized human self-sufficiency more highly than dependence upon God. They demeaned the life to come by focusing without reservation on this-worldly existence. They defined the human good in terms of public usefulness instead of divine approval. Both Protestants and Catholics, in addition, regularly noted the persistent correlation of republican political convictions and heterodox theological opinions. The discourse of virtue, vice, liberty, and tyranny seemed always to be associated with the rejection of innate human sinfulness, with views on human salvation that dispensed with the substitutionary work of Christ, with opinions about Jesus treating him as no more than an unusual human being, and, in the most extreme cases, with arguments denying the existence of God altogether.

The evidence prompting Christian suspicion of republican traditions was not difficult to find. Machiavelli, for instance, was known to have quoted with approval the words of Francesco Guicciardini: "I love my native city more than my soul." His merciless approach to political enemies—"when the safety of one's country wholly depends on the decision to be taken, no attention should be paid either to justice or to injustice, to kindness or cruelty, or to its being praiseworthy or ignominious"—hardly came up to the standards of Christian charity.[14] In addition, Machiavelli's tendency to speak of a well-ordered state as one where *virtù* overcame the blind forces of *fortuna* was equally far from Christian views of providence.[15]

The seventeenth century presented a mixed picture to the doctrinally orthodox who worried about the religious roots of political innovation. In the Netherlands, self-consciously republican opinions were advanced from the 1650s. When proposed by thinkers like Benedict Spinoza, they were associated with efforts to subordinate traditional religion to the new-model state. Yet other Dutch leaders, like Rabod Scheels (Schelius) of Ofverijssel, who wrote a tract called *Libertas publica* during the first war with Cromwell's England (1652–1654), sounded more like later American Christian republicans in arguing for the necessity of religion as the moral guarantor of political stability.[16]

The years of Civil War and interregnum in England (1642–1660) were as disruptive ideologically as they were politically and militarily. One of the results of the traumas of those years are modern debates among historians as to whether the republican commonwealthmen of the Civil War continued, or departed from, the civic humanism of the Machiavellian tradition, and whether any, some, or all of the reformist political thought between the Restoration (1660) and the end of the century, including Locke's *Two Treatises of Government* from the early 1690s, was continuous with the republicanism of the revolutionary period.[17]

An alliance between orthodox Christianity and republican views arose from the Parliamentary coalition of Puritans and commonwealthmen in the 1640s. In his autobiography, the prolific Presbyterian writer Richard Baxter described "two sorts of Men" who had eventually found themselves in Parliament. One was not particularly concerned about cleaning up the Anglican church but was rather interested in mounting a defense against "Arbitrary Government" that would make them "slaves." These ones, Baxter reported, were "the People called *Good Commonwealth's Men*." The second group "were the more Religious Men," who, while not indifferent to political abuses, concentrated much more on rolling back the monarch's efforts to root out Puritan religious practices. Although the two groups pursued different agendas, they nonetheless found it easy to cooperate "because these later agreed with the former in the Vindication of the Peoples Propriety and Liberties, the former did the easilier concur with them against the Proceedings of the Bishops and High Commission Court."[18] The Puritan-republican cooperation was also based on shared ethical values, which coincided, as Blair Worden has noted, in their emphasis "on frugality, industry and sobriety, on 'honest poverty,' on the fundamental distinction between liberty and license, and on the evils of luxury and of sloth."[19]

However much they agreed in opposing monarchical tyranny and promoting self-sacrificing morality, Puritans and republicans nonetheless inhabited different moral universes. Oliver Cromwell, the greatest lay Puritan, was thoroughly pragmatic in his efforts to heed providence—he could favor republican-like measures when they seemed to work (1649–1653) but just as easily lapse into the quasi-monarchical style of the Protectorate (1653–1658). Most important, the intellectual instincts of Puritans and republicans operated differently. Puritans built their lives around trust in providence, they relied on Scripture and prayer, and they exalted the divine grace that chose the elect for salvation.[20] In their forthright supernaturalism, Puritans were more medieval than modern. While Puritans did promote reason, learning, and careful attention to the world, their main concern was superrational fellowship with God.[21] By contrast, Marchamont Needham, James Harrington, John Milton, and others who in the 1650s created the English republican tradition, trusted preeminently in human reason, relied upon a study of history, Aristotle, and other classical authorities, and relativized religion by treating it primarily as a prop for the virtue required in republican commonwealths. Republicans were modern in their this-worldly rationality. While some did not despise piety, all of them sought classically defined *virtù* above all.

Milton was a special case, but one that demonstrates why later defenders of Christian orthodoxy would be so suspicious of republicanism in whatever shape it appeared. When he was most actively promoting commonwealth convictions as a pamphleteer for Parliament and then Cromwell, Milton was also busy shucking off the orthodox Christian certainties of traditional Reformed Protestantism. The most ardently republican Milton was also the Milton who rejected Calvinism for Arminianism, who gave up Presbyterianism, and who exchanged the Trinity for an Arian or Socinian view of Christ.[22] Blair Worden has pointed out, not only that Satan has the best lines in *Paradise Lost*, but that most of those lines are republican complaints against God's tyrannical power. Worden notes also, however, that most of *Paradise Lost* was written as Milton was disengaging from politics and that *Paradise Regained*, which pictures a Christ who rejected political power of all kinds, testified to a decisive change in Milton's own opinions.[23] In other words, Milton himself came to repudiate the ardent republicanism that the devil of *Paradise Lost* propounded so vigorously.

Milton's Puritanism was ambiguous; Richard Baxter's was not. When in 1659 Baxter published his views on what an ideal "holy commonwealth" should look like, that picture was theocratic and defended pious rule by the saints. Baxter's ideal state was not republican in the least: "In a divine commonwealth the honour and pleasing of God and the salvation of the people are the principal ends, and their corporal welfare but subordinate to these."[24] For Baxter, the proper respect due to divine honor completely superseded republican fixation on human honor.

In a careful analysis of the religion of James Harrington, whose *Oceana* of 1656 was the era's fullest statement of republican principle, Mark Goldie has spelled out the conditions under which republican and Puritan views could move beyond simple cooperation against a common foe. The key, according to Goldie, was the softening of Puritan theological orthodoxy: when Puritans remained committed to traditional Christian ideas of human depravity, the sovereignty of divine grace, and the need for a revelation from God, they also remained antagonistic to republican ideas. But, in Goldie's account, "Wherever puritan thought leaned towards acceptance of the possibility of universal salvation and hence of universal priesthood, or to the Socinian idea that Christ was God-in-humanity, then Puritanism became as intensely secular and naturalistic as it was Biblical and Apocalyptic."[25] Most observers in the seventeenth and eighteenth centuries would have agreed. It was only when Christian orthodoxy gave way that republicanism could flourish.

Whatever possibility may have existed for an orthodox Christian republicanism in the 1640s and 1650s vanished completely by the end of the century. The bond between civic humanism and heresy was cemented in the minds of both proponents and opponents when John Toland (1670–1722) in the 1690s republished the republican tracts of the Civil War era. For our purposes, it is important to note that Toland remains an important figure in the history of thought for his vigorous promotion of rational religion, as in the deist tract *Christianity Not Mysterious* (1696) and in his naturalistic explanations for the miracles of the New Testament. Toland was the ideological bridge between the seventeenth-century commonwealthmen and the eighteenth-century Real Whigs.[26]

The bearing of John Locke's political writings on the genealogy of republicanism as well as on the issue of Christian-political connections should by rights be discussed fully at this juncture. Locke, though an ally of the republican stalwart Algernon Sidney, is famous for developing theories of rights, social contract, and civic individualism that are often held to constitute a liberal alternative to the republican tradition. Since, however, the question of how Protestants in the early United States may have exploited Lockean elements alongside republican principles is treated below in chapter 11, it will be enough here to make only two points. The first is to question whether Lockeanism and republicanism should be regarded as antithetical.[27] At least from the perspective of the late seventeenth century—when Locke was working with those who wanted to prevent the Roman Catholic James II from succeeding to the throne in 1685 (the Exclusion Crisis) and when he moved toward publishing the *Two Treatises of Government*—Locke was pursuing the same goals as the radical republicans. The second point is to observe that some contemporary critics regarded Locke's weakening on traditional views of Christ as connected to the same subversion of godly social order as republicans were accused of promoting.[28] In their original contexts, the distinction between Lockean liberalism and seventeenth-century republicanism may have been a matter of emphasis rather than a sharp antithesis.

Contributions to republican thinking in the early eighteenth century did nothing to assuage orthodox Christian concerns. Thomas Chubb (1679–1747), the English radical artisan whose assertions about human freedom were the target for the crushing response of Jonathan Edwards's *Freedom of the Will* (1754), was notorious at the start of the century as both an antitrinitarian and a Real Whig.[29] In the 1720s the publicists John Trenchard and Thomas Gordon provided a version of Real Whig ideology that came to be well known in the colonies. Among the major principles of their newspaper, the *Independent Whig*, was straightforward advocacy of human reason over religious authority: "Why did we, or how could we, leave *Popery*, and embrace the *Reformation*, but because our own *private Reason* told us; and *Scripture*, of which we made *our selves the Judges*, told us? . . . As we must judge from Scripture what is Orthodoxy; so we must judge from Reason, what is Scripture."[30] Into the mid-nineteenth century it remained a staple of religious history to regard the injurious influence of the *Independent Whig* and to note that these tracts were "manifestly written by a man [*sic*] of no religion."[31]

An even more influential text was the Baron de Montesquieu's *Spirit of the Laws*, which became prominent in the republican canon after its publication in 1748. In the opening assertions of this work, Montesquieu went out of his way to set his ideals apart from traditional religion: "What I distinguish by the name of virtue, in a republic, is the love of one's country, that is, the love of equality. It is not a moral, nor a Christian, but a political virtue; and it is the spring which sets the republican government in motion, as honor is the spring which gives motion to monarchy. . . . [T]he honest man of whom we treat . . . is not the Christian, but the political honest man, who is possessed of the political virtue there mentioned."[32] Montesquieu's disavowal was no surprise in the mid-eighteenth century, since it seemed only another illustration of the elective affinity between republican politics and heterodox religion.

Observers from the early sixteenth century through the eighteenth took it for granted that such sub-Christian understandings of the political world would naturally coincide with suborthodox understandings of Christianity itself. A long line of distinguished modern historians—including Caroline Robbins on the English commonwealthmen, J. G. A. Pocock on Machiavelli, Paul Rahe on the republican traditions more generally, J. C. D. Clark on eighteenth-century English society, and J. B. Schneewind on the rise of moral philosophy—has documented the persistent link between republicanism and such heterodox views as Socinianism, Arianism, Unitarianism, and atheism.[33] Of special note is the tie between republican views of human nature that transferred responsibility for the health of society from God to humanity and unorthodox views (whether Socinian or Arian) of the person of Christ. For the latter, Jesus was a good man and valuable for his example of personal morality, but he was not the Son of God, whose saving work opened the only door to human salvation.

It is not necessary to agree completely with Jonathan Clark, who has drawn the strongest conclusions about such links, to recognize that Clark has done historians a great service by documenting the strong bond between political and religious radicalism that many observers perceived in the early modern period. In Clark's view, "all forms of radicalism in early-modern England had a religious origin,"[34] and the presence of radical politics inevitably signaled the presence of theological heterodoxy. By noting "the association of radical contractarian and even republican politics with religious heterodoxy," Clark has generalized the specific insights of a number of historians, including J. G. A. Pocock, who once remarked on the "high degree of correlation in the early eighteenth century between neo-Harringtonian republicanism and deism."[35] Clark's full statement of the logic he finds at work in the opposition between republican tradition and Christian orthodoxy is worth quoting at length, however, since it reveals what the later American ease in merging republicanism and traditional religion has obscured:

> Arianism and Socinianism shared with Deism one novel consequence. The more unnecessary the doctrine of the atonement, the more it could be presumed that man was inherently benevolent; it followed that he was corrupted, or enslaved, only by outside forces (that is, by other people). Nurture rather than nature was prioritised; and the more that the human condition or the workings of divine Providence were excused, the more the blame for society's ills had to be laid at the door of minorities of wicked individuals. The tyranny of sin was subtly transformed into the tyranny of kings and bishops. It was a trope of eighteenth-century historiography that detailed, inner knowledge of public affairs disclosed how great events were the result of small and personal causes; the heterodox imagination seized on this insight and inflated it into self-sustaining conspiracy theories. . . . Even in the absence of formal theological millenarianism, the discourse of late-eighteenth-century heterodox Dissent became increasingly preoccupied with threats of persecution in its perceptions of slavery and corruption, increasingly strident in its invective against civil and ecclesiastical tyrants. To interpret this construction of a social demonology as part of a process of the secularisation of politics is to miss the doctrinal origins of these secular commitments and the theological context in which these social dramas were played out.[36]

If, as I hope to show, the course of American circumstances overrode the internal logic that Clark documents, his rendering of the affinity between republican politics and heretical theology faithfully identifies the religious reasons why so many proponents of classical Christianity so often bemoaned the advance of dissenting political opinions.

This link between republicanism and theological heresy provoked a steady drumbeat of criticism from major religious leaders throughout the early modern period. In the mid-sixteenth century, John Calvin, almost certainly with Machiavelli in view, blasted "the flatterers of princes, immoderately praising their power, [who] do not hesitate to set them against the rule of God himself."[37] Later that century the chief intellectual architect of Anglicanism, Richard Hooker, expressed similar opinions. In the summary statement of Paul Rahe, "Above all else, Hooker feared the influence of 'wise malignantes' such as Niccolò Machiavelli and other 'godless' men who treat religion as 'a meere politique devise' and therefore 'extoll the wisdom of Paganisme.'"[38]

This expressly religious suspicion of republican ideas continued in the new world. The American Samuel Johnson was outraged when Trenchard and Gordon's *Independent Whig* was reprinted in New York City at midcentury. To Johnson as a traditional Anglican, the Real Whig arguments were "pernicious" outbursts from "famous infidel authors."[39] He was not alone in these opinions. Other New Yorkers accused the sponsors of the *Independent Reflector*, where Trenchard and Gordon were reprinted, of being atheists and noted that its publisher, James Parker, had been indicted for "blasphemous libel" against Christianity only shortly before reprinting these English Real Whig opinions.[40]

The perception of a natural connection between republican views of the political world and heterodox opinions in religion long remained a constant on the Continent.[41] Even in the English-speaking world, the older instincts died hard. In the 1830s the British visitor Richard Gooch had nothing but scorn for America's vaunted republicanism, since he thought the fact of slavery instantly revealed the hypocrisy of American ideology.[42] When after Europe's convulsive revolutions of 1848 a number of German socialists migrated to the United States, some American ministers commented with worry on how eagerly these antireligious newcomers embraced the nation's historical language of republican liberty. In the days before the Civil War, John Hughes, Roman Catholic bishop of New York, was distressed by what he regarded as the atheistic republicanism of extreme antislave groups. About the same time, a high-church Anglican, looking across the Atlantic from England in 1863, sniffed that the North was nothing but "a lawless military republic"—that is, as defender of godlessness and vice.[43]

The history of antagonism between republicanism and traditional Christianity therefore poses a major interpretive problem, since, in the carefully chosen words of philosopher Charles Taylor, "for all the well-documented tensions between Christianity and the republican tradition, the United States starts its career by linking the two closely together."[44]

America Contrasted with Britain and Canada

The most notable fact about the ideology of the early United States is not that well-known founders like Benjamin Franklin and Thomas Jefferson, or even George Washington and James Madison, advocated republican politics. These statesmen, though in many ways profoundly religious, did not uphold traditional Christian convictions. On the contrary, their high opinion of unredeemed human nature (or at least of the elite, who cultivated the classical traits of honor, magnanimity, and *virtù*), as well as an exalted understanding of their own reasoning capacity, were the kind of heterodox religious opinions that had long been associated with republican views.

Rather, the remarkable development was that these deists and Unitarians were joined in embracing republicanism by Protestant theological conservatives representing the older British churches, by rambunctious promoters of new-breed evangelicalism, by spokesmen for traditional Protestant faiths from the Continent, by Roman Catholics, and even by representatives of what was then the tiny community of American Jews. In other contexts, these believers in traditional religion might have been expected to repudiate the republican convictions of Jefferson, Franklin, and the other heterodox founders. In fact, they did not. Rather, they set aside the antirepublican convictions that usually (when found outside the United States) accompanied their religious beliefs in order to embrace the republican politics of the founders, whose religion they rejected.

Congregationalists, Presbyterians, Anglicans, and Methodists

Historians have long recognized the Christian republicanism of American Congregationalists and Presbyterians, the denominations that ardently favored the Revolution and that furnished the most visible spokesmen after the war to explain the religious meaning of what had transpired.[45] The 1783 Connecticut election sermon by Congregationalist Ezra Stiles, president of Yale College, was one of the most dramatic expressions of the Christian-republican synthesis. To Stiles, "true religion" was necessary to perfect "our system of dominion and civil polity." In turn, "the diffusion of virtue" provided "the greatest secular happiness of the people." New England, with its relative equality of condition, had led the way in "defence of our property, liberty and country," and by so doing had "realized the capital ideas of Harrington's *Oceana*," the great defense of commonwealth principles published in 1656.[46]

Stiles's exuberant linkage of Christianity and republicanism marked out a path that many others followed. Presbyterian Elias Boudinot of New Jersey was Washington's commisary of prisoners during the war, a president of the Continental Congress, director of the Mint, and the first president of the American Bible Society. In an address for the Fourth of July, 1793, Boudinot advanced from where Stiles had left off: the War for Independence, "our miraculous deliverance from a second Egypt," had made "freedom and independence . . . the most invaluable gem of our earthly crown" and established "the rational equality and rights of men, as men and citizens." Boudinot's hope for the future was expressed as an injunction compounding Christian and republican imperatives: "On your virtue, patriotism, integrity, and submission to the laws of your own making, and the government of your own choice, do the hopes of men rest with prayers and supplications for a happy issue."[47]

Benjamin Rush (1745–1813), a leading Philadelphia physician, a signer of the Declaration of Independence, and a tireless reformer, maintained close connections to Presbyterian interests throughout a long life of spiritual searching. As a young adult, Rush was trained in revivalistic New Side Presbyterianism; at the age of twenty he also rejoiced in the efforts by Philadelphians to repudiate the Stamp Tax and so "to put a stop to arbitrary power."[48] Rush journeyed to Europe (first Edinburgh, then London and Paris) for medical training, where he also undertook a parallel education in dissenting politics. Through systematic reading of Algernon Sidney, hero of resistance to the Catholic James II in the 1680s, and conversation with several of the major republican figures of his era—Tom Paine, John Wilkes, Catherine Macaulay, James Burgh, Joseph Priestley, Adam Ferguson, and the Frenchman Jacques Barbeu Dubourg—Rush's republican leanings expanded into settled convictions.[49] In the crucible of Revolutionary America, Rush's political and religious faiths became one. From the mid-1770s into the early nineteenth century, no one in North America was a more eloquent advocate for the Christian republican synthesis. To John Adams he wrote in July 1789, "The precepts of the Gospel and the maxims of republics in many instances agree with each other." Two years later he expressed the same to the Baptist minister Elhanan Winchester: "Republican forms of government are the best repositories of the Gospel." To Thomas Jefferson in 1800, Rush was even more emphatic: "I have always considered Christianity as the *strong ground* of republicanism. The spirit is opposed, not only to the splendor, but even to the very forms of monarchy, and many of its precepts have for their objects republican liberty and equality as well as simplicity, integrity, and economy in government. It is only necessary for republicanism to ally itself to the Christian religion to overturn all the corrupted political and religious institutions in the world." In 1775 Rush had supplied Tom Paine with the title for his tract *Common Sense* and arranged for its publication. Never once did Rush doubt that his promotion of Paine's radical republicanism was a specifically Christian deed. As he wrote to Granville Sharp in England in 1783, the "language" of American independence "has for many years appeared to me to be the same as that of the heavenly host that announced the birth of the Saviour of mankind. It proclaims 'glory to God in the highest—on earth peace—good will to man.'"[50] Rush put matters as clearly as they could be put, but he was joined in such sentiments by a very wide range of influential leaders among the Congregationalists and Presbyterians.[51]

Yet even while American Congregationalists and Presbyterians articulated so strongly this Christian republicanism, their denominational contemporaries elsewhere in the English-speaking world were retreating rapidly from these same principles. In England, Independents (i.e., Congregationalists), Presbyterians, and Baptists had displayed considerable sympathy for both the American cause and republicanism during the 1770s, and some continued to do so throughout the next decade.[52] But events in the 1790s rapidly weaned old Dissenters from such convictions. The publication of Edmund Burke's *Reflections on the French Revolution* in 1790, the rapid response to Burke by Tom Paine in his *Rights of Man* (1791, 1792), which combined an ardent antimonarchism with an equally stout deism, followed almost immediately by the outbreak of war between England and France in February 1793, recalled the older British Dissent as a nearly unanimous force for the political status quo.[53]

More directly religious factors also affected Dissenting politics. In the midst of political turmoil during the century's last decade, many of the older English Dissenters began to imitate the upstart Methodists by turning to itinerant preaching as a way of reviving their churches. When Anglican leaders attacked such itineration as politically radical, Baptist and Congregational ministers vigorously affirmed their loyalty to the king and the traditional British Constitution. In 1798, for example, the Independent minister William Kingsbury wrote that village preachers were concentrating only on the doctrines of the New Testament; this kind of preaching, moreover, reinforced "good order and subordination in society, from the highest to the lowest; and [was] an utter enemy to a rebellious and levelling spirit." At almost the same time, the minister of Surrey Chapel in Southwark, Rowland Hill, went into print to defend the new Dissenting Sunday schools and to deny flatly that anyone of republican sympathies was associated with that work.[54]

Presbyterianism was the established church in Scotland and also enjoyed considerable support in the north of Ireland. Among Presbyterians in both places, a minority had been receptive to radical politics from the early eighteenth century. A large proportion had also been kindly disposed to the American Revolution. During the 1770s and 1780s broadening republican sentiments became all too visible to the authorities. Throughout most of the eighteenth century, however, the more orthodox parties in the Church of Scotland (whether confessional traditionalists or new evangelicals) did little to promote civic humanism. By contrast, links between heterodox theology and republicanism were stronger among the Moderates, who not only held their orthodoxy lightly but also promoted the new moral philosophy as a commonsense alternative to the rigors of confessional Calvinism.[55] In all Scotland, the ideological situation changed with dramatic speed following the beginning of the French Revolution and the outbreak of war between England and France. Support for Parliament rapidly became a religious duty, republicanism was interpreted as atheism, and leaders of the established Kirk vied with upstart evangelicals outside the state church to see who could disavow radical political principles with greater fervor.[56]

An indication of the shifting climate in the politics of Scottish Presbyterianism is provided by the curious career of the Reverend Charles Nisbet. In his native Scotland Nisbet had preached courageously against the British government during the American War. So strong was his attachment to republican principles that he eventually migrated to the new world. But it took only a few months on the Pennsylvania frontier as the president of struggling Dickinson College to turn Nisbet into an embittered cynic about the American experiment. When he left Montrose, Scotland, in 1785, Nisbet told his friends that America was a land of "liberty and Plenty" where people were free "from the shackles of authority" and open to persuasion by reason. Before long he had his fill of such liberty. By 1800 he was informing Scottish correspondents about how Americans construed the Bible: "In the Beginning the Sovereign People created Heaven & Earth." And he was bemoaning "the Political Errors of our Citizens" and "their Errors in Religion," which arose from "an over-weaning Conceit of themselves, or an extravagant opinion of their own wisdom."[57] Nisbet, a dangerously advanced thinker in his native Scotland, had been shaken loose from radical views by the disillusionment of actual American experience.

An even sharper reversal took place among Irish Presbyterians. Until the rebellion of 1798, both orthodox and heterodox elements in this communion had expressed some support for republican ideals, as well as considerable sympathy for the promoters of American independence.[58] But when the rebellion failed, Irish Presbyterians of all sorts fled from radical politics with dramatic finality. American Presbyterians were also chastened by the careening course of events at home and abroad in the late 1790s. But their characteristic response was to urge earnest religiosity as a way of making republican government work. Thus, in a fast-day sermon of May 1798, the rising young New York minister Samuel Miller could describe how proper religious observance ensured the health of a republican polity: "The native tendency of this divine system is, to check the insolence of power; to restrain the encroachments of oppression; to give energy to the wise prescriptions of government; to secure liberty with order."[59] Later that same month the Presbyterian General Assembly, while complaining shrilly about the decline of godliness in America, nonetheless paused to give thanks for a governmental system created by "the laws of our own making and government of our own choice" and for the blessings of "a representative government."[60]

By contrast, when the General Presbyterian Synod of Ulster gathered in late August of that same year, it took pains in three extraordinary addresses to disavow all hints of republican self-government. The first address, to King George III, rued "the Convulsions of this Skeptical and Revolutionary aera [era]" and urged him to look kindly on those loyal Presbyterians who had so recently suffered to defend "their King and Country, their Liberty, and Religion." To Ireland's lord-lieutenant, the Presbyterians reprobated "the late Attempts which have been made at Home to subvert our Government, under the specious pretext of Reforming it." And to the people at large, the Assembly urged loyalty to the king, while it expressed the hopes that the Irish in general would repudiate "the views of those who would involve this country in the incalculable Horrors of a Revolution."[61]

The contrast between American Protestants embracing a republican outlook and their fellow-Protestants outside America, who either repudiated republicanism or disavowed politics altogether, extended much further than the Congregationalists and Presbyterians. Predictably, leaders of the English state church were in the forefront of those who promoted a politics of subordination, hierarchy, and inherited prerogative.[62] To such ones the sentiments of Americans like James Madison, cousin of the president, who in 1790 became bishop of Virginia in the new American Episcopal Church, were simply incomprehensible. Bishop Madison also preached on the same fast day in early May 1798 that Samuel Miller observed. On this occasion, Madison made full use of a republican vocabulary to promote "Christian Liberty," to decry "the Filth which Ambition, Avarice, and Ignorance was heaping up around" the

Constitution, and to warn, in fine "country" fashion, of "continuous Extensions of power in the Federal Legislature & Executive, [and] the mad ambition of forming standing Armies & Navies."[63]

Anglicans outside the United States operated with very different principles. Nowhere is the contrast more pronounced than in Canada, where, though lacking a true establishment, Anglican leaders took pains to distance themselves from any hint of republicanism. The first Anglican bishop in Nova Scotia was Charles Inglis, who had been rector of Trinity Church in New York City before loyalty to the Crown made him an exile. When early in the War for Independence Inglis prepared an account of events for British officials, it was clear to him that the conflict arose from the "prevalence of Republican or Democratic, Levelling Principles" that had seduced the colonists away from the security of the British Constitution. After the publication of Tom Paine's *Common Sense* in January 1776, Inglis sought to enlist "the English Constitution," "the principles on which the glorious Revolution in 1688 was brought about," Scripture, as well as "Reason, Argument, Common Sense," to defend a moderate Whig view of monarchy and the superiority of "cool reason and judgment." To Inglis, Paine's pamphlet illustrated nothing more strongly than "the violence and rage of a republican." The republicanism that Paine promoted was especially suspect because of its ties to false religion: "It is a most notorious, undeniable fact, that the ancient republics—Rome, Carthage, Athens, &c. were as infamous for every species of the grossest and most abominable idolatry, as any monarchies whatever."[64]

During his service in Nova Scotia, Inglis had ample opportunity to restate his opinions on the connection between republicanism and irreligion. When he received news in 1793 of war between France and Britain, Inglis perceived a reprise of his earlier American experience, with "the same spirit of enthusiasm and conquest attached to a levelling system of Atheism." Somewhat later, when aggressive Baptists and Methodists were winning converts in the Maritimes, Inglis could only conclude that these American-connected Protestants were "engaged in a general plan of total revolution in religion and civil government."[65]

Inglis's identification of true Christianity with moderate, monarchical, antirepublican government was also a staple among the early leaders of what would become Ontario. The presuppositions of a royal Anglican establishment shaped perceptions, like the fear expressed in 1801 as the number of American immigrants increased, that Upper Canada was becoming "an asylum to *exiles* and *aliens*, to *atheists* and to *prawling democrats*." The next year the worry was that American schoolmasters were using "their efforts to poison the minds of the youths, by teaching them in republican books." By 1810 the young cleric and educator John Strachan, who would soon be recognized as the most influential Anglican in British North America, was convinced that the traditional partnership of church and state was an ideal system because it embodied "a constitution of free and equal laws, secured on the one hand against the arbitrary will of the sovereign, and the licentiousness of the people on the other." Just such a constitution was needed to counteract what

Strachan saw as the evil character of the United States, where "licentious liberty" keeps citizens "at a constant boil."[66] The viewpoint of Anglicans in the Maritimes and Upper Canada highlights the contrast with American Episcopalians, who by the 1790s had made their peace with a republican political system and, in so doing, deviated substantially from the norm elsewhere in the North Atlantic region.

Contrasts were even clearer between American Methodists and their counterparts elsewhere. Where in America the commitments of Methodists ranged from pious apoliticism to ardent republicanism, the spectrum moved the other way in Britain and Canada—from pious apoliticism to ardent monarchism. John Wesley set the tone. In 1775, his biting pamphlet, *A Calm Address to Our American Colonies*, explored at length why the American republican course was so dangerous. In Wesley's opinion, the search for a republican government was bound to descend into either chaos or despotism. Yet even if Americans were to secure a stable form of republicanism, Wesley did not think they would like what they found: "Republics shew no mercy." For expressing such opinions, copies of Wesley's address that reached the colonies were destroyed by American Methodists.[67]

Such disdain for republics and their principles remained the Methodist norm outside the United States. One of Wesley's key lieutenants, John Fletcher, summed up the American situation in 1776 by asking why it was not appropriate to use governmental force against the continental army and so, in a turn of phrase that must have fallen strangely on patriot ears, "to assert the liberty of our American fellow-subjects, who groan under the tyranny of republican despotism."[68] Four months after the French Revolution began, the *Arminian Magazine*, in an attempt to curb Methodist sympathy for the Revolution, reprinted a letter of Wesley's that declared, "A republican spirit is injurious to religion among Methodists: as I find most fallen Methodists . . . are Republicans."[69]

By the mid-1770s, Protestant Americans in several churches were already singing the hymns of Charles Wesley. This Wesley, though, was just as sour on Christian use of radical principles as his brother. Employing the language of republicanism with self-conscious derision, Charles Wesley held that the patriots were guilty of trampling underfoot the gifts of God, including the special gift of a benevolent king:

> Thy gift the Rebels spurn,
> With enmity extreme
> His patience mock, his virtues scorn,
> And Thee reject in Him.
>
> Virtue and Him they hate,
> Implung'd in every vice,
> And vow t'or'eturn the British state,
> That they themselves may rise, . . .
> Emerging from the people's lees
> To fill the vacant throne.[70]

The one exception outside the United States to suspicion of radical politics was found among the Methodists of Sierra Leone. In that recently settled West African colony, whose leaders included slaves whom the British had freed and first settled in Nova Scotia before transporting across the Atlantic, the American spirit prevailed. In the early years of the new century, the Methodists of Sierra Leone rejected at least one missionary from England because he was "too proud for a Methodist preacher." That preacher, in turn, thought that the African and African-American Methodists had been corrupted by an "American Republic [*sic*] spirit."[71] Much more typical was the rejection of republican thinking among Methodists in England, Ireland, and Canada. That rejection remained a fixture in the public discourse of Methodism's most important national leaders of the next generation, like Jabez Bunting in England and Egerton Ryerson in Canada.[72] Ryerson's opinions were unusual only for putting so sharply what other Methodists outside the United States also believed: In America, "the origin of republicanism and hatred of monarchy . . . this sudden and marvelous revolution in the American mind" was "produced chiefly" by "the blasphemous infidel and beastly drunkard," Tom Paine.[73]

Sentiments were otherwise in the United States. To be sure, early American Methodists shared with Methodists in Britain and Canada an earnest piety that often left scant room for political considerations of any sort. But as we see in greater detail in chapter 17, when American Methodists did become political, it was always in the direction of republican commitment.

Dutch Reformed, Lutherans, Roman Catholics, and Jews

The American exception in joining republicanism with traditional Christianity was most apparent in the contrast between the older British denominations and their American offspring. Yet it may have been even more impressive that American representatives of the Continental European churches, and of Roman Catholicism, also were busy domesticating republican language for their own purposes in the last decades of the century. The religious experience of the Netherlands might lead one to expect that the Reformed Dutch in America would promote Christian republicanism. One faction of Dutch Reformed in America had in fact been moving in just such a direction throughout much of the eighteenth century.[74] But resistance from the mother church in Holland to notions of American autonomy was also strong. The result was division in America. In the early 1770s defenders of the tie with Amsterdam drew on polar fears to accuse their enemies of pursuing "jesuitical" as well as "republican" plots.[75] After the Revolution, however, the Dutch Reformed churches moved quickly to incorporate themes of the reigning political ideology into their religion. When, for example, John Henry Livingston was installed as the denomination's theological professor in 1785, his address, though declaimed in Latin, revealed a thorough accommodation to the new political world. It was, in other words, filled with phrases that were not difficult to translate back into English: "nostrae libertati . . . libertatis ardor . . . virtutis stimulus . . . beatam rempublican . . . Christianae republicae."[76]

Of even more interest was the way in which republican concepts began to be used by leaders of the Lutheran churches in America. Unlike the Dutch Reformed, these predominately German churches were the product of European regions where advanced politics were almost never linked with traditional religion. The situation in the German-speaking lands was much closer to that in France, where republicanism almost always meant heresy or worse. Something strange was happening, however, even to the Lutherans in America. By the 1770s the most influential American pastor was J. H. C. Helmuth of the St. Michael's and Zion parish in Philadelphia, where he busied himself promoting both Lutheranism and the well-being of his parishioners. As a product of both orthodoxy and pietism, Helmuth took seriously his duties as guardian of pure doctrine. So it was that he preached and wrote against the era's well-known heretics, including Tom Paine and the German thinker Carl Friedrich Bahrdt (1741–1792).[77] Yet his attacks on Paine, Bahrdt, and other heterodox thinkers did not employ, as his orthodox colleagues in Germany would certainly have employed, the charge that Paine and Bahrdt were notorious republicans as well as dangerous infidels. Instead, Helmuth's own politics began to assume a dissenting hue. While never as ardent in his promotion of Christian republicanism as many of his American contemporaries, Helmuth nonetheless employed several genres to sanctify Real Whig principles. In 1785 he published a celebratory ode on the Fourth of July that included thanks to God for freeing Americans from the tyranny of Britain: "The scornful cry of the proud Briton does not bother us any longer, for we are free. God has done it."[78] A few years later when Helmuth published warnings about becoming consumed with affairs of this world, he nonetheless was at pains to approve the establishment of republican self-government in the United States: "The spirit of civil freedom has now and again spread much happiness, and our states have received the first portion of these advantages; whoever would underestimate them is thereby clearly proved to be extremely unworthy of them; we do not underestimate them; we treasure them and justly praise the Lord for them."[79] Helmuth was never as thoroughly politicized as many of his peers, but even among a religious community that could have been isolated from broader American trends, the same move toward linking republicanism and religion was taking place.

It was also taking place among the new nation's still small body of Roman Catholics. What might be called the American church's first lay movement was a concentrated drive by trustees of local congregations to exert independent control over their own fiscal affairs. This effort, which drew heavily on the republican vocabulary of the Revolution but which contradicted long-standing Catholic practice concerning the centralized ownership of property, arose shortly after the Revolution and remained an issue for two full generations.[80] In the debate over church property, lay Catholics were in general arranged against clerics, but this fact did not lead American clerics to oppose republican principles. In fact, it was just the reverse. The American situation, that is, presented a sharp contrast to contemporary Catholic developments in Quebec, where the arrival of émigré priests, forced out of France by the Revolution, lent great support to a monarchical, antirepublican, and politically conservative politics.[81] The American contrast is nicely illustrated by a sermon that John Carroll, the first American bishop, preached upon the death of George Washington. To Carroll, the conceptual discourse of republicanism came easily. Washington had played the key role in "maintaining the liberty . . . of his country on the foundation of order and morality, and guarding it against the turbulence of faction, licentiousness, foreign hostility, and artifice." He deserved praise for his "virtue," for his emancipation of the country "from vassalage," and for his efforts at making the United States "the refuge of true liberty." Among Washington's greatest achievements, according to Carroll, was his guidance of the new governing system of the United States: "Wisdom and experience combined to blend in a republican form of government all the advantages, of which other forms are productive, without many of their evils."[82] In Europe at the time that Carroll spoke these words the papacy was being humiliated by the armies of Revolutionary France and then of Napoleon. In those circumstances European Roman Catholicism was shying away from all species of republicanism, even the sort that Bishop Carroll was hailing in the new United States.[83]

The even smaller community of Jews in Revolutionary America also took to itself the language of liberty. In December 1783 five members of the Philadelphia Synagogue, including the patriot financier Haym Salomon, petitioned the state of Pennsylvania for full civil rights under the new regime. Pennsylvania had decreed that belief in the New Testament, as well as the Old, should be a qualification for holding office. The memorialists responded with republican language to suggest that, "although the Jews in Pennsylvania are but few in number," yet they were "as fond of liberty as their religious societies can be." Moreover, Jews throughout the states had "always tallied with the great design of the Revolution," and the Jews of Pennsylvania especially could count as many "Whigs" as any other group "in proportion to the number of their members."[84] This Jewish use of the new nation's common political language to plead for full civil rights is yet another indication of how widely the intersection of religion and republican concepts had advanced.[85]

The biographer of Jonathan Mayhew posed the question well: "Why was the radical Whig political philosophy of Milton, Sidney, and Locke that was so readably summarized in *Cato's Letters*, widely accepted in the colonies but scorned as a product of a lunatic fringe in the mother country?"[86] The answer does not lie in any intrinsic meaning of this whig philosophy but in the circumstances of American history. Intellectual commitments in the United States were different than in Europe because of the circumstances of American settlement, the absence of a vigorous church establishment, the contingencies of imperial conflict, and the particular circumstances of individual lives. Exceptional American circumstances not only joined together what elsewhere remained apart, they also set the stage for the appearance of a distinctly American theology.

5

Christian Republicanism

In the thirteen colonies that became the United States, republican and Protestant convictions merged as they did nowhere else in the world. That merger was not a random happenstance. Rather, from the mid-1740s Protestant believers actively embraced republican ideals, emphases, habits of thought, and linguistic conventions, and they did so by folding them into their traditional theologies. Patterns of thought that were almost inconceivable from European pulpits became commonplace because of American circumstances, particularly the circumstance of war. This chapter presents specific evidence to detail the progressive stages through which American "Christian republicanism" came into existence. The effect on theology of this new and, to the old world, almost unimaginable construct is a central theme in everything that follows.

By the early decades of the nineteenth century, it had become a matter of routine for American believers of many types to speak of Christian and republican values with a single voice. In 1816 the radical populist Elias Smith, whose movement, the Christian Connection, existed to protest the corruption of traditional denominations, published a manifesto. The Connection, Smith averred, stood for "One God—one Mediator—one lawgiver—one perfect law of Liberty—one name for the children of God, to the exclusion of all sectarian names—A Republican government, free from religious establishments and state clergy—free enquiry—life and immortality brought to light through the gospel."[1] In 1822 James Smith, a former Methodist minister who, on seeing the light of Unitarian faith, had abandoned the ministry, wrote on religious matters to Thomas Jefferson. Smith reported that he had given up on "priestly" religion but had found "shelter under the mild and peaceable Gospel of Jesus Christ, the most perfect model of Republicanism in the Universe."[2] Only a few years later, a well-educated, conservative Presbyterian clergyman, John

73

Breckinridge, who regarded Elias Smith's ecclesiastical democracy and James Smith's Unitarianism with equal disdain, nonetheless joined them in linking Christian truth and republican liberty. Breckinridge noted the way in which similar words hid contrasting realities: "What do the *rights of man* mean, at Vienna, or St. Petersburg? What does *sovereign* mean in America? . . . What does freedom, or liberty of the press, or Christianity mean at Rome, at this day? Our freedom is our peculiarity, as it is our glory."[3]

Because such statements uniting Christian and republican values had become so routine, it was difficult at the time to realize what a great reversal had taken place from less than a century before. The emergence of a republican Christian vocabulary requires, therefore, an explanation. That explanation is found in historical circumstances from the imperial wars of the 1740s through American reactions to the French Revolution of the 1790s. A rehearsal of events in these decades is important for the history of theology, since the rendering of Christian claims in a republican vocabulary contributed so directly to the American cast of theology written during the half century before the Civil War.

Before the 1740s connections between radical political discourse and the main Christian traditions did exist as a minor theme in colonial life. A number of historians have perceptively charted the general bond that linked dissenting Protestantism and colonial wariness of British power.[4] By its nature, Protestant Nonconformity was sensitive to the exercise of any authority preferentially linked to the Anglican establishment. Edmund Burke featured this sensitivity in his famous appeal before Parliament for conciliation with the colonists on 22 March 1775: they were, Burke argued, "protestants; and of that kind, which is the most adverse to all implicit submission of mind and opinion." Moreover, "this averseness in the dissenting churches from all that looks like absolute government" was a fundamental reality of "their history."[5]

In that history, however, dissenting wariness about British power only occasionally drew on civic humanist, republican, or Real Whig thinking. Among all colonial religious traditions, concern for divine revelation, attention to eternal life, and a belief in God's direct control of quotidian existence ensured that the temporal concerns of republicanism enjoyed, at most, a secondary place. After Massachusetts lost its original charter in the mid-1680s, Puritan leaders like Cotton Mather did show that they were aware of commonwealth ideology. Mather's Massachusetts Election Sermon for 1692, as an example, illustrated the amalgamation of religious and political vocabularies. When, as he described ancient history, the Israelites turned from God, "they were punished with a *Slavery* to *men*; a cruel *Shishak* had got them under the Yokes of his Arbitrary Government." By contrast, when things were going well in Israel, "there was no *Law*, and no *Tax*, imposed upon them, except what their own Acts concurred unto." Mather's conclusion was to pose rhetorical questions of the sort that many others would also ask over the course of the next century: "Is it not *Well*, that all *Christian Liberties*, and all *English Liberties*, are by the Royal Charter effectually Secured unto us? . . . [and that] no *Judges*, or *Counsellors*, or *Justices* can ever hereafter be Arbitrarily Imposed upon us?"[6]

A similar familiarity with "country" rhetoric informed the writing of John Wise (1652–1725), the minister of Ipswich, Massachusetts, who otherwise shared almost nothing with Cotton Mather.[7] Wise's protests against the Mathers and others whom he regarded as elite oppressors of the people, like *A Vindication of the Government of New England Churches* (1717), drew on English commonwealth and country authors. But Wise was a maverick; his writings have meant much more for modern students excavating the origins of American democracy than for his contemporaries; his opinions did not represent a groundswell of support for republican convictions.

Despite these early indications of shared Protestant-republican perception, colonists until the middle of the eighteenth century were more likely to view radical Whig principles as opposed to religion than supporting it. The record of the *New-England Courant* is instructive. This newspaper was owned by James Franklin and was the first outlet for the published writings of James's younger brother, Benjamin. The *Courant* was famed, or notorious, as a forum for radical ideas in both politics and religion. It reprinted *Cato's Letters* by John Trenchard and Thomas Gordon, the clearest articulation in its day of Real Whig sentiments. It also ran Benjamin Franklin's *Silence Do-Good Papers*, with their biting satire on the traditions of New England Puritanism. For its combination of radical politics and heterodox religion, the paper was attacked as a licentious opponent of good order in church and state. As the *Boston News-Letter* charged in August 1721, the *Courant* was "full freighted with Nonesense, Unmannerliness, Railery, Prophaneness, Immorality, Arrogancy, Calumnies, Lyes, Contradictions, and what not, all tending to Quarrels and Divisions, and to Debauch and Corrupt the Minds and Manners of New England."[8] The general situation, even in New England, where radical political views were best known, has been well summarized by Richard Bushman: "For fifty years after the issuance of the second charter [in 1691], Massachusetts Bay politicians kept the English radicals at a distance."[9]

The Politics of Revivalism

The situation during the colonial revivals of the period 1735–1745 was similar to the situation under the Puritans. If evangelists like George Whitefield, Gilbert Tennent, and Jonathan Edwards knew how to use the vocabulary of dissenting politics, they were nonetheless mostly interested in eternal matters. In 1737 Tennent could tell his Presbyterian congregation in New Brunswick, New Jersey, that nothing mattered more than coming to experience "everlasting Liberty" from "Bondage and Servitude." But this injunction served spiritual purposes as clarified by the full context of the exhortation: "Are ye in Bondage and Servitude? here is a spiritual, noble, and everlasting Liberty offered to you, in the Riches of CHRIST! Oh! if the Son of the Father's Love do but make you free, ye will be free indeed."[10] Similarly, in New England a long train of private study and public exposition led Jonathan Edwards to call the summary work of his entire career *The Nature*

of True Virtue. But although Edwards doubtless knew by then about the crucial place of "virtue" in republican theory, his understanding of that critical
term was thoroughly and exclusively religious.[11] When Edwards wrote at
length in 1745 about the successful New England expedition against the French
on Cape Breton, his response did not stress the preservation of Whig liberty.
Instead, it was "the late wonderful work of God in America . . . a remarkable
favor of providence."[12] Edwards, with Tennent and most other revivalists in
the 1740s, was not unaware of the republican language of liberty, but that
language remained superstructure over a foundation of traditional Protestant
pietism.

Whitefield presents a more complicated case. As several have argued persuasively, Whitefield certainly plowed a cultural terrain in which republican
Christianity would later flourish.[13] Whitefield's preaching broke traditional rules;
it called for direct, immediate response; it encouraged the laity to perform
Christian services that were the historical preserve of the clergy. Whitefield and
his imitators did not read their sermons like most of the colonies' settled ministers of the early eighteenth century but declaimed them extemporaneously in
order to maximize their power. Whitefield's speech drove home the lesson that
it was not formal education or a prestigious role in the community that ultimately mattered but the choice of an individual for or against God. Whitefield
was the colonies' most visible symbol of changing conceptions of hierarchy;
he represented a new confidence in the religious powers of the people and a
sharp, if implicit, rebuke to the authority of tradition.

Yet what Whitefield said was another matter. While he was familiar with
the newer language of liberty, he usually employed that language for limited
purposes. Thus, in a sermon from 1746 commemorating the recent defeat in
Scotland of Bonnie Prince Charles and the Jacobite challenge to the Hanoverian monarchy, Whitefield condemned Charles's grandfather King James
II for his "arbitrary and tyrannical government, both in church and state."[14]
Yet when Whitefield described spiritual transactions in this sermon, he did
so in spiritual terms; for the most part his religious language was innocent of
political connotations.

Twenty years later Whitefield was making greater use of a republican
framework. In 1766 he published a sermon originally preached in response
to news that France was about to invade Britain. The sermon claimed that
"our civil and religious Liberties are all, as it were, lying at Stake" and that
"in respect to our civil and religious Liberties, we are undoubtedly the freest
People under Heaven." What most threatened the nation, however, was not
France but the ones who had "grown wanton with Liberty," that is, "Men of
such corrupt Minds."[15]

On rare occasions Whitefield did employ the language of Whiggery at a
deeper level to supply metaphors for his spiritual message. His journal for 16
March 1740, as an example, recorded a bit of doggerel—warning against the
evil effects of lordly, unconverted ministers—that merged the political and
the religious:

> Must we submit to their commands,
> Presumptuously they say?
> No, let us break their slavish bands,
> And cast their chains away.[16]

In sermons from the 1740s and 1750s he could also ask those who were "wedded to the world" whether "the poor slaves in the galleys" were not "as reasonably . . . wedded to their chains" as sinners were to their lusts. And he could say that Satan intended to make unwary people "his subjects, his servants, his slaves."[17]

All such Real Whig instincts duly noted, however, Whitefield's politics throughout his career were much more determined by anti-Catholicism than by republicanism. In 1746 he may have been bothered by the threat of political tyranny from the Jacobites, but the spiritual tyranny of Rome loomed much larger. If the Pretender had triumphed, he thundered, "How soon would our pulpits every where have been filled with these old antichristian doctrines, free-will, meriting by works, transubstantiation, purgatory, works of supererogation, passive-obedience, non-resistance, and all the other abominations of the whore of Babylon?"[18]

In sum, Whitefield throughout his career remained primarily a preacher of spiritual liberty. At its most characteristic, Whitefield's language soared above worldly calculation to an apolitical gospel. The sermon warning listeners of Satan's power to enslave was typical in the forthrightness of its appeal: "Come to Christ . . . he will . . . receive you . . . accept salvation . . . [God will] bring you home to his sheepfold . . . choose Christ for your Lord . . . Christ will manifest himself unto you . . . the Lord Jesus Christ will gather you with his elect . . . accept of mercy and grace while it is offered to you . . . come and accept of Jesus Christ in his own way."[19]

The contrast with Whitefield's own disciples was striking. When Whitefield died in 1770 during his seventh trip to the colonies, he was memorialized more intensely than any figure to that time in colonial history. One of the addresses published from that outpouring of grief came from Nathaniel Whitaker, who was serving as the Presbyterian minister in Salem, Massachusetts, but who had earlier been an assistant with Whitefield on a lengthy tour in Britain.[20] For Whitaker the discourses of politics and religion that Whitefield had mostly separated were now thoroughly mingled: "He was a warm friend to religious liberty," said Whitaker, but "he was no less a friend to the civil liberties of mankind. He was a patriot, not in shew, but reality, and an enemy to tyranny. He abhorred episcopal oppression." Whitaker could even stretch the truth to contend that "under God it was in no small measure owing to him that the Stamp-act, that first attack upon our liberties in these colonies, was repealed." The evangelist "had a quick sense of the liberties of his fellow subjects. . . . And thousands of happy souls here own him as the instrument in God's hand of their freedom from the insupportable tyranny of sin and satan."[21] Whitefield had used the charged language of his day differently; for him liberation from terrestrial tyranny loomed much less prominently than it did for Nathaniel Whitaker.

The contrast between Whitefield's cautious and Whitaker's all-out use of republican language helps define a turning point.[22] Revivalists in the first enthusiasm of the Great Awakening had begun to employ words like "liberty," "faction," and "virtue," but at least into the 1750s, their usages were still defined primarily by spiritual purposes. Until about midcentury Protestant theology and republican discourse remained mostly distinct. After that point the situation changed rapidly in response to a singularly American set of circumstances that included at least the following: religious interpretations of the midcentury Anglo-French wars, employment by religious figures of republican arguments for specifically religious purposes, the ready use of traditional religion by the political leaders of the Revolution, the multifaceted impact of the Revolution itself on religious believers, the reactions of religious Americans to the French Revolution, the importance of personal experiences for key religious leaders, and the flexibility of ideologies in America during the second half of the eighteenth century. Attention to these matters cannot adjudicate the much-debated issue of what religion contributed to the American Revolution, but it will cast considerable light on the question of what the American Revolution contributed to religion.

War with France

Suspicion of republican ideas as intrinsically antireligious did not fade easily. But when war with papist France broke out once again in the mid-1740s, the ideological situation underwent a dramatic change. King George's War (1744–1748), encompassing New England's assault in 1745 upon the French fortress at Louisbourg on Cape Breton Island, prompted the first hints of what rapidly became standard religious politics. In the crucible of imperial struggle, a number of colonial ministers from across the theological spectrum began to link the fate of genuine Christianity to hopes for the future of liberty. Most of these ministers were from New England, but significant voices from other colonies followed along as well. Gilbert Tennent in New Jersey, for instance, hailed the reduction of Louisbourg as the rescue "of our civil and religious Liberties" from an enemy "who unweariedly labours to rob us of our civil and religious Liberties, and bring us into the most wretched vassalage to arbitrary Power and Church Tyranny."[23] In Virginia, it was probably William Stith, the Anglican chaplain of the Virginia House of Burgesses, who published two articles showing how biblical precedents helped explain the struggle of freedom and tyranny being played out in conflict between Britain and France.[24]

In New England, most religious commentary on the Louisbourg expedition echoed Jonathan Edwards by stressing traditional religious categories, especially concern for the spiritual character of the colonies and the prerogatives of God's providence.[25] But the liberal Charles Chauncy of Boston was starting to mix once-separated categories by referring to the "Salvation" that God had secured for the colonies in the defeat of the French.[26] The theological moderate Nathaniel Walter of Roxbury went even further by finding biblical prototypes for the "good Commonwealth's Man" of New England, who had fought so valiantly at Louisbourg. As Walter saw it, Moses was "the brave Soldier, expiring in the Cause of Liberty and Virtue." Even more strikingly, Jesus was one who had carried "every Virtue to the highest Pitch," including "that Devotedness to the publick Service, and those other Virtues which render Antiquity venerable."[27] A promoter of revivals, Thomas Prince, chimed in with Chauncy and Walter to employ a full country vocabulary in describing the conflict with France. Prince preached a memorable sermon at Boston's South Church on 14 August 1746 as part of a dual celebration. While continuing to rejoice over the colonists' triumph at Louisbourg, he was also responding joyously to news of the destruction of Bonnie Prince Charles's Highland, Roman Catholic army at the Battle of Culloden in the far north of Scotland earlier that same year. The printed version of Prince's sermon contained a sharply contrasting pair of definitions that came right out of the republican bible: Tories, according to Prince, were "for the absolute, hereditary, and unalienable Right of Kings ... tho' they are *Papists* and rule *arbitrarily*, illegally, tyrannically and cruelly; and they are also for the *Persecution* of Protestant Dissenters." Whigs, by contrast, "are only for the hereditary Right of Kings ... as long as they are *Protestants* and rule according to the *Laws*; but when they are *Papists* or *Tyrants*, then to set up the next *Protestant* of the *Royal Line*, who is like to govern legally and preserve the Constitution; they are also against *persecuting* any Protestant."[28]

Real Whig ideology had obviously arrived in America. Yet an older ideology was still more prominent in these sermons from the mid-1740s—hereditary, if now inflamed, anti-Catholicism. Phrases used by Massachusetts ministers Charles Chauncy and Joseph Sewall revived that spirit by referring to the pope as "Antichrist" and the "Man of Sin" as they rejoiced over the defeat of the French.[29] Several of their colleagues were only slightly less aggressively anti-Catholic.[30] The importance of such anti-Catholic convictions must be stressed.[31] If the American colonists, especially orthodox and evangelical Protestants, were now innovating in beginning to rely on a republican picture of the world that their spiritual predecessors (as well as religious contemporaries outside the colonies) associated with heresy, the colonists' vigorous anti-Catholicism both maintained an older tradition and may have obscured innovations taking place in the use of a new political vocabulary.

The ideological transformation of colonial religious discourse in 1745 and 1746 provides the necessary context for interpreting the phenomenon of Jonathan Mayhew.[32] Mayhew's famous sermon from 30 January 1750, *A Discourse concerning Unlimited Submission and Non-Resistance to the Higher Powers*, has been widely cited as a key document in the colonial appropriation of "country" principles.[33] Historians are entirely correct in regarding this sermon, an exposition of Romans 13:4 ("For he [the ruler] is a minister of God for thee to good"), as an important statement about when it was appropriate to resist the tyranny of arbitrary rule. On such questions, Mayhew well illustrates the mingling of Christian and republican values: it would be, he claimed, "more rational to suppose, that they that did NOT *resist*, than they who did, would *receive to themselves damnation."*[34] The discourse closed with scornful fury at the Anglican practice of honoring 30 January in memory of Charles I, the so-called martyr executed in 1649, whom Mayhew thought had received only the just deserts of his tyranny.

Mayhew's full articulation of republican ideology might seem to support the interpretation of Jonathan Clark that progressive politics grew from heterodox theology, since his contribution to political debate in early 1750 did follow the earlier publication of sermons marking him as a daringly radical theologian.[35] Mayhew's earlier *Seven Sermons* revealed, in fact, everything that Clark has argued could be expected from the promoters of Real Whig politics. They show Mayhew opposing traditional Protestant notions of original sin and de-emphasizing salvation by divine grace through faith, while contending for the sort of universal religious sensibility that had been a staple of English deism.[36]

By putting Mayhew's discourse in the context of colonial agitation over war with France, however, a slightly different picture emerges. Mayhew actually supported the radical politics of his *Discourse* at least in part with a traditionally Protestant appeal against Rome. As he put it, "The hereditary, indefeasible, divine right of kings, and the doctrine of non-resistance, which is built upon the supposition of such a right, are altogether as fabulous and chimerical, as transubstantiation."[37] On this score, Mayhew the political innovator was also repeating time-worn conventions of standard anti-Catholic ideology.

In addition, when the religious politics of war with France are in view, it is evident that Mayhew, however advanced in his theology, represented only one more political voice in what was rapidly becoming a chorus. Mayhew's *Discourse*, in other words, followed a path of religious republicanism that others had opened up during King George's War, and the religious republicanism he promoted in the *Discourse* was just one of many such statements to appear in this period. Considered in the fuller context of North Atlantic religious history, Mayhew was most important for the religious and political convictions he shared with a wide variety of other Americans from many points on the theological spectrum. Regarded in American terms, Mayhew's own linkage of radical politics and heterodox theology was more eccentric than typical.

The way in which Mayhew's religious republicanism was typical became apparent once orthodox and evangelical clergymen began to weigh in with religious commentary after the renewal of hostilities against France in 1754.[38] During this new imperial crisis, the Real Whig vocabulary spread everywhere. It was, for example, already integral to the Connecticut Election Sermon of 1753—"Without Vice supprest, Vertue encouraged, and Learning promoted, a civil Government can't subsist long, the Foundations will sap, and the whole Frame of Government must fall."[39] In 1755 Samuel Davies of Virginia preached the first of his several stirring war sermons that dressed orthodox theology in the garments of Whig liberty. The ostensible purpose of the sermon was to exploit the calamities of war as an appeal for repentance and the new birth, but Davies's analysis of the war was thoroughly republican: "Our religion, our liberty, our property, our lives, and everything sacred to us are in danger," especially of being "enslaved" by "an arbitrary, absolute monarch" enforcing conformity to "the superstition and idolatries of the church of Rome."[40] Although historians have focused mostly on New England as a center of religious republicanism in this period, the same conjunction was present elsewhere in the colonies as well.[41]

Several circumstances explain why evangelical and orthodox clergymen throughout the colonies deviated so readily from earlier Protestant patterns in embracing a republican analysis of the imperial wars with France. The sense of apocalyptic struggle between the forces of godly liberty and satanic slavery, which was a major theme in the revivalistic preaching of the 1740s, certainly played a role.[42] Almost as certainly, the unfolding of the French war revived hereditary Protestant fear of Catholicism and also linked that fear with a rising spirit of nationalism.[43] In addition, republicanism itself may have been losing its tinge of radicalism by the 1750s. Blair Worden has speculated that the influence of Montesquieu was moving some influential Englishmen to regard monarchy as compatible with republican government.[44] Students of the New Englanders' Louisbourg campaign of 1745 have also described its course as promoting secularization in a situation where increasing concern for the wider worlds of commerce, diplomacy, and war was edging out concerns for providence.[45] And because notions of virtue in the colonies had always been defined by religious standards, as opposed to the secular norms of English radicals, it was less of a step for colonists to unite secular and religious meanings of the term than was in the case in Great Britain.[46]

Whatever the exact cause, by the end of active fighting against the French in 1760, an unusually strong bond had emerged in the American colonies between republican political ideology and traditional religious convictions. The crisis over the Stamp Act that followed immediately—and then the spiraling process of alienation from Britain—deepened, expanded, and sharpened American Christian republicanism. In particular, that process turned a rhetoric with British origins into a powerful protest against the British king and Parliament. But in ideological terms, the turn against Britain as villain represented only an extrapolation of what was already in place by 1760. The importance of the religious-republican synthesis was its usefulness for explaining so much of how the world seemed to be working for so many Americans—whether Protestant, deist, or nonreligious—over the last third of the eighteenth century. Specifically religious events, like protests over plans for a colonial Anglican bishop, which increased throughout the 1760s, or over the Quebec Act of 1774, reinforced the validity of the republican categories. It was not, however, conflict with Britain over specifically religious matters that encouraged colonial Protestants to accept Real Whig republicanism; rather, the mingling of what had been previously antagonistic concepts took place in the traumas of war with France well before overt hostility flamed against the mother country.

In at least one case, a colonial minister seems to have been dimly aware of the novelty of the American situation. During a trip to Britain to raise money for the College of New Jersey in the mid-1750s, the Presbyterian revivalist Samuel Davies enjoyed many opportunities to sample the political as well as the religious opinions of his hosts. On one occasion, Davies expressed chagrin at discovering that "the dissenting Ministers," though they were "Friends of the Liberty of Mankind," also "generally embibed Arminian or Socinian Sentiments." The conjunction of opposition politics and heterodox theology so natural to many in Britain was also apparent to Davies: "It is Matter of Complaint, that the Deists generally, if not universally, are of the Whigg-Party, and join the low-Churchmen. Alas! how are the Principles of Liberty abused!"[47] After he returned to Virginia, Davies took time to read a three-volume set of the philosophical works of Henry St. John, Lord Bolingbroke (1678–1751), whom contemporaries recognized as one of the sharpest exponents of Real Whig opposition to the regime of court manager Robert Walpole. Davies roundly criticized Bolingbroke for presenting "a horrendous Deity" and for trivializing the ancient truths of Christianity.[48] Yet he made no reference to the harmony that Bolingbroke's British contemporaries saw between Bolingbroke's heterodox religious views, which Davies rejected, and their political opinions, which paralleled so closely Davies's own reading of the public sphere.

Republicanism in Service to Religious Reform

One of the reasons that republican reasoning became so solidly fixed among a certain class of American revivalists was its utility for advancing religious reform.[49] Isaac Backus, spokesman for New England Baptists, who pursued a mostly apolitical course in prodigious efforts on behalf of his coreligionists, nonetheless was himself adept at using the language of civic humanism for distinctly religious purposes. In 1770 Backus enlisted Whig rhetoric against a Massachusetts legislature that was continuing to enforce legal restrictions against the Baptists. Particularly obvious to him was the incongruity that "many who are filling the nation with the cry of LIBERTY and against oppressors are at the same time themselves violating the dearest of all rights, LIBERTY OF CONSCIENCE."[50] Three years later Backus published a more comprehensive argument for freedom of conscience, a case he presented in person at Philadelphia several months later to the slightly incredulous Samuel Adams and John Adams. This *Appeal* of 1773 showed how arguments of the Whig patriots against Britain could easily be transformed into weapons of religious reform.[51]

Another example of the same process took place in New Jersey, where an independent-minded Presbyterian, Jacob Green, put republican language to use in order to attack slavery. This former colleague of George Whitefield was an enthusiastic supporter of the war, but he was also a determined opponent of chattel bondage. To Green, republican discourse was ideal for promoting what was at root a Christian reform: "It is demonstrable that . . . slave holders are friends to slavery, ergo are enemies to liberty, ergo are enemies

to our present struggle for liberty, ergo are enemies to these United States. . . .
These slavish slave holders will watch for an opportunity to establish slavery
and bondage in the United States: ergo they will, as they have the opportunity, join with our enemies who are attempting this same thing. . . . [Slave-
holders are] tories of the worst sort."[52]

With specific reference to Isaac Backus, Bernard Bailyn has accounted for
such religious use of republican language as "the contagion of liberty."[53] This
is a plausible metaphor, though it is also possible that the ideological osmosis moved the other way as well. Rather than a rhetoric of republican civic
humanism spreading out into the religious backwaters of colonial society, the
religious backwaters may have been rising to carry republicanism where its
leading theorists had not intended it to go. Whatever metaphor is more appropriate, the sectarian use of republican concepts not only enabled these
Protestants to prosecute their reforms but also made these concepts habitual
for themselves.

Christian Language as Republican Disinfectant

Traditional religious believers who might still have worried about the corrupting effects of republican principles could only have been reassured when
leading patriots went out of their way to employ traditional religious language
in supporting their Whig policies. From the time of the Stamp Act crisis to at
least the end of the War for Independence, for example, patriot publicists
skillfully and repeatedly linked Parliamentary actions to the devil.[54] But patriot appropriation of traditional religion to support a republican rebellion went
much further and had wider-ranging consequences.

Tom Paine's *Common Sense*, the dramatic tract from 1776 that did so much
to mobilize colonial opinion against the British crown, was a particularly
clever example of such appropriation. When in the pamphlet Paine urged
Pennsylvania's Quakers to live up to their religious principles and forsake
conservative allegiance to the king, he presented himself as "one of those few,
who never dishonours religion either by ridiculing, or cavilling at any denomination whatsoever." In fact, it is likely that when Paine published *Common Sense*, he had already come to the conclusion, as he put it later in *The
Age of Reason*, that most of the Old Testament, with "a few phrases excepted
. . . deserves either our abhorrence or our contempt." Yet this private opinion
did not prevent him from citing the Hebrew scriptures at great length as part
of his attack on monarchy and the hereditary succession of rulers.[55]

Paine's skill at marshaling biblical narratives for republican ends was
masterful, as in the following précis of ancient Jewish history:

> Near three thousand years passed away from the Mosaic account of the cre-
> ation, till the Jews under a national delusion requested a king. Till then their
> form of government (except in extraordinary cases, where the Almighty inter-
> posed) was a kind of republic administered by a judge and the elders of the
> tribes. Kings they had none and it was held sinful to acknowledge any being

under that title but the Lord of Hosts. And when a man seriously reflects on the idolatrous homage which is paid to the persons of kings, he need not wonder that the Almighty, ever jealous of his honor, should disapprove of a form of government which so impiously invades the prerogative of heaven.[56]

The end to which Paine's biblically flavored reasoning led, however, was a long ways from traditional Protestant faith. Paine's disregard of classic Christian doctrines on the universality of sin, on God's control over human affairs, and on God's equally firm control over the timing of the millennium fairly blazed out from his most memorable assertions: "We have it in our power to begin the world over again. A situation, similar to the present, hath not happened since the days of Noah until now. The birthday of a new world is at hand."[57] Yet because the reasoning leading to this conclusion was so artfully decorated with a traditional Protestant deference to Scripture, Paine's pamphlet worked as effectively upon traditional religious communities as on other colonists.

If Paine's *Age of Reason* (with its dismissive attitude toward the Old Testament) had been published before *Common Sense* (with its full deployment of Scripture in support of republican freedom), the quarrel with Britain may have taken a different course. It is also likely that the allegiance of traditional Christian believers to republican liberty might not have been so thoroughly cemented. And it is possible that the intimate relation between republican reasoning and trust in a traditional Scripture, which became so important after the turn of the new century, would not have occurred as it did.

In the actual unfolding of events, however, the usage provided by Paine was perfected by other patriot leaders. The Continental Congress showed it had taken Paine's rhetorical lessons to heart, for example, when on 1 November 1777 it proclaimed a day of public thanks for the recent victory at Saratoga. Samuel Adams, who composed the resolution, was a more traditional believer than Tom Paine, which probably made it easier for him to use a fully orthodox theology in calling the patriots to prayer. The resolution began by reminding the colonists that it was "the indispensable duty of all men to adore the superintending providence of Almighty God; to acknowledge with gratitude their obligation to him for benefits received, and to implore such further blessings as they stand in need of." But it went on to say that similar adoration was due to God for his providential aid "in the prosecution of a just and necessary war, for the defense and establishment of our unalienable rights and liberties." Congress was calling the people to prayer on the eighteenth of December so that they might "consecrate themselves to the service of their divine benefactor; and . . . join the penitent confession of their manifold sins, whereby they had forfeited every favour, and their humble and earnest supplication that it may please God, through the merits of Jesus Christ, mercifully to forgive and blot them out of remembrance." Congress also asked the people to pray for material prosperity but ended by stressing the need to cultivate "the principles of true liberty, virtue and piety, under his nurturing hand, and to prosper the means of religion for the promotion and enlargement of that kingdom which consisteth 'in righteousness, peace and joy in the Holy

Ghost.'"[58] Whatever the degree of religious sincerity in such statements, they could only have reassured traditional Protestants that in the new United States republican allegiance did not subvert true religion.

As Tom Paine and the leaders of the Continental Congress deployed a vocabulary of traditional religion in support of the war, they were joined by many religious leaders who also described the struggle for independence as an intensely religious cause. Religious use of the republican vocabulary may, in fact, have been more important than any other factor in drawing believers from throughout the new nation's various regions into support of the war effort. Many religious patriots from the middle colonies, for instance, were not as ready to embrace the notion commonly held in New England that the Americans constituted a "new Israel" with their own special covenant with God.[59] Yet in putting to use just-war arguments, especially against Quaker or Anabaptist pacifism, republican concepts worked as powerfully for the religiously plural middle colonies as for Congregational New England. Thus, when the Presbyterian minister John Carmichael from Forks of Brandywine, Pennsylvania, preached a sermon on 4 June 1775 in order to prove, as his title put it, "A Self-Defensive War Lawful," he proceeded to the task with a fully republican arsenal. Carmichael echoed the Congregational patriots of New England by expressing his fear of "the galling yoke of *perpetual slavery*" and in the conviction that there was "nothing that can befall you, so ruinous to yourselves and posterity in this life, as *slavery*."[60] Anti-Catholic and chosen-nation vocabularies were absent from this sermon, but Carmichael's Christian republicanism was more than enough to link him with other believers who supported the patriot cause.

In their shared efforts, both political and religious figures were tailoring the project of republican independence to fit the language of traditional Protestant religion. After only a few years, America's religious population, with Protestant evangelicals in the forefront, began in similar fashion to tailor their religious projects to fit the language of republicanism. The implications for both politics and religion from this tailoring were momentous. In the immediate context, the argument against Parliament acquired the emotive force of revival. In the longer term, religious values migrated along with religious terms into the political speech and so changed political values. But the migration also moved the other way: a religious language put to political use took on political values that altered the substance of religion.[61]

The Multifaceted Impact of the Revolution

The events of the war itself did much to cement the Christian-republican alliance. In an important instance, Real Whig concepts offered a vocabulary that could be shared by Protestant sectarians and heterodox founding fathers like Thomas Jefferson and James Madison in their Revolutionary struggle for the separation of church and state.[62] The Revolution also forced patriots to change their minds about the identity of the colonies' primary enemy. Together they made a move from fearing Continental, papal tyranny to fearing British, perhaps cryptically, papal tyranny,[63] and finally to fearing a negative abstraction of tyranny compounded of all the worst that Americans could imagine about the decrepit authorities of the old world. In this transformation the constant remained a republican conception of power and its effects.

In addition, the war also seemed to make Christian republicanism the only possible option for linking the religious and the political spheres. The success of the patriots led to the literal banishment of traditional divine-right establishmentarians like the Anglican Jonathan Boucher; it also pushed out of sight the pacifists who had considered both warring sides guilty of great sin.[64] More important, it silenced the considerable number who shared the patriots' republican outlook but who did so in a moderate form joined with loyalty to the British crown. William Smith, provost of the College of Philadelphia, preached a sermon on 23 June 1775 in the wake of Lexington and Concord that showed he had mastered the republican calculus: "Illiberal or mistaken plans of policy may distress us for a while, and perhaps sorely check our growth; but if we maintain our own virtue; if we cultivate the spirit of Liberty among our children; if we guard against the snares of luxury, vanity and corruption; the Genius of America will still rise triumphant, and that with a power at last too might for opposition. This country *will be free*—nay for ages to come, a chosen seat of *Freedom, Arts*, and *heavenly Knowledge*: which are now either drooping or dead in most countries of the old world."[65] Smith, however, continued to value his attachment to the king, which meant that his tempered appropriation of republicanism would have no hearing in the wake of the war.

It was the same with Charles Inglis, who, in preaching to Loyalist troops in September 1777, showed that he had also mastered the republican catechism. As Inglis saw the American situation, "popular Tyranny" had turned America into a "bleeding Country, through which Destruction and Ruin are driving in full career, from which Peace, order, Commerce, and useful Industry are banished." Loyalists should offer their all to defend "your Families, your liberty, and Property . . . against the Violence of usurped Power." It was obvious that Inglis remembered the rhetoric of the French and Indian War, for he was willing to contend that if the patriots won the conflict, his auditors would be torn "from the Protection of your parent State, and eventually . . . [come] under the despotic Rule of our inveterate Popish Enemies [i.e., the French], the inveterate Enemies of our Religion, our Country and Liberties."[66] Yet though he knew the language of Whig republican resistance, loyalty to the inherited constitution of king-in-Parliament was stronger.

Outside of the new United States, moderate Whig Loyalism would become the main political resting place for many evangelical, liberal, and traditionalist Protestants, as well as for many Roman Catholics and members of minority faiths. What it meant for that stance to be excised from the religious and political history of the United States could only be ascertained by a full evaluative comparison of the United States on one side with Canada and the various kingdoms of Great Britain on the other.[67] The Revolutionary War not only solidified, but also perpetuated, a singularly American union of religion and political principles.

Far Enough Away from France

The American confluence of Christian and republican reasoning also involved an event that did not happen. For most traditional believers in Britain—Anglicans, Old Dissenters, Methodists, and others—political crises in the 1790s drove a wedge between republican and Christian convictions.[68] The two-part publication of Tom Paine's *Rights of Man* in February 1791 and February 1792 worried British Christians, not just for Paine's arguments against orthodox Christianity, but also because the work promoted an even more radical assault on traditions of all kinds than had Paine's celebrated *Common Sense* of 1776. For most British Christians, the rising carnage of the French Revolution and the outbreak of war between Britain and France in February 1793 underscored the link between infidelity, radical assaults on inherited order, and revolutionary disruption.

In the new United States, by contrast, while many Christian believers were soon alienated from Revolutionary France, that alienation actually strengthened attachment to republican principles, at least of the right sort.[69] The ability to disentangle abhorrence of French excesses from ongoing loyalty to republican values is nicely illustrated by speeches from New Jersey's William Paterson, a signer of the Declaration of Independence, who by the 1790s had become both an active Presbyterian layman and a justice of the United States Supreme Court. To a jury in 1795, Paterson offered a primer in republicanism to explain why American law was so much superior to the British. American citizens were "surrounded . . . with a blaze of political illumination," they enjoyed "republican governments, and written contributions, by which protection and enjoyment of property are rendered inviolable."[70] Only a few years later in a Fourth of July address, Paterson celebrated again the "Freedom and independence our fathers fought for and obtained." But this time he reminded his hearers that there was "no virtue so sublime . . . as to escape the malignant breath of faction." And he praised "schools and seminaries of learning" as one of the best means for preserving "social order . . . national liberty . . . [and] genuine republicanism." Paterson's worry in this address grew out of his reading of Europe, where "the demon of false philosophy, vain and proud, and covered with the spoils and blood of the fairest part of Europe," was reaching out to threaten America.[71] Paterson was as appalled by events in France as any British traditional Christian, but his reaction to those events was not the British tendency to link infidel religion and republication aspirations.

Even more directly relevant for theological history was the reaction of Samuel Miller, a New York City Presbyterian minister who later occupied an influential position at Princeton Theological Seminary. Miller, unlike many formalist evangelicals of the early 1790s, was a Jeffersonian and an enthusiast for the first phases of the French Revolution. But as the French turned violent and Miller turned against the Revolution, his loyalty to republican institutions and republican political vision grew rather than diminished. Thus, in 1795, he instructed a Jeffersonian audience in "all those genuine republican principles" that American independence had brought, like equality of rights and obligations, civil and religious freedom, and the reign of law, "which are calculated to call forth the best energies of man . . . and to build up the fabric of national happiness."[72] Within three years, Miller's Jeffersonianism was rapidly vanishing, but not his republican loyalties. On the occasion of a fast day proclaimed by President John Adams, Miller recoiled from what he described as "the awful derangement of the old world," with "the growing atheism, the profaneness . . . the progress of luxury . . . the dissolution of social ties . . . the rapid strides which all these evils are making." As an antidote for these horrors, Miller offered the religion of Christ. Yet when Miller described "the native tendency of this divine system," it was a religion defined by republican instincts: "to check the insolence of power; to restrain the encroachments of oppression; to give energy to the wise prescriptions of government; to secure liberty with order."[73]

Paterson and Miller did not speak for all Americans, but they were nonetheless typical in combining abhorrence of French infidelity with allegiance to Real Whig political principle. That combination ensured that American Christianity would continue to use, and to be shaped by, a moral language of liberty, an interpretation of virtue as proper public-spiritedness, and an innate suspicion of power. The French trauma that solidified the British disjunction between traditional Christian faith and advanced republican politics worked differently across the Atlantic.

Personal Contingencies

The shape of political-religious connections was also often related to personal experience. To observe the many such connections that were shaped by personal experience also moves the ideological story from the abstract to the concrete: American religious leaders with different theological convictions were pushed together by their support for the American Revolution toward a Christian-republican synthesis; religious leaders in other parts of the North Atlantic region were just as regularly pushed in the opposite direction by negative experiences of revolution.

It was especially significant that a number of individuals who became important Protestant leaders in the early decades of the United States experienced life-shaping conversions in the midst of revolutionary tumult. Without claiming too much for these experiences, the catalog is still impressive. Timothy Dwight, who would later preside over a phalanx of ardently patriotic, establishmentarian Calvinists in New England, professed personal faith and joined the college church in New Haven, Connecticut, in January 1774. The step was taken in extraordinary political times, for it occurred when all New England was ablaze with the news of the Boston Tea Party and when Yale students were forming themselves into a troop to defend their homeland against British invaders. Dwight's own father became a Loyalist, but for Dwight a second conversion (to the patriot cause) followed naturally from his first conversion (to Christ).[74] Only a few months later in 1774, the six-year-old Elias Smith was jolted by the "terrifying report" of the Battle of Bunker Hill and began to pray "with weeping, hoping that by this my sins which were committed against my parents, and others, might be forgiven."[75] Although Smith later became one of Dwight's great nemeses as a promoter of dissenting, antiestablishment evangelicalism, he like Dwight was thoroughly converted to the union of revivalist religion and American republicanism. Barton W. Stone, who became a powerful advocate in the Upper South of an antitraditional evangelicalism similar to Elias Smith's, was not converted until after the Revolution. But firmly lodged in his memory was a life-shaping conjunction of experiences related to the war. These included the bloody battle of Guilford Courthouse, North Carolina, in March 1781 (with its "profane swearing, debauchery, drunkenness, gambling, quarreling and fighting"); his own baptism "into the spirit of liberty," which made it impossible for Stone to "hear the name of British, or tories, without feeling a rush of blood through the whole system"; and his first introduction to the itinerations of Baptists and Methodists that he would later imitate.[76] Ashbel Green, who became a moving spirit among Presbyterians at Princeton College and Princeton Seminary, was permanently marked by his teenage experience as "a flaming whig," his militia duty during the war, and his personal contact with fifteen or sixteen signers of the Declaration of Independence.[77] The earliest memories of Green's Presbyterian colleague Samuel Miller were of public celebrations for the signing of the Declaration and the death of his brother, a physician with the patriot troops.[78] Because the Revolutionary experience of these American Protestant leaders coincided with critical events in their religious formation, it was almost second nature for the significance of these experiences, as well as the language in which they were expressed, to converge in one language made up of both religious and political themes.[79]

Similar conjunctions of formative religious and political experiences outside the United States often had the opposite effect. Henry Alline, whose evangelistic message blazed brightly in the Canadian Maritimes and the New England back country, experienced a traumatic conversion in Nova Scotia on 26 March 1775, three days after Patrick Henry had proclaimed in Virginia, "Give me liberty, or give me death"; less than one month before American patriots captured Fort Ticonderoga; and, more to the point, while Nova Scotia was rife with rumors about an invasion led by George Washington and the possibility of an indigenous rebellion against British rule.[80] Although Alline used a republican language to describe his turn toward God ("whom I saw I had *rebelled* against and been *deserting* from all my days"), his conversion eventually led him to conclude that politics of any sort subverted the purity of Christian faith.[81] The same kind of life-transforming experiences in the context of revolutionary agitation—and leading to the rejection of republican values—also took place in other regions. Robert and James Haldane, whose careers were nearly synonymous with the rise of evangelical Dissent as a powerful force in Scotland, were both won to evangelical faith in early 1793 at the very time that Scotland awoke to the perils of the French Revolution. For the Haldanes, this conjunction of events weaned them from politics and set them on a course of determinedly apolitical pietism.[82] The Haldanes' establishmentarian counterpart in the Church of Scotland, Thomas Chalmers, was drawn back to a communal Christian ideal embracing evangelical piety and parish virtues as a direct result of Scotland's mobilization in 1803 to ward off an anticipated invasion by Napoleon.[83] A few years earlier, in 1798, Henry Cooke, who would become the great spokesman for Northern Ireland's public evangelicalism in the middle decades of the century, was won over to his life's antirepublican Christian outlook by witnessing the march of Ulster rebels against the British king.[84] A few years later, Egerton Ryerson, who helped Upper Canadian Methodists create a Loyalist evangelical society in mid-Victorian Ontario, was movingly converted immediately after his family had been traumatized and the property of friends had been destroyed by invading American troops in the War of 1812.[85]

Outside the United States, in other words, personal engagement with Christianity often meant disengagement from republican political principles. Geography is not always destiny. But for religion in the North Atlantic religion, the places where Protestants experienced radical political events meant a very great deal indeed.

The Flexibility of American Ideologies

Finally, the Christian republicanism of the early United States was possible only because of considerable ideological flexibility. Two critical ambiguities were of supreme importance: one concerning the "virtue" without which republican polity could not succeed, and the other concerning the role of "the people" in the proper functioning of republican institutions.

The willingness of Americans to include several not altogether compatible ideals under the notion of virtue was essential for the flourishing of religious republicanism.[86] Almost all Americans came to agree that the health of a republic required the exercise of virtue by its citizens. Most of the founding fathers thought of that virtue in classical, Machiavellian terms as disinterested service to the common good. Most American practitioners of traditional religion, however, defined virtue in biblical terms as life guided by God's will and cultivated in personal and domestic devotion. By the end of the eighteenth century, a gendered meaning of virtue—as the ethics of female, domestic, private morality—was added to the Roman and theological usages.[87] The result was common use of a single term that masked varied understandings. The political conflict created by this situation lasted until at least the Civil War, when Northern armies enforced the meaning of virtue as defined by latter-day Whigs and the Republican Party on a South, where classical, Roman, honor-driven ideals remained much stronger.

For religious history, the amalgamation of meanings into a single term folded public life into the drama of redemption. Three examples, from multitudes, illustrate this Christian appropriation of republican habits of thought. In 1755, after the defeat of General Braddock, Samuel Davies exhorted Virginians to keep their courage. The slipperiness of the notion of virtue was the key to his logic: "I would rather fly to the utmost end of the earth, than submit to French tyranny and Popish superstition. . . . Shall slavery here clank her chain, or tyranny rage with lawless fury? . . . Therefore, if you would save your country, repent and be converted."[88] In 1780 the New Jersey Presbyterian Jacob Green used the same amalgam of classical and Christian concepts to explain the dynamics of the Revolutionary situation: "Vice," he averred, "is the general, radical cause of this loss [of liberty]." Vice had a double tendency to undermine liberty: "It provokes God to withhold his protection, and punish a sinning people by permitting usurpers and tyrants to seize on their natural rights, and reduce them to a state of bondage. . . . Vice has a *natural* tendency to the loss of freedom. . . . Vice enfeebles the mind, unmans human creatures, and many ways puts them into the power of those who watch for an opportunity to subjugate them."[89] Eighteen years later in a fast-day sermon, Green's son, Ashbel, carried out the same intellectual maneuver. First came the republican calculus: "The established connexion between virtue and prosperity, vice and ruin, . . . is much closer, and more powerful, in relation to communities than to individuals. . . . It is, indeed, the grand tendency of virtue to produce happiness, and of vice to beget misery. . . . When a nation *as such* becomes abandoned to vice, there is no longer any suitable tie by which it can be holden together." With that basis established, Green then reverted to the form of the jeremiad by enumerating a number of religious duties—repentance, prayer, the pursuit of holiness—that had to be practiced if God was to spare the land.[90] In these cases, and many more like them, ambiguity about the meaning of virtue provided just the flexibility necessary for religious believers to become full participants in the American national drama and for the American national drama to be incorporated into the history of redemption.

A similar ambiguity attended conceptions of "the people." The ability of flexible republican categories to accommodate varying attitudes toward democratic politics was matched by a similar ability of flexible Protestant loyalties to empower contrasting religious attitudes. As historians like Nathan Hatch, Curtis Johnson, and Richard Carwardine have shown, the intrareligious debates of antebellum America were severe in large part because both the more populist, democratic churches and the more traditional, hierarchical churches sought the republican high ground for advocating their particular visions.[91]

For clarity of thought, it was not necessarily beneficial that American religious republicanism rested on such ambiguities. But rest on them it did, and with a power that remained a marvel to foreign visitors like Alexis de

Tocqueville. The character of the country that de Tocqueville visited in the 1830s seemed compounded of what he called "two perfectly distinct elements that elsewhere have often made war with each other, but which, in America, . . . they have succeeded in incorporating somehow into another and combining marvelously. I mean to speak of the *spirit of religion* and the *spirit of freedom*."[92] De Tocqueville's observation succinctly summarized the product of a complex history. For theology in the new United States, the shaping power of that complex history was enormous.

6

Theistic Common Sense

The startling reversal in which America's religious leaders took up the language
of republicanism was the most important ideological development for the future of theology in the United States. That reversal, however, was not the only
intellectual surprise of the period. The turn by Protestants to the language of
the eighteenth century's new moral philosophy represented as much a break
from historic associations as did the turn to republicanism. Moreover, the two
turnings took place in similar fashion. Where once the commonalities between
Protestantism and either republicanism or the new moral philosophy were in-
cidental and far less prominent than the differences, during the second half of
the eighteenth century the commonalities loomed ever larger, while points of
tension rapidly faded away. A theological Rip Van Winkle falling asleep in the
early 1740s and waking up half a century later would have found Americans
speaking his language with such a decidedly strange inflection as to constitute
a new dialect; yet those Americans would have been hard-pressed to tell him
why and how their speech had grown so different from his own. Just as combat
with Roman Catholic France and the political firestorm of Revolution may be
said to have created American Christian republicanism, so also the course of
events in the wider world of late eighteenth-century American history is the
key to explaining the rise of theistic common sense. In turn, theistic common
sense would exert a tremendous influence on theology in the nineteenth century. The force of what simply had to be taken for granted was precisely the
force that changed how Americans thought about human character, the nature
of salvation, and the relationship of God to the world.

Terms and Definitions

The form of ethical reasoning that became nearly universal in the new United
States, which was promoted with special vigor by Protestant evangelicals, is

known by several names. It was, first, a localized example of the "new moral philosophy" of the seventeenth and eighteenth centuries, whose proponents set aside Aristotelian and scholastic Christian authorities in search for what they considered better axioms upon which to base theories of human nature, psychology, and morality. In the words of Norman Fiering, the premier student of the subject, "The guiding assumption behind almost all of the new work was the belief that God's intentions for man, His expectations of human beings as moral creatures, could be discovered independently of the traditional sources of religious authority, through a close investigation of human nature."[1] Generically considered, this new moral philosophy promoted "commonsense moral reasoning," or an approach to ethics self-consciously grounded upon universal human instincts. It received fullest formal exposition from the great flourishing of creative thought in Scotland from the time of Francis Hutcheson's professorship at Glasgow (1730–1746) to the death of Thomas Reid in 1796. The fullest popular spread of this commonsense reasoning, albeit in terms considerably altered from their Scottish origin, occurred in the early United States.

"Theistic mental science" is another useful term for the new form of ethical reasoning. It describes especially the books and curricula that popularized commonsense moral philosophy among American believers of all sorts, from deists to Baptists, with many Presbyterians, Anglicans, Episcopalians, and Congregationalists in between. In the typology of D. H. Meyer's *Instructed Conscience*, such ethical investigations could be teleological and utilitarian (i.e., oriented toward the achievement of human happiness), teleological and not utilitarian (i.e., guided by a standard of disinterested benevolence), or deontological (i.e., searching for right action from a grasp of the way things or ethical laws really are).[2] In every case, however, the effort was to construct ethics as Francis Bacon had defined the doing of science—by examining one's own consciousness as an object, treating the deliverances of consciousness as data, and gathering these data inductively into broader conclusions (even "laws") about the nature of human existence itself.[3] Through books by well-known authors like the Anglican clergyman William Paley (teleological and utilitarian), the followers of Jonathan Edwards (teleological and nonutilitarian), or the Unitarian Harvard moral philosopher Francis Bowen and the leading Baptist intellectual of the antebellum period, Francis Wayland (deontological), theistic mental science exerted a nearly pervasive influence on formal American thought.[4]

A final term, the "evangelical Enlightenment," describes the absorption of the new moral philosophy by Protestant evangelicalism, which in the early nineteenth century became so important in Britain and Canada as well as the United States.[5] The American appropriation of Enlightenment reasoning has been the subject of considerable historical inquiry, with Henry May's 1976 study still the defining work.[6] The key to May's argument is the realization that eighteenth-century Americans perceived several Enlightenments. In chronological order, Americans responded calmly to forms of modern thought from late seventeenth-century England but proceeded from ambiguity to disgust for the Enlightenment as defined by Continental Europeans early in the eighteenth century and then English radicals at the end of the century. Americans held in high regard what May calls the *moderate* Enlightenment exemplified by Isaac Newton and John Locke. By contrast, Protestants in America came especially to repudiate two other forms of European Enlightenment: *skeptical,* as defined by Voltaire and David Hume: and *revolutionary,* as in the work of Rousseau, William Godwin, and (after 1780) Tom Paine. A fourth variety of Enlightenment thought, however, received a very different reception in Protestant America. What May calls the *didactic* Enlightenment was largely a product of Scotland, where three generations of philosophers and moralists—among whom Francis Hutcheson (1694–1747), Thomas Reid (1710–1796), Adam Smith (1723–1790), and Dugald Stewart (1753–1828) were the leaders—struggled to show how Enlightenment ideals could restore intellectual confidence and promote social cohesion. In the United States this form of modern thought provided theologians with an intellectual lingua franca for nearly a century.[7]

However described—as the new moral philosophy, theistic mental science, or the evangelical Enlightenment—these patterns of commonsense moral reasoning shaped theology just as distinctly as did assumptions of republican politics. In the decades between the Revolution and the Civil War, almost all Americans, especially Christian ministers who ventured into print, relied strategically on the weight of "self-evident truths" or "intuitive truths," even as they expressed repeatedly the conviction that "the best reason which anyone can have for believing any proposition is that it is so evident to his intellectual faculty that he cannot disbelieve it."[8] So self-evident were these mental procedures that few paused to realize how different they were from earlier habits of mind, especially in the earlier history of Protestantism.

American Opposition to the New Moral Philosophy before ca. 1760

The historical problem is to discern how a Protestantism rooted in the Reformation, descended from Puritanism, and renewed in the 1740s by the New Light revivalism of John Wesley, George Whitefield, and Jonathan Edwards came to take up so thoroughly the new moral philosophy. These three phases of Protestant development—Reformation, Puritanism, and revival—had stressed human disability as much as human capability, noetic deficiency as much as epistemic capacity, and historical realism as much as social optimism. By contrast, the newer reasoning featured the construction of ethics on the basis of science, it insisted upon the universal character of ethical intuitions, and it favored these intuitions over traditional, historic, or ecclesiastical authority as the ideal basis for morality.

The first Protestants had not been quite as eager as the early church father Tertullian (ca. 160–ca. 225) to pose an antithesis between Athens and Jerusalem, but they were nonetheless definite about proper intellectual procedure.

Luther and Calvin were able casuists, but they also consistently bemoaned the damage wrought by unchecked reason or the presumption that merely human learning could dictate to revelation. Luther, when he called reason "the devil's whore," was characteristically more flamboyant. But Calvin could be no less direct: for "knowing God" and "knowing his fatherly favor in our behalf," he held that "the greatest geniuses are blinder than moles."[9] This earliest Protestant conception of intellectual life came much closer to medieval postures (*credo ut intelligam, fides quaerens intellectum*) than to the eighteenth-century confidence in human reason. These early Protestants were also dedicated followers of the church father Augustine. In their minds, this great theologian of the fourth and early fifth centuries had been entirely correct in his most important theological assertion: A sharp divide did separate the elect from the lost, with implications, however imprecisely detailed, for ethics, epistemology, and metaphysics, as well as soteriology.[10] As they saw it, whether one stood in God's grace (and fellowship with the church) or in sinful resistance to that grace (and alienated from the church) was critical for the ability to act morally. In all of its most important instincts, early Protestant theology opposed the ethical universalism that would rise to prominence in the *common* sense of the eighteenth century.

Puritans were heirs of this Augustinian Reformation.[11] Like the earliest Protestants, the Puritans also campaigned against human self-sufficiency in epistemology and ethics. With them, the Puritans expected divine revelation to provide the starting place for all forms of thought. And again, the symbol of arrogantly self-sufficient rationality was Aristotle. How could a pagan philosopher of nature, they wondered, properly comprehend that truly virtuous action flows only from a heart renewed by God's grace? William Ames (1576–1633), foremost among the early Puritans' systematic thinkers, illustrated a common attitude that combined a measure of respect for Aristotle's natural intellectual gifts with a forceful rejection of what Ames considered his dangerous anthropocentricism. On the crucial concept of virtue, Ames was explicit: where "Aristotle holds . . . that the judgment of prudent men is the rule for virtue," Ames responded that "there are nowhere such wise men under whose judgment we might always stand." Put positively, Ames argued that "right reason" was found only "in the Scriptures." The contrast was absolute: "When the imperfect notions about honesty and dishonesty found in man's mind after the fall are truly understood, they will be seen to be incapable of shaping virtue. . . . Therefore, there can be no other teaching of the virtues than theology which brings the whole revealed will of God to the directing of our reason, will, and life."[12]

With Ames, the New England Puritans took virtue, properly so called, to be a fruit of election. Boston's leading minister in the first generation, John Cotton, cited with approval the views of William Perkins, foremost teacher of the leaders who founded New England: "The word, and scriptures of God doe conteyne a . . . platforme, not onely of theology, but also of . . . ethicks, economicks, politiks, church-government, prophecy, [and] academy."[13] Cotton Mather, nearly a century after Ames, was still expressing the same distrust of natural or Aristotelian moral philosophy, which he called "a *Sham*" that "pretends to give you a Religion without a CHRIST, and a *Life* of PIETY without a *Living Principle*; a *Good Life* with no other than Dead Works filling of it. . . . Study no other *Ethics*, but what is in the *Bible*."[14] Mather's testimony on the question of ethical reasoning is especially important, since, like later American evangelicals, he was committed to pietistic activism and intrigued by the potential of natural theology.[15] Yet Mather's opposition to any intellectual move that universalized natural ethical instincts at the expense of electing grace was unremitting. Thus, in 1717, he repeated Ames's phrases by contending that "in *Academics*" it was essential to cultivate first "the Art of *Living* to God." Moreover, "the *Languages* and the *Sciences* should be brought into a due subserviencey unto PIETY. What is not subservient, but rather inimical to the MAXIMS OF PIETY should be laid aside. And the common *Ethicks* especially thrown into the Rubbish. . . . The *Philosophy* is but a *Morosophy*, which does not help to Restore fallen Man unto the *Image* and *Service* of GOD."[16] Mather, almost the last of the Puritans, resolutely maintained the priority of revelation over reason, of grace over self-assertion, of conversion over good taste.

By the early eighteenth century, this Puritan distrust of autonomous reason was encountering serious opposition in the broader English-speaking world. The new thought of the eighteenth century was turning against both authoritarian tradition and Puritan biblicism. For moral reasoning, the rational and intellectualist ethics of Aristotle were giving way to the affectional and volitional sensationalism of the third earl of Shaftesbury (1671–1713) and Francis Hutcheson. The impressionistic essays of Shaftesbury and the more systematic treatises of Hutcheson shared a common reliance upon universal human nature as the starting point for ethics and a tendency to treat morality as a foundation for religion rather than the reverse. Later in this chapter, we pause to unpack the ideas of Hutcheson in an effort to explain their appeal in Revolutionary and post-Revolutionary America. Here it is important to note their importance as an alternative to both Aristotelian and Reformed Puritan reasoning.

To heighten the anomaly of what happened later in America, it is important to note that the new moral philosophies met considerable resistance in the British circles that were most closely connected to the colonies. In Scots-Irish Presbyterianism, which was a fruitful source of immigration to America throughout the eighteenth century, there was as much resistance to Hutcheson as acceptance. A story survives that when the young Francis Hutcheson preached as a licentiate for his father at Armagh in Northern Ireland, a Scottish-born elder expressed informally what learned clerics like Cotton Mather were writing in formal treatises at the same time. After listening to the sermon on a Sunday in 1719, the elder took Hutcheson's father aside to complain: "Your silly loon, Frank, has fashed a' the congregation wi' his idle cackle; for he has been babblin' this 'oor aboot a gude and benevolent God, and the sauls o' the heathens themselves will gang tae Heaven if they follow the licht o' their ain consciences. Not a word does the daft boy ken, speer nor say about the gude auld comfortable doctrines o' election, reprobation, original sin and faith."[17] In Ireland, Hutcheson's type of moral reasoning advanced only among those Presbyterians who also drifted toward theological heterodoxy. Irish Presbyterians who rejected Calvinist teachings on original sin and favored a Socinian conception of Jesus were known as New Lights (a usage confusingly at odds with the use of the term in the colonies for supporters of revival). By the mid-eighteenth century, the modernizing theologians in Ireland were also the ones who constituted the party of Hutcheson and the new moral philosophy.[18]

In Scotland, resistance to the new moral philosophy was located primarily among ministers adhering aggressively to the Westminster Confession and among the era's new evangelicals. John Witherspoon (1723–1794), who would later enjoy a momentous American career, was at midcentury the most visible leader of the Popular Party, which opposed the patronage system of the Scottish state-church. Although some of his colleagues in that faction, like William Wishart (d. 1753) of Edinburgh, employed Hutcheson and Shaftesbury to posit a more optimistic view of human nature, Witherspoon did not.[19] For him it was a major failing of the Moderates, who defended patronage, that they were so uncritically enthusiastic for Hutcheson. In a widely noticed satire from 1753, *Ecclesiastical Characteristics*, Witherspoon spoofed the Moderates for promoting what "has been . . . well licked into form and method by the late immortal Mr. Hutcheson."[20] A sermon from January 1758, preached ten years before leaving Scotland to become president of the College of New Jersey at Princeton, reiterated Cotton Mather's complaint against "the unnatural mixture . . . of modern philosophy with ancient Christianity."[21] Theologically conservative Scottish Presbyterians were not quite as antagonistic to the new moral philosophy as American Puritans, but their opposition was sufficiently strong to raise questions about later theological developments in America. In particular, why did American Presbyterians come to have such enthusiasm for the new moral philosophy? Why did John Witherspoon, once he migrated to America, become such a strong advocate of ethical positions he had attacked while in Scotland?

In eighteenth-century England the place of the new moral philosophy was more complex. The tradition of Anglican reasonableness established by Richard Hooker in the late sixteenth century, the failure of the Puritan Revolution, the restoration of Anglicanism as the state church in 1660, the search at many levels during the last third of the seventeenth century for alternatives to "religious enthusiasm" and "monarchical absolutism," the Glorious Revolution of 1688 with its triumph of Whig Anglicanism over Tory extremism, and the mutually profitable alliance between Newtonian science and Anglican social order—all resulted in a religious situation with more toleration for the exercise of human reason and more reliance on the internal moral sense than found elsewhere among English-speaking Reformed Protestants.[22] Nonetheless, if the specific proposals of Hutcheson and Shaftesbury, as well as the more general tendencies of the new moral philosophy, enjoyed some currency among English intellectuals, they did not fare well with orthodox or evangelical groups. Against the newer teachings of a universal, natural moral sense, traditional Anglicans offered the external authorities of a God-ordained monarch, Christianized Aristotelian philosophy, and the sanctions of the church itself.[23] Among the new evangelicals, the sharper the sense of God's grace, the more skepticism about the supposedly innate powers of human nature. As late as the 1770s, John Wesley blasted Francis Hutcheson almost as aggressively as Cotton Mather had done more than fifty years earlier. After reading Hutcheson's *Essay on the Passions*, Wesley conceded that he "is a beautiful writer." But that was the limit of Wesley's appreciation: "His scheme cannot stand unless the Bible falls. I know both from Scripture, reason, and experience that his picture of man is not drawn from life. It is not true that no man is capable of malice, or delight in giving pain; much less that every man is virtuous, and remains so as long as he lives; nor does the Scripture allow that any action is good which is done without any design to please God."[24]

Even before considering major theologians in the colonies, this rapid survey suggests that the more Protestants inclined to theological orthodoxy or evangelicalism, the less likely they were to embrace the new moral philosophy. Not only did the Puritans offer an opposing ethical system, but those British Protestants who most nearly resembled America's dominant parties shied away from commonsense ethical reasoning.

When we turn to the colonies, that general picture of antagonism is sharpened. As late as the middle of the eighteenth century, America's two most important philosopher-theologians, Jonathan Edwards and Samuel Johnson, had become familiar with the new moral philosophy, but neither was pleased with what he was reading. That these divines were the leading intellectuals in the colonies' two largest and most visible denominations adds greater weight to their complaint against the philosophical drift of the age.

For Samuel Johnson to pursue essentially the same course in ethics as Edwards is all the more striking because of their serious theological differences. To be sure, Johnson's conception of how human knowledge fit together moved tentatively away from the sort of theological grounding approved by William Ames and renewed by Edwards. Johnson did lean toward a more modern conception in which the various enterprises of thought, including theology, were subsumed into a moral philosophy constructed from deliverances of the moral sense.[25] Nonetheless, for all Johnson's move toward the modern, he remained an intellectual conservative. When he innovated intellectually, it was usually, like Edwards, to save aspects of traditional theology that he felt the new learning imperiled. Despite ecclesiastical differences, the two leading colonial divines shared a thorough resistance to what they considered the materialistic implications of Newton and Locke and the anthropocentric tendencies of Hutcheson and Shaftesbury.

In natural philosophy, Johnson was a follower of John Hutchinson (1674–1737), a Yorkshire tutor and author who developed biblical views of the material world to counter what he saw as materialistic implications of Newton's gravitational mechanics.[26] From a painstakingly detailed study of the linguistic roots, without vowel points, of Old Testament Hebrew, Hutchinson thought he had discovered an alternative, Bible-based science to the mechanics of

Newton, where, in his opinion, there was no room for God. More generally, Johnson built his metaphysics from Bishop George Berkeley's immaterialism, a scheme that held matter to be God's ideas that he willed humans to perceive in regular, systematic order. For Johnson, Hutchinsonian science and Berkeley's metaphysics were the divinely given antidotes to the poison of the new moral philosophy.

Although Jonathan Edwards's convictions in natural philosophy were developed more systematically, they were similar to Johnson's. Samuel Johnson's idealism was a product of his direct acquaintance with George Berkeley. Jonathan Edwards's idealism grew from a nearly mystical wonder at the perfections of God: "That which truly is the substance of all bodies is the infinitely exact and precise and perfectly stable idea in God's mind, together with his stable will that the same shall gradually be communicated to us, and to other minds, according to certain fixed and exact established methods and laws."[27] In opposition to his era's rising philosophy of nature, Edwards held that the physics of Newton (which he greatly admired) required an idealistic metaphysics everywhere dependent on God. Edwards would have agreed wholeheartedly with a proposition from a sermon by Johnson in 1731, that "this mighty and magnificent show of nature" is, "as it were, the language of Almighty God, whereby He is continually seeking to imprint a sense of Himself, his wisdom, power, and goodness upon our minds."[28]

The objection of Johnson and Edwards to the new moral philosophy followed exactly their objection to the new natural philosophy: it reduced the agency of God by exalting the self-sufficiency of humanity. As is well known, Edwards's mature work drew on a number of intellectual traditions, but all to the same end. His writings were a final stage in Puritan efforts to reconstruct formal thought on the basis of revelation, but they were also the culmination of his own efforts to blend acceptable aspects of the Enlightenment with the new evangelical piety. Several of Edwards's most important works—his books on free will and original sin, and especially his *Two Treatises* (*The Nature of True Virtue* and *The End for Which God Created the World*)—called into question the natural moral capacities that were foundational to the new moral philosophy.[29] Instead, they reasserted in language drawn from an intriguing mix of Puritan, evangelical, and Enlightenment sources the orthodox Protestant insistence on the centrality of God in the moral as well as the physical universe.

Johnson's ethical reasoning is not as well known, but it moved in the same direction. The first edition of his *System of Morals* (1746) had appropriated much of the new moral philosophy. But the 1752 revision included in Johnson's *Elementa Philosophica* was nearly Edwardsean in the care he took to situate the moral deliverances of general human nature within a God-centered framework. In that version, Johnson conceded that "the law of our nature" is "the same thing which some have called the moral sense—*Vide* Shaftsbury [and] Hutcheson." This moral sense was "a kind of quick and almost intuitive sense of right and wrong." Yet Johnson held that if "we rest here" with such notions, ethical reasoning was fatally incomplete. Unless ethics is comprehended under the sovereignty of "the great Author of our

Being, on whom we do entirely depend, and to whom we are therefore, in all reason, accountable," it falls short of "the just and complete notion of morality."[30] Without the subtlety of Edwards's *Nature of True Virtue*, Johnson yet seconded Edwards's conclusion that traditional Christian morality and the new moral philosophy were antagonistic ethical systems.[31]

Despite the stature of Johnson among the Anglicans and Edwards among the Calvinists, their philosophical orientation soon vanished, leaving barely a trace behind. As a modern student of Johnson put it, "From a philosophical standpoint Johnson had no direct disciples."[32] Followers of Edwards did retain some of his ethical precepts—especially by positioning benevolence as both spring and goal of virtue—but none of them thought it was important to resist systematically the new moral philosophy.

The colonial stance toward ethics cannot be reduced to just Jonathan Edwards and Samuel Johnson, influential though they were. A tiny clique of liberal Congregational ministers in and around Boston by no means agreed with the way Edwards, or for that matter Johnson, construed "true virtue." Because the liberal ministers—especially Jonathan Mayhew and Charles Chauncy of Boston and Ebenezer Gay of Hingham—were capable speakers and effective writers, their thought mattered in the environs of Boston and beyond.[33] In general, the Arminians, Universalists, and proto-Unitarians among liberal Congregationalism were united at midcentury in opposing the dualism that the Calvinist revivalists saw in both salvation and morality. They did not believe that redemption divided the world as Edwards and like-minded preachers thought it did. The Boston ministers were not, however, unanimous in support of the new moral philosophy. Jonathan Mayhew was typical. In sermons from the late 1740s and 1750s, he could appeal to a "moral sense" given to humans by God "to distinguish betwixt moral good and evil." But Mayhew also proclaimed that "the law of nature" and "the light of nature" were especially important as guides to behavior.[34] The latter phrases were intellectualist rather than affectional; they bespoke an ethic more aligned with Aristotle and classic views—where reason was to govern passion—than with the new moral philosophers' understanding of affection intuiting the truth. Something of the same combination was found in Ebenezer Gay's Dudleian Lecture at Harvard in 1759, *Natural Religion as Distinguished from Revealed*, where he appealed to the need for "a Rule of Action within [humankind's] own Breasts," but also to "Reason" and "Revelation" as the basis for proper religion and proper behavior.[35] Charles Chauncy seems to have read Shaftesbury, Hutcheson, and other new moral philosophers by the 1740s and 1750s, but he did not publish his views on the universal power of a natural moral sense until the 1780s.[36] For interpreting the rapid shift of American theologians to commonsense moral reasoning in the second half of the century, therefore, these Boston-area ministers are important because they show that opponents of the opponents of the new moral philosophy were not necessarily all-out proponents of the newer views.

If a few colonial divines in the vicinity of Boston were adding newer ethical thinking to a mix of traditional principles, many more at midcentury from throughout the colonies were mobilized for religious causes that implicitly denied the new theories. The surge of evangelical Calvinism in the Great Awakening was led by effective communicators in all colonial regions who to a person repudiated the high view of natural moral capacities underlying the new moral philosophy. Jonathan Dickinson and Gilbert Tennent of New Jersey, Samuel Davies of Virginia, the New England Baptist Isaac Backus— all were aligned with Edwards (and Samuel Johnson) in how they reasoned about morality. Their ethic was conversionist; it divided sharply the whole of humanity between the redeemed, in whom God had implanted a "new sense of the heart" to know and love the ultimately virtuous, and the rest of human- kind, which had to be content with self-centered or self-serving imitations of true virtue. Jonathan Dickinson, the most respected colonial Presbyterian theologian, was typical in a sermon from 1741 that summed up ethical duty in revivalistic rather than commonsensical terms: for entering into "the Way of Duty," he proclaimed, "you can't trust too little your selves; nor too much to him [God]."[37] This Augustinian picture of human morality was the concep- tual engine that drove the preaching of the New England revivals and spread awakened Calvinism into the middle and southern colonies.

A Historical Problem

A problem, therefore, exists in explaining why, from the 1760s onward, American Protestants generally, and American evangelicals in particular, came so rapidly and so thoroughly to embrace the new moral philosophy of com- mon sense, especially in Scottish forms. The Reformation in which Ameri- can Protestantism was rooted, the Puritan tradition that provided Americans their most articulate theological heritage, the revival tradition of the 1730s and 1740s, the arrival in the colonies of immigrant Scots who had opposed Hutcheson in their homeland, and even the mixed sources of liberal Congre- gationalist ethical theory—all make it harder rather than easier to understand why Protestants by 1800 would so wholeheartedly accept the new moral philosophy's appeal to universal human experience. Intellectual developments within late-colonial Protestantism therefore need to be explained, especially since America's two most important Christian thinkers at midcentury, Jonathan Edwards and Samuel Johnson, shared much more with their Euro- pean Protestant predecessors—that is, with William Ames, who held that secularized forms of "metaphysics and ethics" would "vanish spontaneously" when a proper theology prevailed, and with Cotton Mather, who called the eighteenth century's new moral philosophy "a vile Peece of Paganism"—than with their American Protestant successors.[38]

Despite this earlier Protestant history, by the first decades of the nineteenth century, commonsense moral reasoning employed for constructing theistic mental science prevailed everywhere in the new United States, among both laity and clergy, inside the colleges and far beyond. The influence of this di- dactic Enlightenment stretched broadly, from Jefferson and Madison in the

White House to the first professional scientists and the literary pioneers of the new nation.³⁹ But the most articulate spokesmen for the commonsense moral reasoning of the American Enlightenment were Protestant educators and ministers. These principles provided the basis for collegiate instruction at Unitarian Harvard, Baptist Brown, Congregationalist Yale, Presbyterian Princeton, Lutheran Gettysburg, and the rest of the nation's rapidly growing network of colleges, still at this stage almost all connected to denominations. They defined mental habits for Protestants North and South, for dignified urban ministers and enterprising preachers on the frontier, for sober doctrinal conservatives and populist democratic polemicists.⁴⁰

In the absence of sermons promoting military activity, dramatic public controversy, and formal Congressional proclamations, it is more difficult to chart with precision the rise of commonsense ethics than the parallel rise of republican thinking. Yet the big picture is clear. Protestants did journey from militant opposition against the new moral philosophy to nearly universal approval, and that journey coincided with the crises of independence and the establishment of the new United States. If it is not possible to document the exact course of this momentous intellectual transition, circumstantial evidence of many kinds is enough to suggest an explanation.

Internal developments in theology, epistemology, and political theory did not convert Americans from the idealism, Augustinianism, and conversionist ethics of Puritanism to the realism, optimism, and universalistic ethics of theistic mental science. It was rather that the principles of the new moral philosophy, especially in forms close to what Francis Hutcheson first proposed, offered Americans exactly what they needed in order to master the tumults of the Revolutionary era. In the midst of what Nathan Hatch has called "a cultural ferment over the meaning of freedom," an intuitive, universal, natural ethic provided the most intellectually respectable way to secure public virtue in a society that was busy repudiating most of the props upon which virtue had traditionally rested—tradition itself, history, social hierarchy, inherited government, and the authority of state churches.⁴¹ By the mid-eighteenth century, the new moral philosophy began to seem "uniquely suited," as Norman Fiering put it, "to the needs of an era still strongly committed to traditional religious values and yet searching for alternative modes of justification for those values."⁴² For Protestants who wanted to preserve traditional forms of Christianity without having to appeal to traditional religious authorities, commonsense reasoning of the sort provided by Francis Hutcheson was the answer. The Scottish perspective, informed first by Hutcheson and then by Reid, thrived in America, not for narrowly intellectual reasons, but because it suited so perfectly the needs of the emerging nation.

The New Science in Philadelphia, 1787

Two programs of study that came to fruition in the same place at nearly the same time illustrate the intellectual trajectory of the era. The first was the labor of James Madison during the months before the opening of the Philadelphia Constitutional Convention in May 1787. Madison prepared for that gathering by conducting a private historical seminar that resulted in two memoranda, "Of Ancient and Modern Confederacies" and "Vices of the Political System of the United States."[43] Both were products of what we would today call social science, that is, systematic reflection on past and present circumstances for the purpose of establishing reliable conclusions about the political tendencies of human beings in general. Significantly, Madison undertook this historical study not to find out what past actions American patriots should imitate, but in order to make his own independent judgments about conditions under which societies flourished. In the face of a national crisis, he was turning instinctively to a systematic, or scientific, study of political behavior to find assistance for guiding the uncertain destiny of the United States. He was doing so self-consciously as his own master.

The second course of study lay behind the annual oration at Philadelphia's American Philosophical Society on 27 February 1787, three months before the Constitutional Convention convened on 25 May. The speaker was Samuel Stanhope Smith, the professor of moral philosophy and theology from the College of New Jersey in Princeton. Smith (1751–1819), a Presbyterian minister, was one of America's first professional academics to study the ethics of Francis Hutcheson and also one of the first Americans to incorporate the insights of Thomas Reid into his own work.[44] Smith's address, "Essay on the Causes of the Variety of Complexion and Figure in the Human Species," took up recent proposals from Europe that humanity was made up of several different species. Against such views, Smith contended that climate and geography were enough to explain the differences of skin color and bodily form that had developed within a common human stock. Smith offered a full catalog of learned evidence to support his thesis, but his greatest concern was not in the least ethnographic. As he put it toward the end of his address, those who "deny the unity of the human species" introduce tremendous "confusion." If there really were a plurality of human types, he concluded, "the science of morals would be absurd . . . no general principles of human conduct, of religion, or of policy could be framed."[45] Without the unity of humanity, no science of morals. Without a science of morals, total anarchy. Smith's philosophical study ended at the same terminus as Madison's political inquiry. Useful knowledge—scientifically ascertained—put those who discovered it in a position to frame systems and so fend off chaos.

The ways in which James Madison and Stanhope Smith were putting to use the new moral philosophy help explain its rise in America. The idealistic metaphysics and theocentric ethics of Jonathan Edwards and Samuel Johnson, which fifty years before were central in colonial American thought, were now everywhere in retreat, precisely because they offered so little for meeting the crises of American public life. A new social setting demanded a new form of ethical reasoning. The process by which the new moral philosophy, heavily indebted to models from the Scottish Enlightenment and useful for constructing ethics scientifically, became the regnant American philosophy owed more

to the usefulness of its ideas in the American context (an "external" explanation) than to its triumph in the sphere of merely intellectual reasoning (an
"internal" explanation).

As it happens, Smith, like Madison, was a student of John Witherspoon,
the dynamic Scot who had taken up the presidency at Princeton in 1768 just
as Smith was finishing his college career and Madison was beginning his.[46]
Witherspoon was not the first proponent of the Scottish science of morals in
America, but he was soon the most influential. In early 1787 both Smith and
Madison were putting to use general habits of mind they had first learned as
a part of Witherspoon's course in moral philosophy at Princeton. For both,
the most useful element of this teaching was its guidance concerning universal human nature and the methods by which to discover such universals—for
Smith it was directly a "science of morals," for Madison it was the "science
of politics," or the "science of government," about which he and Alexander
Hamilton would write in *The Federalist*.[47] In turn, both expected the findings
of "science" to meet the crises of the hour. Madison's "political science" would
show the way out of the impasse brought on by the weaknesses of the Articles of Confederation. Smith's "moral science" would rescue a culture threatened by infidelity, moral decay, and the excesses of egalitarianism.

The fact that thinkers like Madison and Stanhope Smith were students of
Witherspoon and that Witherspoon was the leading proponent of Scottish
moral philosophy in the Revolutionary era helps show why the new ethical
reasoning advanced so readily. Examining Witherspoon is important, but not
because Witherspoon's intellect itself was so powerful. Witherspoon clearly
played a major role in spreading Scottish principles through his instruction
of an influential generation of Princeton students, and then to a wider audience through his published lectures. Yet Witherspoon's intellectual influence
rested more on the magnetism of his personality than on the power of his
reasoning. He was a forceful, shrewd leader, but not a particularly astute
philosopher. He composed his lectures in moral philosophy on the run during his first months in America, and he regularly used rhetoric rather than
argument to overcome opposing views.[48] Witherspoon's earliest biographer,
Ashbel Green, passed on firsthand reports of how Witherspoon won his way
at Princeton in 1768: "The Berklean system of Metaphysics was in repute in
the college when he entered on his office. The tutors were zealous believers
in it, and waited on the President with some expectation of either confound-
ing him, or making him a proselyte. They had mistaken their man. He first
reasoned against the System, and then ridiculed it, till he drove it out of the
college."[49] Witherspoon was no buffoon. But it was not his abilities as a dia-
lectician that secured a Scottish perspective in America.

Something Witherspoon once said does, however, suggest why the stance
he promoted became so prominent in America. As an old man, Witherspoon
reflected on the Scottish perspective he had provided to his Princeton students
but denied that he had ever been influenced by Thomas Reid. Witherspoon
specifically groused that one of his own earlier writings, an essay from 1753,
had anticipated the key points that Reid used in his refutations of David Hume

from the mid-1760s.[50] The claim is interesting. Witherspoon's 1753 essay did move in the general direction of Reid's efforts, which was to reestablish epistemology on a firm basis by arguing that "the ideas we receive by our senses, and the persuasions we derive immediately from them, are exactly according to truth, which certainly ought to be the same with philosophic truth."[51] It is also true that Witherspoon's lectures on moral philosophy at Princeton, which were substantially complete by 1772, did not refer at all to Reid or his writings and only incidentally to other Scottish thinkers directly influenced by Reid.[52]

Yet Witherspoon's sensitivity about what he was *not* borrowing from Scotland did not obscure what he *was* taking over from his native land, which was mostly from Francis Hutcheson. Witherspoon in fact incorporated so much material from Hutcheson's writings that, in the opinion of the most careful modern student of the subject, Witherspoon's work "borders on plagiarism."[53] Significantly, what Witherspoon drew from Francis Hutcheson in the early 1770s was exactly what James Madison and Stanhope Smith would later employ to construct public policy and moral guidelines in the late 1780s: the treatment of ethics as a moral science analogous to the physical sciences, a conception of morality as ascertained through study of universal human nature, and a repudiation of the older, more strictly Christian ethics of the Puritans, Jonathan Edwards, and Samuel Johnson, with their restriction of true virtue to the elect.[54] Witherspoon's unacknowledged use of Hutcheson's ethical principles, along with the distinction between Hutcheson and Reid, offers critical insight for understanding the American appropriation of theistic common sense.

Commonsense Ethics in a Rapidly Changing America

A great social transformation lay behind the shift in ethical axioms. That shift began in the religious and domestic circumstances of the 1730s and 1740s before it took political shape a generation later. The colonial revivalists, who were conservative in doctrine, nonetheless helped create the social conditions in which a new intellectual perspective could flourish. The revival compromised the traditional importance of inherited structures by placing more emphasis on the individual's reception of God's grace than on the individual's place in an inherited ecclesiastical order. Its ideal of the pure church hastened a sectarian fragmentation of the traditionally inclusive state churches. Its fervent millennialism encouraged a negative opinion of the theological past. Its extemporaneous mode of address undercut traditional reliance upon classical norms of public speech. In each of these ways, the Awakening loosened the bonds of tradition that had survived the migration from old world to new. The Awakening also contributed to the general breakup of family cohesion that increasingly characterized eighteenth-century colonial life.[55] Land shortages in older communities, the enticement of unsettled terrain in the West, and increasing opportunities for social advancement all militated against the authority of the past. The end of conflict with France in 1763 only accelerated the forces working against traditional social order. Large-scale migrations westward added to worries on the coast about the loss of social control in the hinterlands. Eighteenth-century colonial society was not anarchical, but it was a place where ingenuity in meeting present needs paid greater rewards than simple deference to tradition. In this new-world environment, traditional or external authorities were increasingly on the defensive.

Effects of revival and rapid westward migration, however, are not enough to explain the loss of confidence in traditional ethical authorities and the rapid acceptance of commonsense moral reasoning. Rather, it was the political crises after midcentury that sealed the connection between American social realities and Scottish forms of Enlightenment thought. The Stamp Act struggle of 1764–1765 mobilized colonial opposition against the sovereignty of Parliament, a mobilization that advanced through heightened stages of intensity until the outbreak of hostilities in 1775. A bitter war—as much a civil conflict between colonial factions as between colonists and the mother country—followed. Then, before patriots could savor the success of arms against Britain, they faced the stupendous tasks of reorganizing their own society, crafting workable instruments of government, and restraining the centrifugal forces released by the war.[56]

Against this background the kind of reasoning promoted by Francis Hutcheson was a godsend. But to show why it became significant for America—and so a significant force in altering the assumptions brought to the writing of theology—it is necessary to detour slightly in order to review Hutcheson's life in the context of eighteenth-century Scottish intellectual history. To view Hutcheson in his social context is to see why ideas like his made such an impression in Revolutionary America.

Francis Hutcheson was born in County Down, now Northern Ireland, in 1694.[57] He followed his father and grandfather into the Presbyterian ministry but early on found his vocation as professor rather than pastor. Hutcheson studied at a Presbyterian academy in Ireland before entering Glasgow University in 1711. As a theological student he was influenced by John Simson, one of the first Church of Scotland ministers to question traditional accounts of sinful human nature and Christ's substitutionary atonement for human sin.[58] Also very early, Hutcheson began to defend the principles of Whig liberty that became an abiding passion throughout his career. Despite questions about his theological orthodoxy, he was licensed in 1719 by the General Synod of Ulster but almost immediately began to teach, first at a private academy in Dublin and then from 1730 to his death in 1746 at the University of Glasgow.

Hutcheson published his earliest works, on beauty and the passions, in the 1720s. His more general moral philosophy was communicated in teaching at Glasgow and then brought out in final form after his death.[59] It represented a comprehensive system built on sensationalist, or affectional, ethics—that is, replacing Aristotle's and the scholastic tradition's grounding of morality in reason with a reliance on an innate moral sense of beauty, fitness, or goodness as the true foundation of ethics. Hutcheson died not long after David Hume (1711–1776) brought out his *Treatise of Human Nature* in 1739 and shortly before the 1748 publication of Hume's *Enquiry concerning the Human Understanding* (with its skeptical treatise "On Miracles") and the 1751 appearance of Hume's *Enquiry concerning the Principles of Morals*.

To oversimplify a complex picture, the extreme skepticism of Hume transformed Hutcheson's ethics, hitherto of interest only to a small coterie, into a major defense against moral anarchy. Hutcheson's insistence that an innate, universal moral sense could reliably determine the good and the true made his thought naturally attractive to those who were disconcerted by Hume's arguments. Hutcheson seemed to provide a scientific defense of what Hume attacked, especially the connection between causes and effects, cosmological proofs for the existence of God, and the truthfulness of testimony in support of miracles. Against Hume's assaults, the readers of Hutcheson could deploy the secure testimony of the moral sense. Also important for an age growing in its respect for science was the Hutchesonian claim that, by attending systematically to what that moral sense communicated, it was possible to construct a Baconian ethical science.

Thinkers in America were among the first to exploit Hutcheson's ideas as an antidote to Humean and other forms of instability. By the 1750s, even as Witherspoon was chastising Hutcheson in polemics directed against the Scottish Moderates, Hutcheson's moral philosophy had been introduced at Harvard, it was being taught at the College of Philadelphia by the Scottish immigrant Francis Alison, it had made an impression at the College of William and Mary on the young Thomas Jefferson, and it was being read by students of Jonathan Edwards like Joseph Bellamy in Connecticut.[60]

Thomas Reid would offer an even more substantial response to Hume, but his major study, the *Inquiry into the Human Mind on the Principles of Common Sense*, appeared only in 1764, more than a decade after Hutcheson's work had been widely publicized in the colonies.[61] For its part, Reid's response to Hume's epistemological skepticism featured subtle arguments concerning how ordinary human experience simply required people to take for granted the existence of an external world, real connections between causes and effects, and other commonplaces that Hume had questioned. Reid held that such principles of universal common sense were so basic to human experience that even skeptical arguments casting them into doubt could not even be proposed without implicitly confirming the reality of those principles. In particular, Reid attacked Hume for radicalizing the notion of "ideas" that had come through John Locke and Bishop George Berkeley. According to Reid, it was not the case—as Locke, Berkeley, and Hume assumed—that human perception rested on mental "simple ideas" caused by sensations of the external world. Reid flatly denied that senses "caused" ideas in the way that Hume and Locke proposed. The absurdity of this notion of ideas was the doorway through which Hume had blundered. Rather, Reid held that the human mind perceived directly the objects of sense, especially complex states of being, and that the mind did not require the unnecessary notion of intermediate "simple ideas." Hence, for reasons having to do with the epistemological weakness of Hume's proposals, skepticism was not the major threat it appeared to be.

Reid's work eventually became the definitive statement of Scottish commonsense philosophy, but he was not read widely in America until after the Revolutionary period.[62] Only then did a new intellectual generation, with leaders like Stanhope Smith at Princeton, Timothy Dwight at Yale, and David Tappan at Harvard, put to use Reid's mature works or, more often, those of Reid's colleague and popularizer, James Beattie.[63] It was not until the 1790s, when Dugald Stewart brought out his *Elements of the Philosophy of Mind*, a popularization of Reid's more recondite studies, and when Stewart solicited philosophical articles in accord with Reid's ideas for the third and fourth editions of the *Encyclopedia Britannica* (1788–1794, 1801–1810), that what we could call the American school of commonsense philosophy was linked conclusively to Reid.

In sum, the beachhead in America for the principles of the Scottish Enlightenment was provided by the sentimentalist ethics of Francis Hutcheson rather than the realist epistemology of Thomas Reid.[64] In addition, these Hutchesonian ideas received their most effective promotion from John Witherspoon, a busy college president, national legislator, and ecclesiastical politician, rather than through careful intellectuals like Hume or Reid. This chronology explains why American defense against the skeptical and irreligious radicalism of the eighteenth century first rested on an innate moral sense (Hutcheson) and then only later on attacks against the concept of simple ideas (Reid). When accounts of the Scottish philosophy leap over Hutcheson to concentrate on Reid, as was already happening by the early nineteenth century, the circumstances under which theistic mental science won its way in America are obscured.[65]

The cachet of Hutcheson's kind of moral philosophy was its adaptability to the pressing dilemmas of the American experiment. The two great intellectual tasks confronting political leaders of the Revolutionary generation were matched by a challenge of equal gravity for Protestants who joined the patriot cause. The first need was to justify the break from Great Britain with ideology strong enough to overcome the weight of legal precedent, the venerated traditions of British constitutionalism, and the sacred aura of British liberty that had enraptured the colonists only short years before. The second need was to establish principles of social order for a new nation that, in its repudiation of autocratic government, hierarchical political assumptions, and automatic deference to tradition, was repudiating the only props for social order that the world then knew. The third, specifically Protestant task was to preserve the hereditary position of Christianity in a culture that was turning against the structures of traditional religion (like the political episcopate or the Congregational establishment in New England) as actively as it was turning against other inherited authorities. Moreover, patriots, both political and religious, needed not merely moral and intellectual justifications but justifications untainted by old world traditions associated with the corrupting forces of "tyranny."

For each of these tasks, the kind of reasoning promoted by Francis Hutcheson proved irresistible.[66] The critical requirement was to find a scientific, universal, and optimistic ethical theory that did not require the sanction of tradition. Whether colonists cited his name or not, Hutcheson's work showed the way, first, by demonstrating the value of the new moral philosophy for justifying colonial resistance to an unjust mother country. Second, he provided up-to-date arguments, not themselves dependent upon theological tradition, that traditional Protestants could use in defending the Christian faith. Hutcheson, in other words, illuminated the path that American Protestants trod to the evangelical Enlightenment.[67]

Hutcheson found for ethics the scientific credibility that the age of Newton required by drawing an analogy between the "moral sense" and the external senses that drove Locke's psychology and Newton's physics. The "moral sense," according to Hutcheson, was as much a part of the "frame of our nature" as the physical senses.[68] Just as the physical senses made possible knowledge of the laws of physical nature, so the moral sense made it possible to understand the natural laws of virtue and vice. Such a mental science was particularly useful for considerations of public life because it revealed the existence of certain natural rights of liberty. In Hutcheson's words, "This right of natural liberty is not only suggested by the selfish parts of our constitution but by many generous affections, and by our *moral sense*, which represents our own voluntary actions as the grand dignity and perfection of our nature."[69]

Of critical importance, Hutcheson's ethical theory was also universalistic. It did not depend upon an Augustinian or Puritan view of virtue, in which the action of God's grace was restricted to the elect. "Each one," as Hutcheson defined the moral sense in his *System of Moral Philosophy*, may recognize that there is "a natural and immediate determination to approve certain affections, and actions consequent upon them."[70] Third, reliance on the moral sense provided a way to escape the anarchy that in the seventeenth century Robert Filmer and Thomas Hobbes had predicated for nonauthoritarian societies. Moral perceptions of virtue and vice, honor and shame, were fully capable of leading to personal goodness and social harmony.[71]

Finally, Hutcheson argued that citizens could safely rely upon the communications of the moral sense without needing the sanctions of traditional authorities or the hoary dictates of the past. Hutcheson's ethics, like those of the Puritans or Edwards, were affectional. They looked to the heart, or to the affections, as the surest ground for honorable behavior. Unlike these Calvinist systems, however, Hutcheson required no special place for revelation from beyond the individual, or even for authoritative direction from other human sources. Humans—if they exercised their inherent (albeit God-given) faculties in a disciplined, responsible way—could know ethical maxims simply by nature and could by nature will the good that harmonious human existence required.

On the basis of such reasoning, which Hutcheson himself linked to the political ideology of the British Real Whigs, American Revolutionaries both justified their rebellion against the Crown and set about constructing a new social order. What weight could the traditional authority of the king in Parliament carry against the "self-evident truths," the "unalienable rights," or the "laws of nature" heralded by the Declaration of Independence? Behind these Revolutionary ideas lay not just the political theories of Locke and other political Whigs. Just as much they drew on the capital that a Hutchesonian ethics had piled up in America. What need was there for a careful rebuttal of authorities, or even a careful perusal of Scripture, to justify rebellion, if it was transparent to the properly exercised moral sense that such a rebellion was necessary?[72]

In America, republican theory shared fully the general spirit of the new moral philosophy. Real Whig thought was predicated upon a defense of natural rights. In America it sustained a continual optimism concerning capacities to create the world anew. It also staked its future on an ability to discover natural resources for pressing social needs.[73] Political realists like James Madison, Alexander Hamilton, and John Adams might temper in different ways Enlightenment optimism concerning the new order, but they never doubted that the secret of the Revolution's success lay in discovering the moral laws of human behavior through "the science of politics" and putting them to use in creating a new age, a process that historian Gordon Wood has called "the consuming passion of the Enlightenment."[74]

Similarly, the new guardians of American public virtue could rely on the "moral sense" to restate traditional morality in scientific form without needing to call on the traditional props for ethics, including sometimes even the special revelation of the Bible. Witherspoon could say in his lectures, for example, that, although depravity makes it difficult to understand human nature, and although "the whole Scripture is perfectly agreeable to sound philosophy," nonetheless, when we study ourselves, we end up with the principles for a just and stable society. In his words, "The principles of duty and obligation must be drawn from the nature of man."[75]

So much a follower of Hutcheson did Witherspoon, the old-world opponent of Hutcheson, become, he could even claim that when humans studied their own minds, they could find the proper basis for a just and stable society. In fact, Witherspoon hoped that "a time may come when men, treating moral philosophy as Newton and his successors have done natural [philosophy], may arrive at greater precision" on ethical principles.[76] These were principles, moreover, which everyone who harkened to the moral sense would also find convincing. Thus, Americans had close at hand—within themselves—the resources to bring social order out of the rootlessness of eighteenth-century colonial life and the confusion of the Revolution.

The deliverances of the moral sense became just as important for religious leaders in their search for an anchor for stabilizing faith. It was precisely the "sublimity" of "the doctrines contained in Scripture concerning God, his works, and creatures, and his relation to them" that Witherspoon advanced as the first proof of Christianity, since it "must necessarily have the approbation of unprejudiced reason."[77] American Protestant thinkers did not use extensively the categories of the new moral philosophy until the 1790s, at which time apologists once again were able to take up theistic proofs as refurbished by commonsense epistemology.[78] But even these arguments continued to make much of the innate communications of the moral sense. In the words of one opponent of Tom Paine, nothing worked better at squelching Paine's deism than simple "common sense."[79]

Stanhope Smith's great effort to systematize morality, which lay behind his address in 1787 and everything else he taught and published in a long career, was a specific instance of a general trend. As a Presbyterian minister, Smith naturally defended the harmony of old theology and new moral philosophy, as in his Philadelphia oration in 1787: "I am happy to observe . . . that the most accurate investigations into the power of nature ever serve to confirm the facts vouched by the authority of revelation. A just philosophy will always be found to be coincident with the true theology."

The force a "just philosophy" could exert on a "true theology" was indicated by the movement of Smith's thought. He was contending earnestly for the unity of humanity, since only by presuming that unity could the new moral philosophy move from an examination of one's own heart to universally valid principles of social order. This power would be destroyed if humanity did not constitute a unified species. If humanity were indeed made up of different species, it would be disastrous for society as well as for the reconciliation of religion and science: "Human nature . . . could not be comprehended in any system. The rules which would result from the study of our own nature, would not apply to the natives of other countries who would be of different species. . . . Such principles tend to confound all science, as well as piety; and leave us in the world uncertain whom to trust, or what opinions to frame of others."[80]

Such an investment in the era's commonsense ethics marked a fundamental reversal of earlier positions, a fact that at least a few observers noted at the time. John Trumbull, who later became a renowned Connecticut litterateur, published as a twenty-year-old a series of newspaper essays in early 1770 that spoofed the confusion at work. As he described the "New System of Logic," it contained a fatal contradiction. On the one hand was traditional Christian ethics: "First, That the common sense and reason of mankind is so weak and fallacious a guide, that its dictates ought never to be regarded." But on the other hand was the new moral philosophy: "Secondly . . . nothing is so great that it can surpass, or so perplexing that it can entangle, the understanding of a true metaphysician." Trumbull understood the logic of the age and so was able to poke fun at the reasoning processes that were just beginning to exert their sway: "I can take these points to be so nearly self-evident that although I can say very little in proof of them, the reader ought for this very reason the more firmly to believe them. For such is the nature of every self-evident proposition that no arguments can be brought to prove it."[81]

The self-evidence of consciousness was for the young Trumbull an object of satire. By contrast, it was the way of the future for people who thought like Witherspoon and Stanhope Smith. Their fusion of traditional religion and the new moral philosophy was in fact the path followed by most of the country's Christian intellectuals over the next seventy-five years.[82] Explicit in the lectures and textbooks of the nation's leading intellectuals was the

Enlightenment belief that Americans could find within themselves resources, compatible with Christianity, to bring social order out of the rootlessness and confusion of the new nation.

Most Protestants in Revolutionary America did not rely on Hutcheson explicitly for their opinions, though a few like Witherspoon did so. Appeal to an authority like Hutcheson would, however, have missed the point, since the key to knowledge (as in fact Hutcheson argued) was study of one's own consciousness. Protestant commitment to theistic common sense became deeply ingrained because it seemed so intuitive, so instinctive, so much a part of second nature. As a result, many Protestants denied that they had a philosophy or deferred to an intellectual authority; they were merely following common sense.

Connections among events, ideologies, personal biographies, and religion are complicated, but in this instance, also clear. The great influence of the Revolution on American thought meant that the form of reasoning by which patriots justified their rebellion against the Crown became also the form of reasoning by which worried public men sought a stable social order for the new nation and which Protestant leaders used to defend the place of traditional faith in a traditionless society.

The strength or weakness of commonsense moral philosophy as a narrowly conceived intellectual system was never at issue in Revolutionary and post-Revolutionary America. Rather, the establishment of commonsense moral reasoning as the dominant conceptual language for Protestant discourse was a by-product of larger cultural transitions. The enduring shape that theistic mental science assumed in the nineteenth century owed a great deal to Thomas Reid and his immediate disciples, Beattie and Stewart. But Reid's commonsense epistemology gained its place in large part because it extrapolated for narrower concerns a means of solving intellectual problems—first promoted by Francis Hutcheson—that had already enjoyed momentous success in politics, society, and religion. In Revolutionary America, the cry everywhere was for independence, practicality, self-sufficiency, and universal political empowerment. For the traditional Christian ethics of Jonathan Edwards or Samuel Johnson, there was now scant room, since Americans required ethical guidelines available to all and reliably persuasive for all.[83]

Theologians, as is made clear in the next two chapters, were relatively slow in adjusting inherited convictions to the new moral philosophy. But by the early nineteenth century the infectious language of theistic common sense was everywhere affecting the languages of traditional theology. Of course there always remained much more to theological construction, including Scripture, the practices of worship, some lingering influence of historic confessions, and more. Yet when the cross-pollination between inherited doctrines and new moral philosophy began to bear fruit, the result could truly be called an American theology, since the reasoning of theistic common sense had contributed so integrally to the creation of the government of the new United States and, even more, of the new nation's intellectual culture.

Colonial Theologies in the Era of the Revolution

During the half century between George Whitefield's first arrival in the colonies (1738) and the ratification of the Constitution (1788), the ground was shifting under theology, yet most practitioners on the surface seemed hardly to notice. Before the War for Independence proceeded very far, the alliance between republican and Protestant worldviews was solid. By the mid-1780s a similar alliance of comparable strength joined Protestantism and the new commonsense moral philosophy. Both of these alliances were remarkable for how they reversed intellectual standoffs dating from the Reformation. A third alliance, between Protestant dogma and a belief in the messianic destiny of the new United States under God, had been anticipated by much Anglo-American history, but it too would have an effect on theology. These alliances set the stage for the emergence of an America where the values of evangelical Protestantism shaped public life and where, in turn, the evolution of public life shaped theology.

Into the 1790s, however, and despite an ideological cauldron on the boil, theological affirmation remained for the most part as it had been. Besides the new moral philosophy and a full spectrum of competing republicanisms (classical, deferential, democratic, self-assertive, liberal), the conceptual languages at play in this period also included Newtonian science, new notions of state sovereignty, and the common law.[1] Despite this profusion of aggressive ideologies, however, theology remained remarkably constant. Where theological innovations did take place, they came mostly from importing British progressive opinion or from the extrapolation of themes indigenous to the Protestant pietist tradition. The half century before 1790 thus features "theological development in America" more than "American theologies." Theologians were maneuvering through cultural turbulence, but their thought remained inner-directed, guided primarily by the internal logic of inherited traditions. Only after about 1790 came the self-conscious accommodation of inherited beliefs to norms generated by experience in the new nation, creative new religious expressions in which themes from the national culture bulked large (as with Mormons and the Churches of Christ), or self-conscious moves by conservatives enlisting aid from outside the United States in order to resist accommodation to American popular culture. Before the end of the eighteenth century, in other words, and despite the massive intermingling of conceptual languages that had been going on since the 1750s, Christian theology was still determined more by European and colonial experience than by the events of the American founding. Theology in the United States into the 1790s resembled theology as it would remain in Canada throughout the nineteenth century, where theologians interacted with local environments but still took their bearing from English, Scottish, Ulster, and anti-Revolutionary French sources.[2]

A survey of the main ecclesiastical traditions in the Revolutionary period is required to demonstrate this stability on the surface as well as to notice where subterranean forces were building up below. The relatively static character of theology during this age is most clearly visible in colonial traditions that maintained close contact with the old world—namely, the Lutherans, the Dutch Reformed, the Anglicans (or Episcopalians, as they became in the 1780s), and the Roman Catholics. The situation for the two largest and most articulate Protestant bodies—Congregationalists, concentrated almost exclusively in New England, and Presbyterians, who were much more widely dispersed in the colonies but strongest along the New York–Philadelphia axis—is somewhat more complicated. Although Presbyterians and traditional Congregationalists engaged in lively intramural debates, those debates took place largely within inherited frameworks. Only a small band of liberal Congregationalists in and about Boston may be said to have undertaken significant theological innovation during the period, but those innovations sprang more directly from British ideas imported to America than from the conscious appropriation of American circumstances.

The two other groups that witnessed some theological innovation during the period were free-thinking deists and populist theologians of the people. Deists, however, even more than the liberal Congregationalists, took their cues from Europe. For their part, America's growing number of Christian populists, though breaking the mold of inherited church tradition, proved remarkably conservative through the 1780s. Such populists turned out to maintain traditional theological doctrines, or they innovated with resources drawn from revivalism rather than from the Revolutionary creation of the United States of America.

In all denominations, the vast changes at work under the surface did not appreciably alter the shape of dogma until the decisive decades following the implementation of the Constitution. From that time, however, a singularly evangelical contribution to the forging of national culture began to be matched by singular American influences on the nation's theologians. This chapter treats the theological traditions where dogma remained mostly unchanged during the Revolutionary era. In the next we examine the communities where innovation, though not necessarily innovation driven by distinctly American experience, occurred.

Lutherans

In the century before the ratification of the Constitution, about 120,000 German-speaking immigrants arrived in the thirteen colonies.[3] By the 1790s there were nearly 250 Lutheran congregations in Pennsylvania, a scattering of other Lutherans in New York, Maryland, Virginia, and the Carolinas, and a rapidly multiplying array of German sectarian churches. From the beginning of immigration, ministers of German congregations, no less than their people, were adjusting old-world expectations to circumstances in the new. For Lutherans, who represented the largest group of German immigrants as well as the strongest theological tradition, that process was complex. Lutherans brought with them at least two distinguishable notions of liberty, though both were shaped by the pietist revival of the eighteenth century. From the missionary-minded pietist institutions at Halle in Prussia came a positive notion of freedom as the potential for philanthropic service to God and fellow humans. From southwestern Germany, by contrast, came a negative idea of freedom as liberation from external coercion, alongside the promotion of inner godliness. Both notions, moreover, sustained variable associations with assumptions about property that did not square easily with British or colonial practice.

By the time of the Revolution, a full generation of conceptual evolution had drawn German-speakers closer to the web of political and social conceptions sustained by English-language colonists. Pious promoters of godliness as well as the more active philanthropists had begun to incorporate British notions about the protection of property into inherited German conceptions of freedom. By the 1760s a second printer to serve German-Americans had become a competitor to the Sower (or Sauer) family, who through the Revolution would promote a more strictly pious agenda through publications from their press.[4] This second printer, Henry Miller (Anglicized from Heinrich Möller), later published German translations of Tom Paine's *Common Sense* and the Declaration of Independence. As early as 1765, Miller was freely using the standard Whig vocabulary of "slavery" and "liberty" to describe the contemporary Stamp Act crisis. A decades-long dispute in Philadelphia's St. Michael's Church between a wealthier group of earlier immigrants and a number of later, poorer arrivals also led to the interchange of German and English political concepts. The reactions to which this process of acculturation led can be illustrated by the family of Henry Melchior Mühlenberg (1711–1787), patriarch of American Lutheranism, who, after arriving from Halle in 1742, oversaw the organization of a viable Lutheran presence in North America. During the War for Independence, Mühlenberg himself remained neutral, one son (Friedrich) hesitated before leaving his pulpit to serve with the patriots, while another son (Peter) leaped readily to the cause of independence, because, as he put it to his reluctant brother: "I am a Clergyman, it is true, but I am a member of Society as well as the poorest Layman, & my Liberty is as dear to me as to any Man."[5]

Even those German-American Lutherans, like Peter Mühlenberg's father, who could not so easily speak the Whig language of liberty, often made a self-conscious accommodation to American assumptions. The senior Mühlenberg, who clung to neutrality during the Revolution despite buffeting from both sides, nonetheless counseled his fellow Lutherans to learn from their new environment. In 1763 he reported on how some parties in the Lutheran churches were insisting upon an "American liberty" to select their own pastors. Soon he passed from acknowledgment to acceptance, as in counsel to a fellow pastor in New York: "The English Constitution, the American climate, and many other considerations, demanded . . . that each member in each community must have the right to vote or at least have a hand in voting."[6] By the 1770s, in other words, German-speaking Lutherans, while not abandoning the social and political inheritance of their homelands, had begun to adjust to American political realities.

What they had not yet adjusted, however, was theology as such. Not until the 1790s did American Lutherans turn in any significant degree from the confessional assumptions of their tradition—that is, from theological fidelity to the Augsburg Confession and the liturgical practice of sacramental realism (belief in the saving power of baptism and communion that other Americans have always had difficulty distinguishing from Roman Catholic sacramental realism). In his dealings with German immigrants who were drifting away from their hereditary church, Mühlenberg consistently upheld his own seamless brand of pious orthodoxy. On the Lord's Supper, he warned against the extremes of Roman Catholic transubstantiation and against Reformed or Baptist memorialism. Especially in America, those who in celebrating the Lord's Supper wanted to "exchange the real for the shadow" became a major problem. Baptism, Mühlenberg insisted with equal loyalty to Lutheran tradition, was genuinely "a rebirth." Although baptism was not conversion, it did mean "being cut off from the guilty and corrupt family of Adam and being translated, ingrafted, or incorporated into Christ's kingdom of grace."[7] Mühlenberg eventually became a skillful speaker of English, but the conceptual languages of the colonies did not exert a noticeable effect on the traditional language of his faith.

Movement toward a more distinctly American form of Lutheran theology did not take place until, after Mühlenberg's death in 1787, the social revolution of the 1780s and 1790s began to do its work. The Reverend J. H. C. Helmuth was the pastor from 1779 to 1820 of the St. Michael's and Zion Lutheran Church in Philadelphia, which for much of this period was the largest congregation of any kind in the city. As we have already seen, Helmuth accepted the logic of political independence and welcomed a degree of democratic experimentation in the expression of faith. By the 1790s, however, Helmuth was becoming alarmed at what seemed to him a heedless rush by his fellow Lutherans to sacrifice their theological heritage on the altar of democratic individualism.[8] The nature of Helmuth's complaint, especially on the deployment of the Bible in the period after the Revolution, will require further examination in chapter 18 below. Here it is important to make a chronological point. Until well after independence was secured, Lutheran theology per se remained largely what it had been. Whatever forces were drawing the traditional vocabularies of central European Lutheran pietism toward the political assumptions of the new world, those forces had no obvious impact upon Lutheran theology itself until the 1790s. At that time, however, a battle would begin—precisely over how much Americanization could be accepted in traditional Lutheran teachings about the meaning of baptism, the practice of the Lord's Supper, and the interpretation of the Augsburg Confession— that continued for more than half a century. However weak or insecure Lutheran theology was before the 1790s, it remained the theology of Lutheran orthodoxy as defined by its pietistic exponents in the new world.

Dutch Reformed

The Reformed Dutch, who made up a considerable presence in New York and New Jersey, counted as a significant theological force in the middle colonies during the Revolutionary period because of their place among the region's hereditary elite and the resilience of their ethnic communities.[9] By the 1780s there were about 125 Dutch Reformed churches in the new United States.[10] In that decade the Dutch also became the first American denomination to institute formal theological education for its ministerial candidates when it commissioned for the task John Henry Livingston (1746–1825), an American-born, Yale- and Utrecht-educated scion of an old New York family. As with German Lutherans, the decades surrounding the Revolution were years of linguistic transition for the Reformed Dutch in two senses. They were moving from the use of a European language to English, which perhaps explains the cloud of controversy that surrounded the first minister called to preach in English, the Scottish-born Archibald Laidlie, who began his service in 1764. By 1803 regular preaching in the language of the old country had ceased in New York City's Dutch Reformed congregations.[11] They were also moving from inherited conceptions of human nature, God, and the social order to more American expressions. Yet despite significant changes on both linguistic fronts from the 1760s, the Reformed theology inherited from the Netherlands and enlivened during the colonial period by the revivalism associated with Theodorus Frelinghuysen (1691–1747) remained firmly in place.[12] In their basic theology the Reformed Dutch again resembled the German Lutherans, for that theology represented a subtle blend of orthodox and pietist elements.

Partly as a result of Frelinghuysen's active evangelical preaching, the Reformed Dutch underwent a schism between an American-leaning *Coetus* (synod) and a Dutch-anchored *Conferentie* (conference). The schism, which lasted form 1754 to 1772, formed the backdrop for the introduction of Whig political language. (Some offshoots of the Reformed Dutch, for whom the process of Americanization seemed too slow, joined Presbyterian or Anglican churches, where the absorption of British conceptual languages occurred much more rapidly. William Livingston, editor of the *Independent Reflector* during the 1750s, is the prime example of a child of the Dutch Reformed whose transfer to the Presbyterians coincided with an early and earnest embrace of a republican picture of the world.)[13] In June 1765 the Classis of Amsterdam, which remained the official supervisor of Reformed Dutch churches in the new world until the 1790s, responded to a Coetus memorial filled with the language of republicanism. The Coetus had complained that its relation with the Amsterdam Classis was threatened by "an unlawful exercise of tyranny"; it asked for a "Constitution" to ensure its "inherent rights"; it claimed the prerogatives of "a free people"; it spoke much of "liberty"; and it reflected colonial opinion in the midst of the Stamp Act crisis by contending that it "must have a right to a seat in the session of Classis" if it was to remain subordinate to Amsterdam. The Classis responded with an argument that had little future in America but that in 1765 still carried some weight: "In this business, 'right' is founded on 'history,'" that is, the history that had established the Amsterdam-American connection.[14] During the Revolution the Dutch churches were divided, with Coetus elements leaning toward independence and Conferentie toward Loyalism, but with also a large neutral group in the middle.[15] By the time the denomination reorganized in the early 1790s and reached an amicable parting of the ways with Amsterdam, its American credentials were obvious.

Theologically considered, however, the church stood where it had been. When John Henry Livingston was installed as the denomination's theological professor in 1785, his address did echo with themes of republican nationhood. But the echoes were in a self-consciously classical Latin and expressed very much a deferential republican conception of American experience. Moreover, the address as a whole was a traditional argument for the truths of Christianity against Socinian, deistic, and rationalistic foes.[16] Eight years later when Livingston compiled a constitution for the newly independent Reformed Dutch church, it was a conservative document that defined the church in terms of its old-world doctrinal standards (the Belgic Confession, the Heidelberg Catechism, and the Canons of the Synod of Dort). This constitution also mandated a formal liturgy adhering to historical usage, and it assumed a firm conception of ecclesiastical authority (e.g., "No Psalms or Hymns may be publickly sung in the reformed Dutch Churches, but such as are approved and recommended by the general Synod").[17]

Only after the turn of the century did intimations of American influence appear in the denomination's formal theology. As an example, Livingstone himself in 1804 preached a widely reprinted sermon to encourage missionary activity. To make his point, Livingston exchanged traditional Dutch reticence on apocalyptic questions for an enthusiastic interpretation of a passage from the book of Revelation that shared the heady American confidence in being able to read the signs of the times.[18] Nonetheless, as a corporate body, it was only in the 1820s that the denomination confronted disputes over free will, the native powers of unregenerated humanity, and the extent of Christ's atonement.[19] For the Dutch Reformed these disputes arrived a full generation after similar issues had already greatly disturbed Congregationalists, Baptists, and Presbyterians.

Anglicans/Episcopalians

The Episcopal church experienced such severe trauma in the Revolutionary decades that its continued existence as a major Protestant tradition was in doubt. Although lay Anglicans probably supported the Revolution in greater proportions than the colonial population as a whole (over half the signers of the Declaration of Independence were at least nominally Anglican), the senior and most articulate clergy of the church remained loyal to George III. As a consequence, it was vilified as a remnant of tyrannical imperialism. Not surprisingly, the church also experienced grave difficulties in adjusting to independence. The first General Convention of what would become the Protestant Episcopal Church in the United States of America was held at Philadelphia in September 1785. It began the process of accommodating to unavoidable realities by giving lay delegates—and republican instincts—a much larger part in its deliberations than had ever occurred anywhere in Anglicanism before.[20] By the time a second General Convention convened in 1789, the church had succeeded in securing its own bishops, a critical step for assuring the future of an episcopal church. Many difficulties remained, however, not least the fact that the two bishops who had secured ordination with the consent of Britain's Parliament (William White of Philadelphia and Samuel Provoost of New York) enjoyed a rocky relationship with Bishop Samuel Seabury of Connecticut, who had been ordained by bishops of the nonjuring Scottish Episcopal Church. The organizational turmoil, which came hard on the heels of Revolutionary disruption, explains why Episcopalianism faded so rapidly in the early republic. In its earlier Anglican guise, the church had been the most widely distributed of all colonial denominations, and until well past the mid-eighteenth century, it had numbered more adherents than any Protestant body except the Congregationalists. But between 1780 and 1820, while the American population multiplied threefold, the number of Episcopal churches increased by only 50%, and while falling further behind the Congregationalists and Presbyterians, it was also overtaken in numbers by Baptists, Methodists, Lutherans, and Roman Catholics.[21]

The general fate of Episcopalianism is significant for its theological history, because the four decades between 1760 and 1800 were marked by what Episcopal historians have called "suspended animation."[22] If that phrase does not describe every aspect of American Episcopalianism of the period, it certainly applies to its theology.

The effect of the war was to fix Episcopal theological loyalties in the two overlapping positions that had been developed during the era of Samuel Johnson. These two positions were Johnson's own dedicated high church-manship and a more latitudinarian vision promoted by William Smith (1727–1803). As Johnson used his clerical connections in Connecticut and his teaching post in New York City to promote his views, so too did Smith from educational and ecclesiastical positions in Philadelphia propound the supernatural rationalism of the moderate Enlightenment as exemplified by preacher John Tillotson and ethicist Samuel Clarke. The common points in the two Anglican visions were their anti-Calvinism and a shared respect for the new science of the eighteenth century. Johnson's theological vision remained, however, much more conservative than Smith's, for, as we have seen, Johnson seasoned his anti-Calvinism with a high view of grace, retained a full sense of the divine mystery, and followed Bishop Berkeley (eventually in the extreme form of John Hutchinson's anti-Newtonianism) by advocating stern Christian boundaries to the sway of the new science.[23] For his part, Smith clung to the traditions of Anglican moderation but sailed blithely past the perils that Johnson perceived in modern thought.[24]

The key points for a history of American theology are, first, that Johnson, Smith, and their students at Kings in New York and the College of Philadelphia deliberately took their cues from English or Scottish authorities and, second, that their positions guided Episcopal theology in America until after the turn of the century—until, that is, the church accepted, in Nancy Rhoden's words, "traits entirely antithetical to traditional Anglicanism," and until a self-consciously high-church party inspired by John Henry Hobart of New York and a determinedly evangelical Episcopalianism guided by Charles McIlvaine of Ohio imparted fresh energy to the tasks of theology.[25] During the years of the Revolution and of reorganization after the war, Episcopal theology simply remained what it had been.

In the postwar years, publications of leading Episcopalians continued the earlier mix: pragmatic moderation from Bishop William White, Whig but latitudinarian platitudes from Bishop Samuel Provoost, and earnest high churchmanship in the line of Samuel Johnson from Bishop Samuel Seabury. In 1790 Seabury extended a quixotic invitation to New England's Presbyterians and Congregationalist to forsake their errors and rejoin the Episcopal Church. His reasons featured the same sort of appeal that had moved Samuel Johnson and his Yale colleagues to forsake Congregationalism nearly seventy years before:

> Returning to the Episcopal Church is not giving up the religion of your forefathers. . . . It is only relinquishing those errors which they, through prejudice most unhappily imbibed. You would give up an ill-founded church government, and an unauthorised ministry and sacraments, and you would obtain a government, ministry, and sacraments, according to the institution of Christ, the example of his holy apostles, and the practice of the primitive church, in its purest period.[26]

Through the 1790s, in other words, Episcopal theology took the path of the Lutherans and the Reformed Dutch. While not oblivious to American circumstances, the church maintained a theology still largely defined by its inherited traditions. Only after the turn of the century would Episcopal theology be shaped more directly by local conditions, in one case (high church) in order to shelter religion from American ways, in the other (evangelical low church) to adapt to American circumstances.

Roman Catholics

Before 1800 Roman Catholic theology was barely a recognizable category in America. For one thing, the number of Catholics remained very small. In 1785 John Carroll, newly appointed superior of the Mission to the Thirteen United States of North America, reported to Rome that the fledgling nation contained less than 30,000 Catholics.[27] Size, however, may have been the least important barrier to the development of American Catholic thought. The civil right to practice Roman Catholic faith was only barely secured in the new state constitutions and by the first amendment to the Constitution, and these newly minted civil liberties were still not enjoyed universally.[28] Still more detrimental to the development of an American Catholic mentality were decades of unremitting anti-Catholic polemic that for many Protestants had sealed associations between Roman teaching and intellectual servility, and also between the claims of Catholicism and the exercise of tyranny. These ancient and still widely circulated prejudices did not encourage Roman Catholics to articulate their theology with the assistance of the new nation's intellectual traditions.

To be sure, signs of adjusting old-world theology to new-world realities were far from absent. Through the 1780s John Carroll moved American Catholics toward a series of accommodations with the new environment. Jay Dolan has conveniently summarized these accommodations as a desire to be free from foreign jurisdiction, an effort to establish a national church, an acceptance of the separation of church and state, and a willingness to offer the laity greater weight in ecclesiastical decision-making.[29] The first full defense of Catholicism in the new United States likewise deferred significantly to American ways. In 1784 John Carroll took in hand to answer a pamphlet by a former priest from Maryland, Charles Henry Wharton, who deployed Protestant and Enlightenment cudgels to challenge Roman Catholicism. Carroll went out of his way to write a reply that could be heard in America. He began and ended with citations from the Scriptures; he argued that Catholic submission to church authority was always intended to be "reasonable"; and he praised "the harmony now subsisting in all christians in this country, so blessed with civil and religious liberty."[30]

For the purposes of Catholic theology, however, accommodations to America remained superficial. Carroll's apology of 1784 employed a tone befitting the spirit of Enlightenment, but it gave way not at all in defending the authority of pope, magisterium, and councils. After his consecration as the United States' first Catholic bishop in 1790, Carroll himself came to govern the church as a deferential hierarchy rather than a gathered democracy. His own sermons and the official publications of the church early in his episcopal tenure likewise confirmed traditional Catholic doctrine, promoted traditional Catholic devotion, and even introduced some older liturgical practices from Europe.[31] During the first decades of the nineteenth century, American Catholic thinking would respond directly to the American environment, sometimes by taking deliberate steps to avoid contamination from that environment, other times by adjusting Catholic teaching in deference to powerful principles of American thought. But as it entered those decades, Catholic theology had adjusted hardly at all to its American setting.

Mainstream Calvinists

The reasons that the history of theology in the early United States has so often been written as the history of Congregational theology are neither sinister nor complex. Although Presbyterians by the 1780s were nearly as active intellectually as the Congregationalists, the latter still defined the nation's most substantial theological tradition. Congregationalists enjoyed America's only multigeneration heritage of substantial theological writing. In pastoral education sponsored by Harvard and Yale, as well as in a well-established practice of pastoral apprenticeship, they benefited from the most concentrated system of theological training on the continent. And they were the new world's most industrious producers and most assiduous consumers of theological literature. Moreover, the burden that Congregationalists had taken up to act as theological arbiters for all of New England, a burden not laid down until well into the next century (if then), bequeathed a widely perceived significance to theology that was unique in any region of the United States until the rise of Mormonism in the Rocky Mountain West. The notable theological achievements of New England's Congregationalists, their eagerness to speak for the region and then for the whole nation, along with the willingness of historians to cede them the hegemony to which they aspired—all create a historical problem quite different from the problems confronted by students of the Lutherans, Reformed, Anglicans/Episcopalians, Roman Catholics, sectarian groups, and even eighteenth-century Presbyterians. For the latter it is a struggle to show that meaningful theology was being written. For the former, the task is to simplify a lavish documentary record.

Despite historiographical imbalance, a good case can be made that by the last years of the eighteenth century, American Presbyterians were reaching the theological maturity of their Congregational kin. The Presbyterians could reflect back on two generations of active publication. They were benefiting from sturdy educational efforts at the College of New Jersey and several classical academies, as well as from a far-flung system of ministerial apprenticeships; they enjoyed respect as cultural arbiters for at least some parts of New Jersey, eastern Pennsylvania, Delaware, and a few regions in Virginia, North

Carolina, and South Carolina; the number of their churches was increasing so much more rapidly than the Congregationalists that by 1800 there were about equal numbers in the two denominations; and the Presbyterians' location in the religiously diverse middle and Southern states provided constant occasions to sharpen theological tools in the sort of vigorous interchurch debates still at the time comparatively rare in New England. If scholarship on eighteenth-century Presbyterian theology has been much less significant than on the Congregationalists, the reasons have something to do with later academic fashions as well as with the importance of what was happening on the ground.

The sections that follow benefit from much of the fine scholarship on Congregational developments, even as they constitute an implicit plea for more serious attention to the theology of late-colonial and early-national Presbyterianism. In both cases, however, a similar situation prevailed during the era of the Revolution. Despite the tumult of the times, theology for the Presbyterians and trinitarian Congregationalists, America's largest and most articulate theological traditions, remained relatively stable.

Presbyterians

The seriousness of theology for these earnest Calvinists is illustrated by an incident from the 1860s. Even during the darkest days of the American Civil War, the nation's Reformed theologians did not abandon the theological battles that had been raging for several decades before the firing on Fort Sumter. The main issues, which had been setting Presbyterian upon Presbyterian, and Presbyterians upon Congregationalists, in a series of bruising battles, involved standard theological cruxes like the nature of human guilt before God, the character of divine justice, and the meaning of Christ's atonement. Debate over these questions made for an intellectual amphitheater in which champions of competing positions had been dueling since at least a decade before the much-watched schism between the Old School and New School Presbyterians in 1837–1838. New Schoolers like Albert Barnes of Philadelphia prided themselves on their ability to communicate a modified Calvinist message to an America in desperate need of evangelism and reform; Old Schoolers like Charles Hodge of Princeton Seminary, on an ability to meet the needs of the hour with a Calvinism hewing strictly to ancient confessional standards.

For theological battle at the time of the Civil War, the testimony of honored predecessors from the era of the Revolution was not a trivial detail. Thus it was that when George Duffield, a New School Presbyterian from Detroit and the offshoot of a distinguished Presbyterian family, made a casual historical assertion in the July 1863 number of *Bibliotheca Sacra*, the nation's most able defender of "moderate Calvinism," theological sparks flew. According to Duffield, "The renowned, learned, and patriotic Dr. John Witherspoon, President of Princeton College, and a member of Congress and signer of the Declaration of Independence," had provided support for "the theological views of New School Presbyterians, on the subject of regeneration especially."[32]

To Lyman Atwater of Princeton Theological Seminary, Duffield's contention was outrageous. Atwater, who had grown up in Connecticut under the preaching of Yale's Nathaniel W. Taylor, the most impressive champion of moderating New England Calvinism, had long before rejected Taylor's opinions in favor of what he and his colleagues at Princeton considered the good old Calvinist faith. Stung by Duffield's claim, Atwater snatched up a set of Witherspoon's collected works and fired off a response in the October issue of the *Princeton Review*. With an impressive catena of quotation, Atwater demonstrated to his satisfaction that Witherspoon had actually taught doctrines much more in line with Princeton's Old School confessionalism than with Duffield's New School modified Calvinism. According to Atwater, Witherspoon held that (1) Adam was the representative head of all humanity and hence that all people were born with the guilt of Adam's sin, (2) sinners had no ability in themselves whatsoever to enter the path of salvation, (3) the new birth occurred when God bestowed a new principle of life into the sinner's soul, (4) Christ's suffering for sin represented a penal substitution whereby Christ took upon himself the Father's wrath that otherwise would have fallen on sinners, (5) sinners were redeemed through the imputation of Christ's righteousness, and (6) the saving effects of Christ's atonement worked specifically for the elect and not for all of humanity.[33] Atwater may have used quotations selectively to make Witherspoon speak a little more clearly in death than he had in life, but the torrent of citations did strongly suggest that Witherspoon maintained several doctrines that New School Presbyterians were either moderating or had abandoned.

Since Witherspoon, from his arrival in America in 1768 to his death in 1794, was far and away the most influential Presbyterian in Revolutionary America, Atwater's polemical essay constitutes a strong testimony about the stability of Presbyterian theology during that earlier era. On the surface at least, Presbyterian theology—rooted in the confessional documents drawn up by the Westminster Assembly in the 1640s and self-conscious in adhering to classic Calvinism—remained as it had been. Witherspoon's centrality as president of Princeton ensured that his personal theological convictions would exert a deep influence at large. During his first seven years in New Jersey, Witherspoon personally trained approximately 30% of all the colonial college students of those years who later became clergymen (not just Presbyterian clergymen).[34] When the Presbyterians in 1789 created a General Assembly, Witherspoon looked out over the gathered throng and marveled at the large proportion whom he had personally instructed.

Whatever else was happening to American Presbyterians and whatever theological choices they were facing, dogma was holding steady. Yet Witherspoon's adherence to theological traditions did, nonetheless, mask a dramatic transition in Presbyterian intellectual life. Theological stasis during the 1760s, '70s, and '80s was hiding, first, a shift in demography—both ethnic and religious—and, second, a contest for the future of new-world Presbyterianism.

Into the 1760s the dominant note in colonial Presbyteriansism was eager pursuit of "true religion" as defined by revivalistic Calvinists.[35] As we have seen, this note was sounded with two accents, by transplanted New Englanders led by Jonathan Dickinson of Elizabethtown, New Jersey, and by a party of Scotch-Irish immigrants led by Gilbert Tennent, Samuel Blair Sr. (1712–1751), Samuel Finley, Aaron Burr Sr. (1716–1757), and Samuel Davies. One of the factors making the immigrant party more sensitive to church order was their ties to ecclesiastical developments in Scotland and Ireland. Throughout the century serious struggles were taking place in both homelands between doctrinal traditionalists and liberalizers (often aligned with the party of Francis Hutcheson) who were drifting toward Unitarianism. No matter how devoted they were to piety, the Scotch-Irish in America retained substantial interest in formal doctrine and the niceties of church order. Yet individuals trained at the senior William Tennent's academy in Neshaminy, Pennsylvania, and then at several schools organized in imitation of his "Log College," were also active pietists. They led Presbyterian participation in the awakenings of the 1740s, which most of the New England–born Presbyterians supported as well.

The subordinate note in colonial Presbyterianism was an old-world commitment to ecclesiastical order. That note was strong enough to create a faction ("Old Side," as opposed to the "New Side" alliance of the Dickinson and Tennent circles) and eventually to split the church.[36] But the Old Sides' doubts about revival and their investment in old-world proprieties—especially their reluctance to ordain graduates of academies like the Tennents' Log College—made them an increasingly beleaguered remnant. When the denomination reunited in 1758, the Old Side concern for ecclesiastical decorum revived somewhat, but it remained a secondary concern. The pious Calvinists, who shared much with the awakeners of New England, Wales, and Scotland, as well as with the new party of Calvinistic evangelicals in England, dominated American Presbyterianism at the time of the reunion. Their form of faith stressed especially the need for heart religion and the power of divine grace.

Secure as this awakened Calvinism seemed in the late 1750s, the tide of events soon worked considerable change. In little more than a decade after the reunion of 1758, death, immigration, and the recruitment of Witherspoon drastically restructured Presbyterian religious thought. The often premature mortality of the most influential Calvinist revivalists soon left awakened "true religion" bereft of influential leaders. Jonathan Dickinson's death at age fifty-nine in 1747 began the dismal parade; soon followed Samuel Blair (age thirty-nine) in 1751, Aaron Burr Sr. (age forty-two) in 1757, Samuel Davies (age thirty-eight) in 1761, Gilbert Tennent (age sixty-one) in 1764, and Samuel Finley (age fifty-one) in 1766.[37]

As the flower of awakened Presbyterianism was being laid in the grave, a new surge of immigration began from Ulster that rose steadily from the 1750s to a peak annual rate of roughly 10,000 for each of the five years before the outbreak of the Revolution.[38] A Presbyterian church that had been busy proselytizing the public at large, working at amalgamating New England and Scotch-Irish elements, and adjusting to the distinctive religious pluralism of the middle colonies, suddenly found itself compelled to service a burgeoning immigrant population, redirect its evangelistic energies to that immigrant community, and concentrate on providing ecclesiastical structures for a population that, though often callously unconcerned about Christianity, still looked to the church as an agency of civilization.

The recruitment of John Witherspoon as president of Princeton, at the time the denomination's only substantial institution, completed the intellectual transformation. The college's first five presidents (Dickinson, Burr, Davies, and Finley, the leaders of awakened Presbyterianism, and Jonathan Edwards, great light of New England's revivalistic Calvinism) survived a total of only twenty-one years. Witherspoon himself served twenty-six years. He was, moreover, a commanding presence in public life and the church. Most significantly for Presbyterian theological history, Witherspoon, though orthodox, redirected his coreligionists away from the practices, habits, and metaphysics of the revivalistic Calvinism that had prevailed through the 1750s. During his first weeks as president in 1768 Witherspoon cleansed Princeton of all idealistic philosophy, whether from Bishop Berkeley or from Jonathan Edwards. This action showed where Witherspoon intended to go.[39] Within two years he brought in an entirely new junior faculty, which he himself had trained, and then oriented instruction toward the principles of Scottish moral philosophy and away from the metaphysical Calvinism of Dickinson and Edwards.[40] For the purposes of theological instruction, Witherspoon replaced the books of Edwards and Edwards's disciple Joseph Bellamy with his own lectures and the writings of the Scottish moralists. At the outbreak of the war, he took the steps that would transform the college from its historic balance between piety, learning, and public service into a more straightforward "school of statesmen."[41]

Witherspoon, as Lyman Atwater demonstrated several decades later, did not deviate from traditional Presbyterian dogma. In addition, the immigrants, cast loose in the wilds of central Pennsylvania and the back country of Virginia and North Carolina, often put to use the Westminster Confession and Catechism more faithfully for family instruction than they ever had done in the old country.[42] Nonetheless, an era was over. The midcentury engine of revivalist Calvinism was no more. In its place arose a new theological creature that for many years wandered uncertainly in search of stability.

One of the options opened by the seachanges of the 1750s and 1760s was the chance to modify inherited faith along lines pursued by liberals in the old country and the advanced Congregationalists of Boston. This possibility was the direction pursed by at least some descendants of the midcentury pietists, for example, Samuel Blair Jr. and Samuel Stanhope Smith. The younger Blair's father, founder of a notable academy in Fagg's Manor, Pennsylvania, not only trained a generation of leaders in his image, including Samuel Davies, but was himself an active revivalist. In the early 1740s he reported on an awakening in Fagg's Manor that had arisen in response to his own efforts: "The main scope of my preaching through that summer, was, laying open the deplorable state of man by nature since the fall, our ruined, exposed case by the breach of the first covenant, and the awful condition of such as were not in Christ."[43] Blair's son Samuel Jr. (1741–1818), by contrast, took a more liberal view of those who "were not in Christ." After a period of residence in Boston and years of reading England's most up-to-date ethicists—and only three years after Charles Chauncy published his defense of universalism, *The Mystery Hid from Ages* (1784)—Blair also proclaimed, only from a Presbyterian pulpit in Pennsylvania, that God provided salvation for all.[44]

A similar movement away from strict Calvinist orthodoxy can be charted in the theological relationship between another father and son. Robert Smith (1723–1793), who was one of the senior Samuel Blair's students and a brother-in-law of the junior Samuel Blair, was converted at about the age of fifteen through the preaching of George Whitefield. Robert Smith sustained the revivalistic Calvinism of his mentors through a long life in Pequea, Pennsylvania, as a pastor, an organizer of a classical academy, and an influential figure on the boards of several Presbyterian institutions. Yet the son whom he personally trained for the ministry, Samuel Stanhope, followed the Enlightenment path of his uncle, Samuel Blair Jr., rather than the evangelical path of his father. In the late 1770s Samuel Stanhope Smith exchanged two lengthy letters on the subject of human free will with James Madison, a friend from his student days at Princeton. The notable feature about these letters is that Madison, the man of public affairs who always remained exceedingly private about his own faith, advanced Jonathan Edwards's view on the subordination of will to character, while Smith, himself at the time already a Presbyterian minister, argued for the more modern, less orthodox principle of the will's indeterminacy.[45] When, a decade later, Smith's friend and uncle Samuel Blair Jr. proclaimed his views on universal salvation, Smith (although reserving judgment on the issue itself) waxed indignant at Blair's critics, who wore "a shroud of orthodoxy with lifeless acquiescence in established systems." Smith, who by this time was serving as Witherspoon's vice president at Princeton, did not publish such views, but they filled his correspondence with Blair as also with the Philadelphia physician and reformer Benjamin Rush.[46]

The speculations entertained by Samuel Blair Jr. and Samuel Stanhope Smith, especially as expressed in the orbit of a Greater Philadelphia that was advancing rapidly in wealth and cosmopolitan pretension, were moving toward a Presbyterian equivalent of the liberal Congregationalism that was being advanced at the same time by the elites of cosmopolitan Boston. The tide of circumstances, however, once again prevented the maturation of such a party among the Presbyterians. Deep commitments to the republican principles of the new United States united the generation of the liberalizing Stanhope Smith with that of his more orthodox father, as Presbyterians of all sorts supported the war with great fervor. Into the 1770s and 1780s, it was not clear which direction Presbyterian theology would go. But then the fear of postwar radicalism flushed the liberalism represented by Samuel Blair Jr. and Samuel Stanhope Smith out of the Presbyterian system. The external threat was the French Revolution. The internal threat was the Democratic-Republican political party. Against these perils, Presbyterians rallied around classical, conservative views of the republic, and also classical, conservative conceptions of the Christian faith. The horrific prospect of electing Thomas Jefferson as president put the liberal Presbyterians of Philadelphia, New York, and Princeton on the defensive. Among Presbyterians, theological opinions that were associated with either the bloodshed of Revolutionary France or the infidelity of Jefferson were doomed. Whatever easy confidence in the perfectibility of human nature survived the election of Jefferson was laid to rest by Presbyterian participation in the Southern revivals that were already beginning by the time of his inauguration in 1801. For the Presbyterian generation after Witherspoon, in other words, the combination of cultural fright and revivalistic fervor closed down the option of a liberalizing theology.[47]

But what was left? The revivalists' way of combining pietism and traditional dogma from midcentury was now only a distant memory. The present need was to adjust to the new intellectual and political circumstances of a chaotic new nation. A theological move imitating Boston's liberal Congregationalists was now impossible. By 1800, three alternatives could be glimpsed. One was another effort at mediation, this time between traditional Calvinism and an active evangelism aimed at the conversion of both Americans and American civilization. These mediators did not move as rapidly away from traditional Calvinism as did the younger Blair and Smith, but they were willing to join forces with New England's moderate Calvinists in doing what needed to be done—intellectually and ecclesiastically—to meet the religious needs of a rapidly expanding country. The 1801 Plan of Union with the Congregationalists that led to missionary cooperation on the frontier was the principal institutional expression of this spirit. With leaders like Albert Barnes, George Duffield Jr., and Lyman Beecher, this kind of Presbyterianism eventually became known as the New School.

The second option was a full and frank promotion of historic Calvinist confessionalism. The theology of what became known as the Old School adjusted consciously at only a few points to American experience, like accepting the separation of church and state, though there were also several unconscious adjustments, like the deployment of the new moral philosophy or the discovery of a biblical defense of slavery. This kind of confessional movement looked back to conservative parties in Ulster, Scotland, and the Continent, although it resembled less the first American generation of immigrant Presbyterians than it did the confessional revivals underway in both Ulster and Scotland as the Presbyterian churches also reacted against the French Revolution. Leaders of this form of Presbyterianism included Ashbel Green, who replaced Stanhope Smith and reversed Smith's intellectual leadership when he became president of the College of New Jersey in 1812, the theologians of Princeton Seminary (Archibald Alexander, Samuel Miller, Charles Hodge), and important Southerners like James Henley Thornwell of South Carolina.

The third Presbyterian option was a turn more completely to revivalistic primitivism, especially as practiced on the southern and southeastern frontiers. This was the choice that in 1810 led revivalists who rejected strict Calvinist views of predestination to found the Cumberland Presbyterian Church.[48] It was the course pursued as well by charismatic leaders like Barton W. Stone, Thomas Campbell, and Alexander Campbell, who, though trained as Presbyterians, turned aside in the effort to "restore" an ecumenical form of New Testament Christianity in the "Disciples" and "Christian" movements.

Presbyterian theology after the death of Witherspoon in 1794 would be intensely American. In many formal ways it resembled the theology of American Roman Catholics at the same period by defining itself self-consciously over against prominent patterns of American thought—sometimes aligning, sometimes dissenting, sometimes ambiguous. From engagement with these American circumstances came the New School–Old School schism of 1837, as well as the battle between Duffield and Atwater in 1863 over the right to claim Witherspoon. For the history of Presbyterians in the Revolutionary period, however, the important conclusion must be that during the half century before the nearly simultaneous promulgation of the United States Constitution and the creation of the Presbyterian General Assembly, theology was stable and largely unchanging. Beneath the surface Presbyterian theology was being moved by two important transitions—from a pious metaphysics influenced by New England to a practical ethics molded by Scottish commonsense teaching in American circumstances, and from a broad range of engagements with modern thought, including the option of liberalizing theology, to a much more selective use of principles from the Enlightenment. After 1800 the effect of these shifting positions would be manifest in wide-ranging theological controversy within Presbyterianism and between Presbyterians and other American theologians. Before 1800, however, Presbyterian theology remained deceptively calm.

Trinitarian Congregationalists: New Divinity and Old Calvinists

During the half century before 1790, and in the shadow of Jonathan Edwards's powerful body of writing, New England's trinitarian Congregationalists were already well on the way to creating what historian Bruce Kuklick has called "the most sustained intellectual tradition in the United States."[49] It was anything but a placid theology in that period. In the 1750s these Congregationalists battled each other over the meaning of original sin; in the next decade they contended over the nature of justifying faith and the value of religious actions pursued by the unregenerate; in the 1770s questions of true virtue, human free will, and the church roiled the theological waters; and in the 1780s cautious exploration of the proposition that all humans might someday be redeemed evoked another storm of controversy.[50] As the most self-conscious descendants of the seventeenth-century Puritans, these Congregationalists were as eager as their forefathers to set other people straight on the principles of theology; like their ancestors they also simply assumed that all New England would read, mark, and inwardly digest what they wrote.

Conflicted as Congregational theology was in the decades after the Great Awakening, those tensions were relatively restrained by comparison to what came later in the half century after the Constitution. In that subsequent period ensued what Frank Hugh Foster once called "the great controversies" (within New England) over Unitarianism and (extending well beyond New England) over rival versions of Calvinism.[51] In addition, the period witnessed an even more intense strife between "elite" and "democratic" interests, between "formalist" and "antiformalist" Protestants, who battled each other with abandon through the early national period. The conflicts that resulted would transform Congregational theology in a way that the debates of the Revolutionary period did not.

A full generation of recent historians, as alert to fresh readings of old texts as they are critical about unexamined conventions of traditional interpretations, has reevaluated the achievements of the two main bodies of orthodox Congregationalists who emerged from the revivals of the 1740s.[52] First were the New Divinity theologians who regarded themselves as followers of Jonathan Edwards. In the able accounts of these recent scholars, the New Divinity theologians appear as subtle casuists working simultaneously at appropriating the major insights of Edwards, adjusting with considerable discernment to the evolving political economy of their region, and at the same time dealing with hordes of theological enemies (Anglicans, Sandemanians, Separates, and the contradictory positions promoted by liberal Congregationalists and reactionary Congregationalists).

The other main body of trinitarian Congregationalists, the conservatives, are usually referred to as the Old Calvinists. They have not received such focused attention from historians, partly because of their status, in Allen Guelzo's words, as "the center party" made up of "an amorphous and almost undefinable assortment of New England Calvinists who represented solid Trinitarian orthodoxy."[53] But even in what historians sometimes describe as their frightened attachment to New England traditions, these Old Calvinists tacked much more skillfully against the winds of change than casual accounts of the period have appreciated.

If neither placid nor static, New England's trinitarian Congregationalists were nonetheless upholding with remarkable consistency the main lines of older doctrine. Deep into the Revolutionary period, as Harry Stout's study of the New England sermon demonstrates, nearly the whole spectrum of Congregational clergy, with only a tiny fringe of the most advanced rationalists excepted, continued to organize weekly Sunday sermons around traditional themes of human sin and divine grace, the necessity of faith, and the divine provision of redemption. Even when special discourses for fasts, thanksgivings, militia musters, and election days were taken over by the political jargon of republican liberty, weekly Sunday sermons betrayed very little change from what had gone before. As Stout puts it: "Throughout the periods of crisis and calm, regular preaching retained its subject matter of salvation, self-examination, and godly living. . . . However much themes of civil liberty and resistance to tyranny dominated the occasional pulpit, they did not come at the expense of personal salvation, nor did they signal a new 'civil religion' replacing the old otherworldly religion."[54] To be sure, those who took part in the sharp conflicts between the New Divinity and Old Calvinism almost always assumed that some misstep of the opposition was undercutting a vital principle of New England's hereditary religion. Yet stereotypes of Old Calvinist intransigence and New Divinity hyperorthodoxy obscure the fact that they were equally committed to that religion. New Divinity theologians and the Old Calvinists differed on the best means for expounding the old faith, and those differences loomed large in their own eyes. What is much clearer to a later observer of their quarrels is how much they together embraced the main Christian teachings of that old faith.

Yet as with the Presbyterians, so also with New Divinity and Old Calvinist Congregationalists, intellectual moves made during the Revolutionary period would materially affect theological formulation in the early decades of the nineteenth century. Those moves included especially the incorporation of civic humanist concepts into theological reasoning and a bending toward the ethical imperatives of the eighteenth century's new moral philosophy. These developments deserve at least summary treatment, but before they are sketched, it is important to outline the broader and deeper framework of orthodoxy sustained within both the New Divinity and the Old Calvinists.

The New Divinity was defined first by Joseph Bellamy (1719–1790) and Samuel Hopkins (1721–1803), both of whom had studied with Edwards and to whom the master entrusted his manuscripts. Their most substantial works, Bellamy's *True Religion Delineated* (1750) and Hopkins's *System of Doctrines* (1793), did advance modifications to the older theology, but only as what they considered necessary extensions of the inheritance from Edwards. These works defined a theological era. Hopkins's controversial arguments that a sinner should be willing to be damned for the glory of God, that strivings toward God by the unregenerate were themselves sinful, and that God ordained the fall directly for the greater happiness of humankind were meant to refine an Edwardsean deposit rather than strike off into the unknown.[55] The same purpose was sought through the painstakingly precise but also suspiciously abstract style of theological reasoning practiced by almost all New Divinity theologians.

Bellamy, the most influential of the New Divinity clergy because of his service as theological teacher to upwards of sixty aspiring ministers, did undergo a significant theological modification from preacher of revival in the early 1740s to careful exponent of divine law later in the same decade.[56] Yet even in this transition Bellamy did not waver from the Calvinist doctrines he felt had been properly restored in the revivals. With Edwards, Bellamy held to the glory of God as the key to religion. In his first published work he set out a characteristic challenge: "Many seem to leave the moral excellency of the divine nature out of their idea of God; and consider him as only the author of their happiness, as one disposed to exert his infinite wisdom and almighty power to promote their best good."[57] In *True Religion Delineated*, a precocious tome published in 1750 when Bellamy was barely thirty years old, he urged his readers to "labor after determinate ideas of God, and a sense of his infinite glory." He reminded them that "never is a poor sinner savingly brought home to God and trained up for heaven, but that, from first to last, it was absolutely and entirely owing to the infinite goodness, free grace, and almighty power of God."[58] In an exaggerated comment that yet spoke for the importance of this volume, Harriet Beecher Stowe gave it a prominent role in her novel *Oldtown Folks*, where she commented that this book was "heedfully and earnestly read in every good family of New England; and its propositions were discussed everywhere and by everybody."[59] *True Religion Delineated* was Bellamy's attempt to extend the influence of Edwards's *Treatise on Religious Affections* (1746), with its soul-searching discrimination between genuine piety and its artful imitations. Throughout his career, Bellamy taught from pulpit, desk, and page the Edwardsean version of historic Calvinism—true virtue as ultimate love to God, moral and natural inability as explaining both divine sovereignty and human responsibility, original sin as part of God's permissive will for his own ultimate glory, and justifying faith as a supernatural gift of the Holy Spirit by which a person closes with Christ. Grounded in such views, the New Divinity theologians were not deluding themselves in thinking they stood for orthodoxy.

Though never with the same devotion to metaphysical subtlety, so too did the vast majority of Old Calvinists maintain what they considered the historic doctrines of their faith. Two examples from the traditionalist middle can make this point clearly. The Reverend Nathanael Taylor (1722–1800) of New Milford, Connecticut, is of interest in the larger story of New England theology as the grandfather and first theological teacher of Nathaniel William Taylor, the leading voice of modified Calvinism in the generation after 1810. The older Taylor was a representative Old Calvinist who resolutely opposed the distinctives of revivalistic New Light Calvinism throughout his long career, but he did so calmly and with a studied desire to get along as well as possible with his clerical neighbors. He published only a few short works, but one of them was a defense of Stoddardean church membership that greatly played down the distinction between the elect and the nonelect.[60] Yet although Taylor was anti-Edwardsean, he was not theologically progressive. His published and manuscript sermons reveal a warm, theocentric piety. Victories over the French in the late 1750s and early 1760s were trophies not for those who fought but for God's glory and for the carrying on of "his great Designs, especially respecting the Advancement of the Redeemer's Kingdom."[61] Taylor declared at an ordination sermon in 1764 that the ministerial qualification "which crowns all others" is that of being "experimentally acquainted with the Lord Jesus Christ."[62] And in a sermon preached in January 1767, he counseled his congregation not to be distressed by observing that the wicked prosper, but "having no confidence in ourselves we must trust and depend upon the Lord Jesus Christ alone for salvation and happiness."[63]

Even more traditionally pious in the foundation of his faith was the best-known Old Light of his generation, Ezra Stiles (1727–1795), who in 1778 left an influential charge in Newport, Rhode Island, to become president of Yale College.[64] As a young student at Yale, Stiles turned decisively away from the tumult and zealous revivalism of the Great Awakening. His father, the Reverend Isaac Stiles, had warned Connecticut about the disruptive potential of enthusiastic religion, and Ezra Stiles faithfully followed his advice. After graduating, serving as a tutor, and vacillating between a legal and clerical career, Stiles for a short period drifted away from the hereditary faith. But by the early 1750s he had come to embrace the tolerant but decisive evangelical Calvinism that marked the rest of his career. Stiles never became a friend of the New Divinity. Once after visiting Bellamy, he could only shake his head in dismay at the intellectual stubbornness of Bellamy's party: "My Idea is that all Calvinists should unite. But I find they [the New Divinity theologians] require . . . a Union in their Idea of the divine Moral Character with respect to several of their favorite *eurekas* [,] which they hold the Christian World never knew anything of till [after] President Edwards' Death."[65]

Nonetheless, Stiles did eventually come to a wholehearted affirmation of classic Puritan doctrines, as enumerated in letters from the mid-1760s: "human Nature in Ruins, the Divinity[,] Incarnation[,] and Atonement of the Redeemer, Justification thro Affiance in his Righteousness and vicarious Sacrifice, Regeneration by the Spirit, the nature[,] precepts[,] and motives of Sanctity and Virtue, Immorality and its Retributions . . . the tremendous Torments of Damnation."[66] In 1775 Stiles wrote to the divinity professor at Harvard, "I fear . . . a loss of the Evangelical Doctrines, the Doctrines of Grace as held by the good Old Puritans and by our Ancestors."[67] Although Stiles was an ardent patriot, he worried in the run-up to the struggle with Britain (as only a few of his colleagues did) that preoccupation with politics was displacing a proper emphasis on the minister's duty to preach the gospel: "I am a Friend to American Liberty; of the final prevalence of which I have not the least doubt. . . . I am a Spectator indeed of Events, but intermeddle not with Politics. We [ministers] have another Department, being called to an Office and Work, which may be successfully pursued (for it has been pursued) under every species of *Civil Tyranny* or *Liberty*. We cannot become the Dupes of Politicians without Alliances, Concessions and Connexions dangerous to evangelical Truth and spiritual Liberty."[68] In sum, though a Calvinist of New Divinity predilections he was not, Stiles remained a faithful exponent of traditional Calvinist dogma. Moreover, as the hub of a vast circle of correspondence and clerical intelligence, he promoted that dogma far and wide.

The maintenance of traditional teaching by New England's trinitarian Congregationalists was indeed not the whole story. Again, beneath the surface, theories of society and human nature, as well as new epistemological principles, were gaining strength and would do anything but confirm traditional theological formulas. Such movement may even have been more pronounced among the self-consciously orthodox New Divinity stalwarts than among the Old Calvinists.

As early as 1750, for example, Bellamy gently modified earlier Calvinistic conceptions of the atonement along lines suggested by the era's ethical conventions. The work of Christ, for Bellamy, became not the placation of divine wrath (as had been traditional) but the restoration of moral order in the universe—a "sufficient salvo to the divine honor" was the bloodless phrase he used.[69] Because Christ's death met the divine requirement for a perfect fulfilling of the law, God—as "the supreme governor of the world," "the great Governor of the world," "the infinitely wise and good Governor of the world"—could be approached by all who would trust in him.[70] Bellamy's proposal came close to saying that the work of Christ merely established the conditions for salvation, a transaction now dependent upon human exertion to complete: "A way is opened, wherein the great Governor of the world may, consistently with his honor, and to the glory of his grace, pardon, and receive to favor, and entitle to eternal life, all and every one of the human race, who shall cordially fall in with the gospel design; believe in Christ, and return home to God through him."[71] In addition, Bellamy held that Christ did "design, by his death, to open a door for all to be saved conditionally, that is, upon the condition of faith," and so offered a formula that de-emphasized the divine glory in favor of human efforts to achieve salvation.[72] The restatement of divine sovereignty from an older language of deferential hierarchy to a newer language of egalitarian contractualism represented a significant new emphasis. Bellamy's stress on the divine government was a particularly important step away from notions of God grounded in personal relationships toward understandings defined by general principles. Such moves, as Conrad Wright has helpfully noticed, put Bellamy closer to his liberal contemporary Charles Chauncy than to his mentor, Edwards, on at least some questions, like the nature of benevolence.[73] To Edwards, true goodness flowed from the glory of God; to Bellamy and Chauncy, it was more likely to be described as belonging to the right-living human. Mark Pattison's judgment on the British theology of Bellamy's period came close to applying across the Atlantic as well: "It is this anthropomorphic conception of God as the 'Governor of the universe,' which is presented to us in the theology of the Hanoverian divines, a theology which excludes on principle not only all that is poetical in life, but all that is sublime in religious speculation."[74]

The theology of Samuel Hopkins, Bellamy's friend and fellow student of Edwards, reflected additional traces of a more progressive theology. Hopkins, who pastored churches in Barrington, Massachusetts, and Newport, Rhode Island, innovated by arguing that human sinfulness was the result only of the sins of individuals. No corporate solidarity with Adam such as Edwards had proposed in his treatise *Original Sin* (1758) could account for the guilt and punishment sinners justly deserved. The responsibility for sin was an individual matter.[75] Sinfulness, Hopkins was also eager to point out, did not conflict with God's design for the world but actually increased the quality and quantity of human happiness by triggering the divine plan of redemption.[76] In addition, Edwards's conception of virtue as affectional love to Being in general proved too impractical for Hopkins. His 1773 essay *An Inquiry into the Nature of True Holiness* made ethics more concrete by defining it as benevolence "to God and our neighbors . . . or friendly affection to all intelligent beings."[77] The sphere of benevolence, of virtue, had moved from a state of being to a form of activity, from contemplation to action.

Bellamy and Hopkins by no means repudiated the Calvinism they received from Edwards. They continued to insist that people contributed nothing of their own to salvation. Yet their theology had become, as Joseph Conforti well describes it, "Janus-faced." Hopkins especially "endeavored to revive a strict Calvinist theological perspective by reaffirming the Reformed interpretation of the covenant as an unconditional promise" at the same time that he "advanced a liberal Calvinist concept of the benevolence of the Deity."[78] Even by the 1780s, new intellectual conventions were having their effect. Bellamy and Hopkins had seen their mentor employ modern conceptions (Locke's sensationalism and Hutcheson's moral philosophy) to restate traditional faith, but their own efforts—using this time the imperatives of human happiness and individual prerogative—were not as successful. The difference was that Edwards had translated the new languages back into the old dogma, while Bellamy and Hopkins had begun the process of translating the old dogma into a new language. They did so, in large part, because they were now out in the open without a theological canopy and increasingly exposed to a language of rights, reason, and universal moral intuitions.

Old Calvinists, who eschewed as a point of principle the vagaries of speculation, and who fretted over the health of the social organism also as a matter of principle, were more susceptible to the allure of reasoning from the political arena. Thus, Nathanael Taylor of New Milford, preaching to English and American troops at Crown Point only shortly after the French were ousted during the Seven Years' War, had already made the blithe identification of civil freedom and American millennialism that would became a new context for theology in English-speaking America. What Taylor expected if French Catholicism had prevailed was "nothing but intolerable Tyranny . . . Not only our civil Liberties taken away, and our private Property seized; but we ourselves obliged to yield an implicit Faith and blind Obedience to the Dictates of spiritual Tyrants." With Taylor, however, physical escape from Rome occasioned intellectual capture by the categories of civic humanism: "O happy Nation we, highly favoured of the Lord! Who still full enjoy our Liberties and Property, and have our Enemies subdued under us. Glory be to that God, who is justly to be praised for all the Dispensations of his Providence and Grace."[79] The Separates of New Milford, who had left Taylor's church to seek a more robust gospel, retained a sharper sense of difference between national covenant and church covenant. They complained that in Taylor's church "the civil authority is so much blended with our Ecclesiastical constitution."[80] Like his New Light and New Divinity opponents, Taylor too called for a change of heart in response to God's grace, but he was preoccupied as much with shoring up the social fabric as with pressing home a spiritual message. Taylor remained essentially conservative, but in his thought one can glimpse a move away from theology as master in its own house to theology as a servant of New England's traditional social order.

Ezra Stiles was almost exactly the same. Over the course of his long career, Stiles regularly waxed eloquent about the blessings of a republican system. In an effort to promote the harmonious cooperation of Presbyterians and Congregationalists from 1761, Stiles contended, "In more things than one, that of exile, our New England churches may resemble God's antient chosen people. I apprehend God has great things in design for this vine which his irresistible arm has planted: and that he purposes to make of us a great people and a pure and glorious church."[81] In 1783, when Stiles was asked to preach Connecticut's election sermon, his earlier subjunctive voice was transformed into an emphatic indicative. Now Stiles saw the new country perfected in holiness, he described Washington as a "man of God, greatly beloved of the Most High," he reasoned that the cooperation of "Moses and Aaron . . . the magistracy and priesthood" constituted the United States "the happiest on earth," and he told how God's special and particular blessings were directly the cause of success in the late war.[82]

Old Calvinists assimilated the language of American messianism as readily as the proponents of the New Divinity absorbed the moral conventions of the Enlightenment. Neither adoption, however, had yet made much of an impact on the specific doctrines inherited from the Puritans. After about 1795—after reaction against the French Revolution, in the heyday of explicitly American ideology, and with the widespread social transformations of the new republic—it would be a different theological story. But if a period's history may be written for itself and not for what came later, the verdict for the period 1740 to 1790 is clear: while American political and social life may have been undergoing revolutionary change, the theology of traditional Congregationalism was not.

Although theology was not impervious to the dramatic tumolts of the day, Lutherans, Dutch Reformed, Episcopalians, Roman Catholics, Presbyterians, and trinitarian Congregationalists remained colonial in their theologies for almost two decades after they had become politically independent. Despite being caught up in the convulsions of a political revolution, the theologians of these churches remained remarkably traditional. From the perspective of what came later, it is clear that change was underway, but for these heirs of the European churches, it remained hard to see significant alterations in theology at least into the 1790s.

Innovative (but Not "American") Theologies in the Era of the Revolution

If traditional theology of many sorts was maintained with surprising consistency in the era of the America Revolution, it is also true that significant theological innovation was taking place. Liberal Congregationalists in Massachusetts, Freewill Baptists on the New England frontier, and several other kinds of radical religious thinkers were proposing notable alterations to inherited Protestant theology, even as representatives of the largest traditions were restating what they regarded as orthodoxy. It is important to note the extent of this innovation, and also where it came from. The argument of this chapter is that almost all theological innovation in the Revolutionary period arose either from the importation of progressive European convictions into the colonies or from extrapolations of traditional pietistic themes. This generalization pertains to the learned liberals of Boston as well as for African Americans, Baptists, and radical dissenters. The kind of theological innovation that became much more common after 1790—when theology was adjusted to the dynamics of distinctly American experiences—remained rare in the Revolutionary and constitutional years.

Liberal Congregationalists

The theology of liberal Congregationalism in Boston and its environs was an exception to the rule of relative theological stability during the Revolutionary era. Congregational ministers like Ebenezer Gay (1696–1787), Charles Chauncy (1705–1787), and Jonathan Mayhew (1720–1766) did innovate significantly in the period between Whitefield's first tour and the ratification of the Constitution. The particular circumstances in which that innovation took place, however, meant that theological development among Boston liberals only partially resembled the wholesale Americanization of theology that occurred more generally in the new country from the 1790s. Similar to what happened later was the incorporation of themes from political dissent and the new moral philosophy into the substance of theology. Also similar was the effort to liberate the Scriptures from historic interpretive constraints. The Boston liberals differed, however, in the sources from which they took the new ideas, as well as in their devotion to stratified hierarchy as a guiding model for society.

Boston liberalism broke from the path of Puritan theology in several important particulars. First, its spokesmen self-consciously proclaimed their liberation from Calvinistic dogmas. When in 1747 Ebenezer Gay preached the sermon of installation for Jonathan Mayhew as pastor of Boston's West Church, all who attended knew that Gay was taking aim at traditional Puritan Calvinism when he summarized the message of the apostle Paul as the Christian's "Freedom from the Servitude of the *Mosaic Yoke*, the Bondage of the Ceremonial Law."[1] Second, the Boston liberals exalted the role of natural revelation at the expense of special revelation, and as a consequence greatly minimized the distinction between the realms of grace and nature. Jonathan Mayhew sounded these notes in the sermons that, when published in 1749, established his reputation for heterodoxy: "Although the christian revelation brings us acquainted with [*sic*] many truths besides those which the light of nature suggests, . . . yet the most important and fundamental duties required by christianity are . . . the same which were enjoined as such under the legal dispensation; and the same which are dictated by the light of nature. . . . God is the same in all times and places; . . . as mankind bear [*sic*] the same general relation to him in all times and places."[2]

Third, these same ministers came to be known as Arminians, not because they adopted specific principles from European divines like Jacob Arminius or John Wesley, but because they exalted the human capacity for self-determination. In the words of Sydney Ahlstrom and Jonathan Carey, "Optimistic views about the human condition and prospects provided the most immediate point of departure from orthodoxy."[3] Finally, these Congregationalists also tended toward the belief that God would eventually redeem all of humanity. In 1784 Charles Chauncy published a manifesto to that end, one that also summarized much liberal Congregational conversation of the previous four decades. Its title was *The Mystery Hid from Ages and Generations, Made Manifest by the Gospel Revelation; or, The Salvation of All Men*. Significantly, it was published in London.

The context for these theological innovations was a singular mix of rarefied British thought and pragmatic Boston circumstances. Jonathan Mayhew's most perceptive biographer, Charles Akers, has caught the nature of that context precisely by focusing on the elements Mayhew synthesized in his preaching: "Puritan tradition, science and rationalism, and the enterprising, independent spirit of his townsmen." Mayhew's deliberate eclecticism was intended to fit his environment, and so, in Akers's words, "he saw no problem in mixing the Reformation with the Enlightenment, revelation with rationalism, and individualism with deference to one's betters."[4]

Much more than for later American theologians in the national era, the Boston liberals were still guided by European thought. The theological works of Daniel Whitby (e.g., *Discourse on the Five Points of Calvinism, with Arminian Objections,* 1710; 2d ed., 1735) and John Taylor (e.g., *Scripture Doctrine of Original Sin,* 1740), which Jonathan Edwards and his followers took pains to rebut, Mayhew, Chauncy, and their circle took pains to heed. More general intellectual influences—Newton, Locke, Leibniz, Bolingbroke, and the natural theologians John Ray, John Woodward, and Samuel Clarke, who posed pressing intellectual challenges for Edwards and Samuel Johnson—offered answers to the Boston liberals.[5] In later decades, the most important contextual influences on theology would be contemporary American ideologies and then guidance from the Continent. For the Boston liberals of this period, by contrast, that guidance came most directly from contemporary British thought.

At the same time, intellectual influences that would become central for theologians more generally received their first American airing among these Boston liberals. Mayhew's use of dissenting Whig thought has been widely noted, but Chauncy was not far behind. In addition, Gay, Chauncy, and Mayhew also put considerable stock in the self-evident deliverances of consciousness as instructed by Scotland's leading moral philosophers. When, in 1757, Gay said that God had "designed and framed [human nature] for the Practice of Virtue" and that "the Power of Self-determination, or Freedom of Choice," was "self-evident," he was simply drawing an early payment from what became common intellectual coinage in the 1790s.[6] Finally, the willingness of these supernatural rationalists to be instructed by the Bible—but the Bible liberated from its traditional conventions of interpretation—also anticipated the future. Chauncy's claim in *The Mystery Hid from Ages* that the doctrine of universal salvation came from "studying the *scriptures* in [a] *free, impartial,* and *diligent* manner" anticipated a prominent leitmotif of antebellum theology.[7] Where Chauncy's biblicism did not anticipate later American patterns was his frankness in acknowledging a debt to John Taylor of Norwich, England, for suggesting this way of reading the Bible. That was a confession of intellectual dependency of the sort that became rare in the new republic.

Even in their anticipations of more general American patterns—even, that is, in reliance upon Whig principles, moral-sense intuitions, and the Bible alone—the Boston liberals were not fully aligned with later American norms. In particular, they drew far less from American ideologies than did the most prominent of their intellectual heirs, the Unitarians and the transcendentalists. An analysis of Charles Chauncy's public pronouncements from the 1760s and 1770s illustrates the major differences. Chauncy did have a sense of God's unique dealing with New England and of the indubitable righteousness of Whig principles—convictions that became normative for later theologians— but he used these convictions to argue for an older stratified society and for privileged enjoyment of the fruits of commerce in ways more representative of the mid-eighteenth century than the early nineteenth. By opposing both democratic empowerment and unfettered access to the fruits of new-world capitalism, as well as by defending the prerogatives of Boston's traditional elites, Chauncy showed that theological innovation in America did not have to follow the dictates of emerging American ideologies.[8]

Chauncy's public statements between the Stamp Act and the end of the War for Independence were suffused with two important elements of later American theology: a devotion to libertarian thought and a conviction that God was preoccupied with the welfare of New England. His joyful sermon in 1766 at the repeal of the Stamp Act rang with the praise of "liberties and privileges, valued by us next to life itself," and he maintained this commitment to Whig values throughout the period.[9] When in 1767 Chauncy published a letter against Anglican plans for an American bishop, he did so out of fear of "Church-power, arbitrarily exercised,"[10] a fear that during this period came to include the arbitrary exercise of governmental as well as ecclesiastical power.[11] When in 1774 he broadcast his contention that Boston was being "brought into a state of slavery by the hand of power,"[12] he was only reiterating a libertarian theme that had long been prominent in his work.[13]

Chauncy sanctified his picture of social order as New England's earlier Puritans had also sanctified theirs when he declared that God was behind the Whig struggle against Britain.[14] To hearten his listeners at the election sermon of 1770, held in Boston despite the governor's transfer of the assembly to Cambridge, Chauncy reminded them that "the religious and civil liberties and privileges, both of the mother-country and the American colonies, were nearly and closely connected with the signal interposition of . . . God."[15] And to those suffering because of the Boston Port Bill, Chauncy could declare in 1774 that this circumstance might be God's way of providing a more robust native industrial capacity in America.[16]

The providential nature of Chauncy's Whig views is nowhere more clearly evident than in his perception of analogies between New England and Israel. As the Jews had been miraculously delivered from Egypt and, later, from the destruction of Ahasuerus, so had New England been delivered from the Stamp Act.[17] The founders had been saved from tyranny in England and had been established in a new land just as God had saved his people from Egypt and later established them in Canaan.[18] In short, Chauncy could reassure threatened Americans in 1770 with words that continued to reecho in the national period: "Perhaps, there are no people, now dwelling on the face of the earth, who may, with greater pertinency, adopt the language of king *David*, and say, 'our fathers trusted in thee; they trusted and thou didst deliver them.'"[19]

Chauncy's concern for New England occasionally did touch upon the idea of repentance before God,[20] but he displayed much more interest in the economic than in the directly spiritual betterment of New England. To Chauncy the repeal of the Stamp Act brought good news primarily concerning the "commercial good" and New England's "future prosperity."[21] His argument against the prospect of Anglican bishops in the colonies was also substantially economic. Colonial bishops would draw off inhabitants to the Church of England, disrupt the collection of ecclesiastical taxes, and deprive the Congregationalists of money and power.[22]

As Chauncy's care for the prerogatives of the Congregational establishment suggests, there was, in Clifford Shipton's phrase, "no democracy in his Whiggism."[23] Chauncy tempered his joy at the repeal of the Stamp Act with a careful reminder that now "we may be at peace and quiet among ourselves, every one minding his own business."[24] He denounced the sacking of Lieutenant Governor Hutchinson's home (which occurred at the height of Stamp Act agitation in August 1765) as an outrage and expressed his opposition to "mobbish actions."[25] At the same time, he reminded the colonists to shun "all irregular, turbulent proceedings" and to be "peaceable, loyal subjects."[26] Having secured the continuation of traditional liberties, it was time to settle down and restore the order of New England society that England's arbitrary acts had threatened.

Where Chauncy did call for spiritual reform, his appeals were usually directed more toward the well-ordering of society than toward the salvation of souls. A sermon from 1778 began with an evangelistic denunciation of the "corrupt and degenerate" state of New England: "The *accursed thing* is in the midst of us, impiety towards God, unrighteousness and unmercifulness towards our neighbor, and insobriety with respect to our selves; yea, we have dishonored Christ, neglected his salvation, abused his grace, and grieved his spirit."[27] When Chauncy applied these conclusions to his audience, he also appeared evangelistic: the poor, widows, and the fatherless were being oppressed and needed relief. But when Chauncy began to detail the nature of that oppression as due to "paper currency . . . the undue love of money" and a law forcing individuals "to accept of four or five shillings instead of a pound" on paper issues;[28] when he shifted focus from widows and orphans to "the sad case of *salary-men*, and particularly *the Clergy*";[29] and when he spent twice the time describing their sorry state as he had given to widows and orphans,[30] his more basic interests came to the fore. This jeremiad eventually came to rest on how "the Pastors of the Churches in this State" have been "almost universally wronged, and to an high degree."[31] The lecture concluded by referring to "things pertaining to the kingdom of God, and of Jesus Christ," and with special excoriation of "sordid avarice" and the "unsatiable thirst for money,"[32] but the sting had been drawn from Chauncy's spiritual interest by the realization that his greatest concern was the effects of wartime inflation upon clerical stipends.

Four years later, when Chauncy published a compendium of Scripture texts to defend the idea of a universal salvation, he went out of his way to attack the universalism of John Murray (1741–1815), an English-born, Irish-reared itinerant. Yet Chauncy's reason for attacking Murray's use of the Bible concerned much more its plebeian egalitarianism than its suspect theology: Murray's teaching was "an *encouragement* to Libertinism," whose evil effects among the youth could be seen by their having "by means of it, . . . lost all sense of religion, and given themselves up to the most criminal excesses!"[33]

In a word, Chauncy's defense of New England was infected by none of Bernard Bailyn's "contagion of liberty."[34] His kind of theological liberalism fit well with a gentleman's vision of classical republicanism, but not with the republican liberalism that became so important in the new nation. In this conviction, ironically, Chauncy shared much with exponents of traditional theology, who would also find themselves challenged by antiformalist populists who carried republicanism in the direction of radical individualism.

Chauncy and his liberal colleagues were responsible for some of the freshest theology in the colonies during the middle decades of the eighteenth century. Yet with their self-conscious reliance on British authorities and their marriage to the ideal of a stratified, elite-dominated, mercantile Boston, they were leading where the most important theologies of the American national period did not follow.

Deists

Like the Boston liberals, free-thinking rationalists, or deists, also promoted significant theological innovation during the second half of the eighteenth century. Even more than Boston liberalism, however, deism retained a foreign flavor. Although strands of deist thought (or self-conscious reactions to deism) exerted a noticeable impact in America for nearly two centuries after 1700, and although deist views were very much in the air during the two decades surrounding 1800, deism never succeeded in establishing itself as an *American* theology. Discriminating recent studies by Kerry Walters improve on previous scholarship by clarifying the European roots of deism as well as the contexts in which it burst onto the American landscape in the 1780s, only to fade rapidly away before the War of 1812.[35]

The deism that many saw in the thought of Benjamin Franklin and Thomas Jefferson, and that came to full expression in the writings of Ethan Allen (1737–1789), Tom Paine (1737–1809), Elihu Palmer (1764–1806), and Philip Freneau (1752–1832), was inspired by a characteristically European understanding of the Enlightenment. Where the dominant expressions of the Enlightenment in America were the Christianized forms described in chapter 6 and the politicized versions at work defining independence and promoting the Constitution, deism was inspired by European attempts at constructing a comprehensive religion from the most optimistic of Enlightenment principles.[36] American deists, that is, were keeping alive the effort of earlier English savants—John Toland (1670–1722), Anthony Collins (1676–1729), Matthew Tindal (1657–1733), and to some extent Samuel Clarke (1675–1729)—long after their work had faded in Britain. In the heady wake of the Glorious Revolution and Sir Isaac Newton's scientific triumphs, that earlier generation of freethinkers had proposed a religion of nature as an intellectual and social improvement on traditional Christianity. In particular, these early deists wanted to show that ordinary human intelligence could fully understand God and his ways without the need of special revelation (e.g., Toland's *Christianity Not Mysteri-*

ous, 1696). They also were concerned to cleanse Christianity of its vulgar supernaturalist superstitions (e.g., Tindal's *Christianity as Old as the Creation: or, The Gospel, a Republication of the Religion of Nature*, 1730). It was significant for later American developments that Britain's radical deists were also usually advocates of radical Whig politics.

In America, Tom Paine was the most significant proponent of both kinds of radicalism—deism in religion, Real Whig republicanism in politics.[37] Deist thinking in America was fed further by radical French anticlericalism, a posture that gained momentary credibility in the new United States during the early 1790s. The religious writings of Paine and the widely shared American eagerness to view the Revolution in France as a natural consequence of the American Revolution opened a window of opportunity for deist convictions. Space for deism had also been provided by the decline of Calvinist hegemony in New England and by the general upheavals of the Revolutionary era.

Americans who were willing to call themselves deists in the 1780s (in contrast to Franklin and Jefferson, who remained ambiguously diffident about religious labels) certainly shared much of the American ethos, including a rejection of inherited authorities and a confidence in the human future. But as even brief citation from their landmark works can show, the self-described deists' exaltation of nature and obeisance to reason were at once too abstract and too specifically rooted in European free thought to gain a purchase in the American environment. As troubled as more orthodox Christians were by deist writings, they, and not the deists, remained closely tied to broad public opinion. In hindsight it is apparent that social order in the new republic required sanctions enforced by a much more active God than the deists offered.

Tom Paine might conclude about the Old Testament (after citing passages from the book of Judges) that "when we contemplate the immensity of that Being who directs and governs the incomprehensible WHOLE of which the utmost ken of human sight can discover but a part, we ought to feel ashamed at calling such paltry stories the word of God." Or he might assert boldly a minimalist meaning for the New Testament: "Jesus Christ founded no new system. He called men to the practice of moral virtues, and the belief of one God. The great trait in his character is philanthropy."[38] But the "we" who shared his blithe confidences was rarely more than a hothouse band of intellectual transplants. Similarly, the paeans to reason and nature that inspired Ethan Allen's distillation of earlier English deism in his *Reason the Only Oracle of Man* (1784) might have been shared fairly widely in America: "That mankind are by nature endowed with sensation and reflection, from which results the powers of reason and understanding, will not be disputed. . . . The promulgation of this supreme [moral] law to creatures, is co-extensive and co-existent with reason, and binding on all intelligent beings in the universe; and is that eternal fitness, as applicable to God, by which the creator of all things conducts his infinitude of providence, and by which he governs the moral system of being, according to the absolute perfection of his nature."[39] But America's more orthodox thinkers, who also sensed new authority in reason and nature, were much more convincing than Allen and his deist confreres at demonstrating why historical Christianity provided an entirely more satisfying framework, both intellectual and social, for these natural principles.

Deism, in sum, represented creative new theology, especially in the decades immediately following the war. But like defenders of hierarchical forms of European traditional religion at the other end of the theological spectrum, deists were never successful at translating their essentially European faith into the idioms of American conceptual discourse.

Populist Theologies

Theology of, by, and for the people appeared first in America on a broad scale during the revivals of the 1740s. The conviction of George Whitefield, Samuel Davies, Gilbert Tennent, and other New Light evangelists—that God's grace was no respecter of persons—encouraged ordinary men and women to treat their own religious experience with as much respect as the directives of traditional authorities. This populist effect often surprised the major revivalists, who were themselves representatives of formal authority, but their surprise did not abate the populist consequences of their message. During and after the Revolution, an even broader assertion of rights on behalf of ordinary people—again, often coming as a surprise to the national founding fathers, who assumed that the language of liberty could be contained—had an even broader impact on theology and religion. Rather than defer to the dictates of the better sort, who presumed to speak by right of character or position, populists insisted on the ability of people to think for themselves. Two characteristic assertions from Israel Holly, an able Connecticut Separatist, who broke with New England's church-state establishment in order to found congregations enjoying the freedom of the gospel, illustrate the language of self-assertion that fueled the populist drive.

Holly (1728–1809) was an unusually interesting product of the colonial Great Awakening.[40] Little is known of his background or training, except that it did not include college. It is clear from his publications, however, that he promoted New Light revivalism, read Jonathan Edwards with appreciation, and modeled his pulpit oratory on George Whitefield. From 1763 to 1784, Holly pastored a Separate Congregationalist church in Suffield, Connecticut, only then to return, for obscure reasons, to ministry in the established church. Holly stood out in his age as a pugnacious writer of considerable theological depth. Whatever his theme—defending the laity or the power of a local congregation to ordain its own ministers, defending extempore preaching, attacking New England's traditional Half-Way Covenant, defending infant baptism against the Baptists (including Isaac Backus), promoting the cause of American rights at the time of the Revolution, attacking the innovations of New Divinity theology, or defending historic Calvinism—his writings reveal a keen theological wit.[41]

At least so long as he remained a Separate, Holly was a forceful spokesman for the rights of ordinary people. On 13 June 1776, less than a month before the promulgation of the Declaration of Independence, Holly preached an ordination sermon for a fellow Separate in New Milford, Connecticut, right under the nose of Nathanael Taylor, the Old Calvinist stalwart who presided over New Milford's tax-supported Congregational church. In a mostly apolitical sermon, Holly nonetheless raised a banner against those who would restrict the power of a congregation to regulate its own life. Christ's own "liberty" was contravened, Holly urged, when congregations assumed that their ministers had to be certified by a college or university, the standard requirement for Congregational and Presbyterian ordination in the colonial period. According to Holly, it was a denial of God-given liberty to "say a man can't be a minister of Christ, without having, what is called a *liberal education*."[42] Four years later Holly ended a doctrinal treatise on dogmas debated by New Divinity Calvinists with another populist password. Again, the burden of Holly's effort was remarkably free from the language of politics, but his last words expressed what by then was a credo found nearly everywhere in the new United States: "I profess in reality, and trust I am sincere in the profession, that I mean to yield to the power and force of truth, whenever it appears such to me, let it be advanced by whom it will; but determine to think and judge for myself, and call in religious matters, no man father."[43]

In the history of Anglo-American religion, populist sentiments like those from Israel Holly could be found at least back to the days of Wycliffe and the Lollards. They had then regularly reappeared, especially at times of socio-religious upheaval, like the Protestant reign of Edward VI (1547–1553) or the era of the Puritan Revolution (1640–1660). But they emerged with unprecedented energy in the revivals of the 1730s and 1740s and with epoch-making force during the Revolutionary era.[44] This populism was found first, and most widely, among Baptists, whose protest against the Anglican establishment was their main reason for existence, but also with Separate Congregationalists and then among the lush sectarian outgrowth of the Revolutionary period itself, including Universalists, Freewill Baptists, Shakers, Brethren of several European strains, and some Quakers. The universal foundation of populist self-assertion was a refusal to be dictated to. Populists claimed the right, simply as human beings, to think for themselves.

From a modern perspective, it might seem logical that populist principle would have an immediate effect on doctrine, that the refusal to accept the inherited authority of tradition would lead naturally to a rejection of the dogmas taught by the tradition. In point of fact, however, the situation at least into the 1790s does not follow that logic. Again, the case of Israel Holly illustrates the point. In the ordination sermon preached on the eve of independence, where Holly attacked the monopoly of the colleges over the training of ministers, he also exalted the doctrines he felt any worthy minister should proclaim. These doctrines had a decidedly traditional cast: Real ministers would never "deny original sin, and the imputation of Adam's guilt to his posterity; deny that we are born into the world sinners, and are naturally spiritually dead; deny the doctrines of efficacious grace, and almighty power exerted at conversion; deny that 'tis free and sovereign grace in God, that distinguishes one man from another for the better, but assert that 'tis free-will in man that has made this distinction."[45] Similarly, in the tract where Holly professed to think for himself, the theology he promoted was "the good old way of ancient truth," which Holly defined more particularly as "a good system of doctrines received, and adopted by the church of Christ, even since the reformation from popery; . . . I mean, for substance, the doctrines called Calvinistical: which if we exchange away, for novelties, I apprehend we shall be great losers, and the case of truth must greatly suffer thereby."[46]

Populist theology in the period 1740–1790 must not necessarily be equated with innovative theology. Nor when populist innovations did occur were they necessarily the product of "American" concepts at work on the language of theology—that is, of republican deference to liberty, commonsense reliance on scientific demonstration, the ideological sway of democracy, or the influence of market economy. Each of these "American" predispositions would one day infiltrate populist as well as elite theology, but at least before the 1790s they did not do so. Rather, through the Revolution and the immediate postwar years— and even as the revolt against formal, traditional authority grew dramatically— the newly articulate populist voices were as likely to defend traditional theology as to undermine it, or, if attacking it, to do so from a source within the tradition itself rather than from influences seeping in from the socio-political environment.

The following series of brief accounts supports the same conclusion for theologians of the people as was argued for the for the elites of European-derived denominations—whatever was happening beneath the surface in the exchange between theology and culture, the articulated theologies of the period continued to be remarkably traditional.

African Americans

Perhaps the most striking illustration of the stability in theological statement is the first recorded Christian confessions of African Americans. Themes of liberty were prominent among virtually all black Christians during and after the Revolution, and African Americans rarely embraced formal theology in exactly the form their white instructors intended. But believing blacks whose views were recorded often embraced a very traditional faith. The poems of Phillis Wheatley (ca. 1753–1784), written and published while she was still a slave in a Boston household during the early 1770s, hinted at themes of particular relevance to slaves. She praised Whitefield at his death in 1770 for proclaiming the gospel of an "Impartial Saviour" who "longs for" Africans and is willing to make them "sons and kings, and Priests to God."[47] Wheatley composed republican odes during the Revolution, but in the classical and deferential mode.[48] To the extent that formal theology entered into her pious verse, it was a theology, as in a poem to the students at Harvard, taking for granted doctrines like the substitutionary atonement ("How Jesus' blood for your redemption flows") and eternal punishment ("Let sin . . . By you be shunned. . . . An Ethiop tells you 'tis your greatest foe; / Its transient sweetness turns to endless pain, / And in immense perdition sinks the soul").[49]

The first African American formally ordained by a white denomination exemplified the same convictions. Lemuel Haynes (1753–1833), who pastored a Congregational church for thirty years in Rutland, Vermont, argued during the Revolution for a much broader liberty than the founding fathers envisioned.[50] But in his ministry, he acted the part of a moderate New Light Calvinist by attacking the deism of Tom Paine and Ethan Allen, upholding Calvinist notions of salvation against the Universalist Hosea Ballou, and working faithfully for revival in his own and neighboring towns.[51]

Even more interesting is the record of the Baptist minister David George (1743–1810), who, unlike Wheatley and Haynes, lacked formal education and never enjoyed the traditionalist religious atmosphere provided by New England Congregationalism. George was one of the founders of the black Baptist church in Silver Bluff, South Carolina, which, when constituted in the early 1770s, may have been the first African-American church on the North American mainland. He was converted and instructed by Particular Baptist preachers, black and white, whose view of salvation included the conservative Calvinist conviction that Christ died only—or *particularly*—for the elect. George himself began to exhort before he had learned to read, a skill he later acquired in order to study the Scriptures. During the Revolution George joined the liberating British forces and continued to preach in nearby Savannah.[52] But when his liberators were defeated by the Americans, he accepted a refuge in Loyalist Nova Scotia, where he established the second black church in that province. While in Nova Scotia, George seems to have been touched by the radical evangelicalism associated with the ministry of Henry Alline, which combined mystical God-centeredness with an ardent defense of human free will. In 1792, after a decade in Nova Scotia, George removed to Sierra Leone with part of his congregation and became the leading black minister in that colony on the west coast of Africa. On 25 April 1797 the governor of the colony, Zachary Macaulay, a reformist evangelical of England's Clapham Sect and colleague of abolitionist William Wilberforce, recorded the gist of a twelve-hour conversation during which George expressed his opinions in full. Macaulay had initiated the meeting in order to warn George about the danger of moral lapses and to convince him that holiness of life was essential for all individuals who had been truly born again by the Spirit. The conversation showed the independence of George's theology—only reluctantly did he cave in to Macaulay's barrage of Scripture texts and concede that occasional acts of drunkenness or theft were as important as Macaulay took them to be.[53] George's response was to ask, "But is not God unchangeable, how then can he withdraw his love from his children?"[54] George also relied much more on his experiences of grace than Macaulay thought he should.

What is most intriguing about Macaulay's record of the conversation, however, is his conclusion that George belonged with "those high Calvinists" because of his unshakable commitment to the doctrine of the perseverance of the saints, a commitment that Macaulay felt could lead only to antinomianism.[55] Four years earlier, Macaulay had recorded another incident with a similar conclusion. When a white chaplain preached a sermon suggesting that Christ's death availed for all humanity, George rebuked him with the traditional Calvinist view that this death was intended only for the elect.[56] The conclusion cannot be that George was merely a conventionally traditional Calvinist, but rather that in a faith compounded of Particular Baptist preaching, New Light experientialism, and perhaps elements of African ritual, George also incorporated elements of strongly traditional Calvinist theology. African-American Christians in the Revolutionary age were by no means puppets in the hands of traditionalist teachers, but the experience of Wheatley, Haynes, and George suggests that, however distinctive African-American religious life became in the new United States, African-American theology could make room for large portions of traditional Protestant dogma.

Baptists

The same conclusion, with appropriate adjustments for cultural, regional, and racial differences, pertains to many of the white Baptists of the late-colonial and Revolutionary era, especially Isaac Backus, the key figure in the rise of the Baptist denomination in New England. The history of the Baptists in the eighteenth and nineteenth centuries is a subject as scandalously neglected as had been, until very recently, the history of early American Methodism.[57] Baptists, always of several varieties, grew rapidly in the generation after the Great Awakening and then, in the post-Revolutionary decades, expanded almost as explosively as the Methodists. Populist resentment of hierarchy and pietist assertion of the priesthood of all believers were always significant themes in the Baptist message.[58] Yet even as Baptist forms of populist pietism spread rapidly in the Revolutionary decades, Baptists generally maintained the traditional dogmas of classic Protestant Christianity. One individual's experience cannot verify such a claim adequately, but because Isaac Backus was such a key figure for promoting and recording Baptist faith in this era, his story is unusually important.

Backus (1724–1806) was a child of the colonial revivals. While working in the fields on 22 August 1741, at a time of intense religious excitement in his native Norwich, Connecticut, Backus, as he put it later, "was enabled by divine light to see the perfect righteousness of Christ and the freeness and riches of His grace. . . . My heavy burden was gone, tormenting fears were fled, and my joy was unspeakable."[59] Once having put his hand to the plow of New Light Christianity, Isaac Backus never looked back. After his conversion, Backus held short-term pastorates and then in 1756 helped establish a Baptist congregation in Middleboro, Massachusetts, which he served until his death fifty years later. Backus also played a major role in the influential Warren Association of Baptist churches (founded 1767) and was a diligent historian of the Baptist movement.[60] Something of the dynamism of New England Baptists during Backus's life is indicated by their great growth in New England during the period: from only 25 congregations in 1740 to nearly 24,000 members in 312 churches and 13 regional associations by 1804.

Isaac Backus's mature theology closely resembled the Calvinism of Jonathan Edwards, differing only on questions of baptism, ecclesiology, and the urgency of promoting the separation of church and state. On most other matters, Backus eagerly followed Edwards's lead. With Edwards, Backus rejected "means" as in any sense contributory to salvation, he held to the need for a special work of grace in order to become a child of God, he was committed to the teachings of Scripture understood in a Reformed sense, and he believed that the congregation should reflect the purity of its Head. So close did Backus consider himself to his better-known contemporary that in later life he could refer to "our excellent Edwards."[61] In particular, both Backus's rejection of unregenerate ministers and his argument for a church of professing saints rested on a conception of God's gracious work strikingly similar to that of Jonathan Edwards. As Backus put it in his own words, but with the unmistakable accents of Edwards's *Freedom of Will* and *The Nature of True Virtue*: "The true liberty of man is to know, obey, and enjoy his Creator and to do all the good unto, and enjoy all the happiness with and in, his fellow creatures that he is capable of. In order to which the law of love was written in his heart[,] which carries in its nature union and benevolence to Being in general and to each being in particular according to its relation and connection to and with the Supreme Being and ourselves."[62] On the basis of such reasoning Backus came to define the church as constituted by professing believers only, to deny the validity of infant baptism, and to advocate a full religious liberty. As he saw it, only communion with and among the professedly regenerate reflected the nature of God's holiness and the surpassing beauty of the work of redemption.[63] On these matters, Backus thought he was understanding the implications of Edwards's theology better than Edwards himself.

In the reasoning of Backus and most Baptists, fidelity to this conception of the gospel demanded resistance to the shackles of religious establishment. They perceived a clear dividing line between the church and society; to violate that line ecclesiologically (as nonseparating New Lights like Jonathan Edwards did by baptizing infants who might not be numbered among the elect) or legislatively (as the Massachusetts and Connecticut assemblies did by establishing the Congregational church) was to restrict the work of God and to confuse categories that revivalistic Calvinism had distinguished. Such arguments were radical for New England during Backus's early life, but for him they were put to use on behalf of a traditional doctrine of God as well as traditional doctrines of humanity and salvation. Political involvement, except to fight for ecclesiastical freedom, was usually suspect among Backus and his associates.

John Allen, who arrived from England shortly before the Revolution, was highly unusual in Baptist circles because of his eager participation in political controversy. But in 1773, the very year that Allen published his rousing tract *American Alarm. An Oration upon the Beauties of Liberty*, New England Baptists denounced Allen's theological opinions because they seemed to be departing from historic Calvinism.[64] Such action indicates that New England's

Baptists were able to discriminate between their protests against specific public policies and their defense of traditional Christian doctrines.

During the Revolution, most New England Baptists joined the patriots, but they did not lose sight of their fundamental religious convictions. In fact, they soon were employing the rhetoric of the Revolution's leaders against those leaders themselves. In 1770, even before the Baptists had committed themselves to the patriotic effort, Backus pointed to the incongruity that "many who are filling the nation with the cry of LIBERTY and against oppressors are at the same time themselves violating the dearest of all rights, LIBERTY OF CONSCIENCE."[65] Backus's *Appeal* of 1773 is a classic example of how a revivalist's alchemy could turn patriotic arguments against Britain into attacks on the establishment of religion in New England. Were the colonists concerned about "slavery"? Backus would tell them the real (spiritual) meaning of slavery: "How far have pride and infidelity, covetousness and luxury, yea, deceit and cruelty, those foreigners which came from Hell, carried their influence, and spread their baneful mischiefs in our world! Yet who is willing to own that he has been deceived and enslaved by them?" Did patriots worry about taxation without representation? To Backus a similar question concerned "whether our *civil* legislature are in truth our representation in *religious* affairs or not." Were foes of Parliament mobilizing against a threat to property? Backus would tell them about the colonial governments that seized the property of Baptists, whose only crime was refusing to pay taxes levied to build a Congregationalist church.[66] Backus, in other words, knew how to use the rhetoric of republican civic humanism, but this rhetoric remained the servant rather than the master of his theological vision.

For Backus and most Baptists in the 1770s, the controlling ideas remained the pietistic Calvinism of the revivals. For them, "liberty of conscience" had less to do with the fear of economic or political slavery than with religious, moral, and spiritual freedom. In the terms of Jonathan Edwards's *Freedom of the Will*, the Baptists were concerned with the liberty to act as Christians in accordance with a willing nature regenerated by God (i.e., the freedom to *do* as they willed); they were not overly concerned with political and economic freedoms except where they involved the true, regenerate freedom of the will. These same concerns survived into the 1780s during the struggle over the Massachusetts constitution, when Baptists prodded patriot leaders, now content with the fruits of their victory against Britain, to realize that other expressions of freedom existed besides the political and the economic.

This basic stance—conservative in theology, aggressive in seeking rights for free churches—guided Backus's theological polemics after the war. In 1789 he wrote a tract aimed at the Methodists, reaffirming the dogmas that he had first learned in the midcentury revivals. In this tract, Backus used various episodes of political history to make his theological points, drawing, for example, on American experiences of the 1770s and 1780s to compare the motive power of love and fear. He suggested that when Americans feared "destruction or slavery," they could unite to defeat their enemies. But when Parliament's threat was gone, then "the love of riches, honors and pleasures prevailed," people set to wrangling "over contracts and oaths," and soon the land was filled "with discord, treachery, and infidelity."[67] The language of republican dissent colored this illustration, but it was used to make a theologically conservative point. Likewise, in the opening salvo of the tract, Backus knew how to employ the currently available language, but again for his own religious purposes: "The revealed will of God is the only perfect law of liberty, but how little is it believed and obeyed by mankind."[68] The tract as a whole—in its sturdy defense of predestination, Edwards's account of the will, the particular atonement, and the perseverance of saints—was touched hardly at all by the deep structure of Whig dissent. As late as 1789, the language of Christian freedom was for Backus a deeper, broader reservoir than the language of American liberty.

Radical Dissenters

The situation was somewhat different for two other kinds of populists, those who manifestly imbibed the libertarian spirit of the age and those whose theology innovated, sometimes dramatically, in the Revolutionary era. In the first instance, populist leaders were even more adept than elites at exploring the extended meaning of libertarian and commonsense themes for theology. After the turn of the century, this exercise led to considerable theological innovation. Earlier, however, it was not so clear a case, for at least some populists maintained the central points of inherited dogma, even as they embraced the new age of liberty.

The case of John Leland (1754–1841) illustrates that combination unusually well. Leland was an ardent democrat who preached as a Baptist elder in Virginia and Massachusetts and who became notorious as a vociferous champion of Thomas Jefferson and the Democratic-Republicans.[69] Leland was a determined foe of all hierarchies—social, commercial, medical, and legal, as well as clerical—and of every effort to coerce the conscience. He even took Isaac Backus to task for Backus's willingness to be bound by the words of an inherited creed. Yet on many points of Christian doctrine, Leland remained a traditionalist. As a very old man, he looked back over sixty years of a preaching career that began in the 1770s and said that he had been preaching all those years "to convince men that human powers were too degenerate to effect a change of heart by self-exertion." But now there was "a host of preachers and people . . . risen up, who ground salvation on the foundation that I have sought to demolish." Leland remained, then in his eighties, "open to conviction" and "willing to retract," but nothing yet had convinced him that self-centered approaches to salvation were more truthful than theocentric ones.[70]

In a remarkable statement from a sermon preached some thirty years before this testimony, Leland clearly distinguished between political and religious spheres of life. The subject was the substitutionary atonement, a doctrine that egalitarian and ethical imperatives of the Revolutionary eighteenth century were rendering increasingly suspect. Leland's commentary did show

how fully he had assimilated the age's assumptions about the civil sphere, but also how resilient the old doctrines remained. Leland held that "it would be extremely improper to admit of a vicarious punishment in the governments on earth," since civil government existed "to protect the innocent in their rights, and punish the guilty, and the guilty only." But Christian theology was different. Leland's phrasing of the contrast is worth extended quotation because it reveals self-conscious resistance against the application of republican political principle to theology:

> But in the divine government, where the actions and motives of all men are perfectly known, without evidence—where He that suffered death for the guilty, had power to rise again, and thereby prevent any loss of subjects in the state—where He, who suffered for the guilty, had the power to change the hearts of the transgressors, and make them true men, and thereby prevent future crimes—the objections which forbid a vicarious suffering among men lose all their weight.[71]

Leland was a proponent of what Nathan Hatch has called "a divine economy that was atomistic and competitive rather than wholistic and hierarchical."[72] Such a mind-set would indeed work dramatic changes in the inherited theology as the nineteenth century wore on. But for Leland, as a figure from the transitional eighteenth century, ardent democracy did not yet necessarily mean innovative theology.

By the 1780s innovative theology could indeed be found among other kinds of populists, but the nature of those innovations requires careful scrutiny. Especially in the New England backcountry, radical sectarian movements began to enjoy unprecedented success from the late 1770s.[73] This region was opened to settlement because of the Revolution. It was also open to social reordering beyond anything that had yet been experienced in New England because of frontier circumstances and the weakened capacity of state governments to control the population. The new religious movements, especially those that attracted the most followers—Freewill Baptists, Universalists, and Shakers—made mincemeat of New England's traditional Calvinism. Instead of inherited teachings on divine sovereignty, innate human depravity, a substitutionary and limited atonement, and predestination, the sects taught, in Stephen Marini's summary, "a benevolent God, human perfectibility, universal nonpenal atonement, and free grace for all believers."[74]

When, however, the sources are sought for these distinctive new doctrines, a curious fact emerges. The leaders of the sects were, to an unusual degree, direct converts of George Whitefield or individuals who had been nurtured in a radical evangelical constituency traceable to Whitefield's influence. Thus Ann Lee (Shaker), Benjamin Randel (Freewill Baptist), and John Murray (Universalist) began their careers as populist religious leaders after direct contact with Whitefield. Joseph Meacham (Shaker), Caleb Rich (Universalist), Hosea Ballou (Universalist), Elhanan Winchester (Universalist), and Henry Alline ("New Light" Christian) were products of the radical evangelical constituencies that arose out of the work of Whitefield and similar revivalists.[75]

The religion of these sectarians could not have been more different from the religion of deists and Boston liberals, the era's other most advanced theological innovators. It was based, not on the dictates of eighteenth-century reason, but on a lively, immediate sense of the divine. The sects promoted a religion in which revelation fairly shimmered—through dreams, apparitions, and hermetic, spiritual interpretations of Scripture. It was a religion expecting the most direct kind of divine intervention—in personal life as perfection, in the world at large as apocalypse.[76] This form of religion was given room to develop by the slackening of social bonds in the Revolution. It was also a religion rooted in the extreme revivalism of the 1730s and '40s. It was the religion of radical revivalist James Davenport much more than of cautious politician James Madison.

The ministry of "Nova Scotia's Whitefield," Henry Alline (1748–1754), illustrates the character of extreme dissenting Protestantism.[77] Alline was born in Rhode Island but early moved with his family to Nova Scotia. After a dramatic conversion in 1775, he began to preach a radically evangelical message that influenced both the Maritimes and the New England backcountry. During the War for Independence, he and much of the Maritime and backcountry New England constituency receptive to the sectarian message remained neutral or Loyalist.[78] Alline, to be sure, was not insensitive to the Real Whig rhetoric of the Revolution. In the most succinct summary of his teachings, published shortly before his death under the telling title *The Anti-Traditionalist*, Alline railed against "arbitrary bigots," "arbitrary Power," and "arbitrary Predestinarians."[79] Using populist terms, he appealed to his readers, "chained down by Darkness and Tradition," to join him in breaking free of "the Misery of Man's fallen State, the injury of Tradition, the Prejudice of Education, the Distress and Torment of the Slavery thereby." He urged his readers to find in "some small Experience of Redemption the worth of Liberty, the Sweetness of divine Life, the Joys of Immortal Love."[80]

Yet such use of the age's populist language remained a means to another end. What Alline was trying to communicate was the need for sinners to be "ravished with the meek and lovely Jesus," to be "for ever ravished with the Perfections of such a God," and to "swim . . . in the Boundless Ocean of [God's] uncreated Good."[81] He hoped that his auditors would find, as he had found, the "ONE ETERNAL NOW," which God inhabits, and join "those who have thrown off the Canopy of Matter and Time."[82] Alline, in other words, preached a mystical, Neoplatonic evangelicalism filled with theological innovations— for example, that sinfulness was associated with corporality, that the resurrected body was noncorporeal, and that the atonement was based on Christ's assuming the human "Contrariety" of spirit and flesh.[83] But this religion was a replication of mystical themes that had often appeared in the history of ecstatic Christianity, rather than a reflection of either intellectual Enlightenment or political republicanism. Alline promoted theological innovation with a vengeance, but it was not innovation propelled primarily by American ideological circumstances.

Followers of Alline among the Freewill Baptists, as well as the leading Shakers and Universalists, did not always share his ecstatic ardor, but they took their stand just as clearly on themes derived from earlier expressions of Christian piety. They were most interested in the immediacy of divine action, whether Ann Lee's revelations or the Universalists' claims about the infinity of divine love. They were radicals for whom the American Revolution and the opening of the New England frontier made a real difference, but their religion remained mostly a product of historically recurring impulses.

Thus, populist theology in the Revolutionary period itself was far less influenced by specifically American themes than would be the case in the post-Revolutionary age. If the Revolution made it much easier for people to think for themselves, the theology that many of the people promoted continued along paths defined well before the Revolution. It would not always be so.

Conclusion

During the period from roughly 1740 to 1800, Christian theology remained stable in America even though everything else was in flux. A barrage of conceptual languages—several of them rising to overwhelming importance, and all of them conflicting in some way with the others—swept the colonies even more thoroughly than did the winds of war. Their reach was vastly more extensive than the reach of the continent's new market economy. From the early 1770s the innovative force of these conceptual languages accelerated. Yet through the 1780s conceptual confusion prevailed. Until that confusion eased, traditional theologies, by the very weight of their tradition, prevailed.

Given the uncertainties of the two decades from the Revolution through the presidential administration of George Washington, it is easy to imagine counterfactual national destinies that would have dramatically altered the history of American theology. Had Britain regained control of her lost colonies, it is likely that theology in America would have developed as theology developed in Canada after the War of 1812, the conflict that kept Canada culturally as well as politically British, even as it reconfirmed the independence of the United States. That Canadian pattern witnessed some genuine adaptation to new terrain, but also much more emphasis on tradition, no sharp separation of church and state, much less concern about scientific demonstration, and more reliance on organic instead of individual social bonds.[84] Again, had a Thermidorean reaction occurred, say in a two-term presidency for Alexander Hamilton, the cachet of tradition, ties to Britain, and a hardening of class lines in the British pattern might have been the order of the day.[85] Or, from the other end of the scale of possibilities, it is easy to imagine the United States fragmenting into several national chunks because of crises in 1789 (over the Constitution), the early 1790s (over the Whiskey Rebellion and other agrarian riots), 1800 (over the election of Jefferson), or 1812–1814 (over war with Britain). If fragmentation had occurred, it is doubtful whether a coordinated set of "American" norms

would have exerted a dominant influence; rather, a much broader denominational, regional, and racial spectrum of cultures would have accompanied a
widely variegated theological spectrum.

But none of these possibilities took place. The United States and the American culture, familiar now from a thousand textbooks, did. It is not easy to define the nation and its culture, but at a minimum they incorporated a constitutional theory designed to serve the needs of classical, deferential republicans,
but fleshed out in a political culture following liberal republican impulses. Nation
and culture experienced an unprecedented and largely unexpected social revolution arising from the "expansion of personal choice." They also embodied a
fragile union of Southern, Northern, mid-Atlantic, and Western social vectors—
slavery and honor (South), Puritan conscience (New England and Northwest),
ethnic diversity and commercial energy (mid-Atlantic), and western expansion
as at once highly individualistic and highly communal. In the 1780s practical
needs of great moment called for the creative use of old concepts and the transformation of inherited ideologies. If the first generation of the new republic
endured a turbulent period of ideological strife, it also witnessed social construction on a prodigious scale—expanding commercial and industrial bonds,
the forging of persistent myths about the United States, and hard-won means
of working out political differences.

In these circumstances involving the creation of a new culture as well as a
new nation, the churches also took on a new role. Even as they continued
traditional tasks as organizers of worship, family nurture, and evangelization,
they also became agents of civilization. This role was not new in itself, for so
the churches had always served in Europe. The difference in the United States
was that the churches went about constructing civilization with little assistance from government or the social hierarchies that had been mainstays of
religion in establishmentarian Europe. Only as the churches assumed their
new role in the new nation's new society did theology begin to develop in
response to its American contexts. Only when the churches had begun to do
their part—and it was a very important part—in constructing America did
America decisively shape the churches' theology.

But once the process was underway—a process in which the churches' resources began to make a real difference in organizing the new American society—then the subterranean developments of the late-colonial and Revolutionary periods began to work on the substance of theology. No longer was it merely
a simmering environment for traditional faiths. Now the American ideologies
began to play a role in forging dogma itself. In these terms, George Whitefield's
substantial theological influence may have been greater in the 1790s than in the
1750s. Daniel Pals is only one of many historians who have commented on
Whitefield's "deeply populist frame of mind." But Pals sees also theological
consequences, especially in Whitefield's "fundamentally democratic determination to simplify the essentials of religion in a way that gives them the widest
possible mass appeal."[86] This was a drive that Whitefield himself had no difficulty coordinating with a traditional Calvinist theology. Fifty and more years
later, it would not be so easy to keep such energies together.

A similar conclusion arises from Harry Stout's observations about the nature of New England preaching during the Revolution. While week-to-week sermons retained a traditional Calvinist emphasis on repentance, conversion, and faith, occasional sermons became the vehicle for a sanctified Whig ideology, and these occasional sermons began to be published much more frequently than week-to-week sermons.[87] Stout's observation has greater significance for a history of theology after the sanctified Whig ideology was actually constructing a new society then when it was simple political commentary on a contentious colonial situation. Similarly, slavery would come to mean something far different theologically when it was isolated as a contested factor in a Southern way of life than when it was a more or less inadvertent detail of colonial commerce.

Illustrations of how colonial circumstances began to alter theological formulation only after the former colonists began to construct a national culture point to the following conclusion: From the vantage point of the 1780s and 1790s, the biggest question for the history of Christian theology in the new United States was not how it would develop but whether it would survive. Only in retrospect can we see that there were "givens" in the new American nation. However certain was God's hidden will, the lived world was brimful of contingency. The United States did not have to survive; American culture did not have to develop the way it did; the churches, especially the Protestant evangelical churches, were not fated to be key agents of cultural formation in the two generations between the Constitution and Appomattox Courthouse. Only the story of how and why Protestant evangelical Christianity came to flourish in the new republic can begin to explain the narrower story of how theology in the new United States became American theology.

III

EVANGELIZATION

*Although it formed no part of the design of its [Methodism's] disciples
to enter into the political speculations of the day, nor to intermeddle
with the civil affairs of the country, yet it is thought that its extensive
spread in this country, the hallowing influence it has exerted in society
in uniting in one compact body so many members, through the medium
of an itinerant ministry, interchanging from north to south, and from
east to west, has contributed not a little to the union and prosperity of
the nation.*
    —Nathan Bangs, *A History of the Methodist Episcopal Church*, 1838

The Evangelical Surge . . .

Transplanted European theology became truly American theology when three interrelated developments occurred. First, the significance of Protestant churches increased relative to the significance of other American institutions. Second, within the churches, evangelical influence grew rapidly, especially from groups that rejected ecclesiastical tradition, inherited authority, and historical confessions in order to insist upon the Bible and born-again human conscience as the primary religious authorities. Third, the churches, led by the Protestant evangelicals, adopted forms of the republican and commonsense reasoning that the nation's founders had employed to justify independence and build a new nation. Critical to this sequence was the remarkably effective outreach of Protestant churches and voluntary societies in the years between the Revolution and the Civil War, along with the overwhelmingly evangelical character of that creative energy. Understanding evangelical strength in the new republic first requires, however, some effort at charting evangelical weakness during the preceding half century.[1]

Evangelical Decline ca. 1750–1790

From the standpoint of the 1760s and 1770s, it was almost unthinkable that evangelical Protestantism would soon be expanding rapidly in a new United States. Many years later, voices could still be heard whose assessment of religion continued to speak for this earlier situation. In 1822 Thomas Jefferson predicted to a correspondent that "the present generation will see Unitarianism become the general religion of the United states."[2] Ten years later a French immigrant of noble blood, Achille Murat, said much the same thing in telling a European audience that "the rising influence of the Unitarian sect" now "spreads from one end of the Union to the other."[3] By the time these predictions were made, they were little more than obtuse wishes. Had they been voiced forty years earlier, they would have reflected less Jefferson's and Murat's hopes and more an actual possibility.

In the period from 1740 to 1780 a few denominations were experiencing rapid growth, especially churches fed by strong inflows of immigration (Scots-Irish Presbyterians, German Reformed) and those like the Baptists who had ventured into the southern frontier (table 9.1). But the general rate of church formation was lagging behind the spectacular growth in colonial population. For the period 1760 to 1780, while the number of churches in the colonies/states increased from slightly more than 2,000 to slightly more than 3,000 (roughly a 50% increase), population was rising much faster, from about 1.66 million to 2.67 million (or 61%). The ratio of churches to population was declining gradually throughout the eighteenth century—from 1:598 in 1700 to 1:642 in 1740 to 1:807 in 1780.[4] The revivals of the 1730s and early 1740s did produce a dramatic interest in religion, to which numerous observers attest. Yet after the fires of revival cooled, membership additions dipped below earlier averages, and by the 1750s many churches that had benefited from the revivals were barely adding enough new members to replace those who died.[5] A sustained curve of rising membership does appear among the Baptists in New England and on the southern frontier. But Baptist expansion was slow until the 1760s, and the number of Baptist churches did not come close to the number of Anglican, Congregationalist, and Presbyterian churches until the mid-1770s or later.

Local revivals were occurring throughout the 1770s and 1780s, but these revivals had their greatest impact on frontiers, among African Americans, as

TABLE 9.1. Churches in the Thirteen Colonies, 1740 and 1776

Denomination	1740		1776	
	Churches	% of Total	Churches	% of Total
Congregational	423	33.7	668	21.0
Anglican	246	19.6	495	15.6
Presbyterian	160	12.7	588	18.5
Baptist	96	7.6	497	15.6
Lutheran	95	7.6	150	4.7
Dutch Reformed	78	6.2	120	3.8
German Reformed	51	4.1	159	5.0
Quaker	ca. 50	4.0	310	9.8
German sectarians	ca. 30	2.4	71	2.2
Roman Catholic	27	2.1	56	1.8
Methodist	0	0	65	2.0
Total churches	1,256	100.0	3,179	100.0

Sources: Edwin Scott Gaustad, *Atlas of American Religious History* (rev. ed., New York, 1976), 4; Edwin Scott Gaustad and Philip L. Barlow, *New Historical Atlas of Religion in America* (New York, 2001), 8; Stephen A. Marini, "The Government of God: Religion in Revolutionary America, 1764–1792" (unpublished manuscript).

a result of Methodist itineration, and in response to Baptist antiformalist preaching—in every case, that is, far from the new country's geographic or social centers of power.[6]

Publication records also indicate a proportionate decline in religious vitality during the Revolutionary era. From the beginnings of printing in the English colonies during the 1630s, religious works constituted the backbone of the printing trade. Colonial presses continued through the eighteenth century to issue large quantities of sermons, theological treatises, religious dialogues, contributions to denominational controversies, catechisms, hymnbooks, and reprints of older devotional works. But as with the ratio of churches to the total population, so the number of religious imprints relative to other titles was declining throughout the century. In 1730, for example, 60 out of the 126 (or 48%) separate titles published were religious works; by 1760 that proportion had fallen to 38% (90 out of 238). By 1775, with the burgeoning of political publication, it was down to 16% (122 out of 744). Again, the revival years reversed this trend briefly: in 1740, fully 67% of colonial publications treated religious topics, with 40 of the year's 127 religious imprints contributed by George Whitefield himself. Yet in due course the flood of revival publication ebbed, and the proportionate increase of other publications resumed (table 9.2).

If Protestants in general and evangelicals in particular were not thriving on the eve of the Revolution, neither were they particularly influential among the political activists who guided the colonies to the promised land of self-

TABLE 9.2. Religious Titles as Proportion of All Nongovernmental Publications, 1700–1837

Year	N[a]	% Religious Titles	Year	N[a]	% Religious Titles
1700	61	85	1780	282	24
1710	57	67	1785	543	24
1720	105	53	1790	832	22
1730	126	48	1800	2,334	12
1740	189	67	1810	2,358	25
1750	172	35	1820	3,542	28
1760	238	38	1830	4,337	28
1770	504	31	1837	4,360	26
1775	744	16			

[a] The number of nongovernmental titles excludes publications issued by colonies, the British ministry, states, or agencies of the United States.

Sources: Charles Evans, *American Bibliography* (New York, 1941–67): Clifford K. Shipton and James E. Mooney, *National Index of American Imprints through 1800: The Short-Title Evans* (Worcester, Mass., 1969); Ralph R. Shaw and Richard H. Shoemaker, *American Bibliography: A Preliminary Checklist, 1801–1819* (New York, 1966); M. Frances Cooper, *A Checklist of American Imprints, 1820–1829* (Metuchen, N.J., 1973); Carol Rinderknecht, *A Checklist of American Imprints, 1830–1839* (Metuchen, N.J., 1989); and (for checking general accuracy) G. Thomas Tansell, "Some Statistics on American Printing, 1764–1783," in *The Press and the American Revolution,* ed. Bernard Bailyn and John B. Hench (Boston, 1981), 315–64, esp. 328. I thank David Malone and Kathleen France Beliveau for these enumerations.

government. Although almost all of the new nation's most visible leaders in its founding era were Protestant in some sense of the term, most were formal or detached in their church allegiance, and only a few practiced an evangelical style of religion. Those leaders whose beliefs came closest to evangelical patterns—like Sam Adams of Massachusetts, John Jay of New York, Patrick Henry of Virginia, John Witherspoon and Elias Boudinot of New Jersey, or Roger Sherman of Connecticut—were usually defenders of hereditary church establishments, which they considered essential for the health of religion and society. The founders who mattered most—like the Episcopalians George Washington, Thomas Jefferson, James Madison, and John Wilson; the Congregationalist John Adams; and the unattached Alexander Hamilton and Benjamin Franklin—were either so reticent about their own religious convictions or so obviously deistic as to represent positive opposition to evangelicalism. While such founders have been justly described as sincerely religious, the moralistic and antienthusiastic religions they practiced hardly anticipated an evangelical surge. The founders may have preserved some of the Puritans' moral earnestness and may have borrowed rhetorical strategies from the midcentury revivals.[7] Yet it would be hard to imagine political leaders further removed in religious sensibility from the era's notable evangelical politicians, like William Wilberforce in Britain.

In addition, the language of the nation's founding documents—the Declaration of Independence, the Articles of Confederation, and the Constitution—while respectful of the deity in general, was hardly evangelical in any specific sense. The most careful studies of religion and politics in the founding era make a strong case for the presence of Protestant elements, but none claims for the founding a specifically evangelical influence.[8] The well-documented debates on the ratification of the Constitution were not entirely devoid of interest in religion, since those debates included concern for protecting religious liberty as later specified in the First Amendment.[9] But the overwhelmingly this-worldly character of those debates reveals no preoccupation with explicitly Christian, much less explicitly evangelical, concerns. Political scientist Donald Lutz, who tabulated the citations from 916 separate political publications in the period 1760 to 1805, found the Bible the most cited source. But in the publications of federalists and antifederalists debating the merits of the Constitution in 1787–1789, references to the Bible fade almost to the vanishing point.[10]

The invisibility in high political culture during the late 1780s of the evangelicals who would soon spearhead a national revival is suggested by the scarcity of Methodists and Baptists at the Constitutional Convention. Its members were overwhelmingly establishmentarian (Congregationalists, Presbyterians, some Episcopalians) or nominally religious (the remaining Episcopalians). Although Baptists accounted for about 15% of colonial churches in 1776, and probably close to 20% by 1790, not a single one of the fifty-five members of the Convention was a Baptist.[11]

In discussing specifically the public situation in the late 1780s, John Murrin may overstate matters, but only slightly, when he concludes that "the Federal

Constitution was . . . the eighteenth-century equivalent of a secular humanist text." Murrin points out that Richard Bassett of Delaware, a Methodist who supported Francis Asbury but said nothing during the constitutional debates, was perhaps the only delegate at Philadelphia who would have called him-self "born-again." According to Murrin, "One cliché often applied to the Con-stitution is not correct in any literal sense—that at least the Founders, unlike the wildly optimistic French, believed in original sin and its implications for government and politics. Quite possibly not a single delegate accepted Cal-vinist orthodoxy on original sin—that man is irretrievably corrupted and damned unless redeemed from outside."[12]

Protestants exhibited a full measure of uncertainty in the 1770s and 1780s, not only because of decline relative to population growth and their exclusion from the seats of power, but also because they now lacked a reliable organi-zational compass for navigating through uncharted waters.[13] The principle of church establishment was dead or dying, a fact that may have caused as much uncertainty among traditional dissenters like the Baptists, who had al-ways defined themselves over against the coercive monopoly of public reli-gion, as it did among those, like Congregationalists and Anglicans, who held establishment of religion to be a necessary guarantor of godly order. Protes-tants had long championed their liberties when contending against Roman Catholicism, but throughout Europe and in North America until the 1780s and 1790s, almost all Protestants still instinctively accepted the normative, defin-ing force of ecclesiastical tradition.

As much as the American Revolution occasioned a comprehensive political disruption in notions about who should rule and who should be ruled in the new national republic, so also did the Revolutionary era fundamentally unsettle traditional Protestant assumptions about the social, intellectual, and historical foundations required for personal faith and properly functioning Christian churches.[14] Significantly, the fumbling by national leaders toward workable practices for the political *novus ordo seclorum* took place at the same time that lay and clerical Protestants fumbled their way toward a *novus ordo ecclesiasti-corum*. In Gordon Wood's phrase, "As the Republic became democratized, it became evangelized." Everywhere the two struggles were connected.[15]

A brief account based largely on secondary sources cannot adequately document the extensive transformation that occurred between the Constitu-tional Convention and the start of the Jacksonian era, or provide comprehen-sive interpretation of the relatively more stable regional religious cultures that prevailed from the 1830s into the years of the Civil War. It can, however, sketch enough of the larger picture to illuminate the circumstances that bore most directly on the writing of theology.

The Dramatic Expansion of Evangelical Christianity

The central religious reality for the period from the Revolution to the Civil War was the unprecedented expansion of evangelical Protestant Christianity. No other period of American history ever witnessed such a dramatic rise in religious adherence and corresponding religious influence on the broader national culture.[16] That surge produced a double transformation, first, in the number of religious adherents, and, second, in the denominational affiliation of those adherents. Despite admitted difficulties in measuring such matters, the larger picture is entirely clear. Protestantism boomed in the early United States, and the Protestant bodies that led the way were the most militantly evangelical churches.[17]

Table 9.3, which records the numbers of churches, provides an overview for what was happening on the ground. According to at least some reckonings, these skyrocketing numbers actually undercount the growth in rates of adherence. In one of the most systematic efforts to gauge the expansion, Roger Finke and Rodney Stark have suggested that the proportion of the national population actively associated with churches rose from 17% in 1776 to 34% in 1850.[18] Using figures from an 1848 survey of American denominations, Nathan Hatch has estimated that from 1775 to 1845 the number of Christian ministers increased three times more rapidly than the population.[19]

In 1834 the English Dissenting minister Andrew Reed was dispatched by the Congregational Union of England and Wales to visit American Congregational churches. His report, though no doubt influenced by his own bias as a Nonconformist, became a rousing tribute to the virtues of disestablishment: "The voluntary principle . . . is the only one now for the support of these churches. . . .

TABLE 9.3. Growth in the Number of Churches from 1770 and 1790–1860

Denomination	Number of Churches			Multiple of Growth	
	1770	1790	1860	1770 to 1860	1790 to 1860
Methodist	20	712	19,883	994.1	27.9
Baptist	150	858	12,150	81.0	14.2
Presbyterian	500	725	6,406	12.8	8.8
Roman Catholic	50	65	2,550	51.0	39.2
Congregational	625	750	2,234	3.6	3.0
Anglican/Episcopal	356	170	2,145	6.0	12.6[a]
Lutheran	125	249	2,128	17.0	8.5
Christian/Disciples	0	0	2,100	—	—
Quakers	228	375	726	3.2	1.9
German Reformed	145	236	676	4.7	2.9
Dutch Reformed	100	115	440	4.4	3.8
Total churches[b]	2,481	4,696	ca. 52,500	21.2	11.2
U.S. Population (1,000s)	2,148	3,929	31,513	14.7	8.0

[a] The figure here of 12.6 is artificially high, given the great decline in the number of Anglican churches between 1770 and 1790.

[b] The total number of churches reflects many other, smaller denominations not listed in this table.

Sources: Stephen A. Marini, "The Government of God: Religion and Revolution in America, 1764–1792" (unpublished manuscript); Edwin Scott Gaustad, Historical Atlas of Religion in America, rev. ed. (New York, 1976), 43.

Deliberately, but without hesitation, I say, *the result is in everything and every where most favourable to the voluntary, and against the compulsory principle."* With figures he himself collected, Reed showed that the well-established eastern states of Massachusetts, New York, and Pennsylvania enjoyed many more ministers and churches per capita than even Scotland, which he considered to be the most thoroughly churched region in the British Isles. Reed also marveled at the rapid spread of churches into the newly settled states of Tennessee, Ohio, and Indiana. He was particularly struck by a comparison between numbers of churches and ministers in what he identified as twin British and American cities.[20] In every instance, as table 9.4 indicates, the Americans were more thoroughly churched than the British.

Just as remarkable was the makeup of the freshly Christianized population. All of the churches were doing well in absolute terms, but the largest churches from the colonial period (Congregationalists and Episcopalians), as well as those retaining old-world or colonial habits (Dutch Reformed, German Reformed, Quakers), were not expanding as rapidly as the population. Lutherans and Roman Catholics were growing more rapidly, but both of these communions were still largely immigrant and relatively isolated. The religious wonders of the age were the more aggressively evangelical churches— Presbyterians advancing at or slightly above the rate of the general population growth, Baptists and the new Disciples/Christian Churches far above, and the Methodists off the chart in a class all of their own.

When the 1850 United States census counted "accommodations," or seating capacity, for the nation's churches, it found that in four of the country's five main regions, the Methodists, Baptists, and Presbyterians by themselves had enough space for from 59% to 91% of the population. In New England, the Congregationalists joined Baptists, and Methodists in providing seating

TABLE 9.4. Andrew Reed's Comparisons of U.S. and British Cities, 1834

British/U.S. Cities	Population (1,000s)	Ministers	Churches	Communicants
Liverpool	210	57	67	18,000
New York	230	142	132	31,337
Edinburgh	150	70	65	n.a.
Philadelphia	200	137	83	n.a.
Glasgow	220	76	74	n.a.
Boston	60	57	55	n.a.
Nottingham	50	23	23	4,864
Cincinnati	30	22	21	8,555

Source: Andrew Reed, *American Churches* (1834), in *The Voluntary Church: American Religious Life, 1740–1860, Seen through the Eyes of European Visitors,* ed. Milton B. Powell (New York, 1967), 103–4.

for 69% of the population. Thus, the evangelical churches alone provided enough seating for the vast majority of the national population (table 9.5).

The count of ministers at work in these churches underscores the magnitude of the denominational shift underway. In 1845 the sectarian Freewill Baptists enjoyed almost as many ministers as the Episcopalians. The Christian Churches and Disciples of Christ (a movement officially organized only in 1831 with the merger of groups following Barton W. Stone and Alexander Campbell) employed nearly as many ministers as the Presbyterians. And the number of Methodist preachers was ten times the number of ministers among the Congregationalists, who seventy years earlier had enrolled twice the number of ministers as any other American denomination.[21]

The expansion of the Methodists requires special notice (table 9.6). When Francis Asbury arrived in America in 1771, there were four Methodist preachers caring for about 300 people. By 1813, three years before Asbury's death, the official Methodist minutes listed 171,448 white and 42,850 African-American members "in full society," served by 678 preachers.[22] By that time these itinerants were visiting about 7,000 local Methodist class meetings, each presided over by a local layperson. As many as one million people (or about one out of eight Americans) were attending a Methodist camp meeting each year.[23]

In charting this stunning progress, it is important to remember that American Methodism never enjoyed a serene career.[24] Most damagingly, it was rent by a series of contentious schisms. In the 1790s James O'Kelly's Republican Methodists pulled out. After the War of 1812 the Canadian conferences organized as separate denominations. During the first decades of the new century

TABLE 9.5. Denominational Seating Capacity as Percentage of the Population, 1850

Region[b]	Pop. (1,000s)	Seating Capacity of the Denominations[a]	
		The Three Largest	Others
New England	2,729	Cong (32.1), Bapt (21.3), Meth (16.0) = 69.4	Unit (6.2), Univ (5.9)
Middle	5,899	Meth (26.8), Pres (19.7), Bapt (12.3) = 58.8	Luth (7.6), Epis (7.0)
Southern	4,680	Meth (37.8), Bapt (36.5), Pres (11.0) = 85.3	Epis (5.4), Luth (2.2)
South Western	4,986	Meth (39.6), Bapt (34.2), Pres (17.0) = 90.8	RC (3.5), Chris (1.7)
North Western	4,714	Meth (33.5), Bapt (21.3), Pres (16.7) = 71.5	RC (6.1), Chris (5.5)
California and Territories	185	RC (82.3), Meth (4.6), Pres (1.9) = 88.8	Bapt (1.1), Cong (1.1)

[a] Figures show the percentage of the total regional population that each denomination could accommodate in 1850. Denominations listed are Baptist, Christian/Disciples, Congregational, Episcopal, Lutheran, Methodist, Presbyterian, Roman Catholic, Unitarian, and Universalist.

[b] The 1850 census identified six census regions, encompassing the states and territories as follows:

    New England = Conn., Maine, Mass., N.H., R.I., Vt.

    Middle = N.J., N.Y., Pa.

    Southern = D.C., Del., Fla., Ga., Md., N.C., S.C., Va.

    South Western = Ala., Ark., Ky., La., Miss., Mo., Tenn., Tex.

    North Western = Ill., Ind., Iowa, Mich., Ohio, Wis.

    California and Territories = Calif., Kans., Minn., Nebr., N.Mex., Oreg., Utah, Wash.

Source: Statistical View of the United States . . . Being a Compendium of the Seventh Census (Washington, D.C., 1854), 136–37.

TABLE 9.6. Methodist Growth, 1776–1860

Year	U.S. Population (1,000s)	Methodists[a] (1,000s)	Methodists as Percentage of Population
1776	2,500	5	0.2
1790	3,929	58	1.5
1800	5,297	65	1.2
1810	7,224	175	2.4
1820	9,618	257	2.7
1830	12,901	476	3.7
1840	17,120	795	4.6
1850	23,261	1,185	5.1
1860	31,513	1,744	5.5

[a] Figures, which include members and probationers, show the number of Methodists in the Methodist Episcopal Church and, from 1844, also the Methodist Episcopal Church, South.

Sources: Minutes of the Annual Conferences of the Methodist Episcopal Church for the Years 1773–1840, 2 vols. (New York, 1840); *Minutes of the Annual Conferences of the Methodist Episcopal Church, for the Year 1860* (New York, 1861); *Minutes of the Annual Conferences of the Methodist Episcopal Church, South, for the Year 1860* (Nashville, 1861); and *Historical Statistics of the United States, Colonial Times to 1956* (Washington, D.C., 1960). The Methodist membership figure for 1850 is an estimate based on known Methodist membership in 1860 and in 1853 (the latter in Kathryn Teresa Long, *The Revival of 1857–58: Interpreting an American Religious Awakening* [New York, 1998], 144) and on census data on the number of Methodist churches in 1850 and 1860 (*Statistical View of the United States, ... Being a Compendium of the Seventh Census* [Washington, D.C., 1854] and *Statistics of the United States ... in 1860; Compiled from ... the Eighth Census* [Washington, D.C., 1866]).

the African Methodist Episcopal Church (1816) and the African Methodist Episcopal Zion Church (1821) established separate denominations. In 1830 the Methodist Protestant Church arose as a result of urban protests against episcopal control. Most momentously, the divisive North-South division over slavery in 1844 left a great wound. And in the decades before the Civil War, the hemorrhaging continued with the formation of the Wesleyan Methodist Church (1843) and the Free Methodist Church (1860) as protests against slavery and in favor of older holiness practices.

Yet the juggernaut rolled on. In 1860 the Methodist Episcopal Church (the main Northern body) enrolled 860,000 full members and 135,000 probationers; its 6,987 traveling and 8,188 local ministers baptized 72,366 adults and children in that single year. Its 13,243 Sunday schools enrolled over 790,000 scholars, who were instructed by over 146,000 lay teachers. This Northern denomination contributed $387,000 to missionary and benevolent causes outside their own congregations. Its Southern counterpart, the Methodist Episcopal Church, South, was only slightly smaller, but given the sparser population below the Mason and Dixon Line, even more of a presence: 749,068 members and probationers (including 207,766 African Americans) served by 2,615 traveling and 5,353 settled preachers.[25] From nowhere, in a period of very rapid general growth in church affiliation and over a remarkably short span, Methodism had become the most pervasive form of Christianity in the United States.

For an adequate understanding of American religion in the period between the Revolution and the Civil War, the recent flurry of scholarship on Methodists has been a welcome, if long-overdue, boon.[26] At the same time, much remains to be done on the key question of how the Methodist phenomenon changed the entire American religious landscape, for other religious traditions as much as for themselves. The sort of evidence that awaits systematic study is suggested by the diary of John Mason Peck, a Baptist itinerant in the Mississippi Valley who played an important part throughout the 1820s in keeping slavery illegal in the new state of Illinois. On 6 December 1818 Peck preached a charity sermon in St. Louis and then took up what he thought was the first collection for itinerant missionaries in Missouri. As he did so, he commented on the mistaken notion spreading among his fellow Baptists that "none but pastors . . . are the instrumentalities God has appointed to extend the borders of his kingdom." The way things should go was indicated rather by the Methodists: "*A system of itinerant missions*, or 'circuit-preaching,' as our Methodist friends call it, is the most economical and successful mode of supplying the destitute, and strengthening and building up feeble churches, that has been tried. It is truly the apostolic mode; and if the finger of Divine providence ever pointed out a method adapted to the circumstances of new and sparsely-settled districts, it is itinerating or circuit missions."[27]

When Charles Finney, who was then a Presbyterian, paused to consider the Methodists in his influential *Lectures on Revivals of Religion* from 1835, he echoed Peck's encomium: "Wherever the Methodists have gone, their plain, pointed and simple, but warm and animated mode of preaching has always gathered congregations. . . . We must have exciting, powerful preaching, or the devil will have the people, except what the Methodists can save."[28] What Peck and Finney were recording was the Methodist transformation of American religion as a whole.

The Nature of Evangelical Christianity

Although identifiably evangelical churches by 1860 made up the vast majority of American congregations (at least 85%), these churches did not present a homogeneous faith. In fact, evangelicals fought each other over a host of *Streitpunkte*—over how to interpret the Scriptures; over the definition of many Christian doctrines, including human free will, the atonement, eschatology, the meaning of the sacraments, and the nature of the church; over slavery and other social issues; over the ecclesiastical roles of women and laymen; over whether to sing hymns or psalms only; over whether churches should use creeds; over principles and practices of the market economy; and over every imaginable kind of personality conflict. Yet for all their fissiparous quarreling, Methodists, Baptists, Presbyterians, most Congregationalists, many Episcopalians, Reformed, Friends, and Restorationist "Christians," as well as some Lutherans, were identifiably linked by a relatively common core of belief.

Evangelicals called people to acknowledge their sin before God, to look upon Jesus Christ (crucified—dead—resurrected) as God's means of redemption, and to exercise faith in this Redeemer as the way of reconciliation with God and orientation for life in the world. To evangelicals, the message was validated by their own experience of God's grace, but even more by its centrality in the Bible, which they held to be a unique revelation from God. How such convictions were expressed varied considerably, but not enough to obscure the substantial commonalities. At the risk of repetition, it is important to hear representative figures of the period as they spelled out these convictions.

Francis Asbury, the guiding spirit of the Methodists, often recorded the biblical passages from which he spoke in his life of constant preaching. The texts to which Asbury returned time after time were texts that all evangelicals held dear:

- Luke 11:13 (listed ten times in his journal): "If ye then, being evil, know how to give good gifts unto your children: how much more shall your heavenly Father give the Holy Spirit to them that ask him?"
- Matthew 11:28–30 (fourteen times): "Come unto me, all ye that labour and are heavy laden, and I will give you rest. Take my yoke upon you, and learn of me; for I am meek and lowly in heart; and ye shall find rest unto your souls. For my yoke is easy, and my burden is light."
- Luke 19:10 (sixteen times): "For the Son of man is come to seek and to save that which was lost."
- 2 Corinthians 6:1–2 (twenty-four times): "We then, as workers together with him, beseech you also that ye receive not the grace of God in vain. (For he saith, I have heard thee in a time accepted, and in the day of salvation have I succoured thee: behold, now is the accepted time; behold, now is the day of salvation.)"[29]

Sermons from the learned professor of theology at Congregational Yale, Nathaniel W. Taylor, were more carefully constructed than Asbury's preaching on the run. But the content was remarkably similar:

Merely to provide salvation for men, and to make the offer of it, would, we believe, have never brought the Son of God to die on the cross. We must look for some further and higher end. . . . This end is the actual restoration of a part of mankind to the favor of God. Now, every real Christian is reached by this design of the sacrifice of Christ. He is one of the called, according to God's purpose. That he might be a partaker of the great salvation—that he might be brought into a state of reconciliation with God, and become as really the object of his favor, as if he had never sinned, was the express and ultimate purpose for which God spared not his own Son, but delivered him up to die.[30]

Baptists, who strenuously opposed any one else defining their faith for them, nonetheless wrote a remarkable number of confessions during this early period. In 1833 the Baptist Convention of New Hampshire published a "Declaration of Faith," which in later years many other conventions also adopted. One of its key paragraphs sounded the standard evangelical themes: "The salvation of sinners is wholly of grace; through the mediatorial offices of the Son of God, who took upon Him our nature, yet without sin; honored the law by His personal obedience, and made atonement for our sins by His death; being risen from the dead He is now enthroned in heaven; and uniting in His wonderful person the tenderest sympathies with divine perfections, is every way qualified to be a suitable, a compassionate, and an all-sufficient Savior."[31]

Eight years later, the Presbyterian seminary professor Charles Hodge published a short statement of Christian belief for the American Sunday School Association that, despite his distaste for Methodists, Yankee Congregationalists, and Baptists, sounded in summary very much like what they were saying:

> The divine authority of the Scriptures being established, the great question to be decided by every one by whom they are known is, What do they teach as to the plan of salvation and the rule of duty? . . . the Bible teaches that we are all sinners, and that, being sinners, we have lost the favour of God and are unable to effect our own redemption. When we feel that this is true with regard to ourselves, we are convinced of sin, and are irresistibly led to ask what we must do to be saved? In answer to this question the Scriptures set forth Jesus Christ as born of a woman, made under the law, satisfying its demands, dying the just for the unjust, rising again from the dead, and ascending up on high, where he ever liveth to make intercession for us. They teach us that it is not for any thing done or experienced by us, but solely for what Christ has done for us, that we are justified in the sight of God; and that in order to our being saved through Christ, we must accept him as our Saviour, not going about to establish our own righteousness, but submitting to the righteousness of God.[32]

The era's most widely read female religious writer, Methodist Phoebe Palmer of New York City, recorded in her journal for 27 July 1837 an act of dedication that even Charles Hodge could have approved:

> I also covenanted with God that I would be a BIBLE CHRISTIAN, and most carefully seek to know the mind of the spirit, as recorded in the WRITTEN WORD. . . . The day of the Lord is near in the Valley of *Decision*. This was an important step, and took me much nearer to God, the source of Light and Love. In a manner that exceeded all former perceptions, the living Word said to my heart, "Ye are not your own, ye are bought with a price, therefore glorify God in your body and spirit, which are God's" (quoting 1 Corinthians 6:19–20).[33]

With few exceptions, African-American believers did not formulate their religious convictions in formal ways, but the narratives they left behind spoke of similar convictions. In 1860 a Methodist minister, G. W. Offley, published a memoir in Hartford under a lengthy title that began, "A Narrative of the Life and Labors of the Rev. G. W. Offley, a Colored Man, and Local Preacher, Who lived twenty-seven years at the South and twenty-four at the North; who never went to school a day in his life, and only commenced to learn his letters when nineteen years and eight months old; the emancipation of his mother and her three children; how he learned to read while living in a slave state, and supported himself from the time he was nine years old until he was twenty-one. . . ." This memoir's portraits of believing African Americans included a brief account of "Praying Jacob," a Maryland slave living under a vicious master. "Jacob's rule," according to Offley, was "to pray three times a day, at just such an hour of the day; no matter what his work was or where he might be, he would stop and go and pray." This practice infuriated Jacob's master, who more than once threatened to "blow out his brains" if the praying did not stop. Offley's account went on to record a distinctly evangelical response: "Jacob would finish his prayer and then tell his master to shoot in [and be] welcome—your loss will be my gain—I have two masters, one on earth and one in heaven—master Jesus in heaven, and master Saunders on earth. I have a soul and a body; the body belongs to you, master Saunders, and the soul to master Jesus. Jesus says men ought always to pray, but you will not pray, neither do you want to have me pray."[34] Such varied expressions of personal conviction are the raw material from which general definitions of evangelicalism have been derived.[35]

An important account of basic evangelical convictions was offered in 1844 by Robert Baird in the most comprehensive history published to that date of religion in America. Baird, a Presbyterian who devoted his life to promoting voluntary societies and the principle of voluntarism, highlighted four beliefs as the essence of evangelical Christianity. He enumerated, first, traditional Christian convictions about the Trinity, human sinfulness, "an all-sufficient and only atonement by the Son of God, who assumed human nature, and thus became both God and man in one person; and by his obedience, suffering, death, and intercession, has procured salvation for men." Second was "the necessity of a moral life." Third was the emphasis maintained by "nineteen-twentieths of all the evangelical churches," that it was necessary to experience "being born again," or "born of the Spirit." Fourth, and specifically related to the American environment, Baird insisted that "on no one point are all these churches more completely united, or more firmly established, than on the doctrine of the supremacy of Christ in his church, and the unlawfulness of any interference with its doctrine, discipline, and government, on the part of the civil magistrate."[36] Baird's insistence on what he called "the glorious doctrine of the Headship of Christ" as a defining feature of evangelical religion contrasts nicely with the British situation. There many self-defined evangelicals would have been in full agreement with Baird's first three assertions but, as members of the established churches in England, Wales, Ireland, or Scotland, would not have agreed that resistance to establishment was an essential aspect of Christian faith.

The distinctives of evangelical practice can be discerned even more clearly when compared to the Puritanism of an earlier era. Although Puritans stood against Catholic and Anglican formalism, salvation for the Puritans was still mediated by institutions—family, church, even the covenanted society; in evangelicalism (at least in American forms), salvation was in principle unmediated except by the written Word of God. Puritans protested against nominal ecclesiastical life, but they still treated institutions of church and society as given; American evangelicals created their own communities, at first ecclesiastical, then voluntary. Puritans accepted authority from designated leaders; American evangelicals looked to authority from charismatic, self-selected leaders.

Puritans fenced in enthusiasm with formal learning, respect for confessions, and deference to traditional interpretations of Scripture; American evangelicals fenced in enthusiasm with self-selected leaders, individualistic Bible-reading, local grassroots organizations, and intuitively persuasive reason.

The evangelical churches that flourished in the early United States were deeply indebted to Protestant tradition, especially the historic Protestant attachment to Scripture. That attachment to Scripture was also accompanied by a bias—sometimes slight, sometimes intense—against inherited institutions. American evangelicals also shared a conviction that true religion required an active experience of God, one leading necessarily to discipline. Evangelical experiential biblicism might take converts along many different paths (and leave them with contrasting conclusions) to principles of conduct. But however derived, those principles embodied a common evangelical conviction that the gospel entailed a search for public godliness as well as personal holiness. In sum, they believed that the Bible taught a message of rescue and deliverance, and that this message provided moral guidance, personal empowerment, and direction for self and society.[37]

The Importance of Disestablishment

In the new United States, it was not only the rapid expansion of evangelical churches that changed American society. It was also that the new churches existed in a new ecclesiastical environment. As the expansion of evangelical churches in Britain and Canada demonstrated, the legal separation of church and state was not essential for the flourishing of evangelical religion. In the new republic, however, creative exploitation of institutionalized disestablishment was a significant factor in rapid evangelical growth.[38] For Catholics, Jews, and some sectarian Protestants, religious freedom did not advance nearly as rapidly as it did for the evangelicals. Yet in a situation where, at least by 1800, Protestants of most kinds were effectively free of the legal connections between church and state that had so recently simply been taken for granted, the effect was as far-reaching upon the nation as upon the churches (and their theologians).

From the perspective of American experience, a natural affinity seemed to exist between key evangelical convictions and a polity of disestablishment. To hold that the new birth was a product of the Holy Spirit's action seemed (at least in the United States) irresistibly to trivialize the importance of institutions once held to mediate regeneration. Similarly, to exalt the converted person's use of the Bible as the most important religious authority was implicitly to devalue the elaborate edifices protecting scriptural interpretation within the historic European churches, Protestant as well as Catholic. The institutions compromised by such logic included established churches defined as authoritative communicators of divine grace through word and sacrament, institutions of higher learning monopolized by the establishment, and the monarchy as the primary fount of godly social stability. British Protestant

Dissent may have pointed in the direction of this kind of evangelicalism, but the traumas of the Cromwellian era, the shocks of the Restoration, and the struggle for intellectual and social survival in the century after 1660 had made British Dissent cautiously defensive.

As an important comparative standard against which to measure American developments, it is helpful to remember that many of the key evangelicals outside of the United States in the early nineteenth century remained firmly establishmentarian. This distinguished roster included the Anglicans Hannah More, Charles Simeon, and William Wilberforce; Scottish Presbyterian Thomas Chalmers; and Irish Presbyterian Henry Cooke. In Canada, at least until midcentury, the battle was not so much over the principle of establishment as over which of the major Protestant bodies, including the Methodists and Presbyterians, would share in its fruits.[39] When noting the singularity of the American situation, however, it is important to realize that for most white American evangelicals, a willingness to give up the establishment principle did not mean giving up life in society. It meant, rather, renouncing the traditional mechanisms by which Christian churches (including almost all of the European Protestant churches of the eighteenth century) still protected their social prerogatives and inculcated their traditions. In place of this formal mechanism came informal, voluntary means of exerting social influence that did not require a formal establishment.

This last reminder is essential for understanding American experience between the Revolution and the Civil War. Relinquishing the principle of establishment, which at first looks like a circumstance of greatest importance for the churches, turned out to have an unexpectedly large impact also on the development of the United States. Churches making their way on their own and voluntary associations founded by the energy of their own creators were concerned first about surviving and then about furthering spiritual and benevolent goals. But as a by-product, and because of the unusual barrenness of the post-Revolutionary American cultural landscape, the churches that were liberated from formal establishment ties were also liberated to construct a new nation.

Polarities

Evangelical Christianity never constituted a religious monolith. Neither did coruscating evangelical energy produce a static institutional picture. The denominational traditions marked out the most obvious differences among evangelicals; only nostalgia can blur how deep and wide denominational competition remained in this period.[40] But this competition was not all. Evangelicals were also divided among themselves by four polarities that were as important as the denominational divisions.

Among the most important was the division between "formalists" and "antiformalists."[41] Evangelical formalists—Congregationalists, Presbyterians, Episcopalians, and Reformed—moved only cautiously away from establishment practices, even as they retained some of the proprietary instincts of older European churches. After 1815 or so, these evangelicals were never more than a small minority of the whole, but formalist leadership in education and publishing meant that their views were exceedingly well known. Formalists were the key agents in establishing the most visible voluntary societies, which functioned as a substitute for the paternalistic establishments of the European states. Formalists were more likely to be found exploiting the new markets of commercial America than criticizing expanding national trade. Formalists often took center stage in high-profile religious events like the Businessman's Revival of 1857–1858. They were also the ones who enjoyed the highest profiles in national leadership, for example, the preacher-reformer Lyman Beecher; Beecher's children, the golden-throated Henry Ward and the best-selling author Harriet; Theodore Frelinghuysen, the "Christian Statesman," who stood for vice president on Henry Clay's Whig ticket in 1844; and the abolitionist Theodore Dwight Weld, who was a protégé of the revivalist Charles Grandison Finney. Formalist evangelicals were concentrated in Northern towns and cities. They were natural allies of the Federalist, Whig, and Republican parties. From among them came many leading abolitionists as well as most of the public voices for moderation in the battles over slavery and states' rights.[42]

By contrast, perhaps as many as three-fifths of American evangelicals were antiformalists, generally Methodists, Baptists, and adherents of the newly minted American Restorationist denominations, "Christians," Disciples, and Churches of Christ. They tended to come from middle and lower classes, to be concentrated in the West and South, and to live in small towns and rural areas. They were sometimes opposed to the effects of expanding markets on local religious and social autonomy. Antiformalist religion was frankly sectarian, emotional, apocalyptic, and determinedly conversionist. Representative exemplars were the Baptist preacher John Leland, who was as fervent in his support for Jefferson as he was faithful as an itinerant revivalist; Alexander Campbell, the dominant force in the Restorationist movement; Lorenzo "Crazy" Dow, an energetic itinerant who continued to promote the aggressive evangelism of early Methodism, even after being disowned by the denomination; and the Methodist Nathan Bangs in the earlier, revivalist stage of his career before he settled in New York City as editor, mission-society administrator, and pastor. Because antiformalists were marked by great solicitude for spiritual liberty, they were ranged against the formalists' national plans for promoting education, distributing the Bible, and encouraging social reforms. They tended to be anti-Yankee, anti-Whig, and anti-Republican, and thus Democrats (except in regions where strife with other antiformalist Democrats pushed them into the arms of Whigs or Republicans). This grouping, unfortunately, is less well studied than the formalists.[43]

A second and even more significant polarity was racial. In summarizing a mounting body of evidence, Sylvia Frey and Betty Wood have recently concluded that "the conversion of African Americans to Protestant Christianity was a, perhaps *the*, defining moment in African American history."[44] The form of Protestantism to which African Americans converted was overwhelmingly

evangelical, but it did not necessarily duplicate the religion of white formalists or white antiformalists. After remaining relatively immune to the missionary efforts of formalist Anglicans and Presbyterians, African Americans
responded much more readily to the Baptists and Methodists. Yet African
Americans converted only when, as Michael Gomez has recently written,
Christianity "became useful to the slave's physical and psychological struggle
to be fully human."[45] Distinctive characteristics of African-American Christianity became more obvious only after white Baptists and Methodists grew
more respectable, settled their ministers in towns, and began to provide higher
education for pastoral candidates. African-American Christianity for the most
part remained closer to the enthusiastic Baptist and Methodist religion of the
1790s and the early years of the nineteenth century. It continued to feature
elements that the antiformalist white churches gradually suppressed, including spontaneous, extempore preaching, trances, visions, dance, and prophecy added to biblical sources of revelation.

Some of the racial difference in evangelical experience grew from the strong
bond linking white evangelicals to the republican political principles of the
new United States. African-American believers could share only partially in
an ideology where the discourse of slavery was understood as a metaphor or
as a warning about the future. As a result, the republican impress upon African-American Christianity was quite different than for whites. As Donald
Mathews has noted, it is significant that evangelical preaching typically "broke
down" whites to confess their bondage to sin. Blacks, by contrast, were "lifted
up" to communion with God by the same sort of preaching. The contrasting
environments in which African Americans, slave and free, received the Christian message was decisive. In Mathews's telling phrase, "Blacks . . . found in
Christian commitment and communal identity shelter from the slave system,
an institutional framework to confound the logic of their social condition, an
ideology of self-esteem and an earnest of deliverance and ultimate victory."[46]
If evangelical resources were similar for whites and blacks, both African origins and American circumstances created the contexts for a somewhat different
religion.

A third polarity among evangelicals was created by the division between
slave and free states. Although churches in the North and the South held relatively similar convictions drawn from a common fund of evangelical religion
and republican politics, they constructed different religions because of the local
cultures in which those convictions were incarnated. It was not, for example,
only because of geography that Congregationalists retained visible intellectual leadership among Northern churches, while Presbyterians gained the same
status in the South. Rather, ideals of ecclesiastical order, trajectories of theological development, theories of church and society, and models for the Christian family arose from the fact that Congregationalism was such a thoroughly
Yankee religion, while Presbyterianism had successfully expanded from its
mid-Atlantic base into the South.[47]

A fourth polarity defined differences between men and women.[48] In the
intensity of revival, these differences could recede. "The gendered self," as

Catherine Brekus has concluded, "became meaningless at the moment of union with Christ."[49] Close cooperation between male and female evangelicals— as, for example, the early support provided by women for Methodist itiner- ants—also testified to the way that shared religious purpose could maneuver around gender divisions.[50] At the same time, evangelical Christianity almost always meant something at least slightly different to the men who embraced it than to the women.

During the First Great Awakening, when the paradigmatic language of evangelical experience was taking shape, men and women tended to describe conversions with different vocabularies. Where conversion liberated women from the entanglements of oppressive relationships and bestowed personal agency, for men it provided a countervailing liberation from the excesses of agency and opened the possibilities of relational being.[51] Likewise, conver- sion for women was more likely to free from inherent corruption; for men it freed from the guilt of sinful actions. These contrasts in the experience of conversion were doubtless related to the widespread assumptions of the eigh- teenth and nineteenth centuries that pictured women as both more inherently licentious and more potentially spiritual than men.[52]

After revival fires cleared away the forests of sin, gender distinction of a different form often marked the efforts of evangelical pioneers to construct a Christian civilization. The same evangelical religion that was revolutionary in the boundlessness of regeneration contributed significantly to the stiff boundaries of the nineteenth-century's separate spheres.[53] Evangelical atten- tion to structural personal holiness and systematic social benevolence occurred at different times and in different ways for different groups. It was always in the forefront of consciousness for formalist Congregationalists, Presbyteri- ans, and Episcopalians. For antiformalists, these concerns became more im- portant as the urgent eschatological faith of democratic revivalism matured into steady-state solicitude for the future. Whether formalist or antiformalist, when white evangelicals considered the religious needs of children, the sanc- tifying influence of stable families, the desirability of higher education for clergy, or the creation of institutions to meet far-flung social needs, they in- variably promoted gendered ideals of mature spirituality. Men would speak and so clarify the gospel; they would lead and so mobilize church and home for action. Women would cultivate the passive fruit of the Holy Spirit—love, joy, peace, longsuffering, gentleness, goodness, faith, meekness, temperance— and so build the godly households without which the Christian faith, as well as a Christian republic, would flounder.[54] Especially in the decades after 1830, it became much harder for evangelical women, even from antiformalist tra- ditions, to exercise the gifts of public unction and prophetic exhortation that were witnessed in surprising profusion during the first three decades of the nineteenth century.[55] When in the later period such attempts were made, they regularly required a more labored rationale for female public activity than in the first years of the century.[56]

In sum, polarities within evangelicalism, as well as the more obvious differ- ences created by denominational differences, made up a kaleidoscopic phenomenon quite difficult to define in simple phrases. It was, nonetheless, a form of Christian faith differentiated with utter clarity from Roman Catholicism, establishmentarian Protestantism, pietistic quietism, or rationalistic religions of the Enlightenment.

Periodization

If evangelical religion harbored sharp internal polarities, it also passed through three distinct eras between the Revolution to the Civil War. First was a period of institutional and ideological confusion connected with the traumatic upheavals of the Revolutionary War. Those who had equated establishmentarian Christianity with true religion, as well as the formalists who remained committed to ecclesiastical propriety, experienced the last quarter of the eighteenth century as a disorderly decline. The Presbyterian Robert Baird reported this judgment from his perspective in the 1840s: "The effects of war on the churches of all communions were extensively and variously disastrous. . . . The times immediately following the Revolution were . . . far from favourable to the resuscitation of true religion."[57] By contrast, perspectives from antiformalists were never as doleful. When considering the swelling ranks of Methodist itinerants (from 19 in 1775 to 227 in 1790), the rapid formation of Baptist churches (perhaps as many as 400 or 500 new congregations in that same fifteen years), or the outburst of revivals in Maryland and Virginia among African Americans during the period 1785–1790, "disaster" is the wrong word.[58] Yet with relative weakness among the Protestant traditions that had defined Christianity in the colonial period and expanding vigor limited to forms of the faith that were anything but comfortably familiar, religious life during the Revolutionary and post-Revolutionary years remained in flux.

A second stage, marked by popular and institutional advance on many fronts, began in the 1780s and 1790s. This era witnessed extensive and innovative mobilization—among the denominations, in bursts of revivalistic energy, and with the formation of voluntary societies. The major colonial traditions all took steps to reconstruct themselves as American denominations—the Episcopalians through General Conventions in 1785 and 1789, the Presbyterians by forming a new General Assembly in 1789, and the Congregationalists by establishing new agencies for outreach like the Connecticut Missionary Society (1798) and entering with the Presbyterians into the grand Plan of Union (1801) in order to evangelize the West. These efforts were at best moderately successful. Even after the ordination of American bishops, Episcopalians remained hamstrung, in the authoritative account of Robert Bruce Mullin, by "a paucity of ideas, models, and metaphors that could hold a group together and provide them with a perceived identity and a vision of their role in the new society."[59] Congregationalists generated more energy than they have been credited for showing, but instinctive trust in state-mandated programs kept these traditional New England Protestants on the defensive.[60] The Presbyterians' ability to create new churches and new presbyteries in frontier regions allowed them to expand while maintaining centralized connections. But high educational standards, staunchly middle-class instincts, and inability to exercise a common touch held Presbyterians back. As table 9.7 indicates, Presbyterians lagged behind growth in national population until the second decade of the new century, when, by linking their efforts to the new voluntary societies, they finally found their audience.

The denominational mobilizations that transformed the shape of American religion, even as it supplied religion to an expanding nation, were Baptist and Methodist. For the Baptists, unfortunately, there is not yet an adequate historiography to explore how these self-created, militantly congregational, mostly antiformalist, and yet doctrinally traditional stalwarts performed their marvels in the new republic. Yet marvels they doubtless were, with a net gain in churches between 1792 and 1812 greater than the total number in any denomination existing in America on the earlier date (table 9.8). By 1848 there were at least 200 Baptist churches in each of sixteen states and more than 500 in Virginia (502), Georgia (636), Kentucky (672), and New York (806).[61] Whatever else was at work in this incredible expansion was obviously a deep synergy between the Baptists' message of personal responsibility before God and the specific circumstances of an opening American nation (table 9.9).

For the Methodists, careful connectional records and the welcome attention of recent scholars fills in an even more incredible picture. In late 1784 Methodists in America replaced their cumbersome dependence upon John Wesley with an autonomous national church under the direction of Francis Asbury and Thomas Coke, who—in a typically Methodist balancing act—were both appointed as superintendents by Wesley and elected freely by a congress of American itinerants. Driven by the relentless energy of Asbury and his recruits, Methodism took off almost immediately. The genius of the movement was its unprecedented combination of energy and control. Itinerants were propelled out to where the people were, while a system of record-keeping, exhortation, publications, and spiritual temperature-taking was constituted by interlocking classes, regional conferences, and the nationwide

TABLE 9.7. Presbyterian Growth, 1789–1830

Year	U.S. Population	Churches	Ministers[a]	Presbyteries	Communicants	Communicants as % of Population
1789	3.9 mill.	419	188	17	—	—
1799	5.2 mill.	449	301	25	—	—
1810	7.2 mill.	772	485	36	28,901	0.4
1820	9.6 mill.	1,299	859	—	72,096	0.8
1830	12.9 mill.	2,158	1,711	—	173,329	1.3

Church figures are for only the largest Presbyterian church, the Presbyterian Church in the USA.
[a] "Ministers" includes probationers and licentiates

Source: Robert Ellis Thompson, *A History of the Presbyterian Churches in the United States,* 3d ed. (New York, 1902), 77, 93.

TABLE 9.8. Growth of Regular Baptist Churches, 1784–1848

Year	U.S. Population	Churches	Ministers	Members	Members as % of Population
1784	3.4 mill.	471	424	35,101	1.0
1792	4.2 mill.	891	1,150	65,345	1.6
1812	7.7 mill.	2,164	1,605	172,972	2.2
1832	13.7 mill.	5,320	3,618	384,920	2.8
1840	17.1 mill.	7,766	5,204	570,758	3.3
1848	22.0 mill.	7,920	5,833	664,556[a]	3.0[a]

[a] When 149,355 other Baptists are added to the total members for 1848 (see table 9.9), the percentage of U.S. population that is Baptist becomes 3.7.

Sources: for 1784–1840, Robert Baird, *Religion in the United States* (Glasgow, 1844), 526; and for 1848, John Winebrenner, *History of All the Religious Denominations* (Harrisburg, Pa., 1848), 71, 73.

itinerations of Asbury. In 1784 there were 15,000 Methodist class members; a mere seven years later, 76,000.[62] For most of the next decade, the Methodists marked time, but after the turn of the century the explosion resumed—a net gain of more than 10,000 full class members in 1802, 1803, 1806, 1807, 1811, 1812, and 1813; net additions of more than fifty preachers in 1802, 1807, and 1809; more Methodists in America than in Britain by sometime late in the century's first decade; and African-American membership rising sharply from about 10% of the total in 1786 to 20% by the mid-1790s. To the extent that the United States ever experienced a Second Great Awakening, Methodist expansion was it.

In charting the rise of a much more evangelical America, historians have probably given too much attention to highly visible revival meetings, yet they too played an important part. The restrained, church-centered meetings that began in Congregational New England in the mid-1790s and the rambunctious multiday camp meetings on the frontier, made famous by a memorable gathering in 1801 in Cane Ridge, Kentucky, were important in themselves for quickening interest in religion.[63] For the long term, they were even more

TABLE 9.9. Baptists other than Regular Baptists, 1848

Group	Churches	Ministers	Members
Anti-Mission Baptists	1,968	905	67,340
Freewill Baptists	1,165	771	63,372
Church of God Baptists	130	90	8,200
Seventh-Day Baptists	63	58	6,943
Six-Principle Baptists	20	22	3,500
Total	3,346	1,846	149,355

Source: John Winebrenner, *History of All the Religious Denominations* (Harrisburg, Pa., 1848), 71, 73.

important as recruiting devices for Methodists, the new "Christian" sects, local Baptist churches, and the Presbyterians.

By the early years of the new century, another powerful form of organization, the voluntary society, was added to the evangelical arsenal. The society was a mode of organization found among English-speaking Protestants at least from the late seventeenth century when high-church Anglicans created informal groups to pursue specific devotional or social tasks. The Society for the Propagation of the Gospel and many local voluntary associations were the result. Methodist co-option of the form, as seasoned by Moravian piety and organization, created an engine of great power.[64] From a Britain that was also turning in an evangelical direction, the Religious Tract Society (1799) and, supremely, the British and Foreign Bible Society (1804) offered well-publicized examples for how rapidly, how effectively, and with what reach lay-led, interdenominational societies could address specific needs. A few small-scale voluntary societies had been formed in America before the turn of the nineteenth century, but as self-created vehicles for preaching the Christian message, distributing Christian literature, and bringing scattered Christian exertions together, the voluntary society came into its own only after about 1810. Many of the new societies were formed within denominations, and a few were organized outside the evangelical boundaries, like the American Unitarian Association of 1825. But the most important were founded by interdenominational teams of evangelicals for evangelical purposes. Charles Foster's helpful (but admittedly incomplete) compilation of 159 American societies finds 24 established between 1801 and 1812, and another 32 between 1813 and 1816, with a remarkable 15 in 1814 alone. After a short pause caused by the Bank Panic of 1819, the pace of formation picked up once again through the 1820s.[65] The best funded and most dynamic societies—the American Board of Commissioners for Foreign Missions (1810), the American Bible Society (1816), and the American Education Society (1816), which aimed especially at education for ministerial candidates—were rivaled only by the Methodists in the effectiveness of their national outreach.[66]

To the intimidating challenges posed by disestablishment and the vigorous competition of a rapidly expanding market economy, the combination of denominational mobilization, revival, and the voluntary society offered a compelling response. Observers at the time took note of the innovation. Rufus Anderson, an early organizer of the American missions movement, wrote in 1837 that "the Protestant form of association—free, open, responsible, embracing all classes, both sexes, all ages, the masses of the people—is peculiar to modern times, and almost to our age."[67] Later historians, especially Andrew Walls, have described in more detail "the immense impact on Western Christianity and the transformation of world Christianity which (though its special focus in the missionary society) it [the voluntary association] helped to effect."[68]

Along with denominational mobilization and revival, voluntary agencies transformed the shape of American religion in the half century after the Declaration of Independence. A period of tumultuous, energetic, contentious innovation first reversed the downward slide of Protestantism and then began, as an almost inevitable process, to consolidate. Most remarkably, evangelicals even conquered the South, where an honor-driven culture of manly self-assertion presented a far less propitious field for labor than regions to the North, where the Puritan leaven survived. Although lagging behind the pace of expansion in the Atlantic states, upstate New York, backcountry New England, and the states formed from the Northwest Territory, evangelical growth was significant during the 1790s also in Virginia, Maryland, Kentucky, and the Carolina backcountry. In subsequent decades the Baptists and Methodists were joined by Presbyterians and "Christians" in spreading evangelical religion over the rest of the South. By the 1830s their efforts had proved unexpectedly successful.[69]

The impetus of creative mobilization rolled on into the 1830s as important new movements continued to take shape, like the Disciples or Christians of Alexander Campbell and Barton Stone, the Adventist followers of William Miller, and the Mormons of Joseph Smith. Well-publicized revival meetings continued to be held by Charles Finney in Rochester, New York (1830–1831), and then in Boston (1831–1832) and New York City (1832). Important new voluntary societies, like the American Anti-Slavery Society (1833) and the American Temperance Union (1836), continued to arise.

Yet by the 1830s, and even as the evangelical churches went on expanding in absolute numbers and relative to growth in the national population, a new era had begun.[70] While the single-minded pietism that fueled early evangelical mobilization never passed away, it was increasingly joined by other concerns. The business of organizing Christian civilization took its place alongside the business of saving souls. Steady-state religion began to share space with the revivalistic "one eternal now."

In particular, the great Methodist and Baptist phalanx of eager evangelists and dedicated church planters began to internalize the obligations of success. The Baptists, who had grown in the early republic almost entirely because of the exertions of self-taught farmer-preachers, by the mid-1840s had started at least fourteen colleges and eight theological seminaries.[71] For Methodists, the passing of Francis Asbury in 1816 was a turning point. Not long after he died, there died as well the Methodists' all-out commitment to itinerant ministry. Where once the norm had been for Methodist ministers to itinerate, the standard very soon became the settlement of ministers in single locations. Only a handful of ministers were settled in 1816, but by 1840 the Methodist Episcopal Church counted almost twice as many settled pastors (6,339) as itinerants (3,413). Alongside this formalization of structure came also a formalization of self-consciousness. National and regional periodical publication, which had earlier been left to Congregationalists, Presbyterians, and the voluntary societies, became a big business in the 1820s for almost all Protestants.[72] In sum, enough battles had been won to turn thoughts toward securing a peace. In their trajectory, Baptists and Methodists were following the path of British Dissenters, among whom a period of guarded enthusiasm at the turn of the nineteenth century had also given way to greater concern for social respect-

ability, political propriety, ambitious publication, and attention to the building of institutions.[73]

Evidence for the new situation appeared in many dimensions of religious
life. One important indication that the era of revolutionary evangelical lumi-
nosity had passed was the gradual silencing of women preachers in the
antiformalist denominations that had allowed, or even encouraged, them early
in the nineteenth century.[74] Evangelicals, whose participation in electoral
politics had steadily declined after intense involvement (on both sides) in the
Adams-Jefferson presidential race of 1800 and a spasm of agitation against
Sunday postal service early in the century's second decade, began from the
1830s once again to pay more systematic attention to the political sphere. The
election campaign of 1840, which was pictured in many corners of the land
as a contest between the pious Episcopalian William Henry Harrison and the
conniving political hack Martin Van Buren, set a pattern for engaged evangelical politicking that did not end until after the Civil War.[75]

By the 1830s evangelicals were also faced with dilemmas created by their
own achievement. Most troubling was the fact that successful recruitment among
the general population had not transformed the United States into the kingdom
of Christ. Revival had done wonders, the spread of the major denominations
had created the largest bodies of nonestablished Christians in the world, and
voluntary societies were reaching into almost every nook and cranny of the land.
But the nation, stubbornly, would not be saved. This combination of rising
expectation and intractable resistance set the stage for significant transitions. A
freshened tide of anti-Catholic sentiment was one result.[76] Even more telling
for the course of evangelical history was a geographic relocation by the nation's
leading revivalist. In 1835 Charles Finney, who was at the time one of the nation's
best-known personalities of any kind, moved to Oberlin College in Ohio, which
became his headquarters for the rest of his life. Oberlin—with its promotion of
revival and the Christian "higher life," with its opposition to slavery and its
opening of admissions to women—was the active embodiment of Finney's
revivalism. But the great national transformation, which led Oberlin's founders
to recruit Finney as its leading teacher and which Finney himself preached, did
not take place. The evangelical movement was beginning to fragment. In the
1840s and 1850s Finney became increasingly concerned that the call to conversion was being obscured by efforts to reform society. His own preaching increasingly stressed "Christian perfection"—a transformation of inner life—
rather than the transformation of the broader society.[77]

Strains within evangelicalism, which became apparent in the 1830s, also
pushed the promise of a thoroughly converted country even further into the
future. For some, like veteran Methodist itinerants, consolidations following
the explosion of all-out revivalism were taking place too soon; they could be
understood only as compromise. By contrast, the followers of Alexander
Campbell, Barton Stone, William Miller, and Joseph Smith thought it was
far too soon to consolidate. For them, only compellingly fresh reinterpretation of Scripture (Campbell, Stone, Miller) or even new additions to Scripture (Smith) could rescue what was still a spiritually parlous situation.[78]

Even greater uncertainties were created by the triumph of American experience over evangelical aspiration. The social promise of evangelical mobilization in the early nineteenth century was that, by converting individuals, society could be transformed. Social reform inspired by biblical holiness would grow naturally from the actions of the converted. In the first decades of the nineteenth century this formula seemed to be working. The voluntary societies effectively channeled the religious energies of the converted into the doing of good for the whole society. In the 1830s, however, the dream of a moral Christian society, transformed outwardly by the voluntary efforts of the inwardly converted, began to falter.

Evangelical paralysis in the face of the destruction of the Cherokee Nation by the state of Georgia and the federal government was a harbinger.[79] The tragedy of slavery was broader, deeper, and greater in every respect. Into the 1830s, it seemed possible that the application of conversionist Protestant energy could bring a peaceable end to the slave system. That goal had, in fact, been reached in Britain, where, after intensive efforts sustained impressively by Anglican evangelicals, Parliament in 1833 abolished slavery in the British empire by providing compensation to slaveholders in the West Indies as the price for liberating their slaves. In this instance, however, American experience did not follow the British example.[80]

The Depression of 1837 exacted a special toll on evangelical self-confidence, for it drained away much of the financial support that merchants, like Arthur and Lewis Tappan of Boston and New York, had accumulated from conducting business with evangelical probity and then exploited with evangelical urgency to convert and reform Americans.[81] The division in 1840 of the American Anti-Slavery Society over conflicts about methods and aims was another jolt. The debilitating schism within this society, where evangelicals had joined Unitarians, Quakers, and others to fight the slave system, indicated that the surging tide of revival would not easily dislodge the nation's most deeply entrenched moral problem. Schisms in the major evangelical denominations dramatically underscored the same weakness. Slavery was an ancillary cause of the 1837 separation of the Presbyterians into New School and Old School branches. It was at the heart of the struggles that led to the North-South divisions of both Baptists and Methodists in 1844. In retrospect, these schisms marked the high tide of evangelical outreach. Vital evangelical religion would continue, and the dream of natural redemption did not fail, but never again did the evangelical churches come so close to converting the nation.

Finally, it is germane to note that the years after 1830 were marked by a fresh surge of serious evangelical writing, both historical and theological. Beginning in the early 1840s, a series of substantial histories appeared that chronicled the rise of evangelical America.[82] History writing is not necessarily a sign of stagnation, but it does indicate a self-consciousness about what has been traversed and reveal a felt need for taking stock. Somewhat earlier, a great outpouring of written theology had begun that would make the period from roughly 1825 to 1900 the nation's greatest era in the production of formal Christian thought. As subsequent chapters attempt to show, this theological harvest was closely tied to the transformation of American religion that the evangelical surge first caused and then with which evangelicals were required to live.

Noting polarities within that evangelical surge and also recognizing that it passed through discernible stages should protect observers from at least some errors of imprecision. For the history of American religion, as for all complex movements of thought and practice, it makes considerable difference when a statement was made, who said it, and whence it came.

The larger reality, however, is that in the seventy-five years after the ratification of the Constitution, the religion of the United States underwent a dramatic transformation. The wellsprings of that transformation were Protestant and evangelical. The transformation was big with meaning for the writing of theology, but only first because it was big with meaning for the nation.

. . . and Constructing a New Nation

Why did evangelical churches expand so rapidly in the first decades of the nineteenth century? Responsible historians have provided several different answers to this obviously important question. It is a query, however, that may not be the most relevant one for charting patterns of influence among church communities, intellectual assumptions, political convictions, social experiences, and religious thought. A slightly different question points more directly to the deep interchanges between religion and society that shaped the critical contexts for theological expression: How did a plastic, yet still identifiable, evangelicalism, as it expanded along lines opened up by the circumstances of the new United States, help to build the nation's social and intellectual culture? Answers to this query show, not only how evangelical Christians contributed to the organization of the nation, but also how rendering that help came to exert a material influence on their theology.

Explanations

From within the framework of evangelical belief a good answer to the question of why evangelical churches grew so rapidly was that God chose to bless the labors of those who strove to serve him with all their hearts. In these terms, evangelicalism was a solution for whites and blacks, men and women, farmers, laborers, and capitalists, to perennial human crises of alienation from God, guilt from sin, and desperate longing for grace in Christ—all crises exacerbated by the multiplied strains of a society expanding rapidly in every direction. Wherever one can identify the fervent proclamation of redemption in Christ by dedicated, earnest, and sometimes charismatic preachers, in other words, one can expect to find flourishing Methodist, Baptist, Presbyterian, Restorationist, or other evangelical churches.[1]

A mirror image of this reading is grounded in material rather than spiritual ontology and draws inspiration from Engels, Marx, and E. P. Thompson, instead of John Wesley and Jonathan Edwards. It accounts for the rise of evangelicalism through a narrative of class differentiation, manufacturing growth, and social control. Paul Johnson's influential study of revivalism in Rochester, New York, for the period 1815 to 1837 is a notable representative. To Johnson, "Evangelicalism was a middle-class solution to problems of class, legitimacy, and order generated in the early stages of manufacturing." In this rendering, revivals functioned as tools that entrepreneurs could use for "imposing new standards of work discipline and personal comportment upon themselves and the men who worked for them." Thus, revivals served "as powerful social controls." This service operated at a deep level, for the evangelical belief "that every man was spiritually free and self-governing" allowed entrepreneurs to excuse themselves from interdependent, communal obligations to their employees—and to do so "as the realization of Christian ideals." Evangelicalism opened a way "whereby a particular historical form of domination could assume legitimacy." If workers themselves embraced evangelical religion sincerely, so much the better, since willing participation in this process was "of course . . . the most total and effective social control of all." In this view, the evangelicals' picture of providence is replaced by equally totalistic forces unleashed when labor was separated from ownership of production.[2]

Historical interpretations that bracket ultimate questions about God or the nature of human social organization are more complex.[3] One promising explanation of this sort accounts for the rise of evangelicalism in terms of "commodity exchange and social labor." The phrases are from Jürgen Habermas's description of "the bourgeois public sphere," or "the sphere of private people come together as a public." Although neither religion nor America figures in Habermas's discussion of "bourgeois society," he nonetheless describes a process that fits the American situation well, where, after overthrowing hereditary and aristocratic power, "the [bourgeois] public sphere explicitly assumed political functions in the tension-charged field of state-society relations." Habermas focuses on Great Britain as leading "the developmental history of civil society as a whole in which commodity exchange and social labor become largely emancipated from government directives." But it was the United States, even more than Britain, where a civil society constituted by middle-class participants for their own purposes came to flourish most vigorously during the early years of the nineteenth century. In a setting that, from a traditional European perspective, could only have looked like a nonsystem of competitive chaos, order did emerge. For this process evangelical religion communicated above all a system of inner motivation, at the same time promoting resentment against traditional, aristocratic political authority and imposing self-discipline on the new middle-class managers of social exchange. The alteration required for Habermas's theory to fit American

experience is to add self-regulating religious behavior to economic and ideological forces—to "the fundamental parity among owners of commodities in
the market and among educated individuals in the public sphere."[4]

Just such an addition has been made by the American sociologist George
Thomas in his account of the rise of evangelical Protestantism. For Thomas,
an elective affinity existed between revivalism and "the individualism and
nationalism of political-economic expansion." The affinity was sustained by
three circumstances feeding off each other: the presence of "entrepreneurship
and the small-capital enterprise," the worldview of revivalism, and political
support for the Republican Party and prohibition. In Thomas's picture the
spread of the market was basic, but links to evangelical religion and loyalty
to the Whig and Republican Parties were intrinsic rather than merely mechanical. "Revivalism," he concludes, "was primarily an acceptance of the new
order" that "both legitimated and was legitimated by the individuated market
and the new myth of rational individualism. It comprehensively worked individualism into a unified cosmic order of things, from family relations to
individual action to national growth." By fulfilling this function, in turn, revivalism "became the plausibility structure" for Whig and Republican politics, which, for their part, "constituted a world in which the individual was
autonomous and directly tied to the national state."[5] For Thomas, and by
extension also for Habermas's theory of bourgeois civil society, the rise of
evangelicalism in America was a strategic means for participating in, regulating, and making sense of the new market economy. Compared to Paul
Johnson's materialist explanation, this one allows religious actors both more
self-awareness and more agency.

The most persuasive explanations for the rise of evangelicalism in America,
however, come from historians who try to survey the whole range of relationships dramatically altered by the American Revolution. Gordon Wood,
Robert Wiebe, and Nathan Hatch are not a school of historians, but their
powerful accounts of, first, social dislocation and, then, social reconstitution
in the wake of American independence share enough to be treated as a single
interpretation.[6]

Of first importance is a common narrative of social interaction. Wood,
Wiebe, and Hatch look upon the Revolutionary War as inaugurating a social
as well as a political revolution. It is specifically the war's sanction for liberal, democratic, populist, and (white, male) individualistic constructions of
liberty that is most important. They see such constructions sparked by the
struggle with Britain for independence itself, then gathering force under the
Confederation, and finally breaking loose with abandon shortly after the beginning of constitutional government. In Hatch's terms, the Revolutionary
impetus created "a cultural ferment over the meaning of freedom" and a "crisis of authority in popular culture."[7]

A social revolution spinning out from the vortex of political revolution
had multiplying effects. It first frustrated efforts by the patriotic elites of the
1770s to establish a new American aristocracy in place of the ousted imperial
regime. In Wood's phrase, "Popular principles and popular participation in

politics, once aroused, could not be easily put down."[8] More generally, the social revolution dissolved both external marks and internal acceptance of the deference integral to colonial British society. In addition, it mirrored the opening of American space—at first political, then geographic, then psychological—and so sanctioned competition as a legitimate social mediator. Wiebe's summary draws several of the strands together: "During the early 19th century, space and movement destroyed that hierarchy [which had prevailed into the 1790s]. A dramatic expansion of territory and a perpetual migration of people snapped its networks of personal authority, stretched its base beyond tolerable limits, and finally toppled the entire structure."[9] The "revolution in individual choices" occasioned by the political revolution altered the social environment in such a way as to reward self-exertion rather than the acceptance of station. The consequence was an ideology valorizing the self-made man, described by Alan Taylor as "the enduring potential of the American Revolution to legitimate upstarts unwilling or unable to achieve or endure genteel authority."[10]

For intellectual history, the most important effect of the Revolution was to promote metaphors of self-creation and the market—that is, competitive liberalism—as the favored tropes for describing all arenas of life. Wood catches well what such reasoning meant: "The modern contractual image tended to swallow up the traditional patriarchal idea of authority. It was as if paternalism became so liberal, so republicanized, as to surrender itself willingly to modern legal contractualism." Practical results followed: "In concrete day-to-day terms invocations of the Constitution meant the freedom to be left alone, and in turn that freedom meant the ability to make money and pursue happiness."[11]

In circumstances thus shaped by "the spreading, cumulative effects of a democratic revolution,"[12] successful religious actors were those who knew how to chart their own way, to compete persuasively in the marketplaces of religious belief and practice that were opening up in parallel to the competitions of factional politics and the markets of commercial exchange. To be sure, Wood does slightly oversimplify matters when he says that antiformalist exploiters of the revolution "developed and expanded revivalistic techniques because such dynamic folk-like processes were better able to meet the needs of rootless egalitarian-minded men and women than were the static churchly institutions based on eighteenth-century standards of deference and elite monopolies of orthodoxy."[13] This rendering is an oversimplification because it neglects the fact that formalist churches in the early republic, by democratizing themselves moderately, retained considerable appeal and considerable intellectual prestige. It is also an oversimplification to overlook the nearly uniform propensity of radical antiformalists, however driven by rootless energy and the stirring rhetoric of revolutionary egalitarianism, to move toward churchly, orthodox, and even hierarchical practices once they had successfully broken free from the restrictive paternalism of establishmentarian religion. That was a path navigated rapidly by Methodists (including African-American Methodists), somewhat more slowly by Freewill Baptists and Alexander Campbell's faction in the Disciples movement, and still more slowly by Regular Baptists and the most militant Restorationists—yet embarked upon by all. With these caveats noted, Wood's assessment holds. In Revolutionary America, the churches had to construct revolutionary forms of Christianity or decline.

Nathan Hatch's compelling account of Christian democratization is the best statement of the deep changes that took place as the churches embarked upon that task of internalizing the Revolution. In his picture the ministry of Charles G. Finney during the 1830s climaxed a process begun a half century before by upstart Methodists, Freewill Baptists, African Americans, and radically egalitarian "Christians." Finney, that is, wrought "a Copernican revolution" in making religion "audience centered." He scorned traditional theological study for producing "dull and ineffective communication." His preaching exploited to the full the "language of common life." He eagerly borrowed the techniques of populist politicians in presenting his own message.[14]

The Finney who democratized so much, however, was also the Finney who tamed radical democratization. In Hatch's words, he was "a bridge between cultures" who legitimated revival among the middle classes and "introduced democratic modifications into respectable institutions."[15] In these terms, the Finney who took revivalism to Boston, who accepted a pastorate in New York City, and who became a professor (and then president) of a liberal arts college transcribed in his own life-course the trajectory that many of his loyal converts followed as well. The democratization of American Christianity reflected a revolution in religion but led eventually to consolidation and social reconstruction rather than endless reinvention.

The complementary readings of Wood, Wiebe, and Hatch do not presume to adjudicate ultimate questions of providence or of struggle for control of the means of production. Yet by featuring systematic religious exploitation of revolutionary social change, they do illuminate the interlocking character of religion and society in the early history of the United States. The broad, thorough research undergirding these accounts supports Hatch's careful summary, that the "nonrestrictive environment" of post-Revolutionary America "permitted an unexpected and often explosive conjunction of evangelical fervor and popular sovereignty. It was this engine that accelerated the process of Christianization within American popular culture, allowing indigenous expressions of faith to take hold among ordinary people, white and black. . . . The rise of evangelical Christianity in the early republic is, in some measure, a story of the success of common people in shaping the culture after their own priorities rather than the priorities outlined by gentlemen."[16]

Expanding the Explanations

Yet such accounts may not be comprehensive enough. When, for example, Gordon Wood describes "evangelical religion, utopian communitarianism, millennial thinking, multitudes of dreams and visions by seekers, and the birth of new religions" as "in fact all responses to the great democratic changes

taking place in America between the Revolution and the Age of Jackson";
when he accounts for the rapid increase in alcoholic consumption alongside
the burgeoning of populist churches as "but different reactions to a common
democratic revolution and the chaos it had created"—the causation is too
simple.[17] The "democratic changes" and the "common democratic revolution"
were also in their own way *caused by* religious (and other) forces at their
origin. The American War for Independence precipitated the American democratic revolution but did not by itself constitute it. If the evangelical surge in
the new republic was precipitated by a democratic revolution, religious impulses were also at work to inspire the democratic impulse.[18] Charting a more
complex sequence of causes and effects is necessary for understanding the
depth of connections among the religious, social, and national trajectories.
Such a sequence highlights several "knots" of causation.

First, one of the reasons the War for Independence succeeded was that
Protestants sacralized its aims as from God. The Protestantism that performed
this sacralization did so with fragments of theology left over from the Puritan past. Some of those fragments pointed toward evangelicalism, some did
not. But had not this Revolutionary-era Protestantism already been mostly
cured of historic Christian antagonism toward republican theory and already
mostly won over to commonsense moral reasoning, it would not have been
able to provide such material assistance to the cause of independence. As it
was, however, the patriots' message was embraced by a religious community whose own religious history prepared it for receiving that message. In
turn, the Revolutionary message that precipitated a democratic revolution was
already marked by its associations with a certain kind of Protestant religion,
even as its effects transformed the social, economic, and political axioms by
which Americans ordered their lives.

Second, the refashioning of Protestantism that occurred in response to the
American democratic revolution was part of a longer history. The Christianity that thrived best in the new democratic America had not dropped from the
sky but bore the imprint of its own colonial history. It was the more evangelical forms of faith that survived and then flourished as the democratic revolution did its work on American society; by contrast, elitist forms of Protestantism or the Protestant varieties clinging to establishmentarian habits fell
behind. In other words, the types of religion active in pre-Revolutionary
America were variously disposed toward a democratic revolution. Evangelicalism per se does not fully explain the difference. But an evangelicalism
inspired by face-to-face itinerant preaching, that stressed the all-powerful but
also egalitarian grace of God as the source of salvation, that taught converts
to connect virtue to the exertions of their hearts instead of to mere social
conformity—this was a religion already closer to democracy than the hierarchical establishmentarian communalism of either clerically ordered Congregationalism or inherited Anglicanism. Again, the effects of the democratic
revolution must be understood against a longer, more complex history.[19]

Third, contrasts are important. The flourishing of evangelical Christianity
in post-Revolutionary America created a situation strikingly different from

the difficulties of Christianity in post-Revolutionary France and the flourishing of a different kind of evangelical Protestantism in England. The explanation for these differences is not found in simple contrasts between Catholics and Protestants or establishmentarians and disestablishmentarians. Rather, the contrast with France must take into account the kind of Catholicism rejected in France and the kind of Protestantism accepted in the United States. The particular form of Christianity that flourished in the new United States was an awakened evangelicalism that had abandoned the historic Protestant antagonism to republican politics and was becoming ever more committed to the intellectual procedures of commonsense moral intuition. In France, by contrast, the forces of revolution were historically alien to almost all forms of Christianity, and the activity of the church included much self-conscious opposition to republican principles.[20]

The contrast with England is on a different order, but also instructive. In the United States, evangelicalism provided moral legitimacy for, and was itself enabled to flourish in, a social setting that featured above all the glories of liberty. This evangelicalism stressed the need for moral choice, the capacity of redeemed individuals to create their own nurturing communities, and the image of human existence as a staging ground for personal and social transformation. In England, evangelicalism provided moral legitimacy for, and was itself enabled to flourish in, a social setting that combined traditionally aristocratic instincts, the emergence of new industries, and commitment to laissez-faire economic theory. This evangelicalism featured the sovereignty of God, a divided mind over whether humans could decisively reform the institutions of society, and the image of human existence as a transitory time of moral trial. English evangelicals read Thomas Malthus with a seriousness never found in America; Americans took to Thomas Reid and Dugald Stuart far more seriously than did the English.[21]

Fourth, the churches, especially the evangelical churches that aligned themselves with the forces of America's Revolution, played an extraordinarily significant part in making democracy work. They were key factors in the process by which a people insisting upon their freedom and hypersensitive to the abuses of power (whether those abuses were real or imagined) created from their own inner resources the social structures necessary for survival. If democratization was what the churches needed in order to survive in post-Revolutionary America, then democratized Christianity provided a necessary element of what post-Revolution America itself needed in order to survive.

By the 1830s the competing cultures of the North and the South were both markedly different from predecessor cultures in the Revolutionary era. Antebellum cultures, to be sure, reflected the democratization of American society. But that democratization took a peculiarly Christian form, clearly stamped by the evangelical surge. American public culture was not only more thoroughly democratized than comparable cultures in other North Atlantic societies. Its public space was also more thoroughly evangelicalized.[22] A fully satisfying narrative for how this situation developed must account both for Protestant contributions to the democratic revolution and the interchange of attributes between churches and society as American democracy took shape in the early republic.

Finally, the general development of the American churches was also fully connected with the evolution of American democracy. Fragmenting anti-formalist energy by no means passed away, but by the 1830s both the growing respectability of the revivalist churches and increased public attention to the publications of Presbyterians, Congregationalists, and Episcopalians testified to rising formalist fortunes. The red-hot revivalists who had shown sinners how to be saved now were asked to advise the converted on questions of civilization. The range of questions differed from region to region and from denomination to denomination, but leaders in almost all of the evangelical churches found themselves addressing Cherokee removal and Sunday mails, temperance and the tide of Catholic immigration, slavery, politics, and, finally, war. As that shift took place, so also was a shift visible in the nation as a whole. In the nation's public business it became harder and harder to exclude religious considerations from the debates revolving around the same issues that the churches were addressing. Not only had evangelicals converted individuals; they had also partially converted the nation. But only partially, since the reach of evangelicals always exceeded their grasp, and since the driving engines of democracy and evangelical religion were creating not a single Christian America but Northern and Southern versions of the godly republic.

In sum, while it is true that Revolutionary and post-Revolutionary circumstances stimulated an adaptation of Christianity to America, it is also true that incredible evangelical energy brought about an adaptation of America to Christianity. This second adaptation is the key to the history of theology from the 1790s to the 1860s. Only by seeing how much success the Christian churches, and especially the evangelical churches, had in this work of transforming America is it possible to understand why features of American experience factored so large in Christian theology. Because the churches had done so much to make America, they could not escape living with what they had made.

Evangelicals and the New Nation

The argument that religion, especially as embodied in a full spectrum of evangelical churches, helped create a national culture has two parts. First, more than is usually appreciated, the evangelical churches contributed directly to the networks of institutions and personal relationships that gathered the *disjecta membra* of the former British colonies into a single nation. Second, key elements of American evangelical Christianity again meant more than is often realized in making the ideology of the founding fathers actually work. The argument is not that the other nation-building agents of the early republic—including commerce, political parties, and the national government—were unimportant. It is rather that when the activities of the evangelical churches are compared to the activities of other nation-shaping forces, it be-

comes clear that they were critical. Both arguments—organizational and ideological—depend upon seeing early national culture as politically fragmented,
culturally barren, floundering in unprecedentedly vast amounts of space, and
nearly overwhelmed by fractious local allegiances.

At the close of the Revolutionary War, the United States existed as an independent, republican, antiauthoritarian nation. But it existed also as a society
beset by sharp political, economic, social, and religious division, strain, and
uncertainty.[23] To address these uncertainties, the patriotic republicans who had
directed the drive for independence offered the Constitution. Later historians
properly regard its ratification as a critical step in establishing political and social
stability. At the same time, however, American society was still, in John Murrin's
phrase, "a roof without walls." As Murrin puts it, "American national identity
was . . . an unexpected, impromptu, artificial, and therefore extremely fragile
creation of the Revolution. . . . The Constitution was to the nation a more successful version of what the Halfway Covenant had once been to the Puritans, a
way of buying time."[24] The Constitution secured the promise of a stable political framework, but it did not create a national culture.

Gordon Wood reinforces Murrin's conclusion by stressing how thin the
overlay of national government actually was in the new nation. By the early
nineteenth century, foreign visitors regularly commented on the weakness of
the federal government as a national force: "'It is round you like the air,' said
a startled William Sampson fresh from Ireland, 'and you cannot even feel it.'"
In his own judgment, Wood suggests that "no people in the Western world
ever dismantled its national government more completely than did the Americans of the early republic."[25]

Historians describing the beginnings of national culture quite properly focus upon the local creation of political and social institutions, the rapidly multiplying nexus of commercial connections, a fairly broad respect for the rule of
law, the spread of democratic associations, the burgeoning of newspapers and
a popular press, and the periodic ability of political conflict to galvanize the
whole nation—as in the election of 1800, during the War of 1812, and before
the Missouri Compromise of 1820. Joyce Appleby has recently deepened the
understanding of this process by showing how "a powerful myth about America"
constructed from "repeated messages" describing "effort and accomplishment,
virtue and autonomy, national prosperity and universal progress" created a
widely shared sense of the nation, especially for Northern white men.[26] While
the activities of the churches are regularly included in these accounts,[27] those
activities deserve more attention than they have been given. A fully documented
volume would be necessary to make the case, but a few examples can still suggest why evangelicals were so important for building the walls of nationhood.

Organization

Evangelical contributions to the organization of national culture lay mostly
in industrious efforts out of public view, although participation in spectacular revival meetings—with the conversions, the publicity, and the arguments

such meetings generated—were often a stimulus to that ongoing effort.[28] The often mundane details of denominational history and the almost forgotten course of the voluntary societies reveal most clearly the connecting tissue that evangelicals contributed to the new nation.

Among the denominations the most important agent of cohesion was the Methodists, and the most important Methodist was Francis Asbury. Asbury's itinerations outlined the paths that his many dedicated associates transformed into the circulatory system of an energetic national body. In a characteristically dramatic statement, Perry Miller once claimed that those who gathered at the Cane Ridge revival of 1801 "were not preaching nationalism, they were enacting it."[29] Perhaps that assertion was true for Cane Ridge; indubitably it was true for the work of Asbury. Over a territory the size of continental Europe, Asbury's ceaseless peregrinations took him everywhere—more than fifty times into New York State, more than sixty times into New Jersey, seventy-eight times into Pennsylvania, eighty times into Maryland, sixty-three times into North Carolina, forty-six times into South Carolina, eighty-four times into Virginia, twenty times each into Georgia and Tennessee, twenty-three times into Massachusetts. In the course of one yearly circuit alone (1791–1792), Asbury left New York, passed through the large mid-Atlantic cities (Philadelphia, Wilmington, Baltimore), surveyed Virginia (Alexandria, Petersburg, Norfolk), touched down in North Carolina (Raleigh) and South Carolina (Charleston) and Georgia (Washington), came back through South Carolina and North Carolina, moved west across the mountains into Tennessee, pushed northward into Kentucky as far as Lexington, came back through Tennessee and proceeded north along the western slopes of the Alleghenies through Virginia to Uniontown in Pennsylvania, then traversed the mountains to reach Baltimore, circled back to New York City on the way up to Connecticut and seaboard Massachusetts, then went westward to Northampton, moved south over the Berkshires through Pittsfield and Albany, before returning to New York City eleven and one-half months after departing. The historian who perused Asbury's journal to define this itinerary ended laconically—"In later years his episcopal circuit was even more extended."[30] Asbury was almost certainly known personally to more Americans than any other individual of his age. The Methodist web of classes, circuits, quarterly meetings, conferences, and annual conferences he and his associates established was a marvel of industry as well as a vehicle of redemption.[31] It was also incidentally a system of ligaments tying together the people of a nation. This reality was perceived at the time, as when one of the Methodists' first historians, Nathan Bangs, spoke diffidently yet accurately about what his denomination had accomplished in virtually no time at all. According to Bangs, there was in early Methodism virtually no interest in "political speculations" or "civil affairs," yet he still concluded that "its extensive spread in this country, the hallowing influence it has exerted on society in uniting in one compact body so many members, through the medium of an itinerant ministry, interchanging from north to south, and from east to west, has contributed not a little to the union and prosperity of the nation."[32]

Baptist networking was never developed as fully, but as Baptist churches spread westward, southward, and even northward, Baptist connections drew more and more citizens into Christian fellowship and then cooperative action. Not until 1814 did a national Baptist superstructure come into existence, and that structure, the Baptist General Convention of the United States, was limited by its charter to oversight of foreign missionary activity. Yet well before 1814 Baptists were forming numerous district associations and state conventions. By the mid-1820s even these militant localists had set up other societies promoting cooperative action for home missions, the distribution of tracts, and the education of the poor.[33]

Methodists and Baptists began as antiformalist competitors to the main colonial churches, whose leaders continued to see themselves as the most important agents of national religious direction. On the ground, however, Methodists and Baptists did the work envisioned by the formalist churches. Through their own networks of churches and, eventually, denominational agencies, they were the ones who actually met the formalist challenge of training recruits to construct a national religious culture.

The expansion of evangelicalism was also critical, though more ambiguously, for bridging the racial divide. As Sylvia Frey and Betty Wood have recently pointed out, African Americans played important parts in the developments through which evangelicalism expanded in the early United States. The motive power of revivals, the movement of peoples westward, and the creation of a national Methodist church were all key to the reshaping of American religion from colonial establishments to national evangelicalism. In each of those developments, "the embrace of evangelical Protestant Christianity by African Americans" was centrally important. Most of the leading agents of nation formation, including many white evangelicals, either attempted to exclude African Americans from national culture or worked to minimize their place. The evangelical religion that growing numbers of African Americans embraced alongside growing numbers of Caucasians frustrated, or at least retarded, the creation of racially separate nations.[34]

The cumulative effects of denominational mobilization were manifest by midcentury. The absolute numbers are impressive: even if Robert Baird's contemporary assertion identifying 70% or 80% of Americans as adherents of evangelical churches was much inflated, more conservative estimates still leave, as in Richard Carwardine's conclusion for the mid-1850s, "over 10 million Americans, or about 40 percent of the total population . . . in close sympathy with evangelical Christianity." The important fact here is comparative. Again in Carwardine's summary, "This was the largest, and most formidable, subculture in American society."[35] No other organized promoter of values, no other generator of print, no other source of popular music or compelling public imagery, no other comforter (and agitator) of internal life— none came anywhere close to the organized strength of the evangelical churches in the three-quarters of a century after the dawn of the republic.

The reach of the evangelical denominations was extended many times over by the extraordinary activities of the voluntary societies. Again, it is important to remember that not all voluntary agencies were evangelical and that not all evangelicals supported the voluntary system. With proper qualifications, however, it is still possible to assert that the "epidemic of organization" arising from the evangelical surge worked powerfully to fashion a national culture.[36]

Comparisons are again illuminating. From its beginnings to 1828, the United States government spent nearly $3.6 million on internal improvements (roads, canals, communications). In that same span of years the thirteen leading benevolent societies, overwhelmingly evangelical in constituency and purpose, spent over $2.8 million to further their goals.[37] No broad-based movement, not even the political parties, brought together so many people committed to so much social construction as did the national meetings of the benevolent societies. From the mid-1810s, the societies were sponsoring major local and regional gatherings. By the late 1820s many of the societies were staging their annual conventions as impressive public spectacles. The high point of this visible demonstration of evangelical social construction may have occurred in the first week of May 1834, when at least sixteen different societies gathered in New York City for reports and exhortation relating to their work.[38] The activities pursued by these societies did not by themselves constitute the fabric of the nation. But with their widely ranging interests, they came close:

- six agencies for social benevolence, at a time when neither the states nor the federal government sponsored programs of social welfare;
- four educational societies offering scholarships and other coordinated support for higher learning, at a time when only the most progressive states had only just begun to consider publicly sponsored education;
- three societies for distributing the Bible and religious literature throughout the nation, at a time when American publishing was otherwise mostly carried out by local firms for local audiences;
- two home missionary societies, at a time when there existed almost no other altruistic attention to frontier settlers;
- and one large foreign missionary society, at a time when, after immigration and foreign trade, missionaries represented the United States' primary window to the world at large, and, for the non-Western world, the most important window.

Many have recorded the blow to national unity when the Methodists and Baptists divided North and South in 1844, but an earlier blow of similar proportion may have taken place in the mid- to-late-1830s when the great voluntary societies began to fragment. The societies had always been criticized by sectarian evangelicals. Western and Southern antiformalists attacked them for violating republican precautions against the aggrandizement of power. In 1836 Calvin Colton, a disgruntled former promoter of revivals and institutionalized reforms, published an attack on the societies entitled *"Protestant Jesuitism."*[39] But the dismantling of "the evangelical united front" after 1834 was not in response to such criticism. Contentious disagreements over purposes and strategies in groups like the Anti-Slavery Society caused part of the problem. Even more damaging was the growing tendency of denominations to start their own competitive special-purpose societies. Baptists and Restorations led the pullout—in order, for example, to distribute Bibles that translated relevant New Testament passages as "immerse" instead of simply "baptize."[40] But Methodists, Presbyterians, and Episcopalians also began turning to their own societies, though as often for managerial as for theological reasons. As they did so, they did more damage to the nation's fragile infrastructure of culture than they realized.

Other ways of constructing national culture were also manifest by the 1830s. Evangelical patterns of organization, which drew together contributors and partisans of particular causes from a widely dispersed population and fueled them with enthusiasm for the designated tasks at hand, became a direct inspiration for political organization. The first national political convention, which created the mold that almost all others have imitated, was convened in 1831 by the Anti-Masonic Party, an evangelical voluntary society gone political. Daniel Walker Howe captures the broader influence well: "The hullabaloo of political campaigns in the second party era—the torchlight parades, the tents pitched outside town, the urgent calls for commitment—was borrowed by political campaigners from the revival preachers. Far from being irrelevant distractions or mere recreation, the evangelical techniques of mass persuasion that we associate with the campaigns of 1840 and after provide a clue to the moral meaning of antebellum politics."[41] The appropriate conclusion is not that evangelical causes dominated American politics, though in fact they did exert great influence. It is rather that widely recognized institutions of American national culture very often grew from initiatives pioneered by the era's activistic evangelical Protestants.

Observers at the time did not fail to record the importance of evangelical nation-building. The most direct, and also most poignant, of contemporary testimony came in the early 1850s as sectional antagonisms imperiled the national future. In his famous speech on the Compromise of 1850, read for him in the United States Senate on 4 March of that year, an ailing John C. Calhoun offered passionate testimony to the achievements of evangelicalism. After describing "the great religious denominations" as "the strongest [cords] of . . . a spiritual and ecclesiastical nature" that bound the Union together, he then detailed their forms of organization and the broad sweep of their interests. "All this," Calhoun asserted, "contributed greatly to strengthen the bonds of the Union. The ties which had held each denomination together formed a strong cord to hold the whole Union together." Calhoun's prediction became justly famous—that when all such bonds have snapped, "nothing will be left to hold the States together except force"—but it is his analysis of the structural significance of the denominations on the national stage that illustrates how clearly contemporaries recognized the unitive force of the churches.[42] Two years later, an aged Henry Clay repeated Calhoun's testimony: "I tell you this sundering of the religious ties which have hitherto bound our people together, I consider the greatest source of danger to our country."[43] As later chapters in this book try to show, Clay's words, like Calhoun's, pointed to the tragedy as well as the triumph of the great evangelical surge.

Comparisons are a good way of demonstrating the effectiveness of the evangelicals in helping to organize the new nation. A fine recent book by Richard John has shed much light on the importance of the postal service in the early years of the new nation. John shows that foreigners were amazed at the extent of the U.S. mails, that the United States enjoyed the largest and most productive postal delivery system in the world, that it developed the most elaborate distribution system then existing in the country (interlocking a Washington center, regional depots, and local postmasters), that the postal system was far and away the largest agency of the federal government (much larger, for example, than the military, except during time of war), and that the size of the postal workforce dwarfed the number of employees in any nongovernmental business firm until the expansion of railroad companies in the 1850s.[44] John also demonstrates that contemporaries throughout the early decades of the new century regularly described the work of the postal system as absolutely critical in creating the channels of communication, commerce, and personal contact required for a connected civilization.

Such assertions about the postal service being well made, the comparisons highlighted in table 10.1 speak volumes about the churches. By the 1850s the Methodists by themselves—joined together through an interlocking system of personal and epistolary contact—had constructed almost as many churches

TABLE 10.1. Comparisons between the Postal Service and the Churches

Year	Post Offices	Churches	Postal Employees	Methodist Clergy[a]	All Clergy	Postal Revenue ($1,000s)	Church Income ($1,000s)
1790	75	4,696	—	227	—	37	—
1800	908	—	—	287	—	280	—
ca. 1810	2,300	—	3,341[b]	688[c]	—	551	—
1820	4,500	—	4,766	904	—	1,111	—
1830	8,450	—	8,764	1,900	—	1,850	—
1840	13,468	—	14,290	9,752	ca. 30,000	4,543	—
1850	18,417	34,476	21,391	—	—	5,500	—
1860	28,498	54,009	30,269	23,143	ca. 55,000	8,518	ca. 25,000
1997	38,019	350,000	853,928	39,061	ca. 350,000	$58 bill.	$70 bill.

[a] Before 1837 Methodist minutes record only the number of itinerant preachers, which is shown here for the years 1790–1830. Figures here from 1840 show the total of all Methodist clergy, settled plus itinerant.
[b] The number of postal employees shown here is the number reported for 1816. Subsequent numbers in this column are the totals reported for 1821, 1831, 1841, 1851, and 1861.
[c] This number shows the number of (itinerant) clergy reported for 1812.

Sources: Richard R. John, *Spreading the News: The American Postal System from Franklin to Morse* (Cambridge, Mass., 1995), 4; *Historical Statistics of the United States, Colonial Times to 1957* (Washington, D.C., 1960), 497, 710; *Minutes of the Annual Conferences of the Methodist Episcopal Church for the Years 1773–1840*, 2 vols. (New York, 1840); *Minutes of the Annual Conferences of the Methodist Episcopal Church, for the Year 1860* (New York, 1861); *Minutes of the Annual Conferences of the Methodist Episcopal Church, South, for the Year 1860* (Nashville, 1861); Stephen A. Marini, "The Government of God: Religion and Revolution in America, 1764–1792" (unpublished manuscript); *Statistics of the United States . . . in 1860 . . . Being the Final Exhibit of the Eighth Census* (Washington, D.C., 1866), 497–501; *Statistical Abstract of the United States, 1998* (Washington, D.C., 1998); and (as a basis for projecting the income of the churches) Lewis G. Vander Velde, *The Presbyterian Churches and the Federal Union, 1861–1869* (Cambridge, Mass., 1932), 7–9.

as there were post offices and employed almost as many ministers as there were postal workers. The largest evangelical denominations were each raising almost as much money per year as the postal service took in. Considered together, the evangelical churches employed nearly double the personnel, maintained nearly twice as many facilities, and raised at least three times the money as the Post Office. Moreover, the churches delivered their message to more people in more places than the postal service delivered letters and newspapers. John's figures for number of letters and newspapers delivered per person per year seem small by a modern reckoning, but at the time, they were the most impressive in the world. Yet as table 10.2 suggests, the people of the United States were each hearing several more times the number of Methodist sermons each year than they received pieces of mail.

The last column of table 10.2 points to another level of comparison useful for understanding the place of the evangelical churches in antebellum American society. If my estimates are even approximately correct, there has been a significant decrease in the number of sermons heard by each American per year from 1840 to 1997. At the same time, the number of letters, newspapers, and magazines delivered by the Post Office has increased exponentially. The social situation suggested by these changes is born out by the comparisons in table 10.3. Although some of these figures are admittedly only estimates, the larger picture is entirely clear. As a factor in the organization of day-to-day life, the churches at the end of the twentieth century, while hardly insignificant, cannot begin to compare with the central place they occupied in American society in the mid-nineteenth century. Even with a very conservative estimate for church revenues in 1860, for example, the amount of religious giving proportionate to federal revenues in the late 1990s has shrunk dramatically. The number of evangelical clergy has likewise shrunk dramatically in relation to number of federal employees. The number of other focal points of

TABLE 10.2. Comparison between Mail Received and Sermons Heard

Year	Letters per Person per Year	Newspapers per Person per Year	Methodist Sermons per Person per Year	All Sermons per Person per Year
1820	1.1	0.7	—	—
1830	1.3	1.5	—	—
1840	2.9	2.7	6	20
1997	372.0	38.8	1.5	13

The estimate for Methodist sermons in 1840 is based on the following facts and assumptions: 3,143 traveling Methodist preachers preaching four sermons per week for 50 weeks with 50 auditors per sermon, plus 6,339 local Methodist preachers delivering two sermons per week for 50 weeks with 100 auditors per sermon, divided by a total population of 17,120,000. For national totals in 1840, add to the Methodist numbers the results of 25,000 preachers giving two sermons per week with 100 auditors per sermon. The estimate for sermons in 1997 assumes 350,000 clergy preaching one sermon per week for 50 weeks to an average of 200 auditors, divided by a total population of 268,000,000.

Sources: the same as for table 10.1.

TABLE 10.3. Religion and the Nation, 1860 and 1997

	ca. 1860	ca. 1997
Value of exports	$211 m[a]	$689 b
Value of imports	$275 m[a]	$871 b
Federal receipts	$56 m	$1,579 b
Church receipts	ca. $20–$25 m	$70 b
Federal receipts–church receipts ratio	2.5 : 1	23 : 1
Federal employees	56,065	2,783,704
Active-duty military	27,958	1,056,000
Methodist clergy	23,143	39,061[b]
Total clergy	ca. 55,000	ca. 350,000
Military–Methodist clergy ratio	1.2 : 1	27 : 1
Federal employees–total clergy ratio	1.0 : 1	8 : 1
Banks and branches	1,562	83,911
Number of churches	54,009	ca. 350,000
Church-bank ratio	35 : 1	4 : 1

m = million, b = billion.
[a] Export and import values for ca. 1860 equal the yearly average for the 1850s.
[b] Methodist clergy ca. 1997 is for 1999 (for the sake of comparison, in 1998 there were 139,090 Roman Catholic priests, brothers, and nuns; in 1999 there were 40,887 Southern Baptist churches). Information from the websites for the United Methodist Church, the Southern Baptist Convention, and *Our Sunday Visitor Catholic Almanac 1999* (Huntington, Ind., 1999).

Sources: the same as for table 10.1.

community exchange (like banks) has grown geometrically, while the number of churches has risen only arithmetically. If it were possible to secure reliable figures for periodical publication, leisure time activity, sponsorship of higher education, or other indicators of social organization, doubtless the religious proportion would also be much smaller in 1997 than in 1860.[45]

To the extent that the figures in table 10.3 are even approximately accurate, they might provide grounds for modern jeremiads about the lamentable decline of religion in America. For this book they are meant to serve a historical purpose, which is to indicate the central, indispensable, defining place of the churches—at a time when most of the churches were evangelical—in the organization of American national culture on the eve of the Civil War.

Ideology

In the next chapter we examine two complexities relating to religion in the early national culture: the shifting meanings of the term "republicanism" and the place of market reasoning in religious thought. Here, however, brief consideration of the function that Protestants played in realizing the new nation's republican commitments provides a further indication of the evangelical contribution to American national culture. For this purpose it is necessary to return to the Revolutionary era.

The major founding fathers, though they differed among themselves on many questions of religion as well as politics, did come to a basic agreement on the place of religion in society. A fine recent book by John G. West, for example, documents a wide range of agreement on such questions among John Jay and John Witherspoon, who were evangelicals in something like the modern sense of the term; James Wilson and Alexander Hamilton, whose attachment to Christian orthodoxy fluctuated; George Washington and James Madison, who shared devotion to the republic and an extreme reticence about disclosing their personal religious beliefs; and Benjamin Franklin, John Adams, and Thomas Jefferson, deists or Unitarians who, if only for pragmatic reasons, did not rule out public activities by more traditional believers.[46] All of these major founders wanted the new United States to promote religious liberty, and none wanted the national government to dictate religious beliefs or practices. The surprising degree of agreement among those whose own religious convictions differed so considerably rested on two shared assumptions: first, that the moral goods promoted by the churches largely coincided with the moral goods promoted by the government; second, that the churches had a role to play in making the moral calculus of republicanism actually work.

This moral calculus of republicanism was—indeed, to some extent remains—an extraordinarily significant assumption for many Americans, religious and nonreligious alike. As the calculus was expressed in the first century of the United States, it held that religion could and should contribute to the morality that was necessary for the virtuous citizens, without which a republic could not survive. The practical challenge inherited from the founding era was how a new kind of church, which had given up the rights of establishment, might insert itself as a promoter of morality into a public sphere from which the old form of establishments had been excluded by the founders' commitment to religious freedom.

Especially as the realities of an actual, rather than imagined, democratic republic bore in upon the founders, reluctance to enlist religion as a support for republican virtue nearly vanished. The classic expression of that appeal was Washington's Farewell Address of 1796, but it was made as well by most of the other key founders. Washington's address was a primer in classical republicanism, with warnings about the dangerous public effects of passion, praise for the Constitution as "sacredly maintained," and cautions against standing armies and political factions. Reminding his fellow Americans of the republican calculus was central to Washington's purpose: "Can it be, that Providence has not connected the permanent felicity of a Nation with its virtue?" For maintaining that virtue, Washington evoked religion. That evocation so clearly announced the priority of religion for the future of the republic that it must be quoted in full:

> Of all the dispositions and habits which lead to political prosperity, Religion and morality are indispensable supports. In vain would that man claim the tribute of Patriotism, who should labour to subvert these great Pillars of human happiness, these firmest props of the duties of Men and citizens. The mere Politician, equally with the pious man ought to respect and cherish them. A

volume could not trace all their connections with private and public felicity. Let it simply be asked where is the security for property, for reputation, for life, if the sense of religious obligation *desert* the oaths, which are the instruments of investigation in Courts of Justice? And let us with caution indulge the supposition, that morality can be maintained without religion. Whatever may be conceded to the influence of refined education on minds of peculiar structure, reason and experience both forbid us to expect that National morality can prevail in exclusion of religious principle.

'Tis substantially true, that virtue or morality is a necessary spring of popular government. The rule indeed extends with more or less force to every species of free Government. Who that is a sincere friend of it, can look with indifference upon attempts to shake the foundation of the fabric?[47]

With one exception, the other founders believed much the same thing. As John Adams wrote only five weeks before Washington published his address, "No other Institution" was as effective as "the Christian Religion" in dispensing moral education throughout an entire society, pressing home "the Sanctions of a future Life," and showing how "the Observance of civil and political as well as domestic and private Duties" were "the means and Conditions of future as well as present Happiness."[48] Jefferson was not quite as direct in supporting this equation, but in 1801 after hearing Benjamin Rush expound upon why he "considered Christianity as the *strong ground* of Republicanism," Jefferson himself wrote that "the Christian religion when divested of the rags in which they [the domineering clergy] have inveloped it, and brought to the original purity and simplicity of its benevolent institutor, is a religion of all others most friendly to liberty, science, and the freest expression of the human mind."[49] The one exception to the founding chorus was James Madison, who never commended the churches as providing moral support for the republic but, rather, restricted his comments on religion to the insistence that a society benefits most when churches competed with each other without any governmental support whatsoever.[50]

The position that became canonical in the early republic was, however, not Madison's but the others. A magisterial interpretation of the relationship appeared in Supreme Court Justice Joseph Story's *Commentaries on the Constitution* of 1833. Story fully supported the separation of church and state as defined by the First Amendment, but he also took for granted that "the promulgation of the great doctrines of religion," which included cultivation of "all the personal, social, and benevolent virtues," could "never be a matter of indifference in any well ordered community." So fundamental did Story consider the relationship between religion and the health of American society that he was prepared to make a further assertion: "Indeed, in a republic, there would seem to be a peculiar propriety in viewing the Christian religion, as the great basis, on which it must rest for its support and permanence, if it be, what it has ever been deemed by its truest friends to be, the religion of liberty."[51] This judgment was representative of the vast sweep of American public opinion of this era.

As the evangelical sects expanded in the early years after the Constitution, so also did they rise to the challenge of promoting republican morality. Although evangelicalism in a recognizably modern form contributed only slightly to fashioning the basic guidelines for church-state and religious-social interaction in the founding generation, evangelicals nonetheless committed themselves wholeheartedly to the republican calculus as defined by the founders. In fact, evangelical eagerness to baptize the founders' framework for religious-political interaction became part of the more general process by which they embraced the comprehensive logic of republican politics and commonsense moral reasoning.[52]

The embrace was mutually beneficial. The founders, by using commonsense moral reasoning to justify independence, encouraged the evangelicals, who were beginning to find the same kind of ethical reasoning more broadly convincing than the narrower ethics of Augustinian Calvinism, which held that people must be redeemed before they could be virtuous. Armed with commonsense principles, leading Protestant spokesmen in the 1790s and 1800s offered fresh new apologies for Christianity based on what all people by nature could see to be true. This strategy worked fairly well in the arena of religious discourse, but not nearly as effectively as in the broader public sphere. The climate of the times made it easier for evangelicals to give up their earlier, particularistic picture of virtue as exclusively dependent upon redemption, since that willingness removed one of the principal points of antagonism between republican traditions and classic Reformed Protestantism. For most upholders of republicanism, it was important that virtue *not* be defined exclusively as a product of divine grace, but rather as also a product of self-generated, personally chosen, public self-discipline. To be sure, considerable confusion attended evangelical consideration of the relation among natural endowments, grace, and virtue. Evangelicals never abandoned a central role for grace, but at least in their enthusiasm as patriotic republicans, most played down the role of grace as an absolutely necessary precondition for public virtue. (Only in funeral orations of 1799–1800—when, that is, personal refutation was no longer possible—did evangelicals begin to link George Washington's public virtue to a deep Christian faith.)[53] Once pulled away from Augustinian particularism by the universalism implicit in *common*-sense moral reasoning (as well as by the republican divorce of virtue from grace), evangelicals offered the nation a way of strengthening virtue for the entire populace. Their reasoning amounted to an intellectual half-way house: ordinary people apart from grace could see the truth, and some could even act virtuously as public leaders. But for the deep, pervasive virtue needed to sustain a republic, conversion was still the best bet.

This exchange served to align the trajectories of evangelicalism and republicanism. Patriotic leaders reversed traditional republican suspicion of supernatural religion in order to enlist the churches for help in strengthening virtue among the people at large. Evangelical leaders reversed traditional Augustinian opposition to republican virtue in order to take their place in the public discourse of a republican United States.

During the Revolutionary period and afterward, evangelicals won their right to a public voice by supporting the war and by softening their opposition to the humanism of republicanism and commonsense moral reasoning. By so doing, they helped the republican founding fathers bring the new nation into existence. For their part, the founders soon came to welcome the offer of help from both formalist and antiformalist evangelicals in promoting virtue among the people. This was an offer they needed more than at first they realized. The founders' explanation for why social health required virtue proved much more convincing than their ability to popularize a standard of *virtù* modeled on a noble Roman yeomanry.

The ideological bartering that evangelicals accepted, though it may have been entered into unconsciously, had a very important consequence. By taking on a version of republicanism, evangelicals put themselves in position to offer their religion to the new nation as a competitor to the rational, moralistic faith of the founders. As it turned out, that struggle was almost no competition at all. The new wineskin of a republic without an established church was a secular creation, but the new wine that filled it was evangelical.

Evangelicals also offered the nation a revitalized form of covenant theology. Perry Miller was wrong to conclude that the revival replaced the covenant as a means of mobilizing religious energy behind the new nation.[54] Instead, as indicated by the many days of fasting and thanksgiving called by the Continental Congress, and then by Presidents Washington and Adams, older forms of national covenant were not jettisoned in the early United States but reworded with an evangelical vocabulary of revival.[55]

If for evangelicals during the Revolution "the cause of America" had become "the cause of Christ," as the Pennsylvania Presbyterian Robert Smith put it in 1781, then the achievement of independence meant that, for many patriots, "the cause of Christ" had become also "the cause of America."[56] The belief that the United States was a land chosen and protected by God for special, if perhaps even millennial, purposes may not have been as widely spread during the War for Independence as is sometimes suggested. But it did flourish in the decades after the war.[57] If networks of evangelical denominations and voluntary societies were building national walls under a constitutional roof, so also was the sense of elect nationhood, which was a peculiarly evangelical construction, making a significant contribution as well.

Evangelical political activity in the new dispensation was at first confused. Formalist evangelicals stigmatized Jefferson as a dangerous infidel in the run-up to the election of 1800.[58] This mobilization failed, in part because Jefferson turned out to be a moral president and even supported a wide range of religious practices, like attending Sunday services of Christian worship in the Capitol building and authorizing federal support for military chaplains and Christian missions to the Indians.[59] It failed as well because Jefferson's formalist opponents eventually grasped instinctively that they were treating him as a monarch who might set up an alternative state religion rather than what he actually was, a democratically elected official whose job was to preside over free, competitive public space.

Evangelicals hit their stride politically after about 1812 by turning to voluntary societies as the way of promoting the morality required for a republic. Even when overt political action occurred, like petition drives against Sunday mails and missionary mobilization against Cherokee removal, these efforts meant less than the moral instruction promoted by the voluntary societies and undertaken without formal attention to politics.[60] The fact that evangelicals failed in their efforts to stop the transport of mail on Sunday and to halt the removal of the Cherokee from Georgia does not negate an important fact: these campaigns illustrated successful evangelical adaptation to a nonestablishmentarian polity and to an arena where they understood their job as providing the morality without which a republic would collapse. Because they aimed not at establishment but at providing private moral capital to sustain the republic, evangelicals were largely successful in meeting the challenge posed by the founders.

The success of evangelicals in shaping public morality for a disestablishmentarian republic was widely perceived at the time. Alexis de Tocqueville's comments are best known. As he perceived the American clergy, they "separate themselves carefully from all parties, and avoid contact with them with all the ardor of personal interest." As a result, "one cannot say that in the United States religion exerts an influence on the laws or the details of public opinions, but it directs mores, and it is in regulating the family that it works to regulate the state."[61] De Tocqueville's conclusion on the matter followed exactly the prescriptions of the founders. What had intervened in the generation between Washington's death in 1799 and de Tocqueville's visit to the United States in the early 1830s was the dramatic expansion of the evangelical churches.

Domestic observers said the same thing. A writer in the *Christian Spectator* from 1829 posed a question about connections between religion and the American state. The response: "In the form of ecclesiastical alliances, nothing; but in its operation as a controlling, purifying power in the consciences of the people, we answer, it has every thing to do, it is the last hope of republics; and let it be remembered, if ever our ruin shall come that the questions which agitate, the factions which distract, the convulsions which dissolve, will be but secondary causes: The true evil will lie back of these, in the moral debasement of the people."[62] In a telling aside, Robert Wiebe caught exactly the transition from formal to informal suasion: "The churches added Sunday schools but subtracted election-day sermons."[63]

Further proof that evangelicals had learned how to function as openly Christian advocates in a republic defined by Constitutional freedom of religion is found in the extraordinary role they played in the sectional antagonism leading to the Civil War. That role, which has recently been documented in a magisterial book by Richard J. Carwardine, is the subject of later chapters below.[64] The point to note here is that, as powerful as evangelical public influence became in the three-quarters of a century before Fort Sumter, it was an influence divided starkly by the Mason and Dixon Line.

And the result of the extensive evangelical mobilization? In 1789 Alexander Hamilton could quip that there was no reference to God in the Constitution simply because the framers forgot to put one in.[65] Fifty years later, political parties, like the Whigs, who embodied a general evangelical ethos, and the Anti-Masonic, Liberty, and American Parties, which were founded on specific planks from the evangelical creed, were winning elections throughout New England and the mid-Atlantic states.[66] After only a few more years, Abraham Lincoln, though himself no evangelical, was quoting the Scriptures—in a way unimaginable from the nation's earliest presidents—in order to draw the nation back together after the Civil War.[67]

By the early nineteenth century, evangelicalism was the unofficially established religion in a nation that had forsworn religious establishments. Because of the circumstances before, during, and after the Revolution that led to this informal establishment, republican politics and moral-sense philosophy were both sacralized. More ministers were agreeing with Ezra Stiles's assertion of 1783 that the blessings promised to Israel were "allusively prophetic of the future prosperity and splendor of the United States." When, early in his presidential tenure, Abraham Lincoln, even though he was not a church member, spoke of American citizens as God's "almost chosen people" and of United States freedom as "the last, best hope of the earth," he reflected not simply an extension of Stiles's opinions but their reconstitution in specifically evangelical terms.[68] The significant matter for a history of theology is the reflexive reality: if a confluence of revivalistic Protestantism with republicanism and commonsense moral reasoning helped evangelicals build America, it led as well to the migration of speech about America into their talk about God.

Ideological Permutations

The argument that extensive participation by Protestants in the affairs of the new United States precipitated a decisive shift in theological reasoning can be restated as follows: First, in the struggle for independence from Britain and then the search for national stability, a republican vision of liberty came to the fore of American consciousness. This republican vision entailed certain presuppositions concerning human nature and human relationships, as well as specific ethical ideals about the proper functioning of society. Dedication to the latter ideals led to the development of a republican calculus by which almost all Americans came to view virtue and liberty, as also corruption and tyranny, as mutually reinforcing conditions.

Second, commonsense moral reasoning ratified the universal human validity of what consciousness—in this instance, republican consciousness—perceived to be true. This form of reasoning was partially indebted to the Scottish philosophers who expounded a sophisticated defense of epistemological and ethical realism, but in more instances it was a pragmatic adjustment to politically inspired mistrust of inherited authorities and church establishments.

Third, closely allied to confidence in commonsense moral reasoning was confidence in the natural human ability to perceive clearly the links between moral causes and social effects. This confidence rested in part on presuppositions from the Enlightenment, whereby careful observers assumed that they could explain the connections between public states of affairs and the virtuous or vicious actions that led to these states. It rested as well on a distinctly Christian view of providence, whereby believers assumed they could read the mind of God from the terrestrial occurrences over which he reigned as universal sovereign.[1]

Next, American Protestants, led by the burgeoning evangelical churches, played a critical role for the new United States by putting the republican calculus to work. Personal conversion, the godly discipline of families, the expansion of national denominations, and the flourishing of voluntary societies—all were means of promoting the virtue required to keep the American experiment on a republican course.

Finally, in offering their religious wares to the cultural markets of the new American polity, Protestants—especially the evangelicals—not only exploited but also internalized at least some aspects of the new nation's republicanism, commonsense moral reasoning, and Newtonian-providentialist social theory. Once yoked with political ideology and enlisted as a servant of the national purpose, theology began to be shaped by the churches' own efforts at promoting their message in the new American environment.

As a result, evolution of the new nation's political thought almost necessarily entailed a corresponding evolution in the theological reasoning with which that thought had become so closely entwined. The direction in which political conceptions moved defined also the direction of theological change. In the early years of the new nation, that evolution was away from a republicanism defined largely by civic humanism, with ideals of disinterested public virtue and freedom defined as liberation from tyranny. The movement was toward a republicanism aligned with liberalism, with ideals of individualized private virtue and freedom defined as self-determination. The move was never monolithic, complete, or even irreversible, but it did take place. At the same time, other intellectual resources that Protestant evangelicals were using in the effort to spread the gospel, stabilize the new nation, and subdue the frontier (including commonsense moral reasoning and Newtonian approaches to social theory) were also exerting an influence on the exposition of theology. Each of these resources became important for American theology precisely because in the Revolutionary and post-Revolutionary decades America's religious leaders were such active partners in the creation of American civilization.

Yet exploration of ideology in the early United States cannot rest with consideration of only religious, political, and ethical reasoning. The best discussions of early American ideology are now filled with contentious debates about the role of the market, and reasoning shaped by the market, in the development of thought. It is therefore necessary to ask whether the early republic's rising market consciousness and expanding commercial practices were not as important for theology as republicanism and commonsense ethical principles. Although it is difficult to demonstrate a negative, the last part of this chapter outlines reasons for treating connections between theology and commerce seriously, but not as seriously as connections among theology, political thought, and theistic common sense.

Republicanism

In the early years of the young republic, American political ideology was shifting.[2] That shift was in the direction of liberal individualism, which can be described with varying emphases: for example, as "a continual agrarian and commercial expansion that brought constant pressure for action on the part of the national government"; or as a concentration on "man's natural right to economic as well as political liberty, government's obligation to protect property, [and] the people's opportunity to pursue material happiness"; or "this liberal world of business, money-making, and the open promotion of interests . . . the scrambling, individualistic, acquisitive society."[3] But this movement toward liberalism was not a zero-sum exercise. Even as Americans became more liberal, they retained considerable loyalty to substantial aspects of their republican heritage.

The liberalism of Thomas Jefferson and the Democratic-Republicans was, for example, an ideological compound: it did feature heightened attention to personal rights, economic opportunities, and individual liberty, but it neither reduced concern for the public effects of virtue nor abandoned the perceived bond between liberty and communal well-being.[4] In the late 1790s Jeffersonians attacked their Federalist opponents for letting "the spirit of avarice and corruption" replace "the generous and noble passions," and for allowing a concern for accumulating public offices to drive out concern for the public good.[5] Jeffersonians were almost as convinced that their Federalist opponents were plotting against liberty as American patriots had been in fearing the wily plots of the British ministry during the 1760s and 1770s. During the heightened partisan strife of the John Adams administration, "Tory" was a term of reproach hurled by both parties—Jefferson used it against the Federalists, while Alexander Hamilton used it against the Jeffersonian Democratic-Republicans.[6] In Joyce Appleby's carefully chosen words, "The vitality of republican ideas not only persisted but continued to embarrass the progress of liberal values in America."[7]

Once it is understood that America's increasing liberalism did not necessarily obliterate a broad commitment to republican values—in other words, that a simple antithesis between republicanism and liberalism is a modern construct rather than a historical reality—much else becomes clear about the early national period. Americans of almost all political convictions did embrace stronger notions of individual rights, and most of them also wanted to see the powers of government limited to one degree or the other. But these commitments did not represent a repudiation of the republican heritage of the Revolutionary era. Rather, as Daniel Walker Howe has put it, "Liberalism, far from being a threatening rival to republicanism, became in fact its welcome ally in the task of making free government work."[8] John Murrin skillfully subverts the convention that republicanism and liberalism had to be opposing forces as he makes the same historical point. In an analysis of why concern for corruption was so great in the early United States, Murrin concedes that "we surely ought to see republicanism as the recessive and liberalism as the dominant configuration by 1815." Yet he also insists that "we cannot even begin to make sense of the content of public life unless we see the two as a continuing dichotomy." Murrin argues that "without continuing acceptance of republican values, corruption would not have become a serious issue, much less an obsession, in an environment that was rapidly becoming more participatory and democratic." The result was a situation where actions did not square easily with ideology, but where both were inextricably woven together: "As Jefferson should have said, 'We are all republicans; we are all liberals.' Republicanism remains the political conscience of a liberal society."[9]

To note the substantial overlapping of liberal and republican convictions in the early republic prepares the way for seeing their continual intermingling in the generation before the Civil War. As we note in considerable detail below, a set of republican questions—How do threats against freedom reflect personal corruption? How does the presence of slavery corrupt all involved in the system? How might the cultivation of virtue save the republic?—became increasingly important among religious figures during the middle decades of the nineteenth century. One of the main reasons that these republican queries remained important in the religious sphere is that they also remained very much alive in national public discourse. Illustrations are thick on the ground. Whigs, for example, held that Andrew Jackson's tyrannical instincts threatened the wholesome freedom of the American experiment. In 1833 Henry Clay expressed these fears in well-worn phrases: "We are in the midst of a revolution, hitherto bloodless, but rapidly tending toward a total change of the pure republican character of government."[10] In turn, Jacksonian Democrats could give as well as take. As Martin Van Buren, the successor of Jackson as the Democrats' leader, pictured party conflict of his day, the Whig Party was attacking the ability of local landowners to act with independent integrity. Whigs were the "court" party attacking "country" defenders of liberty. Precisely this Democratic defense of the independent freeholder threatened by the manipulations of a big government (or big bank or big voluntary societies) protected the possibility of "virtue," the ability of ordinary citizens to set self-interest aside and act for the public good.[11] The long life of republican conceptual language in a supposedly liberal America should give pause. If the people of the antebellum period effortlessly conjoined ideological principles that historians in the second half of the twentieth century interpreted as antithetical, the problem is certainly with the historians.

Implications for Theology

For a history of theology in America, these conclusions from recent historical research carry great significance. If ideological streams that historians have treated as distinct entities in fact coexisted, it paves the way for exploring the coexistence of theological beliefs with a variety of other convictions usually studied in isolation from religion. If liberal convictions were increasingly and unmistakably added to American ideology after the War for Independence, it alerts researchers to the need for charting the influence of these additions on theology. If elements of classical republicanism survived even as liberal elements become more prominent in American public discourse generally, it raises the possibility that traditional convictions in theology (like a stress on comprehensive divine agency) may not have simply faded away in the face of newer theological assertions (like a stress on effective human agency). Chapters 12–17 below represent an attempt to read theological history against the background of this broader ideological history.

The most important point concerns chronology. When colonial American Protestants began to employ contemporary political language in the 1740s, their attachments were primarily to classical or civic humanist forms of republican ideology. As one might expect from recent historical insights, this attachment did not necessarily mean a repudiation of all Lockean convictions.[12] The attachment nonetheless grew most directly from parallels between Real Whig commitments and the convictions of late Puritans or early evangelicals.[13] Thus, tyranny was a product of corrupt (or infernal) manipulations of public justice. Liberty was much more a description of ideal social relations (where God's grace was manifestly at work) than of individual rights. Venal (or wicked) conspiracies threatened to impose civil (but also Anglican, or even Roman Catholic) tyranny. Colonials sought relief in a revival of virtue through disciplined public behavior (and through special fasts in repentance before God or celebrations in thanksgiving for the unwarranted blessings of his gracious hand). In short, the early Protestant-republican merger featured classical, organic, and civic humanist associations more than individualized rights, contractual obligations, personal economic opportunities, or a limited view of the state.

From this basis, and precisely because the bond between civic humanism and colonial Puritanism had become so strong, the history of American theology after the Revolution followed the history of political ideology, whereby country or civic humanist convictions gradually gave way to liberal or individualistic convictions. Only because a form of Real Whig republicanism had merged with Protestant thinking during the 1740s would a much more liberal republicanism inform evangelical thought in the 1820s. But precisely these bonds explain why libertarian notions of human freedom, which were held by only a few in the 1720s, became self-evident to many a century later.[14]

Unpacking the tangled conceptual history of republican thinking makes possible at least four important insights concerning religious thought. It reveals how Protestants acted as agents to mediate between republican and liberal convictions that historians have sometimes perceived as simple contradictions. It shows how important religious history was for the migrating meaning of the critical terms "liberty" and "virtue." It explains why antagonistic versions of republican Christianity could emerge in the North and the South, with both fully justified in claiming descent from the founders. And it underscores the elective affinity between the versions of republican politics and commonsense moral reasoning that arose in the early republic.

Protestant Agency

Religious believers were certainly acted upon by the new nation's social and political ideologies. But they also acted—for example, by continuing to bring into public discourse religious language that was shaped primarily by religious experience.[15] They also acted by promoting, or helping to make possible, the liberal republicanism of the early nineteenth century. Evangelicalism, in particular, offered a living demonstration of how the countervailing forces represented by classical and liberal forms of republicanism could coexist. Revivalist conversion was the religious analogue to Lockean individualism. It signaled the freeing of individuals from tradition, family, and inherited authority, even as it allowed believers to take in hand the commerce of their own souls. At the same time, the deeply satisfying communion of the redeemed—whether worshiping together in Methodist class meetings, impromptu venues appropriated by antiformalist sectarians, or the well-built churches of formalist denominations—embodied an altruistic communalism of the sort idealized by civic humanists. Religious community, especially among twice-born evangelicals, pulled individuals away from private concerns into virtuous (or benevolent) willingness to act in public with self-sacrifice for the good of the whole. Evangelical religion, as specified by Catherine Brekus, was a mixture of individualism and communalism: "In many ways, revivalists were conservatives who wanted to subordinate individual selfishness to the greater good of God's new Israel, but their emphasis on religious affections also contained the seeds of a particular kind of individualism."[16] If the American revivalist tradition effortlessly joined together these kinds of individualism and communalism, it illustrates—maybe even explains—why communal and individualistic elements in the American political tradition functioned together with a similar absence of strain. In these terms, the flourishing of Methodism was not only a *response* to radical social and ideological tumults but also the *creator* of a distinct vision of social order that combined principles of self and community that both European traditionalists and modern historians held to be mutually exclusive.

"Liberty" and "Virtue"

Second, once the dramatic changes of the period 1760–1820 are understood, not as coordinated responses to a single Master Ideology, but as intertwined, mutually influencing parts of a multidimensional congeries of causes and effects, it is more evident how religion factored into the era's major ideological transformations. Most straightforward was evolution in the meaning of liberty. If, as in a recent admirable formulation, "the eighteenth century's beau ideal of liberty as the corollary of order yielded to the nineteenth century's liberty as release from custom,"[17] religion was integral to that transformation. The expansion of religious bodies that depicted salvation in Arminian, modified Calvinist, or anti-Calvinist terms assisted in a redefinition of political liberty. In turn, the redefinition of political liberty gave more space for such versions of Christian doctrine, even as it made things difficult for classic Calvinist conceptions of divine sovereignty.[18]

Transformation of the key republican term "virtue" was more complicated.[19] From an ideal of manly, disinterested public action on behalf of the public good (the common weal), "virtue" became increasingly associated with feminine, domestic, private morality. The newer sense of virtue emerged over the second half of the eighteenth century in all western European and North Atlantic societies, but its development in America reflected the particularities of new-world experience. Each of the factors in that development—whether religious, political, social, psychological, economic, or philosophical—influenced and was influenced by the other. They included at least the following:

- *democratization*, whereby the potential for action useful to the public was broadened from an elite, leisured few to a much more numerous democracy of free white men;
- *a liberal concept of government*, whereby, as in arguments for the new Constitution in the *Federalist Papers*, benevolent government was viewed less as a product of disinterested public service of altruistic elites and more as a result of free citizens warily checking each others' propensities for aggregating dangerous quantities of individual power;
- *the new moral philosophy*, whereby the affections were considered a foundation for public ethical behavior and reason was dethroned as the primary arbiter of harmonious social interaction;
- *the spread of sentimental literature*, whereby the epitome of virtuous action came to be seen as the heroic maintenance of female chastity against the conniving conspiracies of aggressive males;
- *evangelicalization*, whereby "a new sense of the heart" became the critical matter in becoming a Christian and the cultivation of "holy affections" became the main end of the religious life;
- *the growth of a republican market mentality*, whereby personal gain could be pursued through commercial channels far beyond the control of local moral regulation and yet still be counterbalanced for the good of the whole by the maintenance of personal virtue cultivated by wives and mothers in homes, schools, and churches.

From these varied sources emerged a new understanding of virtue. The new ideology represented an intellectual evolution in which older ideas—republicanism in general and virtue in particular—were significantly altered, but not left behind. In her attempt to show how tectonic ideological shifts related to the earthquake of the American Revolution, Ruth Bloch summarizes with special clarity the alteration of republican ideals: "What did change as a specific consequence of the American Revolutionary experience was that the feminine notion of virtue took on a political significance it had previously lacked." Americans consistently urged virtue as the basis of a successful republic but increasingly shifted the sphere of virtue to the home, where women presided. "Virtue, if still regarded as essential to the public good in a republican state, became ever more difficult to distinguish from private benevolence, personal manners, and female sexual propriety."[20] Gordon Wood's understanding of this crucial ideological evolution points as well to why it became so important for public religious life: "The importance of this domestication of virtue for American culture can scarcely by exaggerated. . . . It not only helped reconcile classical republicanism with modernity and commerce; it laid the basis for all reform movements of the nineteenth century."[21]

Of greatest significance for a history of theology is the fact that part of the Protestant contribution to the new republic was its contribution to an altered understanding of virtue. That new understanding, which the churches helped to shape, became in turn a great engine driving all kinds of thinking in America, including thought about God in relation to humanity.

North versus South

Religious participation in the era's ideological transformation also helps explain the relationship of theology in the North to theology in the South. Both regions were marked by a common ideological history, but marked in distinctly different ways. Both Northern and Southern cultures were rooted in republican political principles, both experienced a significant degree of Christianization through the agency of evangelical Protestant churches, both underwent economic and psychological transformations that heightened the importance of individual prerogatives and the fruits of individual labor, and both also witnessed a fluid interchange between spheres of public thought and spheres of religious thought.[22] Yet results from these common experiences were markedly different.

By comparison to the North, Southern forms of republicanism remained closer to the deferential, class-stratified, and socially organic civic humanism of the early Revolutionary period.[23] Where Northern citizens in the Whig and Republican Parties came to embrace market values alongside traditional republican concern for public liberty and personal virtue, Southerners of all parties remained more Jeffersonian and tended to regard commercial individualism as the enemy of republican liberty.[24] For the South, republicanism meant more an ideal of social stability than an ideal of individual fulfillment, more an arena to display honor than an opened door for achievement, more an opportunity to save the best of the past than to new-model the future. In describing the differences more generally, Joyce Appleby's conclusions are apt: Southerners "employed a nostalgic imagery and an elegiac tone in their reflections while Northern entrepreneurs and activists imagined a future transformed by their efforts, aided by science and a general receptivity to change."[25]

The ideological consequence of broad regional difference meant that Real Whig commitments to limited government, strict interpretation of founding documents, and separation of powers remained in Southern minds more necessary for the preservation of liberty and social well-being than they did to most Northerners. Northerners were always uneasy with, or came actively to oppose, the argument that slavery was a republican bulwark against tyranny. This conviction, by contrast, was embraced in the colonial South, it was reinforced energetically in the era of the Revolution and the Constitution, and it was consistently maintained to the end of the Civil War and beyond.[26], As only one instance, the Presbyterian theologian Robert Lewis Dabney, at late as the 1880s and 1890s, was still vigorously arguing that slave society had maintained "a real, republican equality of rights" where it was possible to promote "the most perspicacious virtue and self-denial." By contrast, the false republicanism of Northern commercial society was marked by "crimes against liberty and public virtue" and depredations from "the hirelings of political faction."[27]

Dabney's reputation as one of the South's leading thinkers suggests the importance for theology of contrasting Northern and Southern conceptions of republican ideals. Because Southern interpretations of republican freedom never became as democratic, as liberal, or as concerned about individual rights as their Northern counterparts, theology in the South tended not to stress individual spiritual rights and the necessity of personal religious activism as much as theology in the North. In sum, differences in theological emphasis between the North and the South were not the function merely of geography but of ideological convictions that evolved differently in the different regions.

Republican Common Sense

Finally, the debates over republicanism and liberalism clarify one further way in which religion was fully integrated into the ideological history of the new nation. Part of the movement from classical to liberal republicanism was a corresponding movement in ethical reasoning. "The new moral philosophy," which posited a universal moral sense as the basis for personal and social ethics, inspired confidence in the existence of moral absolutes, even after traditional institutions of moral authority like God-ordained monarchy or the established church were cast aside. It provided reassurance that the kind of moral guidance historically offered by social elites could be retained, and even improved upon, in a much more democratic society. It offered reassurance to a restless population that escaping the traditional influence of learning, family authority, and communal guidance did not mean a descent into moral chaos. It offered a defense of political innovation based not on ancient literary authorities but on what a rising people *felt* was right. It gave religious believers, who for both personal and social reasons were committed to traditional faiths—but who with their peers had given up the inherited props for supporting those faiths—a means to retain that allegiance with intellectual self-respect. These contributions from the new moral philosophy were of great significance. Commonsense reasoning as appropriated in America was an intellectual vade mecum for liberal republicanism. It offered the nation as a whole an approach to ethics liberated from the corruptions of authoritarianism and hierarchy. In the early republic the ones who most effectively spread principles of commonsense moral reasoning were not the statesmen but the college presidents, the seminary professors, the stump preachers, the founders of periodicals and learned quarterlies, the authors of religious literature, and the pulpiteers of the nation's churches. The appeal of commonsense ethics was an integral part of America's early republican history. Because it was also so integrally a part of what religious believers offered the nation, it was also a critical factor in the emergence of an American theology.

Instances

The argument that pervasive, multidirectional connections existed between religious and political beliefs remains only speculation unless it can be shown that religious spokespersons unself-consciously employed republican language in talking about their faith and when bringing that faith into the nation's public discourse. In fact, religious use of republican terminology and republican reasoning was a constant in almost all regions throughout the entire period from before the Revolution through the Civil War. Scattered examples cannot carry the weight of demonstration, except that the instances that follow could be multiplied nearly without limit.

Ezra Stiles, president of Yale College, by 1794 had embarked on the project of showing how "a Christian republic" had a responsibility to promote a charitable spirit yet without giving way to a false (and deistic) ideal of charity that led to "the equality, indifference, and nullification of all religions."[28] Seven years after Stiles published these sentiments, his fellow Congregationalist Lemuel Haynes addressed the citizens of Rutland, Vermont, on the twenty-fifth anniversary of American independence. To this New Divinity preacher, the text from Luke 22:26 ("he that is greatest among you, let him be as the younger; and he that is chief, as he that doth serve") "epitomised" the essence of republican government, where "liberty and equality" subdue "a proud ambitious aspiring temper," while supporting "the community at large" and "the interest of the commonwealth." To Haynes, it was "common sense" to realize that "our beneficial creator has furnished us with moral and natural endowments," which were to be used for "the general good." As himself an African American, Haynes did not forbear to describe the "pitiful, abject state" of slaves as resulting from "the effects of despotism."[29] Where Stiles and Haynes as two quite different New England Congregationalists led, Americans of all sort followed.

The era's wars always showed republican Christianity at its most prominent, but also at its most flexible. New England Federalist opponents of James Madison in the War of 1812, like Elijah Perish of Byfield, Massachusetts, denounced the "iron walls" of the Democratic-Republicans, "which have incarcerated your souls and bodies so long." By contrast, religious friends of Madison, found especially among antiformalist Baptists and "Christians," lined up with Elias Smith to praise Madison for making "greater and more successful exertions . . . in favour of civil and religious liberty" than had ever been seen in the country before.[30] It was the same in the Mexican War when friends and foes of James K. Polk assaulted each other with stories of liberty corrupted by vice, and as they demonstrated how wars inevitably undermined (or strengthened) republican liberty.[31] As we will observe, the clash of antagonisms fueled by a common republican vocabulary reached its apotheosis during the Civil War.

The instinctive recourse to varieties of Christian republican jeremiad in times of war grew from steady cultivation of the Christian-republican syllogism in times of peace: Virtue was necessary for public well-being. Tyranny flourished in league with vice. Life-transforming religion was essential for virtue and hence essential also for public well-being. Titles of books and articles from throughout the period hammered home the critical relationships: *The Loving Kindness of God Displayed in the Triumph of Republicanism in America*; *The Connexion of Temperance with Republican Freedom*; *The Republican Influence of Christianity*; or "Republican Tendencies of the Bible."[32]

Leading spokespersons likewise relied steadily upon Christian republican thinking as a critical axiom, whether Robert Baird by describing the "Republican churches" established in new communities of the opening West, or Charles Finney by identifying "intelligence and virtue" and "the fear and love of God" as the only reliable protection for "self-government", or James Henley Thornwell by defining "regulated liberty" as "representative, republican government" proceeding between the contrasting dangers of "the despotism of the mob" and "the supremacy of a single will."[33]

However self-evident the logic of Christian republicanism was to most religious commentators in the United States during this period, it was never universally accepted. Some foreign observers, in particular, never could quite get it. The skepticism about the Christian-republican link that John Wesley, John Fletcher, and Charles Wesley expressed at the time of the Revolution was echoed by many later observers, especially during the Civil War. As an example, Robert Burns of Knox College in Ontario expressed the opinion of many Canadians, who thought that this war was the due payment for a hypocritical history: the United States, "the boasted 'land of the brave and the free,' clung convulsively to the gilded bait [slavery], and is now paying the penalty of her madness."[34] English reactions were, predictably, even harsher. A high-church Anglican magazine expressed contempt for the American churches' vaunted defense of republican liberty by praising the protest of one American Episcopal bishop against the intrusion of political affairs into church business: "It was an act of no small moral courage to make so public and so significant a protest . . . against the manoeuvres of the petted emissary of a lawless military republic."[35] An equally sharp criticism, and one that twisted republican logic back upon the Americans, came from the *British Quarterly Review* when it commented on Northern military strategy: "Nothing but despotism could retain the recovered South, . . . and of all despotisms, a democratic despotism has ever been the worst and the most cruel. The effects upon every part and ramification of the body politic would follow with proportionate rapidity and certainty, and public virtue would as inevitably be depraved as it once was depraved in Rome."[36] In sum, American axioms often remained exclusively American.

In the United States itself, especially after the connotations of republicanism drifted toward individual rights and personal liberties, a few conservatives, committed to the classical ideals of deferential politics, started to worry. In 1808 the prominent Presbyterian patriot Elias Boudinot groused that "many of our mistakes arise from the fashionable principle, that our Government is a Republican one. Altho' this may be true in a strict sense, it is certainly not so, in the popular or democratic Idea of the Term. Our Government was intended by its founders, and is really so in fact, to be a mixed Government, properly balanced, partaking, in a wise proportion, of all the forms of Government[:] Monarchic, Aristocratic & Democratic."[37] His sentiments were echoed shortly thereafter by Thomas Andros, the Congregational minister of Berkley, Massachusetts. In the strife between Federalist New England and the Democratic administration during the War of 1812, Andros lambasted his opponents for descending to the level of "those philosophic fiends who guided [France's] destiny under the abused name of republicans (a name now almost become synonymous with falsehood, tyranny and crime)."[38] Such wariness about the compatibility of Christian and republican traditions lingered throughout the following decades. In 1845, for example, Joseph Tracy concluded his path-breaking history of the Great Awakening by arguing for the demoralizing effects of Whig and Revolutionary thought. For Tracy, the popularity of Tom Paine's writing, "through all of which there runs a secret vein of infidel metaphysics," betrayed the real character of republicanism.[39]

But these were futile protests. Republicanism flourished as an American ideal precisely because it had worked as a system for colonial elites to overthrow the rule of British elites, because it provided a vocabulary for ordinary Americans to protest against the pretensions of American elites, and, not least, because it seemed so clearly to explain the nature of American social experience in the national era and beyond.

Market Reasoning and Theology

Reasoning from economic life never exerted the same sort of influence on theology as reasoning from political ideology, even though money was close to the heart of almost all significant developments in the history of Protestants between the War for Independence and the Civil War.[40] To be sure, visitors to the United States in this period did comment regularly on the close ties they saw between the nation's dominant religious expressions and its economic life. In the early 1840s a Swedish visitor to Rochester, New York, spoke for many others in noting what appeared to be a widespread phenomenon: "Here, as in all of the new cities we passed through, we were surprised to notice the great number of *churches* and *banks*—evidence of the greater intensity of both spiritual and material activity here than in older communities."[41] Anticipating the vocabulary of modern rational-choice theorists, the Austrian Francis Grund thought he knew why religion was faring better in the United States than in Britain during the 1830s. "In America," he concluded, "every clergyman may be said to do business on his own account, and under his own firm." As Grund surveyed the American churches, he was led to expand his metaphor: "The actual stock in any one of those firms is, of course, less than the immense capital of the Church of England; but the aggregate amount of business transacted by them jointly may nevertheless be greater in the United States."[42]

What foreign observers saw as connections between religion and economics reflected an actually existing situation. Disputes over money fueled the era's interdenominational strife, which was often exceedingly fierce. Money was also always a central matter of dispute between formalist and antiformalist believers. Antiformalists distrusted its accumulation and those who sought to harness wealth for broad, national projects; formalists felt a responsibility to use money for such purposes, yet while guarding against greed or the arrogance of power. Money was just as important for the black-white fissure in early American Protestantism. Slavery was never less than a statement about the sovereignty of capital, and its rights, in relation to human rights. In the South, economic restrictions on religious organization by black Christians was part and parcel of the racial system undergirding slavery and the marginalization of free African Americans. Money also defined boundaries in the history of male and female religion. Protestant voluntary societies, by opening up avenues for publishing and public speaking for women like the sisters Sarah and Angelina Grimké, also opened up avenues for relatively independent economic activity. Religious convictions supplied the most powerful impulses for the women's rights movement, and that movement was much concerned about economic matters. In sum, pervasive connections existed between money and religion in the early decades of the United States.

Yet modern conventions that interpret economic relations as primary and all other relations as secondary are misleading. Important statements by Charles Sellers and Paul Johnson, for instance, have tended to treat religious talk instrumentally, as means by which exploiters of the era's opening markets, or their opponents, could work their own economic wills.[43] A much more nuanced conception of religion-market relationships has, however, emerged for the colonial period. George Whitefield, it is now clear, was both a pioneering marketer and a pioneering revivalist. Harry Stout and Frank Lambert, drawing on the scholarship of T. H. Breen, have successfully pictured Whitefield as one who adapted a historic Protestant message to the new dynamics of trans-Atlantic merchandising.[44] The importance of their argument is to show that, quite early on, at least some Protestants in some situations eagerly embraced some aspects of "the market," but for religious rather than material ends (i.e., because they thought such a strategy could enhance the spread of their religion).

In the national period Protestants who published on questions of money and the market seemed prepared to regard religion as base rather than superstructure, or they formulated connections in other ways altogether. In this later period evangelicals especially maintained traditional Protestant attitudes that featured astringent nervousness concerning the accumulation of wealth. When American evangelicals did consider money in larger ideological relationships, they were much more likely to employ standard republican convictions than convictions about the market. Political instincts, that is, bore in much more obviously on theology than did market reasoning. Traditional assessments of power and virtue were more likely to regulate thinking about money than was commitment to market principles.

As an example, an early appeal from 1792 to provide money for young men going into the ministry made wealth subservient to the standard calculus of Christian republicanism through the following syllogism: ministers support religion, religion is essential for a moral social order, therefore giving to support ministers supports a moral social order.[45] The same argument in slightly different form appeared in an 1832 defense of Sunday schools. Since these schools were one of "the great leveling institutions of our age," support for Sunday school teachers amounted to a "more effectual way to banish aristocracy from among us."[46] Although ministers seem to have emphasized the republican significance of money less frequently as the years passed, the fact that economic reasoning was regularly embedded in republican reasoning suggests that market assumptions were not affecting religious convictions as directly as did political assumptions.[47]

The most important conclusion that can be drawn from a survey of writings about money, markets, and the economy in this period is that Protestants regularly, consistently, and without sense of contradiction both enunciated traditional Christian exhortations about careful financial stewardship and simply took for granted the workings of the United States' expanding commercial society.

This standard position appeared from many different kinds of Protestants in many places and in many circumstances. In a Boston sermon of 1813, for example, Joseph Emerson employed his text from John 6:12 ("gather up the fragments that remain, that nothing be lost") to preach on "Christian Economy." According to Emerson, Scripture taught that humanity was to labor primarily for everlasting life, that wealth was fleeting, that money should be used to aid the poor, and that it was sinful to spend so much money on liquor ($33 million annually, at a time when the expenditures of the national government totaled $32 million). Yet Emerson also proclaimed that nothing in the Bible sanctioned disregard for temporal existence and that it was proper to seek prosperity so long as temptation was avoided.[48]

Four years later, a Presbyterian sermon from the as yet unfamous Gettysburg, Pennsylvania, urged traditional Protestant doctrine on the faithful by asking them not to abuse prosperity by indulging in "ease . . . torpid insensibility and luxurious indolence . . . levity, and an excessive love of pleasure . . . vainglory, and presumptuous confidence." Yet after noting how many social, economic, religious, and political advantages God had bestowed upon Pennsylvania, the minister concluded by urging his hearers to learn "how to perpetuate prosperity, and enjoy it with a blessing." Using prosperity for benevolence was the way to keep it from being withdrawn.[49]

In one of the era's most widely read formal introductions to the subject, Francis Wayland of Brown University promoted the same conjunction of traditional Protestant attitudes and acceptance of the modern market. While expatiating at length on the necessity of freedom for economic growth, Wayland was careful to include a moral qualification: "It is almost superfluous, however, to add, that a free constitution is of no value, unless the moral and intellectual character of a people be sufficiently elevated to avail itself of the advantages which it offers."[50] A sermon published just before the outbreak of hard times in 1857 put succinctly what many commentators had said at much greater length during the previous half century: "Our object is to baptize the riches of men with the spirit of the gospel."[51] Even the Restorationist leader Alexander Campbell, who in his extreme antiformalism was so contrary in so many ways, agreed: "There is nothing incompatible with diligence in business and fervor of spirit in serving the Lord."[52]

To be sure, the growing commercializing of American society did exert a gradually more obvious influence on such Protestant writing. The Panic of 1857–1858 elicited a weaker dose of Protestant moralism than had the Panic of 1837; the Businessmen's Revival of 1857–1858 scrupulously avoided the kind of stern injunctions about the misuse of money that had once been more common; and by the 1850s market-savvy treatises on "Systematic Benevolence" revealed the growing influence of commercial reasoning on church practice.[53] Yet even during the 1850s, the basic Protestant stance remained an uncomplicated acceptance of commercial society alongside an extraordinary elaboration of scruple as to how the wealth engendered by modern commerce should be used. The religious contribution to this combination could be explained, in Marx's terms, as one of those "bourgeois prejudices, behind which lurk in ambush just as many bourgeois interests."[54] It is more in keeping with actual developments of America's religious history, however, to explain that contribution as a continuation of historic Christian, Protestant, and Calvinist attitudes as they were adjusted to an American social setting where Protestants had mostly given up aspirations for establishmentarian control.

Better understanding of the influence of market reasoning on religious thought arises from attending to the great religious transformations of the era: the rise of evangelicalism and the abandonment of church-state establishment. For economic concerns, the spread of evangelicalism and disestablishment were factors in the new nation's embrace of the market. A move away from top-down monarchical, hierarchical, and colonial control in religion predisposed many evangelicals in the same direction economically, that is, toward localism and free trade. As antiestablishment evangelicals, these Protestants rejected close regulation of the public spaces in which they hoped to promote their religion, and they were predisposed in favor of situations where individuals could make the choice for God freely. They were also confident in the Spirit-given ability to persuade free agents to close with Christ. Such convictions about religion could only predispose many American evangelicals toward corresponding values in economic practice, including an acceptance of market reasoning.

At the same time, however, evangelicals retained a great deal of hereditary Protestant nervousness about the accumulation of wealth, suspicion about the seductive power of money, and caution about the corrupting influences of economic power.[55] For renovators of Protestantism, there was no contradiction in carrying some of these historic reservations about the accumulation of money into the much looser social environment of Revolutionary and early national America.

The nature of the era's evangelical religion also affected religious-economic connections. European Protestants, who for the most part maintained the ideal of Christendom, regularly thought in terms of all-encompassing models of life-as-a-whole, including economics, But since the United States' disestablishmentarian evangelicals had given up earlier ideals of Christendom, they often found themselves reacting to changes and circumstances in the economic arena over which their religious ancestors had once tried to exert self-conscious control. In their choice for voluntary spiritual suasion, they set aside self-conscious attention to the structures of society. American evangelicals largely stopped trying to construct complete worldviews; in practice, their pietism drove them to a functional division of life into a sacred sphere, which received comprehensive and self-conscious attention, and a secular sphere, which did not.[56] The pietistic instincts of disestablishmentarian evangelicals put them in the position of seeking the transformation of persons and society through revival. Increasingly in the early years of the nineteenth century, these evangelicals were successful beyond hope. Yet by limiting the goals of their activity, the evangelicals also increased the likelihood that dimensions of society they now neglected would influence them unself-consciously.

Disestablishment evangelicals were historical actors who held some of their convictions together loosely. They did not feel compelled to construct grand schemes of economic life under God. They maintained traditional reservations about the entrapping power of money. And they eagerly exploited new market conditions. Such a combination may look incoherent or mystifying to modern interpreters. It was, however, the end point to which the evangelical and disestablishmentarian transformations of the eighteenth century had led a majority of American Protestants by early in the next century. As a consequence, market reasoning never exerted the role in theology that was exercised by republican political commitments or the principles of common-sense moral philosophy, the belief systems that did establish organic bonds with religious life. The latter, rather than the former, are most useful for describing the distinctly American theologies that emerged in the first decades of the nineteenth century.

IV

AMERICANIZATION

New England divinity has been marked by strong, practical common sense. Its framers were remarkable men, invigorated by the scenes of an eventful era, and claiming our deference for their love of plain, wholesome truth.... Our later theologians ... were adepts in the philosophy of Reid, Oswald, Campbell, Beattie, Stewart; and this has been termed the philosophy of common sense. *The tendency of literature, during the last hundred years, has been to develop "the fundamental laws of human belief," and has aided our writers in shaping their faith according to those ethical axioms which so many fathers in the church have undervalued.... There has never been a more independent class of thinkers than our Edwardean theologians. They lived under a free government of church and state.... The metaphysics of New England Theology is such as the yeomen of our fields drank down for the sincere milk of the word. It is the metaphysics of common sense.... The New England system is not only scriptural, but is scriptural* science.

—E. A. Park, "New England Theology," 1852

12

Assumptions and Assertions of American Theology

When Thomas Jefferson held out the olive branch to political foes in his 1801 presidential inaugural by saying, "We are all republicans . . . we are all federalists," he was not thinking about theology. Yet Jefferson's effort to conciliate what political strife had sundered may actually have spoken more accurately for the course of American theology than for American politics. While Jefferson's vision of political harmony was never more than imperfectly realized, American theology was in fact blending a federal aspect and a republican aspect. Continuing through and beyond the Revolution was the powerful biblical theme of covenant (Latin *foedus,* hence "federal"), which had been the central organizing device for the New England Puritans and which also figured in the theologies of other colonial Protestants. Although the integrating power of the Puritans' covenant had collapsed more than a half century before 1800, traditional beliefs about God as the ruler of the universe, humans as responsible moral agents before God, and events as reflecting the disposing hand of providence were maintained vigorously in the new nation. At the same time, American theology was speedily becoming republican. Even as Jefferson spoke in March 1801, the unexpected alliance between Protestant theology and republican politics was advancing with gathering force. The newer Christian republicanism did not repudiate the covenantal past so much as it appropriated selected elements of that past for more distinctly American purposes.[1]

Of course there never was a single American theology, in this or any other period. But especially during the early decades of the nineteenth century, the rapid expansion of the country in combination with the rapid expansion of the churches produced a bewildering appearance of theological diversity. Women, who were almost never regarded as theologians per se, and men, who monopolized almost all formal religious discourse, developed characteristically alternative approaches to religious thought.[2] Class and race produced even stronger disjunctions. The religious discourse of ordinary people remained much more fatalistic, supernaturalist, providentialist—and so in some sense more Calvinist—than the discourse of learned elites who published books and articles.[3] Black religious language differed systematically from white, particularly by employing tropes of liberty literally instead of metaphorically. Creative antiformalists also differed substantially from conservative formalists, and those who sought direct concourse with God ("enthusiasts") produced different theological emphases than those who were content with mediations of the divine presence. As they competed for souls in settled and frontier regions, the denominations developed distinctive doctrines.[4] In addition, geography mattered, with different theological preoccupations dominating New England, the New York–Philadelphia corridor, the urban South, and the opening West. Ethnic communities seasoned their religion with a full range of influences from the old world. And the sum of theological positions was multiplied many times over by the particular considerations of particular individuals speaking out of their own particular times and places. It is this tremendous explosion of individualized, creative, ever-restless, earnest, word-infatuated religious talking and writing that makes any effort at comprehensive theological history so difficult for this period.

Yet even with a great welter of energetic diversity, theology in America from the Revolution to the Civil War shared a great deal more than buzzing confusion. Until the very end of this period, almost all public religious talk in the United States was Christian, even Protestant. Jews and free thinking skeptics were present, but in such small numbers as to remain more important for what came later than for what existed then. Roman Catholic theology was taking shape rapidly from the 1820s, but it remained a thing apart—oriented by Catholic leaders to their separated communities, fenced in by the high walls of Protestant and republican antipapalism, and self-consciously tied to the teachings of the Roman hierarchy. American Protestants were also unified in general terms by common beliefs about religious experience. To be sure, by the early years of the century, serious debate was well begun about what it meant to experience God directly, but almost everyone still believed in the possibility of such experience.[5] The nation's believers also interpreted the Bible with all manner of innovative creativity, and yet Scripture still supplied a common coin for America's multiform religious realms. In a word, it was an expansive period, but with still a relatively cohesive set of widely shared theological convictions and intellectual practices.

With necessary qualifications having been made, it can be asserted that in the early nineteenth century, American theology as a whole was changing rapidly from what it had been in the mid-eighteenth century. It can also be asserted that the most important reason for change was the participation of religious thinkers in the broader movements of American history.

The circumstances that had joined themes of Calvinism to the themes of classical republicanism in the age of Edwards and Whitefield, that had enlisted religious communities in support of the War for Independence, and that then made evangelical Protestants so important in creating an American national culture eventually exerted their influence on formal theology. Not the least important result of change was to render the intellectual assumptions of Edwards and Whitefield foreign to most Americans of the early nineteenth century. The key to understanding such broad developments is to realize that almost all of America's most prominent religious thinkers wanted to preserve the vocabulary of Christianity as an essential part of the language of America. By adopting the conceptual framework of republicanism, theologians ensured that Christian concerns would color the ideology of the Revolution. By then salting republican commitments with the principles of liberal democracy, they guaranteed that Protestant theology would exert a powerful influence on early national America.

America's Christian theologians wanted very much to see people converted, to make their society godly, and to show the rest of the world how the unique blend of Protestant evangelicalism and republican democracy could open the way to the millennium. To reach these goals it was necessary to speak persuasively, to witness with power. For their appeal, the theologians needed a language that could persuade their fellow Americans. Because of a long tradition of interconceptual borrowing between the languages of theology and the languages of public life, it had become second nature to make these appeals in the terms of the dominant public discourse. But since ideologies embedded in cultures have a historical logic of their own, there is scant surprise that as theologians embraced the language of commonsense republican democracy, commonsense republican democracy transformed the expressions of theology.

This chapter and the ones that follow outline the character of that transformation. We begin here with the general situation and then move to more specific considerations, first, of the elite Presbyterians and Congregationalists, who, despite falling far behind Methodists and Baptists in total adherents, continued to dominate formal religious thought; and then of the proliferating Methodists, whose theology underwent a remarkably rapid evolution in the three-quarters of a century between the foundation of the denomination in 1784 and the outbreak of the Civil War.[6] No simple formula can adequately account for the processes of Americanization (and, occasionally, anti-Americanization) at work among these active religious thinkers. Yet general trends were still moving unmistakably in the direction of adjusting inherited religious convictions to the circumstances of the new republic.

Convictions and Assumptions

By the 1790s American habits of mind were beginning to make an obvious difference in propositions about God, human nature, the way of salvation, and other Christian teachings. The contrast between two Connecticut Congregationalists who were both touched by Old Calvinist and New Divinity currents illustrates the progression. James Dana (1735–1812) of Wallingford emerged in the years before the Revolution as the most serious opponent of Jonathan Edwards's account of the human will. Dana's most important reason for disputing Edwards bore the mark of the new moral philosophy: "Let a man look into his own breast, and he cannot but perceive inward freedom—*inward freedom*—For if freedom be not in the *mind*, it is no where. And liberty in the mind implies self-determination." In the heat of the Revolution, Dana was also an effective advocate for the notion that the patriots' republicanism resembled "that of the Hebrews" and was "the only form of government expressly instituted by heaven."[7] Yet despite accepting the republican and commonsense norms that were advancing so rapidly throughout America, Dana's own theological convictions remained mostly traditional. He did not oppose Edwards on the will for reasons drawn from contemporary ideologies. Rather, he held that Edwards's teaching misconstrued the nature of human motives, probed into divine mysteries that should be left alone, and promoted antinomian subversion of the Puritan ideal of an established church-in-society.[8]

With Timothy Dwight (1752–1817) of Greenfield and then New Haven, who was Dana's junior by less than two decades, theological construction proceeded along other paths. Although much in Dwight remained traditional, it was precisely the embrace of newer American norms that best explains his theological innovations. By the turn of the century, Dwight was suggesting that people knew God's benevolence intuitively: the conclusion that God was good came as "the unavoidable dictate of the intellect; of the conscience and understanding." Likewise, it had become second nature for him to describe divine-human relationships with a vocabulary from Francis Hutcheson that combined republican convictions about liberty with notions about the moral sense: God's rule "is a government by motives, addressed to the understanding and affections of rational subjects, and operating on their minds as inducements to voluntary obedience. No other government is worthy of God: there being, indeed, no other, beside that of mere force and coercion."[9] In Dwight's case, these Americanized commitments were linked organically to his theological convictions: that sinfulness came only from sinning itself and not from a hereditary bond with Adam, that salvation required concentrated human activity alongside the gracious action of the Holy Spirit, that Christ's death restored the balance of the moral universe (he did not pay a debt owed by sinners to God), and that God willed the ultimate happiness of sinners as the chief end of the universe.[10]

A similar bond between American commitments and theological expression appeared after the turn of the century in the opening West among the Restorationists, who were otherwise so much opposed to what Dwight stood for. Theirs was a form of Christianity in which themes from the national culture loomed large, as, for example, the republican scorn for inherited authority. That scorn was expressed memorably by two of Barton W. Stone's Restorationist colleagues, Robert Marshall and J. Thompson, who were quarreling with Stone when a third party reprimanded them for disregarding the treasured insights of Calvin and other venerable theologians on questions of salvation and church order. Their reply was classic: "We are not personally acquainted with the writings of John Calvin, nor are we certain how nearly we agree with his views of divine truth; neither do we care."[11] For these Restorationists, a republican understanding of intellectual independence was joined naturally to commonsense confidence in their own ability to understand the Bible in the raw. That combination, in turn, laid the foundation for their ecclesiastical *novus ordo seclorum*, the distinctive Restorationist conviction that the new "Churches of Christ" were simple replications of the churches of the New Testament.[12]

After the turn of the new century, traditionalists also testified to the power of the new American theologies, for the early decades of the nineteenth century witnessed the self-conscious retrieval of old-world norms in order to stand against the onslaught of specifically American innovations. John Henry Hobart and J. W. Nevin were examples of such theologians who testified to the prominence of explicitly American influences by the pains they took to repudiate them. In Hobart's case, it was necessary to affirm the historic authority of the bishops of the Episcopal Church in order to secure true religion against America's ever-proliferating alternatives. For Nevin, who fled Presbyterianism for the German Reformed Church, it was necessary to reassert the power of the sacraments that Americans had discarded in their rage for self-sufficiency.[13] Evidence for the existence of distinctly American theologies accumulated rapidly in the new nation's first decades.

To be sure, American religious thinkers in the early nineteenth century still professed much that earlier theologians also held. Almost all still maintained that humans were sinners in need of salvation, and they continued, with only isolated exceptions like Ralph Waldo Emerson, to think that salvation was provided by God in Jesus Christ. Yet they were much more likely than before to hold that the human will was an active, necessary, and determinative participant in the reception of divine grace, that the human mind played a decisive role in determining the reality of both natural and supernatural phenomena, and that personal apprehension and action were more important than traditional, mediated, or historic authorities in determining the nature of Christian truth.[14] With their Protestant predecessors, American theologians of the early nineteenth century continued to treat the Scriptures as a uniquely inspired revelation from God that provided essential explanations, motives, and guides for life. Much more than their Protestant predecessors, however, they also held that the Bible was the only reliable source of religious authority and that personally appropriated understanding of Scripture was the only reliable means of interpretation. American theologians remained traditionally Christian in beliefs about divine providence. They were, however, less likely to stand in awe of God's mysterious powers and more likely to assume that they could know and adapt themselves clearly, simply, and directly to the ways of God. Finally, American theologians continued to describe the church as the people of God, but they tended to speak instinctively of the church as constructed by those who constituted it rather than as an inheritance from saints of former generations.

The continuity between American theologians of this period and those who had gone before was manifest in the full use of Scripture they employed to propound their doctrines. It was also seen in the traditional language they maintained to describe the Trinity, the person of Christ as both human and divine, the sinful character of humanity, and the activity of God in redeeming sinners. Discontinuities appeared when the vocabulary they had learned in the heat of American experience came to the fore, that is, when they put to use words like benevolence, common sense, conscience, consciousness, freedom, government, interest, justice, power, primitive, reason, science, simple, virtue, or (as negative references) tradition and vice. The appearance of such language almost always signaled new or modified constructions of Christian teaching.

The evolution of theology in America involved differences in underlying assumptions even more than in convictions as such. The nature of those altered assumptions can be illustrated as readily with popularizers as with the learned. George Whitefield, the most popular evangelical communicator in America during the mid-eighteenth century, and Harriet Beecher Stowe, America's most popular evangelical communicator in the mid-nineteenth century, shared much in their religion, as well as in their ability to sway the public at large. But they were also divided by a transformation in assumptions about the character of human experience. Whitefield never deviated from his Augustinian conviction that sinners could do nothing to change their condition until God initiated the work of redemption. For him, the principles of traditional Calvinism—including assertions about the bondage of the human will to its own sinful desires—could be read plainly, not only in the Bible, but also in the human conscience. As he put it in 1741, if the principles of Calvinism are troubling, "Search the Scriptures; search your Experiences." Or again, "Experience, as well as Scripture proves, that we . . . are altogether born in Sin and Corruption, and therefore uncapable, whilst in such a State, to hold Communion with God."[15] Less than a century later, Harriet Beecher Stowe pondered the same question—were sinners entirely helpless until God touched them with his grace? Her affirmation of a natural power of moral action betrayed a revolution in assumptions about human capacity: "If we *know* that we have power to do all that God requires—if we *feel* that we have— nay, more, if we are so made that we never can *help* feeling it—what matter is it if we cannot see *how* it is."[16]

To explain such a shift in assumptions, it is necessary to observe the larger domains in which American religious discourse took place. Whitefield was instrumental in creating the distinctly American idioms that played out in the century after his death, and Stowe, as the child of an unusually prominent early nineteenth-century Congregationalist manse, absorbed those idioms with her mother's milk. But because of larger American events between the time of Whitefield and the time of Stowe, their idioms were not the same.

The assumptions and assertions of American theology were manifest in many ways and in many spheres. In the rest of this chapter we observe how they operated to fuel the appeal to common sense, to provide powerful warrants for debate, and to generate scattered opposition against the movement of Americanization.

The Appeal of Theistic Common Sense

During the early nineteenth century, common sense took on unusual theological importance, for both negative and positive reasons. In Perry Miller's phrase, "Consciousness . . . is a magic word in the early republic."[17] Negatively, common sense was one of the few authorities that survived the Revolutionary assault on inherited privilege. Positively, common sense opened up whole realms of verifiable knowledge to ordinary men (and sometimes women) who had previously been considered incapable of discerning truth for themselves. In such a climate, religious thinkers tailored the presentation of Christianity to the perceptions of free, personally empowered citizens. It was becoming intuitive to think that persuasion should be based on what swayed men who made up their own minds. Influence, interests, factional prejudices, loyalty to the clan, respect for experts, the sacredness of traditional churches, even deference to parents—all had been compromised by the intellectual history of the American founding. What remained was the apprehension and deployment of facts—from observation, the deliverances of conscience, critical study of the past, and the transparently plain meanings of Scripture. Common sense meant something different depending on whether it was applied in the technical discussions of publishing scholars or asserted in the rough-and-ready of plebeian debate. Yet almost everyone agreed with what Timothy Dwight told generations of Yale students: common sense was "the most valuable faculty . . . of man." Most also would have gone alone with Dwight in asserting that "our Saviour treats every subject in the direct manner of Common Sense."[18] Appeals to common sense at all levels also rested on republican assumptions about the corruption of inherited power as well as the confidence of the new moral philosophy in what could be gained from exploring consciousness.

If the discourse of republican common sense was bleeding over into religious discourse, that exchange of rhetorical attributes was part of a larger history. The United States existed as a separate nation because of the persuasive power of republican and commonsense instincts; the Christian believers of the new United States were instrumental in creating a viable national culture; the churches demonstrated their importance for the national project by first embracing the founding ideology and then making it work. The resort by religious thinkers to principles of common sense was anything but a random conceit of the ivory tower.

Commonsense habits of mind that were axiomatic by the first third of the nineteenth century represented a series of overlapping intellectual commonplaces.[19] First was an *ethical* common sense, or the assertion that just as humans know intuitively some basic realities about the physical world, so they may know certain foundational principles of morality by reflecting on their own consciousness. Second was *epistemological* common sense. It was the assertion that under normal conditions, when regulated carefully, human sense impressions revealed the world pretty much as it was. For those versed in formal philosophy this assertion was rooted in Locke but modified by the Scottish school, especially Thomas Reid, to eliminate the confusing mediation of "ideas." The significance of this axiom for theology lay in the conviction that impressions from "the moral sense" and simple ideas from the Bible revealed the moral universe as accurately as impressions from the physical senses revealed the physical world. The third commonplace was a *methodological* common sense, or the assertion that truths about consciousness, the physical world, and religion could be authoritatively built by strict induction from the irreducible facts of experience. In America, this methodological common sense drew strength from the high reputation of Francis Bacon and the stellar achievements of Sir Isaac Newton.

All such commonsense assumptions betrayed the conviction that inherited authority was easily turned to intellectual despotism. Tradition and history, even Christian tradition and Christian history, would have to pass the test of common sense in order to survive in the new American republic. Once having passed that test, however, Christian convictions became an engine of great power in a culture marked by its forward-looking ideology as well as by its widely disbursed remnants of Christendom.

For Protestant leaders in the early republic, Christianized common sense was a godsend. A modern, vigorous defense of the faith was the very thing required for the flourishing of Christianity in the new polity. The American War for Independence differed from the later Revolution in France in part because American Protestants aligned faith in reason with, rather than against, faith in God. The great goal of Protestants in the struggle against the irreligion and disorder of the Revolutionary period was, as John Witherspoon put it in lectures at Princeton, "to meet [infidels] upon their own ground, and to show them from reason itself, the fallacy of their principles."[20] In the 1790s and for several decades thereafter, Protestants relied heavily on the imported apologetics of William Paley to secure their case.[21] Paley's *View of the Evidences of Christianity* (1794) and *Natural Theology* (1802) were welcome because they defended belief in God the creator by appealing to what careful observers could conclude about what they themselves saw in the natural world.

Soon, however, Americans began to develop their own defenses for Christianity; as they did so, they drew even more directly on the principles and methods of theistic common sense. Timothy Dwight became famous for his courage in restoring a lively Christian faith at Yale after his accession as president in 1795. At least as the story came down to later generations, Dwight attacked specifically the charge made by infidel students that "Christianity was supported by authority, and not by argument." In the face of this challenge, Dwight boldly called all comers to debate the question, Are the Scriptures of the Old and New Testaments the Word of God? After appealing for those who doubted the Scriptures to "collect and bring forward all the facts and arguments which they could produce," Dwight "triumphantly refuted their arguments[,] proved to them that their statement of facts was mistaken or ir-relevant," and by "the exposure of argument" recovered the ground for full-blown Christianity.[22]

At the largely Presbyterian College of New Jersey in Princeton, Dwight's contemporary Samuel Stanhope Smith proceeded with slightly less bombast, but along much the same lines. His lectures to students on Christian evidences defined theology as "the science of divine truth." He offered to them "evidence" in order that "our faith may not be merely an enthusiastic and visionary confidence, but a rational offering to truth and reason." He defended the existence of "a Supreme and Intelligent Cause of the universe" as "an intuitive dictate of the understanding." And he elaborated at length on how "the truth of christianity" rested on "evidences which propose themselves directly to the senses, or arise out of the known and immutable laws of human nature."[23]

It was roughly the same at Unitarian Harvard, where the definitive text in this period was Levi Hedge's *Elements of Logick*, a work that grafted Scottish moral philosophy onto New England's traditional concern for intellectual and social order. For Hedge, human reasoning arose from evidence that could be classified as "intuitive," "demonstrative," or "moral." Demonstrative persuasion meant a careful use of deduction and was least important. Moral evidence came from judging the deliverances of sense about the external world and dealt with "matters of fact." Intuitive evidence supplied the most important knowledge about the world and was foundational for all higher understanding. It came from "the evidence of *sense*, of *consciousness*, of *memory*, and of *axioms*, or *general principles*." Of these intuitive sources, the most important was consciousness, which "informs us of our various passions, affections, and mental operations—the whole science of the human mind is built on this evidence; and no branch of knowledge stands on a surer foundation."[24]

For Hedge, as well as for Dwight and Smith, knowledge, especially knowledge of God, had to be pursued carefully. But it was fundamentally the responsibility of individual selves to acquire, judge, and employ that knowledge. Mediation from other authorities did not play a major role for any of these early American apologists. For the purpose of foundational intellectual demonstration, they had dispensed with the Augustinian division of humanity into those enlightened by God and those remaining in the darkness of their sin. That distinction, only two short generations previously, had been critical for the moral reasoning of Jonathan Edwards and Samuel Johnson.

Christian apologetics grounded in common sense rapidly developed into a flourishing of what T. D. Bozeman has helpfully described as Baconian theology.[25] In divinity, a rigorous empiricism resting on facts of consciousness and facts from the Bible became the standard for justifying belief in God, revelation, and the Trinity. In ethics, similar empirical procedures marked out the royal road to moral certainty. The same procedures also provided a key for using physical science itself as a demonstration of religious truths.[26] In every case the appeal was, as Stanhope Smith put it in 1810, "to the evidence

of facts, and to conclusions resulting from these facts which . . . every genuine disciple of nature will acknowledge to be legitimately drawn from her
own fountain."[27] Among theologically articulate Protestants in the early republic, this approach had first been tested in arguments against Tom Paine's
notorious *Age of Reason* in the 1790s. Nothing worked better at squelching
the deism that Paine promoted, said Presbyterian layman Elias Boudinot, than
simply "the rules of common sense."[28] "Supernatural rationalism" of this sort
became especially useful for counteracting the impious use of science; it made
possible the harmonization of first the Bible and astronomy, and then later
Scripture and geology.[29]

So basic did this reasoning become that even self-consciously traditional
Protestants had no qualms about resting the edifice of their faith on the principles of theistic mental science. The conservative Presbyterians at Princeton
Seminary loved to pounce on the theological innovations of their contemporaries. Yet Princeton's founding professor, Archibald Alexander, told first-
year students year by year what very few theologians of any stripe would have
dared assert less than a century before: "To prove that our faculties are not so
constituted as to misguide us, some have had recourse to the *goodness* and
truth of God, our creator, but this argument is unnecessary. We are as certain
of these intuitive truths as we can be. . . . Besides, we must be sure that we
exist, and that the world exists, before we can be certain that there is a God,
for it is from these *data* that we prove his existence."[30]

The domain of commonsense theism eventually comprehended even the
activity of the Holy Spirit. The push, even in a realm where the mysterious
workings of an all-powerful God had once been taken for granted, was toward a scientific predictability accessible to inquiring minds. Charles G.
Finney, the best-known public Protestant in the decades before the Civil War,
did not speak for all Christians, but the elements of commonsense rationality
in his picture of revivalism suggest how pervasive its principles had become.
Finney's *Lectures on Revivals of Religion* (1835), which is discussed at greater
length below in chapter 15, was important for summarizing a new approach
toward reaching the lost. Since God had established reliable laws in the natural world and since humans were created with the ability to discern those laws,
it was obvious that the spiritual world worked on the same basis. Thus, to
activate the proper causes for revivals was to produce the proper effects: "The
connection between the right use of means for a revival and a revival is as
philosophically [i.e., scientifically] sure as between the right use of means to
raise grain and a crop of wheat. I believe, in fact, it is more certain, and there
are fewer instances of failure."[31] Because the world spiritual was analogous
to the world natural, observable cause and effect must work in religion as well
as in physics. The wine of revival—confidence in God's supernatural ability
to convert the sinner—may have looked the same in antebellum America as
it had in earlier centuries, but the wineskin was of recent manufacture.

Reliance on the principles of theistic mental science altered the trajectory
of orthodox Protestant theology in at least two ways. It substituted a measure
of confidence in natural human powers for traditional Protestant suspicions

about what humans could know by nature without God's aid. It also made confidence in human intuitions and the human ability to construe the data of experience, rather than confidence in the being and revelatory acts of God, the foundation for knowledge about the world and about God. This alteration did not take place to the same degree in other historic Protestant regions. But it did take place in the United States, where Americanized habits of mind guided arguments about the Christian faith, even as they shaped the positive articulation of Christian teaching.

The result for religious thinking was not that the theologians of the nineteenth century relied upon widely shared intellectual assumptions, where those of the eighteenth century had not. The result, rather, was that the self-evident deliverances of consciousness were moving theology in new directions. The next three chapters offer a capsule history of Calvinist theology for the three-quarters of a century after the Constitution, but here it is important to underscore the fact that intuitive consciousness was revealing different realities to the generation of Charles Finney than it had disclosed to the generation of Jonathan Edwards.

Edwards had believed that human willing always reflected the religious character of the person, especially the person's relationship with God. By contrast, the great Congregational theologians three generations later—Horace Bushnell, Charles Finney, and N. W. Taylor, all of whom otherwise honored Edwards's memory—held that human will possessed a contrary power to act against the acquired dispositions of character and so could precipitate a change of status before God. Yet the gulf that had grown up over the generations was more evident for what was simply assumed to be the nature of things than it was even for this specific doctrine. For Edwards, "it is in a manner *self-evident*, that there can be no act of will, choice or preference of the mind, without some motive or inducement . . . ; so, *'tis manifest*, there is no such liberty in the universe as Arminians insist on; nor any such thing possible, or conceivable."[32] A century later, habits of mind had changed. For the Hartford pastor Horace Bushnell, simply to note "what *consciousness* testifies" was enough to refute Edwards's belief "that human action is determined uniformly by the strongest motive." Similarly, as Charles Finney saw the world, "*Every one knows with intuitive certainty* that he has no ability to do what he is unable to will to do. . . . The human mind *necessarily assumes* the freedom of the human will as a first truth. . . . [I]n all cases *the assumption* has lain deep in the mind as a first truth, that men are free in the sense of being able to obey God." For his part, N. W. Taylor, the Dwight Professor of Theology at Yale, held that "the *practical belief* of mankind . . . *the decision of common sense*" was that "there can be no sin, or sinfulness, except wrong voluntary action."[33]

Again, Edwards had held that true virtue could exist only among those who experienced the Holy Spirit's regenerating grace. But the Congregationalists of the nineteenth century were joined by most Presbyterians in believing that genuine virtue was best described in relation to a moral sense present universally in all humanity. Here as well, the movement in assumptions was just as important as the movement of doctrine. On the question of virtue, Edwards, after briefly clarifying his terms, had affirmed, "'*tis evident*, that true virtue must chiefly consist in love to God."[34] A century later, for Lyman Atwater of Princeton Seminary, it was "simply part of *the nature of things*" to postulate a universal character to virtue like that belonging to "beauty, truth or happiness."[35] The gap that divided Edwards from his successors was not only a difference in conviction. Even more it was a difference in what could be assumed to be the case about God, humanity, and the human condition. To understand how that gap emerged, it is vital to note the place—and the movement—of commonsense moral reasoning as it developed through an eventful century of American events.

Persuasive Warrants in Disputes

The importance of distinctly American forms of theological reasoning was illustrated sharply in many of the religious conflicts of the national era. When proponents of different forms of Christian or secular faith clashed, they marshaled warrants as soldiers for intellectual battle. These warrants came from far and wide. Many were traditional, and so the American landscape rang with arguments that had been heard of old in Europe as Protestants battled Catholics, immersionists took on pedo-Baptists, and Congregationalists joined Presbyterians and Episcopalians in three-cornered ecclesiological conflict.

Yet with older, customary arbiters came also arguments that took their shape from American circumstances. The latter added distinctly American elements to the construction of theological positions. The way in which newer American warrants were enlisted alongside traditional arguments is well illustrated in the important religious disputes of the period, which together offer revealing insights about the character of religious thought in the early American nation.[36] Even sketchy examination of these disputes shows how prominent the weight of the new commonsense republican synthesis had become.

Episcopalians versus Presbyterians

Among the first serious interconfessional wars embroiling the new nation's formalist churches was the reprise of an issue already much contested in Anglo-American Protestant history. The issue was ecclesiology. In the early nineteenth century the question came again to the foreground, primarily through the enterprising energy of John Henry Hobart (1775–1830).[37] Hobart, a Philadelphia-born Episcopalian, had attended the College of Philadelphia and the College of New Jersey at Princeton, where he was exposed to the era's standard reliance on Scottish commonsense philosophy. But that training did not leave as deep a mark as his own study into the distinctive teachings of the Anglican tradition. As he rose rapidly as a leader of the American church—trustee of Columbia College in 1801, founder of several Episcopal voluntary societies over the next decade, assistant bishop in 1811, bishop in 1816—Hobart also ventured into print on what he considered the unique excellences of

Episcopal church order. His predilection toward the historic episcopacy was fueled by his awareness of strife in Britain, where from 1798 traditionalists battled openly against what they considered the unfortunate incursion into their church of revivalism, individualism, enthusiasm, and evangelical Calvinism. Taking his cue from these defenders of a nearly divine-right Anglicanism, Hobart began to publicize works of the English high-church party in America and to contribute his own offerings supporting historic Christianity as he understood it. The latter included two *Companion*s published in 1804 as guides to devotion, meditation, and church practice. The *Companion*s were classically Protestant in stressing the activity of Christ as redeemer from sin. But they were also notably deferential to the past, as when Hobart, in his *Companion to the Altar*, reminded Episcopalian readers how important it was to maintain "communion with the church by devout submission to the ministrations of its priesthood."[38] Hobart's promotion of such a spiritual vision was assisted by several other able publicists, including Frederick Beasley, an Episcopal priest who served for fifteen years as head of the University of Pennsylvania, and the lawyer Thomas Yardley How, a talented advocate for his denomination. Against the background of the new national culture emerging in the United States, the insistence by such capable spokesmen that genuine Christianity required organic deference to the historic episcopate could only be a provocation.

The Christian groups most offended by high-church Episcopacy were the Reformed, who otherwise shared so much with the Episcopalians—upper-middle-class social location, strength in the New York–Philadelphia corridor and up the Hudson River Valley, commitment to collegiate education, nervousness about the democratic excesses of "the people," and confidence in their own tradition's interpretation of the Scriptures. The predictable response to the moves by Hobart and his high-church colleagues was led by Samuel Miller (1769–1850), a rising Presbyterian star in New York City; John Mitchell Mason (1770–1829), the leading minister of the Scottish-connected Associate Reformed Church, who also actively promoted panevangelical voluntary societies; and William Linn (1752–1808), a minister in the Dutch Reformed church who had been the first chaplain of the United States House of Representatives and later an ardent foe, for religious reasons, of Thomas Jefferson in the presidential election of 1800. After Hobart's two *Companion*s were published in 1804, these three led the charge in reasserting the superiority of the Presbyterians' church order of elders, ministers, and graduated assemblies over the Episcopalians' priests, bishops, and convocations.

For the most part, old-world values wrote the script of this new-world argument. Reformed writers used the Bible to support their conclusions and eagerly pointed out where Episcopalian authorities contradicted themselves, while Hobart with his friends responded in kind. Yet even as these learned antagonists reprised arguments from the tumultuous English clashes of the 1580s, the 1640s, and the 1720s, they also inserted material with a contemporary flavor.

Hobart, for example, did not hide his belief that "Antiquity" demanded respect as a critical aid for interpreting the Scriptures. Yet he also wanted to

claim that "Common sense . . . indignantly rejects the supposition that Episcopacy is an *innovation* or *usurpation*."[39] At least to his own satisfaction, he
also felt he could show that the American Episcopal Church followed generally republican principles by electing its bishops and by allowing the lower
clergy and laity to legislate alongside the bishops.[40]

Predictably, however, it was the Reformed who made readier use of ideological warrants from American experience. In a series of newspaper articles
that sparked intense controversy, pro and con, William Linn gleefully bashed
away with weapons of American manufacture. Presbyterian church government was not just "the true and only one which Christ hath prescribed in his
word," but it was also the form of church government "best adapted to the
temper of the United States and the most conformable to their institutions of
civil government." By contrast, Episcopalianism flourished only "under
Monarchies," Episcopalians could never show anyone where the principles
of their system "are *written*," and they favored practices that were maintained
by no one else except "the Roman Catholics."[41]

Samuel Miller's shafts were subtler, but some of them were just as dependent upon an American vocabulary. Miller began his first major attack on the
high-church party by insisting on the individual character of religion: "Every
man is required to examine, to believe, and to obey the gospel for himself."
Presbyterianism conformed to "apostolic and primitive order," and it mirrored
"the simplicity that is in Christ." High-church episcopal claims, by contrast,
represented "corruptions of apostolic simplicity," they were "of a nature allied to the doctrine of Papal infallibility," and they did not fit well in a polity
where "equal rights and privileges are enjoyed by all."[42] In other contributions to the fray, Miller recommended Presbyterianism because it acknowledged that "the representative principle is a most important one in the constitution of the christian church." He was also at pains to contrast the nonfactional
patriotism of the founders of the Presbyterians' General Assembly with the
party-driven Loyalism of those who had established the American Episcopal
Church.[43]

Hobart and his associates held their own against such onslaughts, but they
were swimming against the tide. As it happened, Presbyterian opposition to
high-church pretensions that seemed to violate republican norms of power,
history, or authority was reinforced by resistance from some Episcopalians
to high-church arguments. As Hobart was defending his principles, an even
stronger movement within his church, guided by rising rectors like Charles
Petit McIlvaine (1799–1873), was moving in a low-church, explicitly anti-
Catholic, quasi-republican, and wholeheartedly evangelical direction.[44] Its
sentiments were well represented by the prominent Episcopal layman William Jay, who was appalled that Hobart and his friends were creating separate
Episcopalian organizations paralleling the Bible, tract, and missionary societies of the more ecumenical evangelicals. In 1815 Jay blasted Hobart's defense of his Episcopal Bible and Common Prayer Book Society for implying
that the Bible's "lucid order" and "embellished simplicity" required authoritarian interpretation, for issuing his own pronouncements as if they were a

"papal bull," and for moving Episcopalians along lines suspiciously similar to "the early stages of Papal usurpation."[45] To Jay and his party among the Episcopalians, the Reformed polemicists were right to be nervous. Many of the worries of the anti-high-church publicists merely repeated what British and American Dissenters had been saying for a very long time about divine-right Anglicans. But some of their worries were being expressed in a new vocabulary that drew its strength from recent American circumstances.

Elias Smith contra mundum

To Elias Smith (1769–1846), one of the era's most irrepressible polemicists, refined, learned dispute over church government, from wherever it came, was a sham. The fundamental problem of the new American nation, considered religiously or politically, was the arrogance of power. On that score there was for Smith not a dime's worth of difference between Samuel Miller and John Henry Hobart. Through a life of energetic peripateticism (from Lyme, Connecticut, to Vermont and then Portsmouth, New Hampshire, later to Boston, Philadelphia, Providence, and Portland, Maine), as well as frequent redirection of career (as minister—successively Baptist, "Christian," Universalist, and "Christian" again—physician, dentist, publisher, and merchant), and in the midst of incessant polemical creativity, one thing remained constant for Elias Smith. His anchor was unshakable belief in a radically egalitarian biblicism. If the religion of formalist Presbyterians and Episcopalians was tinctured with American values, Smith's religion represented a more complete assimilation. That religion was, in the words of a solid recent biography, "a specifically Christian republicanism growing out of a New Light evangelical heritage, conjoined with a rapidly evolving national political culture in a climate of strident partisan conflict."[46] Smith was especially important as a founder of New England's "Christian" movement, a radically antielitist drive that sought a harmonious, unified church for all who wished to live according to the New Testament's "perfect law of liberty." To build such a church, however, it was necessary to clear away traditional biblical interpretations, traditional denominations, and traditional clerical authority.[47]

Smith's many polemics against inherited, learned, or conferred authority—which he abbreviated as "Anti-Christ"—were constructed from his striking knowledge of the Scriptures and an ardent resentment against inherited power. Common sense played a role, especially in conclusions about what ordinary readers would gain from their own unprejudiced reading of Scripture.[48] But Smith's compass was mostly of biblical republican manufacture. For instance, at the end of a sermon series on the doctrine of election, which was jammed with biblical refutations aimed at traditional Calvinist views, Smith paused to explain what the Bible's teaching about election really meant: any one at all who believed in the saving power of Jesus was numbered among the elect, and that was a teaching sufficient "to confound the wise, the mighty, and those who think they are something when they are nothing."[49] "Anti-Christ," according to Smith, had appeared for the first time with the illegitimate opposition to Jesus in his own lifetime and then had continued through a long, sad history of "hereditary and divine right, of unlimited power and passive obedience to *tyrants* and *kings*."[50] Anti-Christ appeared most clearly in the Roman Catholic papacy, but it was also embodied in all Protestant schemes for power. Only in the eighteenth century, when "young people instead of believing on [their?] priests, began to think for themselves," was victory over Anti-Christ possible.[51]

When the respected Congregational minister Jedidiah Morse wrote in his widely distributed *American Geography* that the clergy of Connecticut had acted as a useful "kind of aristocratical balance . . . as a check upon the overbearing spirit of Republicanism," Smith was predictably incensed. In his eyes, the ministers of the traditional churches should indeed fear the rising spirit of the new nation, for "from every appearance they will ere long be *weighed* in the *Republican balance*, and be found wanting. . . . as fast as *Republican principles increase*, so fast *clerical influence* diminishes."[52] Apprehension for Morse was hope for Smith, whose long and clamorous career showed how thoroughly historic Christian and commonsense republican warrants could mingle in the prosecution of a peoples' Christianity.

The Public Debates of Alexander Campbell

Another of the era's great polemicists was Alexander Campbell (1788–1866).[53] In Northern Ireland, where he was born, and during a period of study in Glasgow, Campbell absorbed John Locke, a Scottish commitment to Baconian method, a disillusioned assessment of traditional Protestant churches, and the Bible-onlyism of the Scottish reformers James and Robert Haldane.[54] After arriving in Pennsylvania in 1809, Campbell joined his father, Thomas, who had come to America only shortly before, in preaching the need to dispense with the historic Christian creeds, philosophical speculations (like Calvinism), and unbiblical practices (like the baptism of infants) in order to recover the primitive, nonsectarian, immersionist faith of the New Testament. Thomas and Alexander Campbell were willing to be called Baptists for some time but then moved to establish congregations and associations self-described as Disciples of Christ. After joining in 1832 with Barton W. Stone's followers, who were another body of "Christians" alongside those of Elias Smith, the Restorationist movement was well established, not so much as a denomination in the traditional sense, but as a number of interconnected networks calling themselves Disciples, Christians, or Churches of Christ. Campbell's effectiveness as a leader of the movement rested in large part on his success as editor of two widely read periodicals, the *Christian Baptist* (1823–1830) and the *Millennial Harbinger* (1830–1866). It also rested on a willingness to take his singular set of convictions into the arena of public debate.

Several times from the late 1820s to the early 1840s, Campbell engaged in public disputations, which were as much of a tonic to him as they were compelling entertainment for large and appreciative audiences. In these debates, Campbell argued from principles originating both in his particular religious convictions and in his sense of American cultural values. One exchange with the British socialist Robert Owen in Cincinnati involved twenty-five separate speeches by each antagonist spread out over a week in early April 1829. It featured Owen's defense of his oft-repeated claim that the world's religions were perverse results of destructive child-rearing practices. Campbell's retort presented a brusque Baconian defense of the facts of Christ's life, death, and resurrection as the sure guarantor of the truth of the Christian religion. As he put it, "I aver that the christian religion is founded upon facts, upon veritable, historical, incontrovertible facts—facts *triable* by all the *criteria* known to the courts of law in the ascertainment of what is or is not established in evidence." In making this case, Campbell drew on Lockean concepts of evidence and an encyclopedic grasp of Scripture. But at crucial moments he also thundered forth against "kingcraft and priestcraft," against "the unhallowed alliance between kings and priests, of church and state." As he described how Christianity had been corrupted by principles of hierarchy and deferential authority, Campbell knew well how to play his Cincinnati audience. In the past Christianity had been corrupted, as he put it, by "incorporating . . . the opinions and speculations of Egyptian and Indian philosophy." "The creed system," which was "the fruitful source of all the corruptions in morals, as well as the parent of all the religious discord now in christendom," was the melancholy result. The prevalence of such distorted versions of Christian truth had provided Owen with ample targets for his infidel gibes. Campbell was pleased to announce, however, that Owen had "been fighting against the perversions of christianity, rather than against the religion of facts, of morals, and of happiness which our Redeemer has established in the world." It was "the trinity of nature, reason, and religion" that Campbell was defending in Cincinnati against Owen.[55]

Eight years later, Campbell returned to Cincinnati for another public disputation, this one conducted 13–21 January 1837 with the Roman Catholic bishop of that city, John Purcell. Against Purcell, Campbell showcased again, as he had against Owen, biblical facts and straightforward moral reasoning. For this debate, however, he also added a much more overt appeal to republican values. In conflict with Owen, Campbell had gone out of his way to distinguish between patriotism and Christianity. But against Purcell, an effective builder of Catholic parishes as well as a learned debater, Campbell self-consciously connected biblical religion and proper political values.[56] Campbell's use of such republican warrants came especially in defense of the seventh and last proposition posed for this debate. Where the first six called forth mostly arguments from Scripture and history that were standard in Catholic-Protestant contests, the seventh was a special product of new-world experience: "The Roman Catholic religion, if infallible and unsusceptible of reformation, as alleged, is essentially anti-American, being opposed to the genius of all free institutions, and positively subversive of them, opposing the general reading of the scriptures, and the diffusion of useful knowledge among the whole community, so essential to liberty and the permanence of good government." In defending this proposition, Campbell expatiated at length on how Catholicism made its adherents "abject slaves to their priests, bishops, and popes." Because in Campbell's view, "the benumbing and paralyzing influence of Romanism is such, as to disqualify a person for the relish and enjoyment of political liberty," it was obvious that the Catholic Church did not belong in Cincinnati, since "there never was on earth so free and so equitable an institution as the Protestant institutions of these United States."[57]

Alexander Campbell was not an "American theologian" in the sense that he simply read his convictions off the landscape. For his appeal to Locke and Bacon, his biblicism, and his antisectarian sectarianism there were ample old-world precedents, especially in the reforming activities of the Haldane brothers in Scotland. Yet that Campbell's Restorationist teachings came to enjoy considerable popularity in the opening West and in the border regions between North and South owed more than a little to his ability at presenting Baconian biblicism in the language of antiformalist and republican common sense that was being spoken in the new United States before Campbell arrived on these shores.

Baptists and Methodist Grind the Iron Wheel

From the time of the Methodists' first arrival in North America, contentions with Baptists had existed wherever these two aggressive forms of populist Christianity overlapped. What had been a smoldering set of local feuds burst into flame visible throughout all Tennessee and beyond when in the mid-1850s two redoubtable champions tore into each other with sacred abandon.[58] James Robinson Graves (1820–1893) had been born in Vermont and drifted through teaching positions in Ohio and Kentucky before becoming ordained as a Baptist minister in the mid-1840s and then moving to Nashville.[59] Graves was a primitivist who shared some of the views of Alexander Campbell, especially a conviction that present-day churches needed to disencumber themselves of the corrupt accretions of the centuries in order to recover the purity of New Testament life. He remains a figure of influence among Baptists in the South and border states as the founder of "Landmarkism," a movement that defends local Baptist congregations as the only true churches and the only Christian bodies linked through unbroken historical succession to the churches founded by Jesus himself. In his own lifetime, Graves had a wide regional impact through the pages of the *Tennessee Baptist*, which he dominated from 1848 until crippled by a stroke in 1884. Graves's talent for disputation was visible at its most pugnacious in assaults directed at various times throughout his career against the Methodists. A 600-page brickbat from 1855, *The Great Iron Wheel; or, Republicanism Backwards and Christianity Reversed*, was the most important of these anti-Methodist polemics.

The exchange with an equally forceful Methodist, W. G. Brownlow, that resulted from the publication of Graves's book was especially important for showing how strongly the Christian republican synthesis of the early national period survived into the era of the Civil War, and how much it had come to influence the two great populist churches—Methodist and Baptist—of the era.

Graves's book did repeat many of the standard scriptural arguments for adult baptism, local church autonomy, predestination, and other Baptist distinctives that had been deployed many times before in Britain and America. But even more than earlier doctrinal polemics in the early republic, Graves's attacks on the Methodists came close to being a pure application of American ideological reasoning to Christian doctrine. The nature of his reasoning was clear as soon as a reader opened the book:

Dedication.
To
Every American
who loves our free institutions and scorns to be degraded or
enslaved in church or state;
To Every Christian
who loves the truth, and desires to serve no master but Jesus,
and obey no king or lawgiver but Christ, this
work is most confidently dedicated by
Its Author,
who here, most affectionately acknowledges his indebtedness
for an ardent and early implanted love of republicanism, in
civil and ecclesiastical government, to the faithful,
teachings, and, above all, for his humble hope
in Christ, to the constant prayer, and
pious example, of his mother.

To Graves, the Methodists had absorbed so many principles and practices from Roman Catholics, like the episcopacy, that they deserved to be called "the Popery of Protestantism." John Wesley was doubly condemned, first for starting up a new church, but second for being "a most *militant opposer* of our fathers in their struggle for independence" and for preaching "in scorn against all the principles of liberty, for which Hancock, Washington, and Jefferson contended."[60]

The title of Graves's book came from a description by a Methodist of the interlocking system of connections that made up the denomination. It was "wheels within wheels"—an outer circle made up of the bishops and inner circles representing annual conferences, presiding elders, local conferences, itinerants, class leaders, and local classes. Graves agreed that Methodism worked like a great iron wheel, but to him this was hardly a compliment. His account of how Methodism functioned fairly dripped with republican scorn: "What is Methodism but a perfect system of *passive obedience* and *non-resistance?* . . . *What is it but a monstrous system of clerical absolutism!* The most fearful Hierarchism on the earth." What Graves found hardest to believe was the allegiance that hundreds of thousands of Americans gave to this system: "It *is* astounding to me, beyond my power to describe, how one million of American freemen—patriot Christians—the *sons* and *daughters* of revolutionary heroes, can be made 'to be whirled around every day' at the pleasure of a class of petty spiritual rulers and lordlings?" Graves's conclusion was despair for American and for true religion alike: "Oh, my country,

my country!—how much it is to be feared for thy liberties from these! Oh,
religion—what an astounding machine, managed by ambitious and design-
ing priests, is at work to overthrow thee."[61]

It was a great stimulus to the sales of Graves's *Great Iron Wheel* that this
Baptist barrage was met with even fiercer cannonading from the champion
of the Methodists. There was much in William Gannoway Brownlow's fiery
riposte that rehearsed the Methodists' traditional scriptural and doctrinal support for their distinctive practices. But as in Graves's book, so also in
Brownlow's *Great Iron Wheel Examined*, narrowly religious warrants regularly gave way to reasoning marked by contemporary American ideology.

Brownlow (1805–1877) had been a Methodist itinerant from 1826 to 1836,
after which he became an editor of Whig newspapers in eastern Tennessee.[62]
During the Civil War he was famous as an uncompromising Unionist, but
the ginger of his convictions had been on display long before in fiery publications aimed at Baptists and Presbyterians. Against Graves, Brownlow proceeded as he had against another opponent: "I take the slanderer by the throat,
and drag him forth from his hiding-place, and shake him naked over hell, in
all his deformity!" In 331 vitriolic pages launched against Graves, Brownlow
defended the life and teachings of John Wesley, enlisted testimony from near
and far on the dastardly character of those (especially Calvinists) who opposed the Methodists, and labored diligently to defend Methodist teachings
on baptism, the witness of the Spirit, and the episcopal system. In his torrent
of exposition and abuse, Brownlow paused frequently to defend Methodists
as true American patriots and castigate his foes as Tories or worse. In response
to Graves's charge that Methodists were "death to all the institutions for which
Washington fought and freemen died," Brownlow quoted Washington's letter of high respect to Bishops Coke and Asbury. In response to Graves's claim
that Baptists practiced pure democracy, Brownlow was clever enough to enlist
comments by the eighteenth-century English Baptist Robert Hall, who denied (as was typical of English Dissenters of his time) that Baptists in any
sense supported republicanism. Somewhat smugly, Brownlow asked how the
Methodists could have become twice as numerous as the Baptists in the country if they were so opposed to the founding principles of the United States. In
using warrants from the era's dominant political principles, Brownlow, in a
word, gave as well as he took.[63]

More thoroughly than their populist or learned predecessors in public theological argument, Graves and Brownlow were defending alternative versions
of an American faith. Moreover, they did so during a period when public
religious positions were more closely aligned with partisan political stances
than at any time since the election of 1800. The distinctly American, but also
contradictory, religious positions of North and South during the 1850s and
1860s pointed toward the multiple tragedies (including the theological tragedy) of the Civil War, which is the subject of chapters below. Here it is important to underscore a larger point. The increasing prominence in religious
argument of warrants taken from the realm of American public discourse
spoke eloquently of the impetus that religious movements provided for that

discourse. It also spoke eloquently of the shape that this discourse was giving to religious thought.

Resistance

In the decades between the Revolution and the Civil War, American theology was moving because American ideology was moving. The weight of what could simply be assumed was shifting out of one worldview and into another. The strongest testimony to that shift was the absence of self-consciousness among spokespersons as they used the new moral philosophy and the new nation's political ideology to defend their religious convictions. But there was also a second kind of testimony, which came from those who saw what was going on and did not like it. Resistance to the new intellectual assumptions was fragmentary, often conflicted, and barely noticed during this period. Its existence, however, was yet another gauge of the external influences coming to bear on religious thought.

Spotty and reflexive resistance to the marriage of the new moral philosophy and traditional Christian doctrine appeared early in the nineteenth century but did nothing to stem the tide. At the College of New Jersey at Princeton in the first decade of the new century, at least one Congregational student from Upper New York thought it odd that a purportedly Calvinist institution would be recommending Thomas Reid and Dugald Stewart with such enthusiasm. To William Weeks (1783–1848), what Reid considered to be the self-evident testimony of consciousness, especially concerning the liberty of choice before moral alternatives, contradicted divinely revealed truth: "*Reid* is grossly Arminian, & advocates a *Self-determining* power, which, if it means anything, means that the creature is independent of the Creator."[64] Twenty years later, when Weeks was the minister of a small Presbyterian church in Paris Hill, New York, he tried to mobilize resistance to the "new measures" of Charles Finney's revivalism.[65] Protests on that occasion were as unavailing as his earlier strictures about the embrace of theistic common sense.

In the ranks of leading theologians from the formalist denominations a few also eventually became alarmed at the easy triumph of commonsense principles. At the same time, a somewhat broader range of ministers entertained at least some doubt about the nearly universal synergy of republican ideology and Christian theology. Among the most interesting cases in the former group was James Marsh, an evangelical Congregationalist noteworthy for his efforts at introducing his fellow Americans to the works of Samuel Taylor Coleridge.

Marsh (1794–1842) underwent a conversion experience as a Dartmouth undergraduate, studied for the ministry at Andover Seminary, and then went on to a short but distinguished career at the University of Vermont, where he served from the mid-1820s until his death. Although Marsh was himself a thoroughly evangelical Protestant, he marched to his own drum. In particular, he was suspicious of the claims made for the era's prevailing theistic mental science and wanted to enlist something from Europe's rising romanticism to express his faith. Marsh's place in intellectual history was secured when in 1829 he published the first American edition of Coleridge's *Aids to Reflection*. This work exerted a significant influence on a number of notable American thinkers, including Ralph Waldo Emerson, Theodore Parker, and Horace Bushnell, each of whom heeded Marsh's recommendation of Coleridge without following Marsh's orthodox appropriation of this leading English romantic. For Marsh, direct intuition of the true and the beautiful, rather than Baconian intuition of commonsense facts, was the natural complement to divine revelation. In comments that introduced the *Aids to Reflection*, Marsh analyzed with rare discernment the unself-conscious process by which Americans had forged the strong bond between Christianity and the new moral philosophy: "It is our peculiar misfortune in this country, that while the philosophy of Locke and the Scottish writers has been received in full faith, as the only rational system, . . . the strong attachment to religion, and the fondness for speculation, by both of which we are strongly characterized, have led us to combine and associate these principles . . . with our religious interests and opinions, so variously and so intimately, that by most persons they are considered as necessary parts of that same system." Marsh also echoed the sentiments of Jonathan Edwards and Samuel Johnson from a century earlier by suggesting that the dominance of Baconian common sense was creating a situation "dangerous in its tendency, and at war with orthodox views of religion."[66]

After Marsh published this edition of Coleridge's work, he engaged in an inconclusive, but also telling, correspondence with Charles Hodge, who at the time was just coming into his own at Presbyterian Princeton as a defender of both Baconian method and traditional Calvinism.[67] When he read Marsh's edition of Coleridge, Hodge was worried that this romantic approach subverted orthodox faith. As with so many of his peers, Hodge was greatly concerned about the doctrine of atonement. Coleridge, according to Hodge, was "changing the whole system of the gospel as it has been commonly understood. That instead of the sinner's depending on what Christ has done, as the ground of his acceptance; he is taught to look to himself—to a change wrought in his own heart." Marsh, for his part, wanted to debate perspective with Hodge, as well as doctrine. Rather than teaching error about the objective outworking of the atonement, Coleridge was truthfully dealing with its subjective aspect. In Marsh's opinion, Coleridge was telling the truth about "the activity of rational & spiritual powers consistent in their operation with our own free will."

Yet doctrine per se did not strike Marsh as the sticking point of contention. It was rather that Coleridge was opposing "the mechanical law of cause & effect," and that he was trying to preserve the mystery of God's love for humanity in Christ from simple equation "with a . . . scheme of legal equivalents, a scheme drawn from the analogy of human institutions." What Hodge was viewing as Coleridge's violation of orthodox teaching, Marsh saw as a helpful transcendence of the ordinary categories of republican mental science.

Unfortunately for the future of American religious thought, this discussion seems to have gone no further. Marsh soon died, American followers of Coleridge became increasingly heterodox, and conservatives like Hodge continued to regard deviation from Baconian method as a first-order theological mistake.

Although Marsh's criticism of standard intellectual procedure was unusual, it was echoed by a few others in the antebellum period. Wariness about theistic common sense was usually strengthened by reading in philosophical or theological sources drawn from outside of the United States (or Scotland). In particular, John Williamson Nevin and Henry Boynton Smith emerged as critics of commonsense reasoning as they also moved closer to the moderate pietistic orthodoxy of contemporary Germany.[68] The mature theologies of Nevin, who was located at the German Reformed Seminary in Mercersburg, Pennsylvania, from 1840, and Smith, who taught at the Presbyterian Union Seminary in New York from 1850, were more sacramental, more organic, more self-consciously Christocentric, and less driven by ethical apologetics than the main American theologies of this period. The two were also far less convinced that the natural deliverances of consciousness did as much for theological formation as their American counterparts claimed. When Smith, for example, wrote about the history of theology in New England, he suggested that "on the general basis of the Scotch philosophy," American theologians had constructed "consistent theory." But this reasoning, in his view, led also to "a theory of pure individualism." Smith did not intend a compliment when he claimed that the result amounted to "an ethical and not a theological theory."[69]

For his part, Nevin was characteristically more caustic. A growing attachment to a Christian Platonic understanding of God, matter, and human nature led Nevin to acerbic criticism of what he took to be the unexamined soul-matter dualism of commonsense theism.[70] In 1848 he published "A Plea for Philosophy" in which commonsense Baconian principles were described as "a false empirical scheme of thought" that ruled out genuine philosophy and "all deeper thinking." Nevin's criticism was expressed with some of the metaphysical jargon that his contemporaries found so incomprehensible, but there was no mistaking what he wanted to say:

> The general character of this bastard philosophy is, that it affects to measure all things, both on earth and in heaven, by the categories of the common abstract understanding, as it stands related simply to the world of time and sense. These categories, however, being in themselves the forms or types only of things in this outward world, and representing therefore the conditions merely of existence in space and time—something relative always and finite by the very nature of the case—become necessarily one-sided and false, the moment we attempt to carry their authority beyond these limits, and to apply them to the truths of the pure reason.

Nevin's conclusion about characteristic habits of American thought caught very nicely what mainstream theologians thought they were doing, but also Nevin's own indictment of such ways: "It reasons from time to eternity with vast dexterity and ease; establishing, by strict Baconian comparison and induction, the existence of God, the immortality of the soul, and the truth of revelation; but it is all in such a way as turns eternity itself into time, and forces the whole invisible world to become a mere abstraction from the world of sense."[71] Although Nevin, Smith, and Marsh differed among themselves concerning the nature of a proper theology, they were among the very few in their time to protest the era's general commitment to the new moral philosophy.

Resistance to amalgamating Christianity with republicanism may have been more widely spread, but was in the end just as ineffective as resistance to the Christian embrace of common sense. Historian Mark Hanley has rendered excellent service by gathering into a lucid book widely scattered evidence of uneasiness with Christian republicanism assumptions.[72] By following the lead of Harry Stout's study of manuscript sermons in the Puritan era, Hanley can show that the themes of ordinary, weekly sermons were far less likely to promote a republican civil religion than sermons on Independence Day or other public occasions. In addition, popular publishing enterprises, like the American Tract Society, consistently promoted religious values oriented to theistic and eternal matters as distinct from republican and utilitarian concerns. In other words, for every copy of the Society's *Reward of Drunkenness*, there were two copies of works like *The Lost Soul* and *Sin, No Trifle*, as well as an equal number of substantial evangelistic tomes like Richard Baxter's *Call to the Unconverted,* reprinted from the seventeenth century.

Francis Wayland (1796–1865), president of the Baptists' Brown University in Providence, Rhode Island, was an especially notable figure who, on occasion, distinguished a Christian message applicable to all times and places from a Christian message aimed at guaranteeing the virtue of the American republic. Wayland, an intellectual of consequence but one who has been neglected by historians, was a conflicted figure. He published popular textbooks on mental science and political economy where he aimed to fit the rising generation of young collegiates for the task of maintaining a virtuous republic. Yet he also preached, wrote, and lectured frequently on the need to promote Christianity for the sake of Christianity alone. A sermon to Baptist ministers in Rochester, New York, in 1853 gave him the opportunity to express the latter conviction. On that occasion he reminded his listeners that it was possible to "deliver discourses on subjects associated with religion, without preaching the gospel." In particular, "to show the importance of religion to the temporal well-being of men, or the tendency of the religion of Christ to uphold republican institutions, and a hundred topics of a similar character, may or may not be well; but to do either or all of them certainly falls short of the idea of the apostle, when he determined to know nothing among men but Jesus Christ and him crucified."[73] Some of the Christian resistance to Christian republicanism in the era of Francis Wayland reflected the ideological transitions of the age, for ministers like Wayland who were ill at ease with individualistic, liberal notions of the common good were often more comfortable with deferential, classical models of disinterested public virtue.[74] Yet some doubts about the accepted bond between Christianity and American political values came from the argument that the Christian gospel was of ultimate importance, regardless of its implications for the future of the United States.

It is important to remember the testimony of Francis Wayland, as well as the criticism of James Marsh, Henry Boynton Smith, and J. W. Nevin, when describing the emergence of "American theology." Religious thinkers were not Americanized to the same degree. A few naysayers were always present to question the whole drift of theological development. Testimony from the standpoint of historic Christianity continued to critique the Christian use of commonsense republicanism. Yet once having noticed such criticism, it is important to keep the larger picture in perspective. Critics of the synthesis of republican ideology, commonsense ethical reason, and Christian theology were agitated primarily because they were so ineffective. Tiny minorities objected to the synthesis while vast majorities promoted it.

Testimony from outside the United States again helps to clarify the American picture. Two comments from Britain on the mental habits of the age suggest that the broad intellectual assumptions that meant so much in the United States also had some appeal across the Atlantic. Yet the clarity of these testimonies, though coming from different points on the theological spectrum, also suggests that Britons did not feel the intuitive weight of these mental habits as sharply as their American counterparts.

First was the observation of "Rabbi" John Duncan (1796–1870), student of Hebrew and the Old Testament professor of the Free Church of Scotland's theology college from its founding in 1843. Duncan appreciated the modern philosophical contributions of his native land, especially when figures like Thomas Reid and Dugald Stewart offered reassurances about the reliability of the senses and the trustworthiness of testimony. But to Duncan it was transparent foolishness to think that whole systems of theology could be reared on such a basis: "Does this Reidist solution really satisfy any man? The belief may be false, though we cannot help believing it? . . . Can't-help-myself-ism is to me a very shallow philosophy. . . . Common sense I believe in, but not in a philosophy of common sense."[75]

An even more comprehensive indictment came from John Henry Newman, who in 1836, while still an Anglican, paused to address his age's commitment to Baconian demonstration. For Newman the reliance of Christian apologetics on the conclusions of natural theology was a fundamental error. His specific complaint was about William Paley's *View of the Evidences of Christianity*, which, though published first in 1794, was still required reading in the 1830s at many American colleges, as well as at Oxford and Cambridge. Newman's reasoning, in fact, applied much more to the intellectual situation in the United States than in Britain, where a general deference to tradition continued much more strongly than in the United States: "Nothing is so common," he wrote, "as for young men to approach serious subjects as judges—to study them as mere sciences. . . . The study of the Evidences as now popular (such as Paley's) encourages this evil frame of mind—the learner is supposed external to the system. . . . In all these cases the student is supposed to look upon the system from without, and to have to choose it by an act of reason before he submits to it—whereas the great lesson of the gospel is faith, an obeying prior to reason, and *proving* its reasonableness by making experiment of it, and investigating the truth by practice."[76]

Newman, as did also a few Americans, eventually fled from Protestant doxological science to the historical authority of the Roman Catholic Church. Marsh, Smith, Nevin, and sometimes Francis Wayland were among the few Americans who shared Duncan's or Newman's nervousness about principles of commonsense republican reasoning. The story of American theology in the period between the Constitution and the Civil War did not, however, belong to these lonely critics but to the overwhelming numbers who accepted those principles as if there could be no others.

Interaction between inner theological resources and the dominant American ideologies occurred in myriad forms among the United States' proliferating denominations in the decades after 1800. In the chapters that follow, attention is focused on the main Calvinist churches and the Methodists, not because what happened among other groups was insignificant, but because the Calvinist and Methodist churches were so large, so influential, and so clearly engaged in the Americanization of theology.

13

The Americanization of Calvinism

Contexts and Questions

Commitment to republican understanding of society and commonsense principles of moral reasoning worked most obviously on the theology of the historic Calvinist churches.[1] These were the churches that had rendered the most important religious service to the cause of independence; they took the lead in providing the new country with the institutions of intellectual civilization; from their ranks came the leaders of the voluntary societies; they retained the strongest proprietary concern for the new nation regarded as a moral entity; they (with the exception of the Southern Presbyterians) provided the religious backbone for the Federalist, Whig, and Republican political parties; and they provided most of the spokespersons who explained the ultimate significance of sectional conflict and civil war. In short, they were the churches that on the level of articulated religious discourse were most deeply committed to the project of the new United States; as a consequence, they were the ones most obviously shaped in their theological reasoning by the public discourses of the new nation.

   In the long view it is clear that disestablishment posed a set of difficulties to the Congregationalists of New England that they simply never overcame. It is also clear that the era of Presbyterian leadership in American intellectual life—both church and nation—did not long survive the Civil War, and that the influence of the German and Dutch Reformed was in this era mostly restricted to the ethnic communities served by those denominations. Moreover, during the antebellum decades, the older Reformed churches were falling further and further behind in the search for adherents when compared with the Baptists, the Methodists, and the newly formed sectarian denominations.[2]

Enriched Theological Culture

Despite indications of diminished influence, the older Reformed churches remained central to the nation's formal intellectual life. The rise of the theological seminary, which was of greatest importance for promoting formal religious thought during this period, illustrates the importance of these churches.[3] The founding of Andover Seminary in 1808 was tied closely to the local situation in eastern Massachusetts: when a Unitarian was appointed as the professor of theology at Harvard in 1805, trinitarian Congregationalists of several stripes overcame suspicions of each other to create their own rival institution. Andover, with a curriculum of biblical, systematic, historical, and practical theology designed for students who had completed a collegiate course in the liberal arts, soon became a much-imitated model. It took only a few years for seminaries to exert an influence far beyond the narrow boundaries of the churches, and by the 1830s the seminary movement was well established.

In planting these word-driven institutions, Congregationalists and especially Presbyterians were distinctly the leaders.[4] Elite Calvinists, however, had no monopoly on seminaries, since by 1820 there was also at least one such institution each for the Baptists, Lutherans, Dutch Reformed, Moravians, and Episcopalians. Distinctions between collegiate and seminary instruction remained hazy throughout the period, but by 1860 the national total had risen to more than fifty schools designed primarily for the graduate education of prospective ministers.[5] It is an important indication of more general intellectual trends, however, to note that of this number, only four were Baptist and two Methodist, while five were conducted by Episcopalians and seven by Lutherans. Of the Reformed theological schools in 1860, six were Congregational (Andover, Bangor [Maine], Yale, Oberlin [Ohio], East Windsor [Connecticut], and Chicago), one was Dutch Reformed, two were German Reformed, two were maintained by sectarian Presbyterian bodies, and a full ten—spread from New Jersey to Iowa, from upstate New York to Columbia, South Carolina—were sponsored by either the New School or the Old School Presbyterians. Significantly for public theological guidance during the Civil War, three of the five active seminaries located in the Southern states were Presbyterian.[6] As late as 1860, the only graduate education of any intellectual substance to be found in the United States was theological education, and the four largest seminaries were Presbyterian (Princeton, Union in New York City, Western in Pittsburgh) and Congregational (Andover).[7] Stress on formal education was not a necessary indication of denominational health, but it spoke volumes about intellectual leadership in a society almost otherwise devoid of institutions for graduate learning.

The presence of seminaries influenced the study of theology in several ways. Most important, seminaries created expanding networks of individuals who had been introduced to elite texts, arguments, and formal discourse, and who then made up a market for books, pamphlets, and periodicals that strengthened the ties among those who wrote and those who read. In addition, the existence of seminaries also reawakened American interest in European thought, which had languished from the days of the Revolution. The ones who were called to teach the seminaries' advanced curricula in biblical study and theology were often very much aware of how far short their intellectual accomplishments lagged behind Europeans who performed similar duties. As a direct result, growing numbers of seminary professors and would-be professors traveled to Europe, beginning a few years after the ending of the War of 1812, where they were exposed to modern European opinions and perspectives, as well as to the technical data of theological education.[8] In turn, contact with European education heightened the impression that theologians were an intellectual elite who deserved respect for faithfully pursuing their calling as professionals. In large part because of this seminary culture, the theology of Presbyterians and Congregationalists was more highly developed and became more important for American intellectual life than any form of religious thought would ever be from after the Civil War.

Quite naturally, the expanding network of seminaries fed broadening interests in theological publication. Not at all coincidentally, the golden age of American Reformed theology was also the great age of the learned theological quarterly. During the 1820s almost all religious groups came to sponsor these quarterlies, which were as heavy with print as they were leisurely in argumentation. The monthly *Methodist Magazine*, which had been founded in 1818, was, for example, transformed into a weighty quarterly in 1830. But again the leaders were the Reformed, with each of the most important centers of theological learning sponsoring a quarterly whose articles were read, admired, scorned, and debated to a degree now hard to imagine. The most widely heeded were New Haven's *Quarterly Christian Spectator* (transformed from a monthly in 1829 and giving way to the *New Englander* in 1843), Princeton's *Biblical Repertory* (also in 1829 changed from an eclectic digest providing translations of German works into an organ of definite theological opinions), Andover's *Biblical Repository* (founded in 1831 and then in effect folded into the *Bibliotheca Sacra* in 1843), and the *Literary and Theological Review* (founded in New York City in 1834 by Congregationalists and Presbyterians eager for a vehicle to attack the New Haven theology).[9] As theological argument engendered even more theological argument, many other weighty journals joined in as well, like the Baptists' *Christian Review* (1836), the *Cumberland Presbyterian Review* (1845), the *Southern Presbyterian Review* (1847), the New School *American Presbyterian and Theological Review* (1859), and the Old School *Danville* (Kentucky) *Quarterly Review* (1861). Baptists and Methodists may have been winning the most converts, but in the realm of elite public discourse, Presbyterians and Congregationalists reigned supreme.

Comparison with the Baptists and Methodists does highlight the disparity between an ability to secure adherents and an ability to publish learned quarterlies, but it should be remembered that Reformed theological writing during the first half of the nineteenth century also benefited from an upsurge of Calvinist churches, especially the Presbyterians. During a period when the

Dutch Reformed were fading as a significant religious force (except in New York along the Hudson), as also the German Reformed (except in Pennsylvania), Congregationalists continued to expand modestly and Presbyterians with unprecedented speed. By 1850 the ratio of Presbyterian to Congregational churches was nearing 3 to 1 (4,824 to 1,706).[10] The incredibly rapid expansion of Baptists, Methodists, and Disciples was, to be sure, even more impressive. But during these decades there was no shortage of Reformed churches clamoring for well-trained pastors, no shortage of recruits for the seminaries educating those pastors, and no shortage of interest in sustaining the Calvinist churches as a power in the broader culture.

The story of Calvinist theology in this era is rich, multifaceted, and complex; unlike the story of theology among America's other early religious traditions, it has also been studied in copious detail. Because the writings of the era's Calvinistic theologians and also scholarly works on their theologies are so numerous, it is impossible to provide anything like a systematic survey. What can be attempted is an interpretation, especially concerning how the main theological conclusions of the main Calvinist traditions related to broader American developments. For this effort, the most important inquiry must be why theologians of the period were so preoccupied with questions of human freedom and moral government, and so convinced that answers to these questions would come from the deliverances of conscience and the simple statements of Scripture.

Contexts

The leading Calvinist theologians in the years between 1800 and 1860 knew that they were living in a rapidly changing America. Presbyterians entered this period without strong theological leadership: the tension, described in chapter 7, which divided Presbyterians between those accommodating and those resisting the sprit of Enlightenment rationalism, had not yet been fully resolved. By contrast, Congregationalist theology was a flourishing enterprise, but an enterprise divided into discernibly separate streams. Intellectual descendants of Jonathan Mayhew, Ebenezer Gay, and Charles Chauncy were moving steadily toward a refined, benevolent Unitarianism; Old Calvinist traditionalists were still working for the good of the church and the good of society as a single task; the self-conscious heirs of Jonathan Edwards (the New Divinity men) were trying to promote revival, which Edwards's example inspired, while also exploring problems in metaphysical theology, which were just as much a part of his legacy. Together, representatives of these formalist churches faced a set of national circumstances for which the establishmentarian habits of their earlier histories provided almost no guidance at all.

The first of these circumstances was geographic: the area and population of the body politic over which Calvinist clergy had historically exercised their moral proprietorship were expanding with breakneck speed. In each decade between 1790 and 1860 the population of the new United States

CALVINISM: CONTEXTS AND QUESTIONS   257

rose by at least a third; in the same period the nation's land area more than tripled. These transformations were not as traumatic for the Presbyterians, since whatever establishmentarian pretensions they retained from the old world had already been severely tested by their status as one among several competing denominations in the middle and Southern states. For New England it was different. In 1800 that region had made up nearly a fourth (23.6%) of the new nation's population and 7% of its land area. By 1860 the proportions had fallen to 10% for population and 2% for area. Given these realities, where the Congregational clergy retained the establishmentarian instinct to think that they should exercise determinative moral leadership, the perception of crisis was sure to follow.

With the rapid expansion of the physical country came an even more rapid expansion of the ecclesiastical nation. Congregationalists accustomed to state recognition and Presbyterians accustomed to local deference were forced, willy-nilly, to adjust. More than simply adjusting, they now had to compete for souls, for public allegiance, and for intellectual commitment. As they did so, they increasingly adapted themselves to the methods of the upstart antiformalist churches.

Politically, the Presbyterians and Congregationalists were forced to stand aside as national leadership passed from the kind of sober gentlemen they understood and could sometimes directly influence to a very different species: Southerners, slaveholders, nominal Anglicans, and then rabble-rousing antinomians from the West. Such parvenus were as likely to promote radical democracy and a preference for things French as to favor the Calvinists' balanced republicanism and an inclination to Britain. Midstate Presbyterians recognized that Federalism was a lost cause before their New England Congregationalist contemporaries, but neither group took that political defeat gracefully. Not until the rise of the Whig Party in the early 1830s did national political leaders come onto the scene with whom the leading Calvinists could once again make common cause, but even with these new allies, political success was usually elusive. In practical terms, their position as political "outs" meant that the Reformed clergy were powerless to prevent the election of "infidels" like Jefferson in 1800, to stop the Post Office from carrying the mail on Sunday, to protect the Christianized Cherokee nation from its dreadful fate, and to do much by way of ending the slave system, which from the 1830s many Congregationalists and some Presbyterians agreed was a sinful institution.

Through the voluntary societies, Congregationalists and Presbyterians did mobilize for the promotion of godliness throughout the land. But with due notice taken of the propensity in all ages to consider their own the most evil in recorded history, the Reformed formalists could still point to a set of unusually frightening social conditions. Sabbath observance seemed almost hopelessly compromised. Drunkenness seemed much worse than in previous generations, a supposition that modern historians have confirmed.[11] Rabid money-making increasingly seemed to give markets the kind of authority that once belonged to traditional religion. It is worth repeating that the inability to halt the movement of the mail on Sundays was for many a sign of nearly apocalyptic decadence.[12] If the decay of inherited civilization was not worry enough, defenders of America's Reformed traditions soon had additional cause for concern in the renewal of threats from Europe. Now, however, the source of contagion was more insidious than warfare with a vicious British state. When the trickle of Roman Catholic immigration from Ireland (and then Germany) began to increase, first slowly in the 1820s and then with frightening speed thereafter, the Calvinists' deepest fears for republican government, authentic faith, and biblical civilization awoke once again.[13]

In sum, Congregational and Presbyterian leaders faced a connected series of demographic, social, political, and cultural crises as they tried to guide their churches through the tumultuous decades of early United States history. While Methodists, Baptists, and the sectarians flourished as democratizing, lay-motivating, antielitist movements, the older Calvinist churches adjusted to new American conditions with only mixed success. The combination of altered social circumstances and ever-growing resistance to their once-dominant status provoked a perpetual state of alarm. The church was threatened, godliness was under siege, and society was being cut loose from its moral anchorage. Such perceptions, to Christian republicans, could only mean that the nation as a whole was imperiled.

As the Calvinist clergy were being shaken by the general transformations of American society, so also did they confront intellectual challenges of the same magnitude. In the immediate wake of the Revolution, traditional churches of all kind were drained of European theological ballast. When, especially after the formation of the seminaries, contact was reestablished with European theological opinion, that opinion was more disconcerting than reassuring. Although conservative theological traditions were by no means extinct in Europe, the European voices that drew most American attention in the first half of the century seemed dangerously subjective (Coleridge, and then through Coleridge, Kant and Schleiermacher), dangerously Roman (the Oxford Movement), or dangerously infidel (Auguste Comte).[14] Moderate and conservative Presbyterians struggled to maintain the authority of the Westminster Confession and Catechisms, but American opinion as a whole was not inclined to defer to such traditional formulas. When circumstances demanded that new creeds be written, as was the case at the formation of Andover Seminary in 1808, the resulting documents never attracted wide loyalty.

Because European traditions had been discredited and because Americans were under an ideological obligation to think for themselves, there remained, in effect, only one historical voice with whom the Reformed theologians of the early nineteenth century were compelled to deal. That theologian was Jonathan Edwards. Edwards, who in the history of American theology was both the last of the Puritans and the first of the evangelicals, remained a figure of consequence in part because his students, and then students of those students, were providing the most important formal theology in the new nation's early decades. But Edwards also remained important because he had addressed so powerfully the issues with which Congregationalists and Presbyterians continued to wrestle, especially the freedom of the will, the nature of original sin, and the character of genuine virtue. But apart from Edwards, the theological cupboard of the early republic was largely bare.[15]

The social history of the Reformed clergy in the early years of the United States reveals two matters with greatest clarity: they were in a state that frequently approached panic, and yet they displayed an energetic resolve to do what they could to put things right. The panic and the resolution often went together.

Events

A series of events at the turn of the century reveals the general situation. Atheism and unrestrained militarism in France, the rise of Democratic-Republican political societies, the rapidly opening frontier, apparent paralysis in the historic churches, and the possibility that Thomas Jefferson (whom many of the Calvinists regarded as an infidel) might become president were great causes of alarm. In May 1798 the Presbyterian General Assembly spoke of Europe as beset by "destruction to morals and religion" and "our own country . . . threatened with similar calamities." A few weeks later, Timothy Dwight used a Fourth of July address to hang the sins of French atheism on the party of Jefferson and Madison. In the same months Dwight joined with Jedidiah Morse of Massachusetts to identify a vast conspiracy, spearheaded by the Bavarian Illuminati, as the prime source of the godless disorder sweeping over the United States. Shortly thereafter, Calvinist ministers, including those arch-enemies of the Episcopalians, William Linn and John Mitchell Mason, led the charge against Jefferson's candidacy for president.[16] When Jefferson, despite the prayers and propaganda of the Reformed clergy, was elected, Stanhope Smith of Princeton was not the only one to conclude that Jefferson was promoting policies that led to "national imbecility and disorganization," or to feel that his encouragement of "turbulence and anarchy" would lead the country "from one hotheaded and furious faction to another till we are torn asunder." Little wonder that when, only a few months later, the main building at Princeton burned to the ground, Smith was quick to report to Jedidiah Morse that this fire was "one effect of those irreligious & demoralizing principles which are tearing the bands of society asunder & threatening in the end to overturn our country."[17] To be sure, cooler heads did appeal for calm, as when the Hartford North Association asked fellow Connecticut Congregationalists during the 1800 election campaign to "avoid such an interference as shall tend to destroy their usefulness as ministers of the gospel."[18] Yet the threat of impending chaos remained palpable.

Calvinists, however, had faced dire threats before, and as on previous occasions, the sense of doom proved a marvelous spur to action. Even as public sermons and private correspondence expressed the starkest fears for the future, the Presbyterian General Assembly was setting plans in motion for planting churches on the frontier. In New England, New Divinity clergy created the Connecticut Missionary Society, which from its founding in 1798 became the leading vehicle for Congregationalist missionary work in the opening

West. Three years later the General Association of Connecticut and the Presbyterian General Assembly ratified the Plan of Union, which allowed settlers in the West to organize churches belonging to either or both bodies and likewise to call ministers from either denomination.[19] Calvinist conservatives would later complain that the Plan of Union exposed Presbyterians to the heterodox conclusions of New England theologians, but in the century's first decade the plan was usually regarded as a hopeful means of revitalization.

Events in the tumultuous period from Jefferson's 1807 embargo of British and French manufactured goods through the end of the War of 1812 revealed the same combination of anguished chest-beating and creative activity. When Princeton College students went on a destructive rampage in the spring of 1807, its Presbyterian board shut the school down and then described the riot as a product of "the same mental epidemick which has crazed Europe, and is extending its baleful ravages throughout the civilized world." When the college reopened for classes in the fall, the trustees commissioned their senior member, Elias Boudinot, first president of the Continental Congress and personal friend of George Washington, to warn students away from "these unhingers of human happiness, these presumptuous undoers of the labours of Antiquity" that now threatened America.[20] The next year a leading Philadelphia minister, Archibald Alexander, reminded the Presbyterian General Assembly how desperately the denomination needed to recruit ministers and improve their education, if the tides of undisciplined infidelity were to be subdued.[21]

Calvinist clergy in general were suspicious of James Madison, whose friendship with Jefferson condemned him as fully as did the policies that antagonized Britain and vastly expanded the powers of the national government. The outbreak of war in 1812 sparked another round of fervid clerical reaction, especially in New England, where religious convictions combined with commercial and political interests to foment militant opposition to the Madison administration. In July 1812, when a Democratic-Republican mob trashed a Federalist newspaper in Baltimore, the Reformed clergy to the North responded with a frenzy of concern. As William Gribbin has described it, "Protesting clergymen thought a Jacobin reign of terror was at hand and feared mass martyrdom."[22] As before, there were also moderate voices among the Congregationalists and Presbyterians, but the sense of alarm remained high.

High also was the energy these same Calvinists unleashed in those parlous days. The founding of Andover Seminary in 1808 was a response to what one of its first professors called "the threatening aspects of the times, particularly the wide prevalence of Unitarianism and infidelity." To Jedidiah Morse, the creation of a seminary was a direct response to general deterioration—social and political, as well as religious and theological: "I consider Unitarianism as the *democracy* of Christianity. It dissolves all the bonds of Christian union and deprives religion of all its efficacy and influence upon Society. Our ecclesiastical affairs are fast assuming the portentous aspect and convulsed state of our political affairs."[23] A similar combination of explicitly religious motivation and broadly social urgency fueled the founding of Princeton Theological Seminary four years later.[24] The utilitarian note was even stronger in the flurry of voluntary activity that led to the establishment of the American Board of Commissioners for Foreign Missions (1810), the American Bible Society (1816), and many other national agencies.

Of special note for the history of theology was the founding of another voluntary organization, the Connecticut Society for the Reformation of Morals. It came into existence in 1812 under the chairmanship of Timothy Dwight, but its driving force was the young Congregationalist minister Lyman Beecher, who was already well launched on a career of energetic activism. "It is impossible to make you or any one else understand," Beecher in his old age told his children, "the amount of labor we went through in those days in trying to preserve our institutions and reform the public morals."[25] Conditions might be in extremis, but Beecher and his colleagues were determined to (and the list is nearly endless) outlaw dueling, save the Federalist Party, control the use of alcohol, promote revival, found literary magazines, combat the Episcopal menace, publish books that the public would read, and on and on. Beecher was joined in many of these efforts to save New England by Nathaniel W. Taylor, a fellow-student of Dwight's. It is significant to note that, before either Beecher or Taylor published the theological works for which they became renowned, they had dedicated themselves to the most active kind of service for God, church, and nation.

This is a book about theology, not ecclesiastical activism. But it is imperative to remember that all of the most-read theological writings of the antebellum period were published by ecclesiastical activists. Despite the presence of seminaries, there still existed no "academic" sphere where specialists did their work in isolation while leaving to others the practical translation of scholarly insights for the general public. Theology was being written with the needs of the public in view. Calvinist theologians of this period knew that they were participating in the passing of a religious ancien régime. The guidelines for defining and defending Christianity, for preaching and promoting the godly life, were being refashioned in front of their eyes. They did not want to be left out.

As these theologians spoke, published, and argued about the ways of God and humanity, they were driven by a mixture of motives. They wanted to speak the message of Christian salvation to the growing numbers of Americans who had never heard, or never heeded, that message. They wanted to promote godliness as a response to their own sense of gratitude to God. They wanted to assert the authority of the Bible as they understood it. They wanted to preserve their own authority as leaders who counted in American society. Calvinist theology in this era was written to preserve the best of what had been handed down to its advocates, but it was also written in response to the new shape of American life and the new challenges posed to the traditional status of the Calvinist clergy themselves.

Above all, it was a time for theologizing with effect. During a period when older boundaries had faded and newer boundaries were being erected, words perforce became actions too. What Lyman Beecher once wrote about his own efforts at responding to philosophical objections against Christianity had a much broader application: "Now I rose into the field of metaphysics, and, instead of being simple, I became the philosopher, and began to form my language for purposes of discrimination and power."[26]

Because Presbyterians had not enjoyed the same established status as the Congregationalists and because at the start of this period institutions of Presbyterian intellectual life were less well developed than those for Congregationalists, the burden of reordering the theological cosmos fell at first more heavily upon the New Englanders, but all who wanted to raise a banner for any form of the Reformed faith would soon have to share the weight of that responsibility.

Phases

Calvinist doctrinal development passed through three fairly distinct phases in the years from 1790 to 1860. The first period, to the mid-1820s, was dominated by New England Congregationalist debates set by an agenda inherited from contentions between Jonathan Edwards, Joseph Bellamy, Samuel Hopkins and their opponents in the liberal and Old Calvinist camps, but rapidly being overtaken by fresh concern about the spread of Unitarianism. In this era Presbyterians and Congregationalists both also vigorously pursued polemics against the Episcopalians, which was an indication of how backward-looking their consciousness remained, since these debates featured questions of ecclesiastical authority that had become irrelevant in the free-form religious world of the early republic.

In a second phase from the mid-1820s to about 1850, Calvinists got down to the serious business of beating up on each other. The period was marked by a much-expanded landscape of theological debate. In New England a radical transcendentalist party, whose leading figure was Ralph Waldo Emerson, gave up on traditional theology and sought to define a new, subjective, post-Calvinist religion. But most New England religious thinkers looked upon Emerson with distaste and continued to develop the themes of earlier generations, only in a multiplying number of parties, schools, periodicals, and books.

Of particular significance for mainstream theological development in this period were a Presbyterian recovery of self-confidence and the emergence of a self-consciously revivalistic theology. The founding of Princeton Theological Seminary in 1812, followed in 1825 by the first number of the *Princeton Review*, a theological quarterly that soon became a beacon widely noticed by friends and foes alike, signaled a decisive move in a traditional direction.[27] Growing contact with New England Congregationalists, as brokered especially through the Plan of Union, acted as a stimulus to Presbyterian theological reflection for those who read Edwards, Hopkins, and their successors with appreciation, and even more for those who found the New England theology seriously defective. After 1830 Presbyterians began to divide into a New

School party, which welcomed New England insights, and an Old School party, which did not. For the larger story of Calvinist theology, it was important that Presbyterian discourse had become as vigorous as the Congregationalist and that the two were thoroughly, if not peacefully, intertwined.

The larger story in this period was further complicated when professional revivalists began to publish works of considerable sophistication. Asahel Nettleton, a conservative, was the first revivalist since the 1740s to make a theological impression. But the key figure was Charles Finney, a daring innovator in thought as well as practice. By the late 1820s learned Congregationalists and Presbyterians had taken note of Finney's revivals, and within a short span they were also forced to respond to his very popular writings. While Finney's positions often resembled those of the more advanced New England theologians, his populist instincts and his independent spirit distinguished him clearly from the more cerebral New Englanders. By the 1840s the proliferation of articulate factions led to theological interchange of extraordinary vigor that engaged a full range of teachers, preachers, revivalists, voluntary workers, and a surprisingly vocal contingent of the laity as well.

A last phase of theological development can be discerned during the 1850s, when earlier positions were clarified, revised, and expanded, but when several additional innovations also occurred. Led by the Connecticut Congregationalist minister, Horace Bushnell in professional publications and by Harriet Beecher Stowe, the daughter and husband of Congregationalist clergymen, in popular literature, a significant segment of traditionally Calvinist thinkers gave up on the Baconian methods that had dominated American theology through the preceding two generations in favor of more self-consciously romantic accounts of Christian belief. A few professional theologians, most important of which were John Williamson Nevin of the German Reformed Church's Mercersburg Seminary and the New School Presbyterian Henry Boynton Smith of New York, likewise turned aside from what had been the well-worn traditions of American theological discourse, but in their case they looked to Europe for better expositions of the faith. In yet another development, a few thinkers, like Harriet Beecher Stowe's sister Catherine, found themselves alienated from traditional theological positions precisely because they did not abandon the customary methods, debates, and agendas of the American Calvinist tradition (table 13.1).

In the four decades before the Civil War, a few American Calvinists drifted off to the Episcopal Church or even became Roman Catholics, some continued to dialogue with Episcopalians, more began to notice the Methodists as a theological force, and others took first steps in responding to Roman Catholicism as a religion of American citizens.[28] But for the development of Reformed theology in this period, the overwhelming focus was internal. Resources from within the broadly Reformed tradition were what the Calvinist theologians asserted, redefined, debated, reapplied, and expounded in the oceans of print that set this era apart as the greatest, but also the most self-destructive, era of productive Christian theology in the nation's history.

TABLE 13.1. Main Calvinist Factions, 1790–1860

Faction	Representatives[a]	Predecessors[b]
Unitarians	William Ellery Channing (1780-1842), H 1798 Henry Ware (1764-1845), H 1785	Jonathan Mayhew Ebenezer Gay Charles Chauncy

New Divinity—
Andover
	Edwards Amasa Park (1808-1900),
	    Brown 1826, Andover
	Leonard Woods (1774-1854), H 1796
	Moses Stuart (1780-1852), Y 1799
	Enoch Pond (1791-1882), Brown 1813
		Jonathan Edwards (JE)
		   (revivalist, philosopher)
		Samuel Hopkins
		Nathanael Emmons

New Divinity—
East Windsor
	Bennett Tyler (1783-1858), Y 1804
	Asahel Nettleton (1783-1844), Y 1809
		JE (revivalist,
		   consistent Calvinist)
		Joseph Bellamy
		Timothy Dwight
		   (traditional activist)

New Haven	Nathaniel W. Taylor (1786-1858), Y 1807
	Lyman Beecher (1775-1863), Y 1797 [c]
	Chauncy Goodrich (1790-1860), Y 1810
	Eleazer Fitch (1791-1871), Y 1810
	Catharine Beecher (1800-1878)
		JE (revivalist,
		   philosopher)
		Samuel Hopkins
		Timothy Dwight
		   (modern activist)

New School Presbyterians	Albert Barnes (1798-1870), Hamilton 1820, PTS 1824 George Duffield (1818-1888), Y 1837, Union 1840 Lyman Beecher (1775-1863), Y 1797 [c]	John Witherspoon (statesman)

Old School
Presbyterians
	Charles Hodge (1797-1878), P 1797, PTS 1812
	Samuel Miller (1769-1850), Penn 1789
	Robert Brekinridge (1800-1871), PTS 1832
	Robert Louis Dabney (1820-1898),
	   Virginia 1842, Union Sem. [Va.] 1846
	John Henley Thornwell (1812-1862), S.C. 1831
		John Witherspoon
		   (pastor)
		Archibald Alexander

Finneyite Revivalists	Charles G. Finney (1792-1875)	JE (revivalist)
American Romantics	Horace Bushnell (1802-1876), Y 1827, YDS 1833 Harriet Beecher Stowe (1811-1896) Henry Ward Beecher (1813-1887), Lane 1837	Samuel Taylor Coleridge James Marsh

Christological
Romantics
	John Williamson Nevin (1803-1886),
	   Union 1821, PTS 1826
	Henry Boynton Smith (1815-1877),
	   Bowdoin 1834, Andover, Bangor
		Frederick A. Rauch
		F. A. G. Tholuck

[a] Abbreviations for schools attended are as follows: H = Harvard College, P = College of New Jersey at Princeton, PTS = Princeton Theological Seminary, Y = Yale College, and YDS = Yale Divinity School.
[b] Edwards, Dwight, and Witherspoon each served as a predecessor to more than one faction, with their relevant function(s) indicated in parentheses.
[c] In 1832 Lyman Beecher was ordained as a Presbyterian and thereafter was identified with the New School group.

Sources: ANB; BDEB; William B. Sprague, *Annals of the American Pulpit* (New York, 1857–69); *Appleton's Cyclopedia of American Biography* (New York, 1887); and *The New Schaff-Herzog Encyclopedia of Religious Knowledge* (New York, 1908–14).

The Doctrines at Stake

The doctrines that engaged the era's Reformed theologians can be arranged along a spectrum defined by "traditional" and "American" poles, that is, with a tendency to affirm what respected Calvinist confessions and authorities had historically affirmed opposing a tendency to propose alterations of inherited dogmas in response to questions posed by American experience. None of the important theologians can be placed in exactly the same place with respect to each contested doctrine, but there were characteristic positions. With the exception of some issues of authority, Old School Presbyterians usually were the most conservative, while Unitarians tended to move off the scale on the liberal side. Among the trinitarian Calvinists, New School Presbyterians and the East Windsor branch of the New Divinity were often closest to the middle; the Andover branch of the New Divinity was situated somewhat more toward the American pole, and the New Haven theologians regularly moved furthest in that direction. Because of how much his work continued to influence this era, it is important to note that Jonathan Edwards was a traditionalist on almost all contested doctrines, but also that the creative vocabulary and concepts he employed regularly supplied the starting point for theologians on the Americanist side of the spectrum.

The critical theological issues of the era can be phrased as questions.

1. How did humans discover the truth about God, themselves, the way of salvation, and divine oversight of the world?

This question produced responses that did not necessarily follow the usual conservative or liberal division. All the major theologians in the Reformed orbit trusted Scripture, all agreed that human consciousness clearly revealed some aspects of the moral universe, and until the romantic challenges near midcentury, all expected close reasoning on Baconian principles to elucidate obscurities. From about 1830 Old School Presbyterians began to appeal to what they considered traditional beliefs of the universal Christian church and leading figures in Protestant history. In general, New Englanders deferred most readily to consciousness, Finneyites and Presbyterians were the most Baconian, and Old School Presbyterians looked most self-consciously to history. But these tendencies did not restrain the Andover New Divinity stalwart Edwards Amasa Park from self-conscious appeal to historical precedents, nor did they keep Old School Presbyterians from calling on consciousness when convenient, or New Haven theologians from detailed biblical exegesis. Nowhere as on these questions of authority did the commonsense legacy of the Revolutionary era bear more directly on the expression of theological opinion.

2. Who was God, and how did he accomplish his work?

No theologian of this era insisted upon defining the character of God with Jonathan Edwards, who had pictured an absolutely omnipotent deity who actively ruled the universe for the grand purpose of displaying his own ineffable glory. The most common traditional position emphasized the power of God and his lordship over humanity exercised directly through the work of the Holy Spirit or, more commonly, indirectly through the use of "means" employed for his providential purpose. The more American tendency was to depict God as a benevolent, reasonable facilitator of human happiness who ruled the universe by creating moral structures, establishing moral laws, and ordaining moral consequences to govern the lives of God's human subjects. As an example of the transition from traditional to American notions, Bruce Kuklick has pointed out that theologians in New England during this period gradually came to substitute the language of constitution for the language of covenant when describing God's interaction with his human creatures.[29]

> 3. How were human beings constituted, and what were their capabilities, by nature and by grace?

These questions were among the most contentious of the era. When Charles Hodge as an old man wrote a retrospective history of the *Princeton Review*, he highlighted the issues he and his Old School colleagues had defended as the essence of their Calvinism. They were all related to human nature: "Men are born into the world, since the fall, in a state of sin and condemnation; . . . this fact was due to the sin of Adam; . . . men are dependent on the Holy Spirit for their regeneration; and . . . it is due to the sovereign and supernatural interposition of the Spirit that one man is converted and not another."[30] Hodge's list was contentious, but it did reflect accurately the traditionalist positions:

> a. Humans possessed a sinful nature that they inherited from Adam.
> b. Humans were by nature free, but this was a freedom to do what they chose to do, not a freedom to act contrary to their character as sinners.
> c. Thus, the great problem for humanity was its sinful state, from which came individual acts of sin.
> d. God, who had permitted Adam's sin but was not its author, justly condemned unrepentant sinners because they shared the guilt of Adam, because they were sinners, and because they committed sins.
> e. Individuals were reconciled to God when he initiated a change in their character (or hearts) and they responded with repentance and faith.
> f. Finally, traditionalists also held that since redemption meant that God had forgiven sinners (not made sinners perfect), the redeemed should respond to God's grace by leading holy lives, but they should not expect to be perfected until they were received into heaven after death.

The positions more attuned to American values contradicted each of these assertions. No major theologian affirmed all of these countertraditional positions completely, or without explanation, but Unitarians, Finneyite revivalists, and sometimes New Haven theologians came close.

> a. Humans did not *have* a sinful nature inherited from Adam but were influenced by the overwhelmingly comprehensive influence of fallen humanity to *become* sinners.
> b. Humans were by nature free, which meant an ability to choose with liberty against powerful motives or personal character as it had developed (in-

grained habits could strongly influence choices but never absolutely determine them).

c. Thus, the great problem for humanity was that people chose to sin and, thus, because of those choices, were constituted as sinful.

d. God was in no sense responsible for sins, either Adam's or anyone else's, and so he was completely free to condemn sinners and their sin because he had absolutely nothing to do with how it came about.

e. God redeemed those individuals who, under the prompting of the Holy Spirit yet of their own free will, chose to turn to him in repentance and faith.

f. Finally, since redemption was God's loving response accomplished through the Holy Spirit prompting the sinner's choice, redeemed sinners could and should go on to seek the Christian perfection that God in Scripture promised to believers who sought him with their whole heart.

4. How did God redeem sinners?

From the most traditional Old School Presbyterian through the mainstream of Unitarians, there was general agreement that human salvation came through faith in Jesus Christ, whose passion and resurrection won a victory over sin and death in which humans by God's grace now participated. Beyond this agreement, there were major differences, and the critical divides came on questions concerning the atonement.

Traditionalists held that the atonement was "particular": Christ's death might have a significance for all humanity in some general sense, but from what they thought was stressed most in Scripture, they concluded that the death of Christ was applied with saving effect only to those who were redeemed. The opposite position held to a "general" atonement; Christ's death actually and genuinely made possible the redemption of all humans.

More complicated, and even more divisive, was the question of the nature of the atonement itself. The Christian church has never had a universally agreed upon understanding of the means by which loving fellowship is restored between sinful (and therefore unholy) humans and the righteous (perfectly holy) deity. The person and work of Christ have always been crucial, but the centrality of Christ has been construed in at least four different ways. Proponents of various "theories of the atonement," moreover, regularly proceed as they did in antebellum America with zero-sum reasoning, where the defense of one theory usually entailed arguments against all the others.[31] It simplifies things only slightly to describe the main views as follows:

- *Christus victor*: By defeating sin, death, hell, and the devil, Christ won a way back to God for sinners with whom he had identified in the self-giving act of the incarnation.
- *penal substitution*: By taking on himself the wrath of God otherwise destined to fall justly on sinners for their violation of divine holiness, Christ paid the sinners' debt and took the sinners' penalty. God therefore looks upon sinners as covered by the blood of Christ. Reconciliation results as God imputes (i.e., counts or reckons) Christ's righteousness as belonging to formerly guilty sinners.
- *governmental*: By offering himself freely as a sacrifice in keeping with the laws that God had established for the moral ordering of the universe, Christ

makes it possible for God's justice to be reconciled with his holiness and so opens the way for God to forgive humans for their sin and to call them to himself. The main differences with the penal substitution view is to deny that God is angry with sinners and that Christ's righteousness is imputed to believers; the atonement in this view works a change in God's administration of the moral universe defined by his law.

• *moral influence*: By going willingly to a death he did not deserve, Jesus offers the most moving example imaginable of self-giving sacrifice and thus the strongest model possible for humans to exchange self-seeking for the service of others.

Within Protestantism, penal-substitution views dominated from the sixteenth through the eighteenth centuries, though governmental views were advanced by a few thinkers, as in the work of the Dutch jurist Hugo Grotius (e.g., *De Veritate Religionis Christianae*, 1622). Some modern historians have descried a strong *Christus victor* motif in the early Reformers. In America, governmental views began to appear in the mid-eighteenth century with Joseph Bellamy's *True Religion Delineated* of 1750, the first major American work to promote them, while the Unitarians were among the first in North America actively to promote moral-influence theories.

The crux of debate over the atonement lay in the question of imputation. Traditionalists saw a blessed symmetry in sacred history: as God imputed the sinfulness and guilt of Adam to all humanity, so God imputed the righteousness of Christ to all who put their trust in him. The opposite position contended that this was a symmetry badly askew, for in the traditionalist doctrine all humans fell under the curse of Adam but only some were redeemed in Christ. Moreover, opponents of the traditional position held that the very idea of imputation violated some of the most certain intuitive and scriptural principles about what responsibility, fair play, and just dessert simply had to mean.

Questions of truth, God, humanity, and salvation were at the heart of theological exposition and contention in this era. Reformed thinkers worried them nearly to death because they wanted to know God and his ways aright, but also because as Christian republicans they were convinced that knowing and heeding these truths would keep them free.

14

The Americanization of Calvinism

The Congregationalist Era, 1793–1827

As had not been the case before the formation of the United States, the major Reformed theologians from all regions of the country were now becoming increasingly aware of each other; increasingly they read each others' works, criticized each other, and competed for roughly the same theologically literate constituencies. The end result was intellectual exchange of such vigor that no later period has produced historians patient or sympathetic enough to chart the full ebb and flow of Reformed theological development in this era. The drama of the exchange came from the fact that so many conscientious reasoners, while differing sharply among themselves on critical doctrinal questions, still shared so many convictions about God and the nation and so many instincts about how best to theologize for church and society. Its poignancy came from the fact that the theologians showed more skill at exposing the weaknesses of their opponents than providing convincing demonstrations of their own positions. An even sadder reality was that this theologizing cohort of unprecedented breadth and competence was so adept at putting to use the intellectual conventions of the new United States that they would be rendered marginal when other social, political, and intellectual conventions emerged with great force in the decades following the Civil War.

The history of Calvinist theology in the national period was given a decisive impetus by two events from the early 1790s. First was the publication in 1793 of Samuel Hopkins's *System of Doctrines*, the first such attempt at a comprehensive theological statement in New England since the publication of Samuel Willard's *Compleat Body of Divinity* in 1726. But instead of expound-

269

ing an inherited creed as Willard had done, Hopkins wrote self-consciously to codify the insights of his teacher, Jonathan Edwards. He was also offering an updating of those teachings as adjusted in the nearly four decades since Edwards's death by himself, Joseph Bellamy, and Jonathan Edwards Jr. (who after attending Princeton had returned to New England to study with both Bellamy and Hopkins). The second significant event was the appointment in 1795 of Timothy Dwight, a grandson of Edwards, as president of Yale College. Dwight brought to Yale a singular combination of commitments: he was an Old Calvinist in his desire to preserve a godly social order, he venerated his grandfather so highly that he could never be considered an enemy to the New Divinity of Bellamy and Hopkins, he was dedicated wholeheartedly to the cause of revival and social reform, and yet unlike most other New England theologians, he was willing to leave some perplexing questions as unresolved conundrums.

Hopkins and Dwight have sometimes been regarded as moving in opposite directions—respectively, the intellectual systematizer of the New Divinity and the practical promoter of Old Calvinist community order. But that picture is too simple. The way in which the two represented a merging of Edwardsean theological questions and Old Calvinist social ideals can be illustrated by several particulars. One is the fact that by the 1790s almost all Congregationalists of any consequence had adopted Edwards's views on membership by requiring a profession of saving faith from those who would join the church. But almost all of them also displayed a nearly Puritan desire to keep the church at the heart of the social order. Nathaniel W. Taylor, grandson of a resolute Old Calvinist and the most important theologian among Timothy Dwight's students, was a good example of these streams flowing together, since as a pastor he insisted (against his grandfather) on a professing church membership, but he also was devoted (as had been his grandfather) to the principle that a healthy society required a vigorous church as its moral guide. Even as Taylor worked very hard at promoting revival, he also, in Allen Guelzo's well-chosen phrase, "longed for the church-in-society."[1] Taylor upheld these positions, first by fighting to retain the Congregationalist establishment in Connecticut, and then by promoting revivals and voluntary societies as a substitute for the formal ecclesiastical establishment.

A second indication of New Divinity and Old Calvinist confluence came in the founding of Andover Seminary in 1808.[2] While cooperation between the two factions was never entirely harmonious, Dwight's wholehearted assistance with the project expressed a general feeling among the Congregational trinitarians that, whatever their differences with each other, they were far less important than the need to present a common front against the Unitarians. In a word, the combination of an intellectual agenda set by Hopkins and a social agenda set by Dwight was a natural coalition, and it was critical for almost all theological development in New England for more than half a century.

The Legacy of Samuel Hopkins

Hopkins, especially with his *System of Doctrines*, was the key figure in creating what Douglas Sweeney has called "a uniquely Edwardsian culture," meaning not a uniform acceptance of identical doctrines but a nearly uniform New England concentration on the same theological questions and a nearly unanimous agreement, lasting until the appearance of Horace Bushnell, to labor on these questions with the vocabulary that Edwards had provided.[3] Hopkins's importance for the whole tradition was to inspire confidence in other mere mortals that they could continue along the path the great Edwards had pioneered. In his pastorates at Great Barrington, Massachusetts (1743–1769), and Newport, Rhode Island (1770–1803), Hopkins was never able to inspire the revivals for which he preached, and a stiff personality kept him from making a mark in society. Yet he was a sympathetic individual who, despite long hours of study, enjoyed the tenacious loyalty of many congregants, especially the godly women of Newport.[4]

A significant indication of how Hopkins's social location differed from Edwards's was the fact that, unlike his mentor, Hopkins engaged in active social reform. His particular concern was slavery, against which he spoke and wrote both during the Revolution and after the Constitutional Convention had provided legal protection for the slave system. Hopkins's words on the latter occasion showed that he had learned to appropriate the new national vocabulary for his own concerns. As he put it, "tyranny and slavery" were "these evils" that "the gospel" was especially well suited to root out. Putting an end to slavery was urgent, since, in terms familiar to both Puritans and republicans, it threatened to bring down "the righteous judgment of God . . . Have we not all reason to fear that the vengeance of heaven will fall upon us, as a people, in ways perhaps which are not now thought of, unless we repent and reform?"[5]

If Hopkins's active social concern set him apart from Edwards, his key role for later Calvinist theology nonetheless came as he passed along, revivified, and sometimes adjusted specific aspects of Edwards's theological legacy. What marked off later theological parties in New England from each other was their varied responses to this Edwardsean agenda. What marked all New Englanders off from the Presbyterians was the simple assumption that this agenda was the only possible way to approach the critical theological issues.

First, Hopkins and all who followed in his train treated the Scriptures as the only artifact of past Christian centuries to which automatic respect was due. American loyalty to Scripture hid almost as much as it revealed, as chapters below suggest, but it remained, as it had been for Edwards, an unquestioned foundation for all theological reasoning. How theologians adjudicated the deliverances of Scripture over against the deliverances of consciousness eventually became a matter of considerable contention; in general, later theologians were readier to use conscience to interpret Scripture than either Edwards or Hopkins had been.

Second, Hopkins affirmed the urgency of revival. In the New England construct, revival meant a direct, forthright message of human sin and divine grace, along with an expectation that people could respond to that message without delay. In contrast to the situation from 1740 to roughly 1790, when the New Divinity and Old Calvinism clashed over whether revivalism was a good thing, in the period after the Constitution revival became one of the most powerful means moving the parties back toward each other. New Divinity pastors promoted revival as a spiritual good whose by-products would reform society. Descendants of the Old Calvinists promoted revival as a spiritual way of revitalizing and ordering society.

Hopkins and the New England tradition also followed Edwards by advocating clear philosophical reasoning, pursued with a show of independence from previous authorities, as the only legitimate way of explicating divine revelation and applying it to the human condition. Later proponents of New England doctrinal convictions were often criticized by detractors, especially by Old School Presbyterians, for an excess of metaphysics. They responded in character by arguing that this mode of reasoning, even more than the conclusions they reached through it, marked them as the true descendants of Jonathan Edwards.

Hopkins's restatement of Edwards's specific doctrinal formulations provided the essential background for New England's later divisions. Of questions rooted in Edwards's work, four in particular set the stage for much of subsequent theological history.

On the question of free will, Edwards had made a critical distinction that became even more important for later theologians than it was for him. The distinction was his response to the charge that the traditional Calvinist doctrine of election to salvation amounted to pure fatalism—if God selected those who would be saved strictly from the council of his own will, then surely human beings were little more than passive automatons. Edwards repudiated that conclusion. In his view, human conduct revealed two different ways of defining necessity: "By 'natural necessity,' as applied to men, I mean such necessity as men are under through the force of natural causes; as distinguished from what are called moral causes, such as habits and dispositions of the heart, and moral motives and inducements."[6] People were, in fact, free to do what they wanted to do, and so they really did have a "natural ability." But because people were also born sinners, they inevitably and necessarily chose self and sin over God and so displayed a "moral inability." To Edwards, this distinction was enough to show that people could be both free in their choices and bound in their sin.

As an indication of his standing as still, at least partly, a colonial theologian, Hopkins was content simply to pass on Edwards's construction of free will along with basically Edwards's conclusions about it. Those who came after Hopkins, as one of the strongest indications that they were functioning in a new American environment, were as eager to shift the balance of Edwards's argument as they were to retain his vocabulary. Where for Edwards and Hopkins "natural ability" remained a real, but unexplored, possibility, for many later New Englanders "natural ability" became much more important than "moral inability."

Hopkins himself, however, made an important change in a second doctrine, Edwards's understanding of original sin, and this adjustment led on to even greater changes with later theologians. In writing against John Taylor's attack on the traditional understanding that all people bore the guilt and penalty of Adam's fall (*Scripture Doctrine of Original Sin*, 1740), Edwards felt he had demonstrated the adequacy of what Taylor questioned: "that propensity . . . in the nature of all mankind, must be a very evil, depraved and pernicious propensity; making it manifest that the soul of man, as it is by nature, is in a corrupt, fallen, and ruined state."[7] Edwards's singular contribution to this issue, which later New Englanders worried with all their might, was the suggestion that it was reasonable and just for God to treat all humanity as guilty in Adam because all humanity really was *acting in Adam* when Adam turned away from God. For Edwards, the context for this suggestion was his philosophy of theistic idealism. Things exist because God wills them (or re-creates them) every moment into existence.[8] Scripture, according to Edwards, held that God constructed, or willed, as a product of his "divine wisdom," that "Adam and his posterity are dealt with as one." Therefore, Adam and all humanity, as reflecting the will of God, really were one. As a consequence, "both guilt . . . and also depravity of heart, come upon Adam's posterity just as they came upon him, as much as if he and they had all coexisted." Humans, as a consequence, were justly guilty of sin because they were responsible for their *actions in Adam*; moreover, their own evil inclinations represented a "consent to Adam's sin" in which they had shared by the constituting power of the divine will.[9]

Things were significantly different for Hopkins, who, though he retained a strong view of human solidarity with Adam, stressed more strongly the part played by action and consent as the basis for human sinfulness.[10] So much did Hopkins stress this aspect of Edwards's exposition, while neglecting Edwards's very substantial treatment of the inherited and imputed character of sin, that Hopkins could conclude, "This sin, which takes place in the posterity of Adam, is not properly distinguished into original and actual sin, because it is all really actual, and there is strictly speaking, no other sin but actual sin. . . . All sin consists in the nature and quality of the exercises which take place in a moral agent, and not in any thing which goes before, or follows after them, and which is not of the same kind."[11] Later New Englanders would work even harder to define sin as preeminently the result of human action.

The most important change that Hopkins worked in Edwards's thought concerned the concept of virtue. In *The Nature of True Virtue*, Edwards affirmed that "virtue in its most essential nature, consists in benevolent affection or propensity of heart towards Being in general; and so flowing out to particular beings." For his part, Hopkins in the *System of Doctrine* held that "love to God, and love to our fellow-creatures, is of the same nature and kind. . . . It consists most essentially in benevolence or good will to being in general. . . . Disinterested benevolence is pleased with the public interest,—the greatest good and happiness of the whole."[12] Hopkins began his account of virtue as Edwards had done, by considering attitudes toward Being (i.e., God), but then he moved rapidly to the moral imperative of doing good to others. What was for Edwards an aesthetic principle with ethical implications became for Hopkins a practical principle with aesthetic connotations. In the words of Joseph Conforti, this shift was dictated by Hopkins's conclusion that Edwards's account made "unnecessary concessions to rational moral philosophers, . . . tended toward abstraction, mixed aesthetics with ethics, and did not provide an adequate spur to social action."[13]

A parallel alteration occurred in understanding the place of the Christian's good works. Hopkins and later New Englanders made an Old Calvinist use of Edwards's *Treatise on Religious Affections,* in which Edwards identified good deeds as the twelfth, and conclusive, sign of the regenerate heart: "Gracious and holy affections have their exercise and fruit in Christian practice. I mean, they have that influence and power upon him who is the subject of 'em, that they cause that a practice, which is universally conformed to, and directed by Christian rules, should be the practice and business of life." In later eyes this Edwardsian warrant legitimated mobilization for doing good "as the business of life." What Hopkins and other New Englanders did not stress as much was Edwards's account of the character that produced the true signs of "Christian practice." To Edwards, the secret of a changed heart, and so the secret of godly action, was not exertion by itself, as would become the norm in the early nineteenth century, but a special infusion of grace: "Affections that are truly spiritual and gracious, do arise from those influences and operations on the heart, which are *spiritual, supernatural,* and *divine.*"[14]

On the question of virtue, Hopkins kept Edwards's vocabulary but articulated it in response to a new social setting. For Hopkins much more than Edwards, virtue had tasks to accomplish for the good of a dangerously amorphous social order. In his earlier era, Edwards had no need to labor in order to create a social world from the ground up. The universe he took for granted was governed by an established church, a predetermined parish structure, and a history of deference to the learned clergy. By Hopkins's day all these props of personal godliness were gone or going fast. For Edwards, godly action remained primarily a response to God's action. It was not, as it became for Hopkins and even more for succeeding theological generations, a means to build a world for God.

Finally, Hopkins's picture of salvation was a mixture that revised even as it also reaffirmed his teacher's views. With the whole tenor of Edwards's works, but against what would characterize later New England theology, Hopkins insisted that salvation was a divine work that humans received without exerting themselves at all: "The Spirit of God is the only agent and cause by whose energy the effect [of regeneration] takes place; and, so far as the Spirit of God is the cause and agent, the subject, the heart of man, is passive. . . . the Spirit of God is the only agent, and man is the passive subject."[15] On the question of the atonement, however, Hopkins followed Joseph Bellamy, and not his own mentor, in teaching a general atonement.[16] Without pausing to emphasize it, Hopkins also passed on Bellamy's understanding of the atonement as governmental rather than penal.

In sum, Hopkins's *System of Doctrines* maintained much of Edwards's theocentricity, especially with respect to God's monopoly of the motive power in conversion. But it was also clear that Hopkins was writing for a new generation. The nature of that new generation is suggested by the arguments in a short, but revealing tract from Jonathan Edwards Jr. (1745–1801), written about the time that Hopkins published his *System*. Edwards the Younger was, like Hopkins, an earnest reasoner, a person of integrity, and an ineffective preacher. After a quarter century as the minister at the White Haven Church in New Haven, he was dismissed from his congregation for differences over a number of theological issues. Edwards eventually found his true calling in 1799 as the president of Union College, Schenectady, New York, but then, like his famous father, died before he could show what he could do in a collegiate setting. Edwards's brief essay "Remarks on the Improvements Made in Theology by His Father, President Edwards" in actual fact mostly concerned the alterations his own generation had made in the elder Edwards's thought. Of most note in this reassessment was the younger Edwards's manifest apologetic concerns. He wrote with an eye to critics, primarily the proto-Unitarians, who were already trying to seize the moral high ground from the traditional Calvinists. Thus, for example, on the question of imputation—where he set out Bellamy's governmental view—Edwards repeatedly responded to imagined critics with a new sense of egalitarian morality: "Do the posterity of Adam, unless saved by Christ, suffer final damnation on account of Adam's sin? and, if this be asserted, how can it be reconciled with justice? . . . How shall we reconcile it with justice, that Adam's posterity should be doomed on account of Adam's sin?" The answer to his own questions presented an important alteration of his father's views: "They are damned on account of *their own personal sin merely*, and not on account of *Adam's sin*."[17] Even more, it marked a reconstruction of theological reasoning in response to a moral agenda massively reshaped since the days of the older Edwards by ideologies of liberty and right.

The distinctive theological slogans for which Hopkins was well known even before his published the *System of Doctrine* reflected the same reconstituted landscape of public morality.[18] Hopkins proved himself a faithful student of his esteemed teacher by insisting on a theocentric universe—the true followers of God should be willing to be damned for his glory; the unregenerate who tried to save themselves by performing religious duties were in fact more to be condemned than those who remained indifferent, since the former were blasphemously abusing the glorious means provided by a glorious God. But along with this valiant theocentricism came also indications of a theology directed toward a different moral consciousness—sinfulness meant not what we inherit but what we do; virtue meant love-in-action for "the public interest"; God did indeed ordain that sin should come to pass, but only to increase the quantity of human happiness in the world. Hopkinsianism was still the theology of Jonathan Edwards, but it was now Edwardseanism rewritten for an age sensitive about intimations of inequality, awakened to the pursuit of happiness, and desperate for the moral reconstruction of society.

Timothy Dwight and His Students

Timothy Dwight was moving in the very same direction.[19] What Hopkins bequeathed to later New England intellectually, Dwight bequeathed practically. Dwight's own theology could be picked apart into its constituent parts— with Edwards Sr. he held that true religion was at root a matter of the affections, with Hopkins he held that sin was in the sinning, with the Old Calvinists he repudiated pietistic separatism. But most characteristic was the fact that Dwight often intentionally turned aside from complex philosophical discussion to drive home Christian mandates for action. From first to last, Dwight was a man in motion.

He came of age as an ardent supporter of the War for Independence. During the Revolutionary era, he was one of the "Connecticut Wits," who sought to create a True National Literature, at once the equal of Britain's and yet also proudly American in its themes and values. He was for twelve years the pastor of the Congregational Church in Greenfield, Connecticut, which he memorialized in an epic poem (*Greenfield Hill*, 1794) as a nearly idyllic instantiation of ancient Puritan virtues midst the glories of a godly, free United States of America. At Greenfield, Dwight conducted a coeducational academy that was so successful it became his recommendation for the presidency of Yale when Ezra Stiles died in 1795. At Yale he promoted revivals among the students, devoted himself diligently to the liberal arts, wrote, preached, and repeated a series of 173 sermons that combined moderate Edwardsean Calvinism and opposition to the infidelity of Hume, Voltaire, and Paine. With a desperation verging on panic, Dwight mobilized public opinion and political allies in defense of Connecticut's Congregational establishment. He was a lifelong opponent of slavery. Most significantly, he inspired a generation of students to share his activist commitments to revival, reform, and the discipline of public morals.

Like John Witherspoon at Princeton in the preceding generation, Dwight's political savvy, his demonstration of the compatibility between Christian piety and the liberal arts, and his effectiveness as a mentor of students marked him as the most capable college president of his era. During the first fifteen years of the new century, when a wave of destructive student disorders swept through virtually all corners of American higher education, Yale alone remained steadily and piously on course.[20]

Traditionalists

Also like Witherspoon, Dwight's legacy was carried by two different groups of students in two different directions. In Dwight's case it was not the difference between rationalist and confessionalist tendencies, but between traditional revivalism and modern revivalism. Dwight's more traditional students were represented by Asahel Nettleton (1783–1844), who was himself converted at a revival in 1800 and then later attended Yale, and Bennet Tyler (1783–1858), who was converted under Dwight's influence while a student at Yale in 1802. Nettleton was one of the first New England clergymen to devote himself professionally to revival, while Tyler took the more normal course of aiding voluntary religious efforts from his post as a pastor. Both were schooled mostly in the line of Joseph Bellamy; both were, like Dwight, willing to tolerate intellectual mystery; and both insisted upon a conservative interpretation of New England's Calvinist tradition.

The shape of that interpretation was indicated in 1821 when Nettleton was preaching at Lyman Beecher's church in Litchfield, Connecticut. As Bennet Tyler reported in his memoir on Nettleton, "He brought from his treasure the doctrines of total depravity, personal election, reprobation, the sovereignty of divine grace, and the universal government of God in working all things after the counsel of his own will [decrees]. And these great doctrines did not *paralyze*, but greatly *promoted* the work."[21] The proclamation of "Total Depravity, Regeneration by the Holy Spirit, Divine Sovereignty, and Election" was what Tyler also highlighted as the key matters in his account of later theological controversies in New England.[22] With such views, Tyler and Nettleton became implacable opponents of the Unitarians. When Beecher and Nathaniel William Taylor published opinions that could be construed as drifting in a Unitarian direction, Nettleton and Tyler also mounted literary and institutional opposition to their fellow Yale graduates. In 1834 Tyler became the first president of the Theological Institute of Connecticut in East Windsor Hill (later Hartford Seminary), which was organized explicitly to combat the influence of Taylor's views at Yale. In such labors the traditionalist elements in Dwight's Calvinism continued to exert an influence long after his passing.

The Early Lyman Beecher and N. W. Taylor

Dwight's more famous students, Beecher (1775–1863) and Taylor (1786–1858), took a different course.[23] A key to the trajectory of Beecher's activism and Taylor's theology was their cooperation in harmony with their beloved teacher, Dwight, before either of the younger men won renown on his own. That first mobilization, undertaken while Beecher was a young minister on Long Island (1798–1810) and then in Litchfield (1810–1826), and while Taylor was serving as Dwight's amanuensis (1808–1809) and then as the minister of New Haven's First Church (1812–1822), was the effort to save traditional New England. Enemies were legion, including rabble-rousing Methodists, Democratic-Republican demagogues, and aristocratic Episcopalians. In those early efforts, which included the creation of Connecticut's Society for the Reformation of Morals, Beecher and Taylor both embarked on the work for which they became famous. Beecher's gift lay in his organizational energy, which, if it never stayed focused on any one object for long, was nonetheless a powerful force. Thus, within the space of little more than a decade, this young Boanerges launched powerful blows against vice in general and dueling in particular, he proclaimed the need for a general reformation of manners, he urged the recruitment of young men for the ministry, and he championed both the government of God and the Bible as a source of laws.[24] In these publications, as also in his energetic pastorates, Beecher fleshed out the ideal of godly activity that he had learned from Timothy Dwight.

The counterpart to Beecher's energy was Nathaniel William Taylor's incisive intelligence. Taylor eventually became the major theologian of the New Haven school, a figure of extraordinary renown in his own day, and a voice that inspired both ardent loyalty and fervent opposition. Significantly, his earliest published works revealed his powerful dialectical skills arrayed against the Episcopalians and the Methodists, both still much smaller groups than the Congregationalists. It was not a coincidence, however, that in the Connecticut politics of Dwight's last decade, adherents of these denominations were allies of the populist Democratic-Republicans, who were pushing the hardest to disestablish the Congregational churches. Taylor's positions in his early writings outlined views from which, over the course of an influential career, he never retreated.

Those earliest published writings were part of the scheme backed by Dwight and energized by Beecher to save Connecticut. "Are we to be revolutionized by Churchmen and Democrats?" was how Beecher put it to Taylor in 1816.[25] Taylor's response was to publish a sermon from that same year aimed expressly at the Episcopalians and a pamphlet in 1818 that included also the Methodists as its target.[26] Both reacted to the Episcopalians as teachers of false doctrine as well as the embodiment of selfish elitism. Yet Taylor's deepest theological concern was the notion taught in different ways by the Episcopalians and the Methodists that God had restored a certain degree of holiness to humans before they faced the choice for or against conversion. The Episcopal form of the teaching was that baptism constituted its recipients members of the church and thus in a genuine sense regenerate, even if the baptized ones did not immediately act in a holy manner.[27] The Methodist variant was that human free will was restored to all humanity by the atonement of Christ. Methodists vociferously, and Episcopalians with greater decorum, had developed these teachings against the Calvinist belief that choice was always determined by the moral character of the person. Early Methodists and most Episcopalians agreed with the Augustinian, or Calvinist, picture of unregenerate human nature as free enough in its ability to choose evil. They also agreed that in a natural state people indeed could not choose God, but the reason for that inability was that they did not want to choose God. Where they disagreed with Calvinists was about the means God provided to rectify this situation. Calvinists traditionally taught that God supernaturally changed the character of some individuals by applying to them the benefits of Christ's atoning death. Methodists held, by contrast, that God applied the benefits of Christ's atonement to all people, which meant that all people now had the ability, in response to God's gift of grace, to choose freely the good or, in keeping with old evil habits, to continue choosing against God.

Taylor's response to the challenge of the Methodists and Episcopalians worked on three levels. His first tactic was to expose the Episcopalians' erroneous picture of salvation, a picture that was especially troubling for how Taylor thought it undercut practical godliness. According to Taylor, salvation did not come as he said the Episcopalians taught, from being baptized "by those and those only who have received lawful authority from the bishops of the church to administer it," since that would be a system that "places mankind in a state of salvation without a particle of holiness." Salvation rightly ascertained required conversion, "a change of heart," and this conversion— not baptism—supplied the essential "dividing line between sinners and saints."[28] Against the Methodists, Taylor tried to show how absurd their teaching was. After noting the general belief that if a person is to be held responsible for actions, that person must be free to choose those actions (i.e., Jonathan Edwards's "natural ability"), he suggested the Methodists and Episcopalians actually taught that, in effect, God was the source of evil: "Without free-agency there can be no sinful act. But according to the opinion now opposed, there is no free agency in man, but as the result of supernatural grace. But if there can be so sin, without free agency, and if there can be no free agency without supernatural grace, then there can be no sin without supernatural grace!"[29] This summary was in fact a caricature, for Methodists did not teach that people without grace lost free will entirely (i.e., lost "natural ability"); rather, they taught that (in Edwards's terms) "moral ability" was absent until God applied the benefits of Christ's atonement and, by so doing, restored "moral ability" universally to all humanity. Nevertheless, Taylor shrewdly put his finger on a difficulty in this view by showing how it seemed to make the presence of sin depend upon the prior presence of grace.

Taylor's positive positions in these early tracts revealed, second, a different Calvinist arsenal than had been deployed heretofore. Their modernity was especially clear in the pamphlet from 1818, which made much of "the plain principles of common sense" and of "consciousness" to demonstrate that people could not be held accountable for what they were not free to choose. In addition, when Taylor described the nature of personality, he made use of categories new to New England discourse that he called "the faculties of *understanding, conscience,* and *will.*"[30] Most important, these two works revealed a much higher estimate of natural human capacity than earlier Calvinists admitted. In the 1816 sermon, Taylor expressed sentiments that could be interpreted as traditionally Edwardsean: "Men are as complete moral agents, as able to perform their duty, *if* they would, as Adam was before his fall." Yet his concentration on what humans could do by nature ("a power to understand—a power to choose and refuse—a power to love and to hate. These powers no man wants") was much more obvious than what they chose not to do because of a sinful inheritance from Adam.[31] In the 1818 pamphlet he ventured even further. While Taylor put to use an Edwardsean vocabulary to deny that moral agents were crippled by "natural inability," he employed a new phrase—"the inability of disinclination"—to describe why individuals chose to sin. He also anticipated his later and notorious declaration—that in moral actions people always possessed "power to the contrary"—by asserting that humans in their natural state, without grace, and simply as God had created them, possessed "the power to do otherwise."[32]

In these positive statements of his own position, Taylor knew that he was differentiating himself from Edwards, and going further also than Dwight. Against Taylor's opinions, Edwards had held that consciousness revealed a mixture of ability and inability; that "moral inability" was more than a matter of the inclinations; that "power to do otherwise" was a meaningless phrase; and that human beings did not so much *have* faculties but rather *displayed* various faculties in various forms of their action. Mere months after publishing the 1818 pamphlet, Taylor wrote Beecher about what needed to be done to renovate the theology they had inherited. That letter contained high praise for Edwards as "the chief cornerstone of New England orthodoxy, and an impregnable wall to all its enemies." But then Taylor went on to tell Beecher that he felt Edwards had stumbled in "his definition of moral agency and free will." For Taylor, "If language has any meaning, a free will is a will which is free, and to say that free will is a power to do as we please or as we will [as Edwards had asserted] is saying nothing to the purpose."[33] Although historians have not usually concentrated on these early publications by Taylor, they are aware of them and of the letter to Beecher. From divergent readings of how much Taylor was, or was not, preserving the substance and methods of Edwards have come the great debates over whether Taylor was improving upon Edwards,[34] betraying him,[35] perversely inverting his most important convictions,[36] or simply extending his thought by natural development.[37]

Such debates are important, but they may obscure the burden of Taylor's most basic concern. Why was he deliberately altering what had come to him through Edwards, Hopkins, and Dwight? Why was he turning aside from the terms being put to use in the taste-and-exercise debate (explored below), which was still going strong as he brought these works from the press? The key was Taylor's conviction that true godliness always blended personal holiness and responsible public morality. The doctrines of Methodism and Episcopalianism—and, he would later add, of maladroit Calvinism—were obscuring "the equity of the divine government, and the principles on which man is blamed for disobedience."[38] Taylor wanted people to accept responsibility for their sins. He wanted people to realize that they had no one to blame but themselves for remaining in their sin, that there was no divine logic of things to excuse passivity in those who heard the gospel. He wanted them to seek conversion earnestly and immediately. He wanted them just as zealously to pursue lives of active holiness: "For why call it a *new birth*, if nothing new is born, or a *new creation*, if nothing now is created? And do these terms describe any thing but the production of real holiness?"[39] Taylor wanted them, in brief, to understand and to promote "the government of God."[40] From the start—from the days in and immediately after the War of 1812, when the students of Timothy Dwight were taking up spiritual arms to save their holy commonwealth, and when faulty views of grace from Methodists and Episcopalians were conspiring to dismantle that commonwealth—what mattered most was the vindication of God's moral government as the basis for personal holiness and a godly social order, and the encouragement of holy moral action as the antidote to the poison of moral passivity.

Taylor, in other words, was willing to go beyond Nettleton and Tyler. The latter wanted to use traditional Calvinist theology to save souls and thereby *rescue* a Calvinist social order. Taylor realized that there were adjustments required in the deposit of Calvinist theology if souls were to be saved and one was to *build* a Calvinist social order. In a world riven by crisis and uncertainty, Dwight's Calvinist solution was revival and moral reform. Nettleton and Tyler understood this solution to mean that revival would be sparked by traditional teachings and then would lead by a natural osmosis of godliness to moral reform.

By contrast, Taylor and Beecher were convinced that all goals—personal salvation, church mobilization, social renovation—had to be pursued together and with a coordinated set of well-articulated programs and well-defended doctrines. At first Dwight, Beecher, and Taylor assumed that these goals could be reached only through a revived establishment, so they fought hard in league with the Federalists on behalf of stable deference and urged Yale students to go out into the churches as defenders of cultural holiness as well as Christian truth.[41] But gradually Dwight began to suspect that establishment was not a requirement for the ends they sought, while Beecher and Taylor came to conclude that letting the establishment go would be a positive good. The important thing, it turned out, was not a revived and reformed establishment but revival and moral reform, period. If people were not converted, if they did not become active members of churches, and if the churches did not leaven society, America was doomed.

So motivated, Beecher and Taylor urgently campaigned for conversions, personal holiness, and moral order. Under Dwight's tutelage, Beecher especially became master of the jeremiad, sometimes in the traditional Puritan form of asserting that if the community did not turn from its sins and repent, God would wreak vengeance upon it. But under the influence of Taylor's theology, the jeremiad sounded more modern: if the community did not repent, vice would increase, and because of how God had established the moral order of the universe, that vice would destroy the community.

Lyman Beecher went much further than his mentor in implementing Dwight's convictions, and Taylor went much further in adjusting inherited theology to promote those same convictions. But their vision remained what they had been taught. Together, their great enemies were personal unbelief, disdain for orderly holiness, and the pernicious social effects of infidelity. Together, their great engines for hope were revival and moral reform. Taylor and Beecher began their theology with a vocabulary handed on from Samuel Hopkins, but their social and political course came from Timothy Dwight. As they pursued that course, the newer ideologies of American society exerted a palpable effect on the expressions of their theology.

Controversies

The mélange of influences passed on by Hopkins and Dwight through important leaders like Nettleton, Tyler, Beecher, and Taylor eventually broke apart into several distinct factions during the 1820s and 1830s. But before that fragmentation occurred, theology in New England passed through two important controversies and also began to feel the effects of several subterranean intellectual transformations.

Exercise versus Taste

The first of the controversies took place largely among those who sought a modern restatement of the Edwardsean New Divinity. This desire led to the conflict between "exercisers" and "tasters," a debate that is sometimes treated as proof of the comic irrelevance of New England's abstruse theology, but that actually represented a serious intellectual contest among conservative Edwardseans about how to retain both divine sovereignty and human responsibility as integrated parts of one theological system.[42]

In the background of this dispute were insinuations from eastern Massachusetts concerning the embarrassing immorality of Calvinist theology as it had been taught. These murmurings repeated complaints of the liberals who had opposed the revived Calvinism of the Great Awakening, but also pointed to an even franker Unitarian criticism. Students taught by Hopkins, Bellamy, and Dwight were beginning to feel the sting of liberal jibes—tell us again how God can be the all-wise creator of human beings *and* the sole agent of human salvation *and* the entirely just governor of the moral world! If humans were created so that they could only sin, but if somehow sinful humans were still responsible as free agents for that sin, where was the justice?

The "exercise" solution to this problem arose in a line of descent from Edwards through Hopkins. Its leading proponent was Nathanael Emmons (1745–1840), who served as pastor in rural Franklin, Massachusetts, for well over half a century. Emmons—in Sydney Ahlstrom's phrase, "a highly distinctive, almost eccentric theological genius"—marched boldly onto theological territory that had intimidated almost everyone who preceded him.[43] According to Emmons, people considered as moral agents simply *were* their choices: "As the soul is all spirit, so it is all activity. . . . The heart, which is the seat of all moral exercises, consists in nothing but moral exercises."[44] With such assertions Emmons was carrying further a view of the person as unified actor that Edwards had outlined in his *Freedom of Will*. But then Emmons went beyond Edwards to contend that the exercises defining human beings were both entirely free and directly determined by God. (Edwards had stressed that God worked in people through secondary causes, or means.) The example of biblical figures who chose freely to do what God had ordained was critical to Emmons at this point: "Pharaoh chose to act as God foretold he should act. Judas chose to act as Christ said he would. In all these instances, God operated upon the heart, and made men act so as to fulfill his wise and holy designs." Yet in this divine determination, people were entirely free: "I rest my whole cause upon this single proposition, that the divine influence upon the heart, in producing volitions, does not imply compulsion on the part of God, nor destroy liberty on the part of man."[45] Human salvation worked the same way. When God chose to change a person's character, that person was converted and yet with complete freedom began to practice God-honoring exercises.

Thus construed, Emmons appeared to be a Calvinist of exquisite consistency. God was in complete control of the universe, yet people still acted freely in doing what they chose to do. Other aspects of Emmons's teaching, however, rendered certain traditional Christian teachings unnecessary. Humans, for example, did not come into the world with original sin, no imputation of Adam's guilt or Christ's righteousness was necessary, and Christ's atonement was a general, governmental transaction that occurred so that all could see and applaud the character of God's justice. Emmons did not elaborate a comprehensive metaphysic, but by stressing so intensely that God caused all human exercises, he came close to the philosophical idealism that had provided the larger intellectual framework for Edwards's theology.

In opposition to the "exercise" scheme, which won for Emmons more attention than adherents, "tasters" responded that people did in fact possess some kind of underlying spiritual essence that explained the moral character of their choices. Ministers such as Asa Burton (1752–1836) of Thetford, Vermont, who, like Emmons, trained a number of theological students, argued the more conventional position that God's saving work acted on the individual's underlying "nature," "heart," "relish," "disposition," or "taste." Where for Emmons people *were* their motives, for Burton they *had* motives.

Yet Burton too was an innovator, especially in the psychology he spelled out in his *Essays on Some of the First Principles of Metaphysics, Ethicks, and Theology* (1824). That work spread before a large audience a picture of human nature that N. W. Taylor had advanced in his little-noticed pamphlet from 1818. Edwards, for reasons rooted in his theistic idealism, as also Hopkins, who was not as clear philosophically, had regarded the human personality as constituted by understanding and will. "Understanding" described the person from the angle of thought, desire, and character; "will" described the person from the angle of action. The crux of Edwards's argument in *Freedom of Will* was that the person moved into action (or exercised the will) by following naturally the strongest impression (or motive) of the understanding. Burton altered Edwards's view in order to align it with an increasingly popular psychology—humans possessed not two, but three defining "faculties": understanding (or the mind), heart (or taste), and will (or choice). For a human to act was for the heart, or taste, to present the deliverances of the mind with an affectional force to the will, or in Frank Hugh Foster's summary: "Objects excite our desires, and our desires move our wills."[46] Burton himself held to a traditional view of sin and conversion by maintaining that will always followed taste, and so conversion could only occur when God bequeathed a new principle of holiness to the taste. But he had changed the Edwardsean view of the person as a unified being into a person divided into its three faculties. This change amounted to an open invitation for others to postulate an autonomy of action for the faculty of the will.

What kept the exercise-taste debate from degenerating into abstruse irrelevance was the larger social context in post-independence New England. Principles of human freedom, mandates for individual initiative, and insistence upon egalitarian justice were everywhere ascending. Against this rising tide of rights talk, the Calvinists were trying to stand firm. Although they were being stretched intellectually to ever more extreme formulations, they were not giving up on divine sovereignty, supernatural election, the belief that humanity required a divine salvation, or the definition of freedom as the ability to follow through on choices. It was the last generation to maintain that solidarity.

Unitarianism

Theological development within the Calvinistic mainstream as articulated by Samuel Hopkins and Timothy Dwight was decisively influenced by a second major controversy from a different stream of historic New England religion. The Unitarianism that emerged as a self-conscious theological movement in turn-of-the century New England was an extension of the liberalizing religion of an earlier Enlightenment rationalism.[47] As such, it represented a continuation of theological influence from eighteenth-century refined English thought—trust in reason instead of the practice of enthusiasm, belief in salvation by moral amelioration instead of by a bloody sacrifice, hope for the universal salvation of all people instead of a craven fear of hell, God as benevolent creator instead of providential meddler, and, ultimately, the rational clarity of a unified God instead of the recondite mysteries of the Trinity. Under the leadership of pastors and teachers like Henry Ware Sr. (1764–1845), whose election in 1805 as the Hollis Professor of Divinity at Harvard marked a significant public recognition of liberal strength in Boston and environs, Unitarians promoted a benevolent God, a balanced universe, and a sublime human potential. Unitarians resembled Old Calvinists in their concern for an organic and orderly society, they took their stand with the Protestant formalists in treating the American Revolution as a defense of traditional rights, and their social instincts paralleled those of Dwight and his students in distrusting the populist democracy of Jeffersonianism. Yet when the Unitarian vision came to expression from such leaders as William Ellery Channing, in works like "The Essence of Christianity," the gap separating them from other New Englanders was clear: "The purpose of God is to raise the soul from the power of moral evil to perfection—this is the beginning and end of Christianity. . . . Christianity should now be disencumbered and set free from the unintelligible and irrational doctrines, and the uncouth and idolatrous forms and ceremonies, which terror, superstition, vanity, priestcraft and ambition have laboured to identify with it. . . . in[to] its own celestial splendour, and its divine simplicity."[48] In Daniel Walker Howe's entirely apt phrase, Unitarians promoted "Puritanism without Calvinism."[49]

Unitarianism as it emerged as a distinct denomination was not, however, just an eighteenth-century religion of the Enlightenment carried forward into the next century. Unitarians too had become Americans in the tumults of Revolution, political construction, and social reordering. In fact, the addition of American warrants from republican and commonsense principles made the Unitarian threat much more pressing for the defenders of traditional Christianity in the decades after Ware's election. When Unitarians skillfully augmented the inheritance of English rationalism with conservative versions of Real Whig politics and Hutchesonian moral philosophy, they became a greatly disorienting force. No Unitarian carried out these tasks as skillfully as Channing (1780–1842), pastor of Boston's Federal Street Church from 1803 and the public spokesmen whom, despite his gentle mien and frail physique, orthodox leaders like Jedidiah Morse, Lyman Beecher, and N. W. Taylor feared the most.

Channing's landmark sermon from 1819, "Unitarian Christianity," which provided an unambiguous answer to questions about what the Boston liberals actually believed, was a masterpiece of rhetorical adaptation as well as religious exposition. In it Channing did set forth clearly what Unitarians believed: "We object to the doctrine of the Trinity, that, whilst acknowledging in words, it subverts in effect, the unity of God."[50] But he did so through a masterful deployment of the intellectual warrants that virtually all the more orthodox religious thinkers of his day were also scrambling to enlist for their versions of Christian faith.

Thus, Channing professed to reason from the Bible alone: "Whatever doctrines seem to us to be clearly taught in the Scriptures, we receive without reserve or exception." Furthermore, in defining what the Unitarian God was and was not, Channing skillfully employed a republican vocabulary: "It is not because his will is irresistible, but because his will is the perfection of virtue, that we pay him allegiance. We cannot bow before a being, however great and powerful, who governs tyrannically." He also turned the moral sense against Calvinism, which shocks "the fundamental principle of morality, and by exhibiting a severe and partial Deity, . . . tends strongly to pervert the moral faculty."[51] And he ended the sermon with an evocative flourish of images: Calvinism represented only a partial victory over "the Papal tyranny," because it still needed to escape "those hierarchies, and other human institutions, by which the minds of individuals are oppressed under the weight of numbers, and a Papal dominion is perpetuated in the Protestant Church." Against such perversions, God stood ready to overturn "the conspiracy of ages against the liberty of Christians" and to end "the servile assent so long yielded to human creeds." For those who could practice "honest and devout inquiry into the Scriptures," a great triumph was at hand—"Christianity . . . purified from error."[52] Channing's sermon was as exemplary in using the categories of antitraditional, republican common sense as it was definitive in announcing the tenets of Unitarian faith.

It was no surprise, therefore, that when the orthodox Calvinists responded to Channing, they did so with an equally earnest effort to show how republican common sense actually supported their position. Leonard Woods, the inaugural professor of theology at Andover Seminary, took up that challenge and, in so doing, precipitated a lengthy exchange with Henry Ware that witnessed three substantial blasts from each side in the years 1820 to 1823.[53] Apart from the intensive care each author took to interpret Scripture, the most obvious feature of the exchange was the combatants' appeal to the normative intellectual conventions of the early republic. Woods's initial reply to Channing did make less of the deliverances of consciousness than his Unitarian opponents, but he was also more energetic in claiming the scientific reliability of biblical authority. On all efforts to discover the truth about reality, "the only mode of reasoning, which can be relied upon to lead us to right conclusions, is that which is pursued in the science of Physics." Procedural exactitude would point the way back to the truth: "Regulating ourselves by the maxims of Bacon and Newton, we inquire, not what we should expect the properties and laws of the physical world would be, nor whether this or that thing can be reconciled with the infinite wisdom and goodness of God,— but simply, *what is fact? What do we find from observation and experience, that the properties and laws of nature really are?*" Theology required broadening out the subjects of inquiry to Scripture, as the Unitarians agreed, but the process at work was the same: "*Theology*, as well as *Philosophy* [i.e., science], is founded on facts. . . . In both cases, the chief object of inquiry, and the rule of reasoning are the same. We first inquire for the knowledge of facts; and by reasoning from facts, we arrive at general truths." In a word, admitting "any presumptive or hypothetical reasoning in *Ethics*, or *Theology*" was as damaging as "in the science of *Physics*."[54]

The payoff for Woods was that the Calvinist system, when carefully ascertained by Baconian procedure, resulted in "a scheme of religion" that exhibits "a moral government, marked with holiness and righteousness throughout." Calvinism was not superior to Unitarianism in the abstract. Rather, its superiority was practical and up-to-the-minute, since it pressed upon everyone "a wise and holy love . . . of immutable obligation" and revealed "the Governor of the world" manifesting "an invariable determination to support the principles of a righteous moral government." And so Woods went on, like Channing purporting to show the truth with no dependence on discredited traditional authorities and making free use of phrases from contemporary American ideology, but in order to attack what Channing was defending.

New England Calvinism for more than forty years was fixated upon the Unitarian peril. That danger sparked not only the Woods-'n-Ware exchange and a further tide of publication. It was also the reason that Lyman Beecher left Connecticut in 1826 to take a church in Boston and challenge the enemy in its stronghold. It shaped N. W. Taylor's interpretations of Calvinism in classroom and print from the mid-1820s. And it loomed over the factional maneuvering of the region's orthodox clergy—the founding of Andover Seminary, the creation of periodicals like New Haven's *Quarterly Christian Spectator* (1819) and Beecher's *Spirit of the Pilgrims* (1828), and the establishment of the seminary at East Windsor when Nettleton and Tyler felt that Taylor was giving too much away in his writings against the Unitarians, which Taylor had published because he thought Woods had done such a poor job, and on and on.

Interested parties outside of New England grew more concerned when they thought they saw Unitarian ideas infecting the traditional Christian churches than they were with Unitarianism itself, since the Unitarians never succeeded in reproducing themselves in great numbers beyond eastern New England. Yet the Unitarian controversy was still decisive for the entire era. Just as the more orthodox churches, antiformalist as well as formalist, exerted their telling impact on the shape of early national culture by proclaiming a message attuned in different ways to that culture, so too did Unitarians like Channing successfully reclothe eighteenth-century rational refinement in the garments of commonsense republicanism. Because the Unitarians were also successful at maintaining themselves as the elite bearers of reason, good taste, benevolence, and refined sensibility in Boston, the center of New England's learned culture, they enjoyed an intellectual influence far out of proportion to their actual numbers.

Transformation of Consciousness

Controversy between exercisers and tasters, as also between Unitarians and their foes, was conducted out in the open. Such intellectual sparring charted not only the course of individual contests but also the rise and fall of vocabularies favored for scoring points and countering blows. More difficult to document are the general shifts in consciousness that came into view during the controversial exchanges, yet these assumptions were changing rapidly in the early decades of the nineteenth century, and the effects on theology were pervasive. Of such changes, four bore directly on theological understanding.

Self-determination

First was the assumption that an action could be moral only if it was self-determined, only if it was the result of free agency acting apart from the controlling influence of whatever had shaped the individual character in the past. For the gathering force of this assumption there are several possible explanations, including the simply political and the more complex philosophical. Of the latter, none has been more persuasively argued than by Henry Boynton Smith in what is still one of the most impressive essays ever written on the New England theology. Smith's essay appeared early in the Civil War as a review of Nathanael Emmons's collected works.

To Smith it was clear that theologians like N. W. Taylor could assume that the will had a self-determining power because a momentous shift in philosophical allegiance took place after Emmons had outlined his position in print. Smith recognized that Emmons had done away with the notion of original sin but argued that "he did it on the basis of a wholly different metaphysic and psychology" from the theologians who came later. Because Emmons believed "that there was no soul except in volitions, he could afford to say, there is no original sin, for the conclusive reason that his theory does not recognize any moral and personal being, of whom such original sin could be predicated."[55] For Emmons, sinfulness and grace were manifest in actions. In addition, the continuity of human nature was maintained through God's every-moment re-creation of the world and of all humanity. Emmons opposed the "taste" scheme because it manifested a false philosophy—there simply was no material substratum constituting human existence. Rather, under God's ever-active creative power, to be a human being was to be defined by what one did as a person.

Smith went on to contend that when, after Emmons, New England abandoned idealistic metaphysics for variations of commonsense realism, there broke apart what Edwards and Emmons had held together—sinfulness as inherited from Adam and sinfulness as resulting from the individual's own acts of sin. According to Smith, the crucial change was philosophical: when New England theologians moved from idealism to realism (from believing that humans were every moment re-created by God to believing that humans possessed a substantial nature), then they dropped the unity with Adam. Smith stated his own argument in the following terms:

> The whole state of the case was entirely altered, when Berkeleianism was supplanted by the Scotch philosophy, and the distinctions between the soul and its exercises, between tendencies and voluntary acts, between the heart and the will, were reinstated in their rational right. The Exercise scheme . . . was cut loose from its Calvinistic moorings; it was divorced from the divine efficiency. The divine element [i.e., God's direct cause of human exercises] was eliminated, and the human will, in the construction of the system, took the place of the divine will [i.e., the newly identified "will" of faculty psychology was credited with moving people to action in the way that Emmons had credited God with moving people to action]. Modern Emmonism [or theories that say "sin is in the sinning"] is thus as different from the old scheme as democracy from imperialism.[56]

Smith was shrewdly summarizing a knotty philosophical history. Edwards had attempted to baptize the sensationalist epistemology of Locke by conceding that true knowledge comes only from our ideas, but then by contending that the source of human ideas was God's every-moment will to re-create all of the world (including human minds and their grasp of the world outside of themselves). Emmons took this position of Edwards further by regarding all human action as impelled by God's will. Against such idealist constructions of human nature and human will, the Scots countered with the argument that universal experience (or "common sense") made it impossible to deny the existence of a substantial world (and a substantial self) existing as the source of ideas about the world and about the self. When Americans accepted this realistic depiction of the nature of things, as they did with increasing unanimity from the 1780s onward, they were modifying Lockean epistemology, but also Edwards's theocentricity.

Two consequences with theological implications followed. It was assumed that there existed a substantial self that willed its own actions (rather than, as with Edwards and Emmons, a self revealed by its willing). It was also assumed that consciousness revealed the inner human world of morality as faithfully as sense data did the external physical world. Neither of these consequences determined theological conclusions by themselves, as was illustrated by Asa Burton and the "tasters," who accepted a view of substantial human nature in line with Scottish reasoning while retaining a traditionally Calvinist sense of salvation as the product of God's activity alone. But the Scottish position clearly put humankind in a much more favorable position to determine its own destiny than had Edwards's sophisticated idealism or the cruder but more militantly God-oriented psychology of Emmons.

The political complement to Smith's philosophical explanation for assumptions about self-determination came from the history of American politics in relationship to American thought. Arguments linked to Scottish philosophy contributed critically to the ideology of independence and thus also contributed critically to more general habits of thought. Intellectual assumptions were changed, first, in direct response to the insistent championing of liberty: if self-determination was required for a well-ordered state, perhaps it was also necessary for a fully human person. A second change was less direct but was made possible by the philosophical canopy constructed by the ideology of the Revolution: if consciousness revealed the injustice of civil tyranny, perhaps it showed also the injustice of all-powerful divine constraint as well.

Put more simply as a question, Why did theologians make the move that Smith explained from philosophical idealism to philosophical realism? A plausible answer is that the latter philosophy contributed so substantially to the ideology of the Revolution that it was adopted by a considerable number of Christian believers in their effort to promote the gospel message in the nation created by the Revolution.

Faculty Psychology

A second assumption that also became manifestly more powerful in the theological discourse of the new century was the belief that the person consisted of three discrete faculties: the understanding, the passion, and the will.[57] Edwards and other religious traditionalists had often spoken of the faculties, but their older psychology, especially among Augustinian Calvinists, pictured the divine constitution of the self as the key to the integrity of persons. The newer emphasis took for granted more discrete powers (and also responsibilities) for the individual faculties. In the era of the American founding and for at least two generations thereafter, many Americans regularly looked upon the tripartite self as a model for the world at large. Just as it was necessary to regulate individual action (will) by proper knowledge (understanding) guiding emotional life (passion) toward proper ends, so it was necessary to balance carefully the many interests in a state if it would develop harmoniously and peacefully. This was an era that continued to stress the need for personal discipline—in Daniel Walker Howe's well-supported conclusion, "Among the many identities available to antebellum Americans, one of the most widely acknowledged and celebrated was that of the sound, well-balanced character. To have such an identity was to have all one's faculties properly exercised, developed, and disciplined." But as Howe also points out, a long history of political argument, dating back to the *Federalist Papers*, had used very similar language to talk about a well-ordered state: "A well-structured government would resemble the balanced mind of a wise person, while a poorly constructed government, like a weak mind, was prone to fall under the tyranny of some capricious passion."[58] The usefulness of faculty psychology for understanding the self, for understanding the social order, and for understanding the two in common was everywhere apparent when Americans contemplated the need for order, whether of self or society.

Commitment to faculty psychology was not necessarily a mandate for abandoning traditional theology. Yet to picture a healthy personality and a healthy social order as the product of balanced faculties was to show how one could stress the inbred powers of the faculties, as N. W. Taylor did in 1818, when he made one of the first theological applications of a full modern faculty psychology in describing the nature of human freedom:

> Free agency consists in the faculties of *understanding, conscience*, and *will*
> ... those powers, capacities, or qualities of the soul of man by which he is
> enabled to see the difference between good and evil, to feel accountability, and
> to choose good or evil, or to love one and hate the other. That the being who
> possesses these faculties or qualities is a free agent, is as obvious and undeniable, as that he also can thus perceive the difference between good and evil,
> and can choose between them, is *free*, to choose between them; in other words,
> that he who *can* thus choose, is *free* to choose. Give these faculties to the stones
> of the street, and they become at once free-agents; take them from the angels
> and their accountability ceases.[59]

Taylor's particular use of faculty psychology, which became common among later Congregationalists, some Presbyterians, and eventually also Methodists, brought great pressure to bear on traditional doctrines of divine activity (election) and human passivity (original sin). That pressure was not created by faculty psychology as such, but the process by which such a psychology became important in the nation assured its importance for theology.

Moral Government

A third assumption was that God's rule over the world was best described in terms of "moral government." This trope began with Bellamy, was developed further by Dwight, and came to prevail everywhere among New Englanders in the generation of Beecher and Taylor. Taylor's definitive lectures to Yale Divinity students, which appeared posthumously in two large volumes, defined this theme as the heart of divine revelation. As he put it, "To present God to men as their perfect Moral Governor, and to unfold the nature, the mode, and the issues of his moral administration under its different forms" was nothing less than "the great design of Revelation, and that to which every other is subordinate and subservient." The Bible in its entirety, according to Taylor, was aimed at clarifying the nature of moral government, and it was of supreme importance in understanding moral government to grasp "man's duty, character, and destiny, the influences under which he must act, the progress and results of the system."[60] For his part, Lyman Beecher once summarized the essence of the advance he and Taylor made over their predecessors by referring to the same theme: "Our doctrine was . . . that *God governs mind by motive and not by force*. . . . Edwards did not come up to that fair and square, Bellamy did not, and, in fact, nobody did until Taylor and I did." With this insight, according to Beecher, "We had got through with the slang of Old Side and New Side."[61]

Where did the emphasis on moral government come from? It was never more than a minor theme with traditional Calvinist theologians, and it had hardly any currency among contemporary theologians outside the United States. The simple but also significant answer is that "moral government" became a critical theological category because of the omnipresence of Real Whig discourse in American public life. In writing about Bellamy, Mark Valeri has suggested that "the concept of moral government" was a "republican rendition of providential rule through law," and so also an explanation for why New Divinity theologians like Bellamy supported the Revolution in "alliance with patriots who rejected many of the doctrines central to Calvinism."[62] For later generation, the same reasoning applies, as in George Marsden's description of Lyman Beecher's mental world: his "emphasis on 'the Moral Government of God' was essentially a republican restatement of the Puritan theory of the national covenant."[63] For the generation of Beecher and Taylor, as instructed by Timothy Dwight, God's rule of the world was not only—or even not primarily—immediate through a direct covenantal relationship; rather, it was mediated by principles of personal duty, virtue as the promoter of social order, vice as the assurance of disorder, and checks and balances on power—in other words, the panoply of republican reasoning.

Moral government did not become a central theological category through any simple process of intellectual borrowing. It was, rather, that a vocabulary shaped by the usages of broader public life seemed also ideally suited for the urgent tasks of the churches. If Christianity was to survive with vigor, sinners had to be moved to salvation, redeemed sinners had to become active members of churches, churches had to supply the leadership for upholding public morality, and Christians had to rally against the daunting forces of vice and irreligion. For all these tasks there was no "given" help at hand, no established church to rely upon, no governmental assistance except what the saints could voluntarily elect, encourage, and inspire. Energetic leaders like Dwight and his students sensed that they were living in a new American wilderness, not the barely inhabited terrain that greeted the Puritan fathers, but the morally and religiously denuded landscape of the democratic republic. The chaos threatened by such a brave new world could be overcome only by careful, exacting government of the self, only by the voluntary, freely chosen, self-regulating government of society. Perhaps more than any other subterranean shift in American intellectual life, the appearance of "moral government" at the heart of religious thought testified to the pervasive interplay between private religion and public morality, between the spheres of politics and theology.

Consciousness

Finally, the assumption grew ever stronger through the early years of the nineteenth century that, besides the Scriptures, human consciousness was the only sure authority for grasping securely the ways of God. This assumption was foundational, since discussion of individual free agency, the human faculties, and God's moral government more and more came to rest on appeals to immediate consciousness.[64] Increasingly the New England theologians acted as if they were proposing their ideas for a burned-over intellectual landscape in which the landmarks of the past were obliterated—established church, deference to inherited authority, hierarchy of privilege, classical republican noblesse oblige, time-honored confessions of faith, respected titles of nobility, and all authoritative texts from antiquity except the Bible and Shakespeare. Lyman Beecher recognized this state of affairs when he confessed in June 1829, "If I understand my own mode of philosophizing, it is the Baconian. Facts and the Bible are the extent of my philosophy."[65] Reliance on axioms of common sense was nothing new in Western intellectual history. The difference by the 1830s in the United States was that most of the authorities employed by earlier generations to complement consciousness were passing rapidly from the scene.

Isolated aspects of the theology of Joseph Bellamy and Samuel Hopkins reflected these new assumptions that were themselves linked to new American realities. Dwight's theology came closer to being directed specifically at values—both articulated and assumed—of the new national culture. But Dwight, and even more the earnest pastors who debated the taste-and-exercise schemes, were still in many ways colonialists. They were only occasionally embarrassed at ascribing unlimited power to God, and Nathanael Emmons not at all. By the time the students of Dwight emerged from his shadow, the situation had changed. Persistent sniping by the Unitarians exposed more and more of traditional New England Calvinism to ridicule. The relentless gospel preaching of the Methodists, and of still more radical sectarians like Elias Smith, threatened the Calvinists' traditional leadership of New England society. Democratic-Republican riffraff conspired with quasi-monarchist Episcopalians to overthrow the religious establishments that had symbolized New England's Christian purpose for 200 years.[66] Most important, by the 1830s the radical consequences of the American Revolution—an ever-broadening democracy, the exaltation of liberty, and the paranoia about power—had been at work for more than a full generation. Given these realities, it was not remarkable that New England's hereditary Calvinism Americanized, but that it did so with such a strong residual commitment to its traditional Christian past. During the first quarter of the nineteenth century, Congregational theology in New England provided the new nation with its most articulate Christian theology and also reflected most clearly the effect of that new nation on the assumptions of theology.

15

The Americanization of Calvinism

Explosion, 1827–1860

From a period where the most important theologians came from New England, where their theology reflected the agenda of established Congregationalism, and where the most urgent theological task was to refute the Unitarians, American Calvinist thought in the late 1820s was, with a great rush, broadened, deepened, diversified, and fragmented. Lyman Beecher did not grasp the whole story, but he did sense the magnitude of change underway when as an old man he looked back specifically to the year 1829: "While the campaign against Unitarianism was being prosecuted with full vigor and promising auguries, suddenly there were symptoms of discord among the champions of orthodoxy, unaccountable and perplexing to themselves, and matter of rejoicing and ridicule to their enemies."[1] The rapid proliferation of Reformed theologies represented an explosion in two senses—as the quantity of careful theological publication spiraled upward geometrically, and as the voices contending for the mantle of orthodoxy became a cacophony.

The beginning, the end, and the lingering influence of a distinct epoch in American theological history can be designated with reasonable clarity. It started with a meeting in New Lebanon, New York, on 18–26 July 1827, when Charles Finney and other advocates of an urgent, direct, and immediate revivalism gathered with more self-consciously respectable Presbyterian and Congregationalist pastors to hammer out an agreement on the acceptable boundaries of revival practice.[2] This gathering included not only Finney, rapidly becoming the era's best-known revivalist in the most revivalistic country in the world, but also students of Timothy Dwight (namely, Lyman Beecher and Asahel Nettleton) who represented the diverging commitments of their teacher, as well as other significant figures like Nathan Beman, who became a prominent leader of the New School Presbyterians, and Gardiner Spring, minister of New York City's Brick Street Presbyterian Church, who would play a key role thirty-three years later in rousing the Northern branch of the Old School Presbyterians for the Union. The era came to an end in 1849, when the Hartford Congregational minister Horace Bushnell published a series of sermons entitled *God in Christ,* along with "A Preliminary Dissertation on Language." This work questioned not so much the content of specific doctrines but the methods that had become canonical in American theological discourse for writing and speaking about those doctrines. "Language," averred Bushnell, "has a literal character in regard to physical objects. . . . But, when we come to religion and mental science, our terms are only analogies, signs, shadows, so to speak, of the formless mysteries above us and within us."[3] By no means did Bushnell's argument carry the day among Calvinists, but his willingness to question some of the most basic conventions of standard American procedure—and to do so from within the main tradition of New England Congregationalism—struck a dissident note of enduring significance. After 1849 Calvinist theologians pressed forward with their work along much the same lines as earlier, but increasingly through the 1850s and 1860s, Reformed theology was losing its edge. Acrimonious controversy among the leading Calvinists, preoccupation with sectional conflict and then the Civil War, difficulties in adapting to new intellectual challenges, and the ever-increasing profusion of non-Calvinist Protestants, Roman Catholics, and non-Christians in the burgeoning American population—all of these factors worked to marginalize the once-commanding voices of the Calvinist theologians. Between the New Lebanon Convention and the aftershocks of Bushnell's book was played out both the golden age of American Reformed theology and its self-immolation.

Decisive Events

A number of unusually significant events marked the first decade of this extraordinary theological era. Many of them sparked extensive literary debate; many were the source of anguished ecclesiastical controversy; all occurred in an environment primed for theological productivity. In a setting where Calvinists ranked foremost among the religious leaders concerned about defending the deposit of Christian faith and where Calvinists longed to present that faith to educated audiences with maximum persuasiveness, well-publicized sermons, books, articles, and public disputations easily became flashpoints. So it was with the pivotal theological events from 1827 and continuing for many years. Even brief examination of these events shows how Christian teaching was bending before the weight of American influences, but also bending in different degrees and on different questions, and so encouraging great controversy as well as great labor in expounding the Christian message.

New Lebanon, 1827

For a history of religious thought, the New Lebanon conference provided decisive legitimation for Finneyite revivalism as a recognized contributor to Reformed theology.[4] It was one of the key events extending the domain of socially influential theology beyond New England and the Congregationalists. Charles Finney (1792–1875) had been born in Connecticut but as a very young child was taken with his family to upstate New York.[5] After fragments of education and a brief period as a schoolteacher in New Jersey, Finney apprenticed for the law but then in 1821 experienced a powerful conversion that almost immediately redirected his life. He briefly contemplated formal theological training but then decided to pursue private study with George W. Gale, a local Presbyterian minister. Finney later criticized Gale for his loyalty to the Westminster Confession and its doctrines of predestination and election, but Gale in those early years sped Finney through a course of study, encouraged him as a preacher, and in July 1824 sponsored his ordination as a Presbyterian. Immediately Finney's preaching made a deep impression. He spoke without notes, passionately, directly, and persuasively; he drove home his understanding of biblical religion with the skills of a master attorney at the bar; he got results. The audiences that responded most warmly to his message were in the rising towns and cities along the newly opened Erie Canal, in Utica, Rome, Auburn, and Troy, New York. Finney's "new measures," mostly taken over from the Methodists, convinced his converts that he was a man from God and frightened the wits out of the respectable clergy. Finney held protracted meetings (many days running in a single location), he prayed aloud for the unconverted by name, he took it as a sign of divine blessing when hearers collapsed in response to his message, he allowed women to speak before mixed audiences, he urged the laity to testify, and he called awakened sinners to come forward to the "anxious bench" in order to pray through to an experience of grace. Behind these measures was a theology constructed in full, intentional disregard of the Westminster Confession and moving far to the American side on all of the day's contested doctrines. But it was not that theology so much as the disruption caused by his revivals that led to the New Lebanon Convention in 1827.

At that meeting, twenty or so ministers from western New England and New York State debated propositions like, "Audible groaning, violent gestures, and boisterous tones, in prayer, are improper" and, "In social meetings of men and women, for religious worship, females are not to pray." On such questions there was disagreement, with the Nettleton and Beecher forces opting for decorum, while Finney and his allies wanted to stretch the boundaries of accepted ecclesiastical practices. More important than the disagreements, however, was a different realization that emerged as the meeting progressed. It was the sense that although Finney carried revival practices a step or two further than many of the seminary-trained, respectable ministers did, he was actually doing what they too were attempting in their own settled pastorates. So it was that the convention found itself agreeing unanimously on many more propositions than those over which it divided—agreeing, for example, "That the preservation and extension of true religion in our land has been much promoted by these revivals" and "That great care should be taken to discriminate between holy and unholy affections, and to exhibit with clearness the scriptural evidences of true religion."[6]

Asahel Nettleton, William Weeks, and a few other formalists were not convinced by this show of unanimity, for they sensed—correctly—that Finney's gospel message grew out of a much higher estimation of natural human capacity in the process of salvation and a much greater reliance on human energy in the reform of society than they themselves believed. By contrast, although Lyman Beecher was not won over to Finney immediately, he did come away from the meeting affirming that "it was not a question of orthodoxy, nor of the reality of revivals, but of wrong measures." Shortly before the New Lebanon meeting, Beecher had told Finney what he would do if the revivalist ever tried to preach in Massachusetts: "I'll meet you at the State line, and call out all the artillerymen, and fight every inch of the way to Boston, and then I'll fight you there."[7] By 1831, however, Beecher joined with other Boston ministers in asking Finney to hold revival meetings at Boston's Park Street Church, where Beecher's son Edward was the pastor.[8]

Asahel Nettleton became increasingly embittered as American revivalism moved from the strictly Calvinistic form he had successfully promoted during the first quarter of the nineteenth century to the largely anti-Calvinistic form championed by Finney. As a consequence, by the mid-1830s Nettleton thought he could see a conspiracy among Finney, the active revivalist; N. W. Taylor, the careful theologian; and Beecher, the master strategist, to subvert traditional Edwardsean Calvinism.[9] Nettleton was wrong about the presence of a conspiracy, but he was right in perceiving that the movement of Finney's theology was in the same direction as the New Haven theology, which, albeit with a different tone, nonetheless was also promoting revival with much the same convictions.

Beecher's Six Sermons, 1827

The same year that Lyman Beecher surprised himself by discovering a Charles Finney with whom he could actually get along, he also published a major statement on one of the era's major social problems. The abuse of alcohol was no joke in a society where the expanding production of grain had far outstripped the ability of bulk transport to take harvests to market.[10] Beecher's contribution to a solution was the publication of a rousing set of sermons describing, as his title indicated, "the Nature, Occasions, Signs, Evils, and Remedy of Intemperance." This book joined a growing chorus that was proposing strict limits on drink, or even the total prohibition of alcohol, as a solution to the crisis of overindulgence.[11]

The distinctive note in Beecher's book, and the note that makes it important for a history of theology, was his framing of the problem. As a minister trained by Timothy Dwight, it was not surprising that he complained about the unregulated use of alcohol for "the moral ruin it works in the soul." What may have surprised his teacher, however, is how thoroughly Beecher transferred the language Dwight had used in defending Connecticut's establishment to the task of protecting the United States. For Beecher, beverage alcohol was pernicious for the harm it did to "the health and physical energies of a nation," to the "national intellect," to "the military powers of a nation," to the "patriotism of a nation," to the "national conscience or moral principle," to the "national industry," and to "civil liberty."[12] Beecher, who by 1827 had long since accepted disestablishment as a positive good, was nonetheless steaming on with the moral calculus constructed by formalists like Dwight in the first years of the new republic. With godly living compromised by the evils of drink, the virtue of the citizenry was in doubt, and the nation was imperiled. As he urged revival, reform, and the path of godliness, Beecher, as the Puritan he remained, thought instinctively as well about the well-being and "civil liberty" of the nation. That instinctive bond was the means by which he hoped to see godliness shape the broad American public, but it was also the means by which the broad American public shaped the way Lyman Beecher thought.[13]

N. W. Taylor's Concio ad Clerum, 1828

A sermon that N. W. Taylor preached at the Yale College Chapel on 10 September 1828 performed the same function as William Ellery Channing's famous sermon "Unitarianism," nine years earlier.[14] In each case it was an effort to answer pressing questions about what a major religious leader did or did not actually believe. Murmuring against Taylor, who was always linked by his contemporaries to the activism of Lyman Beecher, had been growing steadily since he had moved in 1822 from New Haven's First Church to become Yale's first Dwight Professor of Didactic Theology. Although Taylor's theological acumen made him famous during his tenure at Yale, he was nominated for that post as much for his success at promoting revivals at the First Church—four separate awakenings and a net increase of 400 members in his ten years as pastor—as for his learning. Taylor, in other words, was not merely an academic theologian but a true disciple of Dwight who wanted the presentation of Christian truth, whether in sermons for parishioners or lectures for students, to change lives and through these changed lives sanctify society.[15] Modern scholarly debates over how much Taylor deviated from earlier New England precedents are not unimportant, for along with what Allen Guelzo calls "Taylor's assaults on Edwardsean theology," almost everyone could recognize that his thinking imitated Edwards's in the breadth of its theological, biblical, and philosophical concerns.[16] What has not been emphasized as much is how directly Taylor was speaking to his times. The *Concio ad Clerum*, or "Advice to the Clergy," was, like Channing's "Unitarianism," the clear statement of beliefs that many had hoped to see, but it was also an address using fully the vocabularies, expectations, and perceived needs of the current American situation.

Right from the start of the sermon, Taylor assumed that his audience was convinced of the decrepitude of traditional authorities and equally confident of its own powers: "The Bible is a plain book. It speaks, especially on the subject of sin, directly to human consciousness; and tells us beyond mistake, what sin is, and why we sin." Human nature was sinful, according to Taylor, not because of "any essential attributes or property of the soul," nor because of possessing "a sinful nature, which [humans] have corrupted by being *one* with Adam, and by *acting in his act*" (which had been Edwards's position), and not because of "*any disposition or tendency* to sin, which is *the cause of all sin*" (which was the position of Asa Burton and the "tasters"). Rather, "moral depravity" should be understood as "man's own act, consisting in a free choice of some object rather than God, as his chief good—or a free preference of the world and of worldly good, to the will and glory of God."[17] Taylor thus transferred the onus of sinfulness from character to actions— people were alienated from God because of their own choices and not because of the sinful nature they shared with all other humans. Taylor was carrying further the teaching of Emmons that all sin was in the sinning, but—as H. B. Smith had noted—with a different view of God.

Taylor's *Concio* was a distinctly American effort in two particulars: its appeal to consciousness as the adjudicator of Scripture and tradition, and its insistence upon human action as the natural outcome of correct theology. In the first instance, the bulk of Taylor's positive argument rested on what he styled "philosophy, reason, or common sense." It was "Common Sense" that allowed him to explain what Calvin, the Westminster divines, Bellamy, and Edwards had really intended to say when they took up the question of sinfulness. "Common sense decides" that "the sum total of all sin" is the "sinful action" that prefers "some private interest, object, or end, rather than God." Taylor's final appeal concerning the nature of sin was "to human consciousness," on the basis of which he affirmed that people "are conscious that in all sin, they do freely and voluntarily set their hearts, their supreme affections on the world, rather than God."[18] To consciousness Taylor then added an appeal to "the stubborn things, called facts." On the basis of what the facts of consciousness revealed, he contended "that sin or guilt pertains exclusively to voluntary action" and also that "the doctrine of imputation" and "our personal identity with Adam" were fictions.[19] As the last in a long line of New England theologians expert in the examination of consciousness, Taylor exceeded them all in the weight he placed on the deliverances of the moral sense.

Second, Taylor in this definitive sermon aimed at purposeful action. According to Taylor, false construals of what Calvinism was supposed to mean were having a deadly affect by promoting the passivity of churchgoers and citizens. "To what purpose do we preach the Gospel to men," he thundered as a revivalist, "if we cannot reach the conscience with *its charge of guilt* and *obligations to duty*?"[20] After he took up his position at Yale, Taylor continued to preach for revival in the churches of Connecticut, although with the decorum his friend Lyman Beecher at first found so lacking in Charles Finney. Even more, the Yale Divinity School under Taylor's leadership was a factory energetically producing pastors, revivalists, missionaries, and the leaders of voluntary societies.[21] The reasoning behind these practical efforts of Taylor's career as preacher and professor was spelled out with precise clarity in the *Concio*. The doctrines of this sermon were to be preached in order to convince sinners that they, and they alone, were "the perpetrators of the deed that deserves wrath," and that they alone "by acting" could receive God's mercy only by "the doing of *the very thing* commanded by God." Taylor summed up his message with a single memorable sentence: "Without derogating from the work of God's Spirit let us urge him [the sinner] to his duty—*to his duty—to his duty*, as a point-blank direction to business now on hand and now to be done."[22] Only with a proper understanding of Christian teaching could there be proper Christian action. Only from proper Christian action could the providential rule of God be spread upon the earth. And so the sermon came to an end: "While the theory now proposed exhibits the providential government of God as the basis of submission, confidence, and joy, under all the evils that befall his dependent creatures; it also presents, as no other theory in the view of the writer does present, the Moral Government of God in its unimpaired perfection and glory, to deter from sin and allure to holiness his accountable subjects."[23]

N. W. Taylor's sermon contained much else, especially a carefully reasoned account of what it really meant for humans to possess a morally depraved nature. Even as he changed many traditional doctrines, he clung tenaciously to the proposition that all people did in fact sin. His explanation for this reality was, not that humankind simply was by nature sinful, but that human "*nature* is the *occasion* of sin, as a free act." If humans are made so that they will sin (not "must" sin), then the proper conclusion may be drawn about both humanity's "formal freedom" and "the moral perfection of God."[24] Taylor's distinctions have not worn well over time—confessional Protestants judged that he ascribed too much to humans, secularists that he ascribed too much to God. But for his own time and place, Taylor's balancing act was impressive. He was jettisoning the parts of the Edwardsean tradition that kept him from saying what he felt had to be said in the hour at hand, namely, that despite what the Unitarians claimed about Calvinist teaching, God was not a tyrant; despite what his audience may have heard from supposedly learned teachers in the past, they could trust their own consciousness as a guide to first-order moral questions; despite the conclusions that were being drawn from a misguided apprehension of Calvinism, people had to act if they wanted to save themselves and preserve a measure of godly order in the world at large. The N. W. Taylor of *Concio ad Clerum* was a preacher for the American hour.

This sermon and similar publications were immediately attacked from all points on the theological compass.[25] Unitarians were mildly upset that Taylor had not carried his renovation of New England principles further, but all of the Reformed positions to the right of New Haven were much more warmly engaged. The literary contest that ensued did not play out until more than four decades later, when the last reviews were written on the two volumes of Taylor's posthumously published *Moral Government of God*.[26]

Reorganization of the Princeton Review, *1829*

American Reformed theology expanded during the years surrounding Taylor's famous sermon primarily because of the intellectual reemergence of the Presbyterians. From the founding of Princeton Seminary in 1812, and with gathering intellectual energy that led to the foundation of seminaries at Hampden-Sydney, Virginia (also in 1812), Auburn, New York (1818), and Columbia, South Carolina (1828), Presbyterians had gradually been recovering their theological voice. By the mid-1810s, skillful but also cautious reasoners like Archibald Alexander and Samuel Miller at Princeton, James Richards at Auburn, and Moses Hoge and John Holt Rice at Union Seminary in Hampden-Sydney had begun to reassert the importance of a theology anchored to the Westminster Confessions and Catechisms and, with less assurance, to John Calvin, John Knox, and the European dogmaticians of the seventeenth century. Although the theological direction that Presbyterians would take was not immediately clear, this new generation certainly had little stomach for the liberalizing Enlightenment thinking offered at the turn of the century by Samuel Stanhope Smith and Samuel Blair Jr. The uncertainty resembled the situation of a century before: the question was not whether the Presbyterians should promote a confessional theology but whether their confessionalism should be strict or moderate. To one degree or another the first leaders of Presbyterian seminaries were all seasoning their confessional loyalty with some alloy—whether an interest in revival and Christian religious experience (Archibald Alexander), a renewed commitment to Presbyterian ecclesiology (Samuel Miller), an eagerness to use Baconian principles to expound "the simple truth of the Bible" (John Holt Rice), or varied interests in the apologetics of natural theology, the dynamics of republican polity, and the reassurances of Scottish commonsense philosophy.[27] As so often in the history of Christian theology, agitation from outside the camp precipitated concentrated efforts to clarify the content of belief. For the Presbyterians in this case, the agitation was coming from the Finneyite revivalists and the mediating Calvinists of New England.

Presbyterian reengagement with broader theological history received a strong impetus when Charles Hodge, a young professor at Princeton Seminary, returned in 1829 from a study sojourn in Europe and as one of his first acts reorganized the theological quarterly sponsored by the seminary's professors and a few of their associates at the College of New Jersey.[28] As a youth, Hodge (1797–1873) had been schooled in both catechetical Calvinism and a moderately enthusiastic revivalism by Ashbel Green, his pastor in Philadelphia and then the president at the College of New Jersey during his years as a student there. But the decisive influence on Hodge's formation was Archibald Alexander, the effective preacher and theological autodidact whom the Presbyterian General Assembly had appointed as Princeton Seminary's first professor in 1812. From Alexander, Hodge learned to respect the importance of personal religious experience, the value of biblical study in the original languages, the wisdom of the Westminster standards, the axioms of commonsense reasoning, and the stabilizing gravitas of classic Reformed dogmaticians. It was not until he studied in Europe (1826–1828) and came back to discover the Presbyterians alarmed at how influences from New England were infiltrating their denomination that his own views were clarified. From Europe, Hodge returned with a deepened appreciation for theological scholarship and a remarkably catholic sense of general Christian orthodoxy, but also with strongly fixed opinions about the most pressing dangers menacing the Christian faith. These dangers were "mysticism," or the claims to inner spiritual resources about which he had heard the elderly Friedrich Schleiermacher lecture; "rationalism," or the use of modern canons of science and reason to revise traditional Christian affirmations; and "ritualism," or the misplaced trust in formal ecclesiastical procedure he associated with Roman Catholicism and later with the Anglican Oxford Movement and the German Reformed romanticism of John Williamson Nevin. In order to speak directly against these dangers, and also to have a forum for correcting New Englanders like N. W. Taylor, Hodge reorganized the journal that, through a succession of official titles, was always called the *Princeton Review*.

As editor of the journal, for which he himself wrote more than 140 substantial articles over four decades, Hodge marked out a set of self-consciously conservative positions that placed him far to the traditional side with respect to the era's controversial theological debates. Earlier we have seen what Hodge considered the most important doctrines that he and his colleagues defended in the journal and his other writings.[29] As an indication of his stance in the late 1820s, the corresponding list of positions that Princeton opposed was, in fact, a rough summary of what N. W. Taylor had advocated in his *Concio ad Clerum*:

> that all sin consists in the voluntary violation of known law; that men, since the fall, are not born in a state of sin; that they are not chargeable with guilt or moral pollution until, having arrived at the years of discretion, they deliberately violate the divine law; that all men have plenary ability to avoid all sin; and, having sinned, to return unto God and do all that he requires at their hands; that God cannot prevent sin, or the present amount of sin, in a moral system; that he cannot effectually control the acts of free agents without destroying their liberty; that in conversion it is man, and not God, who determines who do, and who do not, turn unto God; that election is founded on the foresight of this self-determined repentance on the part of the sinner.[30]

The conservative Presbyterianism of Hodge and like-minded colleagues was influential in this era and later because it was learned, because it had a clear vision of God-centered Christian faith, and because it always kept the larger national picture in view. Near the end of the Civil War, Hodge responded to critics of various positions his journal had taken during that conflict by pointing out what a burden his work as editor had been, but also by affirming the journal's long-term contribution. Hodge reported that he would be greatly relieved if he could give up editing the *Review*, which "he has carried . . . as a ball-and-chain for forty years," but also that he did not begrudge that labor in light of "the high privilege and honour of making it an organ for upholding sound Presbyterianism, the cause of the country, and the honour of our common Redeemer."[31] For Hodge, the interests of church, country, and Christianity more generally were always interwoven. When he and his Princeton allies entered the lists, they brought a conservative counterweight into the unfolding of Reformed theological history, but that counterweight shared almost as much with the era's American ideology as the most self-consciously methodical revivalist or the most deliberate New England reviser of Jonathan Edwards.

Albert Barnes's "Way of Salvation," 1829

The redirection of Charles Hodge's journal was not, however, the only significant event for Presbyterian theology in the year 1829. As Presbyterians regained their public voices, they displayed a variety of interests similar to what had existed within the colonial New Light faction a century before. Hodge, his Princeton colleagues, and the Presbyterian Old School more generally carried on the interests of the Scotch-Irish, Tennent wing of the New Light party by balancing moderate support for revival with strong commitments to the historic confession and a high view of Presbyterian church order. As a countervailing force in the denomination were those who carried on the interests of the New England, Dickinson wing of the colonial New Lights. These "New School" Presbyterians were much more open to theological influence from New England than their Old School peers, they were much more ardent proponents of revival, and they were more willing to play down the prerogatives of Presbyterian order for the sake of joint ventures with other evangelicals. When Lyman Beecher moved to Cincinnati in 1832 and sought ordination as a Presbyterian, he was viewed as the epitome of New School interests. But before Beecher transferred from the Congregationalists, those interests had already been well defended by a number of rising young clergymen.

Among the most prominent of the New School's early leaders was Albert Barnes (1798–1870), who received his primary and college education in Connecticut and New York but then studied with Alexander, Miller, and the young Charles Hodge at Princeton Seminary, from which he graduated in 1824.[32] From his first pastorate in Morristown, New Jersey, where he won renown for successfully closing down the city's taverns, and then when he moved to Philadelphia in 1830, Barnes was widely regarded as a minister to watch—as a leader of pious good sense and exactly the right kind of energetic activism by those who would eventually form the New School, but also as a dangerously uncritical adherent of New England principles and precariously earnest moral reformer by some who would later constitute the Old School.[33] Barnes gained national prominence in 1829 with the publication of a sermon entitled "The Way of Salvation," which to Presbyterian moderates and conservatives sounded suspiciously similar to what New Haven theologians were saying. When Barnes was called to Philadelphia's historic First Presbyterian Church, this sermon became a focus of controversy. To the traditionalists, it seemed to feature most of the errant moves of the most irresponsible New Englanders. There was no federal or organic solidarity with Adam, Christ's atonement created the conditions for all to be saved yet was applied to no one in particular, and humans possessed a power within themselves from their own natural resources to choose God. Barnes did stress the work of the Holy Spirit in the process of conversion, yet not so clearly as to distinguish his views from those of N. W. Taylor, who also spoke regularly of the Holy Spirit as a necessary influence in, but not the fundamental cause of, conversion.

Much of the sermon was given over to biblical interpretation that no Presbyterian would have questioned, but at key points Barnes drew on the era's prominent ideologies to carry his message. As he denied the imputation of Adam's sin, for example, Barnes held up the standard of "moral government" and "the facts" it taught by showing that God was always "equitable" in treating humanity.[34] When he affirmed that the atonement "had not respect so much to *individuals*, as to the *law* and *perfection of God*," he argued that it was "a matter of common sense" that God does not require more of people "than *in any sense* they are able to perform."[35] Barnes's own stress on how the sovereignty of God was the key matter in human salvation reassured Presbyterian readers that he was not simply repeating principles from the New Haven theologians, but to many of those same readers the similarities with New England were too striking to ignore.

Tension within the denomination rose after Barnes was charged by conservatives in the Philadelphia presbytery with false teaching, but he was exonerated at the 1831 General Assembly. That Assembly was the first in which identifiable New School forces had demonstrated their strength by electing as moderator a self-identified New School leader, Nathan Beman. The fact that Beman had left the New Lebanon conference with a moderately favorable view of Charles Finney's work did nothing to assuage the fears of Presbyterian traditionalists that their denomination was being steered rapidly onto perilous shoals.

Moses Stuart on Romans, *1832*

Given the instinctive reverence that almost all Americans, churchgoers or not, maintained for the Bible, it was no surprise that as the seminaries promoted the professional study of Scripture, the publications of biblical exegetes became much more important in serious theological literature as a whole. Nor is it surprising, given the theological climate of the late 1820s and following years, that some of this biblical commentary would become matter for great controversy. No American biblical scholar enjoyed a higher reputation in this era than Moses Stuart of Andover, and no work of early American biblical scholarship generated sharper controversy than Stuart's *Commentary on the Epistle to the Romans,* which appeared in 1832.

Stuart (1780–1852) remains a respected figure as the pioneer of modern academic biblical scholarship in America.[36] To peers, his dedication as a professor at Andover to mastering, teaching, and then promoting biblical Hebrew was legendary. He was honored almost as much for his willingness to study the latest German scholarship while maintaining conservative opinions on the inspiration of the Scriptures, the integrity of the Old Testament, and the reality of biblical miracles. Most Protestants were also grateful for his decades-long efforts against the Unitarians, which included weighty responses to William Ellery Channing in 1819 and to the biblical scholarship of Andrews Norton in 1837. At the same time, however, Stuart was suspect to some New England conservatives and to almost all Old School Presbyterians for his theological pedigree and for what they considered the tendentious theological agenda at work in his commentaries.

Stuart was a student at Yale under Timothy Dwight, and when he was converted a few years after graduating, he returned to Yale in 1803 to study with Dwight for the ministry. From 1806 until his call to Andover in 1810, he served as minister of New Haven's First Church, where his pastorate was notable for its successful revivals and for Stuart's friendship with the young N. W. Taylor, who succeeded him on his removal to Andover. As Taylor's opinions became better known, the friends of orthodoxy were not reassured by Stuart's low-key but unmistakable support for the New Haven theologian.

Although Stuart's commentary on *Romans* was hailed universally as a monument to scholarship, orthodox reviewers were troubled by what seemed to be Stuart's aggressive promotion of New Haven conclusions, especially in commenting on the critical passage in chapter 5 that had usually been read by traditional Protestants, as well as many Roman Catholics, to teach human solidarity with Adam, the doctrine of imputation (both Adam's sin to humanity and Christ's righteousness to the redeemed), and the determinative work of the Holy Spirit in converting the lost. The passage, with italics added for the most contentious segments, appeared as follows in the Authorized Version, which functioned for almost everyone as the standard English translation of the day:

12 Wherefore, *as by one man* sin entered into the world, and death by sin; and so death passed upon all men, *for that all have sinned*:

13 (For until the law sin was in the world; but *sin is not imputed when there is no law*.

14 Nevertheless death reigned from Adam to Moses, even over them that had not sinned after *the similitude of Adam's transgression*, who is the *figure* of him that was to come.

15 But not as the offence, so also is the free gift. For if through the offence of one many be dead, much more the grace of God, and the gift by grace, which is by one man, Jesus Christ, hath abounded unto many.

16 And not as it was by one that sinned, so is the gift: for the judgment was by one to condemnation, but the free gift is of many offences unto justification.

17 For if by one man's offence death reigned by one; much more they which receive abundance of grace and of the gift of righteousness shall reign in life by one, Jesus Christ.)

18 Therefore as by the offence of one judgment *came upon* all men to condemnation; even so by the righteousness of one the free gift *came upon* all men
unto justification of life.

19 For as by one man's disobedience many *were made* sinners, so by the
obedience of one shall many *be made* righteous.

Stuart's learning was on full display as he took up the passage, but so also
was what his biographer calls a weakness for "the push of theological prejudice." In summary, Stuart held that the apostle Paul taught that all humans did
sin as a result of Adam's own transgression but that the connection between
Adam and later humanity was circumstantial rather than federal (as the
Westminster Confession affirmed), organic (as held by Jonathan Edwards), or
imputed (as maintained by traditional theologians generally). In addition, Stuart
maintained that sinfulness and the guilt of sin came to humans only when they
themselves sinned, never as a result of the disposition of an underlying character. The result, in John Giltner's conclusion, was to "provide the New Haven
'liberals,' Taylor chief among them, a solid exegetical ground for their speculative conclusions" and to make Stuart "the first American Calvinist biblical
scholar to offer extended exegetical support for what was perceived to be a
significant divergence from the received theological tradition."[37]

The presence of characteristic "American" reasoning was a notable feature of Stuart's exegesis. He was preeminently the careful scholar, which
meant that the *Romans* commentary reflected prodigious linguistic, philologi-
cal, and lexicographical labors. Yet at critical moments the broader intellectual framework from which he worked was plainly in view. He began, for
example, in the preface with a resolute proclamation of his own intellectual
independence: "What Calvin, or Augustine, or Edwards, or Arminius, or
Grotius, or any other theologian or commentator has taught or said, has been
with me only secondary and subordinate." Stuart might honor past worthies,
"but when explaining the Bible, to call no man *master*, and to bow to no system as such, are sacred principles with me." Stuart disavowed paying any
attention at all to the "systems" of "all *party* men in theology," but rather "made
it my constant and only effort, to follow simply the way in which the apostle
seems to lead me."[38] Although Stuart was in a class by himself as the United
States' most learned exegete, he shared a very great deal with his fellow
Americans in the straightforward Baconianism of his intellectual ideals.

On dogmatic questions, when Stuart expanded upon the interpretive cruxes
of Romans 5:12–19, he used standard warrants of early nineteenth-century
intellectual method to bolster his conclusions. Against Edwards's account of
original sin as the participation of all humanity in Adam, as also against the
traditional idea that the guilt and penalty of Adam's sin were imputed to later
humanity, Stuart claimed that commonly held ideas of "moral government"
could not support the older theories. By contrast, he felt that "the whole doctrine of moral retribution, as built on the principles of moral justice . . . at the
very first view of it which is taken by our conscience and our sense of right
and wrong," supported the notion that sinfulness lay ultimately in sinning

itself.[39] Theologians had been misled by their own "philosophizing," and "the speculations of eighteen centuries" had distorted "the simple facts as stated by the Apostle Paul." As Stuart read those facts, he wanted still to affirm that "Adam involved all his race in a state of sin and death," but he refused to use a stronger word than "involved."[40] As he drew such conclusions, Stuart sounded most like N. W. Taylor. For example, "It is in opposition to the immutable principles of our moral nature, to predicate sin in its proper sense of any being that acts without free choice and knowledge of rule." Furthermore, if humans would only realize that they alone were ultimately responsible for their own offensiveness against God, they would align their doctrines with "an immutable law of moral sense" and let their reasoning rest on "self evident principles."[41]

Stuart was not only America's most professionally adept biblical student of his era; he also probably held more of the Scriptures in his head, and discerned with the eye of his mind more connections among passages of Scripture, than any American since Jonathan Edwards.[42] Yet it shows Stuart's distance from Edwards that Stuart denied imputation because his metaphysical and ethical principles did not allow him to treat actions in the mind of God (like considering, or reckoning, sinners as righteous because of standing in Christ) as fully real.[43] Stuart admitted that it was difficult in the extreme to affirm both that Adam's sin influenced later humanity to scorn God and that later humanity scorned God on its own, but he was also confident that a theological system much more like Taylor's (whom he did not name) than Edwards's (whom he named repeatedly) was in accord "with the Scriptures and with our moral sense and judgment."[44]

Finney's Lectures on Revivalism, 1835

If Moses Stuart added American grace notes to the detailed scholarship of his biblical commentary, the published writings of Charles Finney represented a full-blown chorus of American emphases. Finney had published a number of sermons in the early years of his preaching career, but none that created the sensation caused by his *Lectures on Revivals of Religion*. These lectures were the result of a scheme by Joseph Leavitt, editor of the *New York Evangelist*, to save his magazine, which had been established in 1830 by Congregationalists and Presbyterians to promote both "new measures" revivalism and the newer modifications of traditional Calvinism. When Finney returned to New York after an ocean voyage taken to restore his health from a brush with cholera, he found Leavitt in a panic over the financial embarrassment of the journal, a situation caused by the editor's ardent and quite unpopular abolitionism. Leavitt proposed to the returning evangelist that he write some articles for the paper on revival, which Finney after his fashion agreed to do. The result was a series of twenty-two Friday evening lectures, which Finney declaimed from notes and Leavitt wrote up for publication. The lectures first appeared in the *New York Evangelist* throughout the winter and early spring of 1834–1835 and then were published as a book in May 1835. They were popular from the start, with 2,600 new subscribers to the journal by the time the book appeared, 12,000 copies of the volume sold in three months, large printings appearing rapidly from British publishers, and almost immediate translation into French, German, and Welsh.[45]

William McLoughlin's learned commentary on this volume included his judgment that "the first thing that strikes the reader . . . is the virulence of Finney's hostility toward traditional Calvinism and all it stood for."[46] Anti-Calvinist the lectures certainly were, but even more obvious is the urgency they communicated about the need for revival. Because Finney thought traditional Calvinism was encouraging Americans in spiritual laxity, he opposed it, but the urgency of what he desired was more important than what he opposed.[47]

The American character of Finney's message shone most clearly when he described the duties incumbent on people in their natural state. Lecture 7, on being "filled with the Spirit" (Ephesians 5:18), gave him the clearest opportunity to drive his point home: "When you tell sinners that without the Holy Spirit they never will repent, they are very liable to pervert the truth, and understand by it that they *cannot* repent, and therefore are under no obligation to do it until they feel the Spirit." The truth, by contrast, was that "obligation to perform duty never rests on . . . the influence of the Spirit, but on the powers of moral agency." The duty to repent arises from the fact that people "are moral agents, and have the powers which God requires them to exercise." Similarly, people must pray, not because God has given them the Holy Spirit, "but because they have evidence. . . . They are bound to see the evidence, and to believe." Any other way of reasoning—any suggestion that God has a "right to command, unless we have power to obey"—would require the inevitable "conclusion that God is an infinite tyrant."[48] Rather than looking mistakenly to divine power, Finney urged an alternative course, as he put it at the start of lecture 12, "I aim to show that the Bible ascribes conversion to men" and "that this is not inconsistent with those passages in which conversion is ascribed to God."[49] In sum, humans acted and only then did God respond: "God never will yield nor grant you his Spirit, till you repent."[50]

At several places in his lectures, Finney enlisted Jonathan Edwards to defend his own revival practice, for example, in how to pray during seasons of awakening and why to focus more on a changed life than on "bodily effects."[51] But more relevant to his main themes was material drawn from Finney's understanding of the Scottish moral philosophy, as when he urged his hearers to make "the laws of mind the object of thought." Sinners seeking to find God needed to "go to the common sense way to work, as you would on any other subject." Since God designed consciousness to serve human well-being just as much as he did the physical body, people were supposed to read their "moral feelings by consciousness, just as I could tell my natural feelings by consciousness, if I should put my hand in the fire."[52]

The end to which Finney put his lectures never wavered: "If filled with the Spirit, you will be useful. . . . All preaching should be *practical*. . . . Any thing brought forward as doctrine, which cannot be made use of as practical, is not preaching the gospel. . . . It is not the design of preaching, to make men easy and quiet, but to make them ACT. . . . [Converts should] not rest satisfied till they are as perfect as God."[53] The great bulk of the revival lectures, drawing as they did on Finney's intense desire to see sinners find redemption, concentrated on such spiritual action. But in the later lectures he also considered the need to act in society. As much as his contemporary Alexis de Tocqueville, who was writing about the same relationships at this very time, Finney held that "politics are a part of religion in such a country as this." Beyond his concern that believers vote for honest, God-fearing officials, Finney was most exercised about the evil of slavery. In his mind, ending slavery was not as important as saving souls, but it was nonetheless imperative to recognize that "slavery is, pre-eminently, the *sin of the church.*" As part of his own testimony against this sin, Finney reported that he excluded all slave owners and anyone involved in the slave trade from communion, no doubt in part because on such questions he took for granted the standard republican calculus: "God cannot sustain this free and blessed country, which we love and pray for, unless the church will take right ground." On broad questions of national policy, he was as insistent on the same unlimited possibilities as when he addressed sinners on their desperate need to turn to God: "Let Christians of all denominations meekly but firmly come forth, and pronounce their verdict, let them clear their communions, and wash their hands of this thing, let them give forth and write on the head and front of his great abomination, SIN! and in three years, a public sentiment would be formed that would carry all before it, and there would not be a shackled slave, nor a bristling, cruel slave-driver in this land."[54]

Charles Finney was as much the American evangelist as Taylor was the American theologian. Their work differed in learning, in form, in tone, but above all because Finney possessed more charismatic power in his preaching than Taylor or any of the age's other theoreticians of revival. Where they thought as one was preeminently by folding the axioms of American ideology into their understanding of the Christian faith.

Presbyterian Schism, 1837–1838

In standard histories of American intellectual life, much more attention has been accorded to Ralph Waldo Emerson's address of 15 July 1838 to the graduating class of the Harvard Divinity School than to the two Presbyterian General Assemblies that convened at Philadelphia's Central Presbyterian Church on 18 May 1837 and on 17 May the next year at Philadelphia's Seventh Presbyterian Church. Emerson's speech represented a further installment of his personal declaration of independence from the dead weight of intellectual tradition and as such has been examined carefully by modern cultural historians. The Presbyterian actions, by contrast, have been little studied in the twentieth century but were of immense significance in the intellectual world of the antebellum period.

Emerson's pronouncements were so outrageously egregious in using "American" standards of value that centrist thinkers immediately judged them beyond the pale. Although his address to the Harvard students reflected his reading in Carlyle, Coleridge, and the romantic idealists of continental Europe, Emerson also showed himself thoroughly at home in a vocabulary of republican common sense and even in the expressions of current theological debate. His assertion that "a more secret, sweet, and overpowering beauty appears to man when his heart and mind open to the sentiment of virtue," or that "the intuition of the moral sentiment is an insight of the perfection of the laws of the soul," or that "evil is merely privative, not absolute. . . . Benevolence is absolute and real" were carrying common convictions to extremes.[55] But they did arise directly out of main currents of standard American discourse. When, however, he urged that "the Moral Nature, that Law of laws," provided "revelations" that "introduce greatness—yea, God himself, into the open soul," and when he told the graduates that each of them was "a newborn bard of the Holy Ghost," Emerson took himself beyond what any responsible theologian of his age could possibly affirm.[56] It is significant that although this address won the approval of advanced Massachusetts thinkers like Theodore Parker, George Ripley, and (at the time it was given) Orestes Brownson, it was repudiated by almost everyone else, including the Unitarians of Harvard, who would not invite Emerson to return for more than thirty years.

The decisions of the Presbyterian General Assemblies, which led to a schism, were different in every way. They put the standard repertoire of American intellectual warrants to use for standard purposes. This schism of 1837–1838 was important for the history of American Reformed theology because it revealed a fissure among one of the nation's most widely respected theological elites.[57]

From the time of Albert Barnes's first trial in 1830 and 1831, Presbyterian conservatives had been growing increasingly worried about what they saw as the dangerously expanding influence of New England theology in their church. The most conservative forces were led by Ashbel Green of Philadelphia, former president of the College of New Jersey, leading influence in founding Princeton Seminary, and now the aggressive editor of a popular magazine, the *Christian Advocate*. Green (1762–1848) had shown his mettle many years earlier in 1807 when students at the College of New Jersey fomented a major riot. In writing to President Stanhope Smith, Green affirmed, "I have . . . little concern tho' we should loose one half the present students; & would much rather loose the whole than take them back without a change in their sentiments & practice."[58] These sentiments were prophetic of what his attitude would later be about disciplining intellectual disorder in the Presbyterian church.

The more moderate conservatives were led by the faculty of Princeton Seminary, who, while coming to insist with greater determination on the need for faithfulness to historic confessions, were also willing to negotiate as long as necessary with the New School faction in order to keep the denomination intact. For their part, the New Schoolers were not taking up New England ideas, like the emphasis on human action in salvation or a denial of imputation, simply to fiddle with theological traditions. Rather, as George Marsden has well summarized, "theological innovation was never a primary goal. . . . New doctrines were important only as they served practical ends." Ideas like N. W. Taylor's appealed to New Schoolers because they were as "zealous for revivals in their own congregations" as Taylor was in his.[59]

As tensions escalated rapidly in the early 1830s, it became increasingly difficult to balance the New School's willingness to adjust confessions in order to pursue aggressive action with the Old School's willingness to moderate action in order to preserve the confessions. Ill will increased especially when the New School embraced works like Stuart's commentary on *Romans* and activities like Beecher's ardor against strong drink and the Roman Catholics. From 1832 to 1835, ferment boiled over in several local controversies where traditionalists accused ministers from New England, or influenced by New England, of false teaching. Ecclesiastical trials arising from these charges took place in eastern Pennsylvania, in Indiana, in Illinois (against three Yale graduates, including Edward Beecher, who had moved West from his post at Boston's Park Street Church), and, most spectacularly, for Lyman Beecher in Cincinnati.

For traditionalists, the General Assembly of 1836 witnessed the sad culmination to which acquittals in the earlier trials pointed. Meeting in Pittsburgh that year, the Assembly was under the control of a narrow New School majority that reversed efforts approved by Old Schoolers in previous Assemblies to tighten up doctrinal standards. Even more alarming to Old School conservatives was the 1836 Assembly's ruling in the second trial of Albert Barnes. This procedure had arisen when Barnes in 1835 published his *Notes on the Epistle to Romans*, an addition to his very popular set of commentaries on the books of the Bible. The offense to the Old School was not just that Barnes seemed to have swallowed Moses Stuart's conclusions whole.[60] It was also that he did so with engaging prose and in an accessible format that any literate layperson could read. When the Assembly reversed the Philadelphia presbytery's judgment that Barnes's teaching in this book was dangerous, Old School conservatives were moved to action.

The next two years witnessed the type of factional mobilization that has been commonplace in recent history among Methodists, Presbyterians, Episcopalians, Southern Baptists, and Missouri Synod Lutherans, but which was a novelty in the 1830s. Old School forces were especially effective in electing delegates who shared their views to the 1837 General Assembly. The result at Philadelphia's Central Presbyterian Church was amputation. Against the advice of Old School moderates like Charles Hodge, hard-nosed conservatives enacted a series of Draconian decisions. They ended the cooperative Plan of Union with the Congregationalists, which had existed since 1801. They then made that decision retroactive and also spelled out what this decision meant: the four synods formed with substantial contributions from the Plan of Union (the New York Synods of Utica, Geneva, and Genesee, and the Ohio Synod of Western Reserve) were unceremoniously lopped off the denomination. Gone at a stroke were 28 presbyteries, 509 ministers, and 60,000 communicant members.

Throughout the ensuing year New School forces responded by mobiliz-ing as energetically as the Old School had done. Both factions came armed for combat to Philadelphia's Seventh Church in May 1838, but the Old School got there first. By packing into the front of the sanctuary, Old School dele-gates physically protected the moderator as he pointedly refused to recog-nize delegates from the four excised synods. Pandemonium resulted, and a denomination that prided itself on doing everything "decently and in order" descended into chaos. After a raucous period of angry shoving, shouting, and hot-tempered outbursts, delegates from the New School synods, as well as some supporters from other parts of the church, convened their own counter-Assembly, and the New School–Old School schism, which would not be healed in the North until 1869, was a reality.

The theological importance of this event appears more clearly when com-pared with an equally wrenching schism that took place only a few years later in the Scottish Presbyterian Church.[61] The Scottish "Disruption" occurred when ministers and elders led by the renowned preacher, professor, and urban reformer Thomas Chalmers walked out of the 1843 General Assembly in pro-test over the continuation of patronage in the Scottish church. A decade of intense debate, principled argumentation, backroom maneuvering, and judi-cial process had only shortly before culminated in decisions by the House of Lords and the Court of Sessions that upheld Scotland's historic patronage system for appointing ministers to local parishes. The Scottish and American situations were alike in the intensity of the ecclesiastical disagreements. But the Disruption also differed significantly from the Old School–New School schism, and not only by the fact that the final breach in Scotland on 18 May 1843 was conducted with painful dignity and in grave silence. The even more important difference was that the Scots divided when a formal authority—the British legal system—finally ruled decisively against Chalmers and his colleagues. The American schism, by contrast, occurred when Old School and New School Presbyterians, in effect, admitted that the theological authori-ties they had chosen by themselves to guide themselves had failed.

That failure highlights the most important feature of the schism. New School and Old School Presbyterians, like almost all Americans of their gen-eration, claimed to be following the simple teachings of Scripture and the self-evident deliverances of consciousness. As Presbyterians, they also looked to their confessions, as well as to the Bible, for conclusive facts upon which to base faith and life. They shared, in other words, a commitment to intellectual authorities that were widely considered to be self-interpreting. Until 1837–1838 and the division of the Presbyterians, the reliability of these self-inter-preting axioms—from Scripture, from common sense, from Baconian method—had worked with amazing success as a cohesive force to create the United States, to fill in its constitutional framework with a national culture, and to propel the evangelical churches to national preeminence. For the Pres-byterians in 1837–1838 the power of the self-interpreting axioms faltered, as they would falter soon thereafter for the Methodists and the Baptists, and not too many years later for the nation as a whole.

Varieties of Whig Theology

In a perceptive analysis that has stood the test of time, Daniel Walker Howe once showed how the moderate Calvinism of the 1830s, especially the New Haven theology as encompassing the activism of Lyman Beecher and the ratiocination of N. W. Taylor, paralleled the main emphases of the Whig Party, which emerged as the main opposition to Andrew Jackson and the Democrats during the "second party system" from roughly 1830 to 1855. In Howe's depiction, the ultimate goal of these evangelical Calvinists was "to win souls for Christ," but along the way their efforts also helped "to create a modern capitalist social order." What Howe accurately described was the mix of elements that went into much of the era's Calvinist theology as well as its Whig political ideology: self-realization linked to care for community, personal liberty coordinated with self-discipline, "moral responsibility" existing alongside "moral conditioning"—in a word, "the balancing of freedom and control."[62] Howe also showed how central to the Whig worldview were the instincts of republican political analysis and the intellectual tools of Scottish commonsense philosophy.[63] In speaking specifically about the theological contribution of N. W. Taylor, Howe made the important suggestion that its objective was "to blend the activist, voluntaristic, ambitious, fluid attitudes of nineteenth-century America with the religious doctrines of the Reformation." In other words, "this meant formulating into a religious ideology the culture associated with Whiggery."[64]

When considering the Whig elements found in Calvinist theology from the mid-1820s, it is necessary to remember important distinctions. The theology of Charles Hodge, for example, shared some of the standard elements of Whig ideology, but in a much more traditional framework than advanced by New School Presbyterians and most New England theologians. In addition, many Calvinist Baptists and some Southern Old School Presbyterians, like Robert Dabney and J. H. Thornwell, remained fundamentally distrustful of aggressive personal striving in both theology and society; to them this kind of activism meant a sinful replacement of dependency upon God with idolatrous reliance upon the self.[65] The result for public life was determined apoliticism or allegiance with the Democrats. In theology, these apolitical or anti-Whig Calvinists held to convictions that resembled more the main currents of British evangelical thought at the same period. That thought tended toward a much more passive view of human agency, because it ascribed to God rather than to humans the motive power for social change.[66] The concept of "the spirituality of the church," which can be explained as a convenient doctrine allowing Southern Christians to avoid taking action on slavery, was also in fact a sincerely held religious conviction related to this rejection of Whig and Northern Calvinist activism.[67] Yet for the main body of the most visible Calvinist theologians of the 1830s and 1840s, theology was never less than a decidedly Whig exercise, even if it was always also more.

The critical elements constituting a Whig stance in theology flowed as surely from the unfolding of American history as from the historic resources of traditional Protestantism. Put positively, this stance affirmed that it was possible—indeed imperative—to take purposeful action in the face of personal need and social crisis in order to put oneself right with God and realize a healthier, more godly society. Put negatively, it took for granted that the social landscape contained no historic structures of authority that could be trusted, that no dictate of inherited learning, church tradition, or elite social status was as reliable as the precepts of Scripture and the truths of consciousness. America's main Calvinist theologians, especially in the North, were never Whig to uniform or identical degrees, but as even brief attention to major figures can show, they were nonetheless all still Whig theologians.

Finney

It is easiest to observe the Whig elements in those who sought most aggressively to adjust inherited convictions to the new American situation, like Charles Finney, Lyman Beecher, and N. W. Taylor. Yet even for a figure like Finney, who was so intensely attuned to his audience, it is well to recall his continuities with earlier generations, especially Finney's great respect for Jonathan Edwards the revivalist, and his repeated efforts to ground his own theology in Edwards's account of "natural ability."[68]

Yet the general cast of Finney's thought was relentlessly contemporary. He opened his *Lectures on Systematic Theology* (first published in 1846), for example, with the by-then nearly mandatory statement of ideological liberation: "The truths of the blessed gospel have been hidden under a false Philosophy." He then proceeded immediately to the complaint upon which the 600 pages of his text was strung: "Nearly all the practical doctrines of Christianity have been embarrassed and perverted by assuming as true the dogma of a Necessitated Will."[69] Readers of the 1851 London revision of this work were treated to even stronger medicine when Finney added a blast at the use of confessions as "not only impious in itself, but . . . also a tacit assumption of the fundamental dogma of Papacy" and then singled out those who used the Westminster Standards as "an authoritative standard of doctrine" as having "absurdly adopted the most obnoxious principle of Popery, and elevated their confession and catechism to the Papal throne and into the place of the Holy Ghost."[70] Whether Finney in 1851 was speaking directly to developments since the 1846 edition had appeared, like the rise of the Know-Nothing Party in the United States and the onset of massive Irish immigration into both England and North America, he was certainly exploiting to full advantage the Christian republicanism that meant so much to both Whigs and many of the era's Calvinist theologians.

Just as clearly in tune with the theistic mental science that meant so much to the same constituencies was the capsule account of methods and convictions that Finney also announced in the preface to this same 1851 London edition. The "uninspired religious teachers" Finney had read immediately after his conversion spoke of faith in terms "either of the intellect or of the sensibility," but Finney's "consciousness assured me" that they could not be correct. Soon, however, his own mind was illuminated. On the one hand, "the more I read my Bible, the more clearly I saw that these things were not found there upon any fair principle of interpretation, such as would be admitted in a court of justice." On the other hand, "I could not but perceive that the true idea of moral government had [had] no place in the theology of the church." As Finney kept thinking and reading for himself, he found that "the Spirit of God conducted me through the darkness, and delivered me from the laby-rinth and fog of a false philosophy, and set my feet upon the rock of truth, as I trust." The conclusion to which this process led was the keystone of his theological system: "The will is free and . . . sin and holiness are voluntary acts of mind."[71]

Many of the critical teachings of Finney's mature theology advocated just as clearly the values shared by Whigs and modified Calvinists, especially the insistence on self-realization, self-improvement, and self-control. To take only one of many possible examples, Finney devoted a chapter in his *Systematic Theology* to attacking the Methodist doctrine of "gracious ability," which N. W. Taylor had also challenged in his 1818 pamphlet, *Man, a Free Agent without the Aids of Divine Grace*. Finney saw the same absurdities in the doctrine that Taylor had found, and a few more. He wanted to insist that his theology had full scope for "the Holy Spirit's gracious influence" on free moral agents, but no place at all for the notion that humans were by nature spiritu-ally helpless until God acted on them graciously. For Finney, to say that people have a "natural ability to obey God" was only to affirm the indubitable cer-tainty of "the freedom or liberty of the will." This natural ability, moreover, "is necessarily assumed as a first truth of reason, and . . . this assumption is, from the very laws of mind, the indispensable condition of the affirmation, or even the conception, that they are subjects of moral obligation. . . . If the laws of the mind remain unaltered, this is and always will be so." At the end of his attack on the Methodist doctrine, Finney paused to take a shot at Jonathan Edwards, whom he considered guilty of the same kind of error as burdened the Methodists. To Finney, proper reasoning had shown that "the moral in-ability of Edwards is a real natural inability." Because Edwards had violated "the intelligence" and left preachers unable to persuasively urge "sinners and professors of religion to do their duty without delay," Finney was now offer-ing a better doctrine.[72] It was a doctrine that depended explicitly on an active moral agency and implicitly upon the rejection of all external, coercive, or "physical" authority.

Beecher and Taylor

The more refined theology of N. W. Taylor and the broader social activism of Lyman Beecher moved in the same directions. They urged the full use of human reason and human natural capacities in order to find spiritual life so that holiness might spread throughout the land. The Bible and consciousness were their guides. Again, examples exist without number, but Taylor's meth-odological essays and Beecher's meditations on the safety of republics written during the 1830s show how their understanding of theological principles dovetailed with the kind of responsible self-fashioning characteristic of Whig thought as well.

At his sentinel's post in Cincinnati, Beecher's seriousness of purpose matched the moral and physical uncertainties to which all on the opening frontier were exposed. But Beecher had arrived at the West with solutions he first learned from Timothy Dwight and then practiced himself in the rural and urban East. If Christians acted as they should, they would wholeheartedly promote revivals, since revivals were the premier way of spreading godliness, and "there is no safety in republics but in self-government, under the influence of a holy heart, swayed by the government of God." Likewise, defending the Scriptures against "the crude objections of skeptics" was essential, since the Bible "is the anchor of republics."[73]

N. W. Taylor's rapier was the perfect complement to Beecher's broadsword. When in 1831 he showed how and why to apply common sense to disputed doctrinal questions and in 1837 took up the status of reason in theology, he came to conclusions that fit the Whig agenda well. The disputed doctrines Taylor discussed in 1831 were the Catholic teaching on transubstantiation and three traditionally Calvinist doctrines: human identity in Adam, the notion of a sinful nature, and the belief that "all human action, sinful as well as holy, is *irresistibly* produced or created by immediate divine action."[74] The choice of doctrines may have indicated Taylor's assessment of current difficulties in 1831—a rising threat from Catholic immigration but greater problems with unfortunate teachings from New England's Calvinist past. Against transubstantiation, Taylor assembled an arsenal familiar to liberty-loving Americans: "the *very nature of things* forbids" a literal interpretation of Jesus' words "this is my body"; "the dictates of common sense respecting . . . the nature of things" similarly ruled it out; and no one should stand for "the bands of delusion and oppression" created by Rome's teaching on the subject.[75] Against the older Calvinist teachings, Taylor shifted gears. The fatal flaw in each of the doctrines—as ascertained by "the universal assumption of the competency of common sense" or "common sense, and the bible"—was the same.[76] They gave sinners an excuse not to do what Christianity told them to do. On the question of whether divine action or human action precipitated salvation, for example, "What more could the corrupt heart of man ask to quiet him in any course which his propensities might lead him to pursue" than to believe that one must wait on God to be converted and live a holy life?[77] Similarly, when in 1837 Taylor showed how reason should be used in theology, he defended a thesis proposed to the intellect: "The clear, unperverted deductions of reason, are as binding in their authority, and not less truly to be relied on, than the word of God; and . . . the former can never contradict the latter." But his goal was to get people to act with "the mind" that God had "implanted in the breast of every accountable subject of his righteous government . . . in reference to which such responsibility is involved."[78] Taylor reasoned like a Whig, not in any simple sense, but as he put general philosophical and social principles to work for the sake of purposeful moral action.

There would have been no New Haven theology—no Beecher and Taylor as Mr. Outside and Mr. Inside of late-Congregational moral activism—without the Whig appropriation of the American Revolution. The logic of Taylor's arguments has a very familiar ring to students of Revolutionary ideology and its later career. In particular, Taylor's reason for holding that "the mind of man [was] created to be conformed to the law of benevolent action" was simply self-evident: "It comes to us in the very nature and structure of the mind—it is given to us in the actual cognitions of the inner man, in the knowledge of ourselves; and therefore in a manner not less distinct nor less impressive than were it sent in thunder from [God's] throne."[79] Whence this confidence in the unmediated deliverances of the moral sense? At the very least, such confidence arose in the train of Revolutionary developments—the ethics of Hutcheson provided an indubitable moral ground for resisting British tyranny; the "contagion of liberty" encouraged by the Revolution undercut traditional ways of defending Christianity and social order; then in the post-Revolutionary period, while Christians called on a more general philosophy of common sense (incorporating both Hutcheson and Thomas Reid) to defend their faith and to build a culture, Americans as a whole exalted the ideology of the Revolution (with its deep commitment to self-determination) into the general worldview recorded by de Tocqueville, other foreign visitors, and many Americans. The theologian at the end of this road—who with great conviction restated Christianity in order to align it with the conventions of commonsense republicanism and to equip a voluntary church for the urgent tasks of civilization—was Nathaniel William Taylor. Revivalistic republicanism did not write Taylor's theology, but that theology is very hard to imagine without this American ideological context.

Hodge

The extent to which more conservative figures than Finney, Beecher, or Taylor shared a Whig perspective is suggested by the work of Charles Hodge.[80] There is no doubting the essential conservatism of this Princeton stalwart, who could once seriously joke, "I am not afraid to say that a new idea never originated in this seminary."[81] Hodge was singular in his age, especially for firm convictions about the priority of divine initiatives in salvation. His persistent complaint against the major American theologians of his day was that they de-emphasized the work of the Spirit as a by-product of exalting the natural powers of human beings.[82] Yet a revealing exchange on the eve of the Civil War with Robert Dabney, the Southern Old School Presbyterian, suggested that Hodge was far from a disembodied thinker. After the correspondents had failed to convince each other on the current political crisis, they nonetheless parted amicably, and Dabney thanked Hodge for his "instruction in sound presbyterian and republican principles."[83] Even if we remember that Dabney was committed to a classical, antiliberal version of republicanism, his claim was still telling.

To Hodge as well as to his contemporaries, the judgment of D. H. Meyer is apt: "The philosophy of human nature had to keep pace with the ever-increasing potential of men living in a commercial and democratic society. The nineteenth-century Christian moralist . . . had to balance his theological commitments over against his 'Baconian' spirit and his social concerns."[84] For Hodge, using the standard ideology was the only way that traditional Calvinism, a theology of election tending toward sectarianism and an ecclesiology of hierarchies tending toward oligarchy, could still resonate at the center of an American society defined by republican equality.

Hodge's American idiom was revealed especially in two tendencies of his thought, a sometimes uncritical Baconianism and an equally instinctive, if also selective, reliance on the deliverances of consciousness. With one exception, Hodge usually did not apply Baconian method unreservedly. The exception, which has been much publicized, was his declaration at the start of his three-volume *Systematic Theology* from 1871–1872. "The Bible is to the theologian what nature is to the man of science. It is his store-house of facts; and his method of ascertaining what the Bible teaches, is the same as that which the natural philosopher adopts to ascertain what nature teaches. . . . The duty of the Christian theologian is to ascertain, collect, and combine all the facts which God has revealed concerning himself and our relation to Him. These facts are all in the Bible." On the basis of these assertions, Hodge then went on to suggest that "the Theologian [is] to be guided by the same rules as the Man of Science."[85] Even if Hodge elsewhere usually spoke of Scripture as a volume requiring affection and mind together, these remarks in his *Systematic Theology* reveal how easily he could adopt what every other "American" theologian also adopted to speak convincingly in the absence of inherited intellectual authority.

Hodge's reliance on the deliverances of consciousness was more complicated. His general principle against opponents was that deliverances of philosophical method should first be checked by scriptural authority. Yet, alongside the facts of Scripture, Hodge also sometimes spoke of the facts of human experience or of common consciousness as if they were just as authoritative as the Bible. In the *Systematic Theology*, for example, he averred that to trust the Bible for all the facts of theology was "perfectly consistent . . . with the admission of intuitive truths, both intellectual and moral, due to our constitution as rational moral beings; and . . . with the controlling power over our beliefs exercised by the inward teachings of the Spirit, or, in other words, by our religious experience."[86] On issues where deliverances of the moral sense supported his conclusions (or where he thought they agreed with his interpretations of the Bible), Hodge was more than willing to employ common sense fully. An essay from 1862, for example, suggested that it was not so much the Bible as intuitive knowledge of the "moral and physical nature of man" that could "easily refute all the speculation that has been advanced . . . in favour of a separate and independent origin for his several races or varieties."[87]

The theological issue for which Hodge employed common sense most aggressively was the connection between Adam and the rest of the human

race.[88] Hodge vigorously defended a classic doctrine of the imputation of
Adam's sin precisely because that first imputation was the essential prelude
to the heart of his theology, the redeeming imputation of Christ's righteousness to unworthy sinners. But when it came to how Adam was connected to
the whole human race, such that all humanity bore the guilt of Adam's sin,
Hodge mostly gave up the Bible for common sense. In particular, several times
in his career he was at pains to rebut Jonathan Edwards's theory that all humanity existed in a kind of Platonic unity with Adam. Against this view, Hodge
offered almost no scriptural argument. Rather, as he put it in the *Systematic
Theology*, "This doctrine denies the existence of substance. The idea of substance is a primitive idea. It is given in the constitution of our nature. It is an
intuitive truth, as proved by its universality and necessity."[89]

If, however, Hodge was willing to employ commonsense moral intuition
to defend correct doctrinal propositions, he also wanted to rule out the moral
intuitions of others when their conclusions contradicted his own. At this point,
the difficulty was severe for someone who wanted both to defend traditional
Calvinism and to maintain the truth-telling character of common sense, since
it was primarily on the basis of what were asserted to be universal moral sentiments that Hodge's opponents adduced their strongest arguments against
his views. He was caught out on his effort to have things both ways when in
1874 a reviewer in the *Methodist Quarterly Review* took note of Hodge's *What
Is Darwinism?* The reviewer applauded the book's conclusions on Darwin
but then pointed out that Hodge "repeatedly . . . appeals to our 'intuitions' as
the conclusive stronghold against his materialist opponents." This use of intuition the reviewer thoroughly approved. But then came what, given Hodge's
profession about commonsense intuitions, could only have been an embarrassing series of questions: "But how can Dr. Hodge's own theology stand
before the judgment-seat of our own intuitions? Certain it is, that in the contest between Arminianism and Calvinism, one great power of the former has
been in an appeal to the intuitive pronunciation against the view presented
by the latter of the Divine government. How far can we base our Christianity
on intuitive assumptions, and then reject the intuitive negative upon our special theology?"[90]

Hodge's standard response to such arguments followed a dual course.
Characteristically, he held that the Bible supported what his opponents con-
troverted and also that moral intuition, properly grasped, did too. The latter
assertion was the problem, for Hodge himself on several occasions did precisely what he accused his opponents of doing, namely, use commonsense
intuitions to guide his interpretation of Scripture. Thus, in his commentary
on Romans 5:12, where Hodge was battling what he saw as Moses Stuart's
philosophically driven exegesis, Hodge ended his exposition of the key
phrase—"as by one man sin entered into the world . . . and so death passed
upon all men"—with an unabashed appeal to moral intuition: "It is a monstrous evil to make the Bible contradict the common sense and common consciousness of men. This is to make God contradict himself."[91]

It is an arguable judgment that Hodge performed this kind of legerdemain much less frequently than his New School, New Haven, and Finneyite opponents. But the fact that he did it at all showed that he too was a child of his age. Hodge thus joined theologians whose work he severely chastised, like Finney, Beecher, and Taylor, in using the conceptual language of the times in order to speak to his times. The framework for that effort—massively with Finney, Beecher, and Taylor, more selectively with Hodge—was demonstrably Whig. In their ability to use the dominant concepts of the era, all of these capable theologians proved themselves extraordinarily successful at speaking the Christian message—though with considerable variation—into an American intellectual setting that, at least at elite levels, was attuned to Whig values. One of the main reasons that the influence of evangelical religion remained so strong through the 1860s was precisely because figures like Finney, Beecher, Taylor, and Hodge were able to continue the work of the early-century revivalists—who had both won converts and constructed a national culture—as they too carried out a dual mission by theologizing about the faith once delivered to the saints and showing how that faith could be expressed with the concepts of regnant American ideology.

Endgame, 1849 and After

Powerful as Reformed theology remained through the time of the Civil War, the publication in 1849 of Horace Bushnell's *God in Christ*, with its "Preliminary Dissertation on Language," signaled the beginning of the end of the era in which the nation's leading Calvinist theologians counted as its most widely respected intellectuals. The problems of religious argumentation during the Civil War had more to do with the eclipse of Calvinist preeminence than reactions to Bushnell's work, but that book was nonetheless a literary bombshell whose disorienting effect anticipated the actual explosions of the war. Bushnell's bold arguments about language were the preface to yet another effort at convincing Unitarians of the errors of their ways. As such, it was only one more of many such works in a long line stretching back to the flurry of orthodox tracts that had greeted Channing's famous sermon in 1819. The part of Bushnell's book that came from material first given as an address at Unitarian Harvard, for example, declared that in Christ, "this Word of Life, God has now expressed Himself. He has set forth His Divine feeling even to sense and as a fellow feeling—He has entered into human history as one of its biographic elements."[92] The wording was distinctively Bushnell's, but it conveyed a mostly orthodox message. It was, rather, Bushnell on language itself that created the furor.

By this time in his career, Bushnell (1802–1876) enjoyed a well-earned reputation for contrarian singularity.[93] He had been born in northwestern Connecticut, graduated from Yale College in 1827, then dabbled in journalism, teaching, and the law before a conversion experience in 1831 sent him back to the Yale Divinity School and the teaching of N. W. Taylor. The direction of Bushnell's intellectual career was indicated by an early essay, "On Moral Agency," from 1832, in which he criticized the attempt, for which Taylor was renowned, to build a formal science of morals through Baconian means from the impressions of the moral sense. In 1833 Bushnell became pastor of Hartford's North Church, where he remained until ill health and a burgeoning literary career led to his resignation twenty-five years later. In this Hartford congregation Bushnell distanced himself from the revivalism pursued by other churches in the city. Gradually he came to the opinion, eventually expressed in *Discourses on Christian Nurture* (1847), that slow and steady growth in grace within the confines of a loving family was a path to God far superior to one that included dramatic revival conversions. When with *God in Christ* Bushnell rejected the mechanics of revival, the privileging of Baconian method, and the apologetics of mental science, he was carrying further the emphases of his earlier career.

Bushnell on Language

The argument of his book was not new, for Bushnell was expanding upon a distinction made by Samuel Taylor Coleridge and publicized in America through James Marsh's edition of Coleridge's *Aids to Reflection*. It was the difference between "Understanding" (or pragmatic reason about matters of fact) and the much-to-be-preferred "Reason" (or ideas that communicated higher personal and religious truth). Coleridge, in turn, was the main conduit to America of several forms of Continental idealism, including the philosophy of Kant and the theology of Schleiermacher. Bushnell's account of language also bore some resemblances to Emerson's advocacy of "spirit," with the great difference that Bushnell held that the view of language he proposed confirmed Christian faith rather than superseded it. In many aspects of his thought—like his commitment to republican values, his nervousness about the corrupting effects of what he considered the savage races, his opposition to slavery, and his anti-Catholicism—Bushnell was an entirely conventional mid-nineteenth-century upper-class Northern minister. But in his views of language he was anything but conventional.

Bushnell was as much opposed to the slavish use of historic confessions as Charles Finney, who was making his sharpest anticreedal protests at about the time Bushnell brought out this book. In fact, at the inaugural meeting of the Evangelical Alliance in London (1846), Bushnell balked at the requirement that members of the Alliance be committed to one of the orthodox Protestant creeds. But Bushnell was proposing something much more radical than Finney as he attacked the whole framework of logical, empirical, Baconian, and apologetic discourse that Finney was trying to renovate as an alternative to the inherited authority of the creeds.

Bushnell was still willing to concede that "opinion, science, systematic theology, or even dogma in the best possible sense of the term" were not irrelevant for Christians. They had "their proper place"—aiding education of the young, raising a testimony against unbelief, and initiating contacts with other forms of knowledge. But for religious purposes strictly considered, scientific learning of whatever source paled beside "a knowledge of God and Christian truth, which is of the heart." The latter kind of knowledge was superior beyond question: "What is loftiest and most transcendent in the character of God, his purity, goodness, beauty, and gentleness, can never be sufficiently apprehended by mere intellect, or by any other power than a heart configured by these divine qualities." As Bushnell described it, the message of Christianity was best understood as "a magnificent work of art, a manifestation of God which is to find the world, and move it, and change it, through the medium of expression. Hence it requires for an inlet, not reason or logic or a scientific power so much as a right sensibility."[94]

This line of reasoning led Bushnell to describe "the very great difficulty, if not impossibility of mental science and religious dogmatism." Instead, Bushnell argued for a higher form of knowledge: "The teachings of Christ are mere utterances of truth, not argumentations over it. He gives it forth in living symbols, without definition, without *proving* it, ever, as the logicians speak, well understanding that truth is that which shines in its own evidence, that which *finds* us, to use an admirable expression of Coleridge, and thus enters into us."[95]

Especially upsetting to Bushnell's critics were his statements about the Bible, which maintained an orthodox preeminence for Scripture but with radically altered procedures for interpretation. If one approached the Bible with "constructive logic" uppermost in mind, the only possible conclusion was that "no book in the world . . . contains so many repugnances, or antagonistic forms of assertion." But the person who "wants, on the other hand, really to behold and receive all truth, and would have the truth-world overhang him as an empyrean of stars, complex, multitudinous, striving antagonistically, yet comprehended, height above height, and deep under deep, in a boundless score of harmony," that person would be blessed in reading the Scriptures, for "God's own law-givers, heroes, poets, historians, prophets, and preachers and doers of righteousness, will bring him their company, and . . . shine upon him as so many cross lights on his field of knowledge, to give him the most complete and manifold view possible of very truth." With this new approach, the Scriptures would be studied "not as a magazine of propositions and mere dialectic entities, but as inspirations and poetic forms of life, requiring, also, divine inbreathings and exaltations in us, that we may ascend into their meaning."[96]

Radical as its explicit proposals were, even more radical was what they implied. Of those implications, one of the most important was that Bushnell intended his organic, poetic theory of language to be applied selectively. He did not intend it for the physical sciences, governmental policy, and moral reform, all arenas in which he had definite opinions and where in fact he hoped for a more definite connection between verbal propositions and reality. An example was Bushnell's response to Charles Darwin's proposals concerning evolution, which Bushnell rejected with typical flair as simply preposterous: "If there is no stability or fixity in species, then, for aught that appears, even science itself may be transmuted into successions of music, and moonshine, and auroral fires. If a single kind is all kinds, then all are one, and since that is the same as none, there is knowledge no longer."[97] Critics at the time made much the same complaint about what Bushnell was doing in theology. Charles Hodge, for example, thought that Bushnell's "Preliminary Dissertation on Language" came from a "vague ecstasy of feeling, or spiritual inebriation," that it was "a splendid work of art" by "a poet" but provided no substantive contribution to theological knowledge.[98]

What Charles Hodge did not stress, however, was the momentous change that Bushnell proposed with barely a second thought—a two-tiered world where talk about God, human salvation, and the interpretation of the Holy Bible was intentionally disconnected from the world of means-ends reasoning, practical human decisions, and the interpretation of ordinary human documents. For Bushnell, to make this proposal was to cast an entirely different light on how correct theology and faithful Christian living would stabilize society and shape the national destiny.

One contemporary who did see the broader implications was Enoch Pond (1791–1882), the leading theologian at Bangor Seminary in Maine and a longtime associate with Andover's Edwards Amasa Park in many ventures. Pond did not like what Bushnell proposed, but he liked even less how he was making the proposal: "His theory . . . must be of disastrous influence." Pond had no difficulty conceding that "there are imperfections in language," yet notwithstanding its occasional deficiencies, language was "one of the richest, noblest gifts of God" and was intended precisely for expressing "the nicer shades of thought, and the varied emotions and affections of our souls." To "cast doubt on the settled significance of language, and destroy confidence in it, in its application to the subject of religion," would literally destroy civilization. In Pond's phrase: "The foundations of human intercourse, and with them of society, are disturbed, and a mischief is perpetrated for which there is no remedy." As he read Bushnell's book, he saw the stakes as very high: "If theology cannot be taught in words, no more can psychology, morality, or anything else. If a creed or catechism cannot be understood, no more can the Bible; no more can Dr. Bushnell's discourses; no more can the household words of common life." In words reprising the alarmed warning of Samuel Stanhope Smith a half century earlier—on the devastation that would follow if people believed in multiple origins of the human race and, therefore, the impossibility of moral philosophy constructed from common sense—Pond concluded that if Bushnell's theory prevailed, "We have come to another tower of Babel."[99]

As it happened, Pond saw things clearly, though with some exaggeration. American intellectual life did not as a whole follow Bushnell's lead, but ways of talking about the human spirit did move in that direction, especially from the 1870s. The consequence was not Babel but increasing disengagement between realms of thought oriented toward personal fulfillment or spiritual renewal and realms where discourse was assumed to connect words and things reliably—law, business, medicine, all of the physical sciences, even politics.

Eventually the latter became the arena where debate was expected over general social procedures and universal claims for knowledge that could be discussed by the public as a whole.[100] To the extent that Bushnell's "Preliminary Dissertation" really did point in the direction of a later, American version of C. P. Snow's "Two Cultures," it marked the end of the Christian America that revivalists, agents of voluntary societies, seminary professors, and ordinary ministers had been building since the disorganized confusion of the constitutional era.

Bushnell's theory of language was more denounced in his own day than followed. Even in Hartford, where he was for the most part well liked, he could not carry the day. In 1852 his North Church withdrew from the Consociation in order to spare Bushnell further grief at its hand.[101] Bushnell's influence arrived later in the 1880s and 1890s, when the Social Gospel and new forms of idealistic philosophy became prominent in Northern Protestant churches, often under the influence of thinkers who had read Bushnell seriously, like Theodore Munger and A. C. McGiffert.

Whatever his actual influence in the 1850s, Bushnell's rejection of the standard forms of theological reasoning—and the standard mode of linking theology to other intellectual and practical spheres of life—spoke for a creeping disillusionment with the conventions of theistic common sense as they had been developing for half a century in service to God and country. Of greatest significance was the fact that proposals to radically alter these conventions came not from the fringe—not from immigrants, freed slaves, Roman Catholics, Lutherans, or Jews—but from the heart of the nation's dominant Reformed phalanx of leading intellectuals.

Fragmentation

Signs of intellectual fragmentation grew throughout the 1850s, more, to be sure, as noteworthy, but isolated, departures from earlier intellectual norms than as a great number of defections. But where creative and obviously perceptive thinkers led, elites and the populace were sure to follow. Each significant departure from the axiomatic assumptions of earlier theological practice deserves extended consideration, but even brief accounts can indicate how important was the breach that Bushnell opened and other impressive thinkers also passed through.

Even before Bushnell's widely noted book of 1849, John Williamson Nevin had been fulminating against the hegemony exercised over theology by Scottish commonsense philosophy, Anglo-American confidence in a people's Enlightenment, and Reformed theology adapted to activistic revivalism.[102] From the German Reformed seminary in Mercersburg, Pennsylvania, Nevin (1803–1886) had been sniping away at American intellectual icons since the early 1840s, but with little of the attention lavished so nervously on Bushnell's later work. Nevin, though he had studied at Princeton Seminary, had come to conclude that even the most conservative Presbyterians of his day were giving way too readily to sub-Christian practices undertaken ostensibly for the salvation of American society. In a screed from 1843, *The Anxious Bench*, Nevin blasted popular practices for substituting a man-made faith for what he regarded as the properly balanced, Christ-centered, and genuinely biblical religion set forth in the Heidelberg Catechism of the German Reformed Church. Against common revival practices, Nevin held up "the living Catechism, the Catechism awakened and active . . . the centrality of the church"— by which he meant a historically informed faith that valued properly constituted preaching, sacraments, and doctrine.[103]

Three years later Nevin offered a longer, positive statement of what Christianity should look like. His title by itself was indicative of how poorly his ideas fit into the voluntaristic, low-church, often antisacramental attitudes of his age: *The Mystical Presence. A Vindication of the Reformed or Calvinistic Doctrine of the Holy Eucharist*. As much as Charles Hodge believed in the imputed righteousness of Christ as the key to genuine Christianity, so too did Nevin contend for what he called "original Protestant orthodoxy" in eucharistic belief and practice as the key to religious health against the debilitating errors of "the modern popular view of the Lord's Supper."[104] In this vision, as we have seen above, there was no place for the vaunted deliverances of common sense or the hallowing of Baconian procedure.

Much closer to the main currents of public religious opinion were a number of more widely acknowledged voices who came to share Nevin's disillusionment with America's standard theological procedures, even if they looked in different directions for renovating a system gone wrong. Henry Boynton Smith (1815–1877), whose analysis of New England theological history we have already noted, agreed with Nevin that standard American theology had dangerously thinned out the faith in its excessive zeal to convince, enlist, energize, regulate, and inspire the people.[105] Smith had been converted out of a Unitarian upbringing while a student at Bowdoin College, and then converted again during study in Europe to a moderate form of nineteenth-century pietism as presented by the German theologians J. A. W. Neander and Friedrich Tholuck. Smith became an influential figure through his lectures and writings as professor at Union Seminary in New York City, which had been established as a New School Presbyterian institution only shortly before his arrival in 1850. For the Presbyterians, Smith played a critical role by showing his New School colleagues, and eventually convincing even some very conservative Old Schoolers, that it was possible to differ on details involving the Westminster standards *without* coming under the influence of New England theology. Smith, whose relatively meager literary output featured more criticism of other authors than advocacy of his own views, nonetheless effectively advanced a form of moderately conservative Calvinism—including self-conscious reference to Jonathan Edwards—that relied much less on standard notions of Baconian common sense than most of his contemporaries. In particular, Smith criticized both New Haven moderating Calvinists and Old School traditionalists for subsuming theology to sterile rationalism. His solution was to build, with an "organic method," a theology founded on "Christ, as Mediator," to whom "all parts of theology equally refer."[106] It is a mark of how deeply entrenched the standard procedures of theistic common sense and Baconian apologetics were that Smith found it easier to announce such a theology than actually to write it. Nonetheless, his efforts at breaking loose from the paradigm developed by the signal theological works of the late 1820s and 1830s registered another consequential vote in favor of rethinking the entire theological agenda.

A much more popular, and perhaps even more insightful, voice who moved in much the same direction was Harriet Beecher Stowe (1811–1896).[107] As the daughter of Lyman Beecher, the era's most dynamic moderating Calvinist, a youth with firsthand experience of Calvinist ministry in rural New England (Litchfield, Connecticut), urban New England (Boston), and the opening West (Cincinnati), the wife of a Congregationalist professor of biblical literature, a constant participant in a ceaseless round of intense theological conversation, and a careful reader of learned and popular theology, Stowe was as well situated as any person in her age to take the measure of America's mainstream Reformed theology. There are intimations of such a reckoning in *Uncle Tom's Cabin* from 1851, but Stowe did not offer a full-scale accounting until two later novels that were not only set in the New England of her youth (or shortly before) but that also offered a sensitive interpretation of New England theology from the era of Samuel Hopkins through the flourishing of Nathanael Emmons. The novels are *The Minister's Wooing* (1859), in which Hopkins appears as a central figure during his tenure at Newport, Rhode Island, and *Oldtown Folks* (1869), in which the character of Dr. Moses Stern was a thinly disguised representation of Emmons. These works have been criticized for their deficiencies as fiction, but they remain remarkable theological documents. They are distinguished by Stowe's success in communicating two messages simultaneously—her abandonment, not just of certain Calvinist particulars, but of the whole way of thought that defined mainstream Calvinist debate from the 1790s onward; but also her loving admiration for the theology and the theologians she was leaving behind.

The key element in the plot of *The Minister's Wooing* was a matter of great existential moment for the Beecher clan. It concerned the presumed death of the heroine's much-beloved and entirely upright intended, who is lost at sea while still in a professedly unregenerate state. The book is an imitation of life, for Harriet's sister Catharine found herself in just such a situation in 1822 when her fiancé drowned, and the tragic circumstance was played out again when Harriet's oldest son, Henry, met the same fate in 1857. The theological force of the novel comes from Stowe's sympathetic accounts of several different efforts to cope with a situation where everyone realizes that an unusually good person has died, but also where all the key figures sincerely believe in Christian doctrines decreeing that the dead youth will suffer in hell forever because of his lack of saving faith. The Hopkins figure, true to his theology, can offer no assurance about the young man's eternal destiny, but Stowe nonetheless treats him, his reasoning, and especially his prayer for the bereaved with surpassing tenderness.[108] The novel then proceeds almost immediately to an entire chapter entitled "Views of Divine Government," in which Stowe lauds in terms of highest respect the line of theological descent from the first Puritans, through Edwards, to Hopkins: "The views of human existence which resulted from this course of training were gloomy enough to oppress any heart which did not rise above them by triumphant faith or sink below them by brutish insensibility; for they included every moral problem of natural or revealed religion, divested of all those softening poetries and tender draperies which forms, ceremonies, and rituals had thrown around them in other parts and ages of Christendom."[109] Stowe is then almost as sympathetic with the mother of the dead fiancé, who is moved by the tragedy to denounce the whole system of theology she had learned from Hopkins and his predecessors as a monstrosity: "Dr. Hopkins says that this is all best,—better than it would have been in any other possible way,—that God *chose* it because it was for a greater final good. . . . It is *not* right! No possible amount of good to ever so many can make it right to deprave ever so few;—happiness and misery cannot be measured so! I never can think it right,—never! . . . It is impossible!—it is contrary to the laws of my nature! I can never love God! . . . No end!—no bottom!—no shore!—no hope!—O God! O God!"[110] As much as Stowe had internalized respect for the dominant clerical tradition, so also could she respect estrangement from that tradition.

But then Stowe moved on to articulate her own conviction, expressed most forcefully through the character of an African servant, Candace, who after listening patiently to the conversation about the lost son (Jim) between his mother (Mrs. Marvyn), Hopkins, and other interested parties, breaks in with a statement, at once personal and theological, which deserves to be quoted at length:

> "Come, ye poor little lamb," she said, walking straight up to Mrs. Marvyn, "come to ole Candace!"—and with that she gathered the pale form to her bosom, and sat down and began rocking her, as if she had been a babe. "Honey, darlin', ye a'n't right,—dar's a drefful mistake somewhar," she said. "Why, de Lord a'n't like what ye tink,—He *loves* ye, honey! Why, jes' feel how *I* loves ye,—poor ole black Candace,—an' I a'n't better'n Him as made me! Who was it wore de crown o' thorns, lamb?—who was it sweat great drops o' blood?—who was it said, 'Father, forgive dem'? Say, honey!—wasn't it de Lord dat made ye?—Dar, dar, now ye'r crying'!—cry away, and ease yer poor little heart! He died for Mass'r Jim,—loved him and *died* for him,—jes' give up his sweet, precious body and soul for him on de cross! Laws, jes' *leave* him in Jesus's hands! Why, honey, dar's de very print o' de nails in his hands now!"[111]

Stowe's novelistic theology spoke even more directly than H. B. Smith's academic writing: not only was it necessary to rescue theology by a fresh concentration on the person and work of Christ, but that rescue also involved an almost complete rejection ("jes' *leave* him in Jesus's hands!") of the overwhelming compulsion of America's Reformed theologians—Presbyterians as much as Congregationalists—to figure everything out. Stowe remained lovingly attentive to her father in the last years of his life, which were marked with senility. But soon after Lyman Beecher died in 1863, Stowe joined the Episcopal Church, a decision that meant not a violent repudiation of her past but a respectful setting aside of a whole approach to religion, and especially formal theology, which she simply moved beyond.

Not everyone in the Beecher family was so fortunate. Where Harriet Beecher Stowe bent, her older sister Catharine (1800–1878) broke.[112] Catharine's upbringing as the oldest Beecher sibling was everything that her sister Harriet experienced, and more. She possessed a capacious intellect, she became the successful proprietor of several girls' schools, and in carrying out her educational tasks, she read carefully the same texts that were debated among the nation's elite theologians. For most of two decades after the tragic death of her fiancé she followed the loving, but single-minded, guidance of her father in teaching her students and readers that both Scripture and human consciousness confirmed the basic soundness of the Calvinist system. An extensive book from 1836, entitled *Letters on the Difficulties of Religion*, allowed her to explain why "rules founded upon Christianity and the laws of the human mind" made for the best civilizations, why New England represented "a shining example of the tendencies of the religion of the Bible," why it was that "no doctrine of Christianity [was] contrary to reason," and why revivals so regularly made "vice and folly sink away, and every virtue bloom and flourish"—in other words, exactly what her father Lyman was saying in just about so many words at just about the same time in works like *A Plea for the West*.[113]

Yet beneath her active, dutiful, and efficient exterior, a very different story was being played out that she finally offered to the public in 1857 as a personal account prefacing a very different kind of book.[114] Where the *Letters* of 1836 frequently offered "considerations to meet these difficulties," occasioned especially by questions about eternal punishment, moral inability and natural ability, and original sin (however modified by later theologians), her *Common Sense Applied to Religion* of 1857 gave up the effort. "The common sense and the moral sense of mankind" really did contradict certain repellent dogmas "claimed to be contained in the Bible, which are revolting both to the intellect and to the moral nature of man." And common sense was right. As part of the book's preface, Beecher offered a moving account of her own decades-long struggle to internalize the view of Christian faith she had been taught by her father—to feel herself tainted by original sin, to believe that it was just for individuals living in the nineteenth century to suffer through some kind of connection with the sinful deeds of Adam, to believe that her deceased fiancé deserved to suffer in hell for not being willing (or able) to profess saving faith, to think that God arbitrarily chose who would be redeemed, and to doubt that actions of moral obedience were somehow lacking unless carried out in faith.[115]

Despite her own best efforts, Beecher came to a shocking conclusion: "There must be a dreadful mistake somewhere. . . . My renewed decision was, 'There is some dreadful mistake somewhere.'"[116] Yet unlike Harriet Beecher Stowe's Candace, who uttered almost the same phrase, Catharine Beecher did not turn to a new understanding of divine mercy in Christ but to an alternative solution worked up from the intellectual raw materials of the New England heritage. Through her efforts as an educator, she was led to believe that

true Christianity had very little to do with the dogmas she had been taught
about divine sovereignty, the mysterious work of the Spirit, or the atonement,
imputation, and sanctification. Rather, reinforced by her study of the Scottish moralists Thomas Reid and William Hamilton, she came to a new understanding of Christianity—that the Bible was really about the moral example
of Jesus, that it taught the value of obedience before faith rather than the reverse, and that common sense properly followed could educate youth properly and so "eventually . . . renew the whole race, and bring every human being
to perfect obedience to *all* the laws of the Creator."[117] As surely as Bushnell,
H. B. Smith, and her sister Harriet, Catharine Beecher was giving up on the
axiomatic beliefs of American Calvinism; only in her case she did so by *retaining* a first allegiance to the commonsense readings of Scripture and the
principles of moral sense reasoning that the other innovators of the 1850s had
begun to jettison.

An intelligent appendix treating the history of New England Calvinism
brought her book to a close. Its overarching purpose was to demonstrate the
disasters of sectarian religious anarchy along with the ability of women teachers to provide a much better education—both intellectual and moral—than
the men of the United States had yet been able to offer. Along the way she
took to task Augustine, Edwards, her own brother Edward Beecher's attempt
to resuscitate Augustinianism (*The Conflict of Ages*, 1853), and then, most
poignantly, "the New Haven school of theologians," who had made "another
effort to change the hard features of Calvinism." As Beecher interpreted this
latter effort, by her father and N. W. Taylor, it foundered because these theologians were trying to perform two tasks at once: "The one to maintain the
doctrine that sin consisted solely in wrong *action* and not at all in *nature*, and
the other to show that in this they did not differ from Edwards." Part of her
simply marveled at how it was "possible that men so intelligent and so honored should maintain on this subject they had not departed from the system
of New England divinity as exhibited by Edwards." Another part concluded
that Edwards was to blame for being "contradictory and inconsistent" in holding to a fatalistic view of the will and "the contrary doctrine of *free agency*."[118]
And so Catharine Beecher also bade the great intellectual projects of New
England Calvinism good-night.

Increasingly through the 1850s, the hold of "American theology" was beginning to slip. Yet if a few thinkers were giving it up entirely, the synthesis of
Christian republican common sense still prevailed as the dominant intellectual framework among the public at large. As reactions to the Civil War would
show, even those like Bushnell, Nevin, H. B. Smith, and the Beechers found
it much harder to evade the pull of Christian republicanism than they did to
exchange a commonsense Christian Enlightenment for more romantic, idealistic, and Christocentric views of religion, or, in the case of Catharine
Beecher, a more consistent allegiance to Enlightenment common sense. Besides, even if a few elite Calvinists were beginning to express their doubts
about the nation's prevailing intellectual commitments, whole new armies of

rapidly formalizing sectarians were eager to embrace them. Because the Methodists were such an overwhelming portion of the sectarian horde, and because their intellectual maturation was occurring at such a rapid pace, it is appropriate to balance the frequently told, and admittedly important story of Calvinist theological development with the much less well known, but perhaps equally significant, narrative of Methodist theology in these same eventful decades.

The Americanization of Methodism

The Age of Asbury

Early American Methodism was a spiritual *movement*—in the words of Francis Asbury, "a true missionary, apostolic church"—constituted by its ardent gospel preaching and its personal networks of organization.[1] Although an extensive theology underlay the movement, the articulation and defense of that theology were secondary to its preaching for redemption. Similarly, while the early Methodists were not indifferent to social responsibility, they were organized as a vast engine of salvation and so at first resisted, as a distraction from their mission, the formulation of thought for politics, society, literature, or civilization.

Exemplary recent scholarship has revealed much about the Methodists' remarkable story in the early United States.[2] Yet for the movement as a whole there remain mysteries, which are well illustrated by the career of Francis Asbury. Asbury's single-minded energy and organizational genius were critical for the early expansion of Methodism. Because of his lifetime dedication to itinerant preaching and to encouraging others in the same task, he traveled through every state in the Union annually for more than thirty years. Almost certainly Asbury was the most widely recognized face (or figure on horseback) in the new nation's early decades. Yet since Asbury published almost nothing except hymnbooks and the minutes of Methodist conferences, because he was not particularly interested in politics, and because he was not himself a marginal figure (however dedicated, as few others in his era, to aiding the marginalized), scholars have paid him little serious attention.[3] This neglect is extraordinary, since without sympathetic understanding of Asbury and his fellow itinerants, it has been all but impossible to understand the character, appeal, internal variations, dynamism, and remarkable effects of the movement they led. Hence we have the anomalous situation where, even with the rising tide of exemplary Methodist scholarship, existing work only hints at the religious attraction of early Methodism, even though it was its character as religion that made the movement so important in the early history of the United States. Donald Mathews has put the situation well in talking about recent scholarship on Southern evangelical faith: modern students may not find this religion attractive, or even comprehensible, but the great historical challenge nonetheless remains to understand "the appeal of the salvation [Methodists] preached," and to do so in terms employed by the people who "believed that God did indeed care and that they could be made whole not through correct doctrinal formulae or changing society or killing the master, but through receiving the wholeness of the Transcendent in the Spirit."[4]

The historical problem is heightened for Methodist theology. Although the Methodists were as theological as a primarily experiential movement could be, existing scholarship on Methodist understandings of God, human nature, Christian salvation, and holy living cannot begin to compare with scholarship devoted to the era's Congregationalists and Presbyterians, even though the Methodists represented a great people's movement everywhere on the rise in the early United States while America's hereditary Reformed denominations had already entered into a long decline relative to the general culture. Lack of attention to Methodist theology, whether in the populist, kerygmatic form of its early decades or in the more formal, discursive modes of later generations, means that much remains unknown about how Methodist thinking related to the broader social, political, and intellectual contours of the United States. A mere two chapters cannot remedy all such deficiencies, but by highlighting the stages through which Methodist theology passed from the Revolution to the Civil War, they offer a preliminary assessment of why a theology not particularly influenced by American circumstances was so appealing in the early United States and then why it adapted so rapidly to American norms after the success of those early efforts.

Methodist theology came to North America already fully formed. The doctrines with which Francis Asbury, Thomas Coke, and other emissaries of John Wesley crossed the Atlantic in the 1770s and 1780s had been forged in the contexts of English life, with an assist from pietistic renewal on the Continent.[5] The teaching of John Wesley that so decisively informed early Methodist doctrine both resembled and contradicted the more Calvinist theologies that had prevailed in eighteenth-century North America. Resemblances had much to do with a common rootage in the Protestant Reformation. Differences had almost nothing to do with the American environment. In particular, it is vital to recall that Wesley opposed American independence, reprobated republican politics as inherently sinful, and criticized the era's new moral philosophy as dangerously self-centered, when he took any notice of it all.

Attending to the Methodist story offers a picture of Americanization that parallels in some ways the story of Presbyterian and Congregational theology. As Methodists absorbed American notions of republican freedom and theistic common sense, their view of salvation came to stress the natural and the human alongside the supernatural and the divine, their understanding of atonement shifted from a personal transaction to an ethical abstraction, their reliance on Scripture was filtered more obviously through the norms of regnant moral philosophy, and their intrinsic interest in holiness broadened out toward a utilitarian concern for the social benefits of godliness. But this is also a story with a difference. Methodist theology Americanized primarily through peaceful osmosis—by gradually absorbing the mental habits of the educated elite in a climate of interdenominational dialogue—rather than through the Revolutionary crisis, in which Reformed theologians had absorbed powerful American ideologies in order to play a part in shaping the *novus ordo seclorum*. A Protestant culture was already substantially built by the time Methodists began to adjust their inherited theology to the intellectual norms of the nation's elite thinkers. They did not undertake that adjustment as their Reformed peers had done, in the midst of Revolutionary ideological turmoil. Thus, although the Methodists' original dynamism contributed mightily to constructing Protestant culture in America, the distinctive convictions of Methodist theology never exerted the influence on the nation's intellectual life that its spirituality did on the nation's popular religion. When it matured into formal discourse, Methodist theology became far more derivative than its original proclamation of salvation had ever been.

The Character of Early Methodism

Eighteenth-century Methodism was not the exclusive possession of John (1703–1791) and Charles (1707–1788) Wesley, but their leadership through word, song, and constant hands-on attention was critical. Although his practice often contradicted his precepts, John Wesley was at pains to deny that Methodism constituted a system of religious thought. As he wrote in an early effort to define the movement in 1742, "The distinguishing marks of a Methodist are not his opinions of any sort. His assenting to this or that scheme of religion, his embracing any particular set of notions, his espousing the judgment of one man or of another, are all quite wide of the point." Rather, Wesley held that the best definition was experiential and, if possible, expressed in the words of Scripture: "A Methodist is one who has 'the love of God shed abroad in his heart by the Holy Ghost given unto him' [Romans 5:5]; one who 'loves the Lord his God with all his heart, and with all his soul, and with all his mind, and with all his strength' [Luke 10:27 and parallels]. God is the joy of his heart, and the desire of his soul."[6]

Charles Wesley's hymns were always as important as his brother's dicta in charting the Methodist course, though their influence is harder to document. The hymns that were most sung and most reprinted, even by theological opponents of the Wesleys, were those that stressed Christ-centered Christian experience, as in one of the best-known examples:

> Long my imprisoned spirit lay,
>   Fast bound in sin and nature's night.
> Thine eye diffused a quick'ning ray;
>   I woke; the dungeon flamed with light.
> My chains fell off, my heart was free,
>   I rose, went forth, and followed thee.[7]

The most important thing to remember about early Methodist theology in North America is that its adherents deliberately and self-consciously sought to reproduce on the western side of the Atlantic the religion they learned from the Wesleys.

Francis Asbury (1745–1816) was the key figure in that intellectual migration. A typical exhortation to one of his fellow itinerants in 1788 underscored the decisive Wesleyan emphases: "If possible visit from house to house, and that regularly once a fortnight for no other purpose than to speak to each in the family about their souls. . . . Sermons ought to be short and pointed in town, briefly explanatory and then to press the people to conviction, repentance, faith and holiness. . . . So shall we speak not so much by system but by life and application in the heart, little illustration and great fervency in the spark of life. We have cold weather but we may have warm hearts, faith to head to mountains of sin and rivers of ice."[8] The focus in the age of Asbury was experiential knowledge of God as merciful redeemer known through the justifying work of Jesus Christ.

By the time the Methodist invasion of America began, however, there was no doubt that the godly experiences defining the movement also entailed certain commitments in Christian doctrine. Here the views of the movement's third key theologian were especially timely for American developments. John Fletcher (1729–1785) was a Swiss-born pastor who, after his arrival in England in 1750 and a deep spiritual crisis shortly thereafter, rapidly advanced in the Anglican church and in the councils of Methodism. Fletcher's most widely reprinted work, *Checks to Antinomianism*, was issued serially in the early 1770s as part of yet another public debate between Methodists and Calvinists—colleagues in revival, but also sometimes bitter rivals in specifying the exact nature of the Christian faith. Representing the latter position most prominently in this round of controversy with Fletcher and the Wesleys was Augustus M. Toplady, author of the well-known hymn "Rock of Ages" and also, in contrast to Fletcher and the Wesleys, a supporter of American independence.[9] Yet despite Fletcher's politics, the earliest American Methodists turned for theological guidance to him as well as to the Wesleys.

In defending the principles of Methodism, Fletcher's *First Check to Antinomianism* from 1771 highlighted most of the central affirmations of the Wesleyans' creed:

- the total fall of man in Adam, and his utter inability to recover himself, or take any one step toward his recovery, "without the grace of God preventing [i.e., enabling] him";
- Christ as the only way of salvation;

- holiness of heart and life;
- full sanctification;
- general redemption . . . Christ as the Saviour of *all* men, but especially of them that believe; and
- the moral agency of man . . . upon the principles of . . . natural and revealed religion.[10]

The Methodist message as pioneered by the Wesleys, defended by Fletcher, and then brought to America by the likes of Francis Asbury was preeminently a message of Christian experience. Yet that grasp of experience always included an extensive theology, as illustrated in the lives of Asbury's early colleagues.

The career of Benjamin Abbott (1732–1796) was unusual, since he began itinerating only many years after his Methodist conversion. But Abbott's story illustrates how personal experiences of grace led on to distinctive Methodist doctrines. After his conversion in southern New Jersey, Abbott found that Presbyterian and Baptist elders thought he had become insane and so they urged him to return to the safety of traditional Christian doctrines like predestination. While reading a Calvinist treatise, however, Abbott reported that this "doctrine of decrees and unconditional election and reprobation so confused my mind, that I threw it by, determined to read no more in it, as my own experience clearly proved to me, that the doctrines it contained were false." When Abbott checked the confessions of the Presbyterians and the Baptists against the Scriptures, he "found them . . . unscriptural and repugnant to truth . . . I found the Bible held out free grace *to all*, and *for all*, and that Christ tasted death for *every* man, and offered Gospel salvation to *all*. Therefore, I could not bear those contracted partial doctrines of unconditional election and reprobation." As he engaged in this biblical study, Abbott remembered that when he had been converted, "the Lord showed me that it was his will that I should join the methodist church, and that I had been putting it off for six months trying to join either the baptist or presbyterian church." The result was a revelation: "Such a shock of conviction ran thro' my soul upon this reflection, that on a sudden I cried aloud, several times, '*I am a methodist! I am a methodist!*'"[11]

Freeborn Garrettson (1752–1827) was an even more important witness for how Methodist experience led on to Methodist doctrine. Garrettson came from a wealthy Maryland family that was disconcerted when he became a Methodist in 1775 and then began to itinerate. Through a long and influential career, Garettson, with his wife Catharine (née Livingstone), of New York, faithfully promoted the early Methodist vision. In 1827, the last year of his life, Garrettson preached a sermon that looked back fifty years to the message of Methodism in its original form. To Garrettson it was critical that Methodists had proclaimed "the *essentials* of the gospel." Those essentials were crystal clear in his mind: "The design of preaching is to awaken sinners and to bring them to Christ;—to urge believers to the attainment of holiness of heart and life;—to show sinners the turpitude of their hearts and sinfulness of their practice, and to bring them to the foot of the cross, stripped of self and of all self dependence;—to press the old Methodistical doctrines of justification by faith; the direct evidence from God, through faith in the merits of Christ, of the forgiveness of sin; and the adoption into his family. Nor are we to be ashamed of that unfashionable doctrine, Christian perfection."[12] Methodist theology, in sum, featured the experiential reality of Christian salvation as revealed in the Scriptures, offered to lost sinners, open to every person, always dependent upon God's grace in Christ, and leading to both an assurance of present salvation and manifest holiness (even perfection) in this life.

As children of the midcentury revivals, the Methodists shared many connections with other evangelicals, whether Congregational, Presbyterian, Baptist, or Anglican. Most important, Christianity was to be, in the language of the eighteenth century, an "experimental" reality. Almost as important was the conviction that the Bible revealed the truth about God and, in some general sense, about all else. The commendation of Asbury at his funeral spoke for all of early Methodism: "The bible, to him, was the book of books, and his grand confession of faith. He was careful to regulate, all his religious tenets and doctrines, by the book of God, and to discard everything that was incompatible with the divine law and testimony."[13] Methodists, furthermore, joined other evangelicals of their age in affirming that all humans were lost in their sins and incapable as lost sinners of returning to God or living for God. They also believed that repentant sinners were made into true Christians when they received the justifying grace communicated by Jesus Christ. In these convictions, Methodists were as thoroughly traditional as almost any Calvinist.[14] In fact, on the fall of humanity and its effects, many Methodists continued to hold more conservative views than the moderate Calvinists who had come to deny the transmission of guilt from Adam to his descendants and who avoided speaking of human nature as inherently sinful.

On other issues, however, the Methodists advanced positions that Calvinists looked upon as dangerous innovations. First, they affirmed that Christ's atonement was universal and so opened the way to salvation to all people.[15] Second, they held that because of the universal character of that atonement, God's prevenient grace—a grace that "came before" actual salvation—was communicated to all and so enabled all to turn in faith to God. A particular point of dispute arising from this conviction was, third, the belief that when God communicated prevenient grace to all humanity, it restored a self-determining capacity (or a "free will") and made all people, however burdened by sin, able to choose for God and for a holy life. A fourth Methodist distinctive concerned persevering in faith: although God justified guilty sinners freely, the redeemed retained free will and so needed to work out their salvation in good works; if they chose, they could fall from grace and lose their salvation. Finally, in an affirmation that was as faithfully championed by Methodists as it was derided by their foes, they held that it was possible by God's grace for Christian believers to become perfectly sanctified or, in John Wesley's phrase, to enjoy "a deliverance from inward as well as from outward sin."[16] By traditional Calvinist (and even sometimes Anglican) standards, these five positions were all heterodox. For the history of theology in

America, it is important to note that some of these original Wesleyan doctrines did resemble certain conclusions to which New Haven Congregationalists and New School Presbyterians were coming by the 1820s and 1830s. Yet it is also critical to realize that in no case were these Methodist convictions occasioned by adapting to republican thought, to beliefs about the providential destiny of the United States, or to the principles of commonsense moral philosophy. Rather, the theology that early Methodists proclaimed was the theology they had learned from John Wesley. What was once said about the itinerant Smith Arnold in the early 1790s could be said for the whole Methodist movement: he "read himself full of Fletcher's Checks and Wesley's Sermons, which, besides his Bible, were the only books within his reach."[17]

The most important early literature of American Methodism reflected the shape of the movement. Until after 1810, there was almost no indigenous formal theology. Apart from a short-lived effort (1788–1790) to launch a journal in imitation of the Wesleys' own *Arminian Magazine*, the American Methodists sponsored no periodicals until after Asbury's death in 1816. It was likewise only after Asbury's death that Methodists founded secondary schools and colleges (an earlier scheme to begin a "Cokesbury College" had come to nothing.)

What the early Methodists did publish were memoirs, journals, and especially hymnbooks. The literature of an experiential religious movement was experiential literature. Funeral notices for itinerants, many of whom died young because of their arduous labors, were prime early examples of a favored genre.[18] Asbury carried over into America the practice that John Wesley and George Whitefield had perfected by publishing extracts from his journal at periodic intervals.[19] In this effort, Asbury was followed by many of Methodism's early leaders, who also offered to the world through memoirs or published journals a running account of their struggles for, and sometimes with, God.[20] In 1789 the Methodist conference founded a publishing house, called the Book Concern, which became especially important for itinerants, since they soon became colporteurs as well as preachers. The Book Concern also factored large in the denominational division of 1844, since both Northern and Southern branches of the church were keen to appropriate its considerable capital.[21] In its early days the Concern published mostly hymnbooks, memoirs, catechisms for children, and the works of Wesley and other British authors.

Early Methodist literature was, for a fledgling enterprise, fairly extensive, and it was far from anti-intellectual. In particular, it would be a mistake to underestimate the importance of early Methodist hymnals. Asbury published as many as forty-two editions of various Methodist hymnals during his American career, and these Methodist hymnbooks may have been the most widely distributed religious literature of the era.[22] Methodist devotion to hymnody was, as Dee Andrews has wisely noted, "the evangelical Protestant equivalent of the Catholic reverence for painted and sculpted depictions of Christ."[23] For building community, securing long-term affectional allegiance, and teaching a surprisingly deep reservoir of doctrine, there was no equal in early Methodist history.

Asbury's *Pocket Hymn-Book Designed as a Constant Companion for the Pious* was one of the most widely distributed books in the early United States. It was issued in a fresh printing almost every year but was never more than one of the Methodists' many hymnals. Asbury, with his fellow bishop Thomas Coke, regularly closed the prefaces to the annual editions of the *Pocket Hymn-Book* by exhorting its users to "sing with the Spirit, and with the understanding also" (quoting 1 Corinthians 14:15). The hymns they offered certainly allowed for both, as in Charles Wesley's "O for a Thousand Tongues to Sing," which always led off the volume. Its fourth stanza (as printed in America) amounted to an economical précis of the Methodist theology of grace:

> He breaks the power of cancell'd sin,
> He sets the pris'ner free;
> His blood can make the foulest clean;
> His blood avail'd for me.

The same mixture of heart-felt emotion and cool theological precision marked also the hymn that was usually printed second, Joseph Hart's "Come, Ye Sinners, Poor and Needy," where the sixth stanza underscored the urgency along with the God-centered character of Methodist evangelistic preaching:

> Lo' the incarnate God ascending,
> Pleads the merit of his blood:
> Venture on him, venture freely,
> Let no other trust intrude;
>   None but Jesus,
> Can do helpless sinners good.[24]

And so the *Pocket Hymn-Book* went for hundreds of pages. And so also did the other hymnals Asbury produced, like the "supplement" to the pocket hymnbook, with its hymns keyed to biblical texts like Isaiah 55:1 ("Ho! every one that thirsts draw nigh"), John 6:5 ("O Thou, whom once they flock'd to hear! / Thy words to hear, thy power to feel! / Suffer the sinners to draw near, / And graciously receive us still"), and Ephesians 5:8 ("Jesus beholds where Satan reigns, / Binding his slaves in heavy chains: / He sets the pris'ner free, and breaks / The iron bondage from our necks").[25] Hymns like these displayed the vigor of early Methodist publishing and also demonstrated its reliance on Wesley and the experiential character of the movement.

Formal doctrine among the early Methodists remained even more securely British, since the theological norms set out in the first official denominational publications came from Wesley.[26] After the Baltimore Conference of December 1784 received Wesley's instructions for ordaining Thomas Coke and Francis Asbury as superintendents (soon styled "bishops"), and after Asbury took the prudent step of waiting for the assembled preachers to elect him to that position, the two new American bishops issued the *Minutes of Several Conversations between the Rev. Thomas Coke, LL.D., the Rev. Francis Asbury, and Others*. This publication, the Methodists' first official document as an American denomination, followed the form and content of Wesley's own *Minutes*, which from the 1740s had provided authoritative guidance for the

British Methodists. As its standard for theology, Coke and Asbury's *Minutes* featured an abridgment of the Anglican Thirty-nine Articles prepared by Wesley for the Americans. To the twenty-four articles he supplied, the Americans added one more recognizing the jurisdiction of the United States government, which was a prudent move in light of the Wesleys' well-known opposition to the cause of American independence. The 1784 Conference also implied that Wesley's four-volume collection of standards *Sermons* and his *Notes on the New Testament* were to be received as a recognized part of the church's doctrinal basis.[27] At subsequent General Conventions over the next two decades, six other pamphlets, mostly by Wesley, were added to *The Doctrines and Discipline of the Methodist Episcopal Church in America*, as the *Minutes* came to be called from 1792.[28] Throughout this early period, Asbury and Coke continued to stress that the function of proper doctrine was to undergird the Methodists' evangelistic exertions—the "one thing needful [Luke 10:42]" remained the emphasis on "CHRIST dying for and living in us."[29]

Finally in 1808, with Asbury's concurrence and perhaps acting under a compulsion to tie such matters down before he died, the General Conference acted to secure its theological grounding in Wesley for all time. That year it passed five binding resolutions, the first of which stipulated that "the General Conference shall not revoke, alter, or change our Articles of Religion, nor establish any new standards or rules of doctrine contrary to our present existing and established standards of doctrine."[30] Although modern Methodists argue over exactly what was intended under "our Articles of Religion," there is no doubt that, however construed, the doctrines mandated by the 1808 conference as the constitutional basis of American Methodism came entirely from John Wesley.

The distance separating Methodists from the other churches in America during the 1790s and early 1800s was also underscored by the Methodists' wariness about politics.[31] Although the Methodists did eventually follow the American pattern of joining Christian and republican convictions, the timing of that juncture is significant. Asbury's resolution to live above partisanship— "He never meddled in politicks" was the word at his funeral[32]—was decisive for the whole movement, at least to almost 1810. Asbury for some time even shied away from using political designations for the scenes of his labors, preferring instead to speak of his ministry in a simple geographic context: "I want the continent, the world, to flame with the spiritual glory of God."[33] In 1779 he expressed what long remained his typical attitude toward political preoccupations: "I went to a Presbyterian meeting, and heard a good sermon . . . truly applicable to the unfeeling people, who are so full of politics that they seem to have turned all religion out of doors."[34] In 1784 Asbury wrote that he was "wonderfully entertained with a late publication by Silas Mercer, a Baptist preacher, in which he has anathematized the whole race of kings from Saul to George III." Yet Asbury was hardly sympathetic: "His is republicanism run mad. Why [be] afraid of religious establishments in these days of enlightened liberty?"[35] So long as Asbury exercised the controlling voice in

American Methodism, his kind of apolitical pietism prevailed. A colleague, William Watters, later wrote about his concerns as an itinerant during the first decade of the nineteenth century: "Though a friend to my Country, I left politics to those better qualified to defend and discuss them. Preaching was my business: to teach men how to live and to be prepared to die."[36] As Russell Richey has well summarized, "Early American Methodism . . . lacked a concept of the nation. . . . They simply looked right through the nation. They did not see it."[37] In the face of much American preaching to the contrary, some Methodists even continued to feel, as itinerant John Mann expressed it in 1795, that republicanism "eats [religion] out of many hearts."[38]

The rejection of James O'Kelly, who agitated for republican liberties until he left the Methodists in 1792, was the clearest indication of the early Methodists' singular political course.[39] The episode revealed that the Asbury-led Methodists were holding at bay, not only the tide of republican reasoning, but also several related currents that were rapidly altering the shape of theology for other Christian groups.

After O'Kelly (1738–1826) had been converted and joined the Methodists in 1774, he immediately became a vocal supporter for independence as well as for Methodism. During the Revolutionary War, he was arrested several times by Loyalists or the British army but each time escaped; eventually he joined the Continental Army. The specific issues that O'Kelly and like-minded colleagues contested in 1792 were, first, the power of the bishops (Asbury and Coke) to appoint itinerants to their circuits and, second, the power of itinerants to appeal those appointments. Asbury held firm for the former and against the latter and eventually prevailed. But to do so he had to face down assertions from O'Kelly's supporters that the Methodists were "far gone into POPERY," that Americans had not bled "to free their sons from the British yoke" in order to become "slaves to ecclesiastical oppression," that "it was a shame for a man to *accept* of such a lordship, much more to *claim* it," and that Asbury "through a species of tyranny" was making itinerants "slaves for life."[40]

It was also necessary to turn aside O'Kelly's appeal to resolve the dispute by using the New Testament alone, a stratagem that would have set aside the tradition of following Wesley's original instructions to the American Methodists. In addition, those who stood with Asbury were not willing to follow O'Kelly when he appealed to what sounded very much like the age's new moral philosophy. In earlier complaints against following Wesley's instruction, O'Kelly held up an alternative authority to such traditions—where "Revelation is silent," he urged people to "listen to the voice of reason" as to God himself. This appeal echoed conventional views: "Reason—O what a gift to fallen man? This is the light that dear Jesus gives to all born into the world; if they live to be capable of using of it they find it arising with the light of nature as ideas of good and evil appear."[41] O'Kelly, in short, deployed a full range of American ideological principles in combat with Asbury: "As a son of America, and a Christian, I shall oppose your [Asbury's] political measures and contend for the Saviour's government. I contend for Bible government, Christian equality, and the Christian name."[42] When O'Kelly and his associates broke with the main body, they called themselves the Republican Methodist Church. In 1798 O'Kelly published a full-scale indictment of Asbury that continued to employ a wealth of Real Whig themes: "If Christians are free citizens of Zion, they should prize those liberties, seeing they were purchased with the precious blood of Christ. . . . O heavens! Are we not Americans! . . . And shall we be slaves to ecclesiastical oppression?"[43]

Yet in 1792 and for many years thereafter, the use of such American warrants was unavailing, and O'Kelly, with those who thought like him, left the larger church. In this struggle, the relative ordering of Asbury's priorities was clear: "I am happy in the consideration that I never stationed a preacher through enmity, or as a punishment. I have acted for the glory of God, the good of the people, and to promote the usefulness of the preachers."[44] O'Kelly's cause was defeated because most Methodist itinerants concluded with Asbury that the "sacrifice" of personal rights was not "too great to accomplish the object we had in view, namely, the salvation of souls."[45]

Long after O'Kelly's Republican Methodists had departed, Methodists remained willing to relativize American ideology in the service of eternal verities. William McKendree, who in 1808 became the first American-born bishop to join Asbury as leader of the denomination, was representative when he commented on the excitement generated by the Fourth of July and other such national festivities: "How much more cause has an immortal soul to rejoice and give glory to God for its spiritual deliverance from the bondage of sin."[46] At least until after the turn of the century, it was the norm for Methodists to define liberty in other than republican terms. More than freedom from earthly tyranny, they meant the freedom gained by conversion. As the itinerant Thomas Ware once wrote about his own condition, "My soul was in bondage to sin. Civil freedom I thought I understood, and gloried much in it. But the perfect law of liberty, promulgated by Jesus Christ, the Son of the living God, I understood not."[47] The other common use of the term "liberty" in Methodism's early days was for extraordinary effectiveness in preaching. Thus in his journal entry for 4 July 1790, Asbury ignored entirely the civic meaning of the day in order to record that he "was set at liberty, and there was a little shaking and breathing after God, while I opened and explained, 'And there is none calleth upon thy name, that stirreth up himself to take hold of thee' [Isaiah 64:7]."[48] It is little wonder that, even long after these early uses had begun to give way to the more conventional amalgam of Christian republican liberty, Methodists continued to be suspect as crypto-monarchists, hidden papists, and antirepublicans.[49]

The character of Methodist conviction in its early American expression offers an important counterpoint to the general argument of this book. The Methodist experience shows that it was entirely possible for a traditional Christian message that had *not* been adjusted to the norms of American ideology to flourish in the new American nation. Recent historians have made great strides in understanding the relationship between Methodist religion and the American environment. In Dee Andrews's depiction, Asbury and his colleagues provided a message "separate from the crises and conflicts of the American republic but virtually designed for the nation's evangelization."[50] Lynn Lyerly may capture the complicated relationship even more clearly: "The growth of [Methodist] evangelicalism was not merely a product of the Revolution; it constituted a revolution in itself."[51] Their point is not that Methodism was an otherworldly movement oblivious to concrete local realities; it is rather that the Methodist message was more shaping, than being shaped by, those realities.

In the end, it is difficult to explain early American Methodism without paying primary attention to the religious character of the movement. To be sure, Methodist commitment to the people at large did dovetail with themes of democratic empowerment unleashed by the war against Britain. Methodist admonitions to self-sacrificing exertion did inspire a host of young male itinerants whose vocational choices had been disrupted by all that went into the creation of a new American society. Methodist proclamation of the universality of God's love did offer dignity to women and African Americans, whom the tides of republican freedom were passing by. Yet as the Methodist message went out in town and countryside, to scraggly knots of the curious gathered in private homes as well as to sprawling camp meetings thronged by larger crowds than the continent had witnessed since the war, and also, by the early years of the new century, in recognizable church buildings, and as that message was received—by blacks and whites, females and males, mostly middling sorts but also rich and poor—spiritual implications of the message meant the most. Judged as a historical movement, early Methodism was most basically its message of a loving God able to touch people with his Holy Spirit, able to enfold them into supportive fellowship with others who had also felt the touch of justifying grace, and able to nerve them for lives of self-disciplined service to others.

Theology in the new United States was moving in an Arminian or a Methodist direction at the very time when Methodists were establishing themselves in the new world. Yet the role of Methodism in a situation where many of America's traditionally Calvinist denominations were coming to sound more and more Methodistic is curious. Methodism, which owed almost nothing to distinctly American ideologies, was becoming America's most successful religion in the early decades of the new republic at the same time that the Calvinists were becoming more like Methodists precisely of their adjustment to American ideologies.

Methodist concentration on an experiential message of hope is the indispensable context for understanding Methodist theology during the age of Asbury. Early Methodists defined their beliefs with striking consistency as the central convictions of the Wesleys, albeit modified for the purpose of winning the lost in the vast, disorderly spaces of the new world. Although it is difficult to prove a negative, it is still possible to say that until at least the second decade of the nineteenth century, republican and commonsense themes were conspicuous only by their absence in Methodist theological discourse.

The Death of Asbury and the Redirection of Methodist Theology

Methodist theology began to change as Methodist circumstances began to change. Early American Methodism was a people's movement of missionary and apostolic zeal. When the movement broadened to take on responsibilities for education and civilization, it fairly quickly left behind some of the spiritual insights of its missionary period for the conventional intellectual assumptions of the contemporary world of ideas. The result was an alteration in the theology that had driven the missionary zeal.

An example illustrating the nexus between changes in the movement and changes in thought is provided by Stephen Olin (1797–1851), third president of Wesleyan University. Olin was one of the strongest Methodist supporters of higher education in the 1820s as he challenged his fellows to exert themselves in new directions: "We got along passably well when other denominations were wasting their strength in attempting to explain and inculcate the blind mysteries of Calvinism; but now, when they unite great learning and zeal to as much Arminianism as gives them access to the popular mind, we must educate our ministry better, or sink. We may boast of preaching to the poor, but without the due intermixture of the rich and influential, we cannot fulfill our destiny as a Church. Nothing can save us but an able ministry, and this can not be had but by thorough education." Significantly, however, when Olin specified what a learned Methodist ministry should look like, he sounded pretty much like his Presbyterian and Congregationalist contemporaries, who were all agog over the intellectual potential of disinterested mental philosophy. Olin thus turned from a key assertion of early Methodism—that the sole ultimate desideratum was living to God—by contending that the great need of Methodist theology was for "the reduction of its tenets to a scientific system."[52]

Dating the first important shift in Methodist thinking is a relatively easy matter, for it occurred during the second decade of the century, or about the time that Francis Asbury passed from the scene. Not just Asbury, of course, but a set of attitudes that Asbury embodied and that was shared by his most active colleagues was beginning to fade. Still, Asbury's death on 31 March 1816 marked more than a symbolic transition. As a recent student has recognized, Asbury was not only the leader but the embodiment of the early movement: he "governed entirely at the will of the conference of preachers, but wielded significant episcopal power. Despite his influence as superintendent, Asbury traveled more, worked harder, and lived more simply than any other Methodist itinerant preacher."[53]

Under William McKendree and other succeeding bishops, the Methodists did not lack for competent leaders, but they no longer possessed a figure eager to defend, fiercely if need be, the old ways of itinerancy and the original stress on biblical Christian experience. The accumulating growth of the movement meant that pressures for change were also accumulating. Already in 1813, when Asbury wrote a "Valedictory Address" to McKendree, he was beginning to sound out of touch with the times—"I wish to warn you against the growing

evil of locality [i.e., settling down] in bishops, elders, preachers, or Conferences." And he was beginning to appear casuistic in defense of earlier attitudes: "We may rationally conclude that learning is not an essential qualification to preach the gospel. It may be said no man but a fool will speak against
learning. I have not spoken against learning. I have only said that it cannot be
said to be an essential qualification to preach the gospel."[54]

The processes that drew Methodist theology closer to the theology of other
denominations were the processes altering the face of the movement. In the
decade of Asbury's death, the disposition of the ministry began to shift decisively from its earlier situation where the vast majority itinerated to the new
situation where itinerancy became a minority practice.[55] In the decade of
Asbury's death, opposition to slavery was fast fading into the background of
Methodist consciousness, and Richard Allen, whom Asbury had always supported to at least some degree, pulled out of the larger denomination in order
to found the African Methodist Episcopal Church.[56] Again, in the very year
that Asbury died, the General Conference authorized the publication of a
denominational journal. The *Methodist Magazine*, which eventually appeared
in 1818 and absorbed the *Western Christian Monitor,* which had been published privately by an Ohio minister since 1815, was a middle-brow publication that eventually evolved into a learned theological quarterly.[57] Again, in
the decade of Asbury's death the first Methodist secondary schools were
started, to be followed shortly thereafter in 1831 by the founding of Wesleyan
University in Middletown, Connecticut, the opening salvo in the great can-
nonade of Methodist higher education that rolled across the land for the rest
of the nineteenth century.[58]

The change that indicated theological innovation most directly was the fact
that Methodists began to take part in published controversies with their theological opponents in the decade of Asbury's death. Such controversy worked
differently upon American Methodists than it did upon Wesley and the
Wesleyans in the old country. In England, John Wesley's theology remained
suspended between what he considered two contrasting dangers. Against Anglican latitudinarianism he stressed God's free grace; against Calvinist Dissent
he stressed activity in holiness. As American Methodists began to engage in
formal theological exposition, it appeared at first as if they too were facing the
same kind of balanced opposition. Their course seemed set between the Scylla
of Unitarian rationalism and the Charybdis of predestinarian Calvinism. An
exaltation of divine grace was required to combat the Unitarians, a stress on
universal atonement, free will, and perfection to combat the Calvinists.

Well into the nineteenth century, the testimony against excessive reliance
on autonomous reason remained a staple of Methodist concern. In 1804 the
popular itinerant Lorenzo Dow was, for example, much troubled about conceding too much to the Unitarians (whom he called deists) in their exaltation
of natural human capacities: "These Deists attempt to conceive just and accurate ideas of revealed religion, by natural reason, which leads them into an
absurdity." What they needed was the experiential essence of Methodism—
to become "sincere enquirers after truth"; then they "would feel the spirit of

truth bearing witness to, or of the truth, to convince and correct, &c. and their Deism would flee away."[59] Only a few years later, Nathan Bangs, then in the first stages of his memorable career, remonstrated similarly with a fellow itinerant who seems to have been proposing something like commonsense principles for adjudicating moral and religious questions. In response, Bangs was unequivocating: "I cannot assede [accede] to all you say concerning reason, . . . 'When reason dictates our will we are virtuous, consistent, uniform, wise.' If this were so, what need is there of revelation? . . . I can indeed easily perceive that the religion of Jesus Christ is consistent with the nature and fitness of things. . . . But here scripture, not reason, must be our guide, and reason become its handmaid. . . . It is verry danderous [sic] to exalt human reason so as to abuse revelation. Has it not a tendency to engender pride?"[60]

Soon, however, Methodist nervousness about excessive reliance on reason gave way to a set of concerns promoted by debate with the Calvinists. Nothing in fact seemed to work better for skewering Calvinist inconsistencies and defending Methodist doctrines than a careful use of reason, natural intellectual capacities, and the era's new moral philosophy. As years passed and Methodist theological discussion became more and more oriented to the agenda defined by the Calvinists, Methodists displayed much less concern for arguments against rationalist foes on the other side of the theological spectrum.

Yet the primary factor in changing the shape of Methodism from about the time of Asbury's death was its very effectiveness as an instrument of salvation drawing people by the hundreds and thousands into the church. The settlement of ministers, the construction of church buildings, and the gradual decline of itinerancy all illustrate the movement's development from charismatic liminality to prudent organization. But these same developments also constituted a tribute to the spectacular success of the early Methodist vision. Tens—hundreds—of thousands had been converted and set on the path of sanctification (see table 9.6 in chap. 9). Now Methodists felt constrained to look to the converts as well as those needing conversion.

Once Methodism as a pristine missionary movement of biblical experience began to deal with civilization as well as Christianization, with education as well as evangelism, with disorderly society as well as disordered individuals, with the nurture of children as well as the winning of adult converts, it was only understandable that Methodists would want to address an ever-expanding circle of problems. And it is only understandable why those new explorations took on the coloration of ecclesiastical and theological patterns already in place around them. Almost all of the leaders in the generations after Asbury wanted very much to sustain Methodist preaching focused on the personal experience of God, but they also moved—naturally, it seemed—to expressing new interest in the tasks of education, civilization, and public policy that the main religious traditions from the colonial era had long taken for granted as legitimate concerns.

To be sure, it was not inevitable that, when Methodism matured as a movement, it would imitate the intellectual procedures of its peers who had long been concerned for civilization, education, social order, and the nurture of children. Yet it would have taken an intellectual creativity as great as Wesley's organizational genius—as well as an intellectual resolve as fierce as Asbury's lifelong commitment to itineration—to fashion a second- and third-generation Methodism that did *not* follow the forms of ecclesiastical life, the conventions of theological argument, and the instincts about social well-being that by the 1820s were already well established in America's dominant churches. Even proposing such a second tier of creative resolve, however, was almost unthinkable because of how much the Methodists themselves had contributed in such a very short time toward the ecclesiastical and moral nation that had come into existence by the 1820s.

An appropriate analogy for Methodist developments in theology was Methodist testimony against slavery.[61] Only a very compelling message could have won over slaveholders even as it condemned slavery. Only the winning over of slaveholders could have softened the antislave character of the message. Similarly, only a very compelling Methodist message could have won over such a large portion of early national America. Only the winning over of so much of America can explain how America began to change the Methodist message.

17 ✳

The Americanization of Methodism

After Asbury

As Methodists in the post-Asbury era began to augment the imperatives of apostolic evangelism with the duties of responsible citizenship, many came to embrace both republican political ideology and commonsense moral philosophy. American Methodists had never actively opposed these distinctly American commitments as such, but until about 1815 they had been overwhelmingly preoccupied with other, specifically religious concerns. The embrace of republicanism affected Methodist theology less directly than the embrace of commonsense moral reasoning, since the Methodists long sustained their own, traditional, and British-based conceptions of liberty and virtue. Only after the denomination divided in 1844 would republican commitments, expressed in Northern and Southern variations, exert the same influence on Methodist thought as the new moral philosophy was exerting from the 1820s. Yet the Methodists' deployment of standard republican themes still offers a reliable index of their Americanization.

Methodists Become Republicans

Already in the decade of Asbury's death Methodists were beginning to participate in politics to a degree unknown from earlier days, as the instructive case of Luther Lee (1758–1816) indicates.[1] Lee, who later published the first history of Methodism by an American (1810), was converted in 1774 and three years later became a local Methodist preacher in North Carolina. When the tide of Revolutionary battle rolled through his region, he was drafted for ser-

vice with the patriots but refused out of conscientious scruple against bearing arms. His imprisonment, which became an occasion for preaching to
guards and other prisoners, ended only when Lee agreed to serve as an un-
armed teamster driving wagons for the American army. The evolution of
Methodism can be suggested by the fact that, four decades later, Lee as an
honored Methodist elder was elected chaplain of the United States House of
Representatives (first in 1809 and then four other times in later years) and also
chaplain of the Senate (1814), in which capacity he presumably led prayers
for the success of American arms against the British in the War of 1812. For
his part, Asbury was not pleased by such political recognition of Methodist
success. After the Methodist elder Nicholas Snethen was elected chaplain of
the U.S. House in 1811, and another Methodist to the same office for the South
Carolina legislature, Asbury wrote in his diary: "So; we begin to partake of
the honour that cometh from man [John 5:41, 44], now is our time of danger.
O Lord, keep us pure, keep us correct, keep us holy!"[2]

Republican themes accumulated as Methodists moved on from being recognized by the political realm to actually taking part in it. When a young
Methodist minister was selected to deliver the Vermont election sermon on
12 October 1826, the text was John 18:36 ("My kingdom is not of this world").
He developed his theme in what was by then a familiar style. The separation
of church and state helped end "oppressive and tyrannical" government, but
now political leaders were moving too fast toward forgetting "how much they
are indebted to Christ's kingdom for those excellent principles which form
the basis of our political fabric." With Christian principles, it was possible to
guard against "party spirit . . . ambitious views . . . calumny . . . venality."
Where the Protestant Reformation had witnessed "the dawning of liberty's
luminous ray," France had allowed "infidelity and impiety" to corrupt "her
struggle for liberty." Americans knew "by actual experience" how important
it was to enjoy a liberated Scripture, for the Bible "contains such excellent
sentiments upon the rights of man . . . that it becomes dangerous to the pre-
tended divine right of kings and subversive to the absolute authority of tyrants."[3] In other words, when Methodists in the 1820s were asked to give election sermons, they conformed readily to the Christian republican traditions
of the genre.

By the next decade Methodists, except for some teachers of holiness whom
we examine below, were wholehearted promoters of the commonplace Christian republican vision. It was a new day for Methodists when their own elite
periodicals begin to worry in classic Whig fashion about conceding too much
authority to the "sovereignty of the people"; when they employed the standard republican calculus as a matter of course ("it is unquestionable that virtue is essential to the stability of our institutions"); and when they expressed
concern about the tide of immigrants who were introducing "religious principles, which, in general, are averse to that republican simplicity by which
our nation should be distinguished."[4]

From such statements it was a short step to a full-blown Methodist republican discourse. Signs of this evolution multiplied steadily through the next

quarter century. They could be seen in the effort to sanction republican ideals by Scripture, as occurred in an impressive essay from the mid-1840s that reprised standard themes of Congregational and Presbyterian sermons of the 1770s and 1780s. Against "the horse-leech adhesiveness of party feeling," as well as the radical claim that "the Bible is the foe of genuine freedom, and the ready tool of kingly and priestly tyranny," this author was resolute. Not only did Scripture guide a people who wished "to destroy that luxury that destroys more national strength than gunpowder," it also defined the American polity: the "fundamental doctrines of republicanism may, with scarcely an exception, be found in the Bible."[5] The same thinking was at work when one of the Methodists' leading intellectuals could mention in 1851, as if a foregone conclusion, that "Christianity and Republicanism—faith and freedom—still go hand and hand, yielding each other a mutual support."[6] It was this thinking that made Methodists such active participants in political campaigns between 1840 and 1860, when, in the words of Richard Carwardine, "the world of Methodist revivalism . . . led them to present the election campaign as the means of political redemption."[7] The universe framed by Methodist republican assumptions provided the backdrop for Methodist involvement at the highest reaches of American civil religion during the war, as when the Methodist revivalist Charles "Chaplain" McCabe helped transform Julia Ward Howe's poem "The Battle Hymn of the Republic," with its lush mélange of Christian rhetoric, ardent filiopietism, and evocative republican imagery, into a popular hymn.[8]

It was not the case that Methodist appropriation of republican ideology necessarily entailed theological change. Rather, since traditional Methodist conceptions of freedom, virtue, and responsible public action had been originally defined in a British world dominated by other ideologies, the appropriation of republican political views necessarily created an alternative context for American Methodists to develop, expand, and perhaps alter their theology.[9]

Methodists Adopt Commonsense Moral Reasoning

For Methodist theology, the use of commonsense moral reasoning proved even more important than the use of republican political principles, since the former guided Methodists in the successive stages of their acceptance of general American convictions. The process at work was well illustrated from the first major theological writings that American Methodists published, works that began to appear in the years surrounding Francis Asbury's death.

One of the very first formal Methodist theologies was published by Asa Shinn (1781–1853), who had been converted through Methodist preaching in Virginia at age eighteen and who began to itinerate two years later.[10] In 1813 Shinn published a 400–page book, *An Essay on the Plan of Salvation*, which for the most part explained the Christian faith in traditional Wesleyan terms. Shinn, for example, repeated Wesley's insistence that all humans were by nature lost in their sins, but also that the atoning grace of Christ restored a measure of moral freedom to all people. Yet Shinn's advocacy of Methodist theology partook much more generously of moral-sense reasoning than had the Wesleys, John Fletcher, and the generation of Asbury. In his first chapter, which considered how people could know the truth, Shinn held up "intuitive certainty" as the first means, followed by "the evidence of reasoning," and finally "the evidence of Revelation." Later in the volume he stressed the way in which "our rational and moral faculties" confirmed the truthfulness of the Bible and how the "first principles of morals" demonstrated the innocence of infants before their age of responsible action. In these assertions, Shinn was looking to natural human capacities for the spiritual and intellectual assurance that Wesley, Fletcher, Asbury, and most of Shinn's Methodist contemporaries continued to find in the revealed words of Scripture and the personal witness of the Holy Spirit. He was, in particular, eager to use "the strong weapons of common sense against the venerable hypothesis" that new learning disproved the Christian faith. Shinn's merging of influences showed clearly when he said of his position, "It affords me unspeakable pleasure to find I can screen myself under the authority of a Reid, a Beatty, and a Campbell, among philosophers; and . . . of a Baxter, a Wesley, a Fletcher . . . among divines."[11] Two matters concerning Shinn and his book are of further interest. Shinn eventually found the regimen of the Methodist Episcopal Church too despotic and so became a founder in 1828 of the more self-consciously democratic Methodist Protestant Church. Despite Shinn's move out of the MEC, his *Essay on the Plan of Salvation*, with its strong dose of commonsense moral reasoning, was in 1834 added to the reading list of candidates preparing for the Methodist ministry, where it remained until 1878.

An even better case for illustrating the course of American Methodist theology is provided by Nathan Bangs (1778–1862), the individual who came closest to filling the gap left by Asbury's death.[12] Bangs was born in Connecticut and had been drawn to the Methodists before moving to the Upper Canadian wilderness (modern Ontario) in 1799. Two years later he began to itinerate. After twelve years as a pioneering itinerant in Canada, Bangs returned to the States and soon became the driving force in numerous Methodist enterprises. He was the key figure in founding the Methodist Missionary Society, he was for a time the chief officer of the Book Concern, he edited the denomination's most important periodicals, he eventually wrote a major four-volume history of the movement, and he sustained a very broad correspondence with colleagues in the United States, Canada, and Britain.

Bangs's entry into formal Methodist theology came in 1810, when he was asked to present Methodist positions in debate with a Calvinist minister in Franklin, New York. Ongoing controversy sparked by this public presentation eventually led to a significant trio of works in which Bangs tried to demonstrate that, while Methodism captured the meaning of Scripture and promoted genuine Christian experience, the various varieties of New England Calvinism did not.[13] By featuring an amazingly full range of biblical citation and an equally full reliance on the active presence of God as the key to epistemological and religious certainty, these works were more thoroughly Wesleyan and Asburyan than Shinn's *Essay*. Bangs, for example, repeated Wesley's insistence that human nature could not act by itself to restore fellowship with God: "We wish our opponents in this controversy to know, that we do not believe that man has any inherent power to save himself, without the immediate influence of divine grace." He sounded equally like Wesley when he defended the moral freedom of human choice restored by Christ's atonement: "All *may* be saved; and yet none are saved, but those who are willing to bow with submission to the immutable terms of salvation, become holy in heart, and persevere in well being to the end of life. None are under the *necessity* of being finally lost; and yet all will be so lost, who willfully and finally reject the sincere offers of eternal life."[14] Bangs's most important contribution to the articulation of a Wesleyan position was his use of the term "gracious ability" as a way of specifying the meaning of Wesley's "prevenient grace."

Yet as a minor theme in this work, Bangs also enlisted the same kind of academic authorities that Shinn described as a screen for Methodist teachings. Thus, Bangs quoted Princeton's Samuel Stanhope Smith on the intrinsic powers of the active mind, and he likewise drew on Thomas Reid to attack the analogy frequently used by Calvinists in suggesting that cause and effect worked identically in the moral world as in the physical world.[15] When Bangs quoted these authorities, his insistence on "gracious ability" fell briefly from view. But it did not fall very far or for very long. After Bangs moved to New York City and became the Methodists' leading editor, he read more extensively in the writings of Reid, Beattie, and other promoters of the era's new moral philosophy, but what he learned from these sources remained secondary to what he took from the Scriptures as guided by Wesley and Fletcher.[16] As he accepted assignments in publishing and denominational leadership that drew him closer to centers of American influence, Bangs acquired what might be called a reading knowledge of the philosophical language of his day. But his own religious speech remained mostly unaffected by the concepts and assumptions of the newer language.

For the first twenty years of periodical publication in the *Methodist Magazine* and its successors, American Methodist theology developed between the positions marked out by Shinn (who learned and put immediately to use the categories of moral-sense philosophy) and Bangs (who studied but did not much use those categories). Thus, in its first year of publication, the *Methodist Magazine* included a long series from the *New Edinburgh Encyclopedia* entitled "Evidences of the Truth of the Christian Revelation," fearuing, in the Scottish manner, natural intuition. In its early issues, it also included extracts from the Scot James Beattie and from Samuel Stanhope Smith, where these thinkers found in common human consciousness what Methodists thought they read in the Bible about human free will.[17] By the end of the 1820s longer, more sophisticated articles were appearing with titles like "On the Importance of Common Sense," where Methodists were taught that "a partiality for justice, and an aversion to injustice" were "such necessary ingredients in our nature, that no earthly power can eradicate or supplant them."[18] The strand of commonsense reasoning that was present from the start became gradually more prominent as the magazine drew more and more of its authors from clergy who either had attended college or were reading the works widely used in collegiate moral philosophy.

At the same time, the center of gravity in this important periodical remained the biblical experientialism of Wesley and Asbury. Well into the 1830s, the magazine always included a hefty dose of itinerant testimonies and funeral notices which were uniformly devoted to reciting the course of faithful religious experience. A typical article in the *Methodist Magazine*'s sixth issue took up the theme "Methodist Doctrine," doing so by presenting Wesley's biblicism as the ideal: he made "the Bible his only guide in all the important doctrines which he embraced" and resolved to "abstain from all nice and philosophical speculation; from all perplexed and intricate reasoning . . . unless . . . citing the original Scriptures."[19] Two years later, an essay that was particularly important in light of later Methodist reliance on moral philosophy raised pointed questions about overstressing the natural capacities of the human will, even for polemical purposes. Its theme was the dangers that Methodists courted when they battled Calvinist "fatality" with resources supplied by modern moral philosophers. The particular danger was the latter's stress on "the free and proper exercise of its [the mind's] natural faculties and powers." To this author, that stress "certainly contains the marrow of Pelagianism," it contradicted Wesley's express teaching, and it denied "the first and most important doctrine of revealed religion—the utter moral depravity of man through the fall, by which he is naturally rendered absolutely incapable of any liberty in the actions of his mind, respecting a choice of good in preference to evil."[20]

Similar resolve to preserve Wesley's twin stress on direct biblical faith and the immediate witness of the Holy Spirit was evident in a *Streitschrift* that Nathan Bangs published in 1836 as part of an ongoing battle with New Haven's *Quarterly Christian Spectator*. Earlier the Congregationalist authors of the *Spectator* had insinuated that the Methodists' episcopal system verged perilously close to antirepublican monarchy.[21] When New Haven took a shot at Wesley's doctrine of the witness of the Spirit, even as it continued on in adjusting its own Calvinist inheritance, Bangs fired right back. In defending Wesley, Bangs underscored what he took to be the basis of Methodist theology, namely, "the explicit declarations of God's word [and] . . . the experiences of God's people in every period of the church." By contrast, Bangs held that the New Haven Congregationalists were so infatuated with "consciousness" and "our moral agency" that the work of the Holy Spirit was excluded. To Bangs it was evident that the followers of N. W. Taylor had chosen the way of folly: "If this be not substituting 'a theory' in the place of a plain scriptural 'doctrine,' it is at least transmuting moral consciousness into the blind impulses of a disordered imagination."[22]

By the time Bangs was making this spirited defense of ur-Wesleyanism, however, the burden of Methodist thought was beginning to shift. Indicative was another essay from the same year in the *Methodist Magazine and Quarterly Review*, by Abel Stevens (1815–1897), a rising young minister who would later become a much-respected Methodist author and editor. Stevens's essay in 1836 was a general account of how indulging in speculative philosophy had damaged Christian theology in the Middle Ages, but it ended by deferring to John Locke, rather than, as Bangs may have done, to the Scriptures, for resolving the question of what humans properly could and could not know.[23]

The most important transitional figure for Methodist theology was Wilbur Fisk (1792–1839), one of the first American Methodists to receive a college degree, founder of one of its first academies (Wilbraham, Massachusetts), first president of its first permanent college (Wesleyan), active participant in evangelical voluntary societies, and perhaps for that reason the first American Methodist widely recognized by others as a consequential theologian.[24] Fisk resembled Nathan Bangs in his determination to maintain biblical Christian experience as the heart of Methodism, but he also advanced a step beyond Bangs by allowing the norms of commonsense reasoning to shape his thought. Fisk's moves in this direction were cautious. Shortly after he assumed his position at Wesleyan—just, that is, as he was beginning to teach the comprehensive senior course in moral philosophy—he reviewed several of the standard college textbooks then available for such a class. Fisk had particularly high praise for a text from T. C. Upham, a Congregationalist from Bowdoin College, but nonetheless also complained that it did not sufficiently defer to explicit scriptural precepts.[25] Yet in his own 1831 inaugural at Wesleyan, Fisk gave greater attention to Baconian and commonsense themes than any Methodist had ever done publicly before.[26] Fisk's engagement in controversy with New England Calvinists, which began shortly before he took up his duties at Wesleyan, also revealed the new directions in which he was pointing Methodist theology.

A sermon "Predestination and Election" that Fisk published in 1830 became the precipitate for theological combat when it was handled roughly by several Calvinist reviewers. The episodic character of this debate, spread out over five years, revealed a critical turning point in the development of Methodist theology. When the debate began, Fisk was mostly presenting Methodism as it had been presented before. His original sermon did contain a brief nod toward republican certainties by describing the God of Calvinists as a "most merciless tyrant"; in addition, to a somewhat greater degree than Bangs fifteen years before, Fisk now argued that Calvinism was "utterly irreconcilable with mental freedom." But for the most part, Fisk defended standard Methodist teaching with historic Methodist warrants. Scripture, which was liberally quoted, did not contain even "a single passage" teaching God's absolute foreordination of all events. Scripture likewise taught "a conditional election" by which God's grace met all people in their sin in order to overcome the debilitating effects of the fall. Fisk explained the doctrine of prevenient grace as God's "gracious power" liberating the human will and enabling it to choose life. Unlike Calvinism, which "limits the atonement," Fisk defended a religion where the power of

Christ's death imparted prevenient grace to all humanity. The sermon concluded with a rousing tu quoque in which Fisk, though not mentioning
N. W. Taylor by name, accused New Haven theologians of propounding a
"new doctrine" that depicted depravity not as "any taint or sinful corruption of our moral constitution, but [as residing] exclusively and entirely in
moral exercise."[27] This was a vintage Methodist performance.

As the debate wore on, however, Fisk began to lean away from a scriptural defense of divine grace, universal atonement, and free will toward an
appeal to what he called "the philosophy of mind" and "grand philosophical
principles." Fisk did continue to attack "Dr. Taylor and his associates" for
abandoning grace and promoting a view of humanity akin to "the old Pelagian
system." But in his later contributions, he devoted increasing attention to "my
own reason, and the laws of belief." In almost exact proportion as Fisk's appeal
to Scripture declined, his appeal to two features of modern moral philosophy
increased. First was recourse to "consciousness," which Fisk insisted testified uniformly against the Calvinist notion that the will was determined by
the strongest motives in the mind. Second was an appeal to the human personality defined by three separate powers—will, passions, and judgment (also
labeled consciousness or moral feelings). The modern "philosophy of mind"
to which Fisk referred was this tripartite faculty psychology. For both appeals,
Fisk drew on the work of "Dr. Reid." In a neat merger of traditional Wesleyan
soteriology and contemporary faculty psychology, Fisk argued that prevenient grace subdued the "unholy affections," restored harmony to mind, will,
and passions, and thus enabled the will to choose freely for God. Fisk's concluding word was that this kind of philosophy fit perfectly with the Scriptures, as in Romans, chapters 7 and 8, by describing "the same *division* of the
mind—the same *conflict*—the same *thraldom* of the will, and the same *deliverance*, through faith in Jesus Christ our Lord."[28]

Never before in American Methodist history had a leading thinker drawn
so fully on his age's commonsense psychology to expound foundational
Methodist teaching. Leland Scott, the best student of the subject, has accounted
for Fisk's recourse to Scottish commonsense philosophy by seeing it as "a
point of philosophical confirmation for [Methodism's] own critique of the
doctrines of moral agency as held within Calvinism." This appeal, in his view,
was "one of the most significant developments within early American Methodism." It "served, ultimately, to *exaggerate* an individualistic (nominalistic)
and subjective doctrine of personal responsibility" and led American Methodists "increasingly to appropriate extreme elements of *philosophic* anti-
necessitariansim." For theology, the tendency was "to urge man's present,
constitutional independence—apart from any considerations of sin or grace—
as the ground of present responsibility."[29] With Fisk, the effects of such philosophical moves remained only a tendency mixed in with the more traditional
Wesleyan efforts. But when Fisk died only four years after publishing his
Calvinistic Controversy, so also died the Methodists' most creative effort at
explaining original Wesleyanism in the dominant philosophical concepts of
America's elite intellectual realm.

The New Era for Methodist Theology

Wilbur Fisk's years as president of Wesleyan University were transitional for Methodists in several ways. By the time of his death in 1839, Wesleyan had been joined by many other new Methodist institutions of higher learning, including Randolph-Macon in Virginia (1832), Dickinson and Allegheny in Pittsburgh (both taken over by Methodists in 1833), McKendree in Illinois (1834), Emory in Georgia (1836), DePauw in Indiana (1837), and the Wesleyan Female College in Georgia (acquired in 1839).[30] Also by the time of Fisk's death, conflict over slavery had become more visible, and acrimony on this issue was rising toward the schism of 1844. In the decade of the 1830s Methodist theology was also transformed.

The course of formal, elite theology followed the trajectory from Bangs and Shinn through Fisk to an even more complete intellectual Americanization. But that was not the only significant theological development under way. In this same decade there also arose a countervailing movement spearheaded by leaders who were longing for the experience of entire sanctification as that experience had been taught by the founders of the movement. Both theological developments reflected the changing status of Methodism, which by the 1830s had become the largest Protestant denomination in a national culture substantially created by Protestant forces, and a denomination that was rapidly establishing itself as securely in the nation's cities as in its small towns and countryside. It was an era of refinement, but in contrasting forms. Those who were busy articulating Methodism in the categories of moral-sense philosophy sought consecrated respectability; those who were busy with the pursuit of holiness sought respectable consecration.[31]

Theology in Service to Moral Philosophy

The trajectory that moved on from Fisk to more thorough use of elite philosophical norms was epitomized by Daniel D. Whedon (1808–1885).[32] Whedon, after graduating from Hamilton College in New York, was converted through the preaching of Charles Finney and soon joined the Methodists. In 1833 he was recruited by Fisk to teach ancient languages at Wesleyan, where he worked for nearly a decade. After service as a pastor, a professor of rhetoric at the fledgling University of Michigan, and a proprietor of his own private school, he was named editor in 1856 of the *Methodist Quarterly Review*, a position he held for twenty-eight years and in which he was widely recognized as the most respected Methodist theologian of his era.

Whedon's intellectual leadership was critical both negatively and positively. Negatively, Whedon and like-minded thinkers contained the influence among American Methodists of Richard Watson (1781–1833), the most important English Methodist theologian after John Fletcher.[33] Watson's two-volume *Theological Institutes* (1833) was a careful systemization of Wesley's teaching cast as a comprehensive apologetic. Where it incorporated extra-Wesleyan ideas, they were likely to come from Watson's use of Locke's view of the person as a tabula rasa until visited by outside influences and from Watson's strong doctrine of biblical inerrancy, which paralleled other views of a similar sort then on the rise among British evangelicals. Watson was widely respected in America, but his theology was also persistently criticized by Whedon for its weakness in understanding human psychology. In particular, many Methodist scholars agreed with an associate of Whedon, B. F. Cocker, who felt that Watson had neglected the "faculty of knowing" and "*a priori*, self-evident, necessary truth."[34]

Whedon and like-minded theologians, by contrast, were becoming convinced defenders of the intuitive powers of the mind. The positive direction in which Whedon led Methodist theology was toward a much greater reliance on the deliverances of the moral sense and a much greater willingness to reason from those deliverances, instead of from experiential biblicism, in the articulation of Methodist doctrine. In addition, Whedon was much freer than his predecessors in the use of political tropes of republican freedom and responsibility. These intellectual moves, in turn, brought Whedon's doctrinal convictions much closer to the views of New England's moderate Calvinists.

Whedon offered an unusually clear picture of his intellectual formation, and hence of the intellectual factors that most powerfully shaped his theology, in a Phi Beta Kappa oration delivered at Wesleyan in 1850. The larger point of the address was to demonstrate that a well-functioning human intellect required the same kind of moral and intellectual guidance as a well-functioning republic. Whedon found that guidance in faculty psychology. His argument was that "Intellect," "Heart," and "Will" must be harmonized for both persons and republics. While expounding this prescription, Whedon paused to trace the course of his own philosophical development. As a college student, Whedon reported that he was expected to "understand his soul from Locke, his conscience from Paley, and his responsibility from Edwards." To Whedon, such instruction spelled disaster. But it also pointed by negation to what would become his new intellectual anchorage. If "the indicated materialism of the first, the low expediency of the second, and the granite fatalism of the third, did not prepare me for the atheism of Hume, it was because my own moral sensibilities disbelieved and repudiated the whole system." Whedon's rescue by his "own moral sensibilities" led him eagerly to "the philosophy of the present period," where he felt the impossible positions of Locke, Paley, Edwards, and Hume were thoroughly scotched. As he saw it, the modern philosophy "recognizes in the soul the power of knowing ideas that transcend matter, and so authenticates the belief in a spiritual and immortal nature; it enthrones conscience on the basis of eternal right, and so ennobles the moral and divine law; it holds the free-will of man unbound to any necessity to crime, and so inexcusable for its commission; and thus with an immortal soul, a responsible free-agency, and an eternal law divine, it follows that a judgment and an adjudging God are a matter well-nigh demonstrated."[35] Significant by their absence in this account of Whedon's intellectual *Bildung* were the traditional Methodist keystones of revelation from Scripture and the experience of the Holy Spirit.

Whedon, to be sure, prosecuted study of Scripture, as the publication of multi-volume commentaries on the Old and New Testaments indicates.[36] And he remained an active defender of Methodist doctrines in debate with mid-century New England Calvinists. But despite some signs of continuity with earlier Methodist traditions, Whedon was boldly reformulating the substance of Methodist doctrine.

As the one whom outsiders considered the prime Methodist spokesman of his era, Whedon won special renown for two publications, an essay from 1862 solicited by the Congregationalists' *Bibliotheca Sacra* entitled "Doctrines of Methodism," and a major refutation from 1864 of Jonathan Edwards's *Freedom of the Will*. The distance separating these performances from earlier Methodist expositions, whether Asbury or Bangs or even Wilbur Fisk, was breathtaking.

Against Edwards's conception of human action as governed by the power of the strongest motive to compel action, Whedon began by assuming a tripartite definition of the mind (Intellection, Sensibility, Volition). Self-consciously Whedon reversed what he held to be Edwards's procedure: "We have first assumed the prior validity of the intuitions, and then sought by their guidance to ascertain how our psychology and logic may be brought into harmony with their dicta." On this basis, he then criticized Edwards's notion of freedom (the ability to do what one had chosen to do) with the argument that true freedom required an ability to act in contradiction to the motives of the mind. Whedon was speaking with earlier Methodists by insisting on this conception of freedom. But then he broke cleanly with his predecessors, who had looked to prevenient grace (won for humankind by the atonement of Christ) as the source for moral freedom. Whedon, by contrast, asserted that consciousness by itself attested to the will's "full power of otherwise-doing or not-doing," a "central self-power" in the personality. In Whedon's summary of his position, nature has taken the place occupied by grace in the Wesleyans' earlier conception of humankind: "The doctrine of the freedom of the human will, therefore, is an axiom of the intellect affirmed by the common consciousness of all mankind. It is an in-born self-knowledge."[37] In making these assertions, Whedon was conscious of relying on intuitive sources of knowledge that had become very important for moderate Calvinists as well; to Whedon it seemed obvious that these sources pointed toward the kind of freedom that the Methodists, not the Calvinists, had long defended.

If Whedon's specific rebuttal of Edwards was widely admired, his theological exposition in *Bibliotheca Sacra* was perceived as Methodism come of age. This 1862 article was a bravura performance in which Whedon employed many of the maxims generated by the Calvinists in debate among themselves (e.g., "Power underlies responsibility") to make a case for Methodism. Significantly, where earlier Methodists defined their movement around the power of God working for salvation, Whedon's definition centered on human free-will understood as "the power of contrary choice." In making his case, Whedon enlisted John Fletcher, John Wesley, Wilbur Fisk,

and a few other Methodist authorities, but overwhelmingly the historical figure most in view was, again, Jonathan Edwards.[38] And again, the foundation
for rejecting Edwards was Whedon's reliance on consciousness. His argument hinged on "the ordinary laws of mind," "the natural laws of mind," "the
very nature of free agency," "the reasonableness of the doctrine of the witness of the Spirit," and "a simple, firm assurance, like an intuition."[39] Some
of this vocabulary can be traced back to Wesley's sermons on the witness of
the Holy Spirit, but most came from Whedon's understanding of human psychology obtained from Reid, Stewart, and Victor Cousin, the French student
of Reid's philosophy.

The significance of Whedon's construction of Methodist theology is readily
apparent by comparing his essay from 1862 with what Nathan Bangs wrote
in the Methodists' first sustained public controversy with New England Calvinists. In a characteristic passage from 1815, Bangs set forth the heart of
Methodist doctrine in the following terms:

> So far from believing this sentiment [of a Hopkintonian], we continually main-
> tain that the election of souls to eternal life, is predicated of the goodness of
> God; and that, if it depended wholly upon works, no one would see life. It was
> pure love that moved God to give his Son, and that moved the Son to suffer
> and die for man. It is pure love that moves the Holy Trinity to begin, carry on,
> and perfect the work of salvation in the hearts of sinners. But such is the order
> of God, and the economy of grace, that this work of salvation is not effected
> without the co-operation of the free volitions of man. *Work out your own sal-
> vation with fear and trembling, for it is God that worketh in you, both to will
> and to do of his good pleasure* [Philippians 2:12–13]. Neither are we justified
> here as penitent sinners by works, but by faith. *With the heart man believeth
> unto righteousness* [Romans 10:10]. *He that believeth and is baptized, shall be
> saved* [Mark 16:16].[40]

The contrast with Whedon from 1862 is striking:

> The act of will, put forth with full power otherwise in intentional disconformity
> to the law, is actual or *actional sin*. The resultant ethical quality of *condemnability*,
> which our moral sense sees as inhering in the personality of the agent in conse-
> quence of the commission of such sin, we call *guilt*. And as the moral sense can
> see this guilt solely in the personality of the committing agent, it is impossible
> for this guilt to be transferred to another personality. Correlative to this *guilt*,
> the moral sense sees inhering in the person of the guilty *a just desert of punish-
> ment*. These correlations are fundamental and axiomatic.[41]

The difference between these two utterances is not primarily between
prephilosophical and philosophical discourse, and not even the presence
(Bangs) or absence (Whedon) of Scripture. The great change is that grace and
the Bible defined Bangs's intellectual universe, while natural human ability
and the moral sense did the same for Whedon.

The theology that Daniel Whedon developed from the deliverances of his
moral sense was a new Methodist theology. First, it denied, at least function-
ally, that Adam's sin communicated any hereditary guilt to human nature. In

this instance as in many others, Whedon chimed in with New England Calvinists from Dwight to Taylor in claiming that "all responsible sin, . . . whether
of action or condition, arises from the action of free finite beings, in discon-
formity to the law, and in abuse of their free agency."[42] Whedon's theology,
second, looked to the natural capacities of human nature to perform what
"prevenient grace" or "grace ability" had accomplished for earlier Methodists. So solicitous was he of human freedom that divine grace faded nearly
away: "Man does not thereby receive any new faculty. He is not even organically *made* to be a free agent; for he never ceased to be such; only spiritual
things, and the possibility of pleasing God, are again *brought within reach* of
his free agency. Nor is the Holy Spirit, nor any other influence, normally so
brought to bear upon his free agency as to be *irresistible*, or *secured to be
unresisted*; since that would be to overwhelm his free agency on the other
side."[43] Third, in Whedon's theology a weakened sense of human sin and
human guilt led to a weakened sense of atoning grace, and so he wrote of the
human role in salvation with a confidence unimaginable for Methodists
through the time of Wilbur Fisk: "Upon the decision and choice of the man
as a free agent, it ultimately depends whether the condition be performed and
salvation attained, or rejected and eternal death incurred. This is the *great
alternative point* of man's free probation. From his own essential and central
self is the decision most freely made; upon his own central and essential self
must the eternal responsibility rest."[44]

In a word, Whedon's theology was now as much a function of contemporary moral reasoning as of Wesleyan biblical experientialism. In the very
process of responding to American Calvinists—first Jonathan Edwards and
then the moderating figures of New England—Whedon pushed what Leland
Scott called the "intuitive philosophical categories of volitional responsibility" to the center of Methodist theology.[45]

Such an alteration in Methodist theology was too large to go unnoticed.
Whedon's friend and fellow Methodist Daniel Curry (1809–1887) was one
observer who felt that "a sub-species of philosophic theology" had taken
control of Whedon's thinking. Curry was impressed with Whedon's account
of the moral sense, but not as much as Whedon himself. According to Curry,
"Without denying the force and fitness of this method . . . one may hesitate
to accept it as meeting all the conditions of the case. The law by which responsibilities are determined in the divine government is not so certainly
ascertained that our notions of it may be accepted, and safely built upon as a
postulate for further argumentation."[46] A few outside of Methodism expressed
similar reservations. In the 1830s Nathan Bangs and Wilbur Fisk had argued
that N. W. Taylor's views on human capacity and divine grace amounted to
a form of Pelagianism (or the saving of the self by the self with only minor
help from God). In the wake of Whedon's noteworthy publications from the
early 1860s, the Presbyterian Henry Boynton Smith made almost the same
argument with Whedon in view.[47]

Despite such criticisms, Whedon's theology spoke for a growing portion
of Methodists from the 1850s onward. The theological transformation he pro-

posed was not, however, accepted by all Methodists, for from the 1830s a distinctly different course was being pursued by a very different sort of Methodist theological reasoning.

Theology in Service to Holiness

This other course was "the way of holiness." It was pursued by a cadre of Methodists who, though moving into America's respected classes as defined by wealth and education, nonetheless insisted on a model of spirituality drawn from the itinerating phase of early Methodism. That model focused attention on the need for every justified Christian believer to seek full sanctification. Above all, it represented an attempt to preserve the Wesleys' teaching on Christian perfection. While those who pursued this goal were neither anti-intellectual nor indifferent to politics, the intensity of their search for holiness relativized commitments to republican or commonsense principles. Veterans of early American Methodism who survived into the 1830s and 1840s, like Nathan Bangs, supported naturally this emphasis on entire sanctification, but the impetus for an updated rendition of holiness teaching came from a younger cohort. Among the most active leaders of this new holiness movement were Timothy Merritt (1775–1845), editor of Methodist periodicals in New England and founding editor in 1839 of the *Guide to Christian Perfection*; George Peck (1797–1876), circuit rider, presiding elder, and from 1840 editor of the *Methodist Quarterly Review*; and above all Phoebe Worrall Palmer (1807–1874), who from her home in New York City acted as the majordomo of the movement.[48]

The course of Phoebe Palmer's life reveals the solidly Methodist roots of her convictions.[49] Palmer's father, before emigrating to America, had been converted through the preaching of John Wesley; she herself had been catechized by Nathan Bangs, and reading from the Wesleys (including Susanna Wesley) and John and Mary Fletcher had guided her religious formation. Yet traumas as the young wife of Dr. Walter Palmer (three children died in infancy) and her own unrequited spiritual longings propelled her on a quest for a deeper spiritual life. On 26 July 1837, almost exactly a year to the day from the death in a crib fire of an infant daughter, Palmer experienced entire sanctification: "Between the hours of eight and nine—while pleading at the throne of grace for a present fulfillment of the exceeding great and precious promises; . . . and making an entire surrender of body, soul, and spirit; . . . I received the assurance that God the Father, through the atoning Lamb, accepted the sacrifice; my heart was emptied of self, and cleansed of all idols, from all filthiness of the flesh and spirit, and I realized that I dwelt in God, and felt that he had become the portion of my soul, my ALL IN ALL."[50] Almost immediately Palmer began to relate this experience and her understanding of its biblical foundations at the Tuesday Meeting for the Promotion of Holiness, which she had been conducting from February 1836 with her sister, Sarah Worrall Lankford, in the home they shared in New York. Palmer soon began to write of her experiences, with *The Way of Holiness*

(1843) the first of many widely read and often-reprinted books outlining the path of entire consecration.

Palmer's religion replicated in many ways the religion of an earlier generation. Dreams were an important vehicle of communication from God, the record of Christian experience (her own and then others') was the primary means of expounding and defending this theology, and the Bible was presented as the sum and substance of its content. The latter insistence was particularly important, since it pointed Palmer and like-minded believers away from the self-conscious reliance on formal philosophy. Instead, her scriptural fixation was the fixation of the movement: "I also covenanted with God that I would be a BIBLE CHRISTIAN, and most carefully seek to know the mind of the spirit, as recorded in the WRITTEN WORD, though it might lead to an experience unlike all the world beside. . . . my highest and all-engrossing desire was to be a BIBLE CHRISTIAN."[51]

As Palmer defined the experience of holiness, three steps were most important: "entire consecration," or the self-conscious, total surrender of the self to God; an "altar" faith, whereby believers placed their all "upon the altar" in obedience to such biblical mandates as in Matthew 23:19 or Romans 12:1; and then public testimony, in which those who had made the altar surrender testified to God's fulfillment of the biblical promises upon which they had acted. When this system of holiness was spread—by the thousands who eventually attended the Tuesday Meeting over the four decades of its existence, the tens of thousands who heard Phoebe and Walter Palmer speak, the hundreds of thousands who read her works, and the millions who were touched by other holiness teachers—the inherited Wesleyan vocabulary of "entire sanctification" expanded considerably. Within Methodism and far beyond, phrases like "entire devotion," "entire consecration," "heart purity," "the way of holiness," and "keeping all upon the altar" became commonplace because of Palmer's movement.[52] To Daniel Whedon, all of this smacked of a suspect "hyper-Wesleyanism," but on the ground among ordinary Methodists, such phrases were appropriated probably more widely than his own reformulations of Methodist theology in the language of mid-nineteenth-century moral philosophy.[53]

Holiness theology as formulated by Phoebe Palmer showed that Methodism could take other paths than Whedon's deference to the natural moral sense. At the same time, the holiness emphases of the 1830s and following decades were not simply a replication of earlier Methodism. The important leaders from other denominations who were drawn to the Tuesday Meeting or who came to holiness views on their own usually remained loyal to at least some intellectual commitments of their traditions. For example, the Congregationalist minister and Bowdoin College professor T. C. Upham (1799–1872) was already a widely published moral philosopher before he visited the Tuesday Meeting in December 1839 and soon thereafter experienced entire sanctification. Upham would go on to publish many widely read volumes promoting holiness. But as he did so, he retained the trust in commonsense moral intuitions and the relatively high view of natural human capacities that he had worked out as a moderate New England Calvinist. He also became an enthusiast for seventeenth-century Catholic quietist authors like Madam Guyon, a circle of writers whom Phoebe Palmer never regarded as highly. In these ways and more, Upham's vision of holiness was less strictly Methodist than Palmer's, and it was also more directly shaped by the era's conventions of formal thought.[54]

An important insight concerning the contemporaneity of Palmer's holiness teaching was supplied by the aging Nathan Bangs. Bangs himself was a regular attender of the Tuesday Meeting, and his position as a venerated Methodist elder statesman protected Palmer and her teachings from much criticism. Yet despite his obvious respect for Palmer, Bangs felt that she had moved beyond early Methodism in several important ways. In particular, Bangs held out for John Wesley's and John Fletcher's teaching that a state of entire sanctification had to be verified by the ongoing, long-term evidence of the Holy Spirit's presence in a life. He thus set himself against Palmer's teaching that the act of surrender was itself the key to sanctification, which could be guaranteed as having taken place solely on the basis of a person's trusting the Bible's promises. "We must," Bangs put it at a Tuesday Meeting in March 1857, "be sanctified, and have an evidence of it before we have any scriptural authority to believe it." Bangs expressed this opinion in the original Methodist way, with a fusillade of biblical quotation and an insistence that the authority of the Bible must always be backed with genuine Christian experience. His worry was that self-directed mental activity was taking precedence over the work of God: "If I may believe myself sanctified without any evidence of the Holy Spirit that the work has been wrought, I may believe anything else before I have any evidence of it . . . . I may believe or not, as whim or fancy dictate."[55]

Bangs's complaint here was directed against a process of Americanization, but of a more subtle variety than the political and philosophical forces at work in Whedon's theology. He was finding Palmer's trust in the self and its powers as inadequate for the gaining of holiness as Daniel Curry had found Daniel Whedon's reliance on the self for Methodist doctrine. Genetically considered, the problem was that a democratic view of the self—a distinctly American notion of an unformed plastic world waiting to be shaped by personal initiative—was undermining the historic Methodist position that defined the fully capable self as a gracious gift of the Holy Spirit.

The general point to be made about the thinking of both Whedon and Palmer was that neither was building a theology from the resources of Methodist Christian experience, even though it had been that experience that made Methodism such an explosive force in early United States history. Palmer in effect continued to insist that Wesleyanism had no formal theology. Whedon in effect abandoned Wesleyanism in order to write formal theology. Of the latter move, Leland Scott perceptively noted that "American Methodism—in its own theological presentations—had failed to integrate that emphasis on 'experimental' evidence which had been such a promising aspect of its earlier heritage; its academic apologetics were limited, almost completely, to the methodology of 'natural theology.'"[56] This assessment was not as true

for the teachers of holiness, but in general terms it does speak for a lost theological opportunity.

Assessing Methodist Theology

By the era of the Civil War, Methodist theology was dividing in two. A few
Methodists were abandoning the quest for intellectual relevance in order to
recapture a key conviction of the early movement. Other Methodists were
abandoning the movement's early convictions in order to become intellectually relevant.

The effort by Timothy Merritt, George Peck, and especially Phoebe Palmer
to revive the theme of perfection from John Wesley's and Francis Asbury's
experiential biblicism represented a deliberate turning away from the path
opened up by Shinn, Bangs, and Fisk, and then pursued aggressively by
Whedon. Instead of presenting Methodism in the categories of commonsense
moral philosophy, the teachers of holiness employed, with single-minded
thoroughness, the words of Scripture. As a by-product, their emphasis on
holiness acted as a prophylactic against the force of republican reasoning.
Phoebe Palmer's holiness theology offered comfort to many in the era of the
Civil War but little for the problems leading to the Civil War. She had always
excluded discussion of slavery from her Tuesday meetings, and an evangelistic tour with her husband in Britain kept her out of the country from 1859
until 1863. An appeal to Scripture and to the experiences of faith drove the
teaching of holiness. As it happened, this teaching turned out to possess great
staying power: a concentration on holiness as reconfigured by Phoebe Palmer
and her associates continued to rally substantial allegiance in the main Methodist denominations as well as in many smaller movements through the nineteenth and twentieth centuries.[57]

The Methodist way of holiness entailed less thorough Americanization than
the Methodist choice for intellectual engagement. For Phoebe Palmer and like-
minded thinkers, Americanization was a matter of cultural ethos more than
explicit ideology. To be sure, as a leading historian of the holiness revival
points out, Palmer's movement did promote commitments in tune with the
spirit of the age, since in her teaching holiness appealed to "a simple, literal
Biblicist faith . . . combined with an impatient, American pragmatism that
always seeks to make a reality at the moment whatever is considered at all
possible in the future."[58] By leaving to others the effort to explain their faith
in terms of the era's leading ideologies, this form of Methodism did retain
more control over its own character than did the Methodists who made that
effort.

Yet if turning aside from intellectual Americanization preserved a measure of early Methodist integrity, it also rendered the holiness movement
largely irrelevant to the nation's larger cultural history. By the vigor of its
religious life, early Methodism had transformed American religion as a whole.
That transformation, in turn, set the stage for the engagement by some Meth-

odists with the new nation's reigning intellectual assumptions. After the first decades of the nineteenth century, there were no further Methodist transformations. The ardent pursuit of holiness left the minority stream as the *Stille im Lande,* while the move to the American center by the majority made their voice indistinguishable within the common intellectual discourse.

The course of Methodists who did engage the formal thought of the antebellum period soon came to resemble the path taken by moderating Calvinists among the Presbyterians and Congregationalists. This strand of Methodism contributed to later intellectual history, particularly when the Wesleyan heritage of subjective spirituality opened out into the philosophy of personalism. Borden Parker Bowne, for example, who taught at the Methodists' Boston University from 1876 to 1910, countered materialism, social Darwinism, and absolute Hegelianism with the concept of a Divine Person who oriented all relations in the phenomenal world. The subjectivity of personalism was not a simple romantic centering of all upon the ego but an assertion of the fundamental necessity of personal engagement—of active choice—for epistemology and ethics. Discernible Wesleyan emphases remained in such philosophy, yet the tie to ancestral Methodism was more via an abstracted understanding of subjectivity than through specific teachings on justification, Christian perfection, or the atonement.[59]

Daniel Whedon was the most important figure moving elite, theologically self-conscious Methodists in this direction. The parallel to moderating Calvinists is apt, for a figure like Whedon was much more philosophically astute than the Methodists who chose the way of holiness, just as a figure like N. W. Taylor was more philosophically astute than his Old School opponents. Yet like Taylor's form of Congregationalism, Whedon's Methodism became so well adjusted to the intellectually normative thought forms of the early nineteenth century that when those thought forms evolved, there was very little left of the Methodism that Whedon had tried to express in those terms.

Where the course of Whedon's Methodism differed most from Taylor's Congregationalism was in the form of its Americanization. Almost all Presbyterians and Congregationalists—but especially the Congregationalists of New England—remained more proprietary in their attitudes toward America than almost any Methodist. Timothy Dwight, Lyman Beecher, N. W. Taylor, Charles Finney, and even the Old School Presbyterians of Princeton were always pursuing two related goals—rescuing needy sinners and rescuing the nation. Although Methodists also came to embrace Christian republican thinking, and although Methodists joined vigorously in promoting the rival claims of Northern and Southern Christian republicanism during the crisis of the Union, Methodist intellectual interests were often divided: theology was one thing, reasoning about the nation's future was another. This difference meant that the Americanization of Methodist theology was more strictly an intellectual process—in order to expose the errors of Calvinism and to demonstrate the intellectual maturity of the Methodist movement, nothing worked better than sophisticated deployment of the Calvinists' own tried and true habits of mind. When Methodists took up the Calvinists' own intellectual weapons, they made especially full use of commonsense moral reasoning, even though the Methodists never linked the deliverances of the moral sense concerning personal freedom as tightly to notions of republican liberty and to distrust of inherited authority as did their theological peers. Even if Methodists like Whedon turned to the sort of moral philosophy that Wesley had never used, they retained greater deference to the antirepublican Wesley than any mainstream American theologians did for any other known opponent of the nation's founding ideologies. Methodist theology Americanized as it sought to win respectability and to win over Calvinists, whereas the older traditions from the colonial era had Americanized in order to forge a national destiny under God.

Much more remains to be said about Methodist theology in the great age of Methodist expansion. But a few things are clear. Methodist theology was most creative when it was least philosophical. When the Methodists' all-consuming purpose was to evangelize the nation's restlessly mobile lower and middle classes, their theology cut across the grain of dominant American ideologies with unexpected force. Later, as Methodist attention shifted toward the rising middle classes it had recruited so effectively, Methodist theology began to move with the currents of intellectual fashion. Methodists in the age of Asbury believed in human free will because of what they read in the Bible and because of how the Holy Spirit was making the universal effects of Christ's atonement actual in their lives. Methodists in the age of Whedon believed in human free will because of the intuitive deliverances of human consciousness. Methodists were now at home in America.

V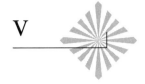

CRISIS

Both read the same Bible, and pray to the same God.
—Abraham Lincoln, Second Inaugural Address, 1865

*Ecco dunque la vera causa del gran fallo: ecco il principio dissolvente
di quella gagliardissima unione. . . . E poichè nè l'uno nè l'atro dei
contendenti oserebbe affermare onesta o iniqua la shiavitù, solo perchè
a lui lucrosa o nociva; amendue ricorrono ad argomenti biblici. . . .
Supponete invece che cotesti diritti fossero assicurati da un'autorità
riverita dai due, e la Bibbia entrasse nella scherma non come per giuoco
di fioretto, ma come per duello di verità che vuole abbattere l'errore
contrario.*

*[Here is then the true cause of their great mistake; here is the principle
that is dissolving such a great union. . . . Since neither side dares define
slavery as either good or unrighteous, simply because it is profitable or
unprofitable, they use biblical arguments to defend their rights. . . . But
supposing that these rights were assured by an* authority *respected by
both parties. Then the Bible could come into the conflict not as a
plaything, but as in a contest of truth over against falsehood.]*
—"La disunione negli Stati Uniti," 1861

18

The "Bible Alone" and a Reformed, Literal Hermeneutic

The American theology that was firmly in place by the 1830s and 1840s among Calvinists, Methodists, and within many other religious traditions did not retain its cultural preeminence for long. The reason was not primarily difficulties in that theology with respect to personal or ecclesiastical religion, but problems with the public alliances that had built the theology. Although by the 1850s questions were being raised about the wisdom of linking Christianity, common sense, and Baconian reasoning as they had been joined for the preceding two generations, the intuitive bond between republican values and Christian faith remained strong. Christian republicanism endured because republican language was developing into something like the language of covenant in the 1770s—a diffuse congeries of morally powerful but somewhat imprecise concepts that could be harnessed to many different political and religious viewpoints.[1] Something of the confusion, but also continuing power, of the language is suggested by an early supporter of the Republican Party who was worried that it had chosen a Roman Catholic, John C. Frémont, as its presidential candidate in 1856. To this observer, some of those who spouted slogans about liberty in favor of Frémont were doing so without the necessary allegiance to evangelical Christianity—that "may be red republicanism, or it may be black republicanism, but it is not American republicanism."[2]

For theology, it was also significant that sectional politics was reconfiguring the shape of republican commitments.[3] While the South was reverting to more classical conceptions, republican ideals in the North were becoming more individualistic. In the North, fragmentation of the Whig Party and the emergence of the Republican Party served to boil down the Whigs' broad understanding of freedom, public virtue, self-fulfilling commerce, and transformative evangelicalism into simpler equations between slavery and vice, free labor and virtue. In the South, criticism from the North stimulated an effort to recast republican values in earlier forms that defined vice as menacing concentrations of alien power, looked upon freedom as the privilege of acting honorably in one's station, and idealized virtue as mutual, organic dependence in communities protected by benevolent patriarchs. Such changes made it easier for Southern theologians to maintain traditional views of divine sovereignty in salvation, but they posed challenges for traditional Calvinists in the North. Significantly, Oliver Wendell Holmes published his poem "The Deacon's Masterpiece," which describes Calvinism as a "wonderful 'one-hoss shay,'" collapsing all of a sudden, in September 1858.[4] The shay ran much, much longer in points west and especially south of Holmes's Massachusetts.

The major theological crux of the period leading up to the war was the interpretation of Scripture. Earlier theological battles—Unitarians versus trinitarians, New Haven versus East Windsor, New School versus Old School—had set the terms of debate on substantive doctrinal questions and allowed the leading theologians to stake out their claims. From the mid-1840s there was little substantial movement on such questions, except from the few critics who were abandoning the era's standard intellectual assumptions. Opposing "American" and traditional positions remained pretty much as they had been. By contrast, questions about how to interpret the Bible now took on special urgency. The success of evangelical religion in the early republic had transformed the public square through its amalgamation of Protestant doctrine and public discourse. Because of that transformation, national conflicts over states rights, slavery, temperance, immigration, and other contentious issues automatically became theological issues as well. Because the Bible had become so much a part of public consciousness, these same debates spurred efforts to use it for adjudicating public controversies. But they also posed grave difficulties. When the nation, which the mixture of commonsense, republican, and Protestant commitments had done so much to create, experienced profound political strain, then tensions also increased about the meaning, use, and interpretation of Scripture.

A comparison between the ideological conflicts of the Revolution and the Civil War sheds light on how the bonds between public life and religious thought had taken shape by the mid-nineteenth century. Religious-political strife during the Revolution occurred between the proponents of what everyone recognized as separate ideologies—between Loyalists, who clung to an early-modern conception of hierarchy, tradition, and monarchical order, against patriots, who contended for a modern understanding of rights, personal capacities, and republican freedom. By contrast, the religious strife of the Civil War occurred between proponents of alternative visions of the same ideology made up of evangelical religion, republican political principles, and commonsense moral reasoning. Religious strife was intense in the earlier conflict but soon faded once the fighting stopped. In the Civil War, religious strife was much more vituperative, there was much more of it, and rather than fading away rapidly after the shooting stopped, religious antagonism continued for a very long time after 1865.[5]

For the middle decades of the century, a history of theology must also be a history of how the theological elements that built the nation fared when the nation came apart. Especially prominent in that history were debates over the interpretation of Scripture.

In 1857 there was published yet another European traveler's account of an American sojourn. This time the author was James Stirling from Britain, who had first journeyed in the North before making his way through the Southern states. Included in the extensive letters that constituted his book was full consideration of Southern arguments for slavery, arguments that had obviously impressed Stirling. Yet although he praised the logic on display particularly in works from George Fitzhugh and Albert Taylor Bledsoe, both of Virginia, Stirling as himself an opponent of slavery was convinced that "the common sense and moral sentiments of mankind" would soon destroy the institution. Nonetheless, Stirling made a special point of commending the skill of the proslavery apologists at "metaphysics," by which he meant also their skill as biblical exegetes. In particular, Bledsoe's 1856 volume *An Essay on Liberty and Slavery* seemed to Stirling an intellectual tour de force: "I must confess that, as against his opponents, the orthodox Abolitionists, he is perfectly triumphant." Stirling felt that Bledsoe's examination of Old Testament passages describing the patriarchs as slaveholders and showing the place of slavery in the Mosaic law, as well as New Testament passages treating the apostle Paul's instructions concerning slaveholding, constituted "irresistible proofs that the institution was recognized by the founders both of Judaism and Christianity." But then Stirling moved from exegesis to hermeneutics, and in so doing opened up the broader intellectual landscape in which debates over the Bible and slavery had become so important. "How," Stirling wrote, "those who adhere to a literal interpretation of the Bible, and consider every direction contained in its pages as applicable at all times to all men, are to reconcile these facts with modern anti-slavery notions, it is, thank goodness, no business of mine to find out."[6]

Stirling's comments pointed to several important realities concerning the use of the Bible in the antebellum period. First, they underscored the grand reliance on Scripture that, as we have seen repeatedly, constituted so much of the theologians' stock-in-trade during this period. But they also underscored the magnitude of the religious crisis at midcentury, since a common trust in Scripture was producing on the subject of slavery anything but a common conclusion. Most important, Stirling's comments pointed toward a distinction perceived by only a few of his American contemporaries, a distinction between the authority of the Bible per se and the axioms of interpretation by which biblical authority was apprehended throughout the United States. Stirling's commentary may have been unstudied, but it was insightful. Not just the Bible, but "a literal interpretation of the Bible" and a belief that "every direction contained in its pages [is] applicable at all times to all men" was winning for proslavery the palm in exegetical battle with its foes.

In order to understand why debates over the Bible and slavery reveal so much about the development of an American theology, it is necessary to sketch the remarkable course of Scripture in the new United States and then to probe in somewhat greater detail the particular hermeneutical conventions that became almost as widespread as trust in the Bible itself. Those conventions, which Stirling caught with unusual economy, may be described as a Reformed and literal hermeneutic. Understanding the prevalence of such a hermeneutic is critical for understanding the debate over Scripture and slavery in the years before the Civil War, which is the subject of the next chapter. An examination of that debate shows, in turn, why the nation's theological crisis grew in magnitude alongside its political crisis. It also reveals how distinctively American the use of the Bible had become, since even sympathetic commentors from outside the United States could no longer fathom what their American peers were now up to as they pondered, debated, and applied the texts of Scripture.

The Bible Alone

As we have seen, the Bible was a given in the history of Protestantism, including Protestant developments in early America. Yet in the immediate aftermath of the decline of Puritanism, the use of Scripture for analysis, argument, and reasoning was more prevalent among individuals and churches than for society at large. The Bible continued to be a presence in the Revolutionary and constitutional periods, but that presence was predominately rhetorical and ornamental. There are few biblical arguments, as such, in these periods like the ones that began to appear after 1800. To be sure, during the 1770s and '80s, the Bible was quoted and biblical narratives were invoked to provide a sacred aura for public actions.[7] But it was rare for political actors to cite chapter and verse as the primary reason for pursuing a particular public policy, and it was even more uncommon for arguments to move from biblical exegesis to direct public advocacy. By contrast, beginning in the 1790s and extending through the Civil War, exactly those sorts of arguments became more and more common, for example, over the transport of mail on Sunday and more general questions of Sabbath observance, over goals and strategies of temperance advocates, over removal of the Cherokee, over the rights of women, and preeminently over the rights and wrongs of slavery.

The Bible became directly important for nineteenth-century public life because, in the great expansion of the evangelical churches, it was becoming so important for private life. The religious revival that filled the churches, that generated such powerful ideals for domestic life, and that created a plethora of voluntary societies led in turn to a much more explicit deployment of the Bible in the public sphere.

Modern historians have recognized the nearly ubiquitous bearing of Scripture on American consciousness in the half century before the Civil War. Joyce Appleby, for example, once observed that the United States Constitution "entered a culture already fully fitted out with symbolic systems and sacred texts." Among these, "the most important source of meaning for eighteenth-century Americans was the Bible."[8] Perry Miller had earlier claimed that "the Old Testament is truly so omnipresent in the American culture of 1800 or 1820 that historians have as much difficulty taking cognizance of it as of the air people breathed."[9] Yet despite such acknowledgment, the cultural role of the Bible has rarely been studied analytically. The result is failure to grasp the immense, and immensely complicated, role of biblical authority in creating the two Christian nationalisms that in 1861 fell on each other with a holy vengeance.

The most striking American development when compared with Europe was that the Bible flourished in the wake of revolution. The presence of Scripture remained strong in western European societies through the first half of the nineteenth century, but without the intense democratization that took place in America. In Europe there was also a strong continuing link between biblical authority and the claims of conservative regimes.[10] Moreover, Hans Frei's description of earlier Bible reading as "strongly realistic, i.e., at once literal and historical," remained true for most Americans far into the nineteenth century, even as that particular way of treating Scripture was fading rapidly from elite and middle-brow circles in Europe.[11]

The striking contrast was that amid America's post-Revolutionary tide of antiformalism, antitraditionalism, democratization, and decentralization, trust in the Bible did not weaken but became immeasurably stronger. It was still "the Bible alone," as proclaimed during the Reformation, that American Protestants trusted. But it was also "the Bible alone" of all historic religious authorities that survived the antitraditional tide and then undergirded the remarkable evangelical expansion of the early nineteenth century. By undercutting trust in other traditional authorities, the power-suspecting ideologies of the Revolutionary and constitutional periods had the ironic effect of scripturalizing the United States. Deference to inherited authority of bishops and presbyters was largely gone, obeisance to received creeds was largely gone, willingness to heed the example of the past was largely gone. What remained was the power of intuitive reason, the authority of written documents that the people approved for themselves, and the Bible alone.

Publishing the Good Book

Up to and through the Civil War, publishing and distribution of the Bible dwarfed all other literary enterprises in the new nation.[12] Because printing of the Bible during the colonial period was restricted by copyrights held in Britain, Scripture publication began slowly in the new nation. Only 22 editions of the Bible appeared before 1790.[13] But then came an explosion. The numbers of editions doubled every decade for thirty years and then leveled off to an average of about 27 new editions each year from 1830 to 1865. In the decade of the 1830s, new editions of the Bible were printed in fourteen different states, led by New York (100 editions), Pennsylvania (65), Massachusetts (58), and Connecticut (57). Thereafter the total number of editions dropped slightly, but larger print runs meant that more actual Bibles were being produced. Many editions in this period represented one-off efforts by struggling printshops, whose efforts were barely noticed in their own locales. But others were publishing juggernauts. A Bible annotated by the Calvinist Anglican Thomas Scott, for example, was first published in America in a five-volume set by William Woodward of Philadelphia over the years 1804–1809. But then in 1827 a consortium of New York and Boston printers brought out a new six-volume edition whose initial print run of over 20,000 copies quickly sold out; this same six-volume edition was reprinted at least ten more times before 1865. The New Testament paraphrase by the eighteenth-century English Congregationalist Phillip Doddridge was republished in 1833 by an Amherst, Massachusetts, firm that recruited Boston scholars to provide additional material on Doddridge and the paraphrase. It passed through at least seventeen printings in the next twenty-three years.[14] During the Civil War, the American Bible Society by itself distributed more than three million Bibles or New Testaments to the North's approximately 2.2 million combatants; something like 300,000 Bibles also passed from Northern publishers into the South (despite a ban on trade between the sections); and Moses Hoge of Richmond by himself braved the Union blockade to smuggle 10,000 Bibles, 50,000 New Testaments, and 250,000 portions of Psalms and Gospels from England back to the South.[15]

The surprising degree of homogeneity that America's heterogeneous religious landscape could produce is indicated by the predominance of the Authorized, or King James, Version in this sea of American Bibles. Fully 90% of the 1,784 separate editions of Scripture published in America from 1776 to 1865 were of the King James Version. Only 6% were Catholic translations, most Douay-Rheims; the rest represented unsuccessful efforts by Protestants to improve upon the King James. The prevalence of this one translation was even greater than these figures suggest, since the larger print runs and the most often reprinted editions were almost always of the Authorized Version.

By the early years of the United States, in other words, Scripture had become the national book par excellence. Confidence in the ability of ordinary people to understand it fueled the formation of many new sects. The revitalization and expansion of Protestantism in the early republic rested upon a widely shared confidence in the trustworthiness of the Bible. Broad familiarity with its contents characterized both ordinary people and elites.[16]

The Bible in a Constitutional Republic

Trust in the Bible was a religious analogue to political trust in the Constitution, and the analogy was sometimes drawn explicitly. William Ellery Channing, for example, said in 1819 that "we reason about the Bible precisely as civilians do about the constitution under which we live."[17] In fact, confidence in the Bible as an authoritative written document from which one could understand practical questions of life may have been one of the impulses that transformed the notion "constitution" from its British meaning of an inherited body of precedents to its American sense of a written document.[18] It was certainly the case that widespread reverence for the written Scripture preceded widespread reverence for the written Constitution. Concentrated attention to the Constitution as such was slow in developing. By the 1830s and '40s, when constitutionalism did emerge as a key concept in political debates and public celebrations, the authority of the written Scriptures had already been long established among the American populace.[19]

To explain why "the Bible alone" in both senses of the term remained so strong in America would require a large book of its own. Here it may be suggested that, among a wealth of inherited Protestant practices, trust in Scripture was the one best suited to the circumstances of the early republic. Reliance on the Bible was a principle that could be easily democratized. Those who trusted the Bible alone found themselves strategically armed for resisting tyrannical abuses of power and soon proved themselves strategically effective in shoring up republican virtue. Religiously considered, reliance on the Bible alone meant that those who had experienced a life-transforming conversion could move immediately to proclamation, even itineration, without waiting for formal institutional or denominational approval. For the millions who purchased, read, pondered, preached, and debated the Scriptures, the principle of *sola Scriptura* constituted an anchor of religious authority in a churning sea of demographic, social, and political turmoil.

Evidence for American allegiance to "the Bible alone" in both senses abounded on every side in the new nation. Because it was hardly a new thing for Protestants to proclaim their loyalty to Scripture, assertions privileging the Scriptures over against all other authorities can be found as far back in the American past as one cares to look. But by the 1770s criticism of other authorities that earlier Protestants had accepted alongside Scripture was becoming more pronounced. Thus in 1775 the learned Congregationalist Ezra Stiles complained that biblical commentaries were "becoming little more than a Vehicle to put off human Systems upon Mankind for the Scripture Verity." Stiles was even nervous about paraphrases of Scripture; he wanted "to have the pure word of God by itself," and to have it in the King James Version, since he felt a better translation had never been prepared for any of the world's main language-groups.[20] Stiles's desire to promote only the Scriptures would be multiplied many times over in the decades that followed.

After the Revolution, Bible-onlyism emerged with great force. In contrast to the late-colonial period, when professions to follow just the Scriptures had been a staple of heterodox exegesis practiced by liberals, now the appeal to Scripture alone was linked closely to traditional theological orthodoxy.[21] What was not traditional, however, was the link between the Bible alone and political republicanism, a link that was especially prominent among the upstart plebeians contending for their place in the public life of the new country. Among the welter of Protestant groups active after the Revolution, the driving force on the question of authority was provided by those who interpreted the founding of the United States as a blow for universal liberation. John Leland, the earnest Baptist itinerant, was seeking souls in Virginia when in 1789 he published *The Bible-Baptist*. It was a tract daring any defender of infant baptism to find anything but nonscriptural support for such practices. Leland elaborated his defense of baptizing adults by immersion through exegesis of biblical texts, but the grounds from which he worked combined religious and political principles of the broadest sort. In contrast to the "lies" that had been allowed to circulate for so long in "the Eastern and European worlds," the new government allowed "the Sons of *America* [to] be free." With that freedom it was the duty of all to abandon "tradition, prejudice, or systematical myths"—to flee the "absurdity" of trusting ancient inherited religious authorities—in order to find the "plain truth" of the Bible.[22]

Four years later, after Leland had returned to his native Massachusetts, the message was the same. For Baptists, "the Bible is the only confession of faith . . . the final umpire they appeal unto for a decision of controversies." What was new in Leland's appeal was not these assertions as such, for they were shared by all kinds of Protestants. The new element, rather, was Leland's vehemence in denouncing the religious authorities from which Baptists were now gloriously liberated: "without pope or king for head—without spiritual or civil courts established by law—without a conclave of bishops, or convocation of clergy—without legalized creeds or formularies of worship—without a ministry supported by law, or any human coercion in discipline."[23]

As a Baptist, and also as a supporter of Thomas Jefferson, Leland stood toward the radical end of American Protestantism, but his willingness to stake all on the Scriptures was an increasingly common theme in the public statements of others. Benjamin Rush, the renowned Philadelphia physician, moved in very different circles from the itinerant Leland, but even as Leland was claiming to base his Baptist preaching on a strict adherence to the Bible alone, so also was Rush saying nearly the same thing, and saying it with even more self-conscious reliance on new political realities. In the spring of 1791, Rush published a letter appealing for the use of the Bible as a set text in the new country's primary schools. More than Leland would do, Rush conceded that God had revealed himself through creation and also in human consciousness, but at the same time he exalted the Bible as a far stronger, purer, and clearer source of divine teaching. Rush's reliance upon Scripture for the health of the nation indicated the singular honor in which he held the Bible (nearly) alone: "We profess to be republicans, and yet we neglect the only means of establishing and perpetuating our republican form of government, that is, the universal education of our youth in the principles of Christianity, by means of the Bible: for this Divine book, above all others, favours that equality among mankind, that respect for just laws, and all those sober and frugal virtues, which constitute the soul of republicanism."[24]

The bond Rush perceived between Scripture (over against other authorities) and republican government (over against other political systems) would be ardently promoted in the years that followed, and by no one more ardently than Elias Smith. Smith—publicist, preacher, and antiformalist par excellence—spoke and wrote many times about the organic connection between trusting only the Bible and enjoying the fruits of republican liberty. One of the most notable of such performances was his Fourth of July address in Taunton, Massachusetts, in 1809. It rang the changes on the "foreign despotic yoke" that had been overthrown on 4 July 1776, and it expatiated at length on why the United States should be recognized as the most prosperous, most equal, and most free country on the earth. For considerations of the place of the Bible in early national America, it is revealing that Smith saw a common set of destructive authorities opposing trust in the Bible alone and also undermining the republican experiment. Religious liberty, that is, meant "being wholly free to examine for ourselves, what is truth without being bound to a catechism, creed, confession of faith, discipline, or any rule excepting the scriptures." But living by no rule but the Bible turned out to be a defense against virtually the same list of enemies as living up to the standards of republicanism: "Many are *republicans* as to *government*, and are yet half *republicans*, being in matters of religion still bent to a *Catechism, creed, covenant*, or a superstitious priest. Venture to be as independent in things of religion as in those which respect the government in which you live."[25] Few Protestants expressed themselves as flamboyantly as Smith in the early republic, but most followed where he led.

So thoroughly did notions of following Scripture alone inform the speech and practice of American churches that by the 1840s observers both American and foreign were able to see, beneath the profusion of the United States' competing sects, a broadly based and widely shared biblicism. The principles of that biblicism were stated by New Hampshire Baptists in 1833 in a much-copied profession: "We believe the Holy Bible was written by men divinely inspired, and is a perfect treasure of heavenly instruction; that it has God for its author, salvation for its end, and truth, without any mixture of error, for its matter; that it reveals the principles by which God will judge us; and therefore is, and shall remain to the end of the world, the true center of Christian union, and the supreme standard by which all human conduct, creeds, and opinions should be tried."[26]

When the English Methodist James Dixon was sent by his denomination to observe the quadrennial conference of the United States' Northern Methodists in 1848, Dixon returned to England with a glowing report on the forces that bound American Protestants together. In his view, the United States was experiencing something quite new. Though there were different groups of Christians with different names, he contended that "there are no sects . . . , no Dissenters, no seceders. . . . They are all alike considered as Christians; and adopting, according to the judgment of charity, with equal honesty the common charter of salvation, the word of God, they are treated as equal."[27] To Dixon, common trust in God's written word provided a common platform of cooperative Christian practice.

Dixon's conclusion was seconded by the era's ablest historian of American religion, Robert Baird. In his explanation for why the "evangelical" denominations of America could cooperate on so many fronts, Baird stressed not merely a common trust in the Bible. Rather, commonality among Protestants existed because "they hold the supremacy of the scriptures as a rule of faith, and that whatever doctrine can be proved from holy scripture *without tradition* is to be received unhesitatingly, and that nothing that cannot so be proved shall be deemed an essential point of Christian belief."[28] Whatever the case may have been with regard to actual practice, the idea that American Protestants followed "the Bible only" was firmly, deeply, and permanently fixed in popular belief.

A Reformed, Literal Hermeneutic

Yet American belief in Scripture was never as simple as believers in the Bible alone assumed. When a perceptive observer like James Stirling could see so clearly that a particular hermeneutic was implicated in arguments over slavery, it is strange that most Americans did not share that recognition.

The reason that very few American could articulate a distinction between the Bible and the Bible-as-read-in-America was precisely because Americans shared so implicitly one particular hermeneutic. The reason they held it so implicitly was precisely because this hermeneutic had unleashed the power of the Bible in the creation of American civilization. Evangelical Protestants contending against each other over the future of the United States were in no position to examine, with critical detachment, the assumptions that had made the fate of the United States worth contending for. Of those assumptions one of the most pervasive was that the people had the right to read all of the Bible for themselves. The assumption behind this assumption was even more widely shared—that the Bible truly revealed God. Such assumptions fed upon the characteristic hermeneutic of the age, for it was compounded of a distinctly Reformed approach to the scope of biblical authority ("every direction contained in its pages as applicable at all times to all men") and a distinctly American literalism that privileged commonsense readings of scriptural texts ("a literal interpretation of the Bible").

Reformed

A Reformed and literal hermeneutic had been emerging in America for two and a half centuries before 1860. On the Reformed side, it was descended from New England Puritans, midstate Presbyterians, and, beyond them, the Scottish, English, Dutch, South German, and Swiss—or broadly Calvinist—forms of the Protestant Reformation. Reformed approaches to Scripture have loomed so large in standard accounts of American religious history that it is easy to forget that they were neither the first nor the only orthodox Protestant ways of appropriating the Bible. A Reformed hermeneutic followed at least three principles that distinguished Calvinists from sixteenth-century Lutherans, as also from the Anglicanism associated with Richard Hooker (ca. 1554–1600) and his *Laws of Ecclesiastical Polity*.[29] Although a full range of internal differ-

ences divided Calvinists against each other, they were united against Lutherans
and high Anglicans in holding the following beliefs about the Bible: First,
Calvinists appropriated the Protestant principle of *sola Scriptura* by perceiving the Bible as an authority set over against other religious authorities. Second, Calvinists often practiced some version of the "Regulative Principle," a
position the English Puritans had developed from general Reformed leanings.
It held that believers were required to do what the Bible commands but were
equally required not to do those things about which the Bible is silent.[30] Last
was the so-called third use of the law, or the belief that, after its twofold use
for restraining sin in society and for showing individuals their need of salvation, the moral teaching of Scriptures existed also (even primarily) to provide a blueprint for how Christians, in grateful obedience to God, should live
their entire lives.[31]

These doctrinal principles of Reformed Protestantism often coexisted with
reinforcing social habits.[32] Reformed Protestantism usually flourished in regions where Calvinists were attacking ecclesiastical tradition, devising efforts
to empower the laity, building institutions to encourage literacy, and promoting the sermon as the central element in communal worship. The hermeneutic inspired by these Reformed practices reverenced the Bible as the supreme
guide to life but also inculcated a suspicion that other authorities beside biblical chapter and verse were not just secondary but dangerous. In other words,
all of the Bible, but only the Bible, for all of life.

Lutherans and high Anglicans shared many of the Reformed attitudes toward Scripture, but they appropriated the Bible with different hermeneutical
practices.[33] Both Lutherans and high Anglicans held to *sola Scriptura,* but in
the sense that the Bible was to be favored *over* all other authorities, rather
than *in place of* all other authorities. Both Lutherans and high Anglicans were
also conservative in the sense that they held traditions to be useful so long as
they did not violate the Bible's message of salvation. Martin Luther repudiated Thomistic definitions of transubstantiation and rejected the sacrifice of
the Mass because he felt these Catholic teachings violated the meaning of the
gospel, but he maintained received traditions on the presence of Christ's body
and blood in the Mass and on the regenerating character of infant baptism.
These traditions, he thought, enjoyed a thorough, implicit sanction, as well
as occasional explicit sanction, in Scripture. High-church Anglicans reasoned
in similar fashion about the divine right of traditional monarchs. Neither group
accepted the Regulative Principle or the desire to find explicit biblical warrant for all contemporary Christian practices, as did the Reformed.[34]

On the relation of the Bible to the conduct of daily life, high Anglicans
like Richard Hooker were not far removed from the Reformed, except that
Hooker felt it was appropriate to allow more authority to reason and Christian tradition in setting norms for Christian behavior. For Lutherans, the law
of God as contained in the Bible was certainly important as a guide for Christian conduct, but it was far more important as the prick of conscience driving
sinners to Christ. It is a small, but telling, difference that in ordering his Small
Catechism of 1529, Luther discussed the Ten Commandments first (as an in-

troduction to the exposition of salvation as explained in the Apostles' Creed), whereas the Reformed Heidelberg Catechism (1563), which otherwise shared so much of the limpid Christ-centered faith of Luther's Small Catechism, discussed the Commandments only after it explained the meaning of Christian salvation. Heidelberg's order, where the commandments guided the believer in godly living, featured a detailed attention to divine law and law-keeping that would be widely imitated in America.

Reformed views of Scripture carried practical implications of extraordinary scope. By the deductive reasoning of some modern intellectuals, as well as to some contemporary Catholics, Lutherans, and high-church Anglicans, Calvinism looks like a thin religion. In point of fact, the Reformed faith was a great fountain of piety. On the ground in early modern Europe and North America, it possessed remarkable social and intellectual power. To be sure, Calvinism was most potent in opposition (as the Dutch against the Habsburgs, John Knox and his associates against Mary Queen of Scots, English Puritans against unfriendly bishops, and Scots-Irish against Anglicans or Roman Catholics). Once having triumphed over their foes, Calvinists were prone to moralism, formalism, and especially schism (as most notably during the English Civil Wars and Commonwealth, 1640–1660). But whether in opposition or in control, when pious Calvinists began to ask, How should we live in the world? they answered by looking to the Bible as a guidebook for life as well as for its message of salvation.

The Reformed hermeneutic became dominant in America in part because the dominant American churches were heirs of this form of Protestantism. The Bible, as read by Reformed hermeneutical principles, fueled the most intensely religious colonial settlements, energized early American higher education, and midwifed the revival tradition of the mid-eighteenth century. It also contributed a full share to the spirit of the American Revolution and to the creation of early American nationalism.[35] It defined as well the approach to Scripture that drove the great voluntary movements in the two generations before the Civil War. Other Christian, and Protestant, groups were present in early America, but for better and for worse, the way they handled the Bible made little public difference.

After the Frenchman André Siegfried visited the United States in the 1920s, he made much of these Calvinist influences in his interpretation of American history. In his opinion, the "religious mysticism and political cynicism" of Lutheranism could not be more different from the characteristic Reformed stance. Siegfried did not refer directly to the use of Scripture, but his general comments accurately described the effects of believing that all of the mandates and sanctions found in the Bible were intended as guides for contemporary action: "Born anew through grace, the Calvinist has a mission to carry out; namely, to purify the life of the community and to uplift the state. He cannot admit two separate spheres of action, for he believes that the influence of Christ should dominate every aspect of life."[36]

When biblical interpretations clashed as they did in the run-up to the Civil War, this Reformed spirit became a liability. Within a Reformed hermeneutical framework, the only possible explanation for an opponent's persistently erroneous use of Scripture was the opponent's malicious intent to pervert the clear word of God. Such clashes led to violent confrontation, but only because the Calvinist use of Scripture provided great energy for religiously inspired social construction.

To illustrate the public weight of Reformed voices during the Civil War, several crude measures are useful. When in April 1863 a convention of Southern ministers appealed to their fellow Christians in the world, 94 of the 96 signers came from Baptist, Methodist, Episcopal, Presbyterian, and Disciples churches, all branches of English-speaking Reformed Protestantism.[37] In David Chesebrough's two compendious books on Northern sermons during the war, well over 90% of the representative texts he selected came from the same ecclesiastical families.[38] A Reformed approach to the Bible had divided into many American variations, but it also defined the theological instincts with which most theologians at the time of the Civil War read, inwardly marked, and outwardly applied the Scriptures. On issues like the morality of slavery, they felt that the Bible spoke just as clearly as it did on questions of eternal life.

Commonsense Literalism

At least two full generations before the Civil War, the prevailing American hermeneutic had also come to embody what James Stirling called "a literal interpretation of the Bible."[39] The literalism that Stirling observed owed more to American historical circumstances than to the Reformed Regulative Principle, for the first Reformed theologians (Calvin, Heinrich Bullinger, Peter Martyr, and many English and American Puritans) had practiced a theological rather than a strictly literal approach to Scripture. That is, their efforts to understand the Scriptures characteristically produced syntheses in which individual biblical texts were subordinated to overarching interpretations, as with Calvin's view of divine sovereignty, the covenant theology of Bullinger, or the ecclesiastical communalism of the Puritans.[40] Yet traditional Reformed hermeneutics connected at a critical point with American popular religion in the early years of the republic. That point was a shared antitraditionalism, long ingrained among the Reformed by struggle against Roman Catholic tradition, and then promoted among early-national Americans by the democratic individualism arising from the Revolution.

The crucial circumstance for later hermeneutical practice was the post-Revolutionary alliance between newly empowered ordinary people and the traditional authority of the Bible. The distinctively American development was the way in which common people appropriated the written Scriptures to create an irrefutable warrant for managing their own lives. As Nathan Hatch has suggested, plebeian trust in the Bible offered "a new ground of certainty for a generation distressed that it could no longer hear the voice of God above the din of sectarian confusion. This approach to Scripture also dared common people to open the Bible and think for themselves. It even challenged them to limit religious discussion to the language of the Bible." So armed with the Bible, ordinary people were liberated from "staid ecclesiastical traditions" and could escape the control of "the respectable clergy."[41]

The Christian antitraditionalism that this use of "the Bible alone" fueled was a commonplace of American religion to and through the Civil War. Its character is illustrated by an outline that Charles Finney prepared for a sermon in 1863:

> Christianity is radically reformatory. Satan has usurped the government of this world. . . . Christ has undertaken the work of counter-revolution . . . to create all things new in the moral order of things . . . to reform or destroy, all governments that dont obey God. . . . It follows that conservatism is its great antagonist. . . . Conservatism is a disposition to preserve the established order. . . . Its law is custom—Precedent—Established usages. . . . It looks back for all that is excellent & counts progress insanity. . . . It is every where & evermore antiChrist.[42]

By the 1860s Finney's animus against conservative religious practice was an American commonplace. Seventy years before, the Connecticut Episcopalian Samuel Seabury had published an appeal for members of the various American churches to unite under the banner of historic Anglicanism, which Seabury tried to defend as the most biblical of all Christian denominations. It was an entirely futile effort, in part because ecclesiastical fragmentation had already advanced too far, in part because Seabury was mistaken in assuming that "the generality of christians," even in America, would "pay a due regard to the traditions of the church."[43]

Much more typical was a particularly American conception of what it meant to think for oneself and thus to read the Bible for oneself. In promoting this distinctly American mandate, upstart Restorationist "Christians" spoke for a much broader audience than did the traditionalist Seabury. Thomas Campbell's early manifesto of American Restorationism, his *Declaration and Address* of 1809, left no doubt about the pillars of the movement. They were self-reliance and the Bible. Campbell was convinced that "it is high time for us not only to think, but also to act, for ourselves; to see with our own eyes, and to take all our measures directly and immediately from the Divine standard." No mere "human interpretation" of the Bible or "human opinions" of any sort should stand in the way of appropriating "the Divine word alone for our rule; the Holy Spirit for our teacher and guide, to lead us into all truth; and Christ alone, as exhibited in the word, for our salvation."[44] Campbell's son Alexander, who brought Restorationism to maturity, professed to steer by the same lights: "I have been so long disciplined in the school of free enquiry, that, if I know my own mind, there is not a man upon the earth whose authority can influence me, any farther than he comes with the authority of evidence, reason, and truth. . . . I have endeavored to read the Scriptures as though no one had read them before me."[45]

This opposition to anything that smacked of interpretive deference with respect to Scripture flourished in the heavily republican climate of early national America. Among the followers of Barton W. Stone, who joined Campbell in creating the Restorationist churches, one writing in 1827 made explicit the connection between politics and hermeneutics: "The present conflict between the Bible and party creeds and confessions, or, in other words, the war between the church and the clergy, is perfectly analogous to the revolutionary war between Britain and America; liberty was contended for on the one side, and dominion and power on the other." It was a question of "Bible government" versus "ecclesiastical despotism."[46] Restorationist hermeneutics represented the extreme statement of a common position. The engine of the era's most active and influential religion was, as proclaimed in 1832 by the *Christian Spectator* of New Haven, "the word of God interpreted by common sense."[47]

The inevitable outworking of populist antitraditionalism was literal interpretation of Scripture. Stripping away the dross of the past enabled present-day readers to grasp what Scripture really meant. What Scripture really meant was exactly what it said. In 1843 a writer in the *Methodist Quarterly Review* expressed this conjunction magisterially in a discussion of biblical eschatology, a theme that regularly produced as much hermeneutical clarity as exegetical confusion: "We claim to be, not only rigid literalists, but unsparing iconoclasts—ruthless demolishers of all theories. We wish to strip the passage of all the superincumbent strata which ingenious men have deposited all round it, and come down to the plainest and most obvious literal reading of the text."[48] Once interpretation had become a democratic enterprise, attempting to understand the Bible literally became the only possible goal.

The assumption that people could see clearly and without ambiguity what the Bible said, and that this biblicistic knowledge qualified one to judge connections between moral cause and moral effect, was the common person's counterpart to the Enlightenment confidence displayed by intellectual elites who employed learned formal moral philosophy to the same ends. Democratic biblicism undercut trust in traditional interpretations of Scripture with the same force that they were being leveled by a reliance on philosophical common sense. In both cases, confidence in present abilities overmastered confidence in what was handed on from the past. In both cases, a liberated modern self was the starting point for biblical interpretation. Populist appropriation of democratic principles and the learned moral philosophy of intellectual elites did not coincide everywhere in the early modern West. But in republican America they provided powerful reinforcement for each other, especially as men and women turned to the sacred page.[49]

A Reformed, literal hermeneutic was the interpretive strategy that evangelical Protestants exploited in winning the new republic for Christ. The social transformation achieved by these evangelicals seemed to validate their approach to Scripture. For reaching the unreached with the Christian message, for organizing congregations and building churches, for creating agencies to construct and reform society, reliance on the Bible alone, literally interpreted, worked wonders. Yet without a principle of revolution—of trust transferred from hereditary, deferential hierarchy to democratic, ideological antihierarchy—this distinctly American form of biblicism could not have come into existence.

Simplicity

By the time of the Civil War, Enlightenment habits of mind were exerting significant influence on the country's theologians. These mental habits fit remarkably well with the Reformed, literal hermeneutic that was being put to use generally as Protestants studied the Bible. A prominent feature common to much of the era's Protestant discourse, whether from high estate or low, was the assumption that life's great issues were simple and could be controlled simply by appeal to simple human exertion and to the simple words of Scripture. Although the complex arguments of confessional theologians and the perplexing religious experiences of many ordinary people forcefully contradicted this assumption, the conventions of pietist-Enlightenment-biblical simplicity circumscribed the known world for much religious thought. Few were capable of the view to which Abraham Lincoln came during the nation's civil conflict, that, as summarized well by Phillip Paludan, "the war had become too complex, too astounding, for him to believe that mere argument made complete sense."[50]

A philosophical tradition reaching back to Locke featured the power of "simple ideas" from sense information. Even as the Scottish moral philosophers removed what they considered the unnecessary fiction of Locke's "ideas," they retained a high opinion of "simple" impressions from whatever source. Thus, to look to Scripture for simple truths of great power was to combine hereditary Protestant trust in the Bible with a modern epistemological stance.

Reliance on what might be called "evangelical Enlightenment simplicity"—of perception and self-assertion—was illustrated in a host of pronouncements throughout this period, some of which were also rooted self-consciously in the rhetoric of the Revolution. John Leland, for example, could summarize his defense of the Baptists from 1789 as faithfulness in following one injunction: "simply regard the bible."[51] To Thomas Campbell, whose program resembled Leland's in many but not all particulars, the goal was to heed "Christ and his simple word" and so "reduce to practice that simple original form of Christianity, expressly exhibited on the sacred page; without attempting to inculcate anything of human authority, of private opinion, or inventions of men."[52]

When Charles Finney, immediately after his conversion in 1821, asked a local minister whether the justice Jesus fulfilled before God the father was "retributive" or "publick," he was not satisfied with the response, so he resolved to solve the issue himself with a self-confidence paralleling the self-confidence of a philosophe. Finney knew he "was but a novice in religion &

in biblical learning." But this fact did not hold him back: "I had read nothing on the subject except my bible, & what I had there found upon the subject I had interpreted as I would have understood the same or like passages in a law book." In presenting his conclusions on the subject, Finney was proud to report, "I do not recollect to have ever read a page upon the subject except what I had found in the bible."[53] A few years after Finney spelled out his method in this way, the Presbyterian John Holt Rice published an extensive consideration of the Christian faith. To Rice, a keystone of proper religion was religious freedom, which he thought had been taught in the Reformation, but which was even clearer on the pages of Scripture: "A remarkably exact proportion [exists] between zeal for freedom of conscience, and conformity of religious doctrine to the simple truths of the Bible."[54]

In 1837 the abolitionist Sarah Grimké sounded a similar note in her own intellectual declaration of independence. For the "important subject" of whether the sexes were equal, she proposed a high standard: "I shall depend solely on the Bible to designate the sphere of woman, because I believe almost every thing that has been written on this subject, has been the result of a misconception of the simple truths revealed in the Scriptures, in consequence of the false translation of many passages of Holy Writ." For Grimké, self-reliance was as much a birthright of biblical interpretation as it was for the men of the period: "I . . . claim to judge for myself what is the meaning of the inspired writers, because I believe it to be the solemn duty of every individual to search the Scriptures for themselves, with the aid of the Holy Spirit, and not be governed by the views of any man, or set of men."[55] The principle of simplicity also featured large when Americans turned to interpreting the prophecies of the Bible. In 1842 the Philadelphia Presbyterian George Duffield claimed to bring no presuppositions with him to that task: "Theory is out of place and unallowable in the study of prophecy. . . . It is a simple question that in all cases must be asked, what is the fair and legitimate meaning of the words—a matter-of-fact investigation—no theorising, no speculations."[56]

Not surprisingly, such views fit well with the age's trust in Baconian intellectual method. When in 1859 the Restorationist James S. Lamar published his *Organon of Scripture; or, The Inductive Method of Biblical Interpretation*, he spoke for many other Americans when he claimed, "The Scriptures admit of being studied and expounded upon the principles of the inductive method; and . . . when thus interpreted they speak to us in a voice as certain and unmistakable as the language of nature heard in the experiments and observations of science."[57] During the years of the Civil War, countless believers extended such convictions by assuming that moral perception could be crystal clear and the means of moral action entirely straightforward. In 1860, the Kentucky Presbyterian Robert Breckinridge told readers how they could discover the essence of a Christian church: "If the world, and more especially the children of Christ, would follow simply and earnestly the light of reason . . . and the teachings of that divine word, which he has given to be a lamp unto our feet . . . , it is not easy to imagine how the least obscurity could hang over such a question."[58] In 1861 the Northern conservative Henry Van Dyke was flabbergasted that abolitionists could read the Bible as they professed to read it: "When the Abolitionist tells me that slaveholding is sin, in the simplicity of my faith in the Holy Scriptures, I point him to this sacred record, and tell him, in all candor, as my text does, that his teaching blasphemes the name of God and His doctrine."[59] That same year the abolitionist Gerrit Smith thought it was just as easy to come to the opposite conclusion: "The religion taught by Jesus is not a letter but a life. So simple is it that the unlearned can both understand and teach it. . . . The true religion is too simple to make the training of a theological seminary necessary for those who teach it. We should allow the wisdom and goodness of God to assure us that the religion which He has given to the world must correspond in its simplicity with the simplicity of the masses."[60] From the South in that same year, the Baptist Thornton Stringfellow expressed the opinion that God's intentions were clearly expressed in the Bible and readily available to all; benevolence was, in Drew Faust's summary, "a 'simple' matter of explicating the Bible and guiding men in following its dictates."[61] In December 1864, the Presbyterian *Independent* of New York felt that the problem of taking care of liberated slaves could be easily solved: "In effect the problem is simple, and its solution comparatively easy." All one had to do was rely on the labor practices, the religious activism, and the educational zeal that had already "raised the american character in the Free States to its present altitude."[62]

This habit of mind—to assume that a simple solution existed for problems in theology, morals, and society—was the mentality that grounded the theologians' approach to Scripture. It is a matter of great historical significance that American Protestants almost never cited biblical chapter and verse to defend their interpretive practices. Precisely as it worked on Scripture, the Reformed, literal hermeneutic revealed most clearly how it arose from the special circumstances of American life. Yet even if this hermeneutic itself was not necessarily rooted in a literal reading of Scripture, it was nonetheless the American norm for the generations between the writing of the Constitution and the end of the Civil War.

In 1865 Phoebe Palmer summed up an era, as well as one of her own arguments, when she wrote, "The Bible is a wonderfully simple book; and, if you had taken the naked Word of God as . . . your counsel, instead of taking the opinions of men in regard to that *Word*, you might have been a more enlightened, simple, happy and useful Christian."[63]

By the early 1860s, however, some Americans might have been forgiven for wondering if things were really that simple. A great difficulty had arisen in simple appropriation of the truth-telling Scriptures. The difficulty was especially troublesome because it grew from the foundational structures of the Christian republican civilization that Protestants had constructed, at the cost of such great effort and with such great success, in the early decades of the century. The extraordinarily potent combination of evangelical fervor, republican conviction, commonsense principle, and the Bible interpreted by the canons of a Reformed, literal hermeneutic had not in fact brought in the millennium. Rather, it was bringing the division of God's chosen nation, a great mobilization of resources aimed at coercing assent, and a staggering death toll of men under arms. Among the most important casualties of the Civil War was American theology as it had developed over the preceding two generations. More than anything else, the crisis that brought this theology down was the inability of Reformed and literal biblical interpretation to handle the reality of black chattel slavery.

19 ✳

The Bible and Slavery

The critical importance of debate over slavery for the course of theology in America lay not only in the fact that fundamental differences so thoroughly divided the era's first rank of Protestant thinkers and denominations. It was even more that the intellectual resources that evangelical Protestants had so eagerly embraced in order to further their efforts of evangelization, church building, and social construction—and that, therefore, had become so important for their own theologies—were powerless in the face of division over slavery. Commonsense moral reasoning perceived directly and intuitively the propriety of the slave system and perceived with equal force its impropriety. Republican principles contradicted slavery and affirmed slavery. Most damagingly, Reformed, literal approaches to the Bible could sanction slavery and also condemn it. The potent tools with which evangelicals had constructed the nation lost their potency when they turned to address this issue. Debates over slavery were critical for American theology because they implicated the intellectual alliances that had made this theology what it was.

An often-quoted observation from Abraham Lincoln's Second Inaugural Address highlighted the theological conundrum of the Civil War. Both North and South, he said, "read the same Bible." The profundity of this statement was twofold. Most obviously, both North and South were well-versed in Scripture and could quote the Authorized Version endlessly. More important for a theological understanding of the period, both were reading Scripture in just about the same way.[1]

The Shape of the Question

The problem of the Bible and slavery was always an exegetical problem, but never only an exegetical problem. If the Bible was God's revealed word to humanity, then it was the duty of Christians to heed carefully every aspect of that revelation. If the Bible tolerated, or actually sanctioned, slavery, then it was incumbent upon believers to hear and obey. The logic was inescapable. By 1861 and the firing on Fort Sumter, the application of that logic had created a theological crisis of the first order. Despite widespread distaste for slavery and a good deal of antislavery activity from some quarters, more and more of the God-fearing in the era's most influential churches had come to believe what almost no Protestants elsewhere in the world still believed—that at least in some senses and with respect to some purposes, the Bible did in fact sanction slavery. If, however, the preponderant view concluded that the Bible allowed or upheld slavery, anything but unanimity existed about how to act upon that conclusion. The crisis of the time was created by the fact that three sizable and vocal constituencies offered conflicting answers to the problem. Each, moreover, was decisively influenced by the effort to interpret the Bible literally and in accordance with Reformed traditions.

Liberation versus the Bible

The first option was to admit that the Bible sanctioned slavery and therefore to abandon the Bible. Given the era's extraordinary exaltation of Scripture, this option was by far the least popular, but it enjoyed widespread publicity, since it was defended by radical abolitionists of great notoriety like William Lloyd Garrison. In 1845 Garrison read Tom Paine's theological works for the first time. The result was electric. Garrison was immediately liberated "from the thraldom of tradition and authority" and so could largely follow Paine's conclusions about the Bible, conclusions that solved the problem of the Bible's support for slavery. But to come to this conclusion, Garrison was forced to abandon the view of Scripture that was everywhere regnant in America: "To say that everything contained within the lids of the Bible is divinely inspired, and to insist upon the dogma as fundamentally important, is to give utterance to a bold fiction, and to require the suspension of the reasoning faculties. To say that everything in the Bible is to be believed, simply because it is found in that volume, is equally absurd and pernicious." In place of implicit trust in an inspired Bible, literally interpreted, Garrison proposed rather "the province of reason" as a way of discriminating in the Scriptures "what in them is true, and what false—what is probable, and what incredible—what is historically true, and what fabulous—what is compatible with the happiness of mankind, and what ought to be rejected as an example or rule of action—what is the letter that killeth, and what the spirit that maketh alive."[2]

   The abolitionist philanthropist Gerrit Smith, who retained a slightly higher view of the Bible than Garrison, came nonetheless to essentially the same position. On 18 November 1860 he explained to a crowd in his native Peterboro, New York, why efforts by Congregational minister George Cheever to show that the Bible condemned slavery were misguided: "Dr. Cheever sees no hope for freedom, if the Bible shall be given to the side of slavery. But I see no hope for the Bible if it shall be proved to be for slavery." Smith's declaration represented a rare instance in this period where trust in commonsense moral reasoning was allowed to contradict trust in Scripture. "All this talk that the Bible is the charter of man's rights is nonsense. His nature is that charter; and his rights are the rights of his nature—no more nor less—every book to the contrary notwithstanding."[3]

The forthrightness with which Garrison, Smith, and a few others made such pronouncements left their position entirely clear. It also had the effect of greatly confusing other efforts to deal with the issue. The dilemma was especially acute for those who disagreed with the radicals about the Bible, while agreeing with them about the evils of slavery, for they were required to show how attacks on slavery could be de-coupled from attacks on the Bible, literally interpreted.

The Bible in Defense of Slavery

The response that most directly contradicted the position of Garrison and Smith was to conclude that, since the Bible sanctioned slavery, faithful Christians should accept the legitimacy of slavery as it existed in the United States out of loyalty to the Bible's supreme divine authority. Because this was the position that seemed most obviously to arise from a Reformed and literal approach to Scripture, it carried great weight. Given (so the Reformed view) that every part of the Bible deserved to be treated as a guide for Christian life and that the privileged interpretation of every biblical passage was the literal reading, any thoughtful believer who could find the word "slavery" in a biblical concordance was a potential convert to this view. As it happened, the position turned out to be the stance of most Southern theologians and a large number of their Northern colleagues as well, however they might differ on the practical questions left in the wake of concluding that the Bible sanctioned slavery. To show what kind of biblical base could be constructed to defend this opinion, it is useful to cite at length the opinion of a Baptist minister from Richmond, Thornton Stringfellow. At the end of an extended exegetical exercise published just before the outbreak of the war, Stringfellow summarized his case by reminding his audience that the issue was a simple one: "My reader will remember that the subject in dispute is, whether involuntary and hereditary slavery was ever lawful in the sight of God, the Bible being judge." To Stringfellow, it was an open-and-shut case:

1. I have shown by the Bible, that God decreed this relation between the posterity of Canaan, and the posterity of Shem and Japheth. [from passages including Genesis 9:25–27]
2. I have shown that God executed this decree by aiding the posterity of Shem (at a time when "they were holiness to the Lord"), to enslave the posterity of Canaan in the days of Joshua. [Genesis 7:5; 12:15–16; 14:14; 23:6]
3. I have shown that when God ratified the covenant of promise with Abraham, he recognized Abraham as the owner of slaves he had bought with his money of the stranger, and recorded his approbation of the relation, by commanding Abraham to circumcise them. [Genesis 17:12–13; 20:14–16]

4. I have shown that when he took Abraham's posterity by the hand in Egypt, five hundred years afterward, he publicly approbated the same relation, by permitting every slave they had bought with their money to eat the Passover, while he refused the same privilege to their *hired servants*. [Exodus 12:44–45]

5. I have shown that God, as their national law-giver, ordained by express statute, that they should buy slaves of the nations around them (the seven devoted nations excepted), and that these slaves and their increase should be a perpetual inheritance to their children. [including Leviticus 25:44–46]

6. I have shown that God ordained slavery by law for their captives taken in war, while he guaranteed a successful issue to their wars, so long as they obeyed him. [Deuteronomy 20:10–11]

7. I have shown that when Jesus ordered his gospel to be published through the world, the relation of master and slave existed by law in every province and family of the Roman Empire, as it had done in the Jewish commonwealth for fifteen hundred years. [citing Gibbon, with Matthew 28:19, 1 Corinthians 7:21]

8. I have shown that Jesus ordained, that the legislative authority, which created this relation in that empire, should be obeyed and honored as an ordinance of God, as all government is declared to be. [Romans 13:7; 1 Peter 2:17–18]

9. I have shown that Jesus has prescribed the mutual duties of this relation in his kingdom. [1 Timothy 6:2–5]

10. And lastly, I have shown that in an attempt by his professed followers to disturb this relation in the Apostolic churches, Jesus orders that fellowship shall be disclaimed with all such disciples, as seditious persons— whose conduct was not only dangerous to the State, but destructive to the true character of the gospel dispensation. [again, 1 Timothy 6:2–5]

At the end of this long parade of exegetical common sense, Stringfellow could afford a succinct conclusion: "He who believes the Bible to be of divine authority, believes those laws were given by the Holy Ghost to Moses [and other biblical authors]. I understand the modern abolitionist sentiments to be sentiments of mortal hatred against such laws; to be sentiments which would hold God himself in abhorrence, if he were to give such laws his sanction; but he has given them his sanction, therefore, they must be in harmony with his moral character."[4]

Stringfellow's status as a local minister who did not enjoy the national repute of the Southern Presbyterian James Henley Thornwell, the Northern Presbyterian Charles Hodge, or the Congregationalist Moses Stuart (luminaries who to one degree or another shared his position) illustrates how powerfully the biblical case for slavery could appear.

Mediating Positions

A full range of spokespersons attempted to stake out their ground in the parlous terrain between the two extreme positions.[5] One type of mediating argument, proposed by some abolitionists and moderate emancipationists, included considerable intellectual complexity. It conceded that, while the Bible did indeed sanction a form of slavery, careful attention to the text of Scripture would show that the simple presence of slavery in the Bible was not a necessary justification for slavery as it existed in the United States. The exegetical argument might be that the biblical Hebrew and Greek for "servant" and "master" did not designate exactly the legal relationships found in the slave states, that the slavery sanctioned in the Old and New Testaments was a different sort of institution than the American peculiar institution, or that the biblical sanction of slavery was localized in its effect (Canaanite and Roman) and therefore was not relevant to contemporary American society. On the eve of the war, both the Lutheran *Evangelical Review* and the Presbyterian *American Theological Review* published an English translation of a learned account by a German Jew of the slavery practiced by the biblical Hebrews. It described a system very different from the one in the South. A comment from the editor of the *Evangelical Review*, however, reveals how much popular opinion resisted such interpretive moves. He reported that, although this essay had been translated in 1859, it could not be published in America until after the war's outbreak because "the dread of giving offence to the South was too strong."[6] Many variations of this argument appeared in the generation before the war, but because it required a movement from the words of the Bible to theories about how the Bible should be applied to modern life, it was not as common as a more direct way of evading the literal meaning of key texts.

This more direct strategy, also promoted by the less radical abolitionists and some moderate emancipationists, was to distinguish between the letter of the Bible (which might be construed to allow slavery) and the spirit of the Bible (which everywhere worked against the institution). The way in which variations of middle positions could evolve over time is illustrated by the career of Albert Barnes, the prominent New School Presbyterian. His *Inquiry into the Scriptural Views of Slavery* (1846), included concentrated study of the Old and New Testament texts that mentioned the institution. Barnes concluded that the realities about which these texts spoke did not correspond to the realities of nineteenth-century American society.[7] Thirteen years later, however, Barnes had come to the conclusion that, in Bruce Mullin's summary, "a clear distinction had to be drawn between the historical facts Scripture attested to, and the moral principles it taught, only the latter were normative and binding."[8] What had intervened between these two publications was the demonstration by Moses Stuart, the North's foremost biblical scholar, that a proper understanding of Scripture ruled out Barnes's earlier position. Stuart's 1850 treatise *Conscience and the Constitution, with Remarks on the Recent Speech of the Honorable Daniel Webster*, had argued that there could be no getting around the fact that the Bible in many places sanctioned the holding of slaves. By adding the scholar's voice to the testimony of the Bible's apparently plain sense, Stuart only made it harder to be both pro-Bible and antislave.

Once the war began, debate on the biblical teaching concerning slavery tailed off dramatically.[9] But when it did continue, Northerners were especially prone to an argument that sought to distinguish the Bible's spirit from its letter. An example appeared in the Baptists' leading theological quarterly, where an author contended that "a hypercritical respect for the ancient Greek, and . . . a misapplication of the strict classic import of words to the New Testament idiom" had been used "to foist slavery upon a Scripture platform." But this effort, in his view, had been "a signal failure." What trumped such craven appeal to scriptural minutiae was "a gradually advancing development of Scripture truth, a steadily increasing knowledge of Bible-teaching, a kind of subjective revelation of the real principles of the divine government to the conscious apprehension of men." This developing sense of what the Bible really meant amounted to a triumph of "the moral convictions of Christians sustained by the majesty and power of God's onward-marching providence" over "such studied efforts to make God the supporter of wrong and oppression."[10]

Conflict

Representatives of the two extreme positions, which were relatively simple, and the middle positions, which were complex, had set out their views fairly completely as early as the 1830s. From that early period, it was evident that, especially given the reigning American conventions governing the interpretation of Scripture, the proslavery argument was formidable. The limited success of abolitionist attention to Scripture testified to the power of proslavery argumentation. In 1837 Theodore Dwight Weld published a much-noticed tract, *The Bible against Slavery*, which was not so much a work of exegesis but, as Robert Abzug once put it, "almost entirely an essay in translation and semantics."[11] When the book appeared, one friendly fellow abolitionist, William Wisner, chided Weld's spotty arguments, which had attempted to define modern Southern slavery as a totalistic institution most unlike Hebrew slavery. Wisner had not been impressed by Weld's exegesis, but he did not think he had to be impressed. In his view, simply noting the existence of slavery among the Hebrews did not mean that God approved the institution.[12] Although a few other abolitionists—and cautious emancipationists—were willing to follow Wisner, far more took Weld's route in trying to best the defenders of slavery at their own game. Many of the latter ended, as Weld himself did, in skepticism or, more commonly, with Albert Barnes, by conceding exegesis of particular passages to proslavery and moving on to show how the Bible's general spirit overcame its occasional letter.

These moves, however, were disconcerting to many Americans, for they shifted the ground on which interpretation took place. The way in which debate over the Bible regularly broke down into conflict between the liberating spirit of Scripture and detailed exegesis of its individual passages was well illustrated in an 1845 debate in Cincinnati between two local Presbyterian ministers. Jonathan Blanchard defended the position that the Bible contradicted slavery, N. L. Rice the opposite. In making his case, Blanchard held that the antislave principle "blazes from every page of God's Book which is a wall of fire around the rights of the poor." The principle of "simple justice to the laboring poor" also "blazes on every page of the Bible from Genesis to Revelation, yet he [Rice] vaunts his eagerness to bring this discussion to the words of Holy Scripture, as if that blessed book contained no justice for men compelled to work without hire!" This chain of reasoning led Blanchard to declaim a great paean to Scripture: "Oh thou blessed charter of human hope! Thou sweet pole-star to the voyager of life! (addressing the Bible which lay on the stand before the speakers,) thou bright beam of the ineffable effulgence of God! would they dive into thy glorious brightness to draw from this charter of human liberty, their title deed of slavery?"[13]

Against this rhetorical onslaught, Rice was entirely unfazed. Instead he stuck to the same texts that Thornton Stringfellow later cited. This strategy allowed Rice to heap scorn on his opponent for Blanchard's supposed "biblical" attack on slavery. Rice was, he said, "disappointed by the course [Blanchard] has thought proper to pursue. . . . I did suppose, that what he calls his 'direct argument' would be a *Bible argument*; but I have heard nothing adduced from the inspired volume." Rice's challenge, to which Blanchard did not rise, was blunt: "Let him shew from the Bible, that the Patriarchs did not hold slaves: let him prove from that authority, that there were no slaves in the apostolic churches; that the Apostles excluded slave-holders from the church of God. Let him prove these things, and we will give up the question. After debating twelve hours, this has not been done. Nothing bearing on the question we are discussing, has been adduced either from the Old Testament or from the New."[14]

In debates like this one between Blanchard and Rice, all-out defenders of American slavery enjoyed several advantages. In a democratic environment where the Bible was widely respected, their first move was to ask people to read individual texts for themselves. They also enjoyed an immense advantage thanks to radical abolitionists like Garrison, who were abandoning the Bible for what he too considered its sanction of slavery. Even if there existed only a few such radicals, their arguments carried great weight because they agreed that proslavery advocates were properly interpreting the Scriptures. Radicals could be easily countered for dismissing the Bible, but they were a treasure to proslavery forces by how they understood the book they dismissed.

All who wished to use the Bible in antebellum America for arguing in any way against slavery faced a double burden of staggering dimensions. It was the same whether they held that the letter of the Bible should give way to its spirit, or if they claimed that what the Bible seemed to teach it did not really teach, or if they suggested that what the Bible taught did not apply to the American situation and its system of slavery. Any who wished to make such arguments first had to execute the delicate intellectual task of showing that literal proslavery interpretations did not adequately exegete the apparently straightforward biblical texts. Then they were compelled to perform an intellectual high-wire act by demonstrating why arguments against slavery should not be regarded as infidel attacks on the authority of the Bible itself. In assessing the nature of biblical arguments on all sides, it is essential to remember that the overwhelming public attitude toward the Bible in the antebellum United States—even by those who neither read it or heeded it—was one of reverential, implicit deference. The moderate Congregationalist Leonard Bacon caught the essential predicament perfectly, as early as 1846, when he wrote that "the evidence that there were both slaves and masters of slaves in the churches founded and directed by the apostles, cannot be got rid of without resorting to *methods of interpretation which will get rid of everything.*" To Bacon, the well-intentioned and even Bible-honoring advocates who "torture the Scriptures into saying that which the anti-slavery theory requires them to say" did more harm to the Bible than "the violence put upon the sacred records by High Churchmen, or by Universalists."[15]

By the start of the war, the question had become acute. The point to which the debate had come is indicated by the collection of fast sermons published in early 1861, which gathered together addresses from both South and North.[16] The book included sermons from leading clergymen like the South's James Henley Thornwell and the North's Henry Ward Beecher, as well as from regional and denominational leaders who were not as well known. From the record of these sermons, it is evident that proslavery advocates had largely succeeded in winning the battle for the Bible.

The South's leading theologian, James Henley Thornwell of Columbia, South Carolina, could treat the matter as a foregone conclusion: "That the relation betwixt the slave and his master is not inconsistent with the word of God, we have long since settled. . . . We cherish the institution not from avarice, but from principle."[17] When theologians did bend to rehearse the exegesis supporting slavery, that exegesis came from *Northerners,* whose fear of the religious havoc wreaked by Bible-scorning abolitionists was greater than their worry about the social damage caused by inappropriate application of a biblically sanctioned slavery. Thus, Henry J. Van Dyke of the First Presbyterian Church in Brooklyn hammered home the relevant texts from Exodus, Leviticus, and the Pauline epistles with one hand. With the other he belted the abolitionists. As Van Dyke saw it, Albert Barnes's efforts to explain away 1 Timothy 6:1–5 ("Let as many servants as are under the yoke count their own masters worthy of all honour. . . . If any man teach otherwise . . . he is proud, knowing nothing") said more about Barnes than about American slavery: "They illustrate the power of fanaticism to embitter the heart. . . . These extracts illustrate most pitiably how fanaticism warps the human intellect." More generally, Van Dyke concluded on the basis of his straightforward biblical interpretation that "this tree of Abolitionism is evil, and only evil—root and branch, flower and leaf, and fruit; . . . it springs from, and is nourished by, an utter rejection of the Scriptures. . . . Abolitionism leads, in multitudes of cases, and by a logical process, to utter infidelity."[18]

Van Dyke's proslavery exegesis received notable support from an unusual quarter. Rabbi M. J. Raphall of the Jewish Synagogue in New York City used the Scriptures to defend not only the propriety of slavery but also the curse of Ham as an explanation for the enslavement of specifically African Americans. According to Raphall, only "the Biblical critics called Rationalists who deny the possibility of prophecy" argued against a modern application of that curse. Raphall felt he was simply following the scriptural evidence where it led: "I do not attempt to build up a theory, nor to defend the moral government of Providence. I state facts." Against arguments by antislave advocates like Henry Ward Beecher, Raphall could only ask, "Is slaveholding condemned as a sin in sacred Scripture? . . . How this question can at all arise in the mind of any man that has received a religious education, and is acquainted with the history of the Bible, is a phenomenon I cannot explain to myself."[19]

In the face of such onslaughts, antislave biblicists continued to struggle. Professor Taylor Lewis of New York conceded that Van Dyke was correct on the superficial exegesis of the Bible. But Lewis thought he could reason his way around superficial conclusions by appealing to the Bible's spirit: "There is, however, something in the more interior spirit of those texts that he fails to see; he does not take the apostles' standpoint; he does not take into view the vastly changed condition of the world; he does not seem to consider that whilst truth is fixed, . . . its application to distant ages, and differing circumstances, is so varying continually that a wrong direction given to the more truthful exegesis may convert it into the more malignant falsehood." Lewis held that slavery in the American South was a very different institution from that which prevailed in ancient Israel, that Van Dyke had missed "the character and purposes of God" in his nearsighted attention to passages from Leviticus, and that the New Testament was speaking about masters "ruling" rather than "owning" slaves.[20]

In its subtlety, Lewis's argument did not represent the main antislave position. That more typical stance, however, entailed the very attitudes toward the Bible that the conservatives feared. In the volume of fast-day sermons, Henry Ward Beecher of Brooklyn's Plymouth Congregational Church was the featured advocate of this position. Through the war years, Beecher (1813–1887), scion of America's most notable Protestant clan, beloved pastor of a thriving middle-class congregation, and a publishing phenomenon with almost as many readers as his sister Harriet, was at the height of his powers.[21] Yet in this instance he faltered. Instead of straightforward exegesis, such as the proslavery defenders presented, or of the subtle hermeneutic of Professor Lewis, Beecher blustered. Although he admitted that professionals should not usually criticize each other publicly, he nonetheless could not resist the urge:

> [I would] lift up my voice, with all my heart and soul, against any man who, professing to be ordained to preach, preaches out of Christ's Gospel the doctrines of human bondage. When the Bible is opened that all the fiends of hell may, as in a covered passage, walk through it to do mischief on the earth, I say, blessed be infidels! . . . Where a man takes the Bible and lays it in the path over which men are attempting to walk from Calvary up to the gate of heaven— I declare that I will do by the Bible what Christ did by the temple: I will take a whip of cords, and I will drive out of it every man that buys and sells men, women, and children; and if I cannot do that, I will let the Bible go, as God let the temple go, to the desolating armies of its adversaries. . . . I should like no better amusement than to answer the sermons of men who attempt to establish the right of slavery out of the Bible. It would be simple butchery![22]

The most telling indication of the weakness of Beecher's own position was that, although he said it would be an easy thing to refute the proslavery biblical arguments, he did not adduce even a single text to that end.

Here, then, was the situation with the Bible and slavery on the eve of the war, and here it stood throughout the war. In theological terms, what was in fact a wide-ranging debate looked like it could be reduced to a forced dichotomy—either orthodoxy and slavery, or heresy and antislavery. On the one side of the forced choice, a theologian could maintain traditional views of the Bible and either actively promote slavery alongside influential Southern voices or, with conservatives North and South, take the slightly more moderate position of simply accepting slavery as reflecting a divine ordinance. On the other side of the forced choice, a theologian could indeed attack slavery as a sin. But this path could be chosen only by advancing one of two unappealing solutions: either abandon the traditional authority of the Bible in favor of the kind of romantic humanism promoted by the radical abolitionists, or—with Albert Barnes, Henry Ward Beecher, Jonathan Blanchard, and like-minded biblicists—drastically modify the hermeneutical practices that had become second nature in much of the United States.

For observers early in the twenty-first century, it might seem that adherents of mediating views should have been in a stronger position. Especially inviting are positions that maintain traditional views of the Bible about kidnapping, the inviolability of marriage, and parental responsibility for children, and then attack slavery as, at the minimum, an inexpedient, sinfully infused institution that, though allowed under the conditions of the biblical worlds, should be ended as soon as possible.[23] But such opinions, though they had noteworthy adherents like Professor Lewis and the early Albert Barnes, carried little weight. The reasons for their ineffectiveness were cultural. They seemed to cede authority to interpretive elites, they privileged nonliteral interpretations over the literal, they called into question the relevance of biblical passages for contemporary moral direction, and they looked like a way station to infidelity. Despite the protests of many at the time, the question was never just the nature of the Bible as such but always and everywhere the nature of the Bible-as-read in the history of a Protestant (and white) America, where during the previous century a massively democratized effort had been carried out to convert the new nation for Christ.

In fact, as described at length in the next chapter, there always existed more than three possible responses to the dilemma posed by the biblical record on slavery. That there seemed to be only three positions shows that the debate over the Bible and slavery was more than an exegetical debate, that it was always a question of who had the power to dictate how the Bible should be interpreted and who had no voice in shaping the accepted canons of interpretation. The issue from first to last was an issue of cultural hermeneutics as well as biblical exegesis.

The hermeneutical situation, in turn, can be explained by reference to the larger history of the early United States. The religious energy of the men and women who had built the evangelical churches and contributed so much to constructing American national culture came from implicit trust in the Bible as the Word of God. It grew from believers who held that all of the Bible's teachings, narratives, and even poetry were directly relevant to their immediate experience. And it was fueled by the conviction that Scripture was best interpreted by ordinary people using their common sense for themselves.

When, however, the crisis over slavery emerged, axioms with respect to Scripture that had provided so much energy and a considerable measure of unity no longer worked. The prime difficulty was that biblical arguments about slavery were taking place in a society where intuitive convictions about racial difference were embraced with every bit of the commonsense certainty as prevailed for the use of Scripture. The effort to square commonsense axioms about race with complete loyalty to the Bible required a choice between common sense and the Bible. This, however, was a choice that the early history of the United States had made very difficult. This antebellum situation illustrates exactly the judgment of a modern philosopher, Nicholas Wolterstorff, that "interpretation of Scripture is always caught up within a broader interpretation of reality and experience and responsibility, in one way or another grounding that larger interpretation. What is handed over and appropriated always constitutes a *vision of meaning*," as well as a set of specific readings from the Bible.[24]

Crisis

The hermeneutical crisis of the Civil War—the crisis arising from the full deployment for more than two generations of a common set of Reformed and literal assumptions about how to read, interpret, and apply the Scriptures— was a crisis on two levels. The obvious crisis that bore directly on the fate of the nation was that "simple" readings of the Bible yielded violently incommensurate understandings of Scripture, with no means, short of warfare, to adjudicate the differences. The more subtle crisis grew from efforts at theological formation and threatened the foundations of American theological reasoning more generally.

Because of the way Reformed and literal interpretations of the Bible had empowered ordinary people and their leaders in creating a Christian civilization, that hermeneutic enjoyed immense implicit authority. An obvious problem by the late 1850s, however, was that this wonderfully energizing use of Scripture had created multiple, conflicting Christian civilizations. Two cultures, purporting to read the Bible the same way, were at each other's throats. Each interpreted Scripture by canons deeply embedded in American experience. Yet interpretive chaos was the result.

If within the dominant interpretative framework of the period, proslavery won the exegetical battle, no Bible-believing abolitionist would admit it. Moreover, many moderates who felt that the Bible tolerated slavery were rapidly and easily converted to some form of abolitionism once war itself was declared and a chorus of influential voices—including President Lincoln and

Protestants from other lands—convinced them that the survival of the Union depended upon the ending of slavery.[25] The Reformed, literal hermeneutic had helped build a biblical civilization—actually, two biblical civilizations. But the hermeneutic itself could not reconcile the divergent interpretations it had produced.

Once again Henry Ward Beecher's assertions from his fast-day sermon of 4 January 1861 are pertinent. At the time he made this speech, the celebrated son of Lyman Beecher and brother of the noted Harriet and Catharine Beecher was the best-known and perhaps the most respected minister in the North. In his address, Beecher gave classic expression to the deeply ingrained belief that the Bible, if simply left alone, would interpret itself. Most of the great themes that had created the dominant hermeneutic underlying the dominant American theology went into his hymn to the liberating power of the Scriptures. His words were thick with the vocabulary of republicanism, fear of Roman Catholicism, pride in American exceptionalism, and confidence in the common sense of ordinary people. It was, in every respect but one, a remarkable statement:

> Now what has been the history of the Book but this: that wherever you have had an untrammeled Bible, you have had an untrammeled people; and that wherever you have had a trammeled Bible, you have had a trammeled people? Where you have had a Bible that the priests interpreted, you have had a king: where you have had a Bible that the common people interpreted; where the family has been the church; where father and mother have been God's ordained priests; where they have read its pages freely from beginning to end without gloss or commentary, without the church to tell them how, but with the illumination of God's Spirit in their hearts; where the Bible has been in the household, and read without hindrancy by parents and children together—there you have had an indomitable yeomanry, a state that would not have a tyrant on the throne, a government that would not have a slave or a serf in the field. Wherever the Bible has been allowed to be free; wherever it has been knocked out of the king's hand, and out of the priest's hand, it has carried light like the morning sun, rising over hill and vale, round and round the world; and it will do it again![26]

The one problem with this paean to the American Bible was that it was not true. Nowhere in the world as of 4 January 1861 was the Bible freer and more open to the public than in the United States of America; nowhere did less authority from tyrants, prelates, or priests constrict the meanings that ordinary men and women took from the Bible; and nowhere in the world did more pious believers hold that the Holy Scriptures sanctioned the institution of slavery.

The theological crisis signaled by antithetical interpretations of Scripture centered on the adequacy of the Bible itself. Although the United States had become one of the most ostensibly Christian societies on the face of the earth, the Civil War's division of the country's ardent Bible believers called into question the reputation of the Bible as an omnicompetent, infallible authority for life now and forever, at least as that adequacy had been formulated by

Protestants since the Reformation. Foreign observers routinely looked upon religion in the United States as the logical end product of this Protestant trajectory. Michael Chevalier, for instance, had observed in 1839 that in the United States, "under the influence of Protestantism and republicanism, the social progress has been effected by the medium of the spirit of individuality; for protestantism, republicanism, and individuality are all one."[27] But some from abroad also wondered if this trajectory was as beneficial as Americans regularly took it to be. For the history of theology, the issue was whether the war offered conclusive demonstration of the Roman Catholic assertion, dating back to the Reformation era, that to give the Bible to everyone was to take it away from everyone.[28]

The Civil War confronted American theologians with the need to show how an authoritative Bible could be retained in a republican, individualistic polity. Given the violently tragic results of the Reformed, literal hermeneutic being played out in the battlefields of the war, it would have seemed natural for serious Protestants to be explaining why efforts at saving the nation (Union or Confederate) should also include efforts at reestablishing the common authority of Scripture. As it happens, sectional controversy and the war did lead to the articulation—or at least the anticipation—of several alternatives to the Reformed, literal hermeneutic. But none of them ever came to enjoy the cultural predominance of the earlier consensus.

The most radical alternative was to abandon, usually by default rather than by direct attack, the Bible in any traditional sense.[29] But this move, though increasingly common among intellectual elites, went far beyond what most Americans could accept.

An attempt that did enjoy considerable support was the move from the Bible's letter to its spirit, which was practiced, to one degree or another, by Jonathan Blanchard, Albert Barnes, Henry Ward Beecher, and Gerrit Smith. The terminus ad quem for such Bible interpreters was the theological liberalism of the last third of the twentieth century. The process was well described by Lyman Abbott, Henry Ward Beecher's assistant and then successor at Brooklyn's Plymouth Church. As an old man, Abbott looked back on the course of his shifting attitudes toward Scripture. Through early years as a pastor in New England, he held to the old view of verbal inspiration. But then he grew increasingly troubled by "the moral problems which this [older] view of the Bible involves." Chief among these moral problems was the question "What answer should I give to the Biblical arguments for slavery and polygamy?" Abbott did have a response—"I could accept Christ's interpretations of the permission of polygamy as a statesman's concession to the passions and prejudices of a primitive people, and could apply the same principle of the permission but curtailment and regulation of slavery." But that process of reasoning about the Bible soon led to a much more liberal understanding of Christianity as a whole: "The foundation of spiritual faith is neither in the Church nor in the Bible, but in the spiritual consciousness of man."[30] The debate over slavery was not necessarily the only factor pushing Abbott in a liberal direction, but it was a factor.[31]

Reasoning that led to such liberal theological conclusions was present in the United States from the 1840s and became even more prominent in the decades after the war.[32] But much more prevalent were efforts by the biblically orthodox to save both traditional views of Scripture and historic theological positions built from a traditional use of the Bible.[33] At least three barriers, however, placed a daunting challenge before such orthodox efforts. Publicity devoted to the liberal move to the Bible's spirit made it seem as if the older literalism was the only alternative to the newer views. Similarly, the orthodox were also daunted by eighteenth-century precedents. In the British world with which American theologians were most familiar, the best-known history of that earlier era (published in 1860) suggested that, when Protestants retreated from literal views of Scripture, their only alternatives were "Church-authority, the Spirit [i.e., enthusiasm], or Reason"[34]—all destinations that orthodox Americans considered abhorrent.

The third barrier to an orthodox, but nonliteral, view of Scripture was the highest. With relentless pressure, skillful defenders of slavery insisted that any attack on a literalist construction of biblical slavery was an attack on the Bible itself. A clear example of this strategy appeared in James Henley Thornwell's fast sermon of 21 November 1860. Thornwell (1812–1862) was widely recognized as a theologian of integrity, probably the South's most highly respected religious thinker.[35] He had been active in his native South Carolina as pastor, college teacher, and seminary professor from the time of his ordination in 1835. Thornwell was an eclectic thinker whose deep grounding in the Scriptures, commitment to the Westminster standards, and suspicion of generically evangelical voluntary societies was combined with a smattering of Scottish philosophy but also serious reservations about the egalitarian tendencies of the new moral philosophy. When he addressed a blue-ribbon audience in Columbia in the immediate aftermath of Abraham Lincoln's 1860 election, a good portion of his sermon was devoted to denouncing the idea that African Americans constituted a species distinct from Caucasians. On this basis he boldly chastised his audience of elite South Carolinians for not treating slaves properly as fellow human beings.

Yet Thornwell's additional concern was to make a point for Northern readers. When he described the opinion that humanity was made up of several species, each with its own origin, and then denounced this view as heresy, his more distant target came into view: "It is as idle to charge the responsibility of the doctrine about the diversity of species upon slaveholders, as to load them with the guilt of questioning the geological accuracy of Moses." He then drove home the polemical dagger. Heretical teachings questioning the Bible's account of a common human origin as well as heretical teachings questioning the Bible's account of the age of the earth indicated clearly the kind of teaching that questioned the slavery found in both Old and New Testaments. Heresies concerning Adam and Eve as well as on the geological record "are assaults of infidel science upon the records of our faith, and both have found their warmest advocates among the opponents of slavery."[36] To audiences predisposed toward biblical literalism, Thornwell's reasoning was persuasive.

To propose for whatever reason that the Bible did not sanction slavery was to attack not just slavery but the Bible as well.

The theological crisis occasioned by reasoning like Thornwell's was acute. Many Northern Bible-readers and not a few in the South *felt* that slavery was evil. They somehow *knew* the Bible supported them in that feeling. Yet when it came to using the Bible as it had been used with such success to evangelize and civilize the United States, the sacred page was snatched out of their hands. Trust in the Bible and reliance upon a Reformed, literal hermeneutic had created a crisis that only bullets, not arguments, could resolve.

Views from Abroad

Powerful as the orthodox defense of slavery seemed in the United States, however, its force came from the specific conditions of American culture. It had virtually no influence outside the country, even among those who shared the conservative theology of slavery's defenders. A preliminary survey of Protestant writings on the American Civil War from England, Scotland, and Canada has turned up almost no support for Thornwell's biblical reasoning on slavery, although the same sources reveal considerable antagonism to the North and much political sympathy for the South.[37] Even among Thornwell's fellow Presbyterians abroad, some of whom held to a form of the Regulative Principle as rigorous as Thornwell's, there was only contempt for efforts to defend Southern slavery on the basis of the Bible.

Canadian Presbyterians, who in this era were usually traditionalist or evangelical, were frankly underwhelmed by the biblical defense of slavery. In September 1864 the main periodical for the largest Presbyterian church in British North America hailed with satisfaction the triumph of radical abolitionist views.[38] Somewhat earlier appeared an even more telling testimony, this time from the Maritimes. In September 1862 a Presbyterian editor went out of his way to describe Southern victories as well-deserved comeuppance for the aggressive North, but this same editor also published a short article on the curse of Ham in order to ridicule it as a justification for slavery.[39]

The clearest Canadian indication of the limitations of Thornwell's reasoning came from the Free Church of Canada, a Presbyterian denomination formed in sympathy with the Free Church of Scotland and very much disposed to the Old School theology provided by conservative American Presbyterians. Canadian Free Presbyterians were wary of American New School Presbyterians because (with objections that Thornwell shared) the New School seemed weak on "the extent of the atonement, and the imputation of guilt and righteousness in the Adamic and Christian covenants." But these conservative Canadian Presbyterians, who hewed so closely to a high view of Scripture in their ancestral confessions, also felt that the American Old School Presbyterians were far too equivocal in their toleration of slavery.[40] Thornwell, the Presbyterian exegete, made sense in Canada, but not Thornwell, the exegetical defender of slavery.

The established Kirk in Scotland remained largely silent on the war, but the two other main divisions of Scottish Presbyterianism—among whom were many whose views on the Bible and the Regulative Principle were as conservative as Thornwell's—scorned the notion that the Bible could justify slavery. As the war began, the journal of Scotland's United Presbyterians lamented the fact that "by neither of the combatants is the cause of negro emancipation adopted. Yet the only hope of good from this fraternal strife would be realized, if the blacks were to obtain their individual freedom and their personal right to claim all the privileges asserted in the American 'Declaration of Independence.'" Early Southern victories were an occasion to state the matter of slavery as clearly as possible. The editor noted that the Confederate states "unblushingly proclaim that slavery is to be the normal condition of this southern millennium which they are about to introduce; and that they, as the superior race, are bound by the law of Divine Providence to keep the sons and daughters of Africa in perpetual bondage." To the Scottish observer, these views were sacrilegious nonsense: "Our sympathies cannot go with the Southern States, who, in the second half of the nineteenth century, are proclaiming a doctrine, the foulest and most revolting that has ever been enunciated since our blessed Redeemer hung upon the cross of shame, and bore away the sins of the world. Sympathy with the Southern States! We have as much sympathy with them as with a gang of robbers or a crew of pirates."[41] Scotland's Free Presbyterian Church joined in almost as energetically to attack the notion that there could be a theological justification for American slavery.[42] The same was true of the English Presbyterians, who viewed the conflict as caused by slavery, for which they had no sympathy whatsoever.[43]

Such foreign Presbyterians reflected little of the Northern moderates' fear that they would look like antibiblical infidels for questioning the legitimacy of slavery. Yet these foreign Presbyterians were also evangelical biblicists who, while sharing Thornwell's theological principles, repudiated the racial, social, and economic contexts upon which the force of Thornwell's hermeneutic depended.

Only in an environment where the principles of the American hermeneutic prevailed could Thornwell's reasoning have carried such weight.[44] The limited appeal of Thornwell's biblical arguments to foreigners does not, however, alter the fact of their power in the United States. Those Americans who attempted to show how one might be both orthodox on Scripture and yet not a practitioner of literalist exegesis had to address the same audiences that Thornwell addressed and also speak out of the same universe of meaning from which he spoke.

To be sure, other Christian constituencies in the United States were trying to evade the forced choice of biblical proslavery versus heterodox antislavery. Their efforts, and the reason for their ultimate failure, are the subject of the next chapter. Here it is important to conclude that the civil war over Scripture did as much to damage the American theology that had taken shape since the early days of the republic as the shooting war did to the body politic.

20 ✴ —————————————————————————

Failed Alternatives

Rivals to the Reformed, literal hermeneutic were always present during the national and antebellum periods. Brief examination of some of those alternatives, along with speculation as to why they could not compete with the dominant mode of biblical interpretation, is useful for several reasons. It reveals from the angle of opposition why the standard hermeneutic was so dominant, but it also suggests something about the great quantity of important theological labor going on outside the mainstream defined by the era's most visible churches and church leaders. Most important, while the crises of the Civil War era revealed how strikingly pervasive Christian public discourse had become since the time of the Revolution, they revealed even more clearly how tightly that Christianity had been linked to commonsense and republican habits of thought. Only that earlier history, as it turns out, can explain adequately why in the anguished and angry debate over Scripture, common sense about race so effectively dominated America's hard-won trust in the Bible.

Doubts about the self-evident character of populist biblical interpretation were not lacking in this period, even if they never were particularly persuasive to most of those who put the Bible to use for public purposes. In 1819 a Methodist complained about effects on the frontier, where religious entrepreneurs without number claimed to follow no creed but the Bible: "It would appear that their bible was to be their only rule and guide in faith and practice; but it was, in fact, turning every one foot-loose, as every individual had an equal right to put his own construction, in order to answer his own purposes, on every question, as to doctrine or government. . . . [T]hey ran wild."[1]

A similar, but more sophisticated, complaint of monograph length came from John W. Nevin in 1849 when he rounded on what he called the sect system. According to Nevin, "This professed regard for the Bible" was what "distinguishes the sects in general." But to Nevin the difficulty in that profession was as manifest as it was stupendous: "If the Bible be at once so clear and full as a formulary of Christian doctrine and practice, how does it come to pass that where men are left most free to use it in this way . . . they are flung asunder so perpetually . . . instead of being brought together?" This anomaly showed that the principle of "no creed but the Bible" was "absurd and impracticable"; it breathed "the spirit of hypocrisy and sham." The end result of acting as if everyone could interpret the Bible simply on their own was irrational excess, hypocritical tyranny where leaders imposed eccentric opinions on followers, and a spirit of rationalism that treated the Bible as a mere compendium of rules.[2] Horace Bushnell was expressing something of the same complaint at just about the same time in his *God in Christ,* when he wrote about the contradiction he saw between American attitudes toward the Bible and American practices with Scripture: "Not allowing ourselves to be rationalists *over* the scriptures, we have yet been as active and confident rationalists *under* them, as it was possible to be."[3]

Only shortly before Nevin and Bushnell aired these opinions, a public voice new to Christian proclamation had chimed in with much the same intent. Orestes Brownson, who was on the verge of leaving behind a checkered career as Protestant, freethinker, and transcendentalist for the Roman Catholic Church, issued a challenge to American Bible-believers in his new role as a Catholic apologist: "We are . . . never in a condition to rely on the Bible alone. We never go to it wholly devoid of preliminary instructions, and therefore of prepossessions." Given this circumstance, as Brownson saw the matter, "for the most part, when we do come to study the Bible, we find little else in it than the faith, we have brought to it, so that we may be said to put our faith into the Bible, not to obtain our faith from it." Thus, Episcopalians find Episcopacy in Scripture, Unitarians do not find the Trinity, and so on. In sum, "Our prepossessions determine, even with the best intentions on our part, the meaning we attach to the words we read."[4] During the Civil War such a mainline figure as Charles Hodge, while not mentioning the Bible explicitly, still made a similar assessment of how geographic and ideological locations predisposed intellectual commitments. "Every man, and every body of men," he concluded when assessing the moral integrity of advocates from both North and South, "are more or less subject to the controlling influence of public opinion, and of the life of the community to which they belong."[5]

Yet all such words were too far from the mainstream, or in Hodge's case too general in their commentary, to revise the dominant hermeneutic. It would be some time before a prominent theologian from the mainstream could affirm as clearly as the conservative Presbyterian William G. T. Shedd would say in 1890: The "appeal to Scripture is only an appeal to Scripture as the reviser understands it. 'Scripture' properly means the interpretation of Scripture; that is, the contents of Scripture as reached by human investigation and exegesis."[6]

If it was difficult in such a setting to gain purchase for orthodox alternatives to the dominant hermeneutic, at least four such alternatives nevertheless existed. None of the four ever exerted much influence on public theology, but each did articulate a hermeneutic that, while at odds with American Reformed literalism, still preserved the authority of the Bible and the orthodoxy of the faith. As such, these alternative hermeneutics also opened possibilities, even for conservatives who were not seeking such a possibility, for using an orthodox, authoritative Bible against, rather than for, slavery.

The most radical alternative to Reformed literalism was offered by the least noticed theological voices of the day, African Americans; the most offensive to Protestant sensibilities came from American representatives of the Roman Catholic Church; the most innocuous arose from Lutheran and German Reformed high-church Protestants; and the one with the most chance of working as an alternative came from Northern and border-state Reformed conservatives caught between asserting and compromising the literalistic hermeneutical principles of their American evangelical confreres. Why all of these alternative hermeneutics gave way before commonsense affirmations about race is the last subject treated in this chapter.

African Americans

African-American Christians were as likely to be champions of the Bible only and of biblical literalism as their white contemporaries. Daniel Alexander Payne (1811–1893), leading bishop of the African Methodist Episcopal Church and the most formidable African-American theologian of his day, gave way to no white preacher in proclaiming the sole sufficiency of Scripture: "The only safe guide for a man or woman, young or old, rich or poor, learned or unlearned, priest or people is the Bible, the whole Bible, nothing but the Bible."[7] When Payne preached in Washington, D.C., on 16 April 1862, to celebrate the ending of slavery in the nation's capital, he exhorted his black congregation in the commonplace terms of the American popular religion: "*Rest not till you have learned to read the Bible.* 'Tis the greatest, the best of books. In it is contained the Divine law. O! meditate therein by day and by night."[8]

Many African-American believers also readily adopted features of the standard hermeneutic, especially its literalism and easy bonding with republican values. As the insurrectionist Nat Turner illustrated, slaves too could take the apocalyptic parts of the Bible as literally as any white.[9] Frederick Douglass, the former slave who became a leading abolitionist orator, journalist, and publisher, resembled the great host of Caucasian believers who held that the United States was a chosen nation and that republican language provided the best way of expressing its privileged status under God.[10] In 1863 a free black from Washington, D.C., John W. Menard, wrote to Douglass's newspaper to argue that republican principles were so interwoven with white American racism that blacks should simply give them up: "The grand plea of the 'great American people' is republicanism and the perpetuity of *white nationality*. . . . Republicanism is the family god of the American people; it is their all—their meat and bread and religion. . . . The inherent principle of the *white majority* of this nation is to refuse FOREVER republican equality to the black minority. . . . The prosperity and happiness of our race and their posterity lay [*sic*] in a separation from the white race." But Douglass would hear nothing of it: "There is the same reason for believing that black and white races of men can live justly and peaceably together in the same country, as that they can so live in the same world."[11]

Similarities to white counterparts notwithstanding, African Americans often deviated from the principles of Reformed, literalist exegesis. The reasons for that deviation were as complex as the general factors shaping African-American religion. For Christians who had regularly been discouraged from efforts to read the Bible, who sustained expressive forms of African ritual practice, and who developed in the spiritual an indigenous narrative theology, habitual use of the Scriptures did not fit easily into the categories of commonsense, republican, nationalistic (and white) exegesis.[12] Rather, the hermeneutical practice of African Americans often featured the Bible as a source of prophecy, magic, conjuring, and dreams; the Bible as a dramatic, narrative book; and the Bible as a volume of grand, inspiring themes instead of ethically oriented verses.

In the first instance, as Theophus Smith has documented, African-American believers retained in their Christian usage features of prophetic religion and formulary magic that adapted the written text to African traditions.[13] It thus posed no difficulty for Daniel Payne, who promoted the Bible as ardently as the strictest Old School Presbyterian, also to find as much inspiration from dreams as the most radical Methodist.[14]

Alternatively, blacks put the Bible to use dramaturgically. Frederick Douglass more than once gave full vent to his frustration with religious reasoning in defense of slavery. In October 1860 he wrote that "the Northern people have but a faint conception of the intensity with which Southern religion clings to the fleshless skeleton of a theological system." In his view the dominant religion combined "now a thread of truth, and then a thread of absurdity in most inexplicable confusion." That confused doctrinal Christianity "has usurped, in the gospel of the South, the place of justice, mercy, and purity. . . . A belief in the five points of Calvin, and in the divine character of slavery is the standard by which every man's godliness is to be tried." Douglass's means of refuting this error, however, was not counterexegesis but a story recounting how a pious slaveholding mistress had unmercifully beat a nine-month-old slave child for a trivial offense.[15] In his Washington, D.C., sermon of 1862, Daniel Payne urged listeners to pray for the success of federal arms so as to hasten total elimination of slavery. But he drove home the point, not by quoting biblical passages commanding the duty of prayer, but by telling the biblical story of Joshua praying for the sun to stand still and the story of John Knox praying for the success of the Protestant gospel in Reformation Scotland.[16]

African Americans also regularly approached the Bible as a source of grand themes rather than for verse-by-verse instruction in experiential particulars—that is, to use white categories, more like Lutherans than the Reformed. So it was that specially preferred biblical passages came to dominate use of the whole Bible, like Psalm 68:31, which has been called "without doubt the most quoted verse in black religious history"—"Princes shall come out of Egypt and Ethiopia shall stretch out her hands unto God";[17] or Acts 17:26 (God "made of one blood all nations of men for to dwell on all the face of the earth").[18]

Frederick Douglass illustrates the way this alternative biblicism could work. Much more than most whites who honored the Bible, he was an apocalyptic, millennial thinker in the mold of Nat Turner or John Brown.[19] When Douglass reviewed G. W. Brownlow's *Ought American Slavery to Be Perpetuated?* (1858) and its use of Scripture to defend the institution, he made a two fold response. He first ridiculed the performance by saying that Brownlow merely "culled out and grouped together sundry passages of Scripture, which, by wresting them from their relations, would seem to countenance slavery." But then he sought to overwhelm Brownlow's exegesis by evoking an absurdity: When Brownlow "sees this noble, Christian missionary institution [of slavery], with all its Christ-like appliances of whips, chains, gags, thumbscrews, cat-o'-nine tails, fetters, and bloodhounds, assailed, he almost stands astonished and appalled by the awful depths of Abolition wickedness!"[20] Douglass did also publish in his newspaper a two-part exegetical refutation of the biblical argument for slavery, but it was a fairly weak example of the type, and it was by a white minister.[21]

In sum, African-American appropriation of Scripture featured (alongside literalist Reformed patterns) narrative, talismanic, and African ways of appropriating the sacred text. These approaches, though they provided great resilience to African-American believers, left the ground of rational exegetical argument to the Reformed literalism that seemed to lean strongly toward the justification of slavery. Even if African Americans had not been socially marginalized, the fact that this pattern of Bible reading diverged from the American norm doomed their biblicism, however orthodox, to irrelevance.

Roman Catholics

Though the numbers of Roman Catholics were rising rapidly by the 1860s, they still stood far from the center of American public influence.[22] Throughout the nineteenth century the Catholic church was oriented more toward sustaining a growing constituency of mixed European origin than toward exerting itself as an intellectual force. Yet as Catholics tended to innumerable practical needs, they also were negotiating with the dominant American ideologies as well. The character of those negotiations is nicely illustrated by positions taken by two of the most important leaders of the antebellum church. When John England (1786–1842), bishop of Charleston, South Carolina, promulgated in 1839 a "Constitution" for the Catholic churches of North Carolina, South Carolina, and Georgia, he led off his preface by asserting that "the positions of our church government are very like to those of the government of the Union" and by stressing that "the general legislative body of the church is a council composed of the representatives of each diocess [*sic*]" acting in proper democratic fashion. Only a few years later, by contrast, Bishop John Hughes (1797–1864) of New York complained about the "passion" and "violence" of America's dog-eat-dog competitive culture and traced the source of the nation's selfish individualism to the principles of Protestantism.[23] Even if such intra-Catholic observations had led to a well-organized, united voice of American Roman Catholic opinion, it is still unlikely that it would have been heard. Systematic Protestant fear of all things Catholic remained strong throughout the period, as anti-immigrant rioting of the 1840s and Catholic-baiting from the Know-Nothing Party indicated. Experiences of American Catholics before and during the Civil War did point to fuller participation in national cultural life but did not yet amount to such participation.[24]

If, however, American Protestants had been able to heed Catholics on the question of religious authority and the Bible, they would have found two different alternatives to the standard Reformed, literal hermeneutic. First, but important more for the twentieth century than the nineteenth, was the effort of John Henry Newman in Britain to show how a traditional doctrine of Roman Catholic permanence could accommodate organic change over time. Newman's *Essay on the Development of Christian Doctrine* was a difficult work when it was published in 1845, but it did offer a means to acknowledge the reality of slavery in the biblical era without holding to its legitimacy in the present. The book's contention for the possibility of change as a form of development might have offered a few American theologians a hint of parallel procedures for Protestants if they had not read the work simply as Roman Catholic propaganda.[25]

Far more common was a Catholic appeal to authority as a way of overcoming Protestant divisiveness. In most cases, to be sure, Catholic responses mostly paralleled Protestant in simply following the dictates of regional practice.[26] But on issues relating to sectional conflict, debate over slavery, and the Civil War, Catholic voices still posed a challenge to received American opinion, even if few public Americans were prepared at the time to notice.[27]

A Roman Catholic stance enabled at least a few Americans to reject what was eventually the common view that saw a benign providence brining good out of the national bloodbath. Shortly after the struggle began, the *Philadelphia Herald and Visitor* asserted boldly that God could not direct a war of this sort, since "God is not the author of sin and misery and therefore God cannot be the author of war." It was blasphemous to claim that God could be responsible for such carnage.[28]

Throughout the conflict several Catholics made more far-reaching claims with direct relevance to the use of Scripture. Such possibilities could be expressed on narrower theological questions by sophisticated thinkers like Orestes Brownson.[29] Or they could be occasions for Catholics to return some of the venom they had long received from American Protestants. The war, in the latter case, was described as arising, not from some grand clash of Right against Wrong, but more basically as an outgrowth from Protestant principles like private judgment, antiauthoritarianism, and the private interpretation of Scripture. In April 1865 the *New York Tablet* made the charge bombastically: "Protestantism is essentially rebellious; . . . its origin is the spirit of secession and revolt, . . . its history is but a chronicle of insurrection, and . . . , in short, sedition and mutiny are but fruits of the Lutheran leaven spreading under the special names of Liberty and Independence into all the ramifications of political, social and domestic life."[30]

The most impressive Catholic commentary on religious authority and the Civil War came, however, from a discerning foreign source as an essay from Rome published in January 1861. It appeared in the Jesuit periodical *Civiltà Cattolica* and may have been meant also as a comment on tumultuous forces then at work in Italian politics. The author expressed considerable sympathy for the United States in its time of trial. But he also highlighted the Protestant character of the United States as a prime factor in explaining the breakdown of political, moral, and social unity. The essay noted that in the crisis of the hour, "suddenly both parties have become theologians, the one side quoting the Pentateuch to justify slavery, the other side quoting the gospel to condemn it." Moreover, the American people had reached a state where they "cannot discuss a political matter without quoting the Old and New Testaments!" American confusion was thus a warning: it "should make those Catholics who want to separate religion from politics think again, as it should those libertines who continuously reproach the church for her interest in political matters." The *Civiltà Cattolica* author was sure he knew "the true cause of their great mistake . . . the principle that is dissolving a great union." Although the United States posesses "many elements of strength and endurance . . . , one element is missing—religious unity." The specifically Catholic convictions of the author pointed to a sure conclusion: "It is therefore impossible to have a reconciliation, because they are divided on a moral question, and moral questions are fundamentally grounded in religious dogma." From Rome, it was a sign of weakness that "both parties use biblical arguments to defend their rights." But the Catholic solution was clear:

> Supposing that these rights were assured by an authority respected by both parties. Then the Bible could come into the conflict not as a plaything, but as in a contest of truth over against falsehood. Would not such an authority perhaps have an almost invincible strength over the two parties, so that one would surrender or that both would be reconciled to each other? But in the States dogmas are very free, as are also moral principles, and everything in these spheres is mere probability. . . . Their independence makes it impossible to find a solution to their quarrel, both because they lack a central religious authority and because they lack moral honesty, which is itself a consequence of not having a central religious authority.[31]

The Roman Jesuit had made a serious point about the need, in the American environment, for a force above the democratic competition. But it was a point no American Protestant was willing to hear, even if *Civiltà Cattolica* was distributed fairly widely in the States, and some American Catholics made arguments of a similar sort. Intrinsic value notwithstanding, Roman Catholicism was too thoroughly "the Other" in an America where public religion was all but monopolized by evangelical, republican, and Catholic-fearing commitments. Whatever the American Civil War may have shown about the desirability of a magisterial interpretation of Scripture, most Americans were hardly in position to consider Rome as the source of that authority.

Churchly Protestants

Immigrant Lutherans and the high-church Mercersburg movement among the German Reformed offered another orthodox alternative to the literal, Reformed understanding of Scripture. By the time of the Civil War, the German Reformed had lost the momentum that for a few decades in the late-colonial period had made them one of the fastest growing denominations in America. Moreover, the self-consciously antirevivalist theology of Mercersburg Seminary, as expressed most sharply by John W. Nevin and then with great learning by his Swiss-born colleague Philip Schaff, never spoke for all, or even a majority of, the German Reformed. Lutheranism, in contrast, was burgeoning by the mid-nineteenth century. Rising tides of German immigration and the firstfruits of an impending Scandinavian harvest joined the increasingly vigorous churches of the colonial period to constitute a substantial Lutheran presence in several American regions by the era of the Civil War. The formation of the Lutheran General Synod in 1820, and then the establishment in 1826 of Gettysburg Theological Seminary, under the dynamic leadership of Samuel Schmucker, testified to the Lutherans' growing institutional maturity.[32]

Both Lutherans and the Mercersburg theologians had access to scriptural traditions that, while orthodox, did not replicate the standard American Reformed literalism. In particular, these "church Protestants" tended to approach the Bible as an organic whole. Following Martin Luther, Lutherans traditionally stressed the exercise of law and gospel in the Bible, thus asking how a passage illuminated the standing of the reader before God in sin or grace, instead of seeking immediately to discover its ethical implications for the believer. On the Continent, Lutherans had also developed a strong two-kingdoms theology in which a sharp divide was drawn between the proper business of the church in announcing sin and grace, and the proper business of the state in maintaining public order.[33] Early polemics with Calvinists over the meaning of the Lord's Supper, and later skirmishing with Anabaptists and Baptists on the question of who should be baptized and at what stage of life, had given the Lutherans, (who could indeed also cite literal chapter and verse when it suited their needs) a habit of defending their distinctive views on the real presence of Christ in the Lord's Supper and baptismal regeneration for infants as much from the general meaning of the whole Bible as from the dictate of any one text.

In America, the foundations for articulating such a hermeneutic had been laid early and well. As we saw in chapter 7, Henry Melchior Mühlenberg, patriarch of Lutheranism in North America, eventually became skilled in the use of English, but he did not Americanize his approach to Scripture or Lutheran traditions. Mühlenberg's successor as the leading American Lutheran, J. H. C. Helmuth, spoke out even more sharply than his predecessor about the need to retain Lutheran hermeneutics as well as Lutheran doctrine in the American sea of democratic individualism. In 1793 he registered a Lutheran protest to what, even at that time, was becoming the characteristic American approach to the Bible. Helmuth thought that it was "altogether harmful when someone reads his whims and fantasies into this holy book." This was, according to Helmuth, "to make a weathervane out of Scripture and so turn it in every direction of the imagination. . . . This is to play with the Bible as children play with a puppet. This is to explain Scripture as if the Holy Spirit must obey the bidding of the imagination of any old person, regardless of how confused. This is to make the Bible into a dark chaos." Treating the Bible like this meant for Helmuth that "the pure religion of Jesus is made an object of scorn and derision."[34]

After Helmuth, however, and before the massive German migrations of midcentury restored a stronger confessional emphasis, American Lutheran theology moved gradually in a more "American" direction.[35] Frederick Henry Quitman of New York City was among the leading American Lutherans in the generation after Helmuth, but he breathed a quite different spirit. Quitman's catechism and hymnal, both published in 1814, revealed much less confessionalism, much more Americanization. Instead of traditional Lutheran insistence on the self-authenticating power of the living Word (Christ) as discovered in the written word (Scripture), Quitman's catechism set out "the grounds that ought to constitute the basis of rational belief" as "either natural perception and experience; or the authority of competent witnesses; or finally, unquestioned arguments of reason." Only later did Quitman bring in the Scriptures, but then insisted that everything having to do with the Bible and its testimony to Jesus as the Son of God needed to "coincide with the dictates of reason."[36] Likewise, Quitman's hymnal featured Anglo-American tributes to the great designer of the moral universe more than the ardently trinitarian hymns that had been customary in hymnals prepared by Mühlenberg.[37]

In local situations during the first decades of the nineteenth century, Lutherans expressed the same tensions as Catholics over how far to follow American norms. On the ground in Pennsylvania, some of the Lutherans and Reformed eagerly embraced a Whig kind of American republicanism, while others held out for a more community-based traditionalism. The latter often were politically Democrats; their solicitude for old-world patterns of communal authority led them to resent the Whig Party's vision of a liberal republican community.[38] Because of these differences, battles among Lutherans over church government often had a thoroughly American sound, as when in 1831 the Western Pennsylvania Synod urged support for the denominational seminary at Gettysburg, since its presence testified "to a church whose organization agrees entirely with the republican principles of your government."[39]

Samuel Schmucker (1799–1873), the most prominent American Lutheran voice from the founding of Gettysburg Seminary until the confessional surge of the mid-1850s, pushed the process of Americanization further. By the mid-1830s Schmucker too was expressing high opinions of republican government and also championing the authority of commonsense reasoning. The work in which such opinions appeared was a popular apology written for those who might be suspicious of the Lutherans. It proceeded in what was by then the common American pattern by first considering "the intellectual structures of man, the extent of the religion of reason, and the evidences of revelation," before beginning "the discussion of the Christian doctrines" proper. The same work also stressed that "the Lutheran divines are strenuous advocates for liberty of thought, and free, untrammeled investigation of God's word," and that principles of "moral government" provided the best possible way of understanding the doctrine of election.[40] In later public appeals on behalf of the Lutheran faith, Schmucker made the same sort of adaptation to the standard American hermeneutic: theology, he held, was "to be governed entirely by the word of God, interpreted according to the correct principles of common sense, which is the only true system of Historical Exegesis." And literal exegesis could be set aside only "when the passage literally interpreted *contradicts natural reason, common sense,* or the testimony of our senses."[41] Schmucker is well known in American religious history for eventually proposing alterations to the Augsburg Confession that would have eliminated, or much reduced, the traditional Lutheran insistence on baptismal regeneration and the real presence of Christ in the Lord's Supper.[42] In making these proposals, he was following an American path that was proving successful in broadening the appeal of Lutheranism beyond its traditional ethnic constituencies. But as the Lutherans in America became more heavily influenced by immigration and by the conviction that Schmucker's moves watered down what was essential in their faith, his views fell from favor. Part of the reason for reaction was the growing unwillingness to give up the traditionally distinctive Lutheran hermeneutic for the more common American pattern.

For their part, the Mercersburg theologians remained sharper critics than Schmucker's Lutherans of American revivalistic individualism and as critics of what they called Puritan (i.e., woodenly literal) approaches to biblical doctrine.[43] As we have seen, Nevin held up an idiosyncratic blend of sixteenth-century Protestant confessionalism and nineteenth-century mediating romanticism as the antidote to American Protestant individualism. After Philip Schaff (1819–1893), fresh from study with Germany's conservative mediating theologians, joined Nevin in Pennsylvania, Mercersburg featured a respect for history and church traditions (including the Roman Catholic) otherwise unusual in American Protestantism.[44]

The result was a theology that, at least in principle, offered a churchly, sacramental, Christ-centered alternative to literal, Reformed exegesis. After Nevin had blasted "the sect system" in 1849/1850, he proposed as "the remedy" and "the only hope" for desperate times "the general resuscitation of a sound church feeling," which began "with its sense of catholicity itself."[45] On the eve of the sectional struggle, an author in the *Mercersburg Review* tried to put Nevin's principles into practice by showing how "synodical church authority" differed from both the Roman Catholic concentration of authority in a single person and the opposite mistake of American individualistic Protestantism, "which makes this power culminate in the people." On the basis of the theological foundation established by Nevin and Schaff, the author claimed that the synod, or corporate mind of a Protestant church, "is the final judge of error in doctrine, and error in conduct."[46]

With both the Mercersburg wing of the German Reformed and still to some extent the Lutherans, therefore, there existed an approach to the Bible and the exercise of Christian authority at odds with the axioms that otherwise prevailed so widely in American Protestantism. As the events of midcentury unfolded, however, this alternative remained hidden away in German-language enclaves or proved far less distinctive in the particular cases of slavery and sectional conflict than the background theories might have led one to expect. The Mercersburg theologians, it turned out, reasoned just like their Protestant fellows when it came to these specific issues—that is, they reasoned from Scripture and intuition rather than from the deliverances of a synod.[47] The presence in the abstract of a theological alternative to the Reformed, literal exegesis was no guarantee that this hermeneutic could actually function in the face of pressing circumstances.

A distinctive Lutheran approach to Scripture also remained virtually mute in public discussion. The process of Americanization had encouraged leaders like Schmucker, but also John Bachman of South Carolina, the leading Lutheran of his region, to adapt Lutheran distinctives for the assistance of broader Protestant purposes of evangelization and Christianization. Such moves came close to leaving Lutherans without a distinctly Lutheran contribution to public debate. Schmucker, for example, was an ardent backer of the Evangelical Alliance, a stalwart defender of temperance, and a consistent advocate of Sabbath observance; his strong antislave stance was of a piece with these Northern Whig positions. By contrast, Bachman, who in 1857 published the strongest Lutheran defense of slavery, reasoned on the issue more like a conservative republican Southern formalist than as a Lutheran.[48] For their part, the newer synods made up of more recent immigrants reasoned like the mainstream American formalists—since the Bible did not directly condemn slavery, neither would the conservative Norwegian Synod nor the Missouri Synod of German Lutherans.[49] Not until after the war did an articulate "old Lutheran" voice emerge. Its insistence upon strict adherence to historic Lutheran confessions in combination with the swelling tides of German and Scandinavian immigrants eventually restored a distinctly Lutheran theology but also removed it almost entirely from meaningful dialogue with American public life.[50] In sum, the churchly Protestant alternative to literal, Reformed exegesis delivered far less at the time of the Civil War than the internal shape and the distinguished heritage of those traditions made possible.

Conservative Reformed

The orthodox alternative to literal, Reformed biblicism with the best chance of securing a hearing during the Civil War era came from within the Reformed tradition itself. It was the confessional Reformed biblicism practiced by Old School Presbyterians of the border and Northern states. In the South, Old School Presbyterians who exploited the literal, Reformed hermeneutic were mounting the era's most effective arguments for slavery. Their counterparts to the North, however, were in a position to show how the Reformed and literal aspects of the standard hermeneutic could be disengaged.

These Northern Old School Presbyterians were the religious thinkers in antebellum America most able to display the intellectual creativity as well as the doctrinal conservatism that had made the Reformed faith the most culturally influential form of Protestantism since the sixteenth century. In Switzerland, the South of Germany, Hungary, southern France, the Netherlands, Scotland, England, and New England, the Reformed commitment to deep piety along with rigorous learning constituted a formidable force. If the Reformed impulse was always threatened by degeneration into mere pietism, mere dogmatism, or mere morality, it also displayed remarkable powers of renewal. Even as the American Civil War unfolded, both degeneration and renewal could be observed in Europe. In Scotland the breakup of the established Kirk in 1843 and the subsequent failure of either Kirk or Free Church to reestablish moral hegemony was leading to the decline of that nation's powerful Reformed civilization.[51] At the same time in the Netherlands, however, the piety of a folk revival was drawing into its ranks some leaders of great intellectual energy—like the young minister Abraham Kuyper, who was being converted from Enlightenment rationalism to Reformed pietism in the little village of Beesd at the very time that the great armies of North and South were facing off against each other in the United States.[52] Soon that mix of piety, intellect, and worldly wisdom would blossom into a renaissance of Reformed cultural influence in Holland.

In America, a similar Reformed energy had made a significant contribution to the Christianization of the nation in the decades after the Revolution. In the South, however, the defense of slavery so co-opted this energy as to leave Reformed leaders with little desire to question the predominant hermeneutic. In the Northern and border states, while the push to conformity was nearly as strong, theologians retained somewhat more room to maneuver. If in America at the eve of the Civil War there would have reemerged the kind of pious, doctrinally rigorous, and culturally encompassing theology that had so strongly shaped Calvin's Geneva, seventeenth-century New England, the Scotland of Thomas Chalmers, or the Netherlands of Abraham Kuyper, it might have come from the conservative Reformed theologians of the North. If it had been possible to rescue the Reformed hermeneutic from proslavery, they were the ones most suited to do so.

Such a breakthrough, however, did not occur. Among Congregationalists, the most able defenders of conservative positions—like Moses Stuart of

Andover Seminary—were gone by the time of the war, and most of their successors had begun to divide historic Reformed understandings of Scripture into a letter that could be held lightly and a spirit to be taken more seriously. Among New School Presbyterians, there was a similar concession to popular practices. In his major writings on the war, for example, Henry Boynton Smith simply proclaimed "the sinfulness of the slave system," without pausing to examine why so many other American Bible-believers disagreed. He was also drawn off from the biblical debate over slavery by his desire to demonstrate for Americans, and especially the British, "the pestilent heresy of *secession*."[53]

Conservative Presbyterians who felt the force of the proslavery biblical argument but who yet retained a desire to shape culture in Christian ways offered the best chance for an orthodox hermeneutic that could escape the proslavery defense championed by their Southern Presbyterian contemporaries. The two most likely candidates for this role were Robert Breckinridge (1800–1871) of Kentucky and Charles Hodge of Princeton.[54] Both Breckinridge and Hodge understood the power of proslavery biblicism, yet both tried to resist the logic of simple literalism. Breckinridge did so as an active minister and seminary professor who served a pastorate in Baltimore (1832–1845) before returning to a distinguished career in his native Kentucky, mostly at the Old School Danville Theological Seminary. His chief contribution to the debate was attempting to define slavery, not in the abstract, but as it existed concretely in the slave states. Breckinridge made this argument most effectively as early as 1833, and despite a gradually weakening position, he continued to maintain this early view for some time. In 1833 he argued boldly that "slavery . . . as it exists among us" was nothing more than a system "in which one portion of the community, called masters, is allowed" to subdue "another portion called slaves." According to Breckinridge, that system was fatally flawed because it allowed masters "to reduce them [slaves] to the necessity of universal concubinage, by denying them the civil rights of marriage; . . . To deprive them of the means and opportunities of moral and intellectual culture . . . ; To set up between parents and their children an authority higher than the impulse of nature and the laws of God."[55] Once having defined slavery in this way, Breckinridge advocated compensated emancipation and the colonization of former slaves as a solution, and he did so despite the most intense public opposition in his native Kentucky, often from members of his extended family and from within his Old School church.

Hodge moved in a different direction. In a series of learned works also dating back to the 1830s, he conceded the biblical grounding for slavery as an institution but argued that a proper understanding of Scripture, as well as a right judgment on American circumstances, should move toward the amelioration of slavery and then its effacement.[56] Unfortunately for Hodge's later reputation, his attack on the biblical exegesis of abolitionists has been remembered more clearly than his defense of gradual emancipation. This attack on the abolitionist effort simply to define slavery as a sinful institution, as well as Hodge's defense of fugitive slave laws, was so effective that two of his earliest essays were incorporated in the compendium *Cotton Is King*, which was published in the South as a major defense of slavery on the eve of the Civil War.[57] What the editor left out of the reprinting from 1860, however, was Hodge's predictions from 1835: "The South, therefore, has to choose between emancipation by the silent and holy influence of the gospel, securing the elevation of the slaves to the stature and character of freemen, or to abide the issue of a long continued conflict against the laws of God. That the issue will be disastrous there can be no doubt."[58]

For both Breckinridge and Hodge, the argument was similar. Both conceded that the Bible sanctioned a kind of slavery, but Breckinridge denied that what the South practiced was biblical slavery, while Hodge felt that the Bible hedged the practice of a legitimate slavery with so many ameliorations that the practice must end when those ameliorations were pursued to their logical "gospel" conclusion.

The specifically hermeneutical stance adopted by both was a tacit abandonment of biblical literalism. Both took for granted that the Bible must be an interpreted book and that the meaning of its words must be conditioned by other realities—with Breckinridge, shifting social conditions over time, with Hodge, the fuller context of the Scriptures themselves. Both retained the Reformed conviction that the Bible provided norms for all of life, but both insisted that these norms be interpreted with respect to the entire message of the Bible, new social conditions, or both.

Their departures from the American hermeneutic were modest. They were, however, doing what most of the leaders of vibrant Reformed cultures had earlier done by applying biblical teaching rigorously defined, and yet applying it with some flexibility to local conditions. In the American situation, they were arguing both that the Bible allowed slavery and that slavery should be eliminated. This was an argument, moreover, that both felt could proceed under warrants derived from the Bible as a whole rather than from individual texts. In their work lay the germ of an orthodox Reformed hermeneutic that could have opposed the much more widely spread literal, Reformed biblicism. Along with hermeneutics from churchly Protestants, Roman Catholics, and African Americans, their stance preserved historic orthodoxy but also defended principles for rescuing the Bible from proslavery.

In the event, none of these hermeneutics prevailed. None influenced in a substantial way theological reasoning during the era of the Civil War. In addition, none was able to compete after the war with the growing strength of the period's two primary Protestant positions—a liberalism that separated biblical letter and spirit, and a revamped biblical literalism that soon reconfigured itself as fundamentalist, dispensational, holiness, pentecostal, and Southern conservative forms of populist Protestantism.

The alternative orthodox hermeneutics failed because the groups that proposed them were culturally marginal. The Catholic hermeneutic was beyond the pale because Catholicism was beyond the pale. Lutherans and German Reformed mediating theologians were not sufficiently American. African-

American hermeneutics shared much with dominant American patterns, but blacks appropriated the American hermeneutic in ways that were ignored when whites read the Bible. The conservative Reformed alternative to literalism was not marginal, but it could not overcome its greatest potential strength—its very similarity to the dominant hermeneutic.

Conservative Reformed thinkers devoted much struggle to whether slavery was an evil in itself (*malum in se*) or a permissible institution that might engender evil if it were not regulated correctly.[59] The importance of the *malum in se* argument was tied up with the hermeneutical question. If one concluded that the Bible did not regard slavery as a *malum in se*, there seemed to be only one practical course. Because of the populist Regulative Principle, in which it was necessary to find a command in the Bible to carry out an action, Bible-believing emancipationists felt they had to find slavery a *malum in se* in Scripture in order to campaign against it.

Conservative Reformed theologians, however, were in position to argue what few other Americans could contemplate—that it was permissible, if reason, prayer, and tradition so indicated, to move from the literal words of the Bible to biblically normed responses to new or developing situations. They were also in position to acknowledge that such movement might entail apparent contradictions between bare words of particular texts of Scripture, but also to show how a larger theological vision might resolve those apparent contradictions.

The standard hermeneutic, with its reliance on "the Bible alone," usually entailed disbelief in prudential arguments arising from Scripture and so made it very difficult to mount a position that combined, as Breckinridge and Hodge attempted, a belief both that the Bible allowed slavery and that slavery should be eliminated. These two positions were not necessarily antithetical, but they certainly looked antithetical in the light of the standard approach to Scripture that had developed in the United States.

In the end, conservative Reformed attempts to mount a mediating argument, on the basis of the Bible as a whole, fell before the residual strength of the literal biblicism that drew such strength from the Reformed themselves. Hodge and Breckinridge were prevented by the influence of the Regulative Principle (and especially in its Southern variation as "the spirituality of the church") from asking what general principles should be sought in a polity determined, not by a Semitic tribe warring against other tribes nor by Romans bent on ruling the world, but in a nation influenced by eighteen centuries of Christian development, in which some of the legislators were themselves Christians. Hodge and Breckinridge seemed to realize implicitly that when conditions in which words were spoken changed, so did the meaning of the words. But unlike their contemporary John Henry Newman, they were never able to justify that implicit sense.

In the end, personal factors also made it impossible to make Newman's case in Presbyterian dress. As the struggle intensified for Breckinridge, he turned increasingly to the merely rhetorical and to a simple filiopietism of the nation.[60] Hodge, in the end, was hamstrung by a constitutional conservatism that left him more troubled by the abolitionist threat to biblical truth than slavery's threat to biblical holiness.

Common Sense about Race

The main reason, however, that alternative hermeneutics failed on the question of slavery was the widespread commonsense consensus about race. Although the Bible and race was never the same question as the Bible and slavery, only African Americans perceived this reality clearly at the time. With white Americans it was virtually impossible to recognize that race and slavery were two distinct issues. One of the strongest reasons for that characteristic Caucasian stance was the intuitive biblical literalism that prevailed among the country's dominant Protestant bodies. What David Brion Davis has written about the economic situation was just as true for the theological situation: "In the United States . . . the problem of slavery . . . had become fatally intertwined with the problem of race. Race had become the favored idiom for interpreting the social effects of enslavement and emancipation and for concealing the economy's parasitic dependence on an immensely profitable labor system."[61] Change "the social effects of enslavement and emancipation" to "the Bible on slavery" and the statement holds equally well for the religious sphere.

Some African Americans, like Frederick Douglass, were certainly able to see the problem. In March 186I he wrote that "nobody at the North, we think, would defend Slavery, even from the Bible, but for this color distinction. . . . Color makes all the difference in the application of our American Christianity. . . . The same Book which is full of the Gospel of Liberty to one race, is crowded with arguments in justification of the slavery of another. Those who shout and rejoice over the progress of Liberty in Italy, would mob down, pray and preach down Liberty at home as an unholy and hateful thing." But Douglass typically responded with arguments of intuitive moral indignation, rather than with exegesis, as, for example, in the same essay, where he claimed, "It would be insulting to Common Sense, an outrage upon all right feeling, for us, who have worn the heavy chain and felt the biting lash to consent to argue with Ecclesiastical Sneaks who are thus prostituting their Religion and Bible to the base uses of popular and profitable iniquity. They don't need light, but the sting of honest rebuke. They are of their father the Devil, and his works they do, not because they are ignorant, but because they are base."[62] With his reference to "Common Sense" and "right feeling," Douglass revealed his knowledge of the standard American hermeneutic, but by so doing, he also exposed the weaknesses of his own arguments in a society where intuitive assumptions about the meaning of race were so strongly contested. In such a situation, the "universal intuitions" of the stronger not only prevailed but effectively wiped clean the slate of all other possible intuitions.

Although debate over exegetical questions had indeed advanced by the time of the war, that advance did not affect the prevailing intuitions about race in mid-nineteenth-century America. Belief that the curse of Canaan from Genesis 9:25–27 applied to blacks still flourished among the people at large but was less prevalent among intellectual elites. Theologians like Philip Schaff or Rabbi Raphal might occasionally be willing to speculate on the relevance of the passage to the modern situation of American slaves.[63] But most elite theologians had long since dismissed that kind of application in favor of a reading that held the Genesis passage to be fulfilled when the children of Israel conquered the Promised Land.[64]

The problem with race and the Bible was far more profound than the interpretation of any one text. It was a problem brought about by the intuitive character of the reigning American hermeneutic. This hermeneutic merged three positions: (1) The Bible was a plain book whose meanings could be reliably ascertained through the exercise of an ordinary person's intelligence; (2) a main reason for trusting the Bible as true was an intuitive sense, sealed by the Holy Spirit; (3) the same intelligence that through ordinary means and intuitions could trust the Bible as true also gained much additional truth about the world through intuitive processes that were also deliverances of universal common sense. The first position was a traditional Protestant teaching intensified by the American environment; the second was historically Protestant and Reformed; the third was simply a function of the American hermeneutic.

In American discussion of the Bible and slavery, these three axioms became one. Exegetes merged their conclusions from the Bible (derived through intuitive literalism) with their conclusions from commonsense intuitions that blacks were an inferior people fit by nature for what Philip Schaff called the "wholesome discipline of slavery."[65] On slavery, exegetes stood for a commonsense reading of the Bible. On race, exegetes forsook the Bible and relied on common sense. Intuitive judgments on American slavery were therefore sanctified by the culture's intuitive biblicism and literally *colored* by the culture's intuitive racism.

Confusion existed between commonsense biblicism and commonsense racism in almost every one of the period's significant writings on the subject. Lay Southern intellectuals, for example, were pleased to repeat the biblical arguments of theologians in defense of slavery, but when they pinpointed Africans as the proper subjects of biblically sanctioned slavery, they were as likely to cite Herodotus, Josephus, or other ancient historians as the Scriptures.[66]

As for the theologians, it is again instructive to single out conservative Reformed leaders, since on Scripture they were the most rigorously and self-consciously orthodox. Philip Schaff, on the eve of the war, published a long article on the question, most of which was given over to exegeting passages from the Old and New Testaments that Schaff felt legitimated slavery. Only at the end did he turn to the American situation, and only then did he abandon his citations from Scripture. Schaff, perhaps because he was an immigrant, could see some things very clearly: "Of all forms of slavery the American is the most difficult to dispose of, because it is not only a question of domestic institution and political oeconomy, but of race. *The negro question lies far deeper than the slavery question."* Yet this solid theologian and shrewd observer of American ways was perfectly content, without adducing a single text, to take for granted that the only slaves in America would be Africans, to conclude that slavery "will no doubt prove an immense blessing to the whole race of Ham," and to urge a cessation of political agitation on the subject, hoping that "Christian philanthropy" and "an all-wise Providence" would bring about the end of slavery and the uplifting of African Americans.[67] By the end of this essay, racial assumptions were crowding out the conclusions of exegesis to such a degree that Schaff had set aside traditional Reformed reliance on "means" to accomplish the revealed will of providence. That is, Schaff was arguing that since providence was responsible for slavery existing in America, God would somehow take care of the problem by himself.[68] Schaff began his essay by hewing strictly to his theme, "Slavery and the Bible," but he ended by importing intuitive conclusions about the character of African Americans and the shape of contemporary contingencies.

Given Schaff's professed willingness to make use of traditions, confessions, and other mediating intellectual authorities for interpreting Scripture, it was perhaps not as much a contradiction for Schaff to import nonbiblical warrants into his argument as it was for others, like the Old School Presbyterians. Among the Old School theologians, Charles Hodge was the most profound reasoner on both slavery and the traumas of the war. His publications on slavery, from the first major essay in 1835, tried consistently to balance biblical reasoning on slavery and biblical reasoning on the God-given dignity of all people. During the war, he was the one major theologian to ponder the way in which multiple cause-and-effect relationships seemed to be at work in American moral, military, social, and religious life.[69] Some of his positions during the war—for example, in attacking the resolution by Gardiner Spring that drove Southern Presbyterians out of the Old School in 1861—were as unpopular as his earlier stand in 1846 that Roman Catholic baptism was legitimate Christian baptism.

But even this consequential theologian—who professed to base his every conclusion on the warrant of Scripture—easily incorporated racial assumptions into the exegetical process as if they carried the same weight as his conclusions from the Bible. To cite examples only from his first major essay on the subject, Hodge insisted that whatever authorities radical abolitionists or proslavery defenders might enlist, he would "recognize no authoritative rule of truth and duty but the word of God. . . . It is our object . . . not to discuss the subject of slavery upon abstract principles, but to ascertain the scriptural rule of judgment and conduct in relation to it." Yet as soon as Hodge left the arena of what could be deduced from Scripture and entered into a discussion of the American situation, other warrants immediately leaped to the fore. Thus, the customary "organization of society" was enough to justify making "the free colored man" at birth "a disfranchised outcast." It was a truth "on all hands admitted" that blacks "could not, consistently with the public welfare, be entrusted with the exercise of political power." It was "the *acknowledged* right of the State to govern them [blacks, slave or free] by laws in the formation of

which they have no voice." And only because "the slaves of this country were
. . . of a different race from their masters" did anyone object to the notion that
slaves might progress from bondage to freedom and eventually even to exercising the rights and privileges of citizenship.[70] So pervasive was the instinct
of racism, even in Hodge's guileless soul, that he seemed not to see how thoroughly he was mixing biblical conclusions with opinions that arose from no
text of Scripture. If Hodge, the most perceptive Old School Presbyterian in
the North, could not tell the difference between slavery in general and the
enslavement of one race in particular, it is little wonder that the distinction
between slavery and the enslavement of African Americans was completely
lost on his Southern counterparts.

Shortly after the conclusion of the war, failure to register the difference
between reasoning from the Bible on slavery and from cultural instincts on
race was illustrated with great force by Robert L. Dabney, a once-generous
theologian of painstaking morality and winning qualities, whom the defeat
of the South turned into an increasingly bitter Jeremiah.[71] When, immediately
after the war, Presbyterians in the Upper South proposed to ordain African-
Americans as clergymen, Dabney opposed the proposal with a spontaneous
speech that both he and observers later called the greatest rhetorical performance in a long life studded with magnificent oratory.[72] Yet when Dabney,
who as an advocate of "the spirituality of the church" had held strongly to
the Regulative Principle, rose to speak in the Synod of Virginia on November 9, 1867, the Bible was not the primary authority. The first half of his speech
offered only intuitive sentiments, especially on the spectre of black-white
intermarriage. This spectre was not, as Dabney described it, a "blind, passionate prejudice of caste, but [came from] the righteous, rational *instinct* of
pious minds." Only after this appeal to intuition did Dabney then turn to arguments from the Bible, but here he reasoned very much as the abolitionists
whose arguments he so abominated had reasoned on the question of slavery—
that the tendency, spirit, or precedents of the Bible spoke against such ordination in a white church.[73]

A final example of race crowding out exegesis came in one of the most
important pronouncements of the South's most respected theologian, James
Henley Thornwell. In May 1861 Thornwell was asked to draft a defense of
secession and the Southern way of life for the new Southern Presbyterian
Church, then meeting in its first General Assembly. When he came to defend
slavery by the Bible, Thornwell began by reiterating a claim associated with
the principle of "the spirituality of the church": "In our ecclesiastical capacity, we are neither the friends nor the foes of slavery." Then he offered the
customary profession that he would reason only from Scripture: "Let it be
distinctly borne in mind that the only rule of judgment is the written word of
God. . . . [The church] is founded . . . upon express *revelation*. Her creed is
an authoritative testimony of God, and not a speculation." Thornwell then
offered an abridged version of the standard biblical defense of slavery.

Yet when, in the course of this discussion, Thornwell began to discuss
slavery in the South, he made—without seeming to notice—the critical shift

from talking about slavery as legitimated in Scripture to African Americans as the only possible slaves:

> We feel that the souls of our slaves are a solemn trust, and we shall strive to present them faultless and complete before the presence of God.
>
> Indeed, as we contemplate their [i.e., African Americans'] condition in the Southern States, and contrast it with that of their fathers before them, and that of their brethren in the present day in their native land, we cannot but accept it as a gracious Providence that they have been brought in such numbers to our shores, and redeemed from the bondage of barbarism and sin.

After this reflexive equation of slaves and African Americans, Thornwell turned explicitly to the intuitions of formal moral philosophy. In this line of argument, he continued to mix categories by talking of "slaves" when he meant "African slaves"—for example, "There are, no doubt, many rights which belong to other men—to Englishmen[,] to Frenchmen, to his master, for example—which are denied to [the slave]." Thornwell's reliance on the intuitive deliverances of moral philosophy sounded pious, but they did not come from Scripture: "The truth is, the education of the human race for liberty and virtue, is a vast Providential scheme, and God assigns to every man, by a wise and holy decree, the precise place he is to occupy in the great moral school of humanity. The scholars are distributed into classes, according to their competency and progress. For God is in history." As a warrant for such conclusions, Thornwell relied on intuition alone: "That test is an inward necessity of thought, which, in all minds at the proper stage of maturity, is absolutely universal. Whatever is universal is natural. We are willing that slavery should be tried by this standard."[74]

One can imagine counterfactually that those who felt the Bible sanctioned slavery in general could also have suggested exegetical arguments from the Bible to justify the enslavement of Africans, and only Africans, in particular. But since there are no arguments in the Bible of the latter kind, a hidden hand had to function in the exegetical process if the Bible were to justify the racial slavery that existed in the United States—and if faith in Bible-only literalism was to be preserved. That hidden hand was the widespread and deeply engrained conviction that among the peoples of the earth only Africans were uniquely set apart for chattel bondage.

The question of the Bible and slavery in the era of the Civil War was never a simple question. The issue involved the American expression of a Reformed, literal hermeneutic, the failure of hermeneutical alternatives to gain cultural authority, and the exercise of deeply entrenched intuitive racism, as well as deep-seated convictions about the Bible as an authoritative religious book and slavery as an inherited socioeconomic relationship. The North—forced to fight on unfriendly terrain that it had helped to create—lost the exegetical war. The South certainly lost the shooting war. But constructive Christian theology was the major loser when American believers allowed bullets instead of hermeneutical self-consciousness to determine what the Bible taught about race and slavery.

Climax and Exhaustion in the Civil War

Three pairs of contrasting statements at the conclusion of the Civil War reveal the theological influences that predominated during the conflict and also the inherited theological reflexes that survived intact throughout the war. They also underscore how reliance on a common stock of ideological resources had created a theological impasse.

The first pair concerns the mingled categories of Christian faith and republican politics that prevailed so widely throughout the whole country. In March 1865, as desperate Southern leaders labored to sustain the fight, the editor of the *Army and Navy Messenger* from Shreveport, Louisiana, exhorted the Confederate troops with a language at once distinctly Christian and American: "Above all, the providence of God has made it their [the Confederate soldiers'] special privilege to defend with their lives the right of freedom of conscience, the essential issue of the war; the right to interpret the Bible for ourselves, without the prescription of creeds for us by synods, councils, or congresses."[1]

A similar ideology spoke to very different ends in the North. On Sunday, 23 April, eight days after the death of Abraham Lincoln, Henry Ward Beecher preached one of that day's most memorable memorial sermons. In it he opined that the disaster of Lincoln's death could yet be overcome, since it occurred after the survival of the nation was secured. According to Beecher, "Republican institutions have been vindicated in this experience as they never were before. . . . God, I think, has said, by the voice of this event to all nations of the earth, 'Republican liberty, based upon true Christianity, is firm as the foundation of the globe.'"[2] The North might still be viewing current events very differently than the South, but for both, Christian republican certainties remained inviolate.

In July 1865 contrasting statements in Connecticut and New Jersey spoke of the profound influence that Christian nationalism exerted on the religious thought of the period. Horace Bushnell, often regarded as the most creative American theologian of the age, was called from Hartford to his alma mater at Yale to deliver a memorial commencement address for alumni who had died in battle. To Bushnell, the war, as by a miracle from God, had brought about a form of national unity unthinkable before it began. This unity was likely "to be more cordial than it ever could have been." And the source of the unity was clear: "It will be no more thought of as a mere human compact, or composition, always to be debated by the letter, but it will be that bond of common life which God has touched with blood; a sacredly heroic, Providentially tragic unity, where God's cherubim stand guard over grudges and hates and remembered jealousies, and the sense of nationality becomes even a kind of religion."[3]

The same month an unnamed Jewish correspondent to New York City's *Occident* begged to differ with Bushnell's assumptions. Jewish leaders had joined the national chorus at Lincoln's death by writing eulogies from texts like Genesis 12:4 ("So Abram departed, as the Lord had spoken unto him"), Genesis 15:1 ("Fear not, Abram: I am thy shield, and thy exceeding great reward"), 2 Samuel 1:14 ("How wast thou not afraid to stretch forth thy hand to destroy the Lord's anointed?"), and 2 Samuel 3:38 ("Know ye not that there is a prince and a great man fallen this day in Israel?"). But at least one Jew from New Jersey took offense. Unlike Bushnell and multitudes of other fellow citizens, it was important for this believer to distinguish between the universal truths of his religion and the contingent events that had occurred in the United States. There was no problem in public expressions of "sorrow at the death of the Chief Magistrate of the country." But there was a problem when those expressions went too far: "Is it necessary for this purpose to run counter to the opinions and religious views of their co-religionists? Is there a Jew in this whole land, educated in the history and traditions of his people, who would consider a Christian deserving of any of the *religious* services appertaining to Jewish worship or who in a moment of calm reflection can find any comparison between the late President and their great law-giver 'whom the Lord knew face to face'?"[4] Unlike Bushnell and many other Americans, the unnamed Jewish correspondent struggled to preserve a separation between God's will as shown in the special revelations of a religious tradition and that same will as displayed in contemporary current events.

Finally, months after the war's completion, deeply rooted, but also deeply divided, convictions about the moral status of slavery still drove religious leaders to get in the last word. To the Reverend G. I. Wood from Guilford, Connecticut, a blessed divine act had been necessary to obliterate the peculiar institution. Before the war, "the Republic was nearly undermined and overthrown by the insidious influence of a social institution, in its very nature antagonistic to the distinctive principles of a free government." Moreover, there seemed to be no way out: "How was the nation to be exorcised of this evil spirit? What human wisdom could devise a way for the solution of this complicated problem? . . . Slavery had a kind of charmed existence." The answer was clear: "The nation could not touch it—the States would not. God only could, and He did."[5]

At just about the same time this verdict was rendered, John Adger, editor of the South's most respected intellectual quarterly, the *Southern Presbyterian Review*, reached a very different conclusion. But in so doing he drew weapons from the same intellectual arsenal that Wood had used. Adger professed to "retain all our former opinions respecting slavery. It was a kindly relation on both sides. It was a good institution, although some abuses were connected with it which demanded reformation, and would have been reformed had the South been let alone of her persecutors." The last thing Adger would admit was that God had brought about the end of this institution, given the fact that the abolitionists betrayed "a rationalistic and practically infidel attitude,—for they have set up a morality better than the Bible's, and are impugning the perfectness of Christ's conduct and doctrine. They claim to be more righteous than God, and wiser than his word."[6] Wood and Adger both saw the will of God clearly, both knew by simple deduction how divine morality related to recent United States history, and both were supremely confident, though with contradictory conclusions, that they could read the mind of God.

As these contrasting testimonies indicate, the most important step in comprehending the Civil War as a theological event is to recognize the continuation of long-standing habits of mind. For more than a century, American theologians had been uniting historic Christian perspectives with specific products of American intellectual life. The ubiquitous Christian reflection on and during the war followed initiatives from the mid-eighteenth century that had been set firmly in place by strategic alliances during the early years of the republic. A powerful combination of intellectual ingredients had given American theologians categories for apprehending sectional controversy and the war itself. Evangelical Protestants in particular provided the religious content for a synthesis of American values that, to one degree or the other, was also accepted by almost all other religious traditions.

The central place of Scripture, theological reasoning, and religiously charged rhetoric during the war grew from the accumulating power of this earlier synthesis. Considered as an episode in the history of theology, the Civil War did occur during a time of transition when questions were being raised about the theological certainties that had prevailed for at least a century. Theological reflection on and during the conflict hastened the transition from those earlier certainties, but they nonetheless provided the framework for most religious thinking during the war and, within many groups, for long afterward as well.

If American theologians were not, for the most part, changing their long-term intellectual commitments during these years, they were called to use them in responding to a full range of difficult theological issues, some imported from Europe and others homegrown. The questions the theologians discussed were weighty, the range of their concerns was considerable, and their responses were learned. Even while preoccupied with the war, they were writing with measured wisdom about major developments in Western theology.[7]

As they wrote voluminously on the American conflict itself, so also did they publish carefully wrought essays in basic theology. For example, several notable essays explored—with far less alarm than would later be the case—the cosmological implications of scientific proposals from Charles Darwin's *Origin of Species* (1859) and Charles Lyell's *Geological Evidence of the Antiquity of Man* (1863).[8] American theologians also canvassed the knotty issues of faith and history raised by Church of England progressives in *Essays and Reviews* (1860) and by Ernst Renan's radical *Vie de Jésus* (1863).[9] They discoursed learnedly on the implications for philosophy, ethics, and Christian civilization of Henry Mansel's Bampton Lectures (1858), with his innovative effort to employ Kant on behalf of Protestant orthodoxy.[10] And in their discussions of these notable European efforts, as well as notice of works by Sir William Hamilton, Herbert Spencer, and others, they probed basic questions of human destiny.[11] In similar fashion, the theologians continued to wrestle with issues of long-standing concern, especially the respective roles of God and humanity in salvation and the workings of providence in historical time and space.[12] On the latter matter, the meaning of America was central, but discussions often went well beyond in efforts to fathom the ways of God more generally.[13]

Before and during the war, in other words, theologians were deeply engaged with a range of traditional religious questions. The conflict itself heightened theological stakes—with its appeal to ultimate loyalties, its ideological intensity, its quickening of religious emotion, and its massive production of death and destruction. Yet as the Civil War proceeded, something very strange was taking place. On issues closest to the conflict itself, the theologians almost always expressed themselves in predictable terms. In its first years, Northerners saw God chastening them for their disobedience when the armies of Burnside, McClellan, Hooker, and Mead faltered; Southerners saw the hand of God mighty to save in the exploits of Lee and Jackson. After Grant took command of the Army of the Potomac, God's designs changed, and now it was the South that endured his cleansing wrath and the North that received the smiles of providence. In the mingled grief, hope, separation, loss, relief, dislocation, boredom, productivity, exaltation, and anguish of the conflict, the Bible spoke with utter clarity about what was going on. Standards of divine morality—on slavery, on the conduct of the war, on the fate of states—remained beacons as clear as the causes of the Union or the Confederacy themselves.

To be sure, occasional notes of ambiguity or doubt could be heard from respected religious leaders, and even more from the laity. But demurrals were far less obvious than clear-eyed moral certainty about God and his will. The great exception to these generalizations was the moral reflections of the sixteenth president of the United States, Abraham Lincoln. To examine his perspective on the mind of God has the significant value of illuminating more clearly the principles, assumptions, and conventional expressions of professional religious thinkers. To make this comparison will also indicate why the Civil War proved to be the climax, but also the exhaustion, of the synthesis of common sense, republicanism, and evangelical Christianity that had exerted such a comprehensive influence in the early history of the United States.

The Puzzles of Lincoln's Religion

Two large questions confront any effort to set Abraham Lincoln's religion in its proper historical context. The first concerns Lincoln and has been a subject of unceasing, if only intermittently fruitful, exploration—how was it that this man who never joined a church and who read only a little theology could, on occasion, give expression to profound theological interpretations of the War between the States?[14] The second question concerns Lincoln's contemporaries and has been the object of relatively scant historical inquiry—how was it that the distinguished theologians of Lincoln's generation, some of whom remain highly honored in various religious communities to this day, were able to offer so little of theological profundity concerning the religious meaning of the Civil War?

The contrast posed by these two questions appears most sharply when considering Lincoln's Second Inaugural Address in its historical context. Throughout the year in which that speech was given, the nation's best theologians, both North and South, took nearly every opportunity imaginable to explain what, under God, the war signified. Yet almost no one today—other than a few historians—has any interest in what this sizable corps of distinguished religious leaders said about the ways of God in the Civil War. By contrast, Lincoln's short address on 4 March 1865 remains an object of intense study and admiration.

The poignancy of this speech, as the martyr-president's last defining utterance on the nation's ultimate defining experience, no less than its magnanimity toward the South and the force of its religious meditation, has placed it among the small handful of semisacred texts by which Americans conceive their place in the world. If, however, we set the address in its own times rather than consider its importance for the Meaning of America, we find it defines a major historical puzzle concerning the character of theology. The puzzle is posed by the fact that none of America's respected religious leaders—as defined by contemporaries or later scholars—mustered the theological power so economically expressed in Lincoln's Second Inaugural. None probed so profoundly the ways of God or the response of humans to the divine constitution of the world. None penetrated as deeply into the nature of providence. And none described the fate of humanity before God with the humility or the sagacity of the president.[15] The contrast has several dimensions.

First, Lincoln expressed remarkable charity to the foe. In hindsight it is clear that, when Lincoln delivered his address on 4 March, the South was tottering on the brink of defeat. But Lincoln himself did not believe that Lee would soon surrender, and the South was still filled with leaders promising to fight on as guerrillas in the mountains or from new bases west of the Mississippi. In these circumstances, after four years of a war in which the South had extracted a terrible toll from the North and in which North and South had both promoted a degree of destructive violence hitherto unknown even in America's never genteel history, Lincoln's magnanimity was as striking as it was singular. Second, almost alone among his contemporaries, Lincoln did not presumptuously assume that the moral high ground belonged to only his side. By questioning the righteousness of the North and by failing to denounce the South in absolute terms, he joined a very small minority in the spring and summer of 1865. If Lincoln's magnanimity and his moral even-handedness were generally religious, his view of providence was distinctly theological. More than any other feature of this address, Lincoln's conception of God's rule over the world set him apart from the recognized theologians of his day.

Charity

Lincoln ended his address on 4 March with one of the most frequently quoted perorations in American public life: "With malice toward none; with charity for all; let us strive to finish the work we are in; to bind up the nation's wounds; to care for him who shall have borne the battle, and for his widow and his orphan."[16] What Lincoln did not say here was as significant as what he did, for the president did not restrict his appeal on behalf of soldiers, widows, and orphans to those who had suffered for the Union.

In sharp contrast to Lincoln's charity, religious leaders were just as prone as the general population to seek retribution. In the wake of Lincoln's assassination, it was understandable for Northerners to display a different spirit than that which their president had voiced only six weeks before. So it was, for example, on 15 April 1865, the day Lincoln died, when three local ministers preached to the assembled citizens of New Haven, Connecticut. Of these hastily composed sermons it was reported that the crowd offered its most fervent applause when Dr. William Patton exclaimed: "Yes, vengeance belongs to God, but he has his human instruments to carry out his vengeance. He will not allow this land to be polluted with the innocent blood unavenged, shed by these rebels. We must wipe it out. . . . If they are not hung, the mildest that we can in justice do them, is to put them on probation for the rest of their lives."[17]

But Dr. Patton was not a household name, and almost anything might be excused in the immediate wake of an assassination. It had been different only one day before, while Lincoln still lived, when the flag of the United States was raised again over Fort Sumter in Charleston harbor, exactly four years and two days after this fort endured the bombardment that began the war. For this triumphant occasion, the Union had called upon Henry Ward Beecher, the Billy Graham of his era. When Beecher addressed his audience at Fort Sumter, he first said what might be expected concerning the victory of the North but soon turned his substantial rhetorical powers in the other direction:

> I charge the whole guilt of this war upon the ambitious, educated, plotting, political leaders of the South. They have shed this ocean of blood. . . . A day will come when God will reveal judgment, and arraign at his bar these mighty miscreants. . . . And then from a thousand battle-fields shall rise up armies of airy witnesses, who, with the memory of their awful sufferings, shall confront these miscreants with shrieks of fierce accusation; and every pale and starved prisoner shall raise his skinny hand in judgment. . . . And, then, these guiltiest and most remorseless traitors . . . these most accursed and detested of all criminals, that have drenched a continent in needless blood, and moved the foundations of their times with hideous crimes and cruelty, caught up in black clouds full of voices of vengeance and lurid with punishment, shall be whirled aloft and plunged downward forever and forever in an endless retribution; while God shall say, "Thus shall it be to all who betray their country"; and all heaven and upon the earth will say, "Amen!"[18]

The contrast between Beecher, the clergyman son of one of the most dynamic religious leaders of his generation, and Lincoln, unchurched son of a hard-shell Baptist layman, could not have been sharper.

Self-Righteousness

Abraham Lincoln's refusal to claim the moral high ground exclusively for the North was even more extraordinary than his charity to a nearly defeated foe. Although sentiments were naturally inflamed after Lincoln's assassination, protestations of good will from both North and South did in fact arise from several quarters. Henry Ward Beecher's vengefulness was common but not universal. At the end of the day, however, the temptation to define the evil of the opponent as the only true evil had become nearly universal. Earlier, when the course of arms went badly, ministers North and South had indeed called their own congregations to repentance. But mostly this was what from a cynical distance we might call utilitarian repentance—God could not grant us victory so long as we continued in our sin. At the conclusion of the war, repentance became overwhelmingly an exercise demanded of the foe.

This climate set the stage, not just for Lincoln's Second Inaugural, but also for much other commentary by American theologians on the relative justice of Northern and Southern action. At Yale in July 1865, Horace Bushnell was atypical only in his rhetorical flamboyance. "'The story of this four years' war," he averred," is the grandest chapter, I think, of heroic fact, and tragic devotion, and spontaneous public sacrifice, that has ever been made in our world." The great epics were but ditties by comparison:

> There never was a better and never so great a cause; order against faction, law against conspiracy, liberty and right against the madness and defiant wrong of slavery, the unity and salvation of the greatest future nationality and freest government of the world, a perpetual state of war to be averted, and the preservation for mankind of an example of popular government and free society that is a token of promise for true manhood, and an omen of death to old abuse and prescriptive wrong the world over; this has been our cause, and it is something to say that we have borne ourselves worthily in it.[19]

Some years ago the historian William Clebsch singled out Bushnell for special commendation as offering an unusually serious theological interpretation of the Civil War.[20] Clebsch saw correctly that Bushnell had pondered deeply the religious meaning of the conflict and that he had done so with concepts appropriated from his faith. To Bushnell the war was a blood sacrifice of atonement that would transform America's fragmented, self-seeking atomism into an organic, redeemed social unity long preserved from the threats of secularism, greed, and disharmony. What seems clearer now than when Clebsch wrote, however, is that Bushnell's romantic nationalism of the redeemed *Volk* was as liable to corruption as it was to promoting the millennium he anticipated.

Robert Lewis Dabney was, like Horace Bushnell, a pastor-theologian much honored in his native region. After the death of James Henley Thornwell in 1862, Dabney was widely regarded as the Southern apologist with the greatest intellectual integrity and the most consistently forceful exposition of orthodox Christian faith. During 1860 and early 1861 Dabney had argued strenuously against secession, but when his state, Virginia, joined the Confederacy, Dabney gave his heart and soul to defend the patriarchal way of life he felt was imperiled by the unchecked currents of Northern mobocracy, Northern industrial capitalism, and Northern religious error. For a time he served as Stonewall Jackson's chief of staff, but his most important service to the Confederacy was constant, passionate, tightly reasoned writing on behalf of the South's way of life.

When Dabney wrote to General Oliver O. Howard, head of the United States Freedman's Bureau, on 12 September 1865, he was already deeply engaged in the effort that would dominate the rest of his long life to defend the antebellum South as a cynosure of divinely ordered civilization devastated by a wantonly vicious North. The burden of the letter was to remind Howard of the responsibility that the North had taken upon itself by conquest to do more for liberated African Americans than the South had done for them when they were slaves. A great mind with great rhetorical skills was on display in this letter, but also a monumental self-righteousness. The South, in Dabney's words, provided for the black slave "universally, such relief for his sickness that every case of serious disease was attended by a physician with nearly the same promptitude and frequency as the cases of the planters' own wives and daughters; and in all the land never was a negro fastened to his bed by illness but he received the personal, sympathizing visits of some intelligent white person beside." And so Dabney's litany went—slaves enjoyed protection against pauperism, there was "not one African poorhouse," and all "African slaves capable of labor" were always given "remunerative occupation" regardless of general economic conditions. The institution had come to the region "at the hands of British and Yankee slave traders," but in generous recompense the South had taught slaves "the rudiments of civilization," it had "diffused among the blacks a pure gospel," it welcomed them to services of Christian worship, and—most important of all—"she has given [the slave] evangelical preaching, unmingled with the poisons of Universalism,

Millerism, Socinianism, Mormonism, or with the foreign and disastrous elements of politics."[21]

Dabney's colleague John Adger was not as well known as Horace Bushnell or as highly regarded as Dabney himself. But this long-time editor of the *Southern Presbyterian Review* was still a formidable figure. He had once been a missionary in Constantinople and would later defend Woodrow Wilson's uncle when James Woodrow was accused of tainting traditional belief with an admixture of evolutionary science. Late in 1865 Adger used the columns of his *Review* to rebut the charge that the Southern pulpit had lapsed into political propaganda during the war. Adger's reply not only defended the South against that particular accusation but also offered a sweeping general defense of the South's Christian rectitude *tout de suite*. All that the ministers had done was "to hold up before their flocks the duty of obeying and supporting the *de facto* government under which they lived" and to preach "hope in God amidst discouragements." If Southern preachers did expound "God's word as it sanctions slavery" and if they "taught their people to commit the cause they were maintaining against a radical infidelity in humble prayer to his wise, and sovereign, and merciful arbitrament," how could anyone condemn those accusations "as a preaching of politics"? Adger knew for a fact that in "the Southern Presbyterian pulpit in general," there was no "other sound than the preaching of the Cross."[22]

Bushnell, Dabney, and Adger were well-trained theologians. Each was a master of the Scriptures. Each was deeply committed to the comprehensive morality of the Christian faith. Each, regrettably, was typical of the moral casuistry of American theologians during and after the Civil War. In volumes of learned, scripturally laden prose, none said anything that approached the sagacity of Lincoln's moral commentary in the Second Inaugural: "Both read the same Bible, and pray to the same God; and each invokes His aid against the other. It may seem strange that any men should dare to ask a just God's assistance in wringing their bread from the sweat of other men's faces; but let us judge not that we be not judged [Matthew 7:1]. The prayers of both could not be answered; that of neither has been answered fully."

Providence

Views of providence provide the sharpest contrast between Lincoln and the professional theologians of his day. Almost alone among public figures, Lincoln's concept of providence combined the conventions of his age with a much more primordial vision.[23]

To be sure, earlier in his presidency Lincoln used a much more common language. At his first inaugural, in 1861, he talked of divine realities as if their main purpose was a utilitarian one to serve the nation. At that time his trust in America had been nearly complete: "Why should there not be a patient confidence in the ultimate justice of the people? Is there any better, or equal, hope in the world?" He even spoke as if God existed as a kind of celestial umpire waiting only to dignify the decisions of U.S. citizens: "If the Almighty Ruler of nations, with his eternal truth and justice, be on your side of the North, or on yours of the South, that truth, and that justice, will surely prevail, by the judgment of this great tribunal, the American people." In that dark hour Lincoln's solution was civil religion pure and simple: "Intelligence, patriotism, Christianity, and a firm reliance on Him, who has never yet forsaken this favored land, are still competent to adjust, in the best way, all our present difficulty."[24]

But before the war had progressed very far, Lincoln evidently began to rethink these conventional views. As early as 1862, another theme rose in Lincoln's consciousness. It was the idea that perhaps the will of God could not simply be identified with efforts to preserve the Union. Such thoughts he committed to paper in September 1862, at one of the darkest moments of the conflict. The North had suffered another defeat at Bull Run, and Lincoln had seriously begun to ponder the radical step of proclaiming the emancipation of Confederate slaves. In response, he penned a "Meditation on the Divine Will," which his secretaries later recalled was meant for Lincoln's eyes alone. It was the most remarkable theological commentary of the war:

> The will of God prevails. In great contests each party claims to act in accordance with the will of God. Both *may* be, and one *must* be wrong. God can not be *for*, and *against* the same thing at the same time. In the present civil war it is quite possible that God's purpose is something different from the purpose of either party—and yet the human instrumentalities, working just as they do, are of the best adaptation to effect His purpose. I am almost ready to say this is probably true—that God wills this contest, and wills that it shall not end yet. By his mere quiet power, on the minds of the now contestants, He could have either *saved* or *destroyed* the Union without a human contest. Yet the contest began. And having begun He could give the final victory to either side any day. Yet the contest proceeds.[25]

The reasoning that led to this private meditation evidently continued, for it was the reasoning that pervaded the Second Inaugural. That reasoning shared the traditional Christian opinion that God ruled over all events. But to this conventional belief Lincoln added two most unconventional convictions. First was the notion that the United States might not necessarily be a uniquely chosen nation, or at least that the moral constraints operating on America were the same as those for other nations, and that these universal standards of justice were of greater consequence than any supposed chosenness of the United States. Second was Lincoln's belief that the ways of providence might be obscure, difficult to fathom, hedged in by contingencies, or otherwise not open to immediate understanding and manipulation.

This combination of convictions—confidence in providence along with humble agnosticism about its purposes—transformed the central section of the Second Inaugural into a theological statement of rare insight. Lincoln began by stating a thesis: "The Almighty has His own purposes." He then quoted Matthew 18:7 to suggest the moral character of life under God: "Woe unto the world because of offences! for it must needs be that offences come; but woe to that man by whom the offence cometh!" Then he looked foursquare into an abyss that few of his contemporaries could bear to contemplate: "If we shall suppose that American Slavery is one of those offences which, in the providence of God, must needs come, but which, having continued through His appointed time, He now wills to remove, and that He gives to both North and South, this terrible war, as the woe due to those by whom the offence came, shall we discern therein any departure from those divine attributes which the believers in a Living God always ascribe to Him? Fondly do we hope—fervently do we pray—that this mighty scourge of war may speedily pass away." The abyss was the suggestion that responsibility for the war must be shared.

Finally, Lincoln concluded by acknowledging that the progress of the United States was as nothing compared to the mysterious will of God: "Yet, if God wills that it continue, until all the wealth piled by the bond-man's two hundred and fifty years of unrequited toil shall be sunk, and until every drop of blood drawn with the lash, shall be paid by another drawn with the sword, as was said three thousand years ago, so still it must be said 'the judgments of the Lord, are true and righteous altogether' [Psalm 19:9]."

America's best theologians joined Lincoln in believing that God was the disposer of all events. But they also continued to affirm the two principles that Lincoln had come to doubt. Almost universally they maintained the long-treasured axiom that the United States had enjoyed, and would continue to enjoy, a unique destiny as a divinely chosen people. The war, they held, had decisively reconfirmed this calling. Second, the theologians continued to speak as if the ways of providence were transparent, as if it were a relatively easy matter to say what God was doing in the disposition of contemporary events. Moreover, what was clearly seen could also be controlled; knowing what God was about gave theologians the confidence that they could determine the course of events. On these points, the chorus of theologians sang with one voice.

At the Yale commencement, Horace Bushnell's confidence concerning what God had done was very strong:

> In these rivers of blood we have now bathed our institutions, and they are henceforth to be hallowed in our sight. Government is now become Providential,—no more a mere creature of our human will, but a grandly moral affair. . . . We have not fought this dreadful war to a close, just to put our government upon a par with these oppressive dynasties [of old Europe]! We scorn the parallel they give us; and we owe it even to them to say, that a government which is friendly, and free, and right, protecting all alike, and doing the most for all, is one of God's sacred finalities, which no hand may touch, or conspiracy assail, without committing the most damning crime, such as can be matched by no possible severities of justice.[26]

John Williamson Nevin of the German Reformed seminary in Mercersburg, Pennsylvania, was given a forum to explain the meaning of the war when he was asked to deliver the Fourth of July address at Franklin and Marshall College in 1865. To Nevin it was as easy as for Bushnell to say what God had been about. The fact that total victory was so unexpected because of Northern unpreparedness, Southern advantages, Lincoln's inexperience, and so forth—"all this goes to establish what we have now immediately in hand, the great thought, namely, that our national deliverance has been wrought out for us, as a world-historical act, by God himself, and that it deserves in this view our most joyful confidence and trust."[27]

For more than a decade, Nevin had been teamed with Philip Schaff at Mercersburg. During the summer of 1865, Schaff presented a view much like Nevin's to the Germans and Swiss who gathered to learn of the religious aspect of the war between the states: "A country—where so many streams of noble blood have flowed, where so many sacrifices were offered by the government and the people, and where the hand of God so visibly and wonderfully guided events to a happy end—must have, according to all human reasoning, a great future. It has passed through the fiery trial and has now entered into the maturity of manly strength and self-sufficiency."[28]

An American thinker who shared much of Nevin and Schaff's romantic view of the world but who had long since passed beyond the boundaries of traditional Christianity nonetheless also saw matters very much as did the Christian theologians. For their annual memorial lecture on 19 April 1865, the citizens of Concord, Massachusetts, called upon native son Ralph Waldo Emerson. As might be expected, Emerson's remarks did not focus so much on the great event that had taken place at Concord Green ninety years before but on the American president who had been slain only five days earlier. In his closing words, Emerson betrayed no doubts about his certainty that Lincoln had been divinity's agent to bring all of the human race toward perfection:

> There is a serene Providence which rules the fate of nations, which makes little account of time, little of one generation or race, makes no account of disasters, conquers alike by what is called defeat or by what is called victory, thrusts aside enemy and obstruction, crushes everything immoral as inhuman, and obtains the ultimate triumph of the best race by the sacrifice of everything which resists the moral laws of the world. It makes its own instruments, creates the man for the time, trains him in poverty, inspires his genius, and arms him for his task. It has given every race its own talent, and ordains that only that race which combines perfectly with the virtues of all shall endure.[29]

The major American theologian who stood furthest removed from the sentiments of Ralph Waldo Emerson was Charles Hodge. As the Civil War unfolded, Hodge had written for the *Biblical Repertory and Princeton Review* the most responsible series of theological reflections to be found anywhere in the United States. His eulogy for Lincoln in the July number shared many of the virtues of his earlier essays, but it could not escape the American quest for beneficent certainty. It was as clear to Hodge as to his theological confreres what God had done and why he had done it:

> The first and most obvious consequence of the dreadful civil war just ended, has been the final and universal overthrow of slavery within the limits of the United States. This is one of the most momentous events in the history of the

world. That it was the design of God to bring about this event cannot be doubted. . . . Almost all foreigners, and a large class of our own people predicted the success of the South. . . . But God has ordered it otherwise. . . . The inevitable difficulties and sufferings consequent on such an abrupt change in the institutions and social organization of a great people, must be submitted to, as comprehended in the design of God in these events.[30]

In the South, the losers naturally read the mind of God differently than did their fellow Christians in the North. But with the theologians of the Union, Southerners thought they could see just as clearly what God was doing and why. So it was with John Adger when in late 1865 he used the columns of the *Southern Presbyterian Review* to reflect on the nature of providence. Southern Christians were not wrong to believe "honestly and earnestly in the justice of the Southern cause." Rather, "the error of some was in allowing themselves to receive the popular idea . . . that God must surely bless the right." But such ones had forgotten that God in his wisdom often allows suffering and sometimes lets "the righteous to be overthrown." The great difficulty in accepting this lesson was because Confederates had defended "a cause which seemed to them so pre-eminently just." Then Adger repeated the standard justification: "Here, in their view, was a cruel, unjust, and wicked war of invasion upon free States, and they sister States also, urged on, in great part, by an infidel fanaticism. They took it for granted that the Almighty would never allow such a cause to triumph. They prayed fervently for the success of the Confederacy, and they never doubted that their prayers would be heard." But it had become obvious that this reasoning harbored "an error." God had not promised victory to his servants; he had retained sovereignty over events. And so Adger concluded: "We accept the failure of secession, as manifestly providential. The overthrow of that just cause made evident not so much the prowess of its foes, nor even their prodigiously superior resources, as it did the direct hand of the Almighty."[31]

The contrast between the learned religious thinkers and Lincoln in how they interpreted the war poses the great theological puzzle of the Civil War. Abraham Lincoln, a layman with no standing in a church and no formal training as a theologian, propounded a thick, complex view of God's rule over the world and a morally nuanced picture of America's destiny. The country's best theologians, by contrast, presented a thin, simple view of God's providence and a morally juvenile view of the nation and its fate.

The theologians talked as if God had accomplished all that had been done, yet they assumed that humans could control their own destinies. Lincoln urged his fellow citizens to seize the opportunities of the moment but did not assume that they could control their own fate. For the theologians there was little mystery in how God dealt with the world; for Lincoln there was awesome mystery. For the theologians, God's power remained securely tethered to the interests of the United States, however differently that interest was perceived. But for Lincoln, God's power was controlled by no one but God. Many of the theologians found only the language of Christian salvation adequate for describing the rescue of the nation; for Lincoln the question of

whether the nation could be rescued evoked the language of Christian sovereignty. For the theologians the end of the war only tightened the bond between God and his American chosen people; for Lincoln the course of the
war injected a doubt about whether America was the people of God.

Qualifying the Puzzle

In actual historical situations dichotomies are rarely as clear as they first appear, and so it is with this one. A few qualifications are necessary. First, some
of the theologians were in fact able to draw on more sophisticated reasoning
to provide less superficial opinions about the meaning of the war. John W.
Nevin, for example, took considerable pains during his address on 4 July 1865
to acknowledge the grievous wrongs of Northern society.[32] By 1867 he was
also displaying considerably more humility in reading the mind of God. It
was still clear to him that "the march of events" spoke of "universal and fundamental changes," but he was no longer as confident about his ability to
fathom the direction of those changes: "We have no assurance in these signs
that the change will move on victoriously in the line of universal righteousness and truth."[33] For his part, if Charles Hodge joined his contemporaries
with a simplistic reading of providence and the war, he nonetheless had begun
his eulogy for Lincoln with a sensitive discussion of the multiple layers of
causation by which any single event could legitimately be analyzed.[34] John
Adger, though firm in his apology for the South, nonetheless saw clearly how
easy it was for passionate politics to devour true religion.[35] And in each of
the other religious thinkers whose simplistic notions on providence have been
cited, there were moments of analysis more faithful to the broader claims of
Christian tradition and less jejune about the contemporary moment.

A second qualification concerns Abraham Lincoln. Although his thoughts
about providence were unusual in their depth, Lincoln nonetheless never
entirely gave up the myth of the chosen nation. Nor was it always easy to see
how his belief in the absolute sovereignty of the divine will differed from sub-
Christian notions of an absolute fatalism. In addition, Lincoln's sense that
God communicated with him intuitively also seems more a product of folk
religion than of traditional Christianity.[36]

Third, it is not entirely true that Lincoln was unique in holding the theological principles expressed in the Second Inaugural. It does, however, seem
that those who shared his perplexity about the ways of providence or who
doubted the automatic connection between divinity and America were not
members of the Protestant mainstream. A number of his contemporaries were
in the process of leaving traditional beliefs behind, and some of that number
expressed their own ambiguous conclusions about the ultimate destiny of
America.[37] Others with some affinities to Lincoln's views remained preoccupied with the Christian God but had abandoned allegiance to traditional
churches. From her retreat in Amherst, Massachusetts, Emily Dickinson seems
to have followed the war closely, with Amherst acquaintances enlisting and

some not returning and with her own father one of Amherst's leading promoters of Union arms.[38] Its events also seemed to have intensified her lifelong struggles concerning death, God, and the tragic character of human existence. Something of the war's stimulus to her kind of religious reflection may be caught in her poems, as perhaps in this one, probably written in 1865:

> Far from Love the Heavenly Father
> Leads the Chosen Child,
> Oftener through Realm of Briar
> Than the Meadow mild.
>
> Oftener by the Claw of Dragon
> Than the Hand of Friend
> Guides the Little One predestined
> To the Native Land.[39]

As it may have been for Emily Dickinson, so it was for Herman Melville, who observed the last half of the war from a new residence in New York City. What he saw seems to have renewed his wrestling with the cosmic themes that had been displayed so powerfully in *Moby Dick* (1851). Words that Nathaniel Hawthorne had written about Melville in 1856 remained true throughout the war: "He can neither believe, nor be comfortable in his unbelief; and he is too honest and courageous not to try to do one or the other. If he were a religious man, he would be one of the most truly religious and reverential; he has a very high and noble nature, and better worth immortality than most of us."[40] In 1864 and 1865 Melville either completed or composed a lengthy cycle of poems entitled *Battle-Pieces,* where there could be heard, even if almost none of his contemporaries were listening, conclusions like those to which Lincoln was also coming. In the words of the prose postscript to this work: "Noble was the gesture into which patriotic passion surprised the people in a utilitarian time and country; yet the glory of the war falls short of its pathos—a pathos which now at last ought to disarm all animosity."[41]

Qualifications, therefore, are necessary in approaching the theological puzzle of the Civil War. The theologians were not entirely superficial; Lincoln was not a theological paragon; and a few parallels can be found to some of Lincoln's most serious theological pronouncements. But necessary qualifications having been made, the puzzle still remains. Abraham Lincoln, and only a few others also beyond the Protestant mainstream, interpreted the war with a theological depth largely absent from the major theologians of the main Protestant churches.

How did this situation come about? Accounting for the singularity of Lincoln's faith must feature the singular combination of his life circumstances and experiences, as these have been described by the best biographies.[42] These circumstances included a life repeatedly scarred by the deaths of his nearest relatives and friends, an arresting conjunction of mental ability and personal insecurity, his thorough acquaintance with strict predestinarian theology (successively in hard-shell Baptist and Old School Presbyterian forms), the quasi-religious views Lincoln held of the American nation, and the strains of his domestic and political existence raised to an extraordinary height by the war itself.[43] To explain the theology of the theologians requires a rehearsal of the main arguments of this book.

Explaining the Theologians

During the two generations following the American Revolution, evangelical Protestants of several varieties undertook the task of evangelizing and civilizing the new United States. In the face of great odds, they succeeded—despite a serious decline in the churches dating from the mid-eighteenth century, an abandonment of traditional Christianity by almost all the nation's revered founding fathers, an overwhelming repudiation of the reverence for tradition that had long been associated with Catholic and Protestant Christianity, a sharp decline in the relative cultural influence of weekly sermons in favor of newspapers and popular print, and a replacement of theology by political ideology as the most prominent form of public discourse. Yet despite these circumstances, evangelical Protestants in the early republic succeeded, not only in winning individuals to Christianity, but in creating a Christian civilization, because they could demonstrate how their form of the faith might vivify, ennoble, and lend transcendent value to the most influential ideological engines of the nation: republican political assumptions themselves, democratic convictions about social organization, scientific reasoning pitched to common sense, and belief in the unique, providential destiny of the United States.

Because of their success in proclaiming the Christian faith in the conceptual languages provided by these ideological themes, evangelical Protestants created a formidable Christian civilization. Church membership, of which nearly three-fourths was Protestant of British heritage, rose sharply. So successful was this Christianization that by at least the third decade of the century, church adherence became the most reliable indicator of voting behavior.[44] In different ways, many parts of the South, New England, and the expanding West were subdued by Methodist piety, joined with a skillful apologetic theology from the older Calvinist churches. The result was the discovery by Alexis de Tocqueville in the early 1830s that "America is . . . the place in the world where the Christian religion has most preserved genuine powers over souls; and nothing shows better how useful and natural to man it is in our day, since the country in which it exercises the greatest empire is at the same time the most enlightened and most free."[45]

God, as defined by the varieties of Protestant evangelicalism, was everywhere ascendant. The Protestant Bible, interpreted in a democratically evangelical fashion, became the nation's book. If Protestant success had its underside—if, for example evangelicals exercised their political influence through "Manicheanism and unforgiving, uncomplicated moralism"—it was still the "golden day of democratic evangelicalism."[46] From many angles, a pinnacle of Christian civilization had been reached where voluntary societies accomplished prodigies of moral discipline and recurring waves of revivals swept more and more individuals into the kingdom.

If, however, evangelical Protestantism was triumphant, it was also domesticated. The religion of evangelicalism was demonstrably shaping the institutions, values, work habits, and self-conception of the new nation. Evangelicals propounded a religion that, before their very eyes, was *working*, both to convert ever greater proportions of the nation and to transform ever more of the society's institutions. For the sake of the theological enterprise, it may have been working too well.

Certainly the evangelical juggernaut was working too well for a few souls who, if they could not stop wrestling with God, still wondered if the energetic God of the Protestant evangelicals was adequate for the complexities of the universe or the turmoils of their own souls. So Emily Dickinson, Herman Melville, and supremely Abraham Lincoln may have been pushed by the successes of "American Christianity" into post-Protestant, even post-Christian, theism. The tragedy of these individuals was that to be faithful to the God they found in their own hearts—or in the Bible, or in the sweep of events— they had to hold themselves aloof from the organized Christianity of the United States and from its preaching about the message of Jesus Christ.

But the American God may also have been working too well for the Protestant theologians who, even as they exploited Scripture and pious experience so successfully, yet found it easy to equate America's moral government of God with Christianity itself. Their tragedy—and the greater the theologian, the greater the tragedy—was to rest content with a God defined by the American conventions God's own loyal servants had exploited so well.

The theological puzzle of the Civil War thus reveals a theological tragedy, both for those who retained profundity at the expense of Christianity and those who retained Christianity at the expense of profundity. In the decades before the Civil War, a Protestant amalgam of traditional faith and public order helped construct a great Christian civilization, but commitment to that very civilization would in the Civil War trivialize the Christian theology that had brought it into existence.

Conclusion

Contexts and Dogma

Theology is about ideas but there can be no ideas without people, no Christian people without churches, no churches without contexts that are political, social, and cultural in nature.
—David Wells, "The Debate over the Atonement in Nineteenth-Century America," 1987

In this book I have tried to describe the migration of meanings attached to a particular set of words—words like freedom, virtue, benevolence, slavery, vice, selfishness—that for the years 1730 to 1865 were as highly charged in public debate as in theological discussion. Almost everyone in those decades believed that these words reflected concrete, universal realities. Most of the time it was assumed that the words referred to matters of ultimate consequence for individuals, communities, and nations. Public spokespersons were convinced that on their controversies concerning the will, the nature of sin, the imputation of Adam's guilt or Christ's righteousness, the nature and extent of the atonement, and related dogmatic questions hung nothing less than eternal life. Their seriousness about how God rescued humans from sin was matched by their seriousness about how rescued sinners might build a peaceful, prosperous, and yet benevolent life for themselves and their nation. They were not playing around. The main burden of the book—besides its history of theological developments themselves—has been to show how the spheres of secular and religious discourse were connected and how the ebb and flow of meanings between these spheres affected efforts to define the central dogmas of Christian faith.

439

Recapitulation

Connections between public life and religious life are not the only way to explain doctrinal change, but for this period they work very well, especially for the most important concepts in American theological life. The migration of meaning for the idea of justice provides a good illustration of a general pattern.

For Jonathan Edwards, justice was one of the divine perfections, ranked in his sermon "The Justice of God in the Damnation of Sinners" with the perfection of the divine "loveliness, honorableness, and authority."[1] A century later, connotations had shifted. For N. W. Taylor, God's justice had become "one specific form or modification of benevolence . . . disapproving, abhorring, and determining to punish sin in the subjects of his government, as that which undermines his authority and tends to destroy the highest happiness, and to produce all evil."[2] For Charles Finney, it was almost the same: "Justice, as an attribute of benevolence, is virtue, and exhibits itself in the execution of the penalties of the law, and in support of public order, and in various other ways for the well-being of mankind."[3] In both cases, an ontological category has been rendered operational, a final value transformed into an instrumental value.

Connections with the evolution of public discourse are both substantial and formal. For a usage close to Edwards's conception, in the classical republicanism that first swept over the colonies in the mid-eighteenth century, justice regularly connoted an abstract, nearly Platonic norm of moral order. By 1820 in liberal America it had come to mean an equipoise of moral principles, a balance, as Isaac Kramnick has put it, in "the Lockean . . . world of personal rights, and most dramatically of property rights."[4] Changes in American society did not dictate what theologians wrote, but they provided a nurturing context for what they wanted to say.

Even more telling was the transformation of the idea of virtue. In the colonies during the 1760s and 1770s, virtue usually implied something close to what it had meant in the civic humanist tradition—a public-spirited attitude that subordinated "personal interest to the public welfare." By 1830 virtue had become a much more private quality, a standard of personal morality, "something that women guarded within the household, something that they protected against lustful males."[5]

For religious thinkers, the parallel shift of meaning was from contemplative theocentricism to activistic anthropocentricism. In Edwards's famous formulation, "True virtue must chiefly consist in *love to God*; the Being of beings, infinitely the greatest and best."[6] A century later, virtue had become an activity. For Taylor, the person of virtue was "the man who governs himself."[7] For Finney, it was important to show "that nothing can be virtue or true religion but obedience to [God's] law," and "that the Government of God acknowledges nothing else as virtue or true religion."[8] The parallel movement between theology and public discourse was from defining virtue as an all-encompassing reality touching the very nature of things to defining it as a quality oriented to the exercise of responsibility by individuals for their own happiness.

The most obvious change in the century under consideration concerned notions of freedom. To early republicans, liberty meant "the right of the people to share in the government." In liberal America, it had become "unrestrained competition and equality, an absence of built-in handicap."[9] The parallel development in theology was just as abrupt. In Edwards's *Freedom of Will*, liberty meant "power, opportunity, or advantage, that anyone has, to do as he pleases. Or in other words, his being free from hindrance or impediment in the way of doing, or conducting in any respect, as he wills."[10] For Taylor, freedom meant "power to do otherwise" in all moral choices—thus, the human being was "a free agent without the aids of divine grace."[11] Finney was even more direct: "The moral government of God everywhere assumes and implies the liberty of the human will, and the natural ability to obey God. Every command, every threatening, every expostulation and denunciation in the bible implies and assumes this. Nor does the bible do violence to the human intelligence in this assumption; for . . . the human mind necessarily assumes the freedom of the human will as a first truth."[12] Once again the parallel was as much formal as substantial, but with immense significance. In 1740 "freedom" was something about which to reason, a quality of human life as a whole to be considered in relation to other aspects of the self, and a positive value that nevertheless needed to be fenced in by other weightier considerations. In 1840 it had become axiomatic, the fundamental defining trait of human morality, and a value than which nothing was greater.

Observing how one perceptive American described the content of Christian belief in his nation's churches offers another testimony to the nature of theological development in the century between Edwards and Finney. Primarily because it was not a work of factional theological argument, Robert Baird's path-breaking *Religion in the United States of America* (from 1843) provides an excellent gauge of continuities and discontinuities at work in the Americanization of theology. Baird (1798–1863) was a centrist figure, a moderate, ecumenically minded Presbyterian, who wrote this book to inform Europeans about the character of church life in the United States. It turned out to be the era's most informative general volume on the subject for his fellow citizens as well.[13]

To follow Baird as he expounded upon what he took to be "the extent of doctrinal agreement and diversity in and among the communions classed together as evangelical" was to see distinctly American habits of mind leading to at least some convictions shaped distinctly by the American setting. Baird, for example, was as casual in his dismissal of theological traditions as he was confident in his own unassisted abilities to interpret the Scriptures: "The questions, What did Edwards hold? What did the Puritans hold? What did the Reformers hold? What did Augustine, Jerome, or the other earlier fathers hold?—though admitted to be important in their place, are regarded as of small importance in comparison with the questions, What said the scripture? What did Christ and the apostles teach?" Not Christianity as "the dead formalism of ecclesiastical institutions—upheld by law, tradition, or the force of fashion," but "the Christianity of the New Testament" prevailed in America. Again, Baird gloried in the fact that "religious opinion and theological science in the United States" were moving "towards a higher appreciation of the simplest and most scriptural Christianity"—"the primitive simplicity of Christian truth." Baird linked his account of true Christianity as intuitively simple with his understanding of how human consciousness functioned. It was a distortion of the faith to feature "speculations about Christianity—remote from any application to the conscience." By contrast, it was proper Christianity to offer a religion "that can be *preached*, and that, being preached, will commend itself to every man's conscience in the sight of God."[14]

Baird's depiction of America's dynamic evangelical religion shared many particulars with pietistic accounts of Christianity found in other traditionally Protestant regions. Yet their American cast was also obvious. Baird distrusted inherited intellectual authority. He expressed great confidence in the individual conscience. He regarded a written document as the cornerstone of his faith and contended that interpreting this document was an inherently simple task. In Baird's account of evangelical Christianity, there is much more than a republican commonsense Enlightenment, but there is also nothing less.

The bearing of such influences on specific Christian doctrines was subtle but manifest. For Baird and for many of his peers, the American setting was especially important for explaining how God was reconciled to sinners and sinners to God—that is, for the doctrine of the atonement. It was Baird's opinion that "the great achievement of American theology" was to clarify "the doctrine of the atonement for sin in the clearest light, by illustrations drawn from the nature of a moral government." Baird's depiction of the atonement in governmental terms was not particularly unusual for Protestant theologies outside the United States during the mid-nineteenth century. What was unusual was Baird's way of setting forth the doctrine. God, for Baird, was primarily "a moral governor of beings made for responsible action." He was not "the God of philosophy," but "a moral governor, . . . a lawgiver, a judge, a dispenser of rewards and penalties." God takes on these roles, moreover, "for the one great end of promoting the happiness of that vast empire." Christ's self-sacrificing death was necessary because God's "law is not arbitrary." Rather, since God's law exists "for accomplishing the greatest good," it cannot merely be set aside. Jesus was sent into the world "to be made a sin-offering for us," by so doing to show that God is righteous. The effect of Christ's action was to enable God to call all sinners to repent and to use "the co-operation of redeemed and renewed men in advancing the work of saving their fellowmen." For Baird, this way of depicting the atonement had the great merit of restoring to Christianity "the freedom, simplicity, and directness" of the early apostolic writings. The result was to show that people were saved, "not by mere power, but by means that harmonise with the nature, and conduce to the ends of God's moral government."[15]

The "American" contribution to this governmental view of the atonement was visible on several levels. As depicted by Baird, God was exonerated from being arbitrary and from exercising power despotically; by contrast, he was praised for administering his duties fairly and for treating humans as the great object of his affections. Baird held that people, while still clearly indebted to God for many mercies, were naturally capable of moral action and cooperation with God in his designs for the world. For Baird, the process of salvation was cleansed of any notion that humans were servilely dependent upon God or bound by the character of their own selves as sinners. The resulting state of Christian redemption was therefore ideal for purposeful, effective, voluntary action in the world, and the Christian message was apprehended best when individuals responded directly, freely, and simply to the straightforward message of the New Testament. In sum, for Baird, the controlling paradigm to explain what was good or evil about the functioning of the universe was the notion of government. To the extent that Robert Baird was correct in claiming that his summary of the Christian faith was shared by most American Protestants, it was to the same extent an indication of theology being tailored to its contexts.

Assessment

The way in which the most widely respected antebellum theologians of the United States engaged in such intellectual tailoring revealed both the success and the failure of Christian thinking in this era when the churches were more central to American culture than ever before or since. Put positively, the theologians translated the historic Christian message into the dominant cultural languages of politics and intellectual life so successfully that these languages were themselves converted and then enlisted for the decidedly religious purposes of evangelism, church formation, moral reform, and theological construction.[16]

Put negatively, the theologians may have been too successful. After he had twice visited the United States in the 1930s, Dietrich Bonhoeffer wrote a perceptive essay contrasting Christian development in America with parallel developments in the parts of Europe most directly shaped by the Protestant Reformation. His assessment included an observation that was as shrewd in its comparative wisdom as it is relevant for the themes of this book: *"The secularization of the church on the continent of Europe* arises from the misinterpretation of the reformers' distinction of the two realms [of church and society]; *American secularization* derives precisely from the imperfect distinction of the kingdoms and offices of church and state, from the enthusiastic claim of the church to universal influence in the world."[17] What Bonhoeffer saw has been described with other terms here: The key moves in the creation of evangelical America were also the key moves that created secular America. If in a great surge of evangelization and moral reform, American Protestants almost converted the nation, so too did the nation mold the Christian gospel in the contours of its own shape.[18]

The gains and loses from the dynamic translations of the era —for the body politic, for the churches, for religion in general, and for the Christian faith in particular—cannot be assessed simply. Attentive readers of these pages will realize that if I had to recommend only one American theologian for the purposes of understanding God, the self, and the world as they really are, I would respond as the Separatist Congregational minister Israel Holly did in 1770 when he found himself engaged in theological battle: "Sir, if I was to engage with you in this controversy, I would say, *Read Edwards!* And if you wrote again, I would tell you to *Read Edwards!* And if you wrote again, I would still tell you to *Read Edwards!*"[19]

Yet the story told in this book cannot be read as decline, for it was a history where every step backward in one sphere of existence was matched by at least one step forward in another. Jonathan Edwards's thought was more rigorously doxological than the thought of any nineteenth-century religious thinker, but evangelists of that latter period did more to Christianize and civilize unchurched Americans in a free-form liberal society than Edwards could ever have done. George Whitefield's picture of human nature was more Augustinian—that is, realistic and traditional—than Charles Finney's, but Finney's democratized theology saw the moral offense of slavery more clearly than Whitefield's pious Calvinism. Puritan theologians possessed a more cohesive ideal of community than did American voluntarists of the 1840s, but voluntarism proved more effective at incorporating strangers and immigrants into communities of faith and service than had the Puritans. It is an oft-stated truism, but worthy of repetition, that if the theological and ecclesiastical changes described here had not taken place, it is not humanly conceivable that American religious beliefs and practices would have remained, by comparison with the rest of the Western world, so relatively vigorous as they remain to this day.[20]

With tradition, hierarchy, and deference to historical precedent discredited by the ideology of the Revolution, religious thinkers in the national period made do with what was left in their efforts to preserve Christian doctrine and inspire Christian practice. The materials at hand were commonsense moral reasoning, narratives of republican liberation, and the Bible. With all thought of a Christian establishment washed away by the republican tide, believers knew it depended upon themselves and the direct ministrations of the Holy Spirit to do what had to be done. An extraordinary mobilization of the churches was the result. The substantial contribution of this religious mobilization to the construction of a national culture—inadvertently from the Methodists, with more forethought from the older formalist churches—was, in nearly literal terms, a gift of grace.

Yet because the churches could make that gift only because they had themselves absorbed the national ideologies so thoroughly, the gift came at a high price. Uniquely in modern Western history, recognizably orthodox theology flourished in the construction of a liberal society. Yet profoundly as that theology flourished and as vitally as it helped build the nation, its inability to grasp as high as it reached was evident by the century's middle decades. As for so much else in American history, so too for theology was the Civil War a grand climax and transition.

Theological debates on the issues that led to the war drew American religious thinking deeper into the intellectual patterns that had been established between the founding of the republic and the outbreak of armed conflict. The cultural influence of those theological habits had been extraordinary, in fact so extraordinary that even the cataclysm of total war could not completely overwhelm them. Yet if these patterns—the merger of Reformed biblicism with principles of American freedom expounded by the canons of common-sense moral philosophy—were too strong to be destroyed, they were nonetheless permanently damaged.

It was thus neither farce nor irony when the religious habits of mind that had built a Protestant Christian America divided and eventually petered out after the war. It was rather a tragedy of worthy thinkers striving faithfully for noble goals who were brought down by the very synthesis of Christian theology and American ideology that had transformed their society and made them its intellectual leaders. As a result of these deeply entrenched patterns of thought, and also because of the way that theological debates over issues like the Bible and slavery were settled by armies instead of arguments, American theology lurched, rather than self-consciously thought, its way into the modern world.

Appendix

Historiography of Republicanism and Religion

Recent historical writing has made abundantly clear that "republicanism" was a multivalent, plastic, and often extraordinarily imprecise term. This large but turbulent stream of contested historiography must be assessed in order to understand what "Christian republicanism" meant in the early history of the United States and, then, how the amalgamation of Christian and republican values affected theological understanding. Such an assessment pays particular dividends, however, since it allows for a fuller integration of religious convictions into the broader national history.

The heated historical debates of the last half century over the place of republican and liberal ideologies in the founding of the United States have produced several important benefits. These benefits come from well-documented attempts to define a single, dominant ideology for American political life. In the years after World War II, the process began with assertions by a Lockean school of political scientists concerning the centrality of a timeless set of liberal principles for the American founding. "The Perspectives of 1776," as described in an influential book by Louis Hartz, came from John Locke's "basic social norm, the concept of free individuals in a state of nature." According to Hartz, "the master assumption of American political thought" was "the reality of atomistic social freedom."[1]

The republican "nay" to this liberal "yea" represented a first-order historical challenge but also eventually became the subject of massive historiographical attention itself.[2] Not modern principles of individual liberty or abstract rights applied in an American setting but ancient commitments to public justice and historically conditioned standards of public virtue were the new keys unlocking the meaning of the American founding. In the influential view of Bernard Bailyn, various historic influences had come to bear on the founding generation, but the writers who "dominated the colonists' miscellaneous learning and shaped it into a coherent whole" reflected "the radical social and political thought of the English Civil War and of the Commonwealth period." That writing, in turn, was given "permanent form . . . at the turn of the seventeenth century and in the early eighteenth century, in the writings of a group of prolific opposition theorists, 'country' politicians and publicists."[3] What these commonwealth or country theorists advocated was a stance that Gordon Wood summarized as a function of republican reasoning: "The sacrifice of individual interests to the greater good of the whole formed the essence of republicanism and comprehended for Americans the idealistic goal of their Revolution."[4]

It was the special contribution of J. G. A. Pocock to trace a pedigree for these republican values deep into early modern Europe. Pocock would later summarize his own understanding of this tradition, first excavated in *The Machiavellian Moment* (1975) and then refined in a series of learned rejoinders to his critics, as preoccupation with a single word: "To be 'republican' . . . was not merely to take up a posture on the left wing of mixed-government doctrine; it was also to commit oneself to engaging, one way or another, in a discourse about 'virtue.'" Pocock, though, repeatedly insisted on the complexity of that engagement: "The reflective discourse of the eighteenth century was deeply concerned with the problematic nature of virtue; with the difficulty of maintaining it and the difficulty of moving away from it; with the gains to human culture that came from specialization, politeness, and enlightenment; with the losses to human culture that came from abandoning the belief that the moral personality expressed itself directly in political activity."[5] To Pocock, grasping the dense complexity of republican (but also liberal) wrestling with "virtue" was critical for understanding the American founding.

The thesis that the new American nation rested on a civic humanist, Real Whig, and republican foundation soon generated a sharply argued antithesis reasserting the central place of a more sophisticated, more democratic, and more historically conditioned liberalism. In revisions proposed especially by Joyce Appleby and Isaac Kramnick, the liberalism of the Revolutionary era was seen as incorporating some of the republican emphases stressed by Bailyn, Wood, and Pocock, but it was defined primarily by concern for personal interests in the new commercial, proto-capitalist contingencies of the late eighteenth century.[6] According to Kramnick, "The radicals of the later eighteenth century, both English and American, were much more likely to base their arguments on natural rights than on historical rights; they were preoccupied less with nostalgic country concerns than with very modern socioeconomic grievances." Again, "the interests of the talented and hard-working middle class" were critical for understanding protests against British imperial authority.[7]

Joyce Appleby's criticism of the republican interpretation has stressed developments in the constitutional period and following years. As Appleby studied the second half of the eighteenth century, she concluded that new possibilities in commerce, science, and psychological self-understanding were defining a propitious moment for the exaltation of personal liberty. An alteration of material conditions was critical for American ideology: "The importance of the free market to this development cannot be reduced to economics. . . . It was the economy's ordering of society with minimal compulsion that stirred the Jeffersonian imagination."[8] In her picture, "This changing balance between the demands of the community and the individual helps explain . . . why liberalism with its core affirmation of the individual's claim upon society to protect his natural rights could so easily have displaced the devotion to order which animated colonial life a half-century earlier."[9] To these critics of a universal republican interpretation, principles of disinterested justice, balanced liberty, and classical virtue may explain some aspects of early American thought, but not nearly as many as individual and individualistic responses to rapidly changing social and economic conditions.

The clash between grand interpretations has given modern students a much broader understanding of the varied communities that participated in political deliberations from the mid-eighteenth century onward. At the same time, even more important benefits have arisen from the realization that this particular historiographical battle is unwinnable. Some of those benefits are unusually useful for a history of theology. It is not as if historians have simply been creating intellectual hegemony where no discernible ebb and flow of ideologies actually existed. It is rather that the clash of interpretations has pushed understanding of the really existing historical situation toward greater flexibility, multivocality, and nuance. Elements that historians once attempted to describe as discrete and competing principles, constructs, or conceptual languages are now much easier to see as overlapping, intermingled, or clashing in ways not conforming to modern categories. For example, Gordon Wood, who still defends the importance of discriminating between republican and liberal perspectives, nonetheless states clearly what many others have also concluded: "Classical republicanism in the eighteenth century was not a clearly discernible body of thought to which people self-consciously adhered. And what we call Lockean liberalism was even less manifest and less palpable." If, in Wood's account, "none of the historical participants, including the Founders, ever had any sense that he had to choose between republicanism and liberalism, between Machiavelli and Locke," then neither should modern historians. "These boxlike categories of 'republicanism' and 'liberalism' are . . . necessarily dangerous distortions of past reality."[10]

Some of what lies behind contemporary understanding of ideological complexity in early America are successful attempts to show that intellectual commitments, once treated as distinct, actually existed together in the integrated thought of important individuals or groups. Thus, principles that later historians described as competitive streams labeled "liberal" and "republican" were actually folded together for Algernon Sidney in the late seventeenth century, as well as for many of those who harkened back to Sidney over the course of the next century. The same conclusion has been reached for the Real

Whig arguments of "Cato" (John Trenchard and Thomas Gordon) from the early 1720s. And John Locke was read with appreciation by many colonists who described themselves self-consciously as republicans.[11] If these demonstrations highlight the danger of letting modern categories tyrannize the thought of historical actors, they also encourage efforts to probe more deeply into other intellectual alliances, including alliances involving religion.

Yet even after artificially reified accounts have been set aside, an overwhelming preponderance of carefully sifted historical evidence still points to the fact that American ideology was shifting during the years of the early republic. That shift was toward ways of thought accommodating to commercial expansion, economic and political rights, and the fulfillment of the individual self.

When and how rapidly that shift took place does remain a historically contested question. A few historians date the transition from the 1760s, a few during the Revolutionary War itself, more in the years immediately following that conflict, and still more in the early years of the nineteenth century.[12] John Murrin's discussion of the historiographical situation summarizes clearly the points of historiographical consensus, as well as the lingering disagreements: Virtually all students "have insisted . . . that there was a transition, a before and after. We do not believe that America was born modern [i.e., liberal]. . . . We probably do agree that the shift to modernity was virtually complete by the 1820s, but no doubt we can still quarrel about how it happened, among whom, and why."[13]

The most direct benefit for a history of theology from the republican-liberal debates has been a broader reconceptualization of intellectual history in the periods of the Revolution and early republic. Recognizing that neither an airtight republicanism nor an equally hegemonic liberalism dominated public intellectual life has led at least some historians to reevaluate the place of religion. Richard B. Morris nicely captured this broader ideological purview by noting that "the Founding Fathers were a product of covenant theology, common-law teaching, of a belief in the supremacy of the parliament over the king, mixed with radical commonwealth thought, plus a heavy dose of Enlightenment thinking, leavened with Hume and Scottish Enlightenment thought, and some unique constitutional ideas of their own."[14] Coming directly from the debate over republican versus liberal paradigms, Isaac Kramnick has contended that a bipolar depiction of early American ideology was simply too simple. Rather, at least four "distinguishable idioms" existed: the republicanism and liberalism familiar from a thousand discussions, but also what Kramnick calls "work-ethic Protestantism" and "state-centered theories of power and sovereignty."[15] John Murrin has gone even further in contending that at least six "discernible value systems" were being put to use by those who formed the American nation: besides civic humanism and liberalism, Murrin cites "Calvinist orthodoxy," "Anglican moralism," "Tom Paine radicalism," and "Scottish moral sense . . . philosophy."[16] Other historians have added still other intellectual streams, like natural-law reasoning and political economy.[17] The important point for this book is that these more comprehensive accounts of American ideology understand religious thought as fully active in the ideological clearinghouse that was the early United States. Rather than assuming that religious belief functioned merely as private opinion or as passively held intellectual convictions reacting to supposedly more basic commitments strewn along the republican-liberal axis, historians now have a new arena opened up for research. Perhaps the ideological balance of trade did flow more strongly from a liberalizing public sphere into religious thought, but by identifying historical religious positions as ideologically potent, the newer picture promotes research rather than gratuitous assumptions.

The general opening up of early American ideological history to the possibility that religious beliefs played an active role is supported by two other historiographical trends. First, a number of researchers have criticized the paradigm-setting discussions for neglecting the ideological force of religion in the early republic.[18] Second, a number of impressive studies have begun to make the case for how that religious influence actually worked.[19] If some of the writing emphasizing the foundational role of religious conviction in the era's most important political conclusions repeats the all-or-nothing tendency of earlier republican-liberal standoffs, most does not. It argues not for the singular domination of religious conviction but its relative importance in relation to other value systems. By making such claims, religious thought not only is restored to its proper historical place in America history but also is opened up for study in relationship to the era's other ideological forces. For understanding the emphases, tone, content, and assumptions of theology during the first two-thirds of the nineteenth century, the inner connections of the nation's early ideological history are of first importance.

Notes

Abbreviations

ANB = *American National Biography*, 24 vols. Edited by John A. Garraty and Mark C. Carnes. New York, 1999.

BDEB = *Blackwell Dictionary of Evangelical Biography: 1730–1860,* 2 vols. (numbered consecutively). Edited by Donald M. Lewis. Oxford, 1995.

Chapter 1

1. For powerful, if also partisan, evocation of the older situation, see two recent books by J. C. D. Clark, *English Society, 1660–1832,* 2d ed. (Cambridge, 2000); and *The Language of Liberty, 1660–1832: Political Discourse and Social Dynamics in the Anglo-American World* (Cambridge, 1994).

2. Outstanding works on different aspects of these large-scale transitions include Paul Hazard, *The European Mind, 1680–1715* (London, 1953); Hans W. Frei, *The Eclipse of Biblical Narrative: A Study in Eighteenth and Nineteenth Century Hermeneutics* (New Haven, 1974); Frank E. Manuel, *The Changing of the Gods* (Hanover, N.H., 1983); James Turner, *Without God, without Creed: The Origins of Unbelief in America* (Baltimore, 1985); Michael J. Buckley, *At the Origins of Modern Atheism* (New Haven, 1987); Charles Taylor, *Sources of the Self: The Making of the Modern Identity* (Cambridge, Mass., 1989); Jaroslav Pelikan, *The Christian Tradition,* vol. 5, *Christian Doctrine and Modern Culture (since 1700)* (Chicago, 1989), 60–226; and J. B. Schneewind, *The Invention of Autonomy: A History of Modern Moral Philosophy* (New York, 1998).

3. Gordon S. Wood, "Intellectual History and the Social Sciences," in *New Directions in American Intellectual History,* ed. John Higham and Paul K. Conkin (Baltimore, 1979), 34.

4. D. W. Bebbington, *Evangelicalism in Modern Britain: A History from the 1730s to the 1980s* (London, 1989), 2–17.

5. As an example, Sydney Ahlstrom's never-bettered collection of texts in *Theology in America: The Major Protestant Voices from Puritanism to Neo-Orthodoxy* (Indianapolis, 1967) includes as representatives of the period from 1730 to 1865 three Congregationalists, one Unitarian, one Presbyterian, one German Reformed, and Ralph Waldo Emerson, a renegade Unitarian whose theological agenda was a product of narrowly regional concerns. Although Methodists, Baptists, and Roman Catholics had each become larger than the Congregationalists and the Presbyterians by the 1820s or 1830s and although they represented the driving religious force in many parts of the United States beyond the Hudson and Susquehanna Rivers, none of them are included.

6. The formalist and antiformalist categories are discussed below in chap. 8. For helpful definitions, see Curtis D. Johnson, *Redeeming America: Evangelicals and the Road to Civil War* (Chicago, 1993), 7.

7. Note, however, Bruce Kuklick's sage caution about rushing to relate "ideas" to "concrete realities" and "a given milieu"; see his, *Churchmen and Philosophers: From Jonathan Edwards to John Dewey* (New Haven, 1985), 254–55.

8. Alexis de Tocqueville, *Democracy in America*, ed. and trans. Harvey Claflin Mansfield and Delba Winthrop (Chicago, 2000), 282. The same observation is made more generally for Europe and America, 43.

9. Murat, *A Moral and Political Sketch of the United States of North America* (1832), in *The Voluntary Church: American Religious Life, 1740–1860, Seen through the Eyes of European Visitors*, ed. Milton B. Powell (New York, 1967), 50.

10. Philip Schaff, *Der Bürgerkrieg und das christliche Leben in Nord-Amerika* (Berlin, 1866), 68: "Ich glaube nicht, daß irgend ein königliches oder fürstliches oder republikanisches [i.e., radical] Staats-Document aus neuerer Zeit dieser Inauguralrede an ächter christlicher Weisheit und Milde zur Seite gestellt worden kann." For similar opinions, see Félix Dupanloup, the Roman Catholic bishop of Orléans, writing in early April 1865, as recorded in John G. Nicolay and John Hay, *Abraham Lincoln*, 10 vols. (New York, 1904), 10:146n1: "Mais quel beau jour déjà lorsque le chef deux fois élu d'un grand peuple tient un langage chrétien, trop absent, dans notre Europe, du langage officiel des grandes affaires." ("What a beautiful day it is when the twice-elected leader of a great people makes use of Christian language, so lacking in our Europe, for the public language of great events.") See also Solomon Schechter, who first heard of Lincoln through Hebrew-language newspapers in Romania, "Abraham Lincoln," in *Seminary Addresses* (Cincinnati, 1915), 156–57: "When reading these lines [of the Second Inaugural] . . . one can scarcely believe that they formed a part of a message addressed in the nineteenth century to an assembly composed largely of men of affairs and representatives of a special political party, surrounded by all the pomp and paraphernalia of one of the greatest legislative bodies the world has ever seen."

11. For the Protestanism of Scotland, see Stewart Mechie, "The Theological Climate in Early Eighteenth Century Scotland," in *Reformation and Revolution*, ed. Duncan Shaw (Edinburgh, 1967); James K. Cameron, "Theological Controversy: A Factor in the Origins of the Scottish Enlightenment," in *The Origins and Nature of the Scottish Enlightenment*, ed. R. H. Campbell and Andrew S. Skinner (Edinburgh, 1982); Leigh Eric Schmidt, *Holy Fairs: Scottish Communion Seasons and American Revivals in the Early Modern Period* (Princeton, 1989), 11–50; and Philip Graham Ryken, *Thomas Boston as Preacher of the Fourfold State* (Edinburgh, 1999). For Northern Ireland, see Peter Brooke, *Ulster Presbyterianism, 1610–1970* (New York, 1987), 66–92. For The Netherlands and Switzerland, see Richard A. Muller, *Post-Reformation Reformed Dogmatics*, 2 vols. (Grand Rapids, 1987–93); the sections fea-

turing Gisbert Boetius (1589–1687, of Utrecht) and Francis Turretin (1623–87, of Geneva) in *Reformed Dogmatics,* ed. John W. Beardslee (New York, 1965); and Timothy R. Phillips, "The Dissolution of Francis Turretin's Vision of *Theologia*: Geneva at the End of the Seventeenth Century," in *The Identity of Geneva: The Christian Commonwealth, 1564–1864,* ed. John B. Roney and Martin I. Klauber (Westport, Conn., 1998), 77–92.

12. Among many helpful works, see Margaret C. Jacob, *The Newtonians and the English Revolution, 1689–1720* (Ithaca, 1976); Michael R. Watts, *The Dissenters,* vol. 1, *From the Reformation to the French Revolution* (Oxford, 1978), 221–393; Gerard Reedy, S.J., *The Bible and Reason: Anglicans and Scripture in Late Seventeenth-Century England* (Philadelphia, 1985); Ernest Gordon Rupp, *Religion in England, 1688–1791* (Oxford, 1986), 5–206; Isabel Rivers, *Reason, Grace, and Sentiment: A Study of the Language of Religion and Ethics in England, 1660–1780,* vol. 1, *Whichcote to Wesley* (Cambridge, 1991), 1–163; Jeremy Gregory, "The Eighteenth-Century Reformation: The Pastoral Task of Anglican Clergy after 1689," and John Spurr, "The Church, the Societies, and the Moral Revolution of 1688," in *The Church of England, c. 1689–c. 1833: From Toleration to Tractarianism,* ed. John Walsh, Colin Haydon, and Stephen Taylor (Cambridge, 1993), 67–85, 127–42; Nicholas Wolterstorff, "Locke's Philosophy of Religion," in *The Cambridge Companion to Locke,* ed. Vere Chappell (New York, 1994); David A. Pailin, "Rational Religion in England from Herbert of Cherbury to William Paley," in *A History of Religion in Britain,* ed. Sheridan Gilley and W. J. Sheils (Cambridge, 1994), 211–33; and Clark, *English Society.*

13. The most important general works on the international scope of those theological changes are W. R. Ward, *The Protestant Evangelical Awakening* (Cambridge, 1992); and Ward, *Christianity under the Ancien Régime, 1648–1789* (Cambridge, 1999). There is also useful material on broader international circumstances in Marilyn J. Westerkamp, *Triumph of the Laity: Scots-Irish Piety and the Great Awakening, 1625–1760* (New York, 1988); Michael J. Crawford, *Seasons of Grace: Colonial New England's Revival Tradition in Its British Context* (New York, 1991); Patrick Streiff, "Der Methodismus bis 1781/1791," and A. Gregg Roeber, "Der Pietismus in Nordamerika im 18. Jahrhundert," in *Geschichte des Pietismus,* vol. 2, *Der Pietismus im achtzehnten Jahrhundert,* ed. Martin Brecht and Klaus Deppermann (Göttingen, 1995), 617–65, 666–700; and Hartmut Lehman, "Die neue Lage," and Ulrich Gäbler, "Evangelikalismus und Réveil," in *Geschichte des Pietismus,* vol. 3, *19. und 20. Jahrhundert,* ed. Gäbler (Göttingen, 2000), 2–26, 27–84.

14. For religious thinkers in the English-speaking world, themes from the Enlightenment were much more likely to be incorporated into traditional Christian understandings than to contradict them. Contrast Bebbington, *Evangelicalism in Modern Britain,* 20–74; and Henry F. May, *The Enlightenment in America* (New York, 1976), 307–57; with Peter Gay's account for the Continent that stresses the opposition of traditional religion and eighteenth-century thought, *The Enlightenment,* vol. 1, *The Rise of Modern Paganism* (New York, 1966). Even Gay's picture of a standoff between traditional religion and Enlightenment convictions can be questioned: see Sheridan Gilley, "Christianity and Enlightenment: An Historical Survey," *History of European Ideas* 1 (1981): 103–21; and Robert Sullivan, "Rethinking Christianity in Enlightened Europe," *Eighteenth-Century Studies* 34 (2001): 298–309.

15. Solid international studies that see somewhat more commonality across national borders than I do are Claude Welch, *Protestant Thought in the Nineteenth Century,* vol. 1, *1799–1870* (New Haven, 1972); and Walter H. Conser Jr., *Church*

and Confession: Conservative Theologians in Germany, England, and America, 1815–1866 (Macon, Ga., 1984).

16. See Richard B. Sher, *Church and University in the Scottish Enlightenment: The Moderate Literati of Edinburgh* (Princeton, 1985); John R. McIntosh, *Church and Theology in Enlightenment Scotland: The Popular Party, 1740–1800* (East Linton, Scotland, 1998); David Alan Currie, "The Growth of Evangelicalism in the Church of Scotland, 1793–1843" (Ph.D. diss., University of St. Andrews, 1990); and Mark A. Noll, "Revival, Enlightenment, Civic Humanism, and the Evolution of Calvinism in Scotland and America, 1735–1843," in *Amazing Grace: Evangelicalism in Australia, Britain, Canada, and the United States*, ed. George A. Rawlyk and Noll (Kingston and Montreal, and Grand Rapids, 1994), 73–107.

17. See Finlay Holmes, *Our Irish Presbyterian Heritage* (Belfast, 1985), 99–112; and David Hempton and Myrtle Hill, *Evangelical Protestantism in Ulster Society, 1740–1890* (London, 1992), 42–44, 62–80.

18. See Roney and Klauber, *Identity of Geneva*, 129–210. For Holland, see Michael J. Wintle, *Pillars of Piety: Religion in the Netherlands in the Nineteenth Century, 1813–1901* (Hull, Eng., 1987); and Ulrich Gäbler, *Auferstehungszeit: Erweckungsprediger des 19. Jahrhunderts* (Munich, 1991), chap. 4, "Isaac da Costa: Die christliche Nation," 86–114.

19. For solid representatives of immense literatures, see Sheridan Gilley, *Newman and His Age* (Westminster, Md., 1991); and Alan Millar, "Mill on Religion," and Wendy Donner, "Mill's Utilitarianism," in *The Cambridge Companion to Mill*, ed. John Skorupski (Cambridge, 1998), 176–202, 255–92.

20. See especially Boyd Hilton, *The Age of Atonement: The Influence of Evangelicalism on Social and Economic Thought, 1785–1865* (Oxford, 1988); and A. M. C. Waterman, *Revolution, Economics, and Religion: Christian Political Economy, 1798–1833* (Cambridge, 1991); as contrasted to the American situation explored by the contributors to *God and Mammon: Protestants, Money, and the Market, 1790–1860* ed. Mark A. Noll (New York, 2001).

21. For early parallels between Canadian and American development, see George A. Rawlyk, *The Canada Fire: Radical Evangelicalism in British North America, 1775–1812* (Kingston and Montreal, 1994); and Nancy Christie, "'In These Times of Democratic Rage and Delusion': Popular Religion and the Challenge to the Established Order, 1760–1815," in *The Canadian Protestant Experience, 1760–1990*, ed. G. A. Rawlyk (Burlington, Ont., 1990), 9–47. For later divergence, see Marguerite Van Die, *An Evangelical Mind: Nathanael Burwash and the Methodist Tradition in Canada, 1839–1918* (Kingston and Montreal, 1989); William Westfall, *Two Worlds: The Protestant Culture of Nineteenth-Century Ontario* (Montreal and Kingston, 1989); and Michael Gauvreau, *The Evangelical Century: College and Creed in English Canada from the Great Revival to the Great Depression* (Kingston and Montreal, 1991).

22. As beginning points for understanding why different national situations led to different theological emphases in North Atlantic societies sharing many similarities, the following are especially useful: Richard B. Sher and Jeffrey R. Smitten, eds., *Scotland and America in the Age of Enlightenment* (Princeton, 1990); Hilton, *Age of Atonement*; Richard Carwardine, *Trans-atlantic Revivalism: Popular Evangelicalism in Britain and America, 1790–1865* (Westport, Conn., 1978); and David Hempton, *Religion and Political Culture in Britain and Ireland: From the Glorious Revolution to the Decline of Empire* (Cambridge, 1996).

23. In the bibliography I have tried to specify the books that have been most helpful in shaping my understanding of this synthesis.

24. For its continuation, see George M. Marsden, *Fundamentalism and American Culture: The Shaping of Twentieth Century Evangelicalism, 1870–1925* (New York, 1980); and Mark A. Noll, *The Scandal of the Evangelical Mind* (Grand Rapids, 1994). For its self-conscious rejection, see William R. Hutchison, *The Modernist Impulse in American Protestantism* (Cambridge, Mass., 1976), 76–110.

25. Article II, amending Article 3 of the 1780 Massachusetts Constitution, in *The Federal and State Constitutions*, 7 vols., ed. Francis Newton Thorpe (Washington, D.C., 1909), 3:1914.

26. Tocqueville, *Democracy in America*, 280.

27. Timothy Dwight, *A Discourse on the Genuineness and Authenticity of the New-Testament, Delivered at New-Haven, September 10, 1793* (New York, 1794), 28–29.

28. Archibald Alexander, *A Sermon Delivered at the Opening of the General Assembly of the Presbyterian Church in the United States, May 1808* (Philadelphia, 1808), 8.

29. Hedge, "Essay concerning Free Agency," *North American Review* 13 (1821): 392, as quoted in Daniel Walker Howe, *The Unitarian Conscience: Harvard Moral Philosophy, 1805–1861* (Cambridge, Mass., 1970), 68.

30. Campbell, "The Foundation of Hope and Christian Union," *Christian Baptist*, 5 Apr. 1824, 178, as quoted in Michael W. Casey, *The Battle over Hermeneutics in the Stone-Campbell Movement, 1800–1870* (Lewiston, N.Y., 1998), 67.

31. For outstanding accounts of religious divisions, see Nathan O. Hatch, *The Democratization of American Christianity* (New Haven, 1989); and Jon Butler, *Awash in a Sea of Faith: Christianizing the American People* (Cambridge, Mass., 1990).

32. All such terms are discussed in considerable detail in chapter 4 below.

33. For women, see Laurel Thatcher Ulrich, "'Daughters of Liberty': Religious Women in Revolutionary New England," in *Women in the Age of the American Revolution*, ed. Ronald Hoffman and Peter J. Albert (Charlottesville, 1989), 211–43; Ruth H. Bloch, "The Gendered Meanings of Virtue in Revolutionary America," *Signs: Journal of Women in Culture and Society* 13 (1987): 37–58; Jan Lewis, "The Republican Wife: Virtue and Seduction in the Early Republic," *William and Mary Quarterly* 44 (1987): 689–721; Susan Juster, *Disorderly Women: Sexual Politics and Evangelicalism in Revolutionary New England* (Ithaca, 1994), 210–17; Cecilia Morgan, *Public Men and Virtuous Women: The Gendered Language of Religion and Politics in Upper Canada, 1791–1850* (Toronto, 1996); and Catherine A. Brekus, *Female Preaching in America, 1740–1845* (Chapel Hill, 1998), 37–43.

34. Outstanding works on that transformation include Donald G. Mathews, *Religion in the Old South* (Chicago, 1977); Fred J. Hood, *Reformed America: The Middle and Southern States, 1783–1837* (University, Ala., 1980); E. Brooks Holifield, *The Gentlemen Theologians: American Theology in Southern Culture, 1795–1860* (Durham, 1978); Bertram Wyatt-Brown, "Religion and the 'Civilizing Process' in the Early American South, 1600–1860," in *Religion and American Politics from the Colonial Period to the 1980s*, ed. Mark A. Noll (New York, 1990), 172–95; and A. Gregory Schneider, *The Way of the Cross Leads Home: The Domestication of American Methodism* (Bloomington, Ind., 1993).

35. See especially Patrick Carey, *American Catholic Religious Thought* (New York, 1987), 5–15, 73–93.

36. Scholarship on both Christian republicanism and Christian common sense is discussed in the appendix, "Historiography of Republicanism and Religion," and also canvassed in the bibliography.

37. On the new interpretive strategies of Alexander Campbell, see Richard T. Hughes and C. Leonard Allen, *Illusions of Innocence: Protestant Primitivism in America, 1630–1875* (Chicago, 1988), 116–19, 157–59; on the revelations to Ellen White, see Ronald L. Numbers, *Prophetess of Health: Ellen G. White and the Origins of Seventh-day Adventist Health Reform,* 2d. ed. (Nashville, 1992), 14–21; and on entirely new Scriptures, see Philip L. Barlow, *Mormons and the Bible* (New York, 1991).

38. Continental influences are understudied for the first half of the nineteenth century, with welcome exceptions provided by Conser, *Church and Confession*; the early sections of Jerry Wayne Brown, *The Rise of Biblical Criticism in America, 1800–1870* (Middletown, Conn., 1969); and Charles D. Cashdollar, *The Transformation of Theology, 1830–1890: Positivism and Protestant Thought in Britain and America* (Princeton, 1989).

39. "Address to the New Jersey Senate at Trenton, New Jersey, Feb. 21, 1861," and "Second Inaugural Address, Mar. 4, 1865," in *The Collected Works of Abraham Lincoln,* 8 vols., ed. Ray P. Basler (New Brunswick, N.J., 1953), 4:236, 8:333.

40. For American examples, see Conrad Cherry, ed., *God's New Israel: Religious Interpretations of American Destiny,* rev. ed. (Chapel Hill, 1998). For reliable historical accounts, see William Haller, *The Elect Nation: The Meaning and Relevance of Foxe's Book of Martyrs* (New York, 1963); and John F. Berens, *Providence and Patriotism in Early America, 1640–1815* (Charlottesville, 1978).

41. For example, the boiling cauldron of religious activity, most of it evangelical, in the 1790s appears hardly at all in the otherwise comprehensive study by Stanley Elkins and Eric McKitrick, *Age of Federalism* (New York, 1993).

42. Thomas L. Haskell, *Objectivity Is Not Neutrality: Explanatory Schemes in History* (Baltimore, 1998), 5.

43. James M. McPherson, *For Cause and Comrades: Why Men Fought in the Civil War* (New York, 1997), 63, and the entire chapter in which this statement appears, "Religion Is What Makes Brave Soldiers."

44. Punctuation and capitalization as originally printed; see David P. McKay and Richard Crawford, *William Billings of Boston: Eighteenth-Century Composer* (Princeton, 1975), 63.

45. Early printings of this poem contained variant spellings and punctuation; this version is from Julia Ward Howe, "Battle Hymn of the Republic," *Atlantic Monthly* 9 (Feb. 1862): 145.

46. Caroline Walker Bynum, *Holy Feast and Holy Fast: The Religious Significance of Food to Medieval Women* (Berkeley, 1987), 8–9.

Chapter 2

1. General treatments of this era are canvassed in the bibliography, especially the section "American Theological History."

2. For expansion on these generalizations, see Michael McGiffert, "Grace and Works: The Rise and Division of Covenant Divinity in Elizabethan Puritanism," *Harvard Theological Review* 75 (Oct. 1982): 463–502; McGiffert, "The Perkinsonian Moment of Federal Theology," *Calvin Theological Journal* 29 (1994): 117–48; J. C. D. Clark, *English Society, 1660–1832,* 2d ed. (Cambridge, 2000), 43–105; and Margaret Jacob, *The Newtonians and the English Revolution, 1689–1720* (Ithaca, 1976). On the complexities of New England's Puritan establishments, see Stephen Foster, *The*

Long Argument: English Puritanism and the Shaping of New England Culture, 1570–1700 (Chapel Hill, 1991), 231–85.

3. In 1740 about one in three of the churches in the colonies was Congregational, about one in five Anglican, and about one in eight Presbyterian. Together Baptists, Lutherans, the Dutch and German Reformed, Quakers, German sectarians, and Roman Catholics combined for about one-third of the churches. For more detail on demoninational distribution, see table 9.1 in chapter 9 below.

4. See J. A. I. Champion, *The Pillars of Priestcraft Shaken: The Church of England and Its Enemies, 1660–1730* (Cambridge, 1992); and Jeremy Gregory, *Restoration, Reformation, and Reform, 1660–1828: Archbishops of Canterbury and Their Diocese* (Oxford, 2000), 181–223.

5. Leonard J. Trinterud, *The Forming of an American Tradition: A Re-examination of Colonial Presbyterianism* (Philadelphia, 1949), 38–52; Thomas Cornman, "Securing a Faithful Ministry: Struggles of Ethnicity and Religious Epistemology in Colonial American Presbyterianism" (Ph.D. diss., University of Illinois at Chicago, 1998); and David W. Hall, ed., *The Practice of Confessional Subscription* (Lanham, Md., 1995). On the rapid drift of English and Irish Presbyterianism toward Unitarianism, see Finlay Holmes, *Our Irish Presbyterian Heritage* (Belfast, 1985), 61–71; and Roger Thomas, "Presbyterians in Transition," in *The English Presbyterians from Elizabethan Puritanism to Modern Unitarianism*, ed. C. G. Bolam et al. (Boston, 1968), 151–74. Scottish Presbyterianism remained creedal, but because subscription to the Westminster Confession and Catechism was required by the Presbyterian establishment, Scotland's theological history took a different course from the places where Presbyterians were not part of an establishment regime; see Andrew Drummond and James Bulloch, *The Scottish Church, 1688–1843: The Age of the Moderates* (Edinburgh, 1973), 34–37, 82–113.

6. For example, "By the decree of God, for the manifestation of His glory, some men and angels are predestined or foreordained to eternal life, through Jesus Christ, to the praise of His glorious grace; others being left to act in their sin to their just condemnation, to the praise of His glorious justice"; or "God, the good Creator of all things, in His infinite power and wisdom doth uphold, direct, dispose, and govern all creatures and things, from the greatest even to the least." See "The Philadelphia Confession of Faith (1742)," in *Baptist Confessions, Covenants, and Catechisms*, ed. Timothy George and Denise George (Nashville, 1996), 61, 62, with background, 10–11.

7. Preliminary guidance for the immense literature on this subject is provided in the bibliography, especially the section "Theology in New England."

8. Outstanding works in showing Puritan theological emphases include Perry Miller, *The New England Mind: The Seventeenth Century* (Cambridge, Mass., 1939); William K. B. Stoever, *"A Faire and Easie Way to Heaven": Covenant Theology and Antinomianism in Early Massachusetts* (Middletown, Conn., 1978); Charles Hambrick-Stowe, *The Practice of Piety: Puritan Devotional Disciplines in Seventeenth-Century New England* (Chapel Hill, 1982); Alan Heimert and Andrew Delbanco, eds., *The Puritans in America: A Narrative Anthology* (Cambridge, Mass., 1985); and Charles Cohen, *God's Caress: The Psychology of Puritan Religious Experience* (New York, 1986).

9. Willard, *Compleat Body of Divinity*, as quoted in Ernest Benson Lowrie, *The Shape of the Puritan Mind: The Thought of Samuel Willard* (New Haven, 1974), 189.

10. Mather, *Benedictus: Good Men Described, and the Glories of Their Goodness, Declared* (Boston, 1715), 5–6. For solid discussion of Mather's incipient

evangelicalism, see Richard F. Lovelace, *The American Pietism of Cotton Mather: Origins of American Evangelicalism* (Grand Rapids, 1979).

11. A useful introduction to Colman is found in John Corrigan, *The Prism of Piety: Catholick Congregational Clergy at the Beginning of the Enlightment* (New York, 1991). On Colman's links to Edwards, see C. C. Goen, ed., *The Works of Jonathan Edwards: The Great Awakening* (New Haven, 1972), 32–45, 112–27. On his remarkable cooperation with Whitefield, see Arnold Dallimore, *George Whitefield*, 2 vols. (Edinburgh, 1970–79), 1:430, 512, 532–37; 2:195–96.

12. For this interpretation of Edwards, see James Ward Smith, "Religion and Science in American Philosophy," in *The Shaping of American Religion*, ed. Smith and A. Leland Jamison (Princeton, 1961), 414–17.

13. This sketch draws on summaries that I have attempted for *The Blackwell Encyclopedia of Modern Christian Thought*, ed. Alister E. McGrath (Oxford, 1993), 145–48; and *Evangelical Dictionary of Theology*, ed. Walter A. Elwell (Grand Rapids, 1984), 343–46. With twenty volumes published as of 2001, the introductions and texts to *The Works of Jonathan Edwards*, ed. Perry G. Miller, John E. Smith, and Harry S. Stout (New Haven, 1957–), are the essential places to begin study of Edwards's thought.

14. "Personal Narrative," in *Works of Edwards*, vol. 16, *Letters and Personal Writings*, ed. George S. Claghorn (New Haven, 1998), 792.

15. Hopkins, preface to *Two Dissertations* (1765), in *The Works of Jonathan Edwards*, Vol. 8, *Ethical Writings*, ed. Paul Ramsey (New Haven, 1989), 401.

16. Edwards, *Concerning the End for Which God Created the World* and *The Nature of True Virtue*, in *Works*, vol. 8, *Ethical Writings*, 526, 550.

17. In *Works*, vol. 8, *Ethical Writings*, 5. For further commentary on the *Two Dissertations* as a summation of Edwards's theology, see Mark A. Noll, "God at the Center: Jonathan Edwards on True Virtue," *Christian Century*, 8–15 Sept. 1993, 854–58.

18. Publication totals are from Leonard J. Trinterud, *A Bibliography of Colonial American Presbyterianism during the Colonial Period* (Philadelphia, 1968), as enumerated by the Reverend Matthew Floding, whom I thank for these figures. Of 483 separate publications, Tennent accounted for 77, Dickinson 38, Davies 36, and Finley 21, or a total of 172 (or 36%). Of 332 individual titles, Tennent accounted for 44, Dickinson 27, Davies 18, and Finley 15, or a total of 104 (or 31%). On these individuals, see Milton J. Coalter, *Gilbert Tennent, Son of Thunder* (New York, 1986); Bruce F. Le Beau, *Jonathan Dickinson and the Formative Years of American Presbyterianism* (Lexington, Ky., 1997); George William Pilcher, *Samuel Davies: Apostle of Dissent in Colonial Virginia* (Knoxville, 1971); "Samuel Finley," in William B. Sprague, *Annals of the American Pulpit*, vol. 3, *Presbyterians* (New York, 1868); and Mark A. Noll, *ANB* 6:159–62 (Samuel Davies), 6:571–72 (Jonathan Dickinson), and 21:443–44 (William Tennent).

19. The hymn was first printed in *Dr. Gibbons's Hymns* in 1769; reprinted from *Trinity Hymnal* (Philadelphia, 1961), 71.

20. For a solid study of how New Sides added aspects of the era's new science to traditional Calvinism, see Nina Reid-Maroney, *Philadelphia's Enlightenment, 1740–1800: Kingdom of Christ, Empire of Reason* (Westport, Conn., 2001). Regrettably, however, there exists no fully satisfying study of colonial Presbyterian theology, which featured several slightly different strands of Calvinist piety, as in the figures of Dickinson, Tennent, Finley, and Davies, as well as several varieties of more moderate Presbyterianism among those who opposed or were cautious toward revival. The best treatment of colonial Presbyterian intellectual history is Douglas Sloan, *The*

Scottish Enlightenment and the American College Ideal (New York, 1971); some of the sources in note 5 above are also helpful.

21. John Frederick Woolverton, *Colonial Anglicanism in North America* (Detroit, 1984), 184.

22. A solid study is Joseph Ellis, *The New England Mind in Transition: Samuel Johnson of Connecticut, 1696–1772* (New Haven, 1973).

23. David C. Humphrey, *From King's College to Columbia, 1746–1800* (New York, 1976), 19–20.

24. Johnson, "A Sermon on the Entire Dependence of the Creature upon God" (first preached 1751), in *Samuel Johnson, President of King's College: His Career and Writings*, 4 vols., ed. Herbert Schneider and Carol Schneider (New York, 1929), 3:543–44. For a solid discussion of theological differences between Johnson and his Anglican colleagues over against the Calvinism of Edwards, see Woolverton, *Colonial Anglicanism*, 180–81, 185–88.

25. Johnson, "A Sermon on the Entire Dependence of the Creature upon God," 540, 546, and again 546. Compare Edwards, "God Glorified in the Work of Redemption, by the Greatness of Man's Dependence upon Him, in the Whole of It" (1731), conveniently available in *The Sermons of Jonathan Edwards: A Reader*, ed. Wilson H. Kimnach, Kenneth P. Minkema, and Douglas A. Sweeney (New Haven, 1999), 66–82.

26. *The Journal of John Woolman*, in *The Journal and Major Essays of John Woolman*, ed. Phillips P. Moulton (New York, 1971), 28. Compare Jonathan Edwards, who in about the year 1739 recorded his spiritual experience from perhaps two decades earlier—"I often . . . spent much time in viewing the clouds and sky, to behold the sweet glory of God in these things"; "Personal Narrative," in *A Jonathan Edwards Reader*, ed. John E. Smith, Harry S. Stout, and Kenneth P. Minkema (New Haven, 1995), 285.

27. *Journal of Woolman*, 83. A catalog of Woolman's relatively limited reading— which featured mostly Quaker standards by George Fox, Robert Barclay, and William Penn; the journals of earlier Quakers; and traditional Protestant classics like John Foxe's *Book of Martyrs*—is found in Edward H. Cady, *John Woolman: The Mind of the Quaker Saint* (New York, 1966), 53–55.

28. Ruth Bloch, *Visionary Republic: Millennial Themes in American Thought, 1756–1800* (New York, 1985), 14; Charles E. Hambrick-Stowe, "The Spirit of the Old Writers: The Great Awakening and the Persistence of Puritan Piety," in *Puritanism: Transatlantic Perspectives on a Seventeenth-Century Anglo-American Faith*, ed. Francis J. Bremer (Boston, 1993), 281.

29. Edmund Morgan, "The American Revolution Considered as an Intellectual Movement," in *Paths of American Thought*, ed. Arthur M. Schlesinger Jr. and Morton White (Boston, 1963), 11.

Chapter 3

1. Richard L. Bushman, *From Puritan to Yankee: Character and the Social Order in Connecticut, 1690–1765* (Cambridge, Mass., 1967); Philip J. Greven, *Four Generations: Population, Land, and Family in Colonial Andover, Massachusetts* (Ithaca, 1970).

2. J. William T. Youngs Jr., *God's Messengers: Religious Leadership in Colonial New England, 1700–1750* (Baltimore, 1976); Stephen Foster, *The Long Argument: English Puritanism and the Shaping of New England Culture, 1570–1700* (Chapel Hill, 1991), 301–9.

462 NOTES TO PAGES 32-35

3. Harry S. Stout, *The Divine Dramatist: George Whitefield and the Rise of Modern Evangelicalism* (Grand Rapids, 1991); and Frank Lambert, *"Pedlar in Divinity": George Whitefield and the Transatlantic Revivals* (Princeton, 1994), both following leads from T. H. Breen, "An Empire of Goods: The Anglicization of Colonial America, 1690-1776," *Journal of British Studies* 25 (1986): 467-99; and Breen, "'Baubles of Britain': The American and Consumer Revolutions of the Eighteenth Century," *Past and Present* 119 (May 1980): 73-104.

4. David W. Bebbington, *Evangelicalism in Modern Britain: A History from the 1730s to the 1980s* (London, 1989), 20-74; W. R. Ward, *The Protestant Evangelical Awakening* (Cambridge, 1992); Ted A. Campbell, *The Religion of the Heart: A Study of European Religious Life in the Seventeenth and Eighteenth Centuries* (Columbia, S.C., 1991).

5. See Patrick Collinson, *The Elizabethan Puritan Movement* (London, 1967), 381-82, 434-35; and Michael McGiffert, "William Tyndale's Conception of Covenant," *Journal of Ecclesiastical History* 32 (Apr. 1981): 167-84.

6. Westminster Confession, 1.6, in *The Creeds of Christendom*, 3 vols., ed. Philip Schaff, 6th ed., (New York, 1919), 3:603.

7. For example, Bernard Bailyn, *The Ideological Origins of the American Revolution* (Cambridge, Mass., 1967), 32-34; Edmund S. Morgan, "The Puritan Ethic and the Coming of the Revolution," *William and Mary Quarterly* 24 (Jan. 1967): 3-18; Charles W. Akers, "Calvinism and the American Revolution," in *The Heritage of John Calvin*, ed. John H. Bratt (Grand Rapids, 1973), 158-76; Sacvan Bercovitch, "How the Puritans Won the American Revolution," *Massachusetts Review* 17 (1976): 597-630; Larzer Ziff, "Revolutionary Rhetoric and Puritanism," *Early American Literature* 13 (Spring 1978): 45-49; Emory Elliott, "The Puritan Roots of American Whig Rhetoric," in *Puritan Influences in American Literature*, ed. Elliott (Urbana, Ill., 1979), 107-27; and Dale S. Kuehne, *Massachusetts Congregationalist Political Thought, 1760-1790* (Columbia, Mo., 1996).

8. George H. Callicott, *History in the United States, 1800-1860* (Baltimore, 1970), 13-23; Lester H. Cohen, *The Revolutionary Histories: Contemporary Narratives of the American Revolution* (Ithaca, 1980), 16.

9. Robert Baird, *Religion in the United States of America* (Glasgow, 1844), 85-121.

10. For the geography of early American printing, see G. Thomas Tanselle, "Some Statistics on American Printing, 1764-1783," in *The Press and the American Revolution*, ed. Bernard Bailyn and John B. Hench (Boston, 1981), 330-40.

11. Foster, *Long Argument*, 311-12.

12. Christopher Dawson, *Religion and the Rise of Western Culture* (New York, 1950), remains a helpful survey of these large-scale events.

13. For the structurally traditional character of the early Reformation, see Euan Cameron, *The European Reformation* (Oxford, 1991), with concluding discussion, 417-22.

14. Lewis W. Spitz, "Luther's Ecclesiology and His Concept of the Prince as *Notbischof*," *Church History* 22 (1953): 113-41; Calvin, *Institutes of the Christian Religion* (1559 ed.), 4.20, "Civil Government."

15. For the general picture, see A. G. Dickens, *The English Reformation*, 2d ed. (University Park, Pa., 1989), 287-315, 339-61.

16. See Ronald VanderMolen, "Anglicans against Puritans: Ideological Origins during the Marian Exile," *Church History* 42 (Mar. 1973): 45-57.

17. This thesis is argued persuasively by Brian A. Gerrish, "John Calvin on Luther," in *Interpreters of Luther*, ed. Jaroslav Pelikan (Philadelphia, 1968), 67-96.

18. Quentin Skinner, *The Foundations of Modern Political Thought,* vol. 2, *The Age of Reformation* (Cambridge, 1978), 2:3–15 (Luther), 189–358 (Calvinists).

19. For the general picture, see John T. McNeill, *The History and Character of Calvinism* (New York, 1954). Specifically, metaphysics, Susan E. Schreiner, *The Theater of His Glory: Nature and the Natural Order in the Thought of John Calvin* (Durham, 1991); epistemology, Walter J. Ong, *Ramus, Method, and the Decay of Dialogue* (Cambridge, Mass., 1958); science, Gary B. Deason, "Reformation Theology and the Mechanistic Conception of Nature," and Charles Webster, "Puritanism, Separatism, and Science," in *God and Nature: Historical Essays on the Encounter between Christianity and Science,* ed. David C. Lindberg and Ronald L. Numbers (Berkeley, 1986); politics, Skinner, *The Foundations of Modern Political Thought,* vol. 2; social and economic theory, W. Fred Graham, *The Constructive Revolutionary: John Calvin and His Socio-Economic Impact* (Atlanta, 1971); painting, John Walford, *Jacob van Ruisdael and the Perception of Landscape* (New Haven, 1991); and poetics, Barbara Kiefer Lewalski, *Protestant Poetics and the Seventeenth-Century Religious Lyric* (Princeton, 1979), 426. The poets Lewalski describe include the American Puritan Edward Taylor.

20. The regional surveys are outstanding in Bob Scribner, Roy Porter, and Mikuláš Teich, eds., *The Reformation in National Context* (Cambridge, 1994).

21. See, for example, Nicholas Wolterstorff, *John Locke: The Ethics of Belief* (Cambridge, 1996), 1–118 ("The Vision: Let Reason Be Your Guide in Believing").

22. On this pietistic move, see especially Ward, *Protestant Evangelical Awakening.*

23. On the fairly rapid slide to rationalism in some forms of Continental pietism, see Martin Brecht, "Der Hallische Pietismus in der Mitte des 18. Jahrhunderts—seine Ausstrahlung und sein Niedergang," in *Geschichte des Pietismus,* vol. 2, *Der Pietismus im 18. Jahrhundert,* ed. Brecht and Klaus Deppermann (Göttingen, 1995), 319–57, esp. "Der Übergang von der pietistischen zur Theologie der Aufklärung," 328–37.

24. Patrick Collinson, *The Elizabethan Puritan Movement* (London, 1967), 12; Charles Cohen, "Puritanism," in *Encyclopedia of the North American Colonies,* 3 vols. (New York, 1993), 3:577–79.

25. Collinson, *Elizabethan Puritan Movement,* 12.

26. Foster, *Long Argument,* 288.

27. This is Christopher Hill's summation of Parker's work, in Hill, *Society and Puritanism in Pre-Revolutionary England,* 2d ed. (New York, 1965), 20.

28. Collinson, *Elizabethan Puritan Movement,* 14.

29. I am relying here on Perry Miller, *The New England Mind: The Seventeenth Century* (Cambridge, 1939), book 4, "Sociology," and appendix B, "The Federal School of Theology"; as modified by George M. Marsden, "Perry Miller's Rehabilitation of the Puritans: A Critique," *Church History* 39 (1970): 91–105; J. W. Gough, *The Social Contract: A Critical Study of Its Development* (Oxford, 1957), chap. 7, "Puritanism and the Contract"; McGiffert, "William Tyndale's Conception of Covenant"; McGiffert, "The Perkinsian Moment of Federal Theology," *Calvin Theological Journal* 29 (Apr. 1994): 117–48; William K. B. Stoever, *"A Faire and Easie Way to Heaven": Covenant Theology and Antinomianism in Early Massachusetts* (Middletown, Conn., 1978), esp. 6, 60, 192–93; and Charles Hambrick-Stowe, *The Practice of Piety: Puritan Devotional Disciplines in Seventeenth-Century New England* (Chapel Hill, 1982), 130–34, 248–55.

30. As explained in Edmund S. Morgan, *Visible Saints: The History of a Puritan Idea* (New York, 1963).

31. Winthrop, "A Model of Christian Charity," in *Puritan Political Ideas*, ed. Edmund S. Morgan (Indianapolis, 1965), 91.

32. John Cotton explained to an English correspondent the logic of the system: because "the best gifts and parts, under a covenant of works (under which all carnal men and hypocrites be) will at length turn aside by crooked ways, to depart from God, and, finally, to fight against God, and are therefore, herein, opposed to good men and upright in heart [,] . . . none are admitted freemen of this commonwealth but such as are first admitted members of some church or other in this country, and of such, none are excluded from the liberty of freemen. And out of such only . . . it is that our magistrates are chosen." Cotton, "Certain Proposals Made by Lord Say, Lord Brooke, and Other Persons of Quality" (1630), in *Puritan Political Ideas*, 166, 165.

33. Unidentified quotation from Perry Miller, *The New England Mind: From Colony to Province* (Cambridge, Mass., 1953), 70.

34. The quotation is from John Winthrop, "Journal," in *Puritan Political Ideas*, 110.

35. Robert G. Pope, *The Half-Way Covenant: Church Membership in Puritan New England* (Princeton, 1967), 261.

36. Williston Walker, ed., *The Creeds and Platforms of Congregationalism* (New York, 1893), 325–28.

37. A superb rendering of "The Devotional Crisis of the Second Generation" is found in Hambrick-Stowe, *Practice of Piety*, 242–77.

38. On Stoddard I have been helped most by James P. Walsh, "Solomon Stoddard's Open Communion: A Reexamination," *New England Quarterly* 43 (1970): 97–114 (which is mostly a correction of Perry Miller, "Solomon Stoddard, 1643–1729," *Harvard Theological Review* 34 [1941]: 277–320); Thomas A. Schafer, "Jonathan Edwards' Conception of the Church," *Church History* 24 (1955): 51–66; Schafer, "Solomon Stoddard and the Theology of Revival," in *A Miscellany of American Christianity*, ed. Stuart C. Henry (Durham, 1963); Patricia J. Tracy, *Jonathan Edwards, Pastor: Religion and Society in Eighteenth-Century Northampton* (New York, 1979); and David D. Hall, "Editor's Introduction," in *The Works of Jonathan Edwards*, vol. 12, *Ecclesiastical Writings* (New Haven, 1994).

39. Stoddard, *The Doctrine of Instituted Churches* (London, 1700), 8, as quoted in Robert Lee Stuart, "The Table and the Desk: Conversion in the Writings Published by Solomon Stoddard and Jonathan Edwards during Their Northampton Ministries, 1672–1751" (Ph.D. diss., Stanford University, 1970), 77.

40. Stoddard, *An Appeal to the Learned. Being a Vindication of the Right of Visible Saints to the Lords Supper, though They Be Destitute of a Saving Work of God's Spirit on Their Hearts; against the Exceptions of Mr. Increase Mather* (Boston, 1709), 69.

41. Stoddard, The *Inexcusableness of Neglecting the Worship of God* (Boston, 1708), 12, 20; also Stoddard, *Appeal to the Learned*, 22, 23, 82–83.

42. Patricia J. Tracy, "Solomon Stoddard," *ANB*, 20:823.

43. For example, Joseph Bellamy, *The Half-Way Covenant* (New Haven, 1769), in *The Works of Joseph Bellamy*, 2 vols. (Boston, 1853), 2:671; versus [Ebenezer Devotion], *Second Letter, to the Reverend Joseph Bellamy* (New Haven, 1770), 10.

44. Exceptions include Youngs, *God's Messengers*; Richard F. Lovelace, *The American Pietism of Cotton Mather: Origins of American Evangelicalism* (Grand Rapids, 1979); Harry S. Stout, *The New England Soul: Preaching and Religious Culture in Colonial New England* (New York, 1986), 127–81; Hall, "Editor's Introduction"; David A. Currie, "Cotton Mather's *Bonifacius* in Britain and America," in

Evangelicalism: Comparative Studies of Popular Protestantism in North America, the British Isles, and Beyond, ed. Mark A. Noll, David W. Bebbington, and George A. Rawlyk (New York, 1994), 73–89; and the forthcoming biography of Jonathan Edwards by George Marsden.

45. Proportions are enumerated in Pope, *Half-Way Covenant*, 272.

46. Outstanding on the prominence of covenant in Willard's theology is Seymour Van Dyken, *Samuel Willard: Preacher of Orthodoxy in an Era of Change* (Grand Rapids, 1972).

47. Insightful scholarship on these changes includes Miller, *New England Mind*, book 3, chap. 20, "A Medium of Trade"; Bernard Bailyn, *The Origins of American Politics* (New York, 1968), x; Stout, *New England Soul*, 127–47; Sydney E. Ahlstrom, introduction to *Theology in America* (Indianapolis, 1967), 35; Norman Fiering, *Moral Philosophy at Seventeenth-Century Harvard* (Chapel Hill, 1981); and the sources mentioned avove in notes 1 and 2.

48. See especially Stout, *New England Soul*, 185–211.

49. Jon Butler, "Enthusiasm Described and Decried: The Great Awakening as Interpretive Fiction," *Journal of American History* 69 (1982–83), 305–25; and Butler, *Awash in a Sea of Faith: Christianizing the American People* (Cambridge, Mass., 1990), 164–65, 177–91. In defense of a more sophisticated understanding of the Great Awakening, see the international perspective provided by Ward, *Protestant Evangelical Awakening*. The most persuasive case for the general significance of Whitefield is in Harry S. Stout, *The Divine Dramatist: George Whitefield and the Rise of Modern Evangelicalism* (Grand Rapids, 1991). For direct response to Butler's challenge, see Frank Lambert, *Inventing the "Great Awakening"* (Princeton, 1999); and the comprehensive analysis of the question in Allen C. Guelzo, "God's Designs: The Literature of the Colonial Revivals of Religion, 1735–1760," in *New Directions in American Religious History*, ed. Harry S. Stout and D. G. Hart (New York, 1997), 141–72, esp. 146–47.

50. Edwards's first work was *An Humble Inquiry into the Rules of the Word of God, concerning the Qualifications Requisite to a Compleat Standing and Full Communion in the Visible Christian Church* (1749). When Solomon Williams replied with *The True State of the Question concerning the Qualifications Necessary to Lawful Communion in the Christian Sacraments* (Boston, 1751), Edwards responded with *Misrepresentations Corrected and Truth Vindicated, in a Reply to the Rev. Mr. Solomon Williams's Book* (1752). These works are cited here from Edwards's *Works*, vol. 12, *Ecclesiastical Writings*. In treating these writings, I am pleased to record a long-standing debt to Joseph Haroutunian, *Piety versus Moralism: The Passing of the New England Theology* (New York, 1960 [orig. 1932]), 97–130.

51. See Hall, "Editor's Introduction"; Tracy, *Jonathan Edwards, Pastor*, 147–94; and George Leon Walker, "Jonathan Edwards and the Half-Way Covenant," *New Englander*, n.s., 7 (Sept. 1884): 601–14.

52. Edwards, *Humble Inquiry*, 189–90, 226; Edwards, *Misrepresentations*, 411. Similarities to the situation that first called Puritanism into existence are striking. In the words of Charles Cohen, "Early Georgian New England's ecclesiastical situation had come to resemble Elizabethan England's: an established church, theologically (and more so liturgically) reformed, incorporating the majority of the population, most of whom fell short of the high piety demanded by the elect"; Cohen, "Puritanism," 591.

53. Edwards, *Humble Inquiry*, 216–19; *Misrepresentations*, 415, 418–19. For one of many possible references to similar reasoning in later works, see *The Works of*

Jonathan Edwards, vol. 1, *Freedom of the Will,* ed. Paul Ramsey (New Haven, 1957), 432.

54. Edwards, *Misrepresentations,* 393.

55. See especially, Schafer, "Edwards' Conception of the Church."

56. Edwards, *Humble Inquiry,* 174, 182.

57. Ibid., 251. The theme of the visibility of godliness is prominent also in *The Works of Jonathan Edwards,* vol. 2, *A Treatise concerning Religious Affections,* ed. John E. Smith (New Haven, 1959), 383 and elsewhere.

58. Edwards, *Humble Inquiry,* 255 (on the Lord's Supper—not quoted here); *Misrepresentations,* 484, 412. For helpful commentary on Edwards's adjustment of the sacraments, see E. Brooks Holifield, *The Covenant Sealed: The Development of Puritan Sacramental Theology in Old and New England, 1570–1720* (New Haven, 1974), 228–29.

59. Edwards, *Humble Inquiry,* 215, 204.

60. Ibid., 206.

61. See especially Hall, "Editor's Introduction," 35–38.

62. On Williams, see Clifford K. Shipton, *Sibley's Harvard Graduates,* vols. 4–14 (Boston, 1933–68), 6:352–59.

63. Williams, *True State,* 23, 24, 75, 139, 141.

64. *Ibid.,* i, v, 134.

65. See Carl Bridenbaugh, *Mitre and Sceptre: Transatlantic Faiths, Ideas, Personalities, and Politics, 1689–1775* (New York, 1962), 83–115.

66. C. C. Goen, *Revivalism and Separatism in New England, 1740–1800* (New Haven, 1962).

67. Williams's fast sermon in February 1750, *The Sad Tendency of Divisions and Contentions in Churches, to Bring on Their Ruin and Desolation* (Newport, 1751), dealt mainly with spiritual matters but also treated the way in which the kind of debates then disturbing the churches "tend to the Ruin of other Societies" (p. 5).

68. See especially Harry S. Stout, "The Puritans and Edwards," in *Jonathan Edwards and the American Experience,* ed. Nathan O. Hatch and Harry S. Stout (New York, 1988), 142–59; and Gerald McDermott, *One Holy and Happy Society: The Public Theology of Jonathan Edwards* (University Park, Pa., 1992), 11–36.

69. H. Richard Niebuhr, *The Kingdom of God in America* (New York, 1959 [orig. 1937]), 123; Perry Miller, "Jonathan Edwards' Sociology of the Great Awakening," *New England Quarterly* 21 (Mar. 1948): 50. See Gerhard T. Alexis, "Jonathan Edwards and the Theocratic Ideal," *Church History* 25 (Sept. 1966): 328–43, esp. 343: "In Edwards the vital link in the theocratic ideal is missing: the agency of the saints in expressing God's will for the whole of the culture."

70. Edwards, *Humble Inquiry,* 215, 269–71. As early as 1744, Edwards was backing away from an eschatology with New England as the center; see his letters of 5 Mar. 1743/44 to William McCulloch of Scotland in *The Works of Jonathan Edwards,* vol. 16, *Letters and Personal Writings,* ed. George S. Claghorn (New Haven, 1998), 135–36. For Edwards's shift from identifying New England as Israel to a more spiritual view, see John Wilson, "History, Redemption, and the Millennium," in *Jonathan Edwards and the American Experience,* 131–41; and McDermott, *One Holy and Happy Society,* 26–36.

71. Edwards, "Farewell Sermon," in *The Works of President Edwards,* vol. 7 (New York, 1968 [London, 1817]), 326, 352.

72. Edwards, *Humble Inquiry,* 170; Edwards, "Farewell Sermon," 325.

73. Alasdair MacIntyre, *After Virtue*, 2d ed., (Notre Dame, Ind., 1984), 236 (emphasis added).

74. Respectively, Nathan O. Hatch, *The Sacred Cause of Liberty: Republican Thought and the Millennium in Revolutionary New England* (New Haven, 1977), 21–54; John F. Berens, *Providence and Patriotism in Early America, 1640–1815* (Charlottesville, 1978), 112–28; and Mark A. Noll, "The American Revolution and Protestant Evangelicalism," *Journal of Interdisciplinary History* 23 (Winter 1993): 615–38.

Chapter 4

1. Linda Colley, *Britons: Forging the Nation, 1707–1837* (New Haven, 1992), 283–319; Bruce Lenman, *Integration, Enlightenment, and Industrialization: Scotland, 1746–1832* (London, 1981), 100–113; Marianne Elliott, *Partners in Revolution: The United Irishmen and France* (New Haven, 1982); E. W. McFarland, *Ireland and Scotland in the Age of Revolution* (Edinburgh, 1994); I. R. McBride, *Scripture Politics: Ulster Presbyterians and Irish Radicalism in the Late Eighteenth Century* (Oxford, 1998); Stanley Elkins and Eric McKitrick, *The Age of Federalism* (New York, 1993); James Roger Sharp, *American Politics in the Early Republic: The New Nation in Crisis* (New Haven, 1993); David Mills, *The Idea of Loyalty in Upper Canada, 1784–1850* (Kingston and Montreal, 1988), 12–33; J. M. Bumsted, *The Peoples of Canada: A Pre-Confederation History* (Toronto, 1992), 166–85, 231–36.

2. For example, see the relatively similar responses to the French Revolution as summarized by James H. Smylie, "Protestant Clergymen and American Destiny, 1781–1800," *Harvard Theological Review* 56 (July 1963): 217–31; Deryck W. Lovegrove, "Unity and Separatism: Contrasting Elements in the Thought and Practice of Robert and James Alexander Haldane," in *Protestant Evangelicalism: Britain, Ireland, Germany, and America, c. 1750–c. 1950*, ed. Keith Robbins (Oxford, 1990), 153–77; and Robert Hole, "English Sermons and Tracts as Media of Debate on the French Revolution, 1789–99," in *The French Revolution and British Popular Politics*, ed. Mark Philp (Cambridge, 1991), 18–37.

3. Bonhoeffer, "Protestantism without Reformation," in *No Rusty Swords: Letters, Lectures, and Notes . . . from the Collected Works of Dietrich Bonhoeffer*, vol. 1, trans. Edwin H. Robertson and John Bowden (New York, 1965), 104–05.

4. Paine, *The Rights of Man*, part 2 (1792), in *Thomas Paine: Political Writings*, ed. Bruce Kuklick (New York, 1989), 167.

5. Hamilton, *The Federalist* (no. 84), ed. B. F. Wright (New York, 1961), 533; Jefferson from autobiographical writings (1821) and Adams, *Defence of the Constitutions of Government of the United States* (1787), both as reprinted in *The Founders' Constitution*, 5 vols., ed. Philip B. Kurland and Ralph Lerner (Chicago, 1987), 1:112a, 1:119a; Madison, *The Federalist*, no. 10, in *The Mind of the Founder: Sources of the Political Thought of James Madison*, ed. Marvin Meyers (Hanover, N.H., 1981), 93; Paine, *Rights of Man*, part 2, 168.

6. Blair Worden, "The Revolution of 1688–89 and the English Republican Tradition," in *The Anglo-Dutch Moment: Essays on the Glorious Revolution and Its World Impact*, ed. Jonathan I. Israel (Cambridge, 1991), 249.

7. I have tried to canvass some of the immense literature on republicanism in the appendix, "Historiography of Republicanism and Religion."

8. Caroline Robbins, *The Eighteenth-Century Commonwealthman: Studies in the Transmission, Development, and Circumstance of English Liberal Thought from the Restoration of Charles II until the War with the Thirteen Colonies* (Cambridge, Mass., 1959).

9. David Wootton, introduction to *Divine Right and Democracy: An Anthology of Political Writing in Stuart England* (London, 1986), 70; all of Wootton's introductory essay (9–86) is helpful.

10. Bernard Bailyn, *The Ideological Origins of the American Revolution* (Cambridge, Mass., 1967).

11. John M. Murrin, "The Great Inversion, Court versus Country: A Comparison of the Revolution Settlements in England (1688–1721) and America (1776–1816)," in *Three British Revolutions: 1641, 1688, 1776*, ed. J. G. A. Pocock (Princeton, 1980), 368–452.

12. On the practice of translation, see Quentin Skinner, *The Foundations of Modern Political Thought*, 2 vols. (Cambridge, 1978), 1:176.

13. See ibid., 159–83; Bailyn, *Ideological Origins*, 55–93; and Alan Craig Houston, *Algernon Sidney and the Republican Heritage in England and America* (Princeton, 1991). A superb book on "the people" that could have lapsed into irony on nearly every page, but did not, is Edmund S. Morgan, *Inventing the People: The Rise of Popular Sovereignty in England and America* (New York, 1988).

14. Quotations are from Paul Rahe, *Republics Ancient and Modern: Classical Republicanism and the American Revolution* (Chapel Hill, 1992), 221; and Skinner, *Foundations*, 1:183.

15. J.G.A. Pocock, *The Machiavellian Moment: Florentine Political Thought and the Atlantic Republican Tradition* (Princeton, 1975), 36–41, 157–58; J. B. Schneewind, *The Invention of Autonomy: A History of Modern Moral Philosophy* (New York, 1998), 38–39; John Milbank, *Theology and Social Theory: Beyond Secular Reason* (New York, 1990), 20–23. For a dissenting view that sees Machiavelli as opposing Savonarola's type of Christianity more than Christianity per se, see Marcia L. Colish, "Republicanism, Religion, and Machiavelli's 'Savonarolan Moment,'" *Journal of the History of Ideas* 60 (Oct. 1999): 597–616 (Colish's extensive notes are useful for cataloging the scholarly consensus that views Machiavelli as basically anti-Christian).

16. Eco Haitsma Mulier, "The Language of Seventeenth-Century Republicanism in the United Provinces: Dutch or European?" in *The Languages of Political Theory in Early Modern Europe*, ed. Anthony Pagden (New York, 1987), 179–95, with 191–93 on Spinoza and 193–94 on Scheels.

17. I am guided in the following paragraphs by a remarkably helpful series of essays from Blair Worden, including "Classical Republicanism and the Puritan Revolution," in *History and Imagination: Essays in Honour of H. R. Trevor-Roper*, ed. H. Lloyd-Jones, V. Pearl, and Worden (London, 1981), 182–200; "Providence and Politics in Cromwellian England," *Past and Present* 109 (Nov. 1985): 55–99; "Milton's Republicanism and the Tyranny of Heaven," in *Machiavelli and Republicanism*, ed. G. Bock, Q. Skinner, and M. Viroli (New York, 1990), 225–45; "Revolution of 1688–89," 241–77; and "Part I" (on English republicanism, 1649–1683), in *Republicanism, Liberty, and Commercial Society, 1649–1776*, ed. David Wootton (Stanford, 1994), 45–193.

18. Baxter, *Reliquiae*, I, I, p. 18 (§27), from Robert S. Paul, *The Assembly of the Lord: Politics and Religion in the Westminster Assembly and the "Great Debate"* (Edinburgh, 1985), 53–54.

19. Worden, "Milton's Republicanism," 230.

20. See especially Worden, "Providence and Politics."

21. An outstanding accounting of the Puritans' restrained enthusiasm is found in John Morgan, *Godly Learning: Puritan Attitudes towards Reason, Learning, and Education, 1560–1640* (New York, 1986).

22. Milton's unpublished work on Christian doctrine from the late 1650s spelled out his objection to "the nonsense of quibbling metaphysicians" that the classic Christian creeds promoted: *Complete Prose Works of John Milton*, vol. 6, *Ca. 1658–ca. 1660: The Christian Doctrine*, ed. Maurice Kelley (New Haven, 1973), 262, with editor Kelley's comments helpful at 68–71. For a recent colloquium that includes contributors who see Milton as more consistently orthodox, see *Milton and Heresy*, ed. Stephen B. Dobranski and John P. Rumrich (Cambridge, 1998).

23. Worden, "Milton's Republicanism."

24. Baxter, *A Holy Commonwealth* (1659), in *Divine Right and Democracy*, 231.

25. Mark Goldie, "The Civil Religion of James Harrington," in *Languages of Political Theory*, 203. "Socinian" and "Arian" were used to describe people who honored Jesus but who did not consider him as fully God. "Arianism" could include a high view of Jesus as a created Son of God but with metaphysical objections to his full divinity; "Socinianism" communicated reverence for Jesus as revealing God but with ethical and rationalist objections to the Trinity. Both were consistent terms of opprobrium.

26. For discussion of organic links between Toland's theology and politics, see J.B. Schneewind, *Invention of Autonomy: A History of Modern Moral Philosophy* (Cambridge, 1998), 297–98; and Robert E. Sullivan, *John Toland and the Deist Controversy* (Cambridge, Mass., 1982), 141–72.

27. For a careful argument that they were not, see Houston, *Algernon Sidney and the Republican Heritage*. See also the pertinent observation by John Marshall, *John Locke: Resistance, Religion, and Responsibility* (New York, 1994), 452: Locke's *Two Treatises* received "only very limited support before the end of the eighteenth century, and the support that they did receive came largely from the critics of the establishment among the theologically heterodox and republican."

28. See J. G. A. Pocock, "Political Thought in the English-Speaking Atlantic, 1760–1790," in *The Varieties of British Political Thought, 1500–1800*, ed. Pocock (Cambridge, 1993), 268 (on Locke's "Socinianism"); and J. C. D. Clark, *English Society, 1688–1832* (New York, 1985), 47 (on his "Arianism"). On the major differences between Locke and earlier Calvinist views of the state and society, see Skinner, *Foundations*, 2:338, 347–48.

29. Paul Ramsey, ed., *The Works of Jonathan Edwards*, vol. 1, *Freedom of the Will* (New Haven, 1957), 66–68; Allen C. Guelzo, *Edwards on the Will: A Century of American Theological Debate* (Middletown, Conn, 1989), 54.

30. From the *Independent Whig*, no. 35, 14 Sept. 1720, as reprinted in *The English Libertarian Heritage: From the Writings of John Trenchard and Thomas Gordon in The Independent Whig and Cato's Letters*, ed. David L. Jacobson (Indianapolis, 1965), 34, 36.

31. Mark Pattison, "Tendencies of Religious Thought in England, 1688–1750," in *Essays and Reviews* (London, 1860), 317.

32. Baron de Montesquieu, *The Spirit of the Laws*, trans. Thomas Nugent (New York, 1949), lxxi.

33. Robbins, *Eighteenth-Century Commonwealthman*, 6, 222; Pocock, *Machiavellian Moment*, 133, 202, 213, 399, 462, 550; Rahe, *Republics*, 220–29, 264, 302–3,

485; Schneewind, *Invention of Autonomy*, 308–9; Clark, *English Society*; Clark, The *Language of Liberty: Political Discourse and Social Dynamics in the Anglo-American World* (New York, 1994), with 38–40 a succinct summary of the major argument of these two books. A useful introduction to Clark's most important theses is A. M. C. Waterman, "The Nexus between Theology and Political Doctrine in Church and Dissent," in *Enlightenment and Religion: Rational Dissent in Eighteenth-Century Britain*, ed. Knud Haakonssen (New York, 1996), 193–218.

34. Clark, *English Society*, 277.

35. Ibid., 294; Pocock, *Machiavellian Moment*, 476.

36. Clark, *Language of Liberty*, 38–39. For almost the same conclusions from Blair Worden, see "Revolution of 1688–89," 252, 273–74; and "Classical Republicanism and the Puritan Revolution," 194–196, 199–200.

37. Calvin, *Institutes of the Christian Religion*, 4.20.1, with the identification of Machiavelli by John T. McNeill, ed., *Calvin: Institutes of the Christian Religion*, 2 vols. (Philadelphia, 1960), 2:1486n4.

38. Rahe, *Republics*, 399.

39. Jacobson, introduction to *English Libertarian Heritage*, liv.

40. Milton M. Klein, introduction to *The Independent Reflector . . . by William Livingston and Others* (Cambridge, Mass., 1963), 18 (quotation from Klein), 19 (unattributed quotation from period).

41. See, among many examples, Groen van Prinsterer's effort as leader of Holland's Anti-Revolutionary Party in 1847 to disentangle Calvinism (which he loved) from republicanism (which he loathed): *Lectures on Unbelief and Revolution*, ed. and trans. Harry Van Dyke (Jordan Station, Ont., 1989), par. 147–49 (e.g., par. 149: "Calvinism assuredly never led to any sort of republicanism"). For a recent French assessment, see Jacques Ozouf and Mona Ozouf, *La république des instituteurs* (Paris, 1992), chap. 7, "Le rejet de la tradition religieuse."

42. Richard Gooch, *America and the Americans in 1833–4, by an Emigrant*, ed. Richard Toby Widdicombe (New York, 1995), 74, 138.

43. On reactions to the Germans, see Mark Y. Hanley, *Beyond a Christian Commonwealth: The Protestant Quarrel with the American Republic, 1830–1860* (Chapel Hill, 1994), 113–14; Hughes cited by Richard J. Carwardine, *Evangelicals and Politics in Antebellum America* (New Haven, 1993), 250; "The American Church in the Disruption," *Christian Remembrancer* 45 (Jan. 1863): 181.

44. Charles Taylor, "Religion in a Free Society," in *Articles of Faith, Articles of Peace: The Religious Liberty Clauses and the American Public Philosophy*, ed. James Davison Hunter and Os Guinness (Washington, D.C., 1990), 101.

45. Alice M. Baldwin, *New England Clergy and the American Revolution* (Durham, 1928); Alan Heimert, *Religion and the American Mind From the Great Awakening to the Revolution* (Cambridge, Mass., 1966); Nathan O. Hatch, *The Sacred Cause of Liberty: Republican Thought and the Millennium in Revolutionary New England* (New Haven, 1977); John F. Berens, *Providence and Patriotism in Early America, 1640–1815* (Charlottesville, 1978); Ruth H. Bloch, *Visionary Republic: Millennial Themes in American Thought, 1756–1800* (New York, 1985).

46. Ezra Stiles, *The United States Elevated to Glory and Honor* (New Haven, 1783), 7–8.

47. Elias Boudinot, *The Life, Public Services, Addresses, and Letters of Elias Boudinot*, ed. J. J. Boudinot, 2 vols. (New York, 1971 [orig. 1896]), 2:358, 341, 365.

48. *Letters of Benjamin Rush*, 2 vols., ed. L. H. Butterfield (Princeton, 1951), 1:18.

49. See the superb monograph by Donald J. D'Elia, *Benjamin Rush: Philosopher*

of the American Revolution, Transactions of the American Philosophical Society, vol. 64, part 5 (Philadelphia, 1974), 20–51.

50. Rush to Adams, 21 July 1789; Rush to Winchester, 12 Nov. 1791; Rush to Jefferson, 22 Aug. 1800, in *Letters of Rush*, 1:523, 1:6111, 2:820–21; and Rush to Sharp, 7 Apr. 1783, in "The Correspondence of Benjamin Rush and Granville Sharp, 1773–1809," *Journal of American Studies* 1 (Apr. 1967): 17, as quoted in D'Elia, *Benjamin Rush*, 52.

51. See also K. Alan Snyder, "Foundations of Liberty: The Christian Republicanism of Timothy Dwight and Jedidiah Morse," *New England Quarterly* 56 (1983): 382–397; Thomas F. Taylor, "Samuel E. McCorkle and a Christian Republic, 1792–1802," *American Presbyterians* 63 (Winter 1985): 375–85; Robert M. Calhoon, *Evangelicals and Conservatives in the Early South, 1740–1861* (Columbia, S.C., 1988), part 2, "Revolution and Republic"; Fred J. Hood, *Reformed America: The Middle and Southern States, 1783–1837* (University, Ala., 1980); and Mark A. Noll, *Princeton and the Republic, 1768–1822* (Princeton, 1989), 8–9, 79–80, 200–205, 220–21.

52. On the substantial, though never universal, earlier sympathy by Dissenters for the American Revolution and republican ideals, see James E. Bradley, *Religion, Revolution, and English Radicalism: Non-conformity in Eighteenth-Century Politics and Society* (Cambridge, 1990); and Bradley, *Popular Politics and the American Revolution in England* (Macon, Ga., 1986).

53. On the shift in Dissenting opinions over the course of the 1790s, see Robert Hole, "English Sermons and Tracts as Media of Debate on the French Revolution, 1789–99," in *The French Revolution and British Popular Politics*, ed. Mark Philp (Cambridge, 1991), 18–37; Hole, *Pulpits, Politics, and Public Order in England, 1760–1832* (Cambridge, 1989), 98–108; and Michael R. Watts, *The Dissenters*, vol. 2, *The Expansion of Evangelical Nonconformity, 1791–1859* (Oxford, 1995), 347–57 (Watts's section is entitled "A Republican Spirit Is Injurious to Religion").

54. William Kingsbury, *An Apology for Village Preachers* (1798), 47, as quoted in Deryck W. Lovegrove, *Established Church, Sectarian People: Itinerancy and the Transformation of English Dissent, 1780–1830* (Cambridge, 1988), 127; on Hill, 128.

55. Peter Jones, "The Scottish Professoriate and the Polite Academy, 1720–1746," in *Wealth and Virtue: The Shaping of Political Economy in the Scottish Enlightenment*, ed. Istvan Hont and Michael Ignatieff (New York, 1983), 89–90, 113, 115; J. G. A. Pocock, "Political Thought in the English-Speaking Atlantic, 1760–1790: Part 1, The Imperial Crisis," in *The Varieties of British Political Thought, 1500–1800*, ed. Pocock (New York, 1993), 249–50; Nicholas Phillipson, "The Scottish Enlightenment," in *The Enlightenment in National Context*, ed. Roy Porter and Mikulás Teich (New York, 1981), 28.

56. G. D. Henderson, *The Burning Bush: Studies in Scottish Church History* (Edinburgh, 1957), 132–33; T. C. Smout, *A History of the Scottish People, 1560–1830* (London, 1969), 441–45; Ian D. L. Clark, "From Protest to Reaction: The Moderate Regime in the Church of Scotland, 1752–1805," in *Scotland in the Age of Improvement,* ed. N. T. Phillipson and Rosalind Mitchison (Edinburgh, 1970), 200–224; and Richard B. Sher, *Church and University in the Scottish Enlightenment: The Moderate Literati of Edinburgh* (Princeton, 1985), 208–11, 305–06.

57. Quoted in James H. Smylie, "Charles Nisbet: Second Thoughts on a Revolutionary Generation," *Pennsylvania Magazine of History and Biography* 98 (Apr. 1974): 191, 195, 200. For treatment of Nisbet as a strong conservative in the American setting, see Gordon S. Wood, *The Radicalism of the American Revolution* (New York, 1992), 254.

58. See Brendan Clifford, ed., *Scripture Politics: Selections from the Writings of William Steel Dickson. The Most Influential United Irishman of the North* (Belfast, 1991); Clifford, ed., *The Causes of the Rebellion in Ireland (1798) and Other Writings by Rev. Thomas Ledlie Birch, United Irishman* (Belfast, 1991); A. T. Q. Stewart, "The Transformation of Presbyterian Radicalism in the North of Ireland, 1792–1825" (M.A. thesis, Queen's University of Belfast, 1956); Stewart, *A Deeper Silence: The Hidden Origins of the United Irishmen* (London, 1993), 51–58, 131, 154; McFarland, *Ireland and Scotland*; and McBride, *Scripture Politics.*

59. Samuel Miller, *A Sermon, Delivered May 9, 1798, Recommended by the President of the United States, to Be Observed as a Day of General Humiliation, Fasting, and Prayer* (New York, 1798), 42.

60. *Minutes of the General Assembly of the Presbyterian Church in the United States of America . . . , 1789–1820* (Philadelphia, 1847), 154.

61. *Records of the General Synod of Ulster. From 1691 to 1820,* 3 vols. (Belfast, 1898), 3:208–11. For the general move of Ulster Protestants away from republicanism, see David Hempton and Myrtle Hill, *Evangelical Protestantism in Ulster Society, 1740–1890* (London, 1992), 24–25.

62. On the sociopolitical conservatism of the most influential Protestant constituencies in England and Scotland during the early nineteenth century, see Boyd Hilton, *The Age of Atonement: The Influence of Evangelicalism on Social and Economic Thought, 1785–1865* (Oxford, 1988); and A. M. C. Waterman, *Revolution, Economics, and Religion: Christian Political Economy, 1798–1833* (New York, 1991).

63. Bishop Madison, *A Form of Prayer to Be Used by the Ministers of the Protestant Episcopal Church in Virginia . . . on the Day to Be Observed as a Day of Solemn Humiliation, Fasting, and Prayer* (Richmond, 1798), as quoted in Charles Crowe, "Bishop James Madison and the Republic of Virtue," *Journal of Southern History* 30 (1964): 61–62.

64. Brian Cuthbertson, *The First Bishop: A Biography of Charles Inglis* (Halifax, Nova Scotia, 1987), 50; Charles Inglis, *The True Interest of America Impartially Stated, in certain Strictures on a Pamphlet, intitled* COMMON SENSE. *By an American* (Philadelphia, 1776), quotations from v-vii, 31–33, and 24. For an account of Inglis as "the most astute of Paine's contemporary critics," see Wootton, introduction to in *Republicanism, Liberty, and Commercial Society,* 30–31.

65. Cuthbertson, *First Bishop,* 178; George A. Rawlyk, *The Canada Fire: Radical Evangelicalism in British North America, 1775–1812* (Kingston and Montreal, 1994), 71.

66. Quotations are from David Mills, *The Idea of Loyalty in Upper Canada, 1784–1850* (Kingston and Montreal, 1988), 22, 21, 18; and Jane Errington, *The Lion, the Eagle, and Upper Canada: A Developing Colonial Ideology* (Kingston and Montreal, 1987), 45. For more general treatment of Canadian rejection of "republican anarchy," see Errington and Rawlyk, "Creating a British-American Community in Upper Canada," in *Loyalists and Community in North America,* eds. Robert M. Calhoon, Timothy M. Barnes, and Rawlyk (Westport, Conn., 1994), 187–200 (quotation 191); and Christopher Adamson, "God's Continental Divide: Politics and Religion in Upper Canada and the Northern and Western United States, 1775 to 1841," *Comparative Studies in Society and History* 36 (July 1994): 417–46.

67. John Wesley, *A Calm Address to Our American Colonies* (London, 1775), as reprinted in *Political Sermons of the American Founding Era, 1730–1805,* ed. Ellis Sandoz (Indianapolis, 1991), 418, with Sandoz's introduction, 412, supplying

the detail on the American fate of the pamphlet. For Wesley's full indictment, see the Epigraph to Part 2, page 51 above.

68. John Fletcher, *The Bible and the Sword or, The Appointment of the General Fast Vindicated: In an Address to the Common People, Concerning the Propriety of Repressing Obstinate Licentiousness with the Sword, and of Fasting when the Sword Is Drawn for That Purpose* (London, 1776), as reprinted in Sandoz, *Political Sermons*, 574. Fletcher (567) was only one of several Methodists, in both Britain and America, to criticize patriots for maintaining black chattel slavery while complaining "absurdly . . . that they are enslaved."

69. *Arminian Magazine* 12 (1789): 614, as quoted in Watts, *Dissenters*, 351.

70. Charles Wesley, "Pharaoh Nechoh [who killed the good King Josiah, 2 Kings 23:29] Hymn XV," in *The Unpublished Poetry of Charles Wesley*, vol. 1, ed. S. T. Kimbrough Jr. and Oliver Beckerlegge (Nashville, 1988), 82.

71. Andrew F. Walls, "The Evangelical Revival, the Missionary Movement, and Africa," in *The Missionary Movement in Christian History* (Maryknoll, N. Y., 1996), 86.

72. See David Hempton, Methodism and Politics in British Society, 1750–1850 (London, 1984), 55–115; Hempton, *The Religion of the People: Methodism and Popular Religion, c. 1750–1900* (London, 1996), chap. 5, "Jabez Bunting: The Formative Years, 1794–1820"; Hempton and Hill, *Evangelical Protestantism in Ulster*, 29–37; Mills, *Loyalty in Upper Canada*, chap. 7, "Born in the Bosom of Loyalty: Egerton Ryerson and the Methodists in Upper Canada." Each of these sources notes the presence of small minority or breakaway groups that were either less opposed or frankly friendly to republican ideas.

73. Ryerson, *The Loyalists of America and Their Times, from 1620 to 1816*, 2 vols. (New York, 1970 [orig. 1880]), 2:66.

74. Randall H. Balmer, *A Perfect Babel of Confusion: Dutch Religion and English Culture in the Middle Colonies* (New York, 1989), 117–56.

75. John W. Beardslee III, "The American Revolution," in *Piety and Patriotism: Bicentennial Studies of the Reformed Church in America, 1776–1976*, ed. James W. Van Hoeven (Grand Rapids, 1976), 28. The accusation of "popish republicanism" was surprisingly frequent in the eighteenth century; it came from those positioned between the perils of old Roman Catholicism and the new tyranny of the mob; see Worden, "Revolution of 1688–89," 262.

76. John H. Livingston, *Oratio Inauguralis de Veritate Religionis Christianae* (New York, 1785), 4–6.

77. For Helmuth's attacks on Bahrdt and Paine, see A. Gregg Roeber, "'Through a Glass, Darkly': Changing German Ideas of American Freedom, 1776–1806," in *Transatlantic Images and Perceptions: Germany and America since 1776*, ed. David E. Barclay and Elisabeth Galser-Schmidt (Washington, D.C., 1997), 27–29. On Helmuth more generally, see Roeber, "J. H. C. Helmuth, Evangelical Charity, and the Public Sphere in Pennsylvania, 1793–1800," *Pennsylvania Magazine of History and Biography* 121 (Jan./Apr. 1997): 77–100; and for an outstanding account of differing assumptions about fundamental social and religious matters among eighteenth-century German immigrants to America, Roeber, *Palatines, Liberty, and Property: German Lutherans in Colonial British America* (Baltimore, 1993), with p. 295 citing an 1823 attack from Germany on the "republican licentiousness" at work in America.

78. J. H. C. Helmuth, "Auf den Tag der Unabhängigkeit der Dreyzehn Staaten von Nord-America, den 4ten Julii, 1785" (broadside); my thanks to A. G. Roeber for

supplying a copy of this ode. "Des stolzen Britten Hohngeschrey / Trift uns nicht länger, wir sind frey, / Er [Gott] hats gethan."

79. J. H. C. Helmuth, *Betrachtung der Evangelischen Lehre von der Heiligen Schrift und Taufe; samt einigen Gedanken von den gegenwärtigen Zeiten* (Germantown, Pa., 1793), 311. "Der Geist der bürgerliche Freyheit hat hin und wieder viel Glück verbreitet und unsere Staaten haben den ersten Antheil an diesen Vortheilen genommen, und wer diese Vortheile verkennen wollte, der wäre derselben höchst unwürdig; wir verkennen sie nicht; wir schätzen sie, und preisen billig den Herrn dafür."

80. Patrick W. Carey, "Republicanism within American Catholicism, 1785–1860," *Journal of the Early Republic* 3 (Winter 1983): 413–38; and Carey, *People, Priests, and Prelates: Democracy and the Tensions of Trusteeism* (Notre Dame, Ind., 1987).

81. Gilles Chaussé, "French Canada from the Conquest to 1840," in *A Concise History of Christianity in Canada*, ed. Terrence Murphy (Toronto, 1996), 83.

82. Bishop John Carroll, *A Discourse on General Washington; Delivered in the Catholic Church of St. Peter, in Baltimore—Feb. 22d 1800* (Baltimore, [1800]), quotations 6, 7, 20, 19.

83. George Rudé, *Revolutionary Europe, 1783–1815* (New York, 1964), 230–41.

84. Jonathan D. Sarna and David G. Dalin, eds., *Religion and State in the American Jewish Experience* (Notre Dame, Ind., 1997), 72–73; this insightful volume reprints other similar documents along with a full discussion, 61–80.

85. For use made of Real Whig argumentation by African-American Christians, who in the 1770s were beginning to form their own congregations, see Sylvia R. Frey, *Water from the Rock: Black Resistance in a Revolutionary Age* (Princeton, 1991), 49–51.

86. Charles W. Akers, "Calvinism and the American Revolution," in *The Heritage of John Calvin*, ed. John H. Bratt (Grand Rapids, 1973), 174.

Chapter 5

1. Elias Smith, *Herald of Gospel Liberty*, 7, no. 181 (22 Dec. 1815): 721, as quoted in Michael G. Kenny, *The Perfect Law of Liberty: Elias Smith and the Providential History of America* (Washington, D.C., 1994), 232.

2. James Smith to Jefferson, 4 Nov. 1822, in *Jefferson's Extracts from the Gospels*, ed. Dickinson W. Adams, The Papers of Thomas Jefferson, 2d ser. (Princeton, 1983), 410.

3. John Breckinridge, *An Address, Delivered July 15, 1835, before the Eucleian and Philomethean Society of the University of the City of New York* (New York, 1836), 34, as quoted in Fred J. Hood, *Reformed America: The Middle and Southern States, 1783–1837* (University, Ala., 1980), 48.

4. See especially Patricia U. Bonomi, "Religious Dissent and the Case for American Exceptionalism," in *Religion in a Revolutionary Age*, ed. Ronald Hoffman and Peter J. Albert (Charlottesville, 1994), 31–51; T. H. Breen, *The Character of the Good Ruler: Puritan Political Ideas in New England, 1630–1730* (New Haven, 1970), chap. 7, "The Country Persuasion"; and Carl Bridenbaugh, *Mitre and Sceptre: Transatlantic Faiths, Ideas, Personalities, and Politics, 1689–1775* (New York, 1962).

5. Edmund Burke, "Speech on Conciliation with America," in *The Debate on the American Revolution, 1761–1783*, ed. Max Beloff, 2d ed. (London, 1960), 208.

6. Cotton Mather, *Optanda: Good Men Described and Good Things Propounded* (Boston, 1692), 32, 33, 86. For outstanding discussion of the political circumstances

of this sermon, see Harry S. Stout, *The New England Soul: Preaching and Religious Culture in Colonial New England* (New York, 1986), 120–21.

7. For a thorough discussion, see Breen, *Character of the Good Ruler*, 251–61.

8. *Boston News-Letters*, 21 Aug. 1721, as quoted in Breen, *Character of the Good Ruler*, 263.

9. Richard L. Bushman, *King and People in Provincial Massachusetts* (Chapel Hill, 1985), 255, with Bushman's entire appendix, "Country Party Rhetoric in Massachusetts," 253–67, an insightful discussion.

10. Gilbert Tennent, *The Unsearchable Riches of Christ* (1737), as reprinted in *The Great Awakening,* ed. Alan Heimert and Perry Miller (Indianapolis, 1967), 19.

11. On the country tone of Edwards's manuscript political sermons, see Gerald R. McDermott, *One Holy and Happy Society: The Public Theology of Jonathan Edwards* (University Park, Pa., 1992), 117–25, and Mark Valeri, "The Economic Thought of Jonathan Edwards," *Church History* 60 (1991): 52.

12. Edwards to unnamed Scottish correspondent, 20 Nov. 1745, in *Works of Jonathan Edwards: Apocalyptic Writings,* ed. Stephen J. Stein (New Haven, 1977), 444–60 (quotations 449, 455).

13. See especially Harry S. Stout, "Religion, Communications, and the Ideological Origins of the American Revolution," *William and Mary Quarterly* 34 (1977): 519–41; Stout, *The Divine Dramatist: George Whitefield and the Rise of Modern Evangelicalism* (Grand Rapids, 1991); and Frank Lambert, *Pedlar in Divinity: George Whitefield and the Transatlantic Revivals* (Princeton, 1994), 204–25. For my own effort at disentangling indirect background influence from direct ideological lineage, see "The Great Awakening and the American Revolution," in Noll, Nathan O. Hatch, and George M. Marsden, *The Search for Christian America,* 2d ed. (Colorado Springs, 1989), 48–69.

14. George Whitefield, "Britain's Mercies, and Britain's Duty" (1746), in *Sermons on Important Subjects* (London, 1825), 56.

15. Whitefield, *A Short Address to Persons of All Denominations, Occasioned by the Alarm of an Intended Invasion* (Philadelphia, 1766), 9–11. In 1768 Whitefield used the same kind of language in a pamphlet protesting the expulsion of six students from Oxford for holding unsupervised religious meetings. In the course of attacking Anglican religious conformity, Whitefield went out of his way to affirm, "What a mercy is it . . . that we live under a free government" and under the rule of George III, who in his first message from the throne pledged to "encourage the practice of true Religion and Virtue, and maintain the toleration inviolable." Yet this pamphlet was more concerned with the spiritual problems created by Anglican formalism than with the limitation of colonial rights or the threat of tyranny; Whitefield, *A Letter to the Reverend Dr. Durell, Vice-Chancellor of the University of Oxford: Occasioned by a Late Expulsion of Six Students from Edmund-Hall* (Boston, 1768), quotation 19.

16. *George Whitefield's Journals*, ed. Iain Murray (London, 1960), 402.

17. Whitefield, "Christ the Believer's Husband" and "Christ the Support of the Tempted," in *Sermons on Important Subjects,* 131, 196.

18. Whitefield, "Britain's Mercies, and Britain's Duty, Preached . . . Sunday, August 24, 1746, and Occasioned by the Suppression of the Late Unnatural Rebellion," in *Sermons on Important Subjects,* 56. For the same kind of anti-Catholic language, see also Whitefield, *A Short Address to Persons of All Denominations,* 3, 10, 11, 15.

19. Whitefield, "Christ the Support of the Tempted," 203.

20. On Whitaker, see Alan Heimert, *Religion and the American Mind from the*

Great Awakening to the Revolution (Cambridge, Mass., 1966), 500–509; and "Nathaniel Whitaker," in *Princetonians, 1748–1768: A Biographical Dictionary*, ed. James McLachlan (Princeton, 1976), 60–63.

21. Nathaniel Whitaker, *A Sermon on the Death of the Reverend George Whitefield* (Salem, Mass., [1770]), 33–35. At this point in the published address Whitaker inserted a footnote (34–35n) taken from "a public press" that was even more thickly studded with a vocabulary of "virtue . . . virtues . . . slaves . . . chains . . . LIBERTY . . . enslave."

22. For the observation that Whitefield's later preaching increasingly stressed Whig and anti-Catholic themes in tandem, see Lambert, *Pedlar in Divinity*, 203, 214–25.

23. Gilbert Tennent, *The Necessity of Praising God for Mercies Receiv'd: A Sermon Occasion'd by the Success of the Late Expedition* (Philadelphia, 1745), 7, 37.

24. Edmund S. Morgan, *American Slavery, American Freedom: The Ordeal of Colonial Virginia* (New York, 1975), 371–72.

25. For example, Samuel Checkley, *Prayer a Duty, when God's People Go Forth to War* (Boston, 1745); Thomas Prentice, *A Sermon Preached at Charlestown, on a General Thanksgiving, July 18, 1745* (Boston, 1745); Thomas Prince, *Extraordinary Events the Doings of God* (Boston, 1745); Samuel Niles, *A Brief and Plain Essay on God's Wonder-Working Providence for New-England, in the Reduction of Louisbourg* (New London, Conn., 1747); Jared Eliot, *God's Marvellous Kindness Illustrated* (New London, Conn., 1745); and Joseph Sewall, *The Lamb Slain, Worthy to Be Praised* (Boston, 1745).

26. Charles Chauncy, *Marvellous Things Done by the Right Hand and Holy Arm of God in Getting Him the Victory* (Boston, 1745), 11.

27. Nathaniel Walter, *The Character of a True Patriot* (Boston, 1745), 17, 10, 18.

28. Thomas Prince, *A Sermon Delivered at the South Church . . . Being the Day of General Thanksgiving for the Deliverance of the British Nations by the Glorious and Happy Victory near Culloden* (Boston, 1746), 20–21n.

29. Chauncy, *Marvellous Things*, 22; Sewall, *Lamb Slain*, 32–33.

30. Tennent, *Necessity of Praising God*, 37; Prince, *Extraordinary Events*, 34; Niles, *Brief and Plain Essay*, 15–16.

31. For background, see especially Mary Augustina (Ray), B.V.M., *American Opinion of Roman Catholicism in the Eighteenth Century* (New York, 1936); and Charles P. Hanson, *Necessary Virtue: The Pragmatic Origins of Religious Liberty in New England* (Charlottesville, 1998), 6–14.

32. For excellent treatment, see Charles W. Akers, *Called unto Liberty: A Life of Jonathan Mayhew, 1720–1766* (Cambridge, Mass., 1964).

33. Mayhew's *Discourse* is, for example, the first item reprinted in *Pamphlets of the American Revolution, 1750–1776*, vol. 1, *1750–1765*, ed. Bernard Bailyn (Cambridge, Mass., 1965), with a full introduction on the wide notice taken of this work, 204–11; see also the prominent treatment of this sermon in Bailyn, *Ideological Origins of the American Revolution* (Cambridge, Mass., 1967), 52, 92–93.

34. Mayhew, *A Discourse, concerning Unlimited Submission and Non-resistance to the Higher Powers* (1750), in *Sermons*, ed. E. S. Gaustad (New York, 1969), 37.

35. For specific discussion of Mayhew, see J. C. D. Clark, *The Language of Liberty, 1660–1832: Political Discourse and Social Dynamics in the Anglo-American World* (New York, 1994), 364–70.

36. Mayhew, *Seven Sermons* (1749), in *Sermons*, e.g., 152: "In short, the whole tenor of our Lord's teaching was *moral* . . . and all his discourses were just as contrary to *solifidian doctrines* which too many have given in to since, as *light* is to *darkness*, or *Christ* to *Belial*."

37. Mayhew, *Discourse*, 33.

38. See especially Nathan O. Hatch, *The Sacred Cause of Liberty: Republican Thought and the Millennium in Revolutionary New England* (New Haven, 1977), 21–54.

39. Ebenezer Devotion, *The Civil Ruler, a Dignify'd Servant of the* LORD, *but a Dying Man* (New London, Conn., 1753), 35.

40. Samuel Davies, "God the Sovereign of All Kingdoms" (5 March 1755), in *Sermons on Important Subjects*, 3 vols., 4th American ed. (New York, 1828), 3:173.

41. For only a few of many more possible examples, see William Hobby, *The Happiness of a People, Having God for Their Ally* (Boston, 1758); Ebenezer Devotion, *Fortitude, Love, and a Sound Judgment, Very Needful Qualifications for the Christian Minister* (New Haven, 1762); Aaron Burr, *A Discourse Delivered at New-Ark, in New-Jersey. January 1, 1755. Being a Day Set Apart for Solemn Fasting and Prayer, on account of the Late Encroachments of the French, and Their Designs against the British Colonies in America* (New York, 1755); and Samuel Finley, *The Curse of Meroz, or, The Danger of Neutrality; in the Cause of God, and Our Country* (Philadelphia, 1757).

42. Ruth Bloch, *Visionary Republic: Millennial Themes in American Thought, 1756–1800* (New York, 1985), 10–21.

43. Linda Colley, *Britons: Forging the Nation, 1707–1837* (New Haven, 1992), 18–30, 328–32.

44. Blair Worden, "The Revolution of 1688–89 and the English Republican Tradition," in *The Anglo-Dutch Moment: Essays on the Glorious Revolution and Its World Impact*, ed. Jonathan I. Israel (Cambridge, 1991), 268–69.

45. George A. Rawlyk, *Nova Scotia's Massachusetts, 1680–1784* (Kingston and Montreal, 1973), 174–75; and Douglas Edward Leach, *Roots of Conflict: British Armed Forces and Colonial Americans, 1677–1763* (Chapel Hill, 1986), 64–75.

46. This suggestion is advanced by Jack P. Greene, "The Concept of Virtue in Late Colonial British America," in *Virtue, Corruption, and Self-Interest: Political Values in the Eighteenth Century*, ed. Richard K. Matthews (Bethlehem, Pa., 1994), 35–42.

47. Davies's diary, 28 July 1745, in *The Reverend Samuel Davies Abroad: The Diary of a Journey to England and Scotland, 1753–55*, ed. George William Pilcher (Urbana, Ill., 1967), 113.

48. Davies, letter of 5 Apr. 1757, in "President Davies on the Works of Bolingbroke," as introduced by Archibald Alexander, *Biblical Repertory and Princeton Review* 9 (July 1837): 349–64 (quotation 354). For Bolingbroke's emphasis on the political centrality of "corruption and decline," see Isaac Kramnick, *Bolingbroke and His Circle: The Politics of Nostalgia in the Age of Walpole* (Cambridge, Mass., 1968), 165–66. On the natural connections British observers saw between Bolingbroke's radical politics and his heterodox theology, see J. C. D. Clark, *English Society, 1688–1832* (New York, 1985), 306–7.

49. See Mark A. Noll, *Christians in the American Revolution* (Grand Rapids, 1976), chap. 4, "The Reforming Response."

50. Backus, *A Seasonable Plea for Liberty of Conscience against Some Late Violent Oppressive Proceedings* (1770), as quoted in William G. McLoughlin, *Isaac Backus and the American Pietistic Tradition* (Boston, 1967), 122.

51. Backus, *An Appeal to the Public for Religious Liberty* (1773), in *Isaac Backus on Church, State, and Calvinism, Pamphlets, 1754–1789*, ed. William G. McLoughlin (Cambridge, Mass., 1968), 311, 332, 340. Separate Congregationalists in Connecticut used these same arguments against the religious establishment in their colony;

see Oscar Zeichner, *Connecticut's Years of Controversy, 1750–1776* (Chapel Hill, 1949), 100.

52. Jacob Green, [letter on slavery], *New Jersey Journal*, 10 Jan. 1781.

53. Bailyn, *Ideological Origins*, 262–67, 305–6.

54. Robert Middlekauf, *The Glorious Cause: The American Revolution, 1763–1789* (New York, 1982), 106, 124, 135, 162, 222, 318.

55. Paine, *Common Sense* (Garden City, N.Y., 1960 [orig. 1776]), 61, with extensive citation from the Old Testament on 19–27; Paine, *The Age of Reason*, part 1 (1794), in *Paine: Political Writings*, ed. Bruce Kuklick (New York, 1989), 218.

56. Paine, *Common Sense*, 20.

57. Ibid., 59.

58. *Journal of the Continental Congress, 1774–1789*, vol. 9, *Oct. 3–Dec. 31, 1777* (Washington, D.C., 1907), 854–55. For expert analysis of the Congress's religious proclamations, see Derek H. Davis, *Religion and the Continental Congress* (New York, 2000).

59. For useful cautions about extrapolating the chosen-nation ideology of a few New Englanders to all colonial ministers, see Melvin B. Endy Jr., "Just War, Holy War, and Millennialism in Revolutionary America," *William and Mary Quarterly* 42 (1985): 3–25; Mark Valeri, "The New Divinity and the American Revolution," *William and Mary Quarterly* 56 (Oct. 1989): 741–69, esp. 765; and Keith L. Griffin, *Revolution and Religion: American Revolutionary War and the Reformed Clergy* (New York, 1994).

60. John Carmichael, *A Self-Defensive War Lawful, Provided in a Sermon, Preached at Lancaster* (Lancaster, Pa., 1775), 6, 22.

61. On the "tailoring" of language from one conceptual sphere to another conceptual sphere, see Quentin Skinner, *The Foundations of Modern Political Thought*, vol. 1, *The Renaissance* (Cambridge, 1978), xi. On the "migration" of speech between spheres, see J. G. A. Pocock, *Politics, Language, and Time* (New York, 1971), 22.

62. For an unusually helpful general picture, see Elizabeth B. Clark, "Church-State Relations in the Constitution-Making Period," in *Church and State in America: A Bibliographical Guide*, vol. 1, ed. John F. Wilson (Westport, Conn., 1986), 151–89.

63. For the surprisingly widespread willingness to see a hidden Catholic hand behind the Parliament's relations to the colonies, see Hatch, *Sacred Cause of Liberty*, 73–74, and Bloch, *Visionary Republic*, 57.

64. Boucher, *A View of the Causes and Consequences of the American Revolution . . . Preached in North America between the Years 1763 and 1775; with an Historical Preface* (New York, 1967 [orig. 1797]); Richard K. MacMaster, with Samuel L. Horst and Robert F. Ulle, *Conscience in Crisis: Mennonites and Other Peace Churches in America, 1739–1789* (Scottdale, Pa., 1979).

65. William Smith, *A Sermon on the Present Situation of American Affairs* (Philadelphia, 1775), 28.

66. Inglis's sermon to the troops at Bridge Head, New York, in September 1777, in John Wolfe Lydekker, *The Life and Letters of Charles Inglis* (London, 1936), 257.

67. Even late in the twentieth century, Seymour Martin Lipset could argue that the most basic differences separating Canada from the United States "stem in large part from the American revolution and the diverse social and environmental ecologies flowing from the division of British North America"; Lipset, *Continental Divide: The Values and Institutions of the United States and Canada* (New York, 1990), 8–13, 22–24, 196–99 (quotation 8).

68. In this paragraph I am following Robert Hole, *Pulpits, Politics, and Public Order in England, 1760–1832* (Cambridge, 1989), 98–108; Hole, "English Sermons and Tracts as Media of Debate on the French Revolution, 1789–99, in *The French Revolution and British Popular Politics*, ed. Mark Philp (Cambridge, 1991), 18–37; and Worden, "Revolution of 1688–89," 272–75.

69. For the importance of the French Revolution in defining the type of republicanism that would be favored in the South through the time of the Civil War, with a stress on checks and balances, an emphasis on the need for private religious virtue to sustain public civic virtue, and a tendency to picture democracy as mob rule, see Elizabeth Fox-Genovese and Eugene D. Genovese, "Political Virtue and the Lessons of the French Revolution: The View from the Slaveholding South," in *Virtue, Corruption, and Self-Interest*, 202–17.

70. William Paterson, *The Charge of Judge Paterson to the Jury, in the Case of Vanhorne's Lessee against Dorrance* (Philadelphia, 1796), 24.

71. Paterson, undated Fourth of July address [ca. 1800], William Paterson Papers—Miscellaneous, Manuscript Division, Library of Congress.

72. Samuel Miller, *A Sermon Delivered in the New Presbyterian Church, New-York. July Fourth, 1795 . . . before, the Mechanic, Tammany, and Democratic Societies, and the Military Officers* (New York, 1795), 15.

73. Samuel Miller, *A Sermon, Delivered May 9, 1798, Recommended by the President of the United States, to Be Observed as a Day of General Humiliation, Fasting, and Prayer* (New York, 1798), 31, 42.

74. Charles E. Cunningham, *Timothy Dwight, 1752–1817* (New York, 1942), 49–51; and John R. Fitzmier, *New England's Moral Legislator: Timothy Dwight, 1752–1817* (Bloomington, Ind., 1998), 33–36.

75. Elias Smith, *The Life, Conversion, Preaching, Travels, and Sufferings of Elias Smith* (New York, 1980 [orig. 1816]), 24.

76. *The Biography of Eld. Barton Warren Stone, Written by Himself* (New York, 1972 [orig. 1847]), 2–5.

77. Ashbel Green, *The Life of Ashbel Green*, ed. Joseph H. Jones (New York, 1849), quotation 44, on war service more generally, 44–97.

78. Samuel Miller, *The Life of Samuel Miller*, 2 vols. (Philadelphia, 1869), 1:28–31.

79. For other examples of the same ideological journey, see K. Alan Snyder, "Foundations of Liberty: The Christian Republicanism of Timothy Dwight and Jedidiah Morse," *New England Quarterly* 56 (1983): 382–97; and Thomas F. Taylor, "Samuel McCorkle and a Christian Republic, 1792–1802," *American Presbyterians* 63 (Winter 1985): 375–85.

80. Rawlyk, *Nova Scotia's Massachusetts*, 230–33.

81. "Alline's Journal," in *Henry Alline: Selected Writings*, ed. George A. Rawlyk (New York, 1987), 87; Maurice W. Armstrong, "Neutrality and Religion in Revolutionary Nova Scotia," *New England Quarterly* 9 (Mar. 1946): 50–62.

82. James Alexander Haldane, *The Lives of Robert Haldane of Airthrey, and of His Brother, James Alexander Haldane* (London, 1852), 82–84.

83. Stewart J. Brown, *Thomas Chalmers and the Godly Commonwealth in Scotland* (Oxford, 1982), 32.

84. R. Finlay Holmes, *Henry Cooke* (Belfast, 1981), 4.

85. R. D. Gidney, "Egerton Ryerson," in *Dictionary of Canadian Biography*, vol. 11, *1881–1890* (Toronto, 1982), 783.

86. On this ideological mixing, see Dale S. Kuehne, *Massachusetts Congrega-*

tionalist Political Thought, 1760–1790 (Columbia, Mo., 1996), 144–51; Bloch, *Visionary Republic*, 60–63; Noll, *Christians in the American Revolution*, 53–58; Hatch, *Sacred Cause of Liberty*, 92–96; and Greene, " Concept of Virtue," 27–54.

87. See especially Ruth H. Bloch, "The Gendered Meaning of Virtue in Revolutionary America," *Signs: Journal of Women in Culture and Society* 13 (1987): 37–58; and Cecilia Morgan, *Public Men and Virtuous Women: The Gendered Languages of Religion and Politics in Upper Canada, 1791–1850* (Toronto, 1996).

88. Samuel Davies, " On the Defeat of General Braddock, Going to Forte-De-Quesne" (20 July 1755), in *Sermons on Important Subjects*, 3:169–71.

89. Jacob Green, "Letter II. On Liberty," *New Jersey Journal*, 10 May 1780.

90. Ashbel Green, *Obedience to the Laws of God, the Sure and Indispensable Defence of Nations* (Philadelphia, 1798), 42.

91. Nathan O. Hatch, *The Democratization of American Christianity* (New Haven, 1989), 23, 28, 32, 69–70, 210, 253; Curtis A. Johnson, *Redeeming America: Evangelicals and the Road to the Civil War* (Chicago, 1993); and Richard J. Carwardine, *Evangelicals and Politics in Antebellum America* (New Haven, 1993).

92. Alexis de Tocqueville, *Democracy in America*, ed. and trans. Harvey Claflin Mansfield and Delba Winthrop (Chicago, 2000), 43.

Chapter 6

1. Norman Fiering, *Jonathan Edwards's Moral Thought and Its British Context* (Chapel Hill, 1981), 6–7. Of almost equal importance for eighteenth-century concerns is Fiering, *Moral Philosophy at Seventeenth-Century Harvard* (Chapel Hill, 1981).

2. D. H. Meyer, *The Instructed Conscience: The Shaping of the American National Ethic* (Philadelphia, 1972), 157–62 ("Varieties of Ethical Theory").

3. On Bacon's skyrocketing reputation in the eighteenth century, see Theodore Dwight Bozeman, *Protestants in an Age of Science: The Baconian Ideal and Antebellum American Religious Thought* (Chapel Hill, 1977); and Brooke Hindle, *The Pursuit of Science in Revolutionary America* (Chapel Hill, 1956), 190, 214–15.

4. The phrase "rational orthodoxy" is nearly equivalent and is used to good effect in E. Brooks Holifield, *The Gentlemen Theologians: American Theology in Southern Culture, 1795–1860* (Durham, 1978).

5. For how that absorption worked in different national settings, see D. W. Bebbington, *Evangelicalism in Modern Britain: A History from the 1730s to the 1980s* (London, 1989), 20–74 (e.g., 74: "The Evangelical version of Protestantism was created by the Enlightenment"); Michael Gauvreau, *The Evangelical Century: College and Creed in English Canada from the Great Revival to the Great Depression* (Kingston and Montreal, 1991), 13–56 ("Between Awakening and Enlightenment"); and Mark A. Noll, "The Rise and Long Life of the Protestant Enlightenment in America," in *Knowledge and Belief in America: Enlightenment Traditions and Modern Religious Thought*, ed. William M. Shea and Peter A. Huff (New York, 1995), 88–124.

6. Henry F. May, *The Enlightenment in America* (New York, 1976). Also discriminating are D. H. Meyer, *The Democratic Enlightenment* (New York, 1976); J. R. Pole, "Enlightenment and the Politics of American Nature," in *The Enlightenment in National Context*, ed. R. Porter and M. Teich (Cambridge, 1981), 192–214; and Robert A. Ferguson, *The American Enlightenment, 1750–1820* (New York, 1997).

7. Among the most helpful recent accounts are Richard B. Sher, *Church and University in the Scottish Enlightenment: The Moderate Literati of Edinburgh* (Princeton, 1985); Istvan Hont and Michael Ignatieff, eds., *Wealth and Virtue: The Shaping of Political Economy in the Scottish Enlightenment* (New York, 1983); and Knud Haakonssen, "Scottish Common Sense Realism," in *A Companion to American Thought*, ed. Richard Wightman Fox and James T. Kloppenberg (Cambridge, Mass., 1995), 618–20.

8. These phrases are from a lecture on epistemology that was first presented to students at Princeton Theological Seminary in October 1812 by the conservative Presbyterian Archibald Alexander, but they were nearly identical with similar expressions from a great array of theologians in the period 1790–1860; Alexander, "Nature and Evidence of Truth," in *The Princeton Theology, 1812–1921*, ed. Mark A. Noll, 2d ed. (Grand Rapids, 2001), 63–65.

9. See the good discussions in Paul Althaus, *The Theology of Martin Luther*, trans. R. C. Schultz (Philadelphia, 1966), 64–71; and William J. Bouwsma, *John Calvin: A Sixteenth-Century Portrait* (New York, 1988), 144–61. Calvin is quoted here from *Institutes of the Christian Religion*, 2.2.18, "The Limits of Our Understanding" (ed. J. T. McNeill, trans. F. L. Battles, 2 vols. [Philadelphia, 1960], 1:277).

10. See especially E. Harris Harbison, *The Christian Scholar in the Age of the Reformation* (New York, 1956), 103–72.

11. On the pietistic character of Puritan epistemology, see John Morgan, *Godly Learning: Puritan Attitudes towards Reason, Learning, and Education, 1560–1640* (Cambridge, 1986), 18–35; and Theodore Dwight Bozeman, *To Live Ancient Lives: The Primitivist Dimension in Puritanism* (Chapel Hill, 1988), 51–80 ("The Protestant Epistemology").

12. Ames, *The Marrow of Theology* (3d Latin ed., 1629), trans. and ed. John Dykstra Eusden (Boston, 1968), 225–26.

13. John Cotton, "Copy of a Letter from Mr. Cotton to Lord Say and Seal in the Year 1636," in *Puritan Political Ideas, 1558–1794*, ed. Edmund S. Morgan (Indianapolis, 1965), 168.

14. Cotton Mather, *Manductio ad Ministerium* (1726), as quoted in Fiering, *Moral Philosophy at Seventeenth-Century Harvard*, 40.

15. See Mather, *Bonifacius: An Essay upon the Good* (1710), ed. David Levin (Cambridge, Mass., 1966); and Mather, *The Christian Philosopher* (1721), ed. Winton U. Solberg (Champaign, Ill., 1994), where texts and introductions both testify to the transitional, but still traditional, character of Mather's thinking.

16. Mather, *Malachi; or, The Everlasting Gospel . . . and Those Maxims of Piety, Which Are to Be the Glorious Rules of Behaviour* (Boston, 1717), 63.

17. From A. T. Q. Stewart, *A Deeper Silence: The Hidden Origins of the United Irishmen* (London, 1993), 72. Stewart calls this "an old, and no doubt much embellished story." The story seems to have appeared in print first in James Stuart, *Historical Memoir of the City of Armagh* (1819), 488–89, where Stuart claimed to have it firsthand from an aged relative of Hutcheson; the archaeology of the story is surveyed in David Stewart, *The Seceders in Ireland* (Belfast, 1950), 39.

18. The theological history of English Presbyterianism is closer to that of Irish than Scottish Presbyterianism. In England over the course of the eighteenth century, Presbyterian tendencies toward Arminianism and Arianism advanced together with a preference for Hutcheson and his ethics; some English Presbyterians attended Hutcheson's instruction in Glasgow; see Jeremy Goring, "The Break-up of the Old

Dissent," in C. Gordon Bolam, Goring, H. L. Short, and Roger Thomas, *The English Presbyterians: From Elizabethan Puritanism to Modern Unitarianism* (Boston, 1968), 178–86, 196–97.

19. John R. McIntosh, "The Popular Party in the Church of Scotland, 1740–1800" (Ph.D. diss., University of Glasgow, 1989), 81–88.

20. John Witherspoon, *Ecclesiastical Characteristics* (1753), in *The Works of the Rev. John Witherspoon*, 4 vols. (Philadelphia, 1802), 3:229. On Moderate use of Hutcheson's and similar ideas, see Sher, *Church and University in the Scottish Enlightenment*, 166–68, 175–78.

21. Witherspoon, "The Absolute Necessity of Salvation through Christ," in *Works*, 2:340. On Witherspoon's theological aversion while in Scotland to the new moral philosophy, see also Thomas P. Miller, "Witherspoon, Blair, and the Rhetoric of Civic Humanism," in *Scotland and America in the Age of the Enlightenment*, ed. Richard B. Sher and Jeffrey R. Smitten (Princeton, 1990), 105.

22. See W. J. Torrance Kirby, *The Theology of Richard Hooker in the Context of the Magisterial Reformation*, Studies in Reformed Theology and History (Princeton, 2000); Daniel Walker Howe, "The Cambridge Platonists of Old England and the Cambridge Platonists of New England," *Church History* 57 (Dec. 1988): 470–85; and Gerard Reedy, S.J., *The Bible and Reason: Anglicans and Scripture in Late Seventeenth-Century England* (Philadelphia, 1985).

23. See J. C. D. Clark, *English Society, 1660–1832: Religion, Ideology, and Politics during the Ancien Regime*, rev. ed. (Cambridge, 2000).

24. *The Journal of the Rev. John Wesley*, 8 vols., ed. Nehemiah Curnock (London, 1911–16), 5:492–95. For superb discussion of this passage and Wesley's general position, see Isabel Rivers, *Reason, Grace, and Sentiment: A Study of the Language of Religion and Ethics in England, 1660–1780*, vol. 1, *Whichcote to Wesley* (Cambridge, 1991), 230; and Rivers, "Shaftesburian Enthusiasm and the Evangelical Revival," in *Revival and Religion since 1700: Essays for John Walsh*, ed. Jane Garnett and Colin Matthew (London, 1993), 21–40.

25. See especially Norman S. Fiering, "President Samuel Johnson and the Circle of Knowledge," *William and Mary Quarterly* 28 (1971): 191–236, which emphasizes Johnson's earliest published and unpublished writing as a moral philosopher; in the latter decades of his life, Johnson increasingly drew back from these early positions.

26. For helpful summaries, see David S. Katz, "The Hutchinsonians and Hebraic Fundamentalism in Eighteenth-Century England," in *Sceptics, Millenarians, and Jews*, ed. Katz and Jonathan I. Israel (Leiden, 1990); and Albert J. Kuhn, "Glory or Gravity: Hutchinson vs. Newton," *Journal of the History of Ideas* 22 (1961): 303–22.

27. Jonathan Edwards, "'The Mind' and Related Papers," in *The Works of Jonathan Edwards*, vol. 6, *Scientific and Philosophical Writings*, ed. Wallace E. Anderson (New Haven, 1980), 344.

28. Johnson, "The Foundation of Our Faith in Christ," in *Samuel Johnson: His Career and Writings*, 4 vols., ed. H. W. Schneider and C. Schneider (New York, 1929), 3:390.

29. The argument on this repudiation in Fiering, *Jonathan Edwards's Moral Thought*, has been modified slightly by Paul Ramsey, introduction to *The Works of Jonathan Edwards*, vol. 8, *Ethical Writings* (New Haven, 1989), 6–7n5, 18n3, and 29nn5–6, to suggest that Edwards was not as directly addressing the Scottish moral philosophy of Francis Hutcheson as Fiering contended.

30. *Elementa Philosophica* (1752), in *Samuel Johnson Writings*, 2:449–50.

31. A third important colonial voice opposing the new moral philosophy was Thomas

Clap, president of Yale College from 1745 to 1766, who was aligned sometimes with the New Light revivalists and sometimes against them. Clap's lectures on ethics that he delivered to seniors at Yale attacked Francis Hutcheson's system of "moral *Taste* and sense" by name and argued that a true understanding of the moral law requires "a *mediator . . . Satisfaction* for sin . . . [and a] Way whereby a sinful Creature might obtain Reconciliation with an *offended* God"; Clap, *An Essay on the Nature and Foundation of Moral Virtue and Obligation; Being a Short Introduction to the Study of Ethics; for the Use of the Students of Yale-College* (New Haven, 1765), 22–25, 53.

32. Theodore Hornberger, "Samuel Johnson of Yale and King's College: A Note on the Relation of Science and Religion in Provincial America," *New England Quarterly* 8 (1935): 390.

33. For background on the individuals, see John Corrigan, *The Hidden Balance: Religion and the Social Theories of Charles Chauncy and Jonathan Mayhew* (New York, 1987); and Robert J. Wilson, *The Benevolent Deity: Ebenezer Gay and the Rise of Rational Religion in New England, 1696–1787* (Philadelphia, 1984). The best general study remains Conrad Wright, *The Beginnings of Unitarianism in America* (Boston, 1955), with 135–45 especially pertinent for the question of ethical reasoning.

34. Mayhew, *Seven Sermons* (1749), in *Sermons*, ed. E. S. Gaustad (New York, 1969), 99, 154. For the context of such statements, see Charles W. Akers, *Called unto Liberty: A Life of Jonathan Mayhew, 1720–1766* (Cambridge, Mass., 1964), 126–27.

35. Gay, *Natural Religion* (1759), reprinted in *An American Reformation: A Documentary History of Unitarian Christianity*, ed. Sydney E. Ahlstrom and Jonathan S. Carey (Middletown, Conn., 1985), 48, 51.

36. For the chronology, see Edward M. Griffin, *Old Brick: Charles Chauncy of Boston, 1705–1787* (Minneapolis, 1980), 112–16.

37. Dickinson, *The True Scripture-Doctrine concerning Some Important Points of Christian Faith* (Boston, 1741), 217.

38. Ames, quoted in Keith L. Sprunger, "Technometria: A Prologue to Puritan Theology," *Journal of the History of Ideas* 29 (1968): 122; *Diary of Cotton Mather, 1709–1724*, Massachusetts Historical Society, *Collections*, 7th ser., 7 (Boston, 1912): 357, as quoted in Fiering, "President Samuel Johnson and the Circle of Knowledge," 201.

39. Helpful accounts are provided by Garry Wills, *Inventing America: Jefferson's Declaration of Independence* (Garden City, N.Y., 1978); but as modified by Ronald Hamowy, "Jefferson and the Scottish Enlightenment: A Critique of Garry Wills's *Inventing America*," *William and Mary Quarterly* 36 (1979): 503–23; Roy Branson, "James Madison and the Scottish Enlightenment," *Journal of the History of Ideas* 40 (1979): 235–50; Herbert Hovenkamp, *Science and Religion in America, 1800–1860* (Philadelphia, 1978); John C. Greene, *American Science in the Age of Jefferson* (Ames, Iowa, 1984), 12–36, 411–12; Wilson Smith, *Professors and Public Ethics: Studies of Northern Moral Philosophers before the Civil War* (Ithaca, 1956); and Terrence Martin, *The Instructed Vision: Scottish Common Sense Philosophy and the Origins of American Fiction* (Bloomington, Ind., 1961).

40. The two most helpful general studies are Sydney E. Ahlstrom, "The Scottish Philosophy and American Theology," *Church History* 24 (1955): 257–72; and Bozeman, *Protestants in an Age of Science*. For the colleges, see Daniel Walker Howe, *The Unitarian Conscience: Harvard Moral Philosophy, 1805–1861* (Cambridge, Mass., 1970); Francis Wayland (president of Brown University), *The Elements of Moral Science* (1837), ed. Joseph L. Blau (Cambridge, Mass., 1963); John R. Fitzmier, *New England's Moral Legislator: Timothy Dwight, 1752–1817* (Bloomington, Ind.,

1998), 83–90; Mark A. Noll, *Princeton and the Republic, 1768–1822* (Princeton, 1989), 36–43, 117–23, 188–91, 284–86; and for collegiate instruction generally, Meyer, *Instructed Conscience*. For the Scottish Enlightenment among Southern Protestants, see Holifield, *Gentlemen Theologians*, 96–101, 110–54; and Fred J. Hood, *Reformed America: The Middle and Southern States, 1783–1837* (University, Ala., 1980), 1–67, 88–112. For its resonance with themes in popular religion, see Nathan O. Hatch, "The Right to Think for Oneself: Enlightenment and Popular Religion in the United States" (unpublished paper, American Historical Association, Dec. 1982); and Richard T. Hughes and C. Leonard Allen, *Illusions of Innocence: Protestant Primitivism in America, 1630–1875* (Chicago, 1988), 79–204.

41. Nathan O. Hatch, *The Democratization of American Christianity* (New Haven, 1989), 6.

42. Fiering, *Moral Philosophy at Seventeenth-Century Harvard*, 300.

43. Marvin Meyers, ed., *The Mind of the Founder: Sources of the Political Thought of James Madison,* rev. ed. (Hanover, N.H., 1981), 47–64.

44. Reid's influence is reflected throughout Smith's textbook *The Lectures, Corrected and Improved, Which Have been Delivered for a Series of Years, in the College of New-Jersey; on the Subjects of Moral and Political Philosophy*, 2 vols. (Trenton, N.J., 1812), the lectures in which were originally composed in the 1770s and 1780s. The role of Hutcheson is discussed below in connection with Smith's teacher John Witherspoon. For Smith in relation to broader ethnographic considerations, see David N. Livingstone, "Geographical Inquiry, Rational Religion, and Moral Philosophy: Enlightenment Discourses on the Human Condition," in *Geography and Enlightenment*, ed. Livingstone and Charles W. J. Withers (Chicago, 1999), 103–13.

45. Smith, *An Essay on the Causes of the Variety of Complexion and Figure in the Human Species* (Philadelphia, 1787), 109.

46. For correspondence between Madison and Smith in 1777 and 1778, which reveals a full immersion in Scottish moral reasoning, see *The Papers of James Madison,* vol. 1, *16 March 1751–16 December 1779*, ed. W. T. Hutchinson and W. M. E. Rachal (Chicago, 1962), 194–212, 253–57.

47. For example, Hamilton in *Federalist* no. 9: "The science of politics . . . like most other sciences has received great improvement"; Madison in no. 37, where he claims that "no skill in the science of government" has yet been able to define exactly the relationships of legislative, executive, and judicial powers; and Madison in no. 47, where he praises Montesquieu for promoting an important precept in "the science of politics"; *The Federalist*, ed. B. F. Wright (Cambridge, Mass., 1961), 125, 269, 337.

48. Witherspoon, "Lectures on Moral Philosophy," in *Works,* 3:367–472. On the haste with which these lectures were composed, see Jack Scott, ed., *An Annotated Edition of Lectures on Moral Philosophy by John Witherspoon* (Newark, Del., 1982); and Ashbel Green, "Dr. Witherspoon's Administration at Princeton College," *Presbyterian Magazine* 4 (1854): 467.

49. Ashbel Green, *The Life of the Revd John Witherspoon* (written ca. 1830), ed. H. L. Savage (Princeton, 1973), 132.

50. Varnum Lansing Collins, *President Witherspoon*, 2 vols. (Princeton, 1925), 1:41.

51. Witherspoon, "Remarks on an Essay on Human Liberty," *Scots Magazine* 15 (1753): 165.

52. For brief references to a 1770 work by Reid's disciple James Beattie, *The*

Nature and Immutability of Truth in Opposition to Sophistry and Skepticism, see Scott, *Annotated Edition of Lectures on Moral Philosophy*, 33, 100n4.

53. Ibid., 27.

54. For fuller treatment, see Noll, *Princeton and the Republic*, 40–43.

55. Historians from different generations account for unsettling conditions differently, but all agree that large changes were under way: for example, Daniel Boorstin, *The Americans: The Colonial Experience* (New York, 1958); Richard L. Bushman, *From Puritan to Yankee: Character and the Social Order in Connecticut* (Cambridge, Mass., 1967); James A. Henretta and Gregory H. Nobles, *Evolution and Revolution: American Society, 1600–1820* (Lexington, Mass., 1987), 103–22; and Frank Lambert, *Inventing the "Great Awakening"* (Princeton, 1999).

56. The political turmoil following the War for Independence is described in Stanley M. Elkins and Eric L. McKitrick, *The Age of Federalism* (New York, 1993); but it is portrayed even more clearly in a creative presentation of populist communications by Richard N. Rosenfeld, *American Aurora: A Democratic-Republican Returns* (New York, 1997).

57. For a solid account situating Hutcheson in his Irish and Scottish environments, see Stewart, *Deeper Silence*, 71–73, 93, 98–100.

58. Anne Skoczylas, *Mr Simson's Knotty Case: Divinity, Politics, and Due Process in Early Eighteenth-Century Scotland* (Montreal and Kingston, 2001), with 221, 337, 345, and 352 on direct connections between Simson and Hutcheson.

59. Hutcheson's major works were *Inquiry into the Original of Our Ideas of Beauty and Virtue* (London, 1725); *A Short Introduction to Moral Philosophy* (Glasgow, 1747), which was an English version of *Philosophiae Moralis Institutio Compendiaria* (Glasgow, 1742); and *A System of Moral Philosophy*, 2 vols. (London, 1755). For helpful commentary, see Elmer Sprague, "Francis Hutcheson," in *The Encyclopedia of Philosophy*, ed. Paul Edwards (New York, 1967), 4:99–101; Mark Valeri, "Francis Hutcheson," *American Colonial Writers, 1735–1781*, ed. Emory Elliott (Detroit, 1984), 310–17; and James Moore, "The Two Systems of Francis Hutcheson: On the Origins of the Scottish Enlightenment," in *Studies in the Philosophy of the Scottish Enlightenment*, ed. M. A. Stewart (Oxford, 1990), 37–59.

60. David Fate Norton (on Alison), "Francis Hutcheson in America," *Studies on Voltaire and the Eighteenth Century* 154 (1976): 1547–68; Wills, *Inventing America*; Mark Valeri, *Law and Providence in Joseph Bellamy's New England: The Origins of the New Divinity in Revolutionary America* (New York, 1994), 45–50.

61. Especially useful for Reid's work in relation to theology are Paul Helm, "Thomas Reid, Common Sense, and Calvinism," and Nicholas Wolterstorff, "Thomas Reid on Rationality," in *Rationality in the Calvinian Tradition*, ed. Hendrick Hart, Johan van der Hoeven, and Wolterstorff (Lanham, Md., 1983); and Wolterstorff, *Thomas Reid and the Story of Epistemology* (New York, 2001).

62. For the constricting effects of the war on intellectual life in the colonial colleges, see Samuel Eliot Morison, *Three Centuries of Harvard, 1636–1936* (Cambridge, Mass., 1936), 151–63; Thomas Jefferson Wertenbaker, *Princeton, 1746–1896* (Princeton, 1946), 57–66; Brooks Mather Kelley, *Yale: A History* (New Haven, 1974), 85–89; David C. Humphrey, *From King's College to Columbia, 1746–1800* (New York, 1976), 153–54; David W. Robson, *Educating Republicans: The College in the Era of the American Revolution, 1750–1800* (Westport, Conn., 1985).

63. Noll, *Princeton and the Republic*, 102, 189–90, 209; Fitzmier, *Timothy Dwight*, 83–88; Howe, *Unitarian Conscience*, 32.

64. For an account of the chronology and the relative influence of Hutcheson and Reid in America that parallels my interpretation, see Peter J. Diamond, "Witherspoon, William Smith, and the Scottish Philosophy in Revolutionary America," in *Scotland and America in the Age of the Enlightenment*, ed. Richard B. Sher and Jeffrey R. Smitten (Princeton, 1990), esp. 115, 118, 122.

65. Samuel Miller, for example, made much of Reid's writing against Hume but did not mention Hutcheson in his wide-ranging *Brief Retrospect of the Eighteenth Century*, 2 vols. (New York, 1803), 2:10-11.

66. Or, as Henry May once put it, "Hutcheson and [Samuel] Clarke [British apologist ca. 1720] early, Reid and Stewart late, seemed to answer the questions Americans wanted to ask"; "The Problem of the American Enlightenment," in *Ideas, Faiths, and Feelings: Essays on American Intellectual and Religious History, 1952-1982* (New York, 1983), 19.

67. The summary of Hutcheson's thought that follows draws upon Jane Rendall, ed., *The Origins of the Scottish Enlightenment* (New York, 1978); L. A. Selby-Bigge, ed., *British Moralists,* vol. 1 (Oxford, 1897); Elizabeth Flower and Murray G. Murphey, *Philosophy in America*, vol. 1 (New York, 1977), 224-81; Valeri, "Francis Hutcheson," 310-17; Fiering, *Moral Philosophy at Seventeenth-Century Harvard*; and Fiering, *Jonathan Edwards's Moral Thought*.

68. Hutcheson, *Essays on the Passions,* 3d ed. (1742), as quoted in Fiering, *Moral Philosophy at Seventeenth-Century Harvard*, 201.

69. Hutcheson, *System of Moral Philosophy* (1755), in Rendall, *Origins of the Scottish Enlightenment*, 86.

70. Ibid., 80.

71. See the discussion in Fiering, *Moral Philosophy at Seventeenth-Century Harvard*, 200-205.

72. On the usefulness of Hutcheson for the justification of rebellion, see Caroline Robbins, "'When It Is That Colonies May Turn Independent': An Analysis of the Environment and Politics of Francis Hutcheson," *William and Mary Quarterly* 11 (1954): 214-51; Scott, *Annotated Edition of Lectures on Moral Philosophy*, 145-46, 149; and Rendall, *Origins of the Scottish Enlightenment*, 95.

73. See Bernard Bailyn, *Ideological Origins of the American Revolution* (Cambridge, Mass., 1967), 184-89; Gordon S. Wood, *The Creation of the American Republic, 1776-1787* (Chapel Hill, 1969), 44; Douglass Adair, "'That Politics May Be Reduced to a Science': David Hume, James Madison, and the Tenth Federalist," in *Fame and the Founding Fathers*, ed. Trevor Colburn (New York, 1974); May, *Enlightenment in America*, 278-304; and especially Wood, "Conspiracy and the Paranoid Style: Causality and Deceit in the Eighteenth Century," *William and Mary Quarterly* 39 (1982): 401-41.

74. Wood, "Conspiracy and the Paranoid Style," 414.

75. Witherspoon, "Lectures on Moral Philosophy," in *Works*, 3:369-70, 368.

76. Ibid., 369, 470. For Witherspoon's use of Hutcheson at this point, see Scott, *Annotated Edition of Lectures on Moral Philosophy*, 26-28.

77. Witherspoon, "Lectures in Divinity," in *Works*, 4:28.

78. An example is Samuel Stanhope Smith, *Lectures on the Evidence of the Christian Religion* (Philadelphia, 1809). On the new style of apologetics, grounded in commonsense principles, see Meyer, *Instructed Conscience*, 7-9; Wilson Smith, "William Paley's Theological Utilitarianism in America," *William and Mary Quarterly* 11 (1954): 402-24; Conrad Cherry, *Nature and Religious Imagination from Edwards to Bushnell* (Philadelphia, 1980), 92-99; and Mark A. Noll, "The Irony of

the Enlightenment for Presbyterians in the Early Republic," *Journal of the Early Republic* 5 (Summer 1985): 149–76.

79. Elias Boudinot, *The Age of Revelation; or, The Age of Reason Shewn to Be an Age of Infidelity* (Philadelphia, 1801), 30.

80. Smith, *Essay on the Causes of the Variety of Complexion*, 109–10.

81. Quoted from the *Connecticut Journal and New Haven Post-Boy*, in Moses Coit Tyler, *The Literary History of the American Revolution*, vol. 1, *1763–1776* (New York, 1957 [orig. 1897]), 206.

82. For the case that religious ethics from Princeton meant more for the entire nation than has been appreciated by historians overfascinated with New England, see Hood, *Reformed America*, 10–46; and Robert M. Calhoon, *Evangelicals and Conservatives in the Early South, 1740–1861* (Columbia, S.C., 1988), 85 (Witherspoon fashioned "a kind of secularized Calvinism that filled a real need in early national political culture"). Yet provenance is not the paramount issue, since roughly the same intellectual movement was taking place in New England.

83. This judgment contradicts the conclusion of James Ward Smith that the reason that neither Edwards's nor Johnson's views "had any significant effect on the American mind of the later eighteenth century" was "primarily religious"; Smith, "Religion and Science in American Philosophy," in *The Shaping of American Religion*, ed. Smith and A. Leland Jamison (Princeton, 1961), 417. While Smith is no doubt correct in the wider sense of the term "religious," it was the particular political and social situation of Revolutionary America that posed the questions common sense was asked to answer.

Chapter 7

1. It is useful to compare also John Murrin's account of six "value systems" affecting Revolutionary America—Calvinist orthodoxy, Anglican moralism, civic humanism, classic liberalism, Tom Paine radicalism, and Scottish commonsense moral philosophy—with John Dwyer's discussion of three active conceptual languages in late eighteenth-century Scotland: civic humanism, the aesthetics of Francis Hutcheson (both of which were reflected in America), and Stoicism (which had only limited impact across the Atlantic). Murrin, "Religion and Politics in America from the First Settlements to the Civil War," in *Religion and American Politics from the Colonial Period to the 1980s,* ed. Mark A. Noll (New York, 1990), 27–28; and Dwyer, *Virtuous Discourse: Sensibility and Community in Late Eighteenth-Century Scotland* (Edinburgh, 1987), 38–65.

2. For that Canadian situation, see Michael Gauvreau, "The Empire of Evangelicalism: Varieties of Common Sense in Scotland, Canada, and the United States," in *Evangelicalism: Comparative Studies of Popular Protestantism in North America, the British Isles, and Beyond, 1700–1990,* ed. Mark A. Noll, David W. Bebbington, and George A. Rawlyk (New York, 1994), 219–52; and A. B. McKillip, *A Disciplined Intelligence: Critical Inquiry and Canadian Thought in the Victorian Era* (Kingston and Montreal, 1979).

3. This section is most heavily indebted to the superb study by A. G. Roeber, *Palatines, Liberty, and Property: German Lutherans in Colonial British America* (Baltimore, 1993), with the number of immigrants supplied at 342n. Additional orientation is offered by Christa Klein, "Lutheranism," in *Encyclopedia of the American Religious Experience*, 3 vols., ed. Charles H. Lippy and Peter W. Williams (New

York, 1988), 1:431–35. A helpful table estimating Lutheran and German-American populations for 1775 and 1790 is found in Theodore G. Tappert, "The Church's Infancy, 1650–1790," in *The Lutherans in North America*, ed. E. Clifford Nelson (Philadelphia, 1975), 37.

4. On these families, see Roeber, *Palatines, Liberty, and Property*, 201, 287; and Willi Paul Adams, "The Colonial German-Language Press and the American Revolution," in *The Press and the American Revolution*, ed. Bernard Bailyn and John B. Hench (Boston, 1981), 151–228.

5. Peter Mühlenberg to Friedrich Mühlenberg, ca. Jan. 1776, as quoted in Theodore G. Tappert, "Henry Melchior Mühlenberg and the American Revolution," *Church History* 11 (Sept. 1942): 292.

6. Quotations from Roeber, *Palatines, Liberty, and Property*, 291, 274.

7. *The Journals of Henry Melchior Mühlenberg*, vol. 2, trans. Theodore G. Tappert and John W. Doberstein (Philadelphia, 1945), 118, 162. For a general picture of Mühlenberg's pious orthodoxy, see Leonard R. Riforgiato, *Missionary of Moderation: Henry Melchior Mühlenberg and the Lutheran Church in English America* (Lewisburg, Pa., 1980), 137–57.

8. See especially A. G. Roeber, "J. H. C. Helmuth, Evangelical Charity, and the Public Sphere in Pennsylvania, 1793–1800," *Pennsylvania Magazine of History and Biography* 121 (Jan./Apr. 1997): 77–100.

9. As late as 1803, the leading Presbyterian layman in the nation, Elias Boudinot, proposed recruiting a Reformed Dutch minister for the College of New Jersey at Princeton as the best solution for solving the Presbyterians' need for reliable theological direction; Boudinot to Elisha Boudinot, 27 Dec. 1803, Thorne Boudinot Collection, Princeton University Library.

10. Edwin Scott Gaustad, *Historical Atlas of Religion in America*. rev. ed. (New York, 1976), 4.

11. Gerald F. De Jong, *The Dutch Reformed Church in the American Colonies* (Grand Rapids, 1978), 223–24.

12. On Frelinghuysen's direct links to Continental pietism, see W. R. Ward, *The Protestant Evangelical Awakening* (Cambridge, 1992), 229–30, 244–46.

13. John M. Mulder, "William Livingston: Propagandist against Episcopacy," *Journal of Presbyterian History* 54 (Spring 1976): 83–105.

14. Classis of Amsterdam to the "so-called Coetus," 3 June 1765, in *Ecclesiastical Records: State of New York*, vol. 6 (Albany, 1905), 391–96.

15. On implications for Coetus-Conferentie divisions for Revolutionary-era loyalties, see Randall H. Balmer, *A Perfect Babel of Confusion: Dutch Religion and English Culture in the Middle Colonies* (New York, 1989), 141–56; and on general reactions to the war, two articles by John W. Beardslee III: "The Dutch Reformed Church and the American Revolution," *Journal of Presbyterian History* 54 (Spring 1976): 165–81; and "The Reformed Church and the American Revolution," in *Piety and Patriotism: Bicentennial Studies of the Reformed Church in America, 1776–1976*, ed. James W. Van Hoeven (Grand Rapids, 1976), 17–33.

16. John H. Livingston, *Oratio Inauguralis de Veritate Religionis Christianae* (New York, 1785), quotations in chap. 4, page 70.

17. [John H. Livingston], *Constitution of the Reformed Dutch Church in the United States of America* (New York, 1793), 348.

18. John Henry Livingston, *A Sermon, Delivered before the New-York Missionary Society . . . April 3, 1804* (New York, 1804; with at least five other editions by 1835).

19. Eugene Heideman, "Theology," in *Piety and Patriotism*, 99–100.

20. Frederick V. Mills Sr., *Bishops by Ballot: An Eighteenth-Century Ecclesiastical Revolution* (New York, 1978), 237–42, 273–77, 298–307.

21. Edwin Scott Gaustad and Philip L. Barlow, *New Historical Atlas of Religion in America* (New York, 2001), 374, 390.

22. The phrase is from Charles Tiffany. On questions of its applicability, see Frederick V. Mills Sr., "The Protestant Episcopal Churches in the United States, 1783–1789: Suspended Animation or Remarkable Recovery?" *Historical Magazine of the Protestant Episcopal Church* 46 (1977): 151–70; and Robert Bruce Mullin, *Episcopal Vision/American Reality: High Church Theology and Social Thought in Evangelical America* (New Haven, 1986), 3–9.

23. Joseph Ellis, *The New England Mind in Transition: Samuel Johnson of Connecticut, 1696–1772* (New Haven, 1973), 132, 140, 234.

24. An excellent summary of Smith's position, as well as a fine overview, is provided by John Frederick Woolverton, *Colonial Anglicanism in North America* (Detroit, 1984), with 208–15 on Smith and 182–219 on general theological patterns in the late-colonial and Revolutionary periods.

25. Nancy L. Rhoden, *Revolutionary Anglicanism: The Colonial Church of England Clergy during the American Revolution* (New York, 1999), 146. For outstanding studies of these later parties, see Mullin, *Episcopal Vision/American Reality*; and Diana Hochstedt Butler, *Standing against the Whirlwind: Evangelical Episcopalians in Nineteenth-Century America* (New York, 1995).

26. Samuel Seabury, *An Address to the Ministers and Congregations of the Presbyterian and Independent Persuasions* (New Haven, 1790), 52. For the recourse to British sources that led Seabury to an increasingly high view of the Eucharist, see Bruce E. Steiner, *Samuel Seabury: A Study in the High Church Tradition* (Columbus, Ohio, 1971), 341–63, and on Seabury's high-church stance more generally, 236–39.

27. James Hennesey, S.J., *American Catholics: A History of the Roman Catholic Community in the United States* (New York, 1981), 73. This volume also provides excellent general context for Catholic theological history.

28. Thomas J. Curry, *The First Freedoms: Church and State in America to the Passage of the First Amendment* (New York, 1986), 119, 218–21.

29. Jay P. Dolan, *The American Catholic Experience* (Garden City, N.Y., 1985), 106–11.

30. [John Carroll], *An Address to the Roman Catholics of the United States of America. by a Catholic Clergyman* (Annapolis, Md., 1784), biblical quotations 3, 116; "reasonable" 6; praise of United States 114; responding to Charles Henry Wharton, *A Letter to the Roman Catholics of the City of Worcester* (Philadelphia, 1784).

31. See the section on Carroll and excerpts from *The Pious Guide to Prayer and Devotion* (1792), in *American Jesuit Spirituality: The Maryland Tradition, 1634–1900*, ed. Robert Emmett Curran, S.J. (New York, 1988), 126–50, 151–68.

32. George Duffield, "Doctrines of the New School Presbyterian Church," *Bibliotheca Sacra* 20 (July 1863): 598.

33. [Lyman Atwater], "Witherspoon's Theology," *Biblical Repertory and Princeton Review* 35 (Oct. 1863): 596–610.

34. John M. Murrin, introduction to *Princetonians, 1784–1790: A Biographical Dictionary*, ed. Ruth L. Woodward and Wesley Frank Craven (Princeton, 1991), xxxv. During the period, admittedly, only a small minority of the clergy attended college.

35. Leonard J. Trinterud, *The Forming of an American Tradition: A Re-examination of Colonial Presbyterianism* (Philadelphia, 1949), remains the essential text.

36. American Presbyterians organized as a formal presbytery in 1706; in 1729 the denomination formally defined the Westminster symbols as their doctrinal standards; in 1741 the Tennent and Old Side factions divided; in 1745 the Tennent New Side group was joined by most of the former Congregationalists under Dickinson; the denomination was reunited in 1758; in 1787–88 it organized itself into a General Assembly and four regional synods. For a fresh interpretation of the midcentury schism, see Thomas Cornman, "Securing a Faithful Ministry: Struggles of Ethnicity and Religious Epistemology in Colonial American Presbyterianism" (Ph.D. diss., University of Illinois at Chicago, 1998).

37. See chap. 2, note 18, on the prominence of these figures among publishing Presbyterians.

38. Maldwyn A. Jones, "Scotch-Irish," in *Harvard Encyclopedia of American Ethnic Groups*, ed. Stephan Thernstrom (Cambridge, Mass., 1980), 896.

39. See page 105 above.

40. Mark A. Noll, *Princeton and the Republic, 1768–1822: The Search for a Christian Enlightenment in the Era of Samuel Stanhope Smith* (Princeton, 1989), 37–38.

41. Thomas Jefferson Wertenbaker, *Princeton, 1746–1896* (Princeton, 1946), chap. 2, "The School of Statesmen," 80–117; and Murrin, introduction to *Princetonians, 1784–1794*.

42. Maurice W. Armstrong, Lefferts A. Loetscher, and Charles A. Anderson, eds., *The Presbyterian Enterprise: Sources of American Presbyterian History* (Philadelphia, 1956), 75, 99; and Ernest Trice Thompson, *Presbyterians in the South*, vol. 1, *1607–1861* (Richmond, 1963), 68, 76.

43. From a report in Thomas Prince's *Christian History* (ca. 1742), as quoted in Trinterud, *Forming of an American Tradition*, 79.

44. James McLachlan, ed., *Princetonians, 1748–1768: A Biographical Dictionary* (Princeton, 1976), 306.

45. Noll, *Princeton and the Republic*, 69–71.

46. Smith to Blair, 27 Jan. 1788, as quoted in Douglas Sloan, *The Scottish Enlightenment and the American College Ideal* (New York, 1971), 169; on Smith's general position, see Noll, *Princeton and the Republic*, 185–213 ("The Republican Christian Enlightenment of Samuel Stanhope Smith").

47. The story is told fully in Noll, *Princeton and the Republic*, 157–291.

48. Ben M. Barrus et al., *A People Called Cumberland Presbyterians* (Memphis, 1972).

49. Bruce Kuklick, *Churchmen and Philosophers: From Jonathan Edwards to John Dewey* (New Haven, 1985), 43. Kuklick's seminal contribution to the study of New England theology represented in this book has been most helpfully augmented by the thirty-two reprinted volumes of his series, American Religious Thought of the Eighteenth and Nineteenth Centuries (New York, 1987), which is mostly given over to New England theologians.

50. I take my roster of disputes from the summaries in Frank Hugh Foster, *A Genetic History of the New England Theology* (Chicago, 1907), 107–269; and Glenn Paul Anderson, "Joseph Bellamy (1719–1790): The Man and His Work" (Ph.D. diss., Boston University, 1971), 510–74, 756–841.

51. Foster, *Genetic History*, 271.

52. Their work is cited in the bibliography in the section "Theology in New England."

53. Allen C. Guelzo, *Edwards on the Will: A Century of American Theological Debate* (Middletown, Conn., 1989), 144.

54. Harry S. Stout, *The New England Soul: Preaching and Religious Culture in Colonial New England* (New York, 1986), 259, 268–71, 375–76 (quotations 268, 271).

55. For a summary of Hopkins's innovations, see Joseph A. Conforti, *Samuel Hopkins and the New Divinity Movement* (Grand Rapids, 1981), 117–24.

56. On Bellamy's students, see Anderson, "Joseph Bellamy," 402–44; and for a general picture of his educational practices, David W. Kling, "New Divinity Schools of the Prophets," in *Theological Education in the Evangelical Tradition*, ed. D. G. Hart and R. Albert Mohler Jr. (Grand Rapids, 1996), 129–47. For authoritative assessment of Bellamy's theological migration, see Mark Valeri, *Law and Providence in Joseph Bellamy's New England: The Origins of the New Divinity Movement in Revolutionary America* (New York, 1994), 50–54.

57. Bellamy, *Early Piety Recommended* (1748), in *The Works of Joseph Bellamy*, 2 vols. (Boston, 1853), 1:536.

58. Bellamy, *True Religion Delineated* (1750), in *Works*, 1:11, 328.

59. Harriet Beecher Stowe, *Oldtown Folks* (1869), ed. Henry F. May (Cambridge, Mass., 1966), 397.

60. On the father, Nathanael Taylor, see Sidney Mead, *Nathaniel William Taylor, 1786–1858: A Connecticut Liberal* (Chicago, 1942), 4–21.

61. Taylor, *Praise Due to God for All the Dispensations of His Wise and Holy Providence* (New Haven, 1762), 14.

62. Taylor, *The Office and Authority of the Gospel Minister* (New Haven, 1765), 8.

63. Taylor, MS. sermon of Jan. 1767, p. 17, Beinecke Rare Book and Manuscript Library, Yale University.

64. An extraordinarily insightful study is Edmund S. Morgan, *The Gentle Puritan: A Life of Ezra Stiles, 1727–1795* (Chapel Hill, 1962).

65. Ezra Stiles, *Literary Diary*, ed. F. B. Dexter, 3 vols. (New York, 1901), 3:4–5.

66. Stiles to Thomas Wright, 18 Nov. 1766, as quoted in Morgan, *Gentle Puritan*, 170–71.

67. Stiles to Edward Wigglesworth, 30 Mar. 1775, as quoted in Morgan, *Gentle Puritan*, 175.

68. Stiles to "Mr. Spencer," 16 Feb. 1773, in *Literary Diary*, 1:351.

69. Bellamy, *True Religion Delineated*, 266, and a nearly identical phrase 271.

70. For a more complete assemblage of such descriptions from Bellamy's *True Religion Delineated* and *An Essay on the Nature and Glory of the Gospel of Jesus Christ* (1762), see Anderson, "Joseph Bellamy," 739–40.

71. Bellamy, *True Religion Delineated*, 292.

72. Ibid., 294.

73. Conrad Wright, *The Beginnings of Unitarianism in America* (Boston, 1966), 183.

74. Mark Pattison, "Tendencies of Religious Thought in England, 1688–1750," in *Essays and Reviews* (London, 1860), 293.

75. Samuel Hopkins, *System of Doctrines* (1793), in *The Works of Samuel Hopkins*, 3 vols. (Boston, 1865): 1:217–19.

76. For example, Hopkins, *Sin, through Divine Interposition, an Advantage to the Universe, and Yet This No Excuse for Sin, or Encouragement to It, Illustrated and Proved; and God's Wisdom in the Permission of Sin . . . Shown and Confirmed, in Three Sermons, from Romans 3:5–8* (1759), in *Works*, vol. 2 (separately numbered pages).

77. Hopkins, *An Inquiry into the Nature of True Holiness* (1773), in *Works*, 3:16.

78. Conforti, *Samuel Hopkins*, 118.

79. Taylor, *Praise Due to God*, 17–18.

80. "New Milford Congregational Church Records," 17 Mar. 1773, vol. A, p. 15, Connecticut State Library, Hartford.

81. Ezra Stiles, *A Discourse on the Christian Union* (Boston, 1761), 108, with 116–18 applying Hebrew history to the colonial situation.

82. Ezra Stiles, *The United States Elevated to Glory and Honor* (New Haven, 1783), 43, 70, 36.

Chapter 8

1. Ebenezer Gay, *The Alienation of Affection from Ministers Consider'd and Improv'd: A Sermon Preach'd at the Ordination of the Reverend Mr. Jonathan Mayhew . . . June 17, 1747* (Boston, 1747), 10.

2. Jonathan Mayhew, *Seven Sermons* (1749), in *Sermons*, ed. E. S. Gaustad (New York, 1969), 154–55.

3. Sydney E. Ahlstrom and Jonathan S. Carey, eds., introduction to *An American Reformation: A Documentary History of Unitarian Christianity* (Middletown, Conn., 1985), 35.

4. Charles W. Akers, *Called unto Liberty: A Life of Jonathan Mayhew, 1720–1766* (Cambridge, Mass., 1964), 226.

5. On the reading of these and similar authors, see Conrad Wright, *The Beginnings of Unitarianism in America* (Boston, 1955), 57 and 80; and John Corrigan, *The Hidden Balance: Religion and the Social Theories of Charles Chauncy and Jonathan Mayhew* (New York, 1987), xi, 33–35, 63, 98–99, and 109.

6. Ebenezer Gay, *Natural Religion, as Distinguish'd from Revealed . . . the Annual Dudleian Lecture at Harvard College . . . May 9, 1759* (Boston, 1759), 12. For Gay's use of Francis Hutcheson and similar thinkers, see Robert J. Wilson III, *The Benevolent Deity: Ebenezer Gay and the Rise of Rational Religion in New England, 1696–1787* (Philadelphia, 1984), 174–77; for the influence of Scottish moral philosophy more generally, see Ahlstrom and Carey, introduction to *American Reformation*, 33–35.

7. Charles Chauncy, *The Mystery Hid from Ages and Generations* (London, 1784), xii, as quoted in Wright, *Beginnings of Unitarianism*, 78.

8. Chauncy's case provides considerable support for Alan Heimert's conclusion that theological liberals were often leading sociopolitical conservatives; Heimert, *Religion and the American Mind, from the Great Awakening to the Revolution* (Cambridge, 1966). The life of Ebenezer Gay, who became a Loyalist during the Revolution, provides even stronger support for this conclusion. At the same time, the cases of Chauncy and Gay argue against J. C. D. Clark's thesis in *The Language of Liberty* (Cambridge, 1994), as well as in *English Society, 1688–1832* (Cambridge, 1985), that theological heterodoxy led to political radicalism, since these proto-Unitarians were more likely to remain Loyalist than their ardently Trinitarian opponents.

9. Charles Chauncy, *A Discourse on "The Good News from a Far Country." Delivered July 24th . . . on Occasion of the Repeal of the Stamp-Act* (Boston, 1766), as found in *The Pulpit of the American Revolution*, ed. John Wingate Thornton, (Boston, 1860), 128. For other expressions of Whig political commitments, see ibid., 129, 135, 137; Chauncy, *A Letter . . . Containing Remarks on Certain Passages in a Ser-*

mon Preached by the . . . Lord Bishop of Landaff (Boston, 1767), 47; Chauncy, *Trust in God, the Duty of a People in a Day of Trouble* (Boston, 1770), 13, 15, 22, 32; and Chauncy, *A Letter . . . Giving a Concise, but Just, Representation of the Hardships and Sufferings the Town of Boston Is Exposed to . . . in Consequence of the Late Act of the British-Parliament . . . Shutting Up Its Port* (Boston, 1774), 25.

10. Chauncy, *Letter [on] Bishop Landaff*, 12.

11. Chauncy, *Good News from a Far Country*, in Thornton, 123; *Trust in God*, 13; *Letter [on] Hardships and Sufferings*, 9, 12–13, 24–26.

12. Chauncy, *Letter [on] Hardships and Sufferings*, 26.

13. Ibid., 15–16; *Good News from a Far Country*, in Thornton, 123, 129, 144; *Letter [on] Bishop Landaff*, 47; *Trust in God*, 12, 15n.

14. Chauncy, *Letter [on] Bishop Landaff*, 47, 52; *Good News from a Far Country*, in Thornton, 141.

15. Chauncy, *Trust in God*, 20.

16. Chauncy, *Letter [on] Hardships and Sufferings*, 28.

17. Chauncy, *Good News from a Far Country*, in Thornton, 129, 137.

18. Chauncy, *Trust in God*, 13, 21.

19. Ibid., 6. See Clifford Shipton, *Sibley's Harvard Graduates*, vols. 4–14 (Boston, 1933–68), 6:451: "For a man who had little interest in miracles in the field of religion, it is amazing to find Chauncy actually believing that if the patriot cause threatened to fail 'a host of angels would be sent to support it.'"

20. For example, Chauncy, *Trust in God*, 10–11, 28, 29–30.

21. Chauncy, *Good News from a Far Country*, in Thornton, 121–22, 136.

22. Chauncy, *Letter [on] Bishop Landaff*, 46.

23. Shipton, *Sibley's Harvard Graduates*, 6:448.

24. Chauncy, *Good News from a Far Country*, in Thornton, 137.

25. Ibid., 132.

26. Ibid., 139n.

27. Chauncy, *The Accursed Thing Must Be Taken Away from among a People, If They Would Reasonably Hope to Stand before Their Enemies* (Boston, 1778), 13.

28. Ibid., 17.

29. Ibid., 18.

30. Ibid., 18–22, as compared with 16–18.

31. Ibid., 20.

32. Ibid., 23.

33. [Charles Chauncy], *Salvation for All Men, Illustrated and Vindicated as a Scripture Doctrine* (Boston, 1782), iii; this pamphlet, published anonymously, anticipated the arguments in Chauncy's *Mystery Hid from Ages* of 1784.

34. Bernard Bailyn, *The Ideological Origins of the American Revolution* (Cambridge, Mass., 1967), 230–319.

35. The paragraphs that follow depend heavily on Kerry S. Walters, ed., *The American Deists: Voices of Reason and Dissent in the Early Republic* (Lawrence, Kans., 1992); see also Walters, *Rational Infidels: The American Deists* (Durango, Colo., 1992).

36. Two books by Morton White—*The Philosophy of the American Revolution* (New York, 1978), and *Philosophy, the Federalist, and the Constitution* (New York, 1987)—document the practical cast of mind with which leading founding fathers appropriated a mélange of ideas from European Enlightenments.

37. See especially Isaac Kramnick, "Religion and Radicalism: The Political Theory of Dissent," in *Republicanism and Bourgeois Radicalism: Political Ideology*

in Late Eighteenth-Century England and America (Ithaca, 1990), 43–70; Clark, *English Society*, 277–348 ("The Ideological Origins of English Radicalism, 1688–1800"); and Edward H. Davidson and William J. Scheick, *Paine, Scripture, and Authority: The Age of Reason as Religious and Political Idea* (Bethlehem, Pa., 1994).

38. Tom Paine, *The Age of Reason: Being an Investigation of True and of Fabulous Theology*, part 1 (1794), in *Paine: Political Writings*, ed. Bruce Kuklick (New York, 1989), 217–18, 222.

39. Ethan Allen, *Reason the Only Oracle of Man* (1784), in *American Deists*, 162, 164.

40. An outline of Holly's career can be traced in *Contributions to the Ecclesiastical History of Connecticut* (New Haven, 1861), 257, 392, 449.

41. Israel Holly, *A Letter, Occasioned by Mr. Beckwith's Second Letter, Upon the Subject of Lay-Ordination* (New London, Conn., 1767); *A Letter . . . upon . . . Qualifications Necessary to a Lawful Profession and Enjoying Special Ordinances* (Hartford, 1770); *The New Testament Interpretation of the Old, Relative to Infant Baptism* (New London, Conn., 1771); *God Brings About His Holy and Wise Purpose or Decree, concerning Many Particular Events, by Using and Improving the Wicked Dispositions of Mankind . . . in a Sermon . . . the Next Sabbath after the Report Arrived, That the People at Boston Had Destroyed a Large Quantity of Tea* (Hartford, 1774); *Old Divinity Preferable to Modern Novelty. A Few Brief Remarks, on Sundry Points, upon What Is Lately Termed,* NEW DIVINITY*; Discerning Somewhat of the Absurd Nature, and Dangerous Tendency of Them* (New Haven, 1780); *and Christ's Righteousness Imputed to Believers as the Only Matter of Their Justification before God; Explained, Proved and Vindicated, in Opposition to the Professed Sentiments of Some Modern Apostates from Genuine Calvinism* (n.p., 1801).

42. Israel Holly, *Boanerges; or, Christ's Ministers Are Sons of Thunder* (New Haven, 1776), 7.

43. Holly, *Old Divinity Preferable*, 67.

44. Essential studies for North America are Stephen A. Marini, *Radical Sects of Revolutionary New England* (Cambridge, 1982); Nathan O. Hatch, *The Democratization of American Christianity* (New Haven, 1989); George A. Rawlyk, *The Canada Fire: Radical Evangelicalism in British North America, 1775–1812* (Kingston and Montreal, 1994); and Susan Juster, *Disorderly Women: Sexual Politics and Evangelicalism in Revolutionary New England* (Ithaca, 1994).

45. Holly, *Boanerges*, 23.

46. Holly, *Old Divinity Preferable*, viii, 9.

47. Phillis Wheatley, "On the Death of the Rev. Mr. George Whitefield, 1770," in *Life and Works of Phillis Wheatley*, ed. G. Herbert Renfro (Washington, D.C., 1916), 51; for the self-consciously Christian contexts of Wheatley's thought, see Phillip Richards, "Phillis Wheatley and Literary Americanization," *American Quarterly* 44 (1992): 163–91.

48. See Wheatley, "To His Excellency, Gen. Washington" and "Poem on the Capture of Gen. Charles Lee by the British," in *Life and Works*, 32–34.

49. Wheatley, "To the University of Cambridge in New England," in *Life and Works*, 46–47.

50. See "Liberty Further Extended" (ca. 1776), in *Black Preacher to White America: The Collected Writings of Lemuel Haynes, 1774–1833*, ed. Richard Newman (Brooklyn, 1990), 17–30. For Haynes's theological interests, see John Saillant, "A Doctrinal Controversy between the Hopkintonian [Haynes] and the Universalist [Hosea Ballou]," *Vermont Historical Review* 61 (Fall 1993): 177–216; and Saillant,

"Slavery and Divine Providence in New England Calvinism: The New Divinity and a Black Protest, 1775–1805," *New England Quarterly* 68 (1994): 584–608.

51. Helen MacLam, "Introduction: Black Puritan on the Northern Frontier. The Vermont Ministry of Lemuel Haynes," in *Black Preacher to White America*, xxiii–xxxi.

52. On George's place in the political, racial, and religious history of the British occupation, see Sylvia R. Frey, *Water from the Rock: Black Resistance in a Revolutionary Age* (Princeton, 1991), 37–39.

53. The conversation is summarized and excerpted in Grant Gordon, *From Slavery to Freedom: The Life of David George, Pioneer Black Baptist Minister*, Baptist Heritage in Atlantic Canada Series (Hantsport, Nova Scotia, 1992), 142–50.

54. Ibid., 145.

55. Ibid., 146.

56. Macaulay's journal, 30 Oct. 1793, in ibid., 340n219.

57. The pioneering scholarship of William McLoughlin is a major historiographical exception. See especially his *New England Dissent, 1630–1833: The Baptists and the Separation of Church and State*, 2 vols. (Cambridge, Mass., 1971). Some help on specifically theological history has been provided by Timothy George and David S. Dockery, eds., *Theologians of the Baptist Tradition*, rev. ed. (Nashville, 2001); Curtis W. Freeman, James W. McClendon Jr., and C. Rosalee Vellos da Silva, eds., *Baptist Roots: A Reader in the Theology of a Christian People* (Valley Forge, Pa., 1999); and William H. Brackney, ed., *Baptist Life and Thought: A Source Book*, 2d ed. (Valley Forge, Pa., 1998).

58. The number of Baptist churches increased from 96 (1740) to 457 (1780) and then 2,700 (1820); see Edwin Scott Gaustad, *Historical Atlas of Religion in America* (New York, 1976), 4, 43. A fine account of Baptist populism is provided in Rhys Isaac, *The Transformation of Virginia, 1740–1790* (Chapel Hill, 1982). But for how populist pietism could wilt before the rhetoric of political liberty, see Juster, *Disorderly Women*.

59. Quoted by William G. McLoughlin, introduction to *Isaac Backus on Church, State, and Calvinism* (Cambridge, Mass., 1968), 2–3.

60. The work of William McLoughlin is especially important for Backus; see *Isaac Backus on Church, State, and Calvinism*; McLoughlin, *Isaac Backus and the American Pietistic Tradition* (Boston, 1967); McLoughlin, *New England Dissent*; and, as editor, *The Diary of Isaac Backus*, 3 vols. (Providence, 1980).

61. Backus, *True Faith Will Produce Good Works* (Boston, 1767), 68. On this relationship, see Heimert, *Religion and the American Mind*, 68; and McLoughlin, introduction to *Isaac Backus on Church, State, and Calvinism*, 16.

62. Backus, *An Appeal to the Public for Religious Liberty* (1773), in *Isaac Backus on Church, State, and Calvinism*, 309.

63. C. C. Goen, *Revivalism and Separatism in New England, 1740–1800: Strict Congregationalists and Separate Baptists in the Great Awakening* (New Haven, 1962), 208–13, 258–64, describes well the logic behind the Separate Baptists' rejection of infant baptism and the traditional way of organizing churches in New England. On issues dividing Separate Congregationalists and Separate Baptists, see McLoughlin, introduction to *Isaac Backus on Church, State, and Calvinism*, 9–10.

64. See John M. Bumsted and Charles E. Clark, "New England's Tom Paine: John Allen and the Spirit of Liberty," *William and Mary Quarterly* 21 (Oct. 1964): 561–70. Allen thus supports J. C. D. Clark's claim that a natural link joined theological heterodoxy and political dissent. Backus, of course, does not.

65. Backus, *A Seasonable Plea for Liberty of Conscience against Some Late Violent Oppressive Proceedings* (1770), in McLoughlin, *Isaac Backus and the American Pietistic Tradition*, 122.

66. Backus, *Appeal*, 311, 332, 340. In Ashfield, Massachusetts, Baptists had been fined and their goods distrained for refusing to pay taxes for the construction of a Congregational meetinghouse.

67. Backus, *The Doctrine of Particular Election and Final Perseverance, Explained and Vindicated* (Boston, 1789), in *Isaac Backus on Church, State, and Calvinism*, 471.

68. Ibid., 451.

69. See Hatch, *Democratization of American Christianity*, 95–101.

70. "Events in the Life of John Leland: Written by Himself," in *The Writings of John Leland*, ed. L. F. Greene (New York, 1969 [orig. 1845]), 39.

71. John Leland, *The Jarring Interests of Heaven Reconciled by the Blood of the Cross* (1814), in *Writings of John Leland*, 399. For the traditional emphases of Calvinism in a similar sermon, see 377, 379.

72. Hatch, *Democratization of American Christianity*, 101.

73. Here I am following especially Marini, *Radical Sects*; George A. Rawlyk, *Ravished by the Spirit: Religious Revivals, Baptists, and Henry Alline* (Kingston and Montreal, 1984); and two volumes edited by Rawlyk in the Baptist Heritage in Atlantic Canada series, *New Light Letters and Songs* (Hantsport, Nova Scotia, 1983) and *The Sermons of Henry Alline* (Hantsport, Nova Scotia, 1986).

74. Marini, *Radical Sects*, 137.

75. Ibid., 154.

76. Ibid., 57.

77. For that title, see George A. Rawlyk, introduction to *Henry Alline: Selected Writings*, Sources of American Spirituality (New York, 1987), 5.

78. Marini, *Radical Sects*, 24, 27, 32, 41, 45, 46; Maurice W. Armstrong, "Neutrality and Religion in Revolutionary Nova Scotia," *New England Quarterly* 9 (March 1946): 50–62; and J. M. Bumsted, "1763–1783: Resettlement and Rebellion," in *The Atlantic Region to Confederation*, ed. Phillip A. Buckner and John G. Reid (Toronto, 1994), 168–72.

79. Alline, *The Anti-Traditionalist* (1783), in *Henry Alline*, ed. Rawlyk, 219, 243, 247.

80. Ibid., 232, 268.

81. Ibid., 247, 248, 229.

82. Ibid., 262, 263.

83. Alline, "Contrariety," in ibid., 249.

84. See the works mentioned in note 2, chap. 7 above, as well as William Westfall, *Two Worlds: The Protestant Culture of Nineteenth-Century Ontario* (Kingston and Montreal, 1989).

85. The way British class lines divided theological perspectives more clearly than in America is nicely illustrated by the contrast between the high-church preoccupations of the elites described in David Newsome, *The Wilberforces and Henry Manning: The Parting of Friends* (Cambridge, 1966), versus the plebeian fixations of those depicted in Deborah M. Valenze, *Prophetic Sons and Daughters: Female Preaching and Popular Religion in Industrial England* (Princeton, 1985). It is as if these British contemporaries inhabited separate planets. Significantly, the Methodists, who bridged traditional class lines more completely than any other Christian tradition of the age, became much more successful in the United States than in Britain; for comparative

analysis, see David Hempton, "'Motives, Methods, and Margins': A Comparative Study of Methodist Expansion in the North Atlantic World, c. 1770–1850," in *The Religion of the People: Methodism and Popular Religion, c. 1750–1900* (London, 1996), 3–28.

86. Daniel L. Pals, "Several Christologies of the Great Awakening," *Anglican Theological Review* 72 (Fall 1990): 426.

87. Harry S. Stout, *The New England Soul: Preaching and Religious Culture in Colonial New England* (New York, 1986), 282–311.

Chapter 9

1. It is important to remember that almost all organized religion in colonial and early-national America was Protestant. At the start of the American Revolution, when there were about 3,200 places of worship in the thirteen colonies, fewer than sixty Roman Catholic churches had been formed, and there were perhaps only five centers of organized Judaism. Throughout the late-colonial period, Protestant churches of British origin constituted about 80% of all places of worship. The remaining 20%— Catholics, Jews, German and Dutch Reformed, Lutherans, Huguenots, Moravians, Mennonites, and German Brethren—were not as visible in public as their proportion of the total might suggest. The first African-American churches were formed only shortly before the Revolution. For these figures and the demography of late-colonial, early-national religion more generally, I am relying especially on an unpublished manuscript by Stephen A. Marini, whose kindness in making it available is much appreciated: "The Government of God: Religion and Revolution in America, 1764–1792." Four other careful accounts are also indispensable for any effort at outlining the broad shape of formal religion in this period: Edwin S. Gaustad, *Historical Atlas of Religion in America,* rev. ed. (New York, 1976); Patricia U. Bonomi and Peter R. Eisenstadt, "Church Adherence in the Eighteenth-Century British American Colonies," *William and Mary Quarterly* 39 (Apr. 1982): 245–86; Rodney Stark and Roger Finke, "American Religion in 1776: A Statistical Portrait," *Sociological Analysis* 49 (Spring 1988): 39–51; and Edwin Scott Gaustad and Philip L. Barlow, *New Historical Atlas of Religion in America* (New York, 2001).

2. Jefferson to James Smith, 8 Dec. 1822, in *Jefferson's Extracts from the Gospels*, ed. Dickinson W. Adams, *The Papers of Thomas Jefferson,* 2d Ser. (Princeton, 1983), 409.

3. Achille Murat, *Esquisse morale et politique des États-Unis de l'Amérique du Nord* (1832), in *The Voluntary Church: American Religious Life, 1740–1860, Seen through the Eyes of European Visitors*, ed. Milton B. Powell (New York, 1967), 54–55.

4. These well-considered estimates are from, respectively, Marini, "Government of God," and Bonomi and Eisenstadt, "Church Adherence," 274.

5. These conclusions are well documented for New England in Gerald F. Moran, "'Sinners Are Turned into Saints in Numbers': Puritanism and Revivalism in Colonial Connecticut," in *Belief and Behavior: Essays in the New Religious History*, ed. Philip R. Vandermeer and Robert P. Swierenga (New Brunswick, N.J., 1991), 38–62, esp. 52–54.

6. On these revivals, see Marini, "Government of God"; Marini, "Religion, Politics, and Ratification," in *Religion in a Revolutionary Age*, ed. Ronald Hoffman and Peter J. Albert (Charlottesville, 1994), 184–217; Sylvia R. Frey and Betty Wood, *Come*

Shouting to Zion: African American Protestantism in the American South and British Caribbean to 1830 (Chapel Hill, 1998), 119–48; Donald G. Mathews, "The Second Great Awakening as an Organizing Process, 1780–1830," in *Religion in American History: Interpretive Essays*, ed. John M. Mulder and John F. Wilson (Englewood Cliffs, N.J., 1978 [orig. 1969]), 210–14; and Russell E. Richey, Kenneth E. Rowe, and Jean Miller Schmidt, eds., *Perspectives on American Methodism* (Nashville, 1993), sec. 1, "The Founding Period."

7. These influences are well charted by, respectively, Edmund S. Morgan, "The Puritan Ethic and the American Revolution," *William and Mary Quarterly* 24 (1967): 3–43; and Harry S. Stout, "Religion, Communications, and the Revolution," *William and Mary Quarterly* 34 (1977): 519–41.

8. The strongest arguments for a Protestant presence are found in Alan Heimert, *Religion and the American Mind, from the Great Awakening to the Revolution* (Cambridge, Mass., 1966); and Barry Alan Shain, *The Myth of American Individualism: The Protestant Origins of American Political Thought* (Princeton, 1994).

9. Bernard Bailyn, ed., *The Debate on the Constitution*, 2 vols. (New York, 1993).

10. Donald S. Lutz, "The Relative Influence of European Writers on Late Eighteenth-Century American Political Thought," *American Political Science Review* 78 (Mar. 1984): 189–97, esp. 194. In reviewing Bailyn's two-volume edition of debates on the Constitution (note 10), Martin E. Marty concludes, "God comes up often, but almost never in biblical terms. . . . The citation of the Bible as authority is extremely rare"; "Religion and the Constitution: The Triumph of Practical Politics," *Christian Century*, 23–30 Mar. 1994, 316.

11. M. E. Bradford, *A Worthy Company: The Dramatic Story of the Men Who Founded Our Country* (Westchester, Ill., 1988), contains capsule biographies of the 55 members of the Constitutional Convention, among whom Bradford finds 27 Episcopalians, 9 Presbyterians, 7 Congregationalists, 3 Quakers, 2 Dutch Reformed, 2 Roman Catholics, 2 Methodists (William Few of Georgia and Richard Bassett of Delaware), and 1 Lutheran.

12. John M. Murrin, "Religion and Politics in America from the First Settlements to the Civil War," in *Religion and American Politics from the Colonial Period to the 1980s*, ed. Mark A. Noll (New York, 1990), 31. An even later indication of the relatively secular character of elite political culture of the period is provided by a diplomatic incident. In 1796 Joel Barlow, a radical deist and friend of Tom Paine, negotiated a treaty with Tripoli in which he inserted an article in the English (but not the Arabic) text asserting that "the government of the United States of America is not in any sense founded on the Christian Religion." Mild protests were heard, but not in the United States Senate, which approved the treaty without a dissenting vote. For a well-documented account, see Paul A. Rahe, *Republics Ancient and Modern* (Chapel Hill, 1992), 753.

13. This metaphor is expanded nicely in Shain, *Myth of American Individualism*, 322: "Revolutionary-era Americans were an uncertain people cast adrift on an unknown sea of material change with an anachronistic intellectual map and a moral compass ill suited for changing times."

14. Insightful writing on connections between political and ecclesiastical turmoil is found in, among other places, Rhys Isaac, "Preachers and Patriots: Popular Culture and the Revolution in Virginia," in *The American Revolution: Explorations in the History of American Radicalism*, ed. Alfred F. Young (DeKalb, Ill., 1976); James D. Essig, *The Bonds of Wickedness: American Evangelicals against Slavery, 1770–1808* (Philadelphia, 1982), chap. 4, "Free Citizens of Zion"; Nathan O. Hatch, *The*

Democratization of American Christianity (New Haven, 1989), chap. 2, "The Crisis of Authority in Popular Culture"; Sylvia Frey, *Water from the Rock: Black Resistance in a Revolutionary Age* (Princeton, 1991), chap. 8, "The Christian Social Order: Reformulating the Master's Ideology"; Alfred A. Young, "Afterword: How Radical Was the American Revolution?" in *Beyond the American Revolution: Explorations in the History of American Radicalism* (DeKalb, Ill., 1993), 322; and Robert M. Calhoon, "The Evangelical Persuasion," and Marini, "Religion, Politics, and Ratification," in *Religion in a Revolutionary Age*.

15. Gordon S. Wood, *The Radicalism of the American Revolution* (New York, 1992), 331.

16. On the extraordinary character of missionary expansion within the United States during this period, see Andrew F. Walls, *The Missionary Movement in Christian History* (Maryknoll, N.Y., 1996), 221–40 ("The American Dimension of the Missionary Movement").

17. Some important groups, especially the Baptists and Restorationist "Christians," looked upon systematic record-keeping with the same suspicion they directed against all top-down instruments of control. Other bodies like the Methodists and Presbyterians were careful, even obsessive, record-keepers, but often without assembling specific information on matters of great interest to modern historians. The most tantalizing of those matters concerns the ratio of adherents to members. Relatively firm information has been preserved for the number of churches, especially after the very early years of the century, and connectional denominations also made an effort to record the number of fully inducted members. All of the churches, however, served a broader population that included nonmembers as well as members. Adherents might hesitate to enter into full membership because of spiritually or psychologically demanding entrance requirements; men were frequently friendly toward the churches of their wives and daughters but without taking out membership themselves; as the decades passed, there was also class dissuasion as city and town churches became more bourgeois in manners, dress, speech, and displays of wealth, and so kept lower social classes at bay; conversely, in frontier and rural regions some who wanted to join churches lay beyond the bounds of regular ministry. These factors, and more, make it necessary always to realize that church adherence was more widespread than church membership, although by how much more remains a puzzle. For one of the most careful discussions of the issue, see Richard J. Carwardine, *Evangelicals and Politics in Antebellum America* (New Haven, 1993), 43–44.

18. Roger Finke and Rodney Stark, "How the Upstart Sects Won America: 1776–1850," *Journal for the Scientific Study of Religion* 28 (Mar. 1989): 30.

19. Hatch, *Democratization of American Christianity*, 4, which employs John Winebrenner, *History of All the Religious Denominations in the United States* (Harrisburg, Pa., 1848).

20. Reed, *American Churches* (1834), as quoted in Powell, *Voluntary Church*, 97.

21. Hatch, *Democratization of American Christianity*, 4.

22. *Minutes of the Methodist Conferences Annually Held in America, from 1773 to 1813, Inclusive* (New York, 1813), 598–99.

23. John H. Wigger, *Taking Heaven by Storm: Methodism and the Rise of Popular Christianity in America* (New York, 1998), 81, 97.

24. In the absence of a comprehensive general history that takes advantage of recent scholarship, the best general account is found in Richey, Rowe, and Schmidt, *Perspectives on American Methodism*.

25. *Minutes of the Annual Conferences of the Methodist Episcopal Church, for the Year 1860* (New York, 1861); *Minutes of the Annual Conferences of the Methodist Episcopal Church, South, for the Year 1860* (Nashville, 1861).

26. Many of the works that have revived Methodist scholarship are listed in the bibliography under "Other Theological Traditions."

27. *Memoir of John Mason Peck, D.D.*, ed. Rufus Babcock, intro. Paul M. Harrison (Carbondale, Ill., 1965 [orig. 1864]), 124.

28. Charles G. Finney, *Lectures on Revivals of Religion* (1835), ed. William G. McLoughlin (Cambridge, Mass., 1960), 273.

29. *The Journals and Letters of Francis Asbury*, 3 vols., ed. Elmer T. Clark (Nashville, 1958), 2:818–24 ("Index of Sermon Texts").

30. Nathaniel W. Taylor, "The Atonement a Pledge to the Christian for Every Real Good" (on Rom. 8:32), in *Practical Sermons* (New York, 1858), 92–93; this sermon was probably preached in the 1820s or early 1830s.

31. "The New Hampshire Confession" (1833), in *Baptist Confessions, Covenants, and Catechisms*, ed. Timothy George and Denise George (Nashville, 1996), 132.

32. Hodge, *The Way of Life* (1841), ed. Mark A. Noll (New York, 1987), 233.

33. From *Phoebe Palmer: Selected Writings*, ed. Thomas C. Oden (New York, 1988), 116

34. Offley, *Narrative of the Life and Labors of the Rev. G. W. Offley* (1860), in *Five Black Lives*, ed. Arna Bontemps (Middletown, Conn., 1971), 135.

35. See page 5 above.

36. Robert Baird, *Religion in the United States of America* (Glasgow, 1844), 414–15, 499

37. The best statement of the connection between personal religion and public responsibility is Daniel Walker Howe, "The Evangelical Movement and Political Culture in the North during the Second Party System," *Journal of American History* 77 (Mar. 1991): 1216–39; for the particular development of that link among Methodists, see Wigger, *Taking Heaven by Storm*, 98–103.

38. A useful summary is Roger Finke, "Religious Deregulation: Origins and Consequences," *Journal of Church and State* 32 (Summer 1990): 609–26.

39. Terrence Murphy, "The English-Speaking Colonies to 1854," in *A Concise History of Christianity in Canada*, ed. Murphy and Roberto Perin (Toronto, 1996), 184–86.

40. See especially Richard Carwardine, "Unity, Pluralism, and the Spiritual Market-Place: Interdenominational Competition in the Early American Republic," in *Unity and Diversity in the Church*, ed. Robert Swanson (Oxford, 1996), 297–335.

41. For careful definition of these terms, see Curtis D. Johnson, *Redeeming America: Evangelicals and the Road to the Civil War* (Chicago, 1993), 18–54. Johnson divides evangelicals in this period into formalists (about one-fifth of all evangelicals), antiformalists (three-fifths), and African Americans (one-fifth). His categories correspond roughly to the "liturgical" versus "pietist" divisions defined by ethnocultural historians of American voting behavior, as summarized in Robert P. Swierenga, "Ethnoreligious Political Behavior in the Mid-Nineteenth Century: Voting, Values, Cultures," in *Religion and American Politics*, 146–71.

42. Among the best accounts of the formalists are Perry Miller, *The Life of the Mind in America from the Revolution to the Civil War* (New York, 1965), 3–95 ("The Evangelical Basis"); Daniel Walker Howe, *The Political Culture of the American Whigs* (Chicago, 1979); and Allen C. Guelzo, *Abraham Lincoln: Redeemer President* (Grand Rapids, 1999).

43. Solid pioneering studies include Hatch, *Democratization of American Christianity;* Richard T. Hughes and C. Leonard Allen, *Illusions of Innocence: Protestant Primitivism in America, 1630–1875* (Chicago, 1988); and William R. Sutton, *Journeymen for Jesus: Evangelical Artisans Confront Capitalism in Jacksonian Baltimore* (University Park, Pa., 1998).

44. Frey and Wood, *Come Shouting to Zion*, xi. Other important treatments of this process include Albert J. Raboteau, *Slave Religion: The "Invisible Institution" in the Antebellum South* (New York, 1978); Mechal Sobel, *The World They Made Together: Black and White Values in Eighteenth-Century Virginia* (Princeton, 1987); Donald G. Mathews, *Religion in the Old South* (Chicago, 1977) 185–236; Christine Leigh Heyrman, *Southern Cross: The Beginning of the Bible Belt* (New York, 1997), 47–52; and Robert M. Calhoon, *Evangelicals and Conservatives in the Early South, 1740–1861* (Columbia, S.C., 1988), 137–41.

45. Michael A. Gomez, *Exchanging Our Country Marks: The Transformation of African Identities in the Colonial and Antebellum South* (Chapel Hill, 1998), 263.

46. Mathews, *Religion in the Old South*, 215, 208.

47. On that expansion, see especially Fred J. Hood, *Reformed America: The Middle and Southern States, 1783–1837* (University, Ala., 1980).

48. Outstanding treatments from a rapidly growing literature are found in Susan Juster, *Disorderly Women: Sexual Politics and Evangelicalism in Revolutionary New England* (Ithaca, 1994); Catherine A. Brekus, *Strangers and Pilgrims: Female Preaching in America, 1740–1845* (Chapel Hill, 1998); Mathews, *Religion in the Old South*; A. Gregory Schneider, *The Way of the Cross Leads Home: The Domestication of American Methodism* (Bloomington, Ind., 1993); Kathryn Teresa Long, *The Revival of 1857–58: Interpreting an American Awakening* (New York, 1998); Heyrman, *Southern Cross*; and Frey and Wood, *Come Shouting to Zion*. It is important to note that these, and almost all other, studies find women as the majority in evangelical churches and denominations.

49. Brekus, *Strangers and Pilgrims*, 42.

50. Heyrman, *Southern Cross*, 161–205.

51. Juster, *Disorderly Women*, 60–68; Brekus, *Strangers and Pilgrims*, 39–43; Mathews, *Religion in the Old South*, 104–5.

52. Brekus, *Strangers and Pilgrims*, 41; Mathews, *Religion in the Old South*, 113.

53. Long, *Revival of 1857–58*, 68–92; Mathews, *Religion in the Old South*, 112.

54. Schneider, *Way of the Cross*, 173.

55. Brekus, *Strangers and Pilgrims*, 267–306.

56. See the defense of women preachers in Phoebe Palmer, *Promise of the Father; or A Neglected Spirituality of the Last Days* (Boston, 1859); and Julia A. Foote, *A Brand Plucked from the Burning: An Autobiographical Sketch* (1886), in *Spiritual Narratives*, ed. Sue E. Houchins, Schomburg Library of Nineteenth-Century Black Women Writers (New York, 1988), 67 .

57. Baird, *Religion in the United States*, 222–23.

58. *Minutes of the Methodist Conferences*; Marini, "Government of God"; Frey and Wood, *Come Shouting to Zion*, 112–20.

59. Robert Bruce Mullin, *Episcopal Vision/American Reality: High Church Theology and Social Thought in Evangelical America* (New Haven, 1986), 9.

60. See especially James R. Rohrer, *Keepers of the Covenant: Frontier Missions and the Decline of Congregationalism, 1774–1818* (New York, 1995).

61. John Winebrenner, *History of All the Religious Denominations in the United States*, 2d ed. (Harrisburg, Pa., 1848), 71.

62. *Minutes of the Methodist Conferences.*

63. See David W. Kling, *A Field of Divine Wonders: The New Divinity and Village Revivals in Northwestern Connecticut, 1792–1822* (University Park, Pa., 1993); John B. Boles, *The Great Revival: Beginnings of the Bible Belt,* (2d ed. (Lexington, Ky., 1996); and Paul Conkin, *Cane Ridge: America's Pentecost* (Madison, Wis., 1990), which makes considerable use of Leigh Eric Schmidt, *Holy Fairs: Scottish Communions and American Revivals in the Early Modern Period* (Princeton, 1989).

64. See John Walsh, "Religious Societies: Methodist and Evangelical, 1738–1800," in *Voluntary Religion*, ed. W. J. Shiels and Diana Wood (Oxford, 1986), 279–302; and on Moravian influences, Colin Podmore, *The Moravian Church in England, 1728–1760* (Oxford, 1998).

65. Charles I. Foster, *Errand of Mercy: The Evangelical United Front, 1790–1837* (Chapel Hill, 1960), 275–79.

66. The best studies of how the societies actually did their work are from David Paul Nord, including "Free Grace, Free Books, Free Riders: The Economics of Religious Publishing in Early Nineteenth-Century America," *Proceedings of the American Antiquarian Society* 106 (1996): 241–72; and "Benevolent Capital: Financing Evangelical Book Publishing in Early-Nineteenth-Century America," in *God and Mammon: Protestants, Money, and the Market, 1790–1860*, ed. Mark A. Noll (New York, 2001), 147–70.

67. Rufus Anderson, "The Time for the World's Conversion Come" (1837–38), as reprinted in *To Advance the Gospel: Selections from the Writings of Rufus Anderson*, ed. R. Pierce Beaver (Grand Rapids, 1967), 65.

68. Walls, *Missionary Movement in Christian History*, 241, with more general discussion including treatment of Rufus Anderson, 223–24, 241–43.

69. For expert discussion, see Heyrman, *Southern Cross*; Calhoon, *Evangelicals and Conservatives*; Mathews, *Religion in the Old South*; Boles, *Great Revival*; and Bertram Wyatt-Brown, "Religion and the 'Civilizing Process' in the Early American South, 1600–1860," in *Religion and American Politics*, 172–95.

70. I rely here especially on James D. Bratt, "The Reorientation of American Protestantism, 1835–1845," *Church History* 67 (Mar. 1998): 52–82.

71. Baird, *Religion in the United States*, 369; Winebrenner, *History of All the Religious Denominations*, 72.

72. For a thorough compilation, see Gaylord P. Albaugh, *History and Annotated Bibliography of American Religious Periodicals and Newspapers Established from 1730 through 1830*, 2 vols. (Worcester, Mass., 1994).

73. See Deryck W. Lovegrove, *Established Church, Sectarian People: Itinerancy and the Transformation of English Dissent, 1780–1830* (Cambridge, 1988); and David Hempton, *Methodism and Politics in British Society, 1750–1850* (London, 1984).

74. Brekus, *Strangers and Pilgrims*, 267–306.

75. Carwardine, *Evangelicals and Politics*, 50–96.

76. Jenny Franchot, *Roads to Rome: The Antebellum Protestant Encounter with Catholicism* (Berkeley, 1994), 99–111, 136–49; and John Wolffe, "Anti-Catholicism and Evangelical Identity in Britain and the United States, 1830–1860," in *Evangelicalism: Comparative Studies of Popular Protestantism in North America, the British Isles, and Beyond, 1700–1990*, ed. Mark A. Noll, David W. Bebbington, and George A. Rawlyk (New York, 1994), 179–97.

77. Finney's career is well charted in Charles E. Hambrick-Stowe, *Charles G. Finney and the Spirit of American Evangelicalism* (Grand Rapids, 1996).

78. Connections among these groups are learnedly discussed in Richard T. Hughes and C. Leonard Allen, *Illusions of Innocence: Protestant Primitivism in America, 1630–1875* (Chicago, 1988), 102–87.

79. See William G. McLoughlin, *Cherokees and Missionaries, 1789–1839* (New Haven, 1984), 239–334.

80. Outstanding on such British-American comparisons is David Brion Davis, *The Problem of Slavery in the Age of Revolution, 1770–1823,* new ed. (New York, 1999).

81. See Bertram Wyatt-Brown, *Lewis Tappan and the Evangelical War against Slavery* (Cleveland, 1969).

82. Israel D. Rupp, *Original History of the Religious Denominations in the United States* (Philadelphia, 1840); John Hayward, *The Book of Religions . . . Particularly of All Christian Denominations in Europe and America* (Boston, 1842); Nathan Bangs, *A History of the Methodist Episcopal Church,* 4 vols. (New York, 1844); Baird, *Religion in the United States;* (1844) and Winebrenner, *History of All the Religious Denominations* (1848).

Chapter 10

1. The last two sentences paraphrase, but also invert, conclusions drawn by Paul E. Johnson, *A Shopkeeper's Millennium: Society and Revivals in Rochester, New York, 1815–1837* (New York, 1978), 138; and George Thomas, *Revivalism and Cultural Change: Christianity, Nation Building, and the Market in the Nineteenth-Century United States* (Chicago, 1989), 7.

2. Johnson, *Shopkeeper's Millennium,* 138, and for theoretical guides, 202–3. Johnson goes on helpfully (139–41) to show why revivalism was "not a capitalist plot," since most of the motives of those who took part in revivals were primarily religious, but he also suggests that, despite their own fixations, participants' actions nonetheless constituted "a crucial step in the legitimation of free labor." Criticism of Johnson's argument, on historical rather than metaphysical grounds, is now extensive. See especially Curtis D. Johnson, *Islands of Holiness: Rural Religion in Upstate New York, 1790–1860* (Ithaca, 1989), 77–80, with crucial questions about the way in which Rochester's extant church records forced Paul Johnson to limit archival correlations to Presbyterians and Episcopalians; Richard R. John, *Spreading the News: The American Postal System from Franklin to Morse* (Cambridge, Mass., 1995), 326n86, who queries Johnson's grasp of the Rochester merchants' sabbatarianism; Thomas, *Revivalism and Cultural Change,* 85–88, where Johnson is criticized for reversing causes and effects with respect to revival and individualist self-assertion in the market economy; Jama Lazerow, *Religion and the Working Class in Antebellum America* (Washington, D.C., 1995), 5–6, who suggests that workers may have turned to religion more for purposes of self-control than as a result of manipulation by entrepreneurs; and William R. Sutton, *Journeymen for Jesus: Evangelical Artisans Confront Capitalism in Jacksonian Baltimore* (University Park, Pa., 1998), who, without mentioning Johnson, nonetheless perceives a small-producer tradition that welcomed revivalism precisely as a means of resisting larger market forces.

3. For my own explanation of evangelicalism as a type of religion ideally suited to revolutionary situations, whether successful or unsuccessful, see "Revolution and the Rise of Evangelical Social Influence in North Atlantic Societies," in *Evangeli-*

calism: Comparative Studies of Popular Protestantism in North America, the British Isles, and Beyond, 1700–1990, ed. Noll, David W. Bebbington, and George A. Rawlyk (New York, 1994), 113–36.

4. Jürgen Habermas, *The Structural Transformation of the Public Sphere: An Inquiry into a Category of Bourgeois Society,* trans. Thomas Berger (Cambridge, Mass., 1989 [orig. 1962]), 27–29, 73–75. I thank Frank Turner for drawing this work to my attention and for indicating how its analysis might fit the situation of Anglo-American societies.

5. Thomas, *Revivalism and Cultural Change,* 7, 162.

6. See especially Gordon S. Wood, "Evangelical America and Early Mormonism," *New York History* 61 (Oct. 1980): 359–86; Robert H. Wiebe, *The Opening of American Society From the Adoption of the Constitution to the Eve of Disunion* (New York, 1984); Nathan O. Hatch, *The Democratization of American Christianity* (New Haven, 1989); and Wood, *The Radicalism of the American Revolution* (New York, 1992). A major difference in the interpretations of Wiebe and Hatch on the one side and Wood on the other is chronological; the former see the momentum of social transformation from the Revolution sustained over a longer period of time than does Wood.

7. Hatch, *Democratization of American Christianity,* 6, 17.

8. Wood, *Radicalism,* 173. Such assertions reprise the argument of Bernard Bailyn concerning "the contagion of liberty" in *The Ideological Origins of the American Revolution* (Cambridge, Mass., 1967), 230–319.

9. Wiebe, *Opening,* 131.

10. Ibid., 129 for "revolution in choices"; Alan Taylor, *William Cooper's Town: Power and Persuasion on the Frontier of the Early American Republic* (New York, 1995), 6.

11. Wood, *Radicalism,* 166, 336.

12. Wiebe, *Opening,* 241.

13. Wood, "Evangelical America," 371.

14. Hatch, *Democratization of American Christianity,* 198.

15. Ibid., 199.

16. Ibid., 9.

17. Wood, "Evangelical America," 361.

18. The best studies of early Methodism repeat this judgment, for example, Cynthia Lynn Lyerly, *Methodism and the Southern Mind, 1770–1810* (New York, 1998), 8–10: and Dee E. Andrews, *The Methodists and Revolutionary America, 1760–1800* (Princeton, 2000), 244: "Wesleyan discourse . . . furnished a powerful alternative to republican civic culture and harnessed the energies of a restless American people."

19. See Daniel Walker Howe, "Religion and Politics in the Antebellum North," in *Religion and American Politics from the Colonial Period to the 1980s,* ed. Mark A. Noll (New York, 1990), 136–37: "the Puritan/evangelical tradition did not simply adapt to, or borrow from, modernity and democracy; it actively helped form them. Individualism, voluntarism, and contractualism were features of the Puritan/evangelical religious tradition before they were taken over by the secular political philosophers of possessive individualism." This entire essay has much useful material on the active role of evangelical agencies and publications in constructing antebellum culture, as does also Howe, "The Market Revolution and the Shaping of Identity in Whig-Jacksonian America," in *The Market Revolution in America: Social, Political, and Religious Expressions, 1800–1880,* ed. Melvyn Stokes and Stephen Conway (Charlottesville, 1996), 259–81, esp. 270.

20. Of great significance for this comparison is the recently published edition of Alexis de Tocqueville, *The Old Regime and the Revolution,* vol. 1, ed. François Furet and Françoise Mélonio, trans. Alan S. Kahan (Chicago, 1998), esp. book 3, chap. 2, "How Irreligion Was Able to Become a General and Dominant Passion among the French of the Eighteenth Century, and What Kind of Influence This Had on the Character of the Revolution," 202–9.

21. See Boyd Hilton, *The Age of Atonement: The Influence of Evangelicalism on Social and Economic Thought, 1785–1865* (Oxford, 1988), especially the influence of Malthus on Thomas Chalmers, 59–67; and A. M. C. Waterman, *Revolution, Economics, and Religion: Christian Political Economy, 1798–1833* (Cambridge, 1991), which also contains extensive discussion of Malthus. For pertinent English-American comparisons, see Howe, "Religion and Politics in the Antebellum North," 133–34.

22. Compare the massive effect of various forms of evangelicalism on American society for the period 1830–60, as described by Richard J. Carwardine, *Evangelicals and Politics in Antebellum America* (New Haven, 1993), with the much more specific, much less comprehensive impact of the Dissenting churches on English society in the same period, as described in Timothy Larsen, *Friends of Religious Equality: Nonconformist Politics in Mid-Victorian England* (Woodbridge, Eng., 1999). The evangelical impress on public life in the north of Ireland was closer to the American situation, although Irish evangelicalism was far less democratized than its American counterpart; see on the leading public evangelical of his day, R. Finlay Holmes, *Henry Cooke* (Belfast, 1981).

23. Accounts that focus narrowly on the politics of the early republic are not as successful at recording the fragility of the early national experiment as those that focus on the stunning dimensions of geographic and cultural expansion, like D. W. Meinig, *The Shaping of America,* vol. 1: *Atlantic America, 1492–1800* (New Haven, 1986), chaps. 14 and 15, "The Problems of Federations" and "Nation-Building," 385–406.

24. John M. Murrin, "A Roof without Walls: The Dilemma of American National Identity," in *Beyond Confederation: Origins of the Constitution and American National Identity,* ed. Richard Beeman et al., (Chapel Hill, 1987), 344, 347.

25. Wood, *Radicalism,* 328.

26. Joyce Appleby, *Inheriting the Revolution: The First Generation of Americans* (Cambridge, Mass., 2000), 266, 263.

27. For exemplary instances, see Wiebe, *Opening,* 228–33, 303–7; and Appleby, *Inheriting the Revolution.*

28. The two most helpful attempts at sketching the larger terrain are Donald G. Mathews, "The Second Great Awakening as an Organizing Process," *American Quarterly* 21 (1969): 23–43, reprinted in *Religion in American History,* ed. John M. Mulder and John F. Wilson (Englewood Cliffs, N.J., 1978), 199–217; and Daniel Walker Howe, "The Evangelical Movement and Political Culture in the North during the Second Party System," *Journal of American History* 77 (Mar. 1991): 1216–39.

29. Perry Miller, *The Life of the Mind in America from the Revolution to the Civil War* (New York, 1965), 11.

30. Ezra Squier Tipple, *Francis Asbury: The Prophet of the Long Road* (New York, 1916), 162–63, cited from L. C. Rudolph, *Francis Asbury* (Nashville, 1966), 72–73.

31. For a sensitive evaluation of the Methodist connections that came together through regional meetings, see Russell E. Richey, *The Methodist Conference in America* (Nashville, 1996).

32. Nathan Bangs, *A History of the Methodist Episcopal Church*, 4 vols. (New York, 1838–41), 1:46.

33. See Gregory A. Wills, *Democratic Religion: Freedom, Authority, and Church Discipline in the Baptist South, 1785–1900* (New York, 1997), 11–36.

34. Sylvia R. Frey and Betty Wood, *Come Shouting to Zion; African American Protestantism in the American South and British Caribbean to 1830* (Chapel Hill, 1998), 120.

35. Carwardine, *Evangelicals and Politics*, 44, with 343n114 and 344n115 containing full assessment of the statistics from which the estimates were made. Carwardine's estimates are quite close to those made by Roger Finke and Rodney Stark, "Turning Pews into People: Estimating Nineteenth-Century Church Membership," *Journal for the Scientific Study of Religion* 25 (June 1986): 180–92, esp. 187–89; and they anticipate as well the careful attention to church membership found in Kathryn Teresa Long, *The Revival of 1857–58: Interpreting an American Religious Awakening* (New York, 1998), Appendix B: "Membership Statistics and Church Growth Rates, 1853–61," 144–50.

36. The phrase is from Mathews, "Second Great Awakening," 208. For an insightful meditation on the significance of these societies in the context of general American life, see Joel L. From, "The Moral Economy of Nineteenth-Century Evangelical Activism," *Christian Scholar's Review* 30 (Fall 2000): 37–56.

37. Charles I. Foster, *An Errand of Mercy: The Evangelical United Front, 1790–1837* (Chapel Hill, 1960), 121. Foster's account remains the most helpful general study of the American voluntary societies.

38. Ibid., 148–53.

39. Colton, *Protestant Jesuitism* (New York, 1836), with discussion in Foster, *Errand of Mercy*, 154–55.

40. The first edition of Alexander Campbell's own translation of the New Testament appeared in 1826, with five more editions in the next thirteen years; Margaret T. Hill, *The English Bible in America* (New York, 1962). For perceptive discussion of this and similar translations, see Paul C. Gutjahr, *An American Bible: A History of the Good Book in the United States, 1777–1880* (Stanford, 1991), 101–9.

41. Howe, "Evangelical Movement and Political Culture," 1231.

42. Richard K. Crallé, ed., *The Works of John C. Calhoun*, vol. 4, *Speeches of John C. Calhoun, Delivered in the House of Representatives and the Senate of the United States* (New York, 1854), 557–58.

43. Clay quoted in C. C. Goen, *Broken Churches, Broken Nation: Denominational Schisms and the Coming of the Civil War* (Macon, Ga., 1985), 106.

44. John, *Spreading the News*, with a summary of these major points on pp. 1–7. John shows (6) that it was not until the reorganization of the Pennsylvania Railroad in the 1870s that any American firm came to employ more workers than the postal service. John's book offers compelling documentation for Gordon Wood's remark that "in time the delivery of the mail was the only way most citizens would know that such a government even existed"; *Radicalism*, 328.

45. As only one example, between 1818 and 1860, Congregationalists and Presbyterians founded 51 colleges; by 1860 the Methodists were sponsoring 34 institutions of higher learning, the Baptists 25, and the Disciples of Christ an additional 6. In other words, with only a very few exceptions, higher education during this period meant simply evangelical-sponsored higher education; for a summary, see Curtis D. Johnson, *Redeeming America: Evangelicals and the Road to Civil War* (Chicago, 1993), 26, 39.

46. John G. West Jr., *The Politics of Revelation and Reason: Religion and Civic Life in the New Nation* (Lawrence, Kans., 1996), with 11–78 on the founding era, and the rest of the book a learned interpretation of evangelical politics in the period 1800–1835, with concentration on Sunday mails and Cherokee removal.

47. "Farewell Address" (19 Sept. 1796), in *Washington: Writings*, Library of America, ed. John Rhodehamel (New York, 1997), 972, 971.

48. *Diary and Autobiography of John Adams*, 4 vols., ed. L. H. Butterfield (Cambridge, Mass., 1961), 241; with discussion in West, *Politics of Revelation*, 51.

49. Rush to Jefferson, 22 Aug. 1800; and Jefferson to Moses Robinson, 23 Mar. 1801; in *Jefferson's Extracts from the Gospels*, ed. Dickinson W. Adams, The Papers of Thomas Jefferson, 2d Ser. (Princeton, 1983), 318, 325.

50. See the discussion in West, *Politics of Revelation*, 67–73. For an account that places Madison closer to the other founders, see Paul Rahe, *Republics Ancient and Modern: Classical Republicanism and the American Revolution* (Chapel Hill, 1993), 763–64.

51. Story, *Commentaries on the Constitution* (1833), cited from *The Founders' Constitution*, 5 vols., ed. Philip B. Kurland and Ralph Lerner (Chicago, 1987), 5:108a, 108b.

52. Evangelical attachment to the Constitution as a divinely provided instrument seems to have arisen only in the 1820s, that is, at about the time that the rise of evangelical churches to new national strength led naturally to an evangelical interpretation of the founders' reliance on religion as a support for republican government. In the late 1780s evangelicals (or at least antiformalist evangelicals) seemed to have sided with anti-Federalists in opposing the Constitution; see Stephen A. Marini, "Religious Revolution in the District of Maine, 1780–1820," in *Maine in the Early Republic: From Revolution to Statehood*, ed. Charles E. Clark (Hanover, N.H., 1988), 129–34; and Marini, "Religion, Politics, and Ratification," in *Religion in a Revolutionary Age*, ed. Ronald Hoffman and Peter J. Albert (Charlottesville, 1994), 184–217. The story that Benjamin Franklin's appeal for prayer at a critical moment during deliberations over the Constitution was the key to agreement on that document began to appear in the 1820s. When the story was given wider circulation in a tract published by Thomas S. Grimké in 1833, James Madison went out of his way to set the record straight: although Franklin had indeed appealed for prayer, his motion was tabled, and the Convention never did gather officially to pray. Franklin's motion is found in *Notes of Debates in the Federal Convention of 1787 Reported by James Madison*, Bicentennial Edition (New York, 1987 [orig. 1966]), 209–10; publication of Grimké's tract and Madison's reaction are treated in *The Records of the Federal Convention of 1787*, 3 vols., ed. Max Farrand (New Haven, 1911), 3:471, 499–500 (Madison to Jared Sparks, 8 Apr. 1831) and 531 (Madison to Grimké, 6 Jan. 1834).

53. See James H. Smylie, "The President as Republican Prophet and King: Clerical Reflections on the Death of Washington," *Journal of Church and State* 18 (Spring 1976): 233–52.

54. Perry Miller, "From the Covenant to the Revival," in *The Shaping of American Religion*, ed. James Ward Smith and A. Leland Jamison (Princeton, 1961), 322–68. For cogent criticism of Miller's argument, see Mathews, "Second Great Awakening," 203; and William Gribbin, "The Covenant Transformed: The Jeremiad Tradition and the War of 1812," *Church History* 40 (Sept. 1971): 297–305.

55. On the precedents in the Continental Congress for calling fast days continued by Washington and Adams, see the summary in James H. Hutson, *Religion and the Founding of the American Republic* (Washington, D.C., 1998), 51–58, 79–82.

56. Robert Smith, *The Obligations of the Confederate States of North America to Praise God . . . for the Various Interpositions of his Providence in Their Favour during Their Contests with Great Britain* (Philadelphia, 1782), 33.

57. For useful cautions against reading Christian support for the American Revolution as necessarily entailing national messianism, see Melvin B. Endy Jr., "Just War, Holy War, and Millennialism in Revolutionary America," *William and Mary Quarterly* 42 (1985): 3–25.

58. See West, *Politics of Revelation*, 79–81; and Mark A. Noll, *One Nation under God? Christian Faith and Political Action in America* (San Francisco, 1988), chap. 5, "The Campaign of 1800." Antiformalist support for Jefferson is noted in Hatch, *Democratization of American Christianity*, 95–96.

59. See Hutson, *Religion and the Founding*, 84–97.

60. See West, *Politics of Revelation*, 137–206.

61. Alexis de Tocqueville, *Democracy in America*, ed., and trans., Harvey C. Mansfield and Delba Winthrop (Chicago, 2000), 278. See also 280: "Religion, which among Americans, never mixes directly in the government of society, should therefore be considered as the first of their political institutions; for, if it does not give them the taste for freedom, it singularly facilitates their use of it."

62. Undocumented quotation in Miller, *Life of the Mind*, 71.

63. Wiebe, *Opening*, 306. See also Perry Miller, *Life of the Mind*, 95: American Protestantism "was committed to the absolute conviction that, amid a multitude of forms, revivalistic piety was the primary force in maintaining 'the grand unity of national strength.' This was the evangelical heritage."

64. Carwardine, *Evangelicals and Politics*.

65. See Douglass Adair, "Was Alexander Hamilton a Christian Statesman?" in Adair, *Fame and the Founding Fathers*, ed. Trevor Colbourn (New York, 1974), 147–48n8.

66. See particularly Daniel Walker Howe, *The Political Culture of the American Whigs* (Chicago, 1979); and Allen C. Guelzo, *Abraham Lincoln: Redeemer President* (Grand Rapids, 1999).

67. Gordon Wood's judgment is pertinent on the state of religion in the nation by this time, *Radicalism*, 333: "Nowhere in Christendom had religion become so fragmented and so separated from society. Yet nowhere was it so vital. By the second quarter of the nineteenth century, the evangelical Protestantism of ordinary people had come to dominate American culture to an extent the founding fathers had never anticipated."

68. Ezra Stiles, *The United States Elevated to Glory and Honor* (New Haven, 1783), 7; Lincoln, "Address to the New Jersey Senate" (21 Feb. 1861) and "Annual Message to Congress" (1 Dec. 1862), in *The Collected Works of Abraham Lincoln*, 9 vols., ed Roy T. Basler (New Brunswick, N.J., 1953), 4:236, 5:537.

Chapter 11

1. The nonpareil exposition of this Enlightenment confidence remains Gordon S. Wood, "Conspiracy and the Paranoid Style: Causality and Deceit in the Eighteenth Century," *William and Mary Quarterly* 39 (1982): 401–41. For thoughtful discussions of providentialism in the early republic, see Lester H. Cohen, *The Revolutionary Histories: Contemporary Narratives of the American Revolution* (Ithaca, 1980), esp. 49–53, who suggests that, while ministers in the Revolutionary era retained a nearly

Puritan sense of providence, lay writers moved toward more humanistic notions of contingency; and George H. Callcott, *History in the United States, 1800–1860: Its Practice and Purpose* (Baltimore, 1970), esp. 183–86, who documents a move back toward providentialism in the leading historians of the Jacksonian era like George Bancroft.

2. For the modern scholarship on which the assertions of this section rests, see the appendix, "Historiography of Republicanism and Religion."

3. Reginald Horsman, "The Dimensions of an 'Empire for Liberty': Expansion and Republicanism, 1775–1825," *Journal of the Early Republic* 9 (Spring 1989): 20; John Patrick Diggins, *The Lost Soul of American Politics: Virtue, Self-Interest, and the Foundations of Liberalism* (New York, 1984), 32; and Gordon Wood, "Ideology and the Origins of Liberal America," *William and Mary Quarterly* 44 (July 1987): 635.

4. For example, Lance Banning, *The Jeffersonian Persuasion: Evolution of a Party Ideology* (Ithaca, 1978), 56–60; Banning, "Jeffersonian Ideology Revisited: Liberal and Classical Ideas in the New American Republic," *William and Mary Quarterly* 43 (Jan. 1986): 8; Drew R. McCoy, *The Elusive Republic: Political Economy in Jeffersonian America* (Chapel Hill, 1980), 84–103; Robert E. Shalhope, "Republicanism, Liberalism, and Democracy: Political Culture in the New Nation," in *The Republican Synthesis Revisited*, ed. Milton M. Klein, Richard D. Brown, and John B. Hench (Worcester, Mass., 1992), 90; James T. Kloppenberg, "The Virtues of Liberalism: Christianity, Republicanism, and Ethics in Early American Political Discourse," *Journal of American History* 74 (June 1987): 19; and John Ashworth, "The Jeffersonians: Classical Republicans or Liberal Capitalists?" *Journal of American Studies* 18 (Dec. 1984): 425–35.

5. Banning, *Jeffersonian Persuasion*, 270.

6. James Roger Sharp, *American Politics in the Early Republic: The New Nation in Crisis* (New Haven, 1993), 174, 176.

7. Joyce Appleby, "Republicanism and Ideology," in *Liberalism and Republicanism in the Historical Imagination* (Cambridge, Mass., 1992), 290. For a learned summary of how thoroughly republican and liberal instincts came to be merged, see Dorothy Ross, "Liberalism," in *Encyclopedia of American Political History,* vol. 2, ed. Jack P. Greene (New York, 1984), 750–63, esp. 751–52.

8. Daniel Walker Howe, *Making the American Self: Jonathan Edwards to Abraham Lincoln* (Cambridge, Mass., 1997), 13, and 10–17 for an excellent general argument along the same lines.

9. John M. Murrin, "Escaping Perfidious Albion: Federalism, Fear of Aristocracy, and the Democratization of Corruption in Postrevolutionary America," in *Virtue, Corruption, and Self-Interest: Political Values in the Eighteen Century*, ed. Richard K. Matthews (Bethlehem, Pa., 1994), 138–39.

10. Quoted in Daniel Walker Howe, *The Political Culture of the American Whigs* (Chicago, 1979), 88. In this book Howe shows how Whigs abandoned earlier republican suspicion about wealth formation, but he also indicates that they retained firm commitments to a largely republican picture of the political world; see 8–9, 32, 44, 48, 67, 77–80, 87, 91, 126, 171, 187, 203, 217, 231, 248.

11. This interpretation follows Major Wilson, "Republicanism and the Idea of Party in the Jacksonian Period," *Journal of the Early Republic* 8 (Winter 1988): 419–42, with 433–34 especially on Van Buren's understanding of the Whigs. For a similar picture of Democratic republicanism, see Charles Sellers, *The Market Revolution: Jacksonian America, 1815–1846* (New York, 1991), 293–96.

12. See especially Steven M. Dworetz, *The Unvarnished Doctrine: Locke, Liberalism, and the American Revolution* (Durham, 1990), chap. 5, "Theistic Liberalism in the Teaching of the New England Clergy."

13. Specific bonds between Real Whig and late-Puritan thought are explored in, among other places, Ruth Bloch, *Visionary Republic: Millennial Themes in American Thought, 1756–1800* (New York, 1985), 53–74; Mark A. Noll, *Christians in the American Revolution* (Grand Rapids, 1977), 52–60; and Steven J. Keillor, *This Rebellious House: American History and the Truth of Christianity* (Downers Grove, Ill., 1996), 86–90.

14. Among the few historians who have traced the parallel evolution of New England theology and the development from classical to liberal republicanism are William Breitenbach, "Unregenerate Doings: Selflessness and Selfishness in New Divinity Theology," *American Quarterly* 34 (Winter 1982): 498–502; and Allen C. Guelzo, "From Calvinist Metaphysics to Republican Theory: Jonathan Edwards and James Dana on Freedom of the Will," *Journal of the History of Ideas* 56 (July 1995): 413–18.

15. Works that insist upon taking that religious experience seriously as a basis for thought include Susan Juster, *Disorderly Women: Sexual Politics and Evangelicalism in Revolutionary New England* (Ithaca, 1994); G. A. Rawlyk, *"Wrapped Up in God": A Study of Several Canadian Revivals and Revivalists* (Burlington, Ont., 1988); Barry Alan Shain, *The Myth of American Individualism: The Protestant Origins of American Political Thought* (Princeton, 1994); and Curtis D. Johnson, *Islands of Holiness: Rural Religion in Upstate New York, 1790–1860* (Ithaca, 1989). In general, however, nineteenth-century religious experience has not been studied as thoroughly in connection with formal dogma as with the Puritans, as in the works noted above, chap. 2, note 8.

16. Catherine A. Brekus, *Strangers and Pilgrims: Female Preaching in America, 1740–1845* (Chapel Hill, 1998), 43. Others who have also seen the mixture of something like republican communalism and liberal individualism in the evangelical tradition include Gordon S. Wood, "Evangelical America and Early Mormonism," *New York History* 61 (Oct. 1980): 361; Rhys Isaac, "Radicalised Religion and Changing Lifestyles: Virginia in the Period of the American Revolution," in *The Origins of Anglo-American Radicalism*, ed. Margaret Jacob and James Jacob (London, 1984), 264–65; Harry S. Stout, "Rhetoric and Reality in the Early Republic: The Case of the Federalist Clergy," in *Religion and American Politics from the Colonial Period to the 1980s*, ed. Mark A. Noll (New York, 1990), 20; Juster, *Disorderly Women*, 20; and especially Daniel Walker Howe, "The Evangelical Movement and Political Culture in the North during the Second Party System," *Journal of American History* 77 (1991): 1216–39.

17. Joyce Appleby, Lynn Hunt, and Margaret Jacob, *Telling the Truth about History* (New York, 1994), 108.

18. Joyce Appleby has caught much of this dynamic exchange in two sentences: "During these same [early national] years evangelical Protestants successfully propagated an individualized Christian message that challenged much of Calvinist orthodoxy. They compared liberation from sin to liberation from tyranny as a kind of individual empowerment, thus providing a Christian foundation for the civil religion forming around natural rights." Appleby, *Liberalism and Republicanism*, 4.

19. I am here mostly following Ruth H. Bloch, "The Gendered Meanings of Virtue in Revolutionary America," *Signs: Journal of Women in Culture and Society* 13 (1987): 37–58. Other pertinent discussions of the meaning of virtue, moving in do-

mestic, female, or democratic directions, include Diggins, *Lost Soul of American Politics*, 164; Kloppenberg, "The Virtues of Liberalism," 20, 29; Lance Banning, "Some Second Thoughts on Virtue and the Course of Revolutionary Thinking," in *Conceptual Change and the Constitution*, ed. Terence Ball and J. G. A. Pocock (Lawrence, Kans., 1988), 194–212; Dale S. Kuehne, *Massachusetts Congregationalist Political Thought, 1760–1790* (Columbia, Mo., 1996), 144; several of the essays in *Virtue, Corruption, and Self-Interest*; Howe, *Making the American Self*, 100; Gordon S. Wood, *The Radicalism of the American Revolution* (New York, 1992), 217; and Derek H. Davis, *Religion and the Continental Congress: Contributions to Original Intent* (New York, 2000), 175–98 ("Virtue and the Continental Congress").

20. Bloch, "Gendered Meaning of Virtue," 56.

21. Wood, *Radicalism of the American Revolution*, 218.

22. On the confluence of republican and evangelical thinking in particular, and for the whole country, see Richard Carwardine, *Evangelicals and Politics in Antebellum America* (New Haven, 1993).

23. This point is made forcefully by George C. Rable, *The Confederate Republic: A Revolution against Politics* (Chapel Hill, 1994), 12–16, 76–77; and Stephanie McCurry, "The Two Faces of Republicanism: Gender and Proslavery Politics in Antebellum South Carolina," *Journal of American History* 78 (1992): 1245–64.

24. In the South, commitment to economic expansion was at least sometimes viewed as intrinsically antirepublican; see James Oakes, "From Republicanism to Liberalism: Ideological Change and the Crisis of the Old South," *American Quarterly* 37 (Fall 1985): 551–71; and Kenneth Moore Startup, *The Root of All Evil: The Protestant Clergy and the Economic Mind of the Old South* (Athens, Ga., 1997), 56–57, 139.

25. Joyce Appleby, *Inheriting the Revolution: The First Generation of Americans* (Cambridge, Mass., 2000), 243.

26. See Edmund S. Morgan, *American Slavery, American Freedom: The Ordeal of Colonial Virginia* (New York, 1975), 384–85; Robert M. Calhoon, *Evangelicals and Conservatives in the Early South, 1740–1861* (Columbia, S.C., 1988), 167 (Sen. Nathaniel Macon of North Carolina); Rahe, *Republics Ancient and Modern*, 753 (the governor of South Carolina); Eugene D. Genovese, *The Slaveholders' Dilemma: Freedom and Progress in Southern Conservative Thought, 1820–1860* (Columbia, S.C., 1992), 18 (T. R. Dew), 47 (John C. Calhoun), 78 (William H. Trescot), and 89–92 (James Henry Hammond).

27. Dabney, "The New South" (1882), in *Discussions by Robert L. Dabney*, vol. 4, *Secular*, ed. C. R. Vaughan (Mexico, Mo., 1897), 2–24 (quotations 8, 17); Dabney, "Wilson's Slave Power in America" (1897), in *Discussions*, 248–59 (quotations, 255, 256).

28. Ezra Stiles, *History of the Three Judges of Charles I* (Hartford, 1794), 308, 314; as quoted in Charles P. Hanson, *Necessary Virtue: The Pragmatic Origins of Religious Liberty in New England* (Charlottesville, 1998), 202.

29. Lemuel Haynes, "The Nature and Importance of True Republicanism" (1801), in *Black Preacher to White America: The Collected Writings of Lemuel Haynes, 1774–1833*, ed. Richard Newman (Brooklyn, 1990), 78, 80, 82.

30. Elijah Perish, *A Protest against the War, a Discourse Delivered at Byfield, Fast Day, July 23, 1812*, 16; and Elias Smith, *Herald of Gospel Liberty*, 11 Dec. 1812, both in William Gribbin, *The Churches Militant: The War of 1812 and American Religion* (New Haven, 1973), 25, 63.

31. Carwardine, *Evangelicals and Politics*, 145–47.

32. Elias Smith, *Loving Kindness* (Taunton, Mass., 1809); Albert Barnes, *Connexion* (Philadelphia, 1835); Benjamin F. Tefft, *Republican Influence* (Bangor, Maine, 1841); Enoch Pond, "Republican Tendencies," *American Biblical Repository* 4 (1848): 283–98.

33. Baird, *Religion in the United States of America* (Glasgow, 1844), 298–300; Finney, "Professor Finney's Lectures. Lecture 34," *Oberlin Evangelist*, 9 June 1841, 90 (my thanks to Allen Guelzo for this citation); Thornwell, "Slavery and the Religious Instruction of the Colored Population" (1850), in *Collected Writings of James Henley Thornwell*, 4 vols., ed. John B. Adger (Richmond, 1871), 4:404–5.

34. Robert Burns, "The Aspect of the Times Practically Considered," *Home and Foreign Record of the Canada Presbyterian Church* 4 (May 1865): 201.

35. "The American Church in the Disruption," *Christian Remembrancer* 45 (Jan. 1863): 181. I thank Terrance K. Mann and Allan Peterson Milne for securing photocopies of these and other British comments on the Civil War.

36. "Moral Aspects of the American Struggle," *British Quarterly Review* 38 (July 1863): 230.

37. Elias Boudinot to Elisha Boudinot, 3 June 1808, quoted in George Adams Boyd, *Elias Boudinot: Patriot and Statesman, 1740–1821* (Princeton, 1952), 277.

38. Thomas Andros, as quoted in Michael G. Kenny, *The Perfect Law of Liberty: Elias Smith and the Providential History of America* (Washington, D.C., 1994), 113.

39. Joseph Tracy, *The Great Awakening: A History of the Revival of Religion in the Time of Edwards and Whitefield* (Boston, 1845), 420.

40. This section summarizes arguments from Mark A. Noll, ed., *God and Mammon: Protestants, Money, and the Market, 1790–1860* (New York, 2001), especially my introduction and "Protestant Reasoning about Money and the Economy, 1790–1860: A Preliminary Probe," where much more documentation can be found. I thank Rachel Maxson for expert help in preparing this material.

41. Gustaf Unonius, *A Pioneer in Northwest America, 1841–1858*, ed. Nils W. Olsson (1950), cited in Marvin Fisher, *Workshops in the Wilderness: The European Response to American Industrialization, 1830–1860* (New York, 1967), 109.

42. Grund, *The Americans* (1837), in *The Voluntary Church: American Religious Life, 1740–1860, Seen through the Eyes of European Visitors*, ed. Milton B. Powell (New York, 1967), 77.

43. Sellers, *The Market Revolution: Jacksonian America, 1815–1846* (New York, 1991); Johnson, *A Shopkeeper's Millennium: Society and Revivals in Rochester, New York, 1815–1837* (New York, 1978), with thesis stated most clearly, 138. In response to Sellers, see especially Daniel Walker Howe, "The Market Revolution and the Shaping of Identity in Whig-Jacksonian America," and Richard Carwardine, "'Antinomians' and 'Arminians': Methodists and the Market Revolution," in *The Market Revolution in America: Social, Political, and Religious Expressions, 1800–1880* (Charlottesville, 1996), which are also reprinted in *God and Mammon*.

44. See Harry S. Stout, *The Divine Dramatist: George Whitefield and the Rise of Modern Evangelicalism* (Grand Rapids, 1991); Frank Lambert, *"Pedlar in Divinity": George Whitefield and the Transatlantic Revivals, 1737–1770* (Princeton, 1994); and as an example of Breen's work, "An Empire of Goods: The Anglicization of Colonial America, 1690–1776," *Journal of British Studies* 25 (Oct. 1986): 467–99.

45. *Congregational Charitable Society. Rev. Sir . . . July 25, 1792* (Boston, 1792).

46. William Henry Seward, "Sunday School Celebration, Staten Island, July 4, 1832," in *The Works of William H. Seward*, 5 vols., ed. G. E. Baker (New York, 1853–54), 3:210.

47. For other examples, see Isaac Hurd, *A Discourse Delivered in the Church in Brattle Street, in Boston, Tuesday, June 11th, 1799, before the Humane Society of the Commonwealth of Massachusetts* (Boston, 1799), 7, 11–14; Abraham Bodwell, *A Sermon, Delivered at the Request of the Female Cent Society, in Sandborn, New Hampshire, December 23, 1812* (Concord, N.H., 1813), 19; and Beriah Green, "Anniversary Address," *Home Missionary* I (1 June 1828): 25–28.

48. Joseph Emerson, *Christian Economy: A Sermon, Delivered before the Massachusetts Missionary Society . . . May 25, 1813* (Boston, 1813).

49. David McConaughy, *The Duties and Dangers of Prosperity: A Sermon . . . Being a Day of Thanksgiving, on account of the General Plenty and Prosperity* (Gettysburg, Pa., 1817), 13–14, 15–16.

50. Francis Wayland, *The Elements of Political Economy* (Boston, 1841), 113.

51. John McFarlane, "Altar-Gold; or, Christ Worthy to Receive Riches," in *Pulpit Eloquence of the Nineteenth Century*, ed. Henry C. Fisk (New York, 1857), 673.

52. Alexander Campbell, "Short Sermons for Business Men," *Millennial Harbinger*, 5th ser., 13 (July 1860): 400.

53. See especially, Kathryn T. Long, "'Turning . . . Piety into Hard Cash: The Marketing of Nineteenth-Century Revivalism," in *God and Mammon*, 236–61.

54. Karl Marx, *Communist Manifesto*, trans. Samuel Moore (Chicago, 1954), 35.

55. On that inheritance, see, for example, W. Fred Graham, *The Constructive Revolutionary: John Calvin and His Socio-economic Impact* (Atlanta, 1971), 65–94; and Gordon Marshall, *Presbyteries and Profits: Calvinism and the Development of Capitalism in Scotland, 1560–1717* (Oxford, 1980), 115–26.

56. The contrast with Britain is again instructive. There is in the United States very little of the self-conscious effort to link theology and political economy described for the late eighteenth and early nineteenth centuries by Boyd Hilton, *The Age of Atonement: The Influence of Evangelicalism on Social and Economic Thought, 1785–1865* (Oxford, 1988); and A. M. C. Waterman, *Revolution, Economics, and Religion: Christian Political Economy, 1798–1833* (Cambridge, 1991). By contrast, self-conscious and comprehensive religious reflection on political economy in the United States did not begin until the 1830s and 1840s. For such comparisons, I am indebted to Stewart Allen Davenport, "Moral Man, Immoral Economy: Protestant Reflections on Market Capitalism, 1820–1860" (Ph.D. diss., Yale University, 2001).

Chapter 12

1. Some of the immense quantity of literature on American religious thought from 1790 to 1865 is surveyed in the bibliography in the general section "American Theological History."

2. For comprehensive orientation, see Catherine A. Brekus, *Strangers and Pilgrims: Female Preaching in America, 1740–1845* (Chapel Hill, 1998), 117–264.

3. This is the well-documented conclusion of Lewis O. Saum, *The Popular Mood of Pre–Civil War America* (Westport, Conn., 1980).

4. One way of schematizing a fairly wide range of theological positions in early national America is to construct a grid along axes defined by formalist-antiformalist and enthusiast-antienthusiast poles. In this scheme, Presbyterians, Congregationalists, German and Dutch Reformed, Lutherans, and Roman Catholics could be grouped as antienthusiast formalists; Baptists would represent the most important antienthusiast antiformalists; Millerites, Mormons, many early Methodists, and most

African-American thinkers could be styled enthusiast antiformalists; a few elite Methodists like Phoebe Palmer could be described by the 1830s as enthusiast formalists; and Methodists as a whole could be grouped in a flexible circle around the intersection of the axes.

5. For expert discussion of how analysis of divine experience advanced alongside manifold claims for its presence, see especially Ann Taves, *Fits, Trances, and Visions: Experiencing Religion and Explaining Experience from Wesley to James* (Princeton, 1999).

6. A comprehensive volume would continue on to consider Lutherans, Unitarians, Catholics, African-American denominations, Jews, and representatives of other religious traditions, but concentration on the largest Protestant traditions will reveal conditions that, to one degree or another, also come to bear on these other groups.

7. James Dana, *An Examination of the Late Reverend President Edwards's "Enquiry on Freedom of Will"* (Boston, 1770), v; Dana, *A Sermon Preached before the General Assembly* (Hartford, 1779), 17.

8. On Dana's positive beliefs, see especially Allen C. Guelzo, "From Calvinist Metaphysics to Republican Theory: Jonathan Edwards and James Dana on Freedom of the Will," *Journal of the History of Ideas* 56 (1995): 399–418.

9. Timothy Dwight, *Theology: Explained and Defended*, 4 vols. (New Haven, 1843), 1:209. These sermons/lectures were originally published in 1818; Dwight had been delivering them on Sundays to Yale students since the 1790s.

10. For summaries of Dwight's theology, see Frank Hugh Foster, *A Genetic History of the New England Theology* (Chicago, 1907), 361–66; and John R. Fitzmier, *New England's Moral Legislator: Timothy Dwight, 1752–1817* (Bloomington, Ind., 1998), 109–26.

11. Robert Marshall and J. Thompson, *A Brief Historical Account of Sundry Things in the Doctrine and State of the Christian, or, as It Is Commonly Called, the Newlight Church* (Cincinnati, 1811), 17. For discussion, see Nathan O. Hatch, *The Democratization of American Christianity* (New Haven, 1989), 174.

12. For a summary of the early Restorationist beliefs, see Richard T. Hughes, *Reviving the Ancient Faith: The Story of Churches of Christ in America* (Grand Rapids, 1996), 56–57.

13. See Robert Bruce Mullin, *Episcopal Vision/American Reality: High Church Theology and Social Thought in Evangelical America* (New Haven, 1986); and James D. Bratt, "Nevin and the Antebellum Culture Wars," in *Reformed Confessionalism in Nineteenth-Century America: Essays on the Thought of John Williamson Nevin*, ed. Sam Hamstra Jr. and Arie J. Grffioen (Lanham, Md., 1995), 1–22.

14. For an unusually clear statement contrasting the older and newer sense of the self, see Bruce Kuklick, "The Two Cultures in Eighteenth-Century America," in *Benjamin Franklin, Jonathan Edwards, and the Representation of American Culture*, ed. Barbara B. Oberg and Harry S. Stout (New York, 1993), 101–13.

15. George Whitefield, *Sermons on Various Important Subjects* (Boston, 1741), iv and 212 (the latter in a sermon entitled "The Marks of the New-Birth").

16. Stowe, undated letter, quoted in Joan D. Hedrick, *Harriet Beecher Stowe: A Life* (New York, 1994), 41.

17. Perry Miller, *The Life of the Mind in America from the Revolution to the Civil War* (New York, 1965), 25.

18. Dwight, *Theology:Explained and Defended*, 4:260–61. For expert discussion of Dwight's appeal to common sense, see George M. Marsden, "Everyone One's Own Interpreter? The Bible, Science, and Authority in Mid-Nineteenth-Century America,"

in *The Bible in America*, ed. Nathan O. Hatch and Mark A. Noll (New York, 1982), 85; and Conrad Wright, *The Beginnings of Unitarianism in America* (Boston, 1955), 92.

19. These distinctions are elaborated in Mark A. Noll, "Common Sense Traditions and American Evangelical Thought," *American Quarterly* 37 (1985): 220–25.

20. Witherspoon, "Moral Philosophy," in *The Works of the Rev. John Witherspoon*, ed. Ashbel Green, 4 vols. (Philadelphia, 1802), 3:368.

21. Wilson Smith, "William Paley's Theological Utilitarianism in America," *William and Mary Quarterly* 11 (1954): 402–24; and Bruce Kuklick, *Churchmen and Philosophers: From Jonathan Edwards to John Dewey* (New Haven, 1985), 53.

22. "Memoirs of the Life of President Dwight," as prefaced to Dwight, *Theology: Explained and Defended*, 1:22–23. For questions about whether things were as seriously anti-Christian when Dwight took over, see Edmund S. Morgan, "Ezra Stiles and Timothy Dwight," *Proceedings of the Massachusetts Historical Society* 72 (1963): 101–17. For Dwight's deployment of these principles, see *A Discourse on the Genuineness and Authenticity of the New Testament, Delivered at New-Haven, September 10, 1793* (New York, 1794), and the series, "Lectures on the Evidences of Divine Revelation," in the *Panoplist and Missionary Magazine United,* which ran from June 1810 through December 1813. For comment, see Fitzmier, *New England's Moral Legislator*, 90, 244.

23. Samuel Stanhope Smith, *Lectures on the Evidences of the Christian Religion, Delivered to the Senior Class, on Sundays, in the Afternoon, in the College of New Jersey* (Philadelphia, 1809), 1, 3, 13, 34. For comment, see Mark A. Noll, *Princeton and the Republic, 1768–1822* (Princeton, 1989), 186–88.

24. Levi Hedge, *Elements of Logick; or, A Summary of the General Principles and Different Modes of Reasoning* (Cambridge, 1816), 85, 78, 79. For the contexts of Hedge's work, see Daniel Walker Howe, *The Unitarian Conscience: Harvard Moral Philosophy, 1805–1861* (Cambridge, Mass., 1970), 33–35.

25. Theodore Dwight Bozeman, *Protestants in an Age of Science: The Baconian Ideal and Antebellum American Religious Thought* (Chapel Hill, 1977), 3–31.

26. For examples in divinity, see John Witherspoon, "Lectures on Divinity," in *Works*, 4:22–75; Samuel Stanhope Smith, *A Comprehensive View of the Leading and Most Important Principles of Natural and Revealed Religion* (New Brunswick, N.J., 1815); Archibald Alexander, *A Brief Outline of the Evidences of the Christian Religion* (Princeton, 1825); and Nathaniel W. Taylor, *Lectures on the Moral Government of God*, 2 vols. (New York, 1859). For ethics, the standard account remains D. H. Meyer, *The Instructed Conscience: The Shaping of the American National Ethic* (Philadelphia, 1972). For science, see note 29 below.

27. Samuel Stanhope Smith, *An Essay on the Causes of the Variety of Complexion and Figure in the Human Species*, 2d ed. (New Brunswick, N.J., 1810), 3.

28. Elias Boudinot, *The Age of Revelation, or, The Age of Reason Shewn to Be an Age of Infidelity* (Philadelphia, 1801), 30. For similar responses elsewhere, see James H. Smylie, "Clerical Perspectives on Deism: Paine's *Age of Reason* in Virginia," *Eighteenth-Century Studies* 6 (1972–73): 203–20.

29. For good discussions of "supernatural rationalism," see Kuklick, *Churchmen and Philosophers,* 87; and more generally in E. Brooks Holifield, *The Gentlemen Theologians: American Theology in Southern Culture, 1795–1860* (Durham, 1978). On the harmonizations, see Ronald L. Numbers, *Creation by Natural Law: Laplace's Nebular Hypothesis in American Thought* (Seattle, 1977), 55–66; Bozeman, *Protestants in an Age of Science*, 71–159; Herbert Hovenkamp, *Science and Religion in America, 1800–1860* (Philadelphia, 1978), 119–46; Walter H. Conser Jr., *God and the*

Natural World: Religion and Science in Antebellum America (Columbia, S.C., 1993); and Rodney L. Stiling, "Scriptural Geology in America," in *Evangelicals and Science in Historical Perspective*, ed. D. N. Livingstone, D. G. Hart, and M. A. Noll (New York, 1999), 177–92.

30. Archibald Alexander, "Theological Lectures, Nature and Evidence of Truth" (1812ff.), in *The Princeton Theology, 1812–1921*, ed. Mark A. Noll, 2d ed. (Grand Rapids, 2001), 65.

31. Charles G. Finney, *Lectures on Revivals of Religion* (1835), ed. William G. McLoughlin (Cambridge, Mass., 1960), 33. A good discussion of the intellectual presuppositions of this new mode of revivalism is found in C. Leonard Allen, Richard T. Hughes, and Michael R. Weed, *The Worldly Church* (Abilene, Tex., 1988), 27–31.

32. *The Works of Jonathan Edwards,* vol. 1, *Freedom of the Will*, ed. Paul Ramsey (New Haven, 1957), 238, and for similar usage, 182–83. Italics in the quotations of this paragraph and the next are added.

33. Horace Bushnell, *Nature and the Supernatural*, 5th ed. (New York, 1860), 49, 47; Charles Grandison Finney, *Lectures on Systematic Theology,* vol. 2 (Oberlin, Ohio, 1847), 14, 17, 19; Nathaniel W. Taylor, "Application of the Principles of Common Sense to Certain Disputed Doctrines," *Quarterly Christian Spectator*, 3d ser., 3 (Sept. 1831): 464.

34. Edwards, *The Nature of True Virtue*, in *The Works of Jonathan Edwards,* vol. 8, *Ethical Writings*, ed. Paul Ramsey (New Haven, 1989), 550.

35. Lyman Atwater, "Outline of Moral Science," *Biblical Repertory and Princeton Review* 25 (1853): 19.

36. Historians have treated New England's theological polemics extensively, but not those in other regions of the country. A persuasive case for the importance of such disputes elsewhere is found in Richard Carwardine, "Unity, Pluralism, and the Spiritual Market-Place: Interdenominational Competition in the Early American Republic," in *Unity and Diversity in the Church*, ed. Robert Swanson (Oxford, 1996), 297–335.

37. The nonpareil study is Robert Bruce Mullin, *Episcopal Vision/American Reality: High Church Theology and Social Thought in Evangelical America* (New Haven, 1986), esp. chap. 2, "The Public Controversies."

38. Hobart, *Companion for the Altar* (1804), 32, as quoted in ibid., 31.

39. John Henry Hobart, *An Apology for Apostolic Order and Its Advocates* (New York, 1807), 219.

40. Ibid. For discussion, see Mullin, *Episcopal Vision/American Reality*, 45.

41. William Linn, *A Collection of Essays on the Subject of Episcopacy, Which Originally Appeared in the Albany Sentinel, and which Are Ascribed Principally to the Rev. Dr. Linn, the Rev. Mr. Beasley, and Thomas Y. How* (New York, 1806), 1–3.

42. Samuel Miller, *Letters concerning the Constitution and Order of the Christian Ministry as Deduced from Scripture and Primitive Usage* (New York, 1807), 3, 7, 11, 19, 354.

43. Samuel Miller, *The Divine Appointment, the Duties, and the Qualifications of Ruling Elders . . . preached . . . May 28, 1809* (New York, 1811), 26; Miller, *Memoirs of the Rev. John Rodgers, D.D., Late Pastor of the Wall-Street and Brick Churches in the City of New York* (New York, 1813), 206–9, 333–37.

44. See Diana Hochstedt Butler, *Standing against the Whirlwind: Evangelical Episcopalians in Nineteenth-Century America* (New York, 1995); and Allen C.

Guelzo, *For the Union of Evangelical Christendom: The Irony of the Reformed Epis-copalians* (University Park, Pa., 1994), chap. 1, "The Evangelical Episcopalians."

45. *Strictures on a Pastoral Letter to the Laity of the Protestant Episcopal Church, on the Subject of the Bible and Common Prayer Book Society by John Henry Hobart . . . by a Layman* (New York, 1815), 8–10; the author is identified as Jay in Mullin, *Episcopal Vision,* 56–57.

46. Michael G. Kenny, *The Perfect Law of Liberty: Elias Smith and the Provi-dential History of America* (Washington, D.C., 1994), 260. Alongside Kenny's ex-emplary study, see also on Smith's importance for general developments in the early republic, Hatch, *Democratization of American Christianity,* 68–70, 73–76, 102–3, 128–30.

47. In a path for which Methodism provided the archetype, however, Smith's "Christian" movement evolved within less than two generations from condemning the payment of ministers to certifying its own pastors, and from blasting the preten-sions of college-trained clergy to founding its own seminaries and colleges (includ-ing Antioch in Ohio, named for the New Testament site where believers were first called Christians).

48. Smith's explanation of the doctrine of election, for example, rested on "the plain declaration of the scriptures" (*Three Sermons on Election* [Exeter, N.H., 1808], 4). His defense of adult, believer baptism paused at several points to highlight what "any person of common sense must know" (*A Sermon on New Testament Baptism, in Distinction from All Others* [Exeter, N.H., 1807], 12).

49. Smith, *Three Sermons on Election,* 99.

50. Smith, *The History of Anti-Christ: In Three Books. Written in Scripture Stile, in Chapters and Verses: For the Use of Schools* (Portland, Maine, 1811), 117.

51. Smith, *Sermon on New Testament Baptism,* 33.

52. Smith, *History of Anti-Christ,* 115, 120.

53. A great desideratum is a full-orbed biography of this important figure. In the interim, solid preliminary work can be found in Richard T. Hughes, *Reviving the Ancient Faith: The Story of Churches of Christ in America* (Grand Rapids, 1996), 21–46; and David Edwin Harrell, *Quest for a Christian America: The Disciples of Christ and American Society to 1866* (Nashville, 1966), with Campbell as public debater, 81–83, 215–16.

54. For the nature of that Scottish precedent, see Deryck W. Lovegrove, "Unity and Separatism: Contrasting Elements in the Thought and Practice of Robert and James Haldane," in *Protestant Evangelicalism: Britain, Ireland, Germany, and America, c. 1750–c. 1950,* ed. Keith Robbins (Oxford, 1990), 153–77.

55. *The Evidences of Christianity: A Debate between Robert Owen, of New Lanark, Scotland, and Alexander Campbell, President of Bethany College, Va., Con-taining an Examination of the "Social System," and All the Skepticism of Ancient and Modern Times. Held in the City of Cincinnati, Ohio, in April 1829* (St. Louis, n.d.), 35, 13, 14, 369, 370, 399.

56. So strongly did Campbell appeal to general American values that historians of the Restorationist movement single out this debate as an important point of tran-sition in Campbell's career when he moved from a primitivist critique of other Prot-estant denominations to stressing pan-Protestant unity against Roman Catholics. See Hughes, *Reviving the Ancient Faith,* 32–37; and L. Edward Hicks, "Republican Re-ligion and Republican Institutions: Alexander Campbell and the Anti-Catholic Move-ment," *Fides et Historia* 22, no. 3 (Fall 1999): 42–52.

57. *A Debate on the Roman Catholic Religion: Held in the Sycamore-Street Meeting House, Cincinnati, from the 13th to the 21st of January, 1837. Between Alexander Campbell of Bethany, Virginia, and the Rt. Rev. John B. Purcell, Bishop of Cincinnati* (Cincinnati, 1851), viii, 311.

58. For expert background, see Carwardine, "Unity, Pluralism, and the Spiritual Market-Place," 317–33; and Carwardine, *Evangelicals and Politics in Antebellum America* (New Haven, 1993), 228–29.

59. See Harold S. Smith, "J. R. Graves," in *Baptist Theologians*, ed. Timothy George and David S. Dockery (Nashville, 1990), 223–48.

60. J. R. Graves, *The Great Iron Wheel; or, Republicanism Backwards and Christianity Reversed* (Nashville, 1855), 169, 154. Other anti-Catholic commentary begins on 239, 327, and 336.

61. Ibid., 160.

62. On Brownlow, see Carwardine, *Evangelicals and Politics*, 85–86, 224–29.

63. William G. Brownlow, *The Great Iron Wheel Examined; or, Its False Spokes Extracted, and an Exhibition of Elder Graves, Its Builder* (Nashville, 1856), quotations 108, 279, with 146–48 and 279–81 as the clearest defense of Methodists as true republicans.

64. William Weeks to Eb. Weeks, 11 Apr. 1808, William Weeks Letters, Sheldon Art Museum, Middlebury, Vt.

65. *The Memoirs of Charles G. Finney*, ed. Garth M. Rosell and Richard A. G. Dupuis (Grand Rapids, 1989), 142–43.

66. James Marsh, preliminary essay to *Aids to Reflection*, by S. T. Coleridge, (Burlington, Vt., 1829), xliv–xlv. I am grateful to Matthew Lundin for drawing my attention to Marsh's commentary.

67. Quotations in the next two paragraphs are from Marsh to Hodge, 4 Nov. 1830 and Hodge to Marsh, 22 Nov. 1830, Charles Hodge Papers, file 28, Speer Archives, Princeton Theological Seminary.

68. The *Vermittlungstheologie* of Isaak Dorner, Ernst Hengstenberg, Johann Neander, and Friedrich Tholuck deserves more study for its bearing on American theology of this period than it has received. A number of these important thinkers had significant contact with Americans, and their thought both resembled (in piety and in basic Trinitarian orthodoxy) and differed from (in being much more philosophically idealist) the mainstream American theology of their era. For solid introduction, see Walter H. Conser Jr., *Church and Confession: Conservative Theologians in Germany, England, and America, 1815–1866* (Macon, Ga., 1984), 13–96.

69. Henry Boynton Smith, "The Idea of Christian Theology as a System" (1855), in *Faith and Philosophy* (New York, 1877), 152.

70. See especially William DiPuccio, *The Interior Sense of Scripture: The Sacred Hermeneutics of John W. Nevin* (Macon, Ga., 1998), 122–35.

71. J. W. Nevin, *Human Freedom and a Plea for Philosophy: Two Essays* [originally in the *American Review*] (Mercersburg, Pa., 1850), 42, 42–43, 44. Nevin's critique in this essay ends with a gibe at the standard collegiate course in moral philosophy, which at the time was taught almost everywhere as a comprehensive exercise in mental and moral philosophy for seniors; these classes were not "the keystone of the academic arch," as claimed, but "at best an outside ornament simply, of most light and airy structure, set loosely on its summit, of which, in a short time, no trace whatsoever is to be found" (45). I thank Bill DiPuccio for introducing me to this essay.

72. Mark Y. Hanley, *Beyond a Christian Commonwealth: The Protestant Quarrel with the American Republic, 1830–1860* (Chapel Hill, 1994).

73. Francis Wayland, "The Apostolic Ministry," in *Sermons to the Churches* (New York, 1858), 18–19; for discussion, see Hanley, *Beyond a Christian Commonwealth*, 38.

74. Hanley, *Beyond a Christian Commonwealth*, 95, 97, 100–101.

75. John Duncan, *Colloquia Peripatetica,* 6th ed. (1907), 2, as quoted in Paul Helm, "Thomas Reid, Common Sense, and Calvinism," in *Rationality in the Calvinian Tradition*, ed. H. Hart, J. van der Hoeven, and N. Wolterstorff (Lanham, Md., 1983), 83.

76. John Henry Newman to Arthur Percival, 11 Jan. 1836, as quoted in Marvin R. O'Connell, *The Oxford Conspirators: A History of the Oxford Movement, 1833–1845* (New York, 1969), 178–79. For an account of Newman's life that stresses his opposition to such characteristically evangelical intellectual habits, see Frank Turner, *John Henry Newman: The Challenge to Evangelical Religion* (New Haven, 2002).

Chapter 13

1. This and the next two chapters offer interpretations growing out of thirty years of reading in the primary and secondary sources of Calvinist theology for the period 1735 to 1865. I have tried to acknowledge the major influences on those interpretations in the bibliography but have mostly refrained in these pages from the weighing of secondary authorities that the rich historiography of the subject so much deserves. Again, however, I must stress the great debt all students of the subject now owe to Bruce Kuklick as editor of the 32-volume series American Religious Thought of the Eighteenth and Nineteenth Centuries (New York, 1987).

2. Baptists were overwhelmingly Calvinist in the antebellum period and, like the Presbyterians and Congregationalists, of several varieties. But their position as antiformalist upstarts meant that it was not until the 1830s that widely recognized theological spokesmen emerged from within the Baptists churches. Because of the individualistic and sometimes militantly localist character of Baptist religion, these spokesmen were sometimes more highly regarded by others than by Baptists themselves. For a solid introduction, see Timothy George and David S. Dockery, eds., *Theologians of the Baptist Tradition*, rev. ed. (Nashville, 2001).

3. For perceptive comments on how the growth of seminary education fragmented as well as encouraged formal thought, see Bruce Kuklick, *Churchmen and Philosophers: From Jonathan Edwards to John Dewey* (New Haven, 1985), 86–87.

4. See especially Glenn T. Miller, *Piety and Intellect: The Aims and Purposes of Ante-Bellum Theological Education* (Atlanta, 1990).

5. It is also worth observing that in 1829, the presidents of forty of the nation's oldest fifty-four colleges were Presbyterian or Congregational ministers. See Charles I. Foster, *An Errand of Mercy: The Evangelical United Front, 1790–1837* (Chapel Hill, 1960), 241.

6. "Theological Seminaries," in *New Schaff-Herzog Encyclopedia of Religious Knowledge*, 13 vols. (New York, 1908–14), 11:343–94.

7. Estimates of size are from Peter Wallace and Mark Noll, "The Students of Princeton Seminary, 1812–1929: A Research Note," *American Presbyterians* 72 (Fall 1994): 205, 215n11. Slightly different totals, which nonetheless reflect the same preeminence of Presbyterian and Congregationalist schools, are found in Miller, *Piety and Intellect*, 201–2. The only postgraduate competition to seminaries were the law schools, which at this time did not enjoy the reach or scope of the seminaries.

8. See Carl Diehl, *Americans and German Scholarship, 1770–1870* (New Haven, 1978), 56–61, 155–59.

9. Frank Luther Mott, *A History of American Magazines, 1741–1850* (New York, 1930), 310, 529–30, 371, 624, and 369–79 on the general vigor of religious periodicals in this era.

10. Edwin Scott Gaustad and Philip L. Barlow, *The New Historical Atlas of Religion in America* (New York, 2001), 374, 400.

11. See especially W. J. Rorabaugh, *The Alcoholic Republic: An American Tradition* (New York, 1979).

12. See especially Richard R. John, *Spreading the News: The American Postal System from Franklin to Morse* (Cambridge, Mass., 1995), 169–205.

13. See Ray Allen Billington, *The Protestant Crusade, 1800–1860* (New York, 1838); Jenny Franchot, *Roads to Rome: The Antebellum Protestant Encounter with Catholicism* (Berkeley, 1994); and for trans-Atlantic comparison, John Wolffe, "Anti-Catholicism and Evangelical Identity in Britain and the United States, 1830–1860," in *Evangelicalism: Comparative Studies of Popular Protestantism in North America, the British Isles, and Beyond, 1700–1990*, ed. Mark A. Noll, David W. Bebbington, and George A. Rawlyk (New York, 1994), 179–97.

14. The fullest treatment of the American response to European theological neology, which concentrates on August Comte, is Charles D. Cashdollar, *The Transformation of Theology, 1830–1890: Positivism and Protestant Thought in Britain and America* (Princeton, 1989).

15. From standard bibliographies it is possible to provide a rough gauge for the currency of theologians from previous eras. During the period 1800–1839, there were 69 works of Jonathan Edwards reprinted in the United States, 15 of Cotton Mather, 2 of Jonathan Dickinson, and none of Benjamin Colman, John Cotton, Thomas Hooker, Increase Mather, Gilbert Tennent, and Samuel Willard. From English Puritans, there were no reprints for William Ames and William Perkins, but 14 for John Owen. John Calvin was reprinted 9 times. The only figures from the English Reformed tradition who were reprinted more frequently than Edwards in these decades were Richard Baxter with 112 and John Bunyan with 169, but Bunyan was represented mostly by *The Pilgrim's Progress* and Baxter by his more devotional works like *A Call to the Unconverted* and *The Saints' Everlasting Rest*. See Ralph R. Shaw and Richard H. Shoemaker, *American Bibliography: A Preliminary Checklist, 1801–1819* (New York, 1966); M. Frances Cooper, *A Checklist of American Imprints, 1820–1829* (Metuchen, N.J., 1973); and Carol Rinderknecht, *A Checklist of American Imprints, 1830–1839* (Metuchen, N.J., 1989). (A slightly higher number of Edwards's reprints is reported in the catalog prepared by Thomas H. Johnson, *The Printed Writings of Jonathan Edwards 1703–1758: A Bibliography* [Princeton, 1940]. In Johnson's listing, 103 of Edwards's titles were reprinted between 1801 through 1850; of that number, 57% were revival-related works, 16% were sermons or sermon collections, and 27% were theological treatises.)

16. *Acts and Proceedings of the General Assembly of the Presbyterian Church in the United States of America, May 11, 1798* (Philadelphia, 1798), 11; Timothy Dwight, *The Duty of Americans at the Present Crisis* (New Haven, 1798); Jedidiah Morse, *A Sermon, Delivered . . . May 9th, 1798, Being the Day Recommended by John Adams, President of the United States of America, for Solemn Humiliation, Fasting, and Prayer* (Boston, 1798); William Linn, *Serious Considerations on the Election of a President* (New York, 1800); John Mitchell Mason, *The Voice of Warning to Christians on the Ensuing Election of a President of the United States* (New York, 1800).

17. Smith to Jonathan Dayton, 22 Dec. 1801, and Smith to Morse, 10 Mar. 1802, Samuel Stanhope Smith Collection, Princeton University Library (the fire was almost certainly the result of poorly maintained chimneys). For expanded treatment of the sense of crisis in these circles at this time, see Vernon Stauffer, *New England and the Bavarian Illuminati* (New York, 1918); Mark A. Noll, "The Campaign of 1800," in *One Nation under God? Christian Faith and Political Action in America* (San Francisco, 1988), 75–89; and Noll, "Fire and Rebuilding, 1802–1806," *Princeton and the Republic, 1768–1822* (Princeton, 1989), 157–84.

18. Consociation Records, Hartford North Association, 1790–1820, 136, Connecticut Library (Hartford), as quoted in David W. Kling, *A Field of Divine Wonders: The New Divinity and Village Revivals in Northwestern Connecticut, 1792–1822* (University Park, Pa., 1993), 56.

19. On these initiatives, see James R. Rohrer, *Keepers of the Covenant: Frontier Missions and the Decline of Congregationalism, 1774–1818* (New York, 1995), 11–13.

20. "Revolt at Princeton College," *Troy Gazette*, 19 May 1807 (copy in Princeton University Archive); Mark A. Noll, "The Response of Elias Boudinot to the Student Rebellion of 1807: Visions of Honor, Order, and Morality," *Princeton University Library Chronicle* 43 (Autumn 1981): 1–22 (quotation 20).

21. Archibald Alexander, *A Sermon Delivered at the Opening of the General Assembly . . . 1808* (Philadelphia, 1808), 30–37.

22. William Gribbin, *The Churches Militant: The War of 1812 and American Religion* (New Haven, 1973), 31.

23. Leonard Woods, *History of the Andover Theological Seminary* (Boston, 1885), 41; Morse to Joseph Lyman, 15 June 1805, as quoted in Richard J. Moss, *The Life of Jedidiah Morse: A Station of Peculiar Exposure* (Knoxville, 1995), 87.

24. Mark A. Noll, "The Founding of Princeton Seminary," *Westminster Theological Journal* 42 (Fall 1979): 72–110; Noll, *Princeton and the Republic*, 258–70.

25. Barbara M. Cross, ed., *The Autobiography of Lyman Beecher*, 2 vols. (Cambridge, Mass., 1961), 1:196. For a general account of the moral urgency of those days, see Sidney Earl Mead, *Nathaniel William Taylor, 1786–1858: A Connecticut Liberal* (Chicago, 1942), 81–84.

26. *Autobiography of Lyman Beecher*, 2:53, writing about his early work after moving to Boston, 1826–27.

27. As an indication of the increasingly traditional character of the denomination, the Presbyterians' seminary founded at Auburn, New York, in 1818, was more accommodating to American values but never exerted anything like the influence of Princeton. For an account featuring James Richards, leading theologian in Auburn's early history, see Laura S. Seitz and Elaine D. Baxter, *Before the Throne of Grace: An Evangelical Family in the Early Republic* (Franklin, Tenn., 1999), 91–117, 172–99.

28. On those explorations, see especially James D. Bratt, "The Reorientation of American Protestantism, 1835–1845," *Church History* 67 (March 1998): 52–82; and Franchot, *Roads to Rome*.

29. Kuklick, *Churchmen and Philosophers*, 60–62.

30. Hodge, "Retrospect of the History of the *Princeton Review*," in *Biblical Repertory and Princeton Review: Index Volume* (Philadelphia, 1870–71), 12.

31. Clear summaries of atonement teaching, along with advocacy for the authors' own views, are found in Gustaf Aulén, *Christus Victor: An Historical Study of the*

Three Main Types of the Idea of the Atonement, trans. A. G. Hebert (London, 1931); Louis Berkhof, *The History of Christian Doctrines* (Grand Rapids, 1937); 165–202; and J. I. Packer, "What Did the Cross Achieve? The Logic of Penal Substitution," *Tyndale Bulletin* 25 (1974): 3–45.

Chapter 14

1. Allen C. Guelzo, *Edwards on the Will: A Century of American Theological Debate* (Middletown, Conn., 1989), 241.

2. The fullest account remains Leonard Woods, *A History of the Andover Theological Seminary* (Boston, 1885).

3. Douglas A. Sweeney, "Nathaniel William Taylor and the Edwardsian Tradition: A Reassessment," in *Jonathan Edwards's Writings: Text, Context, Interpretation*, ed. Stephen J. Stein (Bloomington, Ind., 1996), 141. This essay provides a good introduction to the themes of Sweeney, "Nathaniel William Taylor and the Edwardsian Tradition: Evolution and Continuity in the Culture of the New England Theology" (Ph.D. diss., Vanderbilt University, 1995).

4. The two best, though quite different, portraits of Hopkins are in the memoir by Edwards A. Park that prefaces *The Works of Samuel Hopkins*, 3 vols. (Boston, 1865); and the novel by Harriet Beecher Stowe, *The Minister's Wooing* (New York, 1859). A solid modern interpretation is Joseph A. Conforti, *Samuel Hopkins and the New Divinity Movement* (Grand Rapids, 1981).

5. Samuel Hopkins, *A Discourse upon the Slave-Trade, and the Slavery of the Africans* (Providence, 1793), 8, 18.

6. *The Works of Jonathan Edwards,* vol. 1, *Freedom of the Will*, ed. Paul Ramsey (New Haven, 1957), 156–57.

7. *The Works of Jonathan Edwards,* vol. 3, *Original Sin*, ed. Clyde A. Holbrook (New Haven, 1970), 128.

8. Ibid., 401: "the existence of created substances, in each successive moment, must be the effect of the *immediate* agency, will, and power of God."

9. Ibid., 403, 397, 389, 392.

10. For the emphasis on solidarity with Adam, see Samuel Hopkins, *System of Doctrines* (1793), in *Works*, 1:211–12.

11. Ibid., 224, 231.

12. Edwards, *The Nature of True Virtue*, in *The Works of Jonathan Edwards,* vol. 8, *Ethical Writings*, ed. Paul Ramsey (New Haven, 1989), 557; Hopkins, *System of Doctrines*, 1:236, 379.

13. Conforti, *Samuel Hopkins,* 110.

14. *The Works of Jonathan Edwards,* vol. 2, *A Treatise concerning Religious Affections*, ed. John E. Smith (New Haven, 1959), 383, 197.

15. Hopkins, *System of Doctrines*, 1:367.

16. Ibid., 365. I am led to the conclusion that Edwards taught a mostly traditional view of the atonement (though with his own vocabulary) by the arguments in Christopher A. Mitchell, "Jonathan Edwards' Theology of the Atonement: A Reappraisal" (M.A. thesis, Wheaton College Graduate School, 1986), which concentrates on Edwards's "Miscellany" 779, "The Necessity of Satisfaction for Sin," now readily available in *The Works of Jonathan Edwards,* vol. 18, *The "Miscellanies" 501–832*, ed. Ava Chamberlain (New Haven, 2000), 434–48.

17. Edwards, "Remarks on the Improvements Made in Theology by His Father, President Edwards," in *The Works of Jonathan Edwards, D.D.*, ed. Tryon Edwards, 2 vols. (Andover, 1842), 1:487.

18. See chap. 7, page 132 on Hopkins.

19. On Dwight, I have been most helped by Marie Caskey, *Chariot of Fire: Religion and the Beecher Family* (New Haven, 1978), 37–43; and John R. Fitzmier, *New England's Moral Legislator: Timothy Dwight, 1752–1817* (Bloomington, Ind., 1998).

20. See Steven J. Novak, *The Rights of Youth: American Colleges and Student Revolution, 1798–1815* (Cambridge, Mass., 1977), 129–36.

21. Bennet Tyler, *Memoir of Nettleton* (Hartford, 1844), 48, as quoted in Caskey, *Chariot of Fire,* 44. For an especially shrewd account of Tyler's career, see Allen C. Guelzo, *BDEB,* 1127–28.

22. Bennet Tyler, *Letters of the Origin and Progress of the New Haven Theology* (New York, 1837), 9.

23. On Beecher, see especially Caskey, *Chariot of Fire.* On Taylor, I have drawn most on Sweeney, "Nathaniel William Taylor"; Allen Guelzo's superb capsule biography in *ANB,* 21:396–98; and William R. Sutton, "Benevolent Calvinism and the Moral Government of God: The Influence of Nathaniel W. Taylor on Revivalism in the Second Great Awakening," *Religion and American Culture* 2 (Winter 1992): 23–48.

24. See Lyman Beecher, *The Practicality of Suppressing Vice, by Means of Societies Instituted for That Purpose* (three printings in 1804); *The Remedy for Dueling* (eleven printings, 1807–09); *Reformation of Morals Practical and Indispensable* (nineteen printings, 1813–14); *On the Importance of Assisting Young Men of Piety and Talents in Obtaining an Education for the Gospel Ministry* (ten printings, 1814–20); *The Government of God Desirable* (nineteen printings, 1809–13); and *The Bible a Code of Laws* (six printings in 1818).

25. Barbara M. Cross, ed., *The Autobiography of Lyman Beecher,* 2 vols. (Cambridge, Mass., 1961), 1:219.

26. Nathaniel William Taylor, *Regeneration the Beginning of Holiness in the Human Heart: A Sermon* (New Haven, 1816); Taylor, "Man, a Free Agent without the Aids of Divine Grace," in *Tracts Designed to Illustrate and Enforce the Most Important Doctrines of the Gospel* (New Haven, 1818). I thank Peter Thuesen for securing a copy of the second work for me.

27. Taylor, in *Regeneration the Beginning of Holiness*, 13–14, attacked Bishop John Henry Hobart by name for propounding this doctrine.

28. Ibid., 13, 18 (last 3 quotations).

29. Taylor, "Man a Free Agent," 14.

30. Ibid., 5.

31. Taylor, *Regeneration the Beginning of Holiness*, 11, 12.

32. Taylor, "Man a Free Agent," 7, 12–13, 6n.

33. *Autobiography of Lyman Beecher*, 1:284–85.

34. For example, Frank Hugh Foster, *A Genetic History of the New England Theology* (Chicago, 1907), 245–47; and Bruce Kuklick, *Churchmen and Philosophers: From Jonathan Edwards to John Dewey* (New Haven, 1985), 94.

35. For example, Joseph Haroutunian, *Piety versus Moralism: The Passing of the New England Theology*, (Chicago, 1932), e.g., 282 (with Taylor clearly in view): "They were urging men to believe in 'God, freedom, and immortality'; to be good, to do good, and to live in peace with their fellowmen. They preached these things, and expected men to believe and practice them. They were great optimists."

36. For example, Lyman Atwater, "Taylor's Lectures on the Moral Government of God," *Biblical Repertory and Princeton Review* 31 (July 1859): 489–538; and B. B. Warfield, "Edwards and the New England Theology," in *Encyclopedia of Religion and Ethics*, vol. 5, ed. James Hastings (New York, 1912), 221–27.

37. Edwards A. Park, introductory essay to *The Atonement: Discourses and Treatises*, 3d ed. (Boston, 1863 [orig. 1859]); and Sweeney, "Nathaniel William Taylor."

38. Taylor, "Man a Free Agent," 8.

39. Taylor, *Regeneration the Beginning of Holiness*, 6.

40. Taylor, "Man a Free Agent," 17.

41. On Dwight's purposes, see especially Harry S. Stout, "Rhetoric and Reality in the Early Republic: The Case of the Federalist Clergy," in *Religion and American Politics from the Colonial Period to the 1980s*, ed. Mark A. Noll (New York, 1990), 62–63, 71.

42. I am especially dependent in this section on Foster, *Genetic History*, 214, 243–45; Kuklick, *Churchmen and Philosophers*, 55–59; Guelzo, *Edwards on the Will*, 106–11; James Hoopes, "Calvinism and Consciousness from Edwards to Beecher," in *Jonathan Edwards and the American Experience*, ed. Nathan O. Hatch and Harry S. Stout (New York, 1988), 205–25; and Joseph A. Conforti, *Jonathan Edwards, Religious Tradition, and American Culture* (Chapel Hill, 1995), 126–31.

43. Sydney E. Ahlstrom, *A Religious History of the American People* (New Haven, 1972), 405. An affectionate portrait of Emmons is found in the figure of "Dr. Strong" in Harriet Beecher Stowe's novel *Oldtown Folks* (1869), with illuminating commentary in the edition of this novel by Henry F. May (Cambridge, Mass., 1966).

44. Nathanael Emmons, "Sermon 26: Prayer of Saints for the Constant Exercise of Holy Affections," in *The Works of Nathanael Emmons*, 6 vols., ed. Jacob Ide (Boston, 1863), 4:356–57.

45. Emmons, "Letters on Moral Agency," in *Works*, 6:711–12.

46. Foster, *Genetic History*, 244–45.

47. See the section "Liberal Congregationalists" in chapter 8 above on Jonathan Mayhew, Ebenezer Gay, and Charles Chauncy. The unexcelled account of the path to Unitarianism remains Conrad Wright, *The Beginnings of Unitarianism in America* (Boston, 1955).

48. Channing, "The Essence of the Christian Religion" (from *The Perfect Life*, 1873), in *Theology in America: The Major Protestant Voices from Puritanism to Neo-Orthodoxy*, ed. Sydney E. Ahlstrom (Indianapolis, 1967), 204, 208.

49. Daniel Walker Howe, *The Unitarian Conscience: Harvard Moral Philosophy, 1805–1861* (Cambridge, 1970), 137–38. My picture of Unitarianism in the age of Channing draws heavily on this book.

50. Channing, "Unitarian Christianity" (1819), in *The Unitarian Controversy, 1819–1823*, vol. 1, ed. Bruce Kuklick (New York, 1987), 14.

51. Ibid., 4, 27, 30. Channing, in fact, repeated that last assertion (37): Calvinism "subvert[s] our responsibility and the laws of our moral nature."

52. Ibid., 46–47. For echoes of this argument in Charles Finney's dismissal of creedal Calvinism, see pages 313–14 below.

53. Woods, *Letters to Unitarians Occasioned by the Sermon of the Reverend William E. Channing at the Ordination of the Rev. J. Sparks* (Andover, Mass., 1820); Ware, *Letters Addressed to Trinitarians and Calvinists Occasioned by Dr. Woods' Letters to Unitarians* (Cambridge, Mass., 1820); Woods, *A Reply to Dr. Ware's Letters to Trinitarians and Calvinists* (Andover, Mass., 1821): Ware, *Answer to Dr. Woods' Reply, in a Second Series of Letters Addressed to Trinitarians and Calvin-*

ists (Cambridge, Mass., 1822); Woods, *Remarks on Dr. Ware's Answer* (Andover, Mass., 1822); and Ware, *A Postscript to the Second Series of Letters Addressed to Trinitarians and Calvinists* (Cambridge, Mass., 1823). These tracts are reprinted in the two volumes of *The Unitarian Controversy, 1819–1823.*

54. Woods, *Letters to Unitarians*, 27–29.

55. Smith, "The Theological System of Emmons" (1862), in *Faith and Philosophy* (New York, 1877), 243.

56. Ibid., 244. For Frank Hugh Foster's repetition of Smith's point, though with an opposite judgment, see *Genetic History*, 246: "the final abandonment of the Berkleianism which had been so influential, and so balefully so, up to this time."

57. My comments here depend heavily upon the nuanced discussion of the faculties in Daniel Walker Howe, *Making the American Self: Jonathan Edwards to Abraham Lincoln* (Cambridge, Mass., 1997).

58. Ibid., 127, 91.

59. Taylor, "Man a Free Agent," 5.

60. Taylor, *Lectures on the Moral Government of God*, 2 vols. (New York, 1859), 1:1.

61. *Autobiography of Lyman Beecher*, 2:117.

62. Mark Valeri, "The New Divinity and the American Revolution," *William and Mary Quarterly* 46 (Oct. 1989): 743.

63. George M. Marsden, *The Evangelical Mind and the New School Presbyterian Experience* (New Haven, 1970), 21.

64. See especially James Hoopes, *Consciousness in New England: From Puritanism and Ideas to Psychoanalysis and Semiotic* (Baltimore, 1989), 95–124.

65. *Autobiography of Lyman Beecher*, 2:131.

66. For perspective in understanding the besieged psyche of New England Congregationalism in the first decades of the nineteenth century, it is useful to remember that only in the year 2000 did Connecticut finally accumulate as much history without a religious establishment as it had experienced under an establishment, and that Massachusetts will not reach that divide until the year 2036.

Chapter 15

1. Barbara M. Cross, ed., *The Autobiography of Lyman Beecher*, 2 vols. (Cambridge, Mass., 1961), 2:117.

2. A full record of the convention is found in the *New York Observer and Religious Chronicle*, 4 Aug. 1827, 122–23, which unfortunately does not record the ebb and flow of debate that led to the convention's many resolutions.

3. Horace Bushnell, *God in Christ: Three Discourses, Delivered at New Haven, Cambridge, and Andover, with a Preliminary Dissertation on Language* (Hartford, 1849), 77.

4. For the unfolding of the meeting, see Charles C. Cole Jr., "The New Lebanon Convention," *New York History* 31 (Oct. 1950): 385–97. On the importance of the meeting for aligning both former Federalists of New England and upcoming revivalists from New York State with the early Whig Party, see Daniel Walker Howe, *The Political Culture of the American Whigs* (Chicago, 1979), 160–62.

5. For a shrewd, sympathetic introduction to Finney's life, see Charles Hambrick-Stowe, *Charles G. Finney and the Spirit of American Evangelicalism* (Grand Rapids, 1996). See also the text with very extensive apparatus in *The Memoirs of Charles*

G. Finney: The Complete Restored Edition, ed. Garth M. Rosell and Richard A. G. Dupuis (Grand Rapids, 1989).

6. *New York Observer,* 4 Aug. 1827, 122 (first three quotations), 123 (last).

7. *Autobiography of Beecher,* 2:75 (both quotations).

8. *Memoirs of Finney,* 345–46.

9. On Nettleton's suspicions, see *Autobiography of Beecher,* 2:79–80.

10. See W. J. Rorabaugh, *The Alcoholic Republic: An American Tradition* (New York, 1979), 78–88.

11. Lyman Beecher, *Six Sermons on the Nature, Occasions, Signs, Evils, and Remedy of Intemperance* (Boston, twenty printings from 1827 to 1838).

12. Beecher, *Six Sermons* (Boston, 1827), 8, 48, 49, 51, 52 (both "patriotism" and "national conscience"), 53, 56.

13. Beecher's much-read *A Plea for the West* (seven printings, 1835–45) revealed even more clearly how broad and deep his foundation of republicanism remained; the antiCatholicism of this latter effort powerfully revived another traditional staple of American republican ideology.

14. On Taylor, see the sources from chap. 14, note 23.

15. Taylor prefaced his sermon, *Concio ad Clerum,* with the affirmation that its teaching did not depart "in any article of doctrinal belief, from his revered instructor in theology," that is, Dwight. Taylor, *Concio ad Clerum,* in *Theology in America: The Major Protestant Voices from Puritanism to Neo-Orthodoxy,* ed. Sydney E. Ahlstrom (Indianapolis, 1967), 214n.

16. Guelzo, "Taylor," *ANB,* 21:397.

17. Taylor, *Concio ad Clerum,* 213–17.

18. Ibid., 216, 220 (with quotations from authorities 217–19), 221, 229.

19. Ibid., 231, 234, 235.

20. Ibid., 239.

21. Yale's graduates were not quite as likely as graduates from the East Windsor Theological Institute to serve with voluntary or mission societies, but both schools directed a steady stream of graduates to such pursuits. For this information I thank Bruce Kuklick, along with Margaret Sobcazk, "Ideas and Society in American Religion: A Case Study of the New Haven Theology" (unpublished paper, University of Pennsylvania, 1987).

22. Taylor, *Concio ad Clerum,* 240–41.

23. Ibid., 249.

24. Ibid., 225–26n.

25. From the New Divinity tradition, see Bennet Tyler, *Letters on the Origins and Progress of the New Haven Theology* (New York, 1837); from Old School Presbyterians, see Charles Hodge, "Review of an Article in the 'Christian Spectator' on the Doctrine of Imputation," *Biblical Repertory and Princeton Review* 4 (July 1832): 425–72. On Methodist criticism of Taylor, see page 353 below. For a summary of responses, see Douglas A. Sweeney, "Nathaniel William Taylor and the Edwardsian Tradition-Evolution and Continuity in the Culture of the New England Theology" (Ph.D. diss., Vanderbilt University, 1995), 164.

26. This work appeared in 1859, the year after Taylor's death. Conflict over Taylor lingered for another decade until a final debate between George P. Fisher, "The 'Princeton Review' on the Theology of Dr. N. W. Taylor and Presbyterian Reunion," *New Englander* 27 (Apr. 1868): 284–348; and Lyman Atwater, "Professor Fisher on the Princeton Review and Dr. Taylor's Theology," *Biblical Repertory and Princeton Review* 40 (July 1868): 368–98, who were debating Charles Hodge's charge that

Taylor's theology was still infecting the New School; see Hodge, "Presbyterian Reunion," *Biblical Repertory and Princeton Review* 40 (Jan. 1868): 53–83.

27. Quotation is from Fred J. Hood, *Reformed America: The Middle and Southern States, 1783–1837* (University, Ala., 1980), 58; the best accounts of Presbyterian intellectual life in the first quarter of the nineteenth century are found in this volume; see also Theodore Dwight Bozeman, *Protestants in an Age of Science: The Baconian Ideal and Antebellum American Religious Thought* (Chapel Hill, 1977), 32–38; and Lefferts A. Loetscher, *Facing the Enlightenment and Pietism: Archibald Alexander and the Founding of Princeton Theological Seminary* (Westport, Conn., 1983).

28. The biography by Hodge's son is still the best general study, A. A. Hodge, *The Life of Charles Hodge* (New York, 1880); the most perceptive account of Hodge's intellectual life is John W. Stewart, *Mediating the Center: Charles Hodge on American Science, Language, Literature, and Politics*, Studies in Reformed Theology and History (Princeton, 1995). For my own assessments, see "Charles Hodge," *ANB* 10:907–9; "The Spiritual Vision of Charles Hodge," in *Charles Hodge*, ed. John W. Stewart and James Moorhead (forthcoming); and "The Princeton Review," *Westminster Theological Journal* 50 (1988): 283–304.

29. See the list on page 266 above.

30. Hodge, "Retrospect of the History of the *Princeton Review*," in *Biblical Repertory and Princeton Review: Index Volume* (Philadelphia, 1870–71), 12–13.

31. Hodge, "The Princeton Review on the State of the Country," *Biblical Repertory and Princeton Review* 37 (1865): 657.

32. For helpful treatment of Barnes, see George M. Marsden, *The Evangelical Mind and the New School Presbyterian Experience* (New Haven, 1970), esp. 25–28, 52–55, 110–13. Allen Guelzo's article on Barnes in *BDEB* also situates Barnes' work in his era's broader theological controversies.

33. Barnes's affinity with at least some New Englanders was further suggested by how much the themes of Beecher's *Six Sermons on Intemperance* appeared in his own oration *The Connexion of Temperance with Republican Freedom . . . Delivered on the 4th of July, 1835* (Philadelphia, 1835).

34. Albert Barnes, *The Way of Salvation . . . Together with Mr. Barnes' Defence of the Sermon*, 7th ed. (New York, 1836), 15–16n, 16.

35. Ibid., 21, 24n.

36. See Jerry Wayne Brown, *The Rise of Biblical Criticism in America, 1800–1870: The New England Scholars* (Middletown, Conn., 1969), 45–59; a useful monograph is John H. Giltner, *Moses Stuart: The Father of Biblical Science in America*, Society of Biblical Literature Centennial Publications (Atlanta, 1988).

37. Giltner, *Moses Stuart*, 110, 112–13, 116.

38. Moses Stuart, preface to the first edition, *A Commentary on the Epistle to the Romans with a Translation and Various Excursus*, 2d ed. (Andover, Mass., 1835), v. The commentary appeared in four editions, with at least fourteen printings, between 1832 and 1865.

39. Stuart, *Commentary on Romans*, 585, 593.

40. Ibid., 599.

41. Ibid., 610, 614, 615.

42. The claim for Edwards's biblical expertise is based on *The Works of Jonathan Edwards*, vol. 15, *Notes on Scripture*, ed. Stephen J. Stein (New Haven, 1998).

43. Stuart, *Commentary on Romans*, 585–86, 592–94.

44. Ibid., 616.

45. For publishing details, see *Memoirs of Finney*, 372–77; and Charles Grandison

Finney, *Lectures on Revivals of Religion (1835)*, ed. William G. McLoughlin (Cambridge, Mass., 1960), lviii–lix. The *Lectures* were reprinted at least sixteen times in three decades, 1835–65.

46. McLoughlin, introduction to Finney, *Lectures on Revivals*, ix.

47. As noted on page 314 below, Finney made a similar complaint about Methodist conceptions of grace promoting spiritual passivity.

48. Finney, *Lectures on Revivals*, 107–8.

49. Ibid., 194. Most of the content of lecture 12, "How to Preach the Gospel," was taken over from Finney's sermon entitled "Sinners Bound to Change Their Own Hearts," which he preached first in Boston in 1831 during the campaign assisted by Lyman and Edward Beecher and which he then published as the lead exhortation in a collection that, with slight variation in content, appeared as both *Sermons on Various Subjects* and *Sermons on Important Subjects*, of which there were at least thirteen printings between 1834 and 1839. See McLoughlin's annotation, Finney, *Lectures on Revivals*, 195n1.

50. Finney, *Lectures on Revivals*, 112.

51. Ibid., 67.

52. Ibid., 40.

53. Ibid., 118, 198 ("All preaching" and "Any thing"), 199, 403.

54. Ibid., 297, 301, 297, 302.

55. Ralph Waldo Emerson, "An Address to the Senior Class in Divinity College, Cambridge, July 15, 1838," in *Ralph Waldo Emerson: Essays and Lectures*, The Library of America, ed. Joel Porte (New York, 1983), 75, 76, 77.

56. Ibid., 82–83, 89.

57. The following paragraphs follow the superb account in Marsden, *Evangelical Mind*, 53–69; they have also benefited from Earl A. Pope, "New England Calvinism and the Disruption of the Presbyterian Church" (Ph.D. diss., Brown University, 1962), reprinted in the series Religious Thought of the Eighteenth and Nineteenth Centuries (New York, 1987), edited by Bruce Kuklick.

58. Green to Smith, 5 May 1807, Princeton University Archives, Princeton University.

59. Marsden, *Evangelical Mind*, 87, 52.

60. For example, Barnes on Romans 5:19 ("many were made sinners"): "There is not the slightest intimation that it was by imputation. The whole scope of the argument is, moreover, against this; for the object of the apostle is not to show that they were charged with the sin of another, but that they were in fact *sinners* themselves." Albert Barnes, *Notes on the New Testament* (Grand Rapids, 1949 [orig. 1835]), 141.

61. See Stewart J. Brown, *Thomas Chalmers and the Godly Commonwealth in Scotland* (Oxford, 1982), 296–349; and Brown and Michael Fry, eds., *Scotland in the Age of the Disruption* (Edinburgh, 1993).

62. Howe, *Political Culture of the American Whigs*, 158–61 (quotations 158). Definitive treatment of the political phenomenon is found in Michael F. Holt, *The Rise and Fall of the American Whig Party: Jacksonian Politics and the Onset of the Civil War* (New York, 1999).

63. On the republican, or "commonwealth," values, see Howe, *Political Culture of the American Whigs*, 8, 32, 48, 51, 63, 67, 75, 87, 91, 126, 171–73, 187, 203, 217, 231, 248, 256, 261, 290; and on the use of Scottish moral philosophy, 27–28, 32, 48, 67, 160.

64. Ibid., 159–60. Subsequent scholarship has underscored the wisdom of Howe's analysis. See especially Allen C. Guelzo, *Abraham Lincoln: Redeemer President*

(Grand Rapids, 1999), 63, 72, 138–40, 176, 456–63; and Richard Carwardine, *Evangelicals and Politics in Antebellum America* (New Haven, 1993), 122–23, where it is noted that many of the Calvinist theologians—including Albert Barnes, Lyman Beecher, Nathan Beman, Charles Hodge, Moses Stuart, and N. W. Taylor—were active supporters of the Whig Party. Helpful interrogation of Howe's conclusion is found in Sweeney, "Nathaniel William Taylor," 146–47. For an instructive countercase of an important Whig activist who renounced his earlier evangelical Calvinist revivalism, see James D. Bratt, "From Revivalism to Anti-Revivalism to Whig Politics: The Strange Career of Calvin Colton," *Journal of Ecclesiastical History* 52 (Jan. 2001): 63–82.

65. See Kenneth Moore Startup, *The Root of All Evil: The Protestant Clergy and the Economic Mind of the Old South* (Athens, Ga., 1997), 90–95; James Oscar Farmer Jr., *The Metaphysical Confederacy: James Henley Thornwell and the Synthesis of Southern Values* (Macon, Ga., 1986), 72–75; and Carwardine, *Evangelicals and Politics*, 124.

66. See, for example, the British evangelical reliance on Malthus's demographic determinism, which never was as important in America, as explained in Boyd Hilton, *The Age of Atonement: The Influence of Evangelicalism on Social and Economic Thought, 1785–1865* (Oxford, 1988), 64–76.

67. On the concept, see John H. Leith, "The Spirituality of the Church," in *Encyclopedia of Religion in the South*, ed. Samuel S. Hill (Macon, Ga., 1984), 731.

68. An account of Finney reading Edwards "with rapture" in 1827 is recorded in *Autobiography of Lyman Beecher*, 2:67. On efforts to imitate Edwards, see Finney, *Lectures on Revivals*, 241–42. Finney's attempt at linking his own theology back to Edwards's teaching on "natural ability" is well canvassed in Allen C. Guelzo, "Oberlin Perfectionism and Its Edwardsian Origins, 1835–1870," in *Jonathan Edwards's Writings: Text, Context, Interpretation*, ed. Stephen J. Stein (Bloomington, Ind., 1996), 159–74.

69. Charles G. Finney, *Lectures on Systematic Theology Embracing Lectures on Moral Government, Together with Atonement, Moral and Physical Depravity, Regeneration, Philosophical Theories, and Evidences of Regeneration* (Oberlin, Ohio, 1846), iii.

70. Finney, *Lectures on Systematic Theology* (London, 1851), x–xi. In an appreciative but also patronizing preface, Finney's London editor, George Redford, begged his readers to "suspend your judgment of the Author and his theology until you have gone completely through his work," but he also commended Finney precisely for having been "trained in none of the theological schools of his country" and "therefore" imbibing "no educational preference for one system more than another" (v–vi).

71. Ibid., vii–viii. The list of doctrines that Finney held to contradict "both reason and revelation" has a familiar ring: "The doctrines of a nature, sinful *per se*, of a necessitated will, of inability, and of physical regeneration, and physical Divine influence in regeneration, with their kindred and resulting dogmas."

72. Ibid., 501, 502, 504, 509–10 (on Edwards).

73. Lyman Beecher, "The Necessity of Revivals of Religion to the Perpetuity of Our Civil and Religious Institutions," *Spirit of the Pilgrims* 4 (Sept. 1831): 471; Beecher, "Republicanism of the Bible," *The Hesperian; or, Western Monthly Magazine* 1 (May 1838): 53.

74. N. W. Taylor, "Application of the Principles of Common Sense to Certain Disputed Doctrines," *Quarterly Christian Spectator*, 3d ser., 3 (Sept. 1831): 468.

75. Ibid., 454, 455, 456.

76. Ibid., 458, 467, with similar expressions, 459–60, 460, 463, 467, 472. At the end of the essay, Taylor presented reasons for not using common sense in the same way with respect to the doctrine of the Trinity, even though some of his Unitarian contemporaries claimed that this traditional doctrine offended ordinary human consciousness, 475–76.

77. Ibid., 468.

78. Taylor, "On the Authority of Reason in Theology," *Quarterly Christian Spectator*, 3d ser., 9 (Mar. 1837): 151, 155.

79. Taylor, *Lectures on the Moral Government of God*, 2 vols. (New York, 1859), 1:200.

80. I am here summarizing arguments developed at greater length in my Introduction to *The Princeton Theology, 1812–1921*, 2d ed. (Grand Rapids, 2001), 25–40; and the writing mentioned above in note 28.

81. Hodge in 1872, at the semicentennial celebration of his tenure at Princeton, as quoted in A. A. Hodge, *The Life of Charles Hodge* (New York, 1880), 521. For much the same sentiment, at somewhat greater length, see Hodge, "Retrospect of the Princeton Review," 11.

82. See his criticisms of, respectively, Taylor, Finney, and Bushnell: "The New Divinity Tried," *Biblical Repertory and Princeton Review* 4 (1832): 301; "Finney's Lectures on Theology," ibid. 19 (1847): 241; and "Bushnell's Discourses," ibid. 21 (1849): 273–74.

83. Dabney to Hodge, 23 Jan. 1861, Dabney Papers, Historical Foundation of the Presbyterian and Reformed Churches, Montreat, N.C. My thanks to Skip Stout for a copy of this letter.

84. D. H. Meyer, *The Instructed Conscience: The Shaping of the American National Ethic* (Philadelphia, 1972), 54.

85. Hodge, *Systematic Theology*, 3 vols. (New York, 1871–72), 1:10–11.

86. Ibid., 15. For examples of the many other places where Hodge made the same juxtapositions, see "Beecher's Great Conflict," *Biblical Repertory and Princeton Review* 26 (Jan. 1854): 101; "Salvation by Grace," MS. sermon outline for 20 Mar. 1853, Archives, Princeton Theological Seminary; and *Systematic Theology*, 1:53.

87. Hodge, "Diversity of Species in the Human Race," *Biblical Repertory and Princeton Review* 34 (July 1862): 462. For other examples of the same kind of reasoning, see Hodge, *What Is Darwinism?* (1874), ed. Mark A. Noll and David N. Livingstone (Grand Rapids, 1994), 71–72, 149–52.

88. On the exceedingly complex issues at stake in such discussions, I have benefited greatly from George P. Hutchinson, *The Problem of Original Sin in American Presbyterian Theology* (Nutley, N.J., 1972), with 28–35 on Hodge.

89. Hodge, *Systematic Theology*, 2: 219.

90. *Methodist Quarterly Review* 56 (July 1874): 516.

91. Hodge, *Commentary on the Epistle to the Romans*, rev. ed. (Grand Rapids, 1947 [orig. 1886]), 151. George Hutchinson points out how heavily nineteenth-century sentiment about the innocence of children bore down upon Hodge at this point. As a classic Calvinist, Hodge had to preserve human unity in Adam, but as a sensitive Victorian, he had somehow to get dying infants into heaven. The result was a theory of imputation that made an ingenious distinction between imputed sin (which only grace could overcome) and actual sinning (which condemned people to hell). That Hodge found in Scripture a theology of covenant to support his new position

suggests how complicated the exchange of social conventions and objective research actually was for biblical exegesis. See Hutchinson, *Problem of Original Sin*, 33.

92. There were seven printings of *God in Christ* from 1849 to 1853 and another three in 1851 of Bushnell's *Christ in Theology: Being the Answer of the Author, before the Hartford Central Association of Ministers, October, 1849, for the Doctrines of the Book Entitled "God in Christ."* I am using an 1849 edition of *God in Christ* published in Hartford by Brown and Parsons (quotation 187). (As a gauge of interest in Bushnell, there were more twentieth-century editions of *God in Christ* than appeared in the nineteenth century after the initial flurry of printings from 1849 to 1853.)

93. On Bushnell, I have been guided by the sources in H. Shelton Smith, ed., *Horace Bushnell*, A Library of Protestant Thought (New York, 1965); on his theological contributions, by Conrad Cherry, *Nature and Religious Imagination from Edwards to Bushnell* (Philadelphia, 1980); and E. Brooks Holifield, "Horace Bushnell," *ANB*, 4:86–88; and for his integration into nineteenth-century civic affairs, by Howard A. Barnes, *Horace Bushnell and the Virtuous Republic* (Metuchen, N.J., 1991). I am glad to note that, after finishing this section, my judgments were mostly confirmed by reading the authoriatative forthcoming biography of Bushnell by Bruce Mullin.

94. Bushnell, *God in Christ*, 309, 301, 302 (last two quotations).

95. Ibid., 72, 75.

96. Ibid., 69–70, 93.

97. Bushnell, "Science and Religion," *Putnam's Monthly Magazine of Literature, Science, Art, and National Interests* (1868), 271, as quoted in Jon H. Roberts, *Darwinism and the Divine in America: Protestant Intellectuals and Organic Evolution, 1859–1900* (Madison, Wis., 1988), 44.

98. Hodge, "Bushnell's Discourses," *Biblical Repertory and Princeton Review* 21 (1849): 274, 296, 298.

99. Enoch Pond, *Review of Dr. Bushnell's "God in Christ"* (Bangor, Maine, 1849), 13–14. For Smith's alarm, see page 104. One of the most important discussions on theology itself in American history was a by-product of other negative reactions to Bushnell. Although Andover's Edwards Amasa Park proposed a more modest critique of Bushnell, it was still too radical for Charles Hodge. The result was a seven-part debate in Andover's *Bibliotheca Sacra* and the *Princeton Review* that began with Park's "Theology of the Intellect and That of the Feelings," *Bibliotheca Sacra* 7 (July 1850): 533–69, and ran for almost two more years. On the importance of this debate, see D. G. Hart, "Divided between Heart and Mind: The Critical Period for Protestant Thought in America," *Journal of Ecclesiastical History* 38 (Apr. 1987): 254–70; Hart, "Poems, Propositions, and Dogma: The Controversy over Religious Language in American Learning," *Church History* 57 (Sept. 1988): 310–21; and Noll, *Princeton Theology*, 185–86.

100. On that process, see James Turner, "Secularization and Sacralization: Speculations on Some Religious Origins of the Secular Humanities Curriculum, 1850–1900," in *The Secularization of the Academy*, ed. George M. Marsden and Bradley J. Longfield (New York, 1992), 74–106; Jon H. Roberts and James Turner, *The Sacred and the Secular University* (Princeton, 2000); and D. G. Hart, *The University Gets Religion: Religious Studies in American Higher Education* (Baltimore, 1999).

101. It is a testimony to Bushnell's boundless mental flexibility that, even as he was battling his Consociation, he participated with apparent wholehearted support in an evangelistic campaign mounted by Charles Finney in Hartford; see *Memoirs of*

Charles Finney, 520–22, esp. 522n18, where a contemporary is quoted about the visits Finney paid to Bushnell's home: "There the two grand men would sit and talk, hour after hour, totally disagreeing in their philosophy on certain mooted questions, but agreeing in their aims and burning desires and in their belief that Christians might claim and receive far higher blessings than were usually supposed to be any part of our earthly inheritance."

102. On Nevin, I have been guided by James Hastings Nichols, ed., *The Mercersburg Theology*, A Library of Protestant Thought (New York, 1966); Charles Yrigoven Jr., "Nevin and Methodism," in *Reformed Confessionalism in Nineteenth-Century America: Essays on the Thought of John Williamson Nevin*, ed. Sam Hamstra Jr. and Arie J. Griffioen (Lanham, Md., 1995), 209–31; and especially William DiPuccio, *The Interior Sense of Scripture: The Sacred Hermeneutics of John W. Nevin* (Macon, Ga., 1998).

103. Nevin, *The Anxious Bench* (Chambersburg, Pa., 1843), 56. This work was printed twice in 1843, reprinted twice in an expanded edition in 1844 and twice in a German translation the same year, and then not again until 1892.

104. Nevin, *The Mystical Presence* (Philadelphia, 1846), 53. *The Mystical Presence* was printed two or three times in 1846, once (from two presses) in 1867, and then not until the 1960s.

105. I am guided on Smith especially by Marsden, *Evangelical Mind*, 157–90; and Richard A. Muller, "Henry Boynton Smith: Christocentric Theologian," *Journal of Presbyterian History* 61 (1983): 429–44.

106. Smith, "The Idea of Christian Theology as a System" (address, 1855), in *Faith and Philosophy: Discourses and Essays* (New York, 1877), 137.

107. On Stowe as a religious thinker, I have benefited especially from Charles H. Foster, *The Rungless Ladder: Harriet Beecher Stowe and New England Puritanism* (Durham, 1954); Henry May, introduction to *Oldtown Folks,* by Harriet Beecher Stowe (Cambridge, Mass., 1966); Marie Caskey, *Chariot of Fire: Religion and the Beecher Family* (New Haven, 1978), 169–207; and for a general biography, Joan D. Hedrick, *Harriet Beecher Stowe: A Life* (New York, 1994).

108. Harriet Beecher Stowe, *The Minister's Wooing*, in *Three Novels*, The Library of America, ed. Kathryn Kish Sklar (New York, 1982), 719. In the novel, the young man did not actually die but reappears toward the end of the story, which is one of the reasons the book is less convincing as a novel than for the expressions of theological opinion that Beecher composed from situations where the dead did not return.

109. Ibid., 728.

110. Ibid., 734–35.

111. Ibid., 736.

112. On Catharine Beecher, I have benefited from the clear account of her life in Kathryn Kish Sklar, *Catherine Beecher: A Study in American Domesticity* (New Haven, 1973); and from the theological insight of Beth Anne Johnson, "The Grand Question of Life: An Analysis of the Relationship between Religion and Education in the Life and Thought of Catharine Beecher" (M.A. thesis, Wheaton College Graduate School, 2000).

113. Catharine E. Beecher, *Letters on the Difficulties of Religion* (Hartford, 1836), vi, 20, 74, 327.

114. Beecher, *Common Sense Applied to Religion, or, The Bible and the People* (New York, 1857). The dedications of these two books are telling: from 1836, to "an honored and beloved father"; from 1857, "to the people as the safest and truest interpreters of the Bible, and to woman, as the heaven-appointed educators of mind."

115. Ibid., ix–x, xv–xxxiv.
116. Ibid., xxiv, xxvi.
117. Ibid., xxxiv. For Beecher's reference to Reid and Hamilton, xxxv.
118. Ibid, 306–7.

Chapter 16

1. Asbury, "Valedictory Address" to William McKendree, 5 Aug. 1813, in *The Journal and Letters of Francis Asbury*, ed. Elmer T. Clark et al., 3 vols. (London and Nashville, 1958), 3:477 (cited hereafter as *JLFA*).

2. For the importance of early Methodist mobilization in the general history of the early United States, see chap. 9 above. For this and the next chapter, I am especially indebted to Leland Howard Scott, "The Message of Early American Methodism," in *The History of American Methodism,* vol. 1, ed. Emory Stevens Bucke (New York, 1964), 291–359; and Scott, "Methodist Theology in the Nineteenth Century" (Ph.D. diss., Yale University, 1954).

3. The key work remains *JLFA*.

4. Donald G. Mathews, "The Patriarchs' Conversion," review essay of *Southern Cross: The Beginning of the Bible Belt*, by Christine Leigh Heyrman, *Pew Notes*, Fall 1998, 1–5, (quotation 5). For other analyses of this same sort, see Mathews, "Evangelical America—the Methodist Ideology," in *Perspectives on American Methodism: Interpretive Essays*, ed. R. E. Richey, K. E. Rowe, and J. M. Schmidt (Nashville, 1993), 17–30; David Hempton, "'Motives, Methods, and Margins': A Comparative Study of Methodist Expansion in the North Atlantic World, c. 1770–1850," in *The Religion of the People: Methodism and Popular Religion, c. 1750–1900* (London, 1996), 3–28; and Hempton, "Methodism's Missing Chapter," in *Books and Culture*, March/April 1999, 37: "The Methodist itinerant preachers . . . did not self-consciously apprehend that they were engaged in a mission that perfectly suited their democratic and market-driven times. They set out on their mission because they thought their lives had been transformed by a powerful message of universal grace, and they could not wait to tell anyone else who would spare the time to listen."

5. For Continental connections, see W. R. Ward, *The Protestant Evangelical Awakening* (Cambridge, 1992). Outstanding on Wesley and his theology in the context of his times is Henry D. Rack, *Reasonable Enthusiast: John Wesley and the Rise of Methodism* (Philadelphia, 1989).

6. John Wesley, "The Character of a Methodist" (1742), in *The Works of John Wesley*, 14 vols. (London, 1872), 8:340, 341.

7. *A Collection of Hymns for the Use of the People Called Methodists*, ed. Franz Hildebrandt and Oliver A. Beckerlegge, vol. 7 of *The Works of John Wesley* (Nashville, 1983), 323.

8. Asbury to Ezekiel Cooper, 24 Dec. 1788, *JLFA*, 3:66.

9. The title of Fletcher's work spoke of the Wesleyans' great practical complaint against Calvinism. As they saw it, if humans were as passive in the process of redemption as Calvinists said they were, it was inevitable that they would not be active in love to God and others and so would live in opposition (= *anti*) to God's law (= *nomos*). On opinions regarding the American rebellion among feuding English evangelicals in the 1770s, see Rack, *Reasonable Enthusiast*, 461.

10. John Fletcher, *First Check to Antinomianism* (1771), as excerpted in *Wesleyan Theology: A Sourcebook,* ed. Thomas Langford (Durham, 1984), 25–31.

11. Abbott, *The Experience and Gospel Labours of the Rev. Benjamin Abbott* (New York, 1805), 19–23.

12. Garrettson, "Substance of the Semi-Centennial Sermon" (1827), in *American Methodist Pioneer: The Life and Journals of the Rev. Freeborn Garrettson, 1752–1827*, ed. Robert Drew Simpson (Rutland, Vt., 1984), 399.

13. Ezekiel Cooper, *The Substance of a Funeral Discourse. Delivered . . . the 23d of April, 1816 . . . on the Death of the Rev. Francis Asbury* (Philadelphia, 1819), 40.

14. A striking testimony to the traditional character of Methodist theology can be found as late as 1861 in the self-consciously orthodox pages of the Old School Presbyterian *Biblical Repertory and Princeton Review,* where this judgment was rendered about "the spiritual power which their [Methodist] ministry unquestionably possessed": it "was derived from the earnestness, the plainness, the unction with which they proclaimed the essential doctrines of that very Calvinism which they so frequently and vigorously vituperated. Man's ruin by the fall; his native depravity and alienation from God; his absolute need of a Saviour, and utter inability to save himself; the necessity of regeneration by the Holy Spirit; justification, not by works, but by faith alone in the blood and righteousness of Jesus; the free offer of salvation to every human being, without money and without price; the necessity of holiness, not to merit heaven, but to become meet for it—these articles constituted the very burden of their preaching." "Annals of the American Pulpit," *Biblical Repertory and Princeton Review* 33 (July 1861): 507.

15. Wesley also generally opposed the Calvinist understanding of imputation because he thought this doctrine implied a passivity among Christians that encouraged antinomianism and discouraged actively pursuing holiness of life. Yet Wesley was always much stronger in attacking Calvinist understandings of a limited atonement than Calvinist understandings of imputation. See Rack, *Reasonable Enthusiast,* 452.

16. John Wesley, *Christian Perfection* [Sermon 40] (1741), in *Works* (1872 ed.), 6:17.

17. J. B. Wakeley, *Heroes of Methodism,* 12th ed. (Toronto, n.d.), 318.

18. Much of the annual *Minutes* came to be devoted to the accounts of deceased colleagues.

19. Asbury published parts of his journal in the two volumes of the American *Arminian Magazine* and also as at least one other separate publication during his own lifetime; see introduction to *JLFA,* 1:xv–xxii.

20. Early examples included Freeborn Garrettson (1791), Thomas Coke (1793), William Keith (1806), William Watters (1806), Lorenzo Dow (1814), and *Extracts of Letters Containing Some Account of the Work of God since the Year 1800; Written by the Preachers and Members of the Methodist Episcopal Church to Their Bishops* (1805); see bibliography in *History of American Methodism,* 692–93.

21. See Richard J. Carwardine, "Trauma in Methodism: Property, Church Schism, and Sectional Polarization in Antebellum America," in *God and Mammon: Protestants, Money, and the Market, 1790–1860,* ed. Mark A. Noll (New York, 2001), 195–216; and Carwardine, *Evangelicals and Politics in Antebellum America* (New Haven, 1993), 165–66, 190–91.

22. The first American Methodist hymnal that Asbury did not have a hand in preparing was the forty-third edition of *The Methodist Pocket Hymn-Book. Revised and Improved: Designed as a Constant Companion for the Pious of All Denominations* (New York, 1817).

23. Dee Andrews, *The Methodists and Revolutionary America, 1760–1800: The*

Shaping of an Evangelical Culture (Princeton, 2000), 78. On early Methodist hymnody, see Henry Bett, *The Hymns of Methodism* (London, 1945).

24. *Pocket Hymn-Book, Designed as a Constant Companion for the Pious. Collected from Various Authors*, 23d ed. (Philadelphia, 1800), iii, hymn 1, hymn 2. It is significant that, as in Britain, American Methodists did not scruple about the source of hymns, for Joseph Hart was a staunch Calvinist who from his London Dissenting chapel sometimes preached against the Methodists.

25. *A Selection of Hymns, from Various Authors, Designed as a Supplement to the Methodist Pocket-Hymn Book, Compiled under the Direction of Bishop Asbury, and Published by Order of the General Conference*, 6th ed. (New York, 1813), hymns 1, 3, 5.

26. This account follows Frank Baker, "The Doctrines in the Discipline," in *From Wesley to Asbury: Studies in Early American Methodism* (Durham, 1976), 162–82; Richard P. Heitzenrater, "At Full Liberty: Doctrinal Standards in Early American Methodism," *Quarterly Review* 5 (Fall 1985): 6–27 (these two articles reprinted in *Perspectives on American Methodism*); and Thomas C. Oden, *Doctrinal Standards in the Wesleyan Tradition* (Grand Rapids, 1988).

27. Modern Methodists debate this issue, with Heitzenrater, "At Full Liberty," suggesting that these documents were not included, and Oden, *Doctrinal Standards*, arguing that they were.

28. For a list, see Oden, *Doctrinal Standards*, 49.

29. *The Doctrine and Discipline of the Methodist Episcopal Church, in America. With Explanatory Notes, by Thomas Coke and Francis Asbury*, 10th ed. (Philadelphia, 1798), 113.

30. Quoted in Oden, *Doctrinal Standards*, 54.

31. On the early apoliticism of American Methodists, I have been guided to sources and clarified in my views especially by Mark A. Vanderpool, "Citizens of Zion: Republican Thought and Early American Methodism, 1770–1800" (M.Div. thesis, Asbury Theological Seminary, 1996); and Christian F. Sawyer, "Tyrant or Servant? Religious Authority and Character Among the Methodists in America, 1767–1792" (M.A. thesis, Wheaton College Graduate School, 2001).

32. Cooper, *Substance of a Funeral Discourse*, 83.

33. *JLFA*, 3:130 (22 Sept. 1794).

34. Ibid., 1:310.

35. Ibid., 458. The work was Silas Mercer, *Tyranny Exposed, and True Liberty Described, Wherein Is Contained the Scripture Doctrine concerning Kings; Their Rise, Reign, and Downfall: Together with the Total Overthrow of Antichrist* (Halifax, N.C., 1783).

36. *Short Account of the Christian Experience and Ministerial Labours of William Watters, Drawn Up by Himself* (Alexandria, Va., 1806), 70.

37. Russell E. Richey, *Early American Methodism* (Bloomington, Ind., 1991), 33.

38. John Mann to Daniel Fidler, 19 July 1795, Drew University Library, as quoted in Andrews, *Methodists*, 7.

39. On O'Kelly and his republicanism, see also John H. Wigger, *Taking Heaven by Storm: Methodism and the Rise of Popular Christianity in America* (New York, 1998), 39–43; Nathan O. Hatch, *The Democratization of American Christianity* (New Haven, 1989), 62–82; and Richey, *Early American Methodism*, 88–93.

40. The first two charges were reported by James O'Kelly, *The Author's Apology* (1798), as reprinted in *Sourcebook of American Methodism,* ed. Frederick A. Norwood, (Nashville, 1982), 141; the last two were recorded in Thomas Ware, *Sketches*

of the Life and Travels of Rev. Thomas Ware, Who Has Been an Itinerant Methodist Preacher for More than Fifty Years. Written by Himself (New York, 1839), 221.

41. O'Kelly to unknown correspondent, Apr. 1787, in *JLFA*, 3:52.

42. O'Kelly, *A Vindication of the Author's Apology* (1801), 60–62, as quoted in Hatch, *Democratization of American Christianity*, 70.

43. O'Kelly, *The Author's Apology*, 4, 38, as quoted in Richey, *Early American Methodism*, 88–89.

44. Asbury to "My Dear Brethren," ca. 1 Nov. 1792, *JLFA*, 1:734.

45. Ware, *Life and Travels*, 220.

46. Benjamin St. James Fry, *William McKendree* (1852), 83–84, as quoted in Scott, "Message of Early American Methodism," 299.

47. Ware, *Life and Travels*, 46.

48. *JLFA*, 1:644.

49. See the charges by J. R. Graves in chap. 12, pages 244–46 above.

50. Andrews, *Methodists*, 200.

51. Cynthia Lynn Lyerly, *Methodism and the Southern Mind, 1770–1810* (New York, 1998), 10. These conclusions echo the sage words of Sydney Ahlstrom, *A Religious History of the American People* (New Haven, 1972), 438: "There is no justification for the conclusion of many historians (including the most fervent Methodists) that the Methodist message was a 'democratic theology' or a 'frontier faith.' . . . Arminianism in this [Methodist] context meant not an optimistic view of human nature (as with the Boston liberals), but a reinterpretation of the strict Calvinistic understanding of atonement, grace, and the sanctifying work of the Holy Spirit."

52. *The Life and Letters of Stephen Olin* (1853), 2:385; and B. F. Tefft, *Methodism Successful* (1860), as quoted in Scott, "Methodist Theology," 135, 137.

53. Sawyer, "Tyrant or Servant?" 50.

54. *JLFA*, 3:475, 481.

55. In 1816 there were almost certainly still far more itinerants than settled ministers. The Methodist minutes recorded only itinerating ministers until 1837; in that year the ratio of settled clergy to itinerants was about 5 to 3 (4,954 to 2,933). *Minutes of the Annual Conference of the Methodist Episcopal Church*, vol. 2 (New York, 1840).

56. Asbury did not always actively aid Allen and other African-American Methodists, but he was far more open to their concerns than later generations of white leaders; see Carol V. R. George, *Segregated Sabbaths: Richard Allen and the Rise of Independent Black Churches, 1760–1840* (New York, 1973), 56, 65, 74, 77.

57. On the founding of these magazines, see William R. Cannon, "Education, Publication, Benevolent Work, and Missions," in *History of American Methodism*, 574–78.

58. See especially David B. Potts, *Wesleyan University, 1831–1910: Collegiate Enterprise in New England* (New Haven, 1992), 1–27.

59. Lorenzo Dow, *The Opinion of Dow; or, Lorenzo's Thoughts, on Different Religious Subjects, in an Address to the People of New England* (Windham, Mass., 1804), 121–22.

60. Nathan Bangs to Laban Clark, 18 Jan. 1808, in *Sourcebook of American Methodism*, 302–4.

61. See Donald G. Mathews, *Slavery and Methodism: A Chapter in American Morality, 1780–1845* (Princeton, 1965); James Essig, *The Bonds of Wickedness: American Evangelicals against Slavery, 1770–1808* (Philadelphia, 1982), 67, 120, 143–45; and Christine Leigh Heyrman, *Southern Cross: The Beginnings of the Bible Belt* (New York, 1997), 92–94, 155–56.

Chapter 17

1. On Lee, see Donald W. Dayton, introduction to *Five Sermons and a Tract,* by Luther Lee (Chicago, 1975).

2. *The Journal and Letters of Francis Asbury,* ed. Elmer T. Clark et al., 3 vols. (London and Nashville, 1958), 2:687 (19 Nov. 1811). Snethen's political life was especially noteworthy, for he stood as a Federalist candidate in Maryland elections in 1816 and 1817 and then in 1828 became a leader of the Methodist Protestant Church, which came into existence as a protest against the MEC's restriction of self-determination; see Donald M. Lewis, "Nicholas Snethen," *BDEB,* 1032.

3. Wilbur Fisk, "Christ's Kingdom Not of This World," *Methodist Magazine* 10 (Jan. 1827): 4; (Feb. 1827): 43, 46, 47, 48.

4. "Our Country," *Methodist Magazine and Quarterly Review* 19 (1837): 453, 454.

5. J. V. Moore, "Republican Tendency of the Bible," *Methodist Quarterly Review,* new ser., 6 (Apr. 1846): 203, 207, 211, 213. Moore also made the point (220–21), so beloved of Reformed ministers during and after the Revolution, that the government of Old Testament Israel was thoroughly republican.

6. D. D. Whedon, "The Manly Man" (commencement address, University of Michigan, 1851), in *Public Addresses, Collegiate and Popular* (Boston, 1852), 58.

7. Richard Carwardine, "Methodists, Politics, and the Coming of the American Civil War," *Church History* 69 (Sept. 2000): 588. For the full Methodist participation in the sectional conflicts that ended in war, see also Carwardine, *Evangelicals and Politics in Antebellum America* (New Haven, 1993).

8. Louise Hall Tharp, *Three Saints and a Sinner: Julia Ward Howe, Louisa, Annie, Sam Ward* (Boston, 1956), 246.

9. For an illuminating account of how successive generations of Methodist historians incorporated more and more themes from American civil religion into their narratives, see Russell E. Richey, "Methodism and Providence: A Study in Secularization," in *Protestant Evangelicalism: Britain, Ireland, Germany, and America, c. 1750–c. 1950,* ed. Keith Robbins (Oxford, 1990), 51–77.

10. On Shinn, see Leland Howard Scott, "Methodist Theology in the Nineteenth Century" (Ph.D. diss., Yale University, 1954), 93–94, 562–68; L. Dale Patterson, "Nathan Shinn," *BDEB,* 1008; and for his later career in the Methodist Protestant Church, William R. Sutton, *Journeymen for Jesus: Evangelical Artisans Confront Capitalism in Jacksonian Baltimore* (University Park, Pa., 1998), 106, 113–14.

11. Asa Shinn, *An Essay on the Plan of Salvation: In Which the Several Sources of Evidence Are Examined, and Applied to the Interesting Doctrine of Redemption, in Its Relation to the Government and Moral Attributes of the Deity* (Baltimore, 1812), 16, 23 ("faculties"), 321 ("principles"), 109 (last two quotations).

12. On Bangs, see Abel Stevens, *Life and Times of Nathan Bangs, D.D.* (New York, 1863); Scott, "Methodist Theology," 90–108, 569–89; Charles H. Lippy, "Nathan Bangs," *BDEB,* 53–54; G. A. Rawlyk, *The Canada Fire: Radical Evangelicalism in British North America, 1775–1812* (Kingston and Montreal, 1994), 112–20, 147–55; and Steven W. Lewis, "Nathan Bangs and the Impact of Theological Controversy on the Development of Early Nineteenth Century American Thought" (Ph.D. diss., St. Louis University, 1998).

13. Bangs, *The Errors of Hopkinsianism: Detected and Refuted in Six Letters to the Rev. S. Williston* (New York, 1815); *The Reformer Reformed; or, A Second Part of the Errors of Hopkinsianism Detected and Refuted* (New York, 1816); and *An Examination of the Doctrine of Predestination* (New York, 1817).

14. Bangs, *Examination of Predestination*, 104n, 63.

15. Ibid., 103–16.

16. Especially helpful on Bangs's theological development is Scott, "Methodist Theology," 569–89.

17. The essay from the *Edinburgh Encyclopedia* was spread through all twelve numbers of the *Methodist Magazine*'s first year. See also "Extract from Betty's Essay on Truth," *Methodist Magazine* 1 (Apr. 1818): 129–36; and "Of Volition: From Smith's Lectures on Moral and Political Philosophy, Delivered in the College of New Jersey," ibid. (Aug. 1818): 309–12; (Sept. 1818): 344–48; (Oct. 1818): 388–92.

18. N.B.A., "On the Importance of Common Sense," *Methodist Magazine* 10 (May 1827): 169.

19. "Of the Methodist Doctrine," *Methodist Magazine* 1 (June 1818): 209–10.

20. C.L.K., "Illustration of Romans 6:14," *Methodist Magazine* 3 (1820): 332–35.

21. Lewis, "Nathan Bangs," 105.

22. Nathan Bangs, "*The Christian Spectator* versus John Wesley and the Witness of the Spirit," *Methodist Magazine and Quarterly Review* 18 (July 1836): 262, 263.

23. Abel Stevens, "Of the Connection between Speculative Philosophy and Christian Theology, Particularly during the Middle Ages," *Methodist Magazine and Quarterly Review* 18 (Apr. 1836): 164–76.

24. On Fisk, see Scott, "Methodist Theology," 58–75, 590–604; Scott, "The Message of Early American Methodism," in *the History of American Methodism*, vol. 1, ed. Emory Stevens Bucks (New York, 1964), 291–359; 349–57; Douglas James Williamson, "The Ecclesiastical Career of Wilbur Fisk: Methodist Educator, Theologian, Reformer, Controversialist" (Ph.D. diss., Boston University, 1988); and Charles Yrigoyen Jr., "Wilbur Fisk," *BDEB*, 391.

25. Fisk to M. G. Parks, 27 July 1833, as quoted in Scott, "Methodist Theology," 72–73.

26. See Scott, "Methodist Theology," 59–60.

27. Wilbur Fisk, *Calvinistic Controversy: Embracing a Sermon on Predestination and Election and Several Numbers, Formerly Published in the Christian Advocate and Journal* (New York, 1835), 26, 10n, 16, 35, 44, 53, 60.

28. Ibid., 292, 294, 190 ("Dr. Taylor" and "old Pelagian"), 156, 155, 292, 168 ("Dr. Reid"), 292, 294. For a good, short explanation of Fisk's faculty psychology, see Scott, "Methodist Theology," 122n47.

29. Scott, "Methodist Theology," 93, 95.

30. William R. Cannon, "Education, Publication, Benevolent Work, and Missions," in *History of American Methodism,* 553–60.

31. I borrow these phrases from Kathryn T. Long, who employs them slightly differently, but whose account of Methodist adaptation to refined, urban culture illuminates both moves; see Long, "Consecrated Respectability: Phoebe Palmer and the Refinement of American Methodism," in *Methodism and the Shaping of American Culture*, ed. Nathan O. Hatch and John H. Wigger (Nashville, 2001), 281–307.

32. On Whedon, see especially Scott, "Methodist Theology," 146–221, 607–30.

33. For an introduction to Watson, see Thomas Langford, *Practical Divinity: Theology in the Wesleyan Tradition* (Nashville, 1983), 57–66; and Langford, ed., *Wesleyan Theology: A Sourcebook* (Durham, 1984), 56–64.

34. Scott, "Methodist Theology," 146.

35. Whedon, "The Man-Republic: A Phi Beta Kappa Oration" (1850), in *Public Addresses*, 78.

36. Whedon, *Commentary on the New Testament* (New York, 1860); *Commentary on the Old Testament* (New York, 1873).

37. Whedon, *The Freedom of the Will as a Basis of Human Responsibility and a Divine Government* (New York, 1864), 4, 82, 369. In these claims, Whedon went beyond the critique of Edwards found in A. T. Bledsoe, who with Whedon appealed to "the tribunal of consciousness" against Edwards, but who against Whedon felt that freedom of will was an inference from observation of consciousness; see Albert Taylor Bledsoe, *An Examination of President Edwards' Inquiry into the Freedom of the Will* (Philadelphia, 1845), 224, 229. Bledsoe was not formally a Methodist when he published this book, but he circulated all his life in Methodist orbits and eventually became a Methodist preacher.

38. Whedon, "Doctrines of Methodism," *Bibliotheca Sacra* 19 (Apr. 1862): 242, 243. Edwards is addressed on 242, 243, 244, 250; Fletcher on 43; Wesley on 258n, 271.

39. Ibid., 262, 263, 264, 267 (last two quotations).

40. Bangs, *Errors of Hopkinsianism*, 97-98.

41. Whedon, "Doctrines of Methodism," 252.

42. Ibid., 251.

43. Ibid., 257. See also 259-60, where Whedon doubts if "gracious ability" is any longer a good phrase for describing the power that humans retain by nature.

44. Ibid., 267.

45. Scott, "Methodist Theology," 224; see also 221: Whedon's theology "constitutes a fundamental transition from the broader evangelical norms of earlier Wesleyan theology, a transition effected, in part, under the pressure of the Arminian dialectic with Edwardsean Calvinism."

46. Daniel Curry, *Fragments, Religious and Theological* (New York, 1880), as quoted in Scott, "Methodist Theology," 224, 233n27.

47. Compare Fisk, *Calvinistic Controversy*, 190-91; and Bangs, "*The Christian Spectator* versus John Wesley," 262-63; with Smith, "Whedon on the Will" (1865), in *Faith and Philosophy* (New York, 1877), 359-99, esp. 365-66.

48. For the movement as a whole, see Melvin Easterday Dieter, *The Holiness Revival of the Nineteenth Century* (Metuchen, N.J., 1980).

49. On Palmer, see *Phoebe Palmer: Selected Writings,* ed. Thomas C. Oden (New York, 1988); David Bundy, "Phoebe Palmer," *BDEB,* 852-53; Harold E. Raser, *Phoebe Palmer* (Lewiston, N.Y., 1987); and Charles E. White, *The Beauty of Holiness: Phoebe Palmer as Theologian, Revivalist, Feminist, and Humanitarian* (Grand Rapids, 1986).

50. Palmer, *The Way of Holiness* (London, 1845 [orig. 1843]), 95-96.

51. Richard Wheatley, *The Life and Letters of Mrs. Phoebe Palmer* (New York, 1876), 36.

52. For a discussion of these and other characteristic Holiness phrases, see Oden, *Phoebe Palmer*, 18-19.

53. For Whedon's comment, see Dieter, *Holiness Revival*, 134.

54. For Upham, I have relied on Kathryn Long, "The New England Connection: Thomas Upham and the Nineteenth-Century Holiness Movement" (unpublished paper); Darius L. Salter, *Spirit and Intellect: Thomas Upham's Holiness Theology* (Metuchen, N.J., 1986); and Patricia A. Ward, "Madame Guyon and Experiential Theology in America," *Church History* 67 (Spring 1998): 484-98.

55. Stevens, *Life and Times of Nathan Bangs*, 399, 402.

56. Scott, "Methodist Theology," 159.

57. For an indication of this movement's literature, see "The Higher Christian Life": Sources for the Study of the Holiness, Pentecostal, and Keswick Movements, (New York, 1984), a forty-eight-volume series edited by Donald W. Dayton.

58. Dieter, *Holiness Revival*, 31.

59. On Bowne, the Methodist strand in Boston personalism, and the liberalizing effects of personalism on Methodist theology, see A. C. Knudson, *The Philosophy of Personalism* (New York, 1927); John H. Lavely, "Personalism," in *Encyclopedia of Philosophy*, 8 vols. (New York, 1967), 6:108–9; and Langford, *Practical Divinity*, 119–24 (Bowne) and 177–81 (Knudson).

Chapter 18

1. See William E. Gienapp, *The Origins of the Republican Party, 1852–1856* (New York, 1987), 364–65, who suggests that by 1850 republican reasoning had assimilated several elements that would have been anathema in 1780, like party factions, the benefits of commerce, and white male suffrage (even without property), and virtue now meant as much a vigilance for liberty as a shunning of luxury.

2. The individual was John Inskip of New York; see Richard J. Carwardine, *Evangelicals and Politics in Antebellum America* (New Haven, 1991), 263.

3. Reliance on republican values, broadly construed, through the time of the Civil War is amply documented in the standard literature, for example, Michael Holt, *The Political Crisis of the 1850s* (New York, 1978), 4–6, 8, 16–17, and throughout; James Moorhead, *American Apocalypse: Yankee Protestants and the Civil War, 1860–1869* (New Haven, 1978), 5–6, 55–59, 71–77, 109–10, 118–19, 159–60, 207–9, 224–26, and elsewhere; James McPherson, *Battle Cry of Freedom: The Civil War Era*, Oxford History of the United States (New York, 1988), 48–49, 55–56, 241, and elsewhere; Carwardine, *Evangelicals and Politics*, 18–19, 64, 77–78, 200–201, 248–50, 297–98, 403, and elsewhere; and George C. Rable, *The Confederate Republic: A Revolution against Politics* (Chapel Hill, 1994), 12–16, 76–77, 281–87.

4. Ronald Gottesman et al., comps., *The Norton Anthology of American Literature,* vol. 1 (New York, 1979), 1378–81.

5. At least it did so in the South; see Charles Reagan Wilson, *Baptized in Blood: The Religion of the Lost Cause* (Athens, Ga., 1980); and Gaines M. Foster, *Ghosts of the Confederacy: Defeat, the Lost Cause, and the Emergence of the New South, 1865–1913* (New York, 1987).

6. James Stirling, *Letters from the Slave States* (London, 1857), 117, 118, 120. I was alerted to Stirling's observations by Eugene D. Genovese, *"Slavery Ordained of God": The Southern Slaveholders' View of Biblical History and Modern Politics*, Fortenbaugh Memorial Lecture (Gettysburg, Pa., 1985), 30n58.

7. On the extensive referencing of Scripture by founding fathers in the Revolutionary period, see especially the work of Donald S. Lutz, including "The Relative Influence of European Writers on Late Eighteenth-Century American Political Thought," *American Political Science Review* 78 (1984): 189–97; and *The Origins of American Constitutionalism* (Baton Rouge, 1988), 140–43. A description of the rhetorical, ornamental use of the Scripture in these periods is found in Mark A. Noll, "The Bible in Revolutionary America," in *The Bible in American Law, Politics, and Political Rhetoric*, ed. James Turner Johnson (Philadelphia, 1985), 39–60.

8. Joyce Appleby, "The American Heritage: The Heirs and the Disinherited," *Journal of American History* 74 (Dec. 1987): 809. Appleby does not pursue her insight, perhaps because, as indicated in this essay, she regards the Bible primarily for how it was used to justify racial differences, traditional family structure, sexual taboos, and the inferiority of women, rather than as offering hope, energy, and self-confidence to many—black and white, female and male—who read it.

9. Perry Miller, "The Garden of Eden and the Deacon's Meadow," *American Heritage*, Dec. 1955, 54.

10. For comparison, see the essays on France (20–132), Germany (133–59), and Great Britain (161–86) in *Bible de tous les temps,* vol. 8, *Le monde contemporain et la Bible*, ed. Claude Savart and Jean-Noël Aletti (Paris, 1985).

11. Hans Frei, *The Eclipse of Biblical Narrative: A Study in Eighteenth and Nineteenth Century Hermeneutics* (New Haven, 1974), 1.

12. See especially Paul C. Gutjahr, *An American Bible: A History of the Good Book in the United States, 1777–1880* (Stanford, 1999), with details on publication and distribution, 181–96; and for a helpful study of the American Bible Society, Peter J. Wosh, *Spreading the Word: The Bible Business in Nineteenth-Century America* (Ithaca, 1994).

13. The information in the next two paragraphs is taken mostly from Margaret T. Hills, *The English Bible in America* (New York, 1962), 1–266. I thank Rachel Maxson for assistance in cataloging its contents.

14. Details on these two editions are from ibid., 20–21, 90–91, 125.

15. Hills, *English Bible in America*, 255; Philip Schaff, *Der Bürgerkrieg und das christliche Leben in Nord-Amerika* (Berlin, 1866), 31, 50; and W. Harrison Daniel, "Bible Publication and Procurement in the Confederacy," *Journal of Southern History* 24 (1958): 191–201.

16. Works in which this familiarity is particularly well illustrated are Lewis O. Saum, *The Popular Mood of Pre–Civil War America* (Westport, Conn., 1980); Carwardine, *Evangelicals and Politics*; Eugene D. Genovese and Elizabeth Fox-Genovese, "The Religious Ideals of Southern Slave Society," *Georgia Historical Quarterly* 70 (Spring 1986): 9–14; and Kenneth Cmiel, *Democratic Eloquence: The Fight over Popular Speech in Nineteenth-Century America* (Berkeley, 1990). Reference to the use of Scripture between the Revolution and the Civil War in the testimonials of presidents and other social leaders, by Bible societies, in the naming of children and places, and in public iconography is found in Mark A. Noll, "The Image of the United States as a Biblical Nation, 1776–1865," in *The Bible in American Culture*, ed. Nathan O. Hatch and Noll (New York, 1982), 40–41, 52–53.

17. William Ellery Channing, "Unitarian Christianity" (1819), in *The Unitarian Controversy, 1819–1823,* vol. 1, ed. Bruce Kuklick (New York, 1987), 8 (with following pages showing how Channing thought that the same principles used to interpret the Constitution should lead readers of the Bible to Unitarianism). On the Bible-Constitution analogy, there are also helpful hints in Daniel Walker Howe, *The Political Culture of the American Whigs* (Chicago, 1979), 23–24, 227; and Robert H. Wiebe, *The Opening of American Society: From the Adoption of the Constitution to the Eve of Disunion* (New York, 1984), 308.

18. On how "constitution" came in America to mean a single, written document, see Gerald Stourzh, *"Constitution*: Changing Meanings of the Term from the Early Seventeenth to the Late Eighteenth Century," in *Conceptual Change and the Constitution*, ed. Terence Ball and J. G. A. Pocock (Manhattan, Kans., 1988), 44–48.

19. On the relatively slow process by which the Constitution came to be venerated, see Michael Kammen, *A Machine that Would Go of Itself: The Constitution in American Culture* (New York, 1986), 72–75, and the first part of this book more generally.

20. *The Literary Diary of Ezra Stiles*, 3 vols., ed. Franklin Bowditch Dexter (New York, 1901), 1:556–57.

21. For the way in which Charles Chauncy, Jonathan Mayhew, and like-minded Boston liberals had appealed to just the Scriptures as justification for heterodox teachings like the salvation of all people or a Socinian interpretation of Jesus, see Conrad Wright, *The Beginnings of Unitarianism in America* (Boston, 1955), 187, 194, 209.

22. John Leland, *The Bible-Baptist* (Baltimore, 1789), 4, 5, 24.

23. John Leland, "Circular Letter of the Shaftsbury Association" (1793), in *The Writings of John Leland*, ed. L. F. Greene (New York, 1969 [orig. 1845]), 196.

24. Benjamin Rush, "A Defense of the Use of the Bible as a School Book" (dated 10 Mar. 1791), published as pp. 53–65 in John Eyten, *Our Lord Jesus Christ's Sermon on the Mount . . . Intended Chiefly for the Instruction of Young People*, 2d American ed. (Baltimore, 1810), 65 (quotation) and 55 for Rush's understanding of revelation in creation and consciousness (with quotation from Lord Shaftesbury).

25. Elias Smith, *The Lovingkindness of God Displayed in the Triumph of Republicanism in America: Being a Discourse, Delivered at Taunton (Mass.) July Fourth, 1809 at the Celebration of American Independence* (n.p., 1809), 3, 27, 32. For discussion, see Nathan O. Hatch, *The Democratization of American Christianity* (New Haven, 1989), 69–70.

26. Timothy George and Denise George, eds., *Baptist Confessions, Covenants, and Catechisms* (Nashville, 1996), 131.

27. James Dixon, *Methodism in America* (1848–49), in *The Voluntary Church: American Religious Life, 1740–1860, Seen through the Eyes of European Visitors*, ed. Milton B. Powell (New York, 1967), 174.

28. Robert Baird, *Religion in the United States of America* (Glasgow, 1844), 658 (emphasis added).

29. For general consideration of the many paths explored by Protestants for replacing Roman Catholic norms of authority, see G. R. Evans, *Problems of Authority in the Reformation Debates* (New York, 1992).

30. For modern explanations of this principle, see Ralph J. Gore Jr., "Reviewing the Puritan Regulative Principle of Worship," *Presbyterion* 20 (Spring 1994): 41–50 and 21 (Spring 1995): 29–47; and John Allen Delivuk "Biblical Authority and the Proof of the Regulative Principle of Worship in the Westminster Confession," *Westminster Theological Journal* 58 (Fall 1996): 237–56.

31. See John Hesselink, "Christ, the Law, and the Christian: An Unexplored Aspect of the Third Use of the Law in Calvin's Theology," in *Reformatio Perennis: Essays on Calvin and the Reformation in Honor of Ford Lewis Battles*, ed. Brian A. Gerrish (Pittsburgh, 1981), 11–26; and for a Lutheran perspective, Paul M. Hoyer, "Law and Gospel: With Particular Attention to the Third Use of the Law," *Concordia Journal* 6 (Spring 1980): 189–201.

32. A good survey of local situations is *Calvinism in Europe, 1540–1620*, ed. Andrew Pettegree et al. (Cambridge, 1994).

33. In a discussion of biblical practices, the Anabaptists may be considered as following an extreme Reformed hermeneutic, with a particular emphasis on the New Testament. See, for orientation, the chapter "The Scripture and Mennonite Ethics," in Abraham P. Toews, *The Problem of Mennonite Ethics* (Grand Rapids, 1963), 35–53.

34. As introductions to complicated subjects, see Eric W. Gritsch and Robert W. Jenson, *Lutheranism: The Theological Movement and Its Confessional Writings* (Philadelphia, 1976), esp. 2–15; and Horton Davies, *Worship and Theology in England,* vol. 1, *From Cranmer to Hooker, 1534–1603* (Princeton, 1970), 51–54, 234–37.

35. The multiple and contradictory connections between Scripture and the Revolution are well illustrated in *Political Sermons of the American Founding Era, 1730–1805* ed. Ellis Sandoz (Indianapolis, 1991).

36. André Siegfried, *America Comes of Age: A French Analysis* (New York, 1927), 34.

37. *An Address to Christians throughout the World, by a Convention of Ministers, Assembled at Richmond, Virginia, April, 1863* (Philadelphia, 1863), 17–20.

38. David B. Chesebrough, *God Ordained This War: Sermons on the Sectional Crisis, 1830–1865* (Columbia, S.C., 1991), 297–349 (where identifications of ministers are incomplete); Chesebrough, *"No Sorrow like Our Sorrow": Northern Protestant Ministers and the Assassination of Lincoln* (Kent, Ohio, 1994), xvi, 149–92 (where denominational identification is nearly complete).

39. The best discussions of which I am aware on biblical interpretation in the antebellum period are in E. Brooks Holifield, *The Gentlemen Theologians: American Theology in Southern Culture, 1795–1860* (Durham, 1978), esp. 96–100, "Interpreting the Word: Rational Hermeneutics"; Theodore Dwight Bozeman, *Protestants in an Age of Science: The Baconian Ideal and Antebellum American Religious Thought* (Chapel Hill, 1977), 132–59 ("Baconianism and the Bible"); and George M. Marsden, "Everyone One's Own Interpreter? The Bible, Science, and Authority in Mid-Nineteenth-Century America," in *The Bible in America,* 79–100. For the hermeneutics of the Restorationists, who enunciated general "American" principles with special clarity, see C. Leonard Allen, "Baconianism and the Bible in the Disciples of Christ: James S. Lamar and 'The Organon of Scripture,'" *Church History* 55 (1986): 65–80.

40. Puritans, by calling their initial scheme of government in Massachusetts "Moses' Judicials," sought the biblical high ground for their experiment, but they did not use principles of commonsense literalism in defending the scripturalism of their system. See Edmund S. Morgan, ed., *Puritan Political Ideas, 1558–1794* (Indianapolis, 1965), where the eighteenth-century examples do begin to use those modern principles.

41. Hatch, *Democratization of American Christianity,* 182–83.

42. Charles Finney, sermon outline, 1863, Finney Papers, Oberlin College, courtesy of Allen Guelzo. I have omitted Finney's many italicizations.

43. Samuel Seabury, *An Address to the Ministers and Congregations of the Presbyterian and Independent Persuasion in the United States of America. By a Member of the Episcopal Church* (New Haven, 1790), 12.

44. Thomas Campbell, *Declaration and Address* (1809), introduction by F. D. Kershner (St. Louis, 1972), 23–24. For Restorationism as an extreme example of typical American attitudes, see Richard T. Hughes and C. Leonard Allen, *Illusions of Innocence: Protestant Primitivism in America, 1630–1875* (Chicago, 1988); Richard T. Hughes, ed., *The American Quest for the Primitive Church* (Urbana, Ill., 1988); and Hughes, *Reviving the Ancient Faith: The Story of Churches of Christ in America* (Grand Rapids, 1996).

45. Alexander Campbell, "Reply" (to an Episcopal bishop who had written to reprove Campbell for breaking with tradition), *Christian Baptist* 3 (3 Apr. 1826): 204.

46. T.S., "To the Editor," *Christian Messenger* 1 (25 Sept. 1827): 249–50.

47. As quoted in Perry Miller, *The Life of the Mind in America from the Revolution to the Civil War* (New York, 1965), 47.

48. "The Millennium of Rev. xx.," *Methodist Quarterly Review* 25 (Jan. 1843): 87, as quoted in James Moorhead, "Prophecy, Millennialism, and Biblical Interpretation in Nineteenth-Century America," in *Biblical Hermeneutics in Historical Perspective*, ed. Mark S. Burrows and Paul Rorem (Grand Rapids, 1991), 297.

49. An important statement of connections between populist religion and elite realms of thought has been provided by Gordon S. Wood, "Evangelical America and Early Mormonism," *New York History* 61 (Oct. 1980): 359–86, esp. 378: "The biblical literalism of these years became, in fact, popular religion's ultimate concession to the Enlightenment." "Contribution" might describe what happened better than "concession," but the synergy between spheres of religion and thought was every bit as powerful as Wood suggests.

50. Phillip S. Paludan, "Lincoln and the Rhetoric of Politics," in *A Crisis of Republicanism: American Politics in the Civil War Era*, ed. Lloyd E. Ambrosius (Lincoln, Nebr., 1990), 88.

51. Leland, *Bible-Baptist*, 23.

52. Campbell, *Declaration and Address*, 24–26.

53. *The Memoirs of Charles G. Finney: The Complete Restored Text*, ed. Garth M. Rosell and Richard A. G. Dupuis (Grand Rapids, 1989), 44–45.

54. John Holt Rice, *Historical and Philosophical Considerations on Religion* (Baltimore, 1832), 50–54, as quoted in Fred J. Hood, *Reformed America: The Middle and Southern States, 1783–1837* (University, Ala., 1980), 58.

55. Sarah Grimké, *Letters on the Equality of the Sexes, and Other Essays* (1838), ed. Elizabeth Ann Bartlett (New Haven, 1988), 31–32.

56. George Duffield, *Prophecies Relative to the Second Coming* (New York, 1842), as quoted in Moorhead, "Prophecy, Millennialism, and Biblical Interpretation," 296.

57. Lamar, *Organon of Scripture* (1859), 176, as quoted in Hughes and Allen, *Illusions of Innocence*, 156.

58. Robert J. Breckinridge, *The Knowledge of God, Subjectively Considered* (New York, 1860), 444–45.

59. Henry J. Van Dyke, "The Character and Influence of Abolitionism," in *Fast Day Sermons; or, The Pulpit on the State of the Country* (New York, 1861), 139.

60. Gerrit Smith, "The Religion of Reason," in *Sermons and Speeches* (New York, 1861), 4–5.

61. Drew Gilpin Faust, "Evangelicalism and the Meaning of the Proslavery Argument," *Virginia Magazine of History and Biography* 85 (Jan. 1977): 8.

62. *Independent*, 15 Dec. 1864, 4, as quoted in Moorhead, "Prophecy, Millennialism and Biblical Interpretation," 118.

63. Phoebe Palmer, "Witness of the Spirit," *Guide to Holiness* 47 (June 1865): 137; as quoted in Nancy A. Hardesty, *Your Daughters Shall Prophesy: Revivalism and Feminism in the Age of Finney* (Brooklyn, 1991), 65–66.

Chapter 19

1. The stimulating essays of Eugene Genovese and Elizabeth Fox-Genovese have opened up this subject in an unusually fruitful manner. For citations of their publications, see the bibliography. Of recent writing, I have been helped especially by Mitchell Snay, *Gospel of Disunion: Religion and Separatism in the Antebellum South* (New York, 1993), 53–109; Robert P. Forbes, "Slavery and the Evangelical Enlightenment," and Laura L. Mitchell, "'Matters of Justice between Man and Man':

Northern Divines, the Bible, and the Fugitive Slave Act of 1850," in *Religion and the Antebellum Debate over Slavery*, ed. John R. McKivigan and Mitchell Snay (Athens, Ga., 1998), 68–106, 134–66; and J. Albert Harrill, "The Use of the New Testament in the American Slave Controversy: A Case History in the Hermeneutical Tension between Biblical Criticism and Christian Moral Debate," *Religion and American Culture* 10 (Summer 2000): 149–86. A fine study that appeared too late for me to use is Stephen R. Haynes, *Noah's Curse: The Biblical Justification of American Slavery* (New York, 2002).

2. Quoted from *William Lloyd Garrison, 1805–1879: The Story of His Life Told by His Children* 4 vols. (New York, 1885–89), 3:145–46. On Garrison's abandonment of traditional views of biblical inspiration, see also John L. Thomas, *The Liberator: William Lloyd Garrison* (Boston, 1963), 351–53; and Harrill, "Use of the New Testament," 159–60.

3. Gerrit Smith, "Bible Civil Government," in *Sermons and Speeches* (New York, 1861), 119.

4. Thornton Stringfellow, "The Bible Argument; or, Slavery in the Light of Divine Revelation," in *Cotton Is King, and Pro-slavery Arguments*, ed. E. N. Elliott (Augusta, Ga., 1860), 459–91 (quotation 477).

5. J. Albert Harrill's identification of various hermeneutics adopted by these moderates—of immutable principle, of the seed growing secretly, of moral intuition, and of typology—is especially helpful; see Harrill, "Use of the New Testament."

6. "The Institution of Slavery among the Ancient Hebrews, according to the Bible and the Talmud. By Dr. M. Mielziner. A Contribution to Hebraico-Judaic Archaeology," *Evangelical Review* 13 (Jan. 1862): 311–55; editor's statement, 312n. The article was also printed as "Slavery among the Ancient Hebrews from Biblical and Talmudic Sources," *American Theological Review* 3 (Apr. 1861) and (July 1861).

7. Albert Barnes, *An Inquiry into the Scriptural Views of Slavery* (Philadelphia, 1846).

8. Robert Bruce Mullin, "Biblical Critics and the Battle over Slavery," *Journal of Presbyterian History* 61 (Summer 1983): 226n42; concerning Albert Barnes, *Inquiries and Suggestions in Regard to the Foundation of Faith in the Word of God* (Philadelphia, 1859), esp. 44–53.

9. August Wenzel, "Theological Implications of the Civil War" (mimeograph, Garrett Theological Seminary Library, Evanston, Ill., 1971), 13.

10. M.E.F., "Does the Bible Sustain Slavery?" *Christian Review* 27 (Oct. 1862): 584–85. The year before in the same journal a similar contrast had been drawn between "mere verbal criticism and hair-splitting exegesis" and "the broad catholic spirit of freedom and humanity." This contrast was presented as a definite answer to the problem of slavery and the Bible. [E. G. Robinson, ed.], "The Vital Forces of the Age," *Christian Review* 26 (Oct. 1861): 566.

11. Robert H. Abzug, *Passionate Liberator: Theodore Dwight Weld and the Dilemma of Reform* (New York, 1980), 162.

12. Ibid.

13. *A Debate on Slavery, Held on the First, Second, Third, and Sixth Days of October, 1845, in the City of Cincinnati, between Rev. J. Blanchard, Pastor of the Sixth Presbyterian Church, and N. L. Rice, Pastor of the Central Presbyterian Church* (Cincinnati, 1857), 304–5.

14. Ibid., 218–19.

15. Leonard Bacon, *Slavery Discussed in Occasional Essays, from 1833 to 1846* (New York, 1846), 180 (emphasis added).

16. *Fast Day Sermons; or, The Pulpit on the State of the Country* (New York, 1861).

17. Thornwell, "Our National Sins," in ibid., 44.

18. Van Dyke, "The Character and Influence of Abolitionism," in *Fast Day Sermons*, 129n, 137, 163.

19. Raphall, "Bible View of Slavery," in *Fast Day Sermons*, 234, 236, 236–37. On the controversy in Jewish communities that followed publication of this sermon, see Bertram W. Korn, *American Jewry and the Civil War*, 2d ed. (Philadelphia, 1961), 17.

20. Lewis, "Patriarchal and Jewish Servitude No Argument for American Slavery," in *Fast Day Sermons*, 180, 198, 219. This essay was originally published in the *New York World* as a response to Van Dyke's sermon. The fact that it was the only nonsermon included in the volume suggests the importance of the issue at the time.

21. For the most nuanced study, see Richard Wightman Fox, *Trials of Intimacy: Love and Loss in the Beecher-Tilton Scandal* (Chicago, 1999).

22. Beecher, "Peace, Be Still," in *Fast Day Sermons*, 286, 289.

23. Suggestions for the large modern literature on the subject are found in Willard M. Swartley, *Slavery, Sabbath, War, and Women: Case Studies in Biblical Interpretation* (Scottdale, Pa., 1983); David L. Thompson, "Women, Men, Slaves, and the Bible: Hermeneutical Inquiries," *Christian Scholar's Review* 25 (Mar. 1996): 326–49; and Murray J. Harris, *Slave of Christ* (Leicester, Eng., 1999).

24. Nicholas Wolterstorff, "The Art of Remembering," *Journal of the Irish Christian Study Centre* 5 (1994): 2.

25. Once the war began, Northern moderates and conservatives were often driven to abolitionism by heightened Southern defenses of slavery as a biblical institution. The case of Charles Hodge, who as we see in the next chapter had defended slavery as biblical, is instructive. Southern Presbyterians opined at their General Assembly in 1864, that "We hesitate not to affirm that it is the peculiar mission of the Southern Church to conserve the institution of slavery, and to make it a blessing both to master and to slave." Hodge's reaction showed how far the war had moved him on the question of slavery: "It is enough to humble the whole Christian world to hear our Presbyterian brethren in the South declaring that the great mission of the Southern church was to conserve the system of slavery. Since the death of Christ no such dogma stains the record of an ecclesiastical body." Hodge, "President Lincoln," *Princeton Review* 37 (July 1865): 439. The Southern Assembly is quoted (and Hodge at length refuted) in John Adger, "Northern and Southern Views of the Province of the Church," *Southern Presbyterian Review* 16 (Mar. 1865): 389.

26. Beecher, "Peace, Be Still," 289.

27. Michael Chevalier, *Society, Manners, and Politics in the United States* (Boston, 1839), 368.

28. One of the earliest Catholic polemics against Protestant Bible-only thinking made this argument in classic form, Robert Bellarmine, *Disputationes de controversiis Christianae fidei adversus hujus temporis hereticos*, 3 vols. (1586–93).

29. This response is well illustrated by many of the individuals examined in George M. Fredrickson, *The Inner Civil War: Northern Intellectuals and the Crisis of the Union* (New York, 1965); and Anne C. Rose, *Victorian America and the Civil War* (New York, 1992).

30. Lyman Abbott, *Reminiscences* (Boston, 1915), 447, 448, 451.

31. Another liberal of Abbott's vintage and beliefs, William Newton Clarke, detailed the same sort of journey in his spiritual autobiography, *Sixty Years with the*

NOTES TO PAGES 399–400 547

Bible: A Record of Experience (New York, 1909), where, without specifying the debate over slavery specifically, he yet describes how "the moral difficulties of the Bible" that began to surface in his mind from at least "the Sixties" (226) contributed their share to Clarke's move from "using the Bible in the light of its statements" to "using it in the light of its principles" (120–21) and eventually to giving up "the impossible doctrine of verbal inspiration" (131).

32. For how debate over slavery accelerated the acceptance of critical views of Scripture, see Harrill, "Use of the New Testament." The end to which that acceptance came is well described in William R. Hutchison, *The Modernist Impulse in American Protestantism* (Cambridge, Mass., 1976).

33. On how resistance to Protestant liberalism in the postbellum period drew on the intellectual reflexes of antebellum America, even as it discovered fresh applications of supernaturalist and biblicist convictions, see George M. Marsden, *Fundamentalism and American Culture: The Shaping of Twentieth Century Evangelicalism, 1870–1925* (New York, 1980); and Mark A. Noll, *The Scandal of the Evangelical Mind* (Grand Rapids, 1994), 59–148.

34. This was the picture described by Mark Pattison, "Tendencies of Religious Thought in England, 1688–1750," in *Essays and Reviews* (London, 1860), 328. The presence of Pattison's historical essay in this notorious book ensured that it would be widely read, since the book's modernist proposals (Pattison's piece is much less radical) and the attention it received in England guaranteed also its currency in the United States.

35. There is a growing corpus of solid writing on Thornwell and his intellectual and theological commitments, including Morton Smith, *Studies in Southern Presbyterian Theology* (Phillipsburg, N.J., 1962), 121–82; James Oscar Farmer Jr., *The Metaphysical Confederacy: James Henley Thornwell and the Synthesis of Southern Values* (Macon, Ga., 1986); Luder G. Whitlock Jr., "James Henley Thornwell," in *Southern Reformed Theology*, ed. David F. Wells (Grand Rapids, 1989), 61–74; John H. Leith, "James Henley Thornwell and the Shaping of the Reformed Tradition in the South," in *Probing the Reformed Tradition*, ed. Elsie Anne McKee and Brian G. Armstrong (Louisville, 1989), 424–47; William W. Freehling, "James Henley Thornwell's Mysterious Antislavery Moment," *Journal of Southern History* 57 (Aug. 1991): 383–406; Craig A. Troxel, "Charles Hodge on Church Boards," *Westminster Theological Journal* 58 (Fall 1996): 183–207 (with Thornwell as Hodge's main opponent); and Michael O'Brien, "Calvinism and Intellectual Modernity: James Henley Thornwell's Theology" (unpublished paper, Southern Historical Society, Bloomington, Ind., Spring 2001).

36. Thornwell, "Our National Sins," 50. For a modern explanation of how Thornwell's defense of a common human race (and hence his defense of African Americans as fully human) was linked to his biblical defense of slavery, see Eugene D. Genovese, *A Consuming Fire: The Fall of the Confederacy in the Mind of the White Christian South* (Athens, Ga., 1998), 4, 80–88.

37. Journals sampled include those from Canadian and Scottish Presbyterians, as well as English Anglicans; supporting this conclusion are several essays by W. Harrison Daniel, including "The Reaction of British Methodism to the Civil War and Reconstruction in America," *Methodist History* 16 (1977): 3–20; "The Response of the Church of England to the Civil War and Reconstruction in America," *Historical Magazine of the Protestant Episcopal Church* 47 (1978): 57–72; and "English Presbyterians, Slavery, and the American Crisis of the 1860s," *Journal of Presbyterian History* 58 (1980): 50–62.

38. "Progress of Anti-slavery Views in the American Churches," *Home and Foreign Record of the Canada Presbyterian Church* 3 (Sept. 1864): 295–97.

39. *Monthly Record of the Church of Scotland in Nova Scotia and the Adjoining Provinces* 8 (Sept. 1862): 203–4.

40. Richard W. Vaudry, *The Free Church in Victorian Canada, 1844–1861* (Waterloo, Ont. 1989), 78–79, with quotations from Free Church minutes.

41. "Monthly Retrospect: Foreign," *United Presbyterian Magazine,* new ser., 5 (Aug. 1861): 396; and "The Civil War in America, and Our Present Difficulty," ibid. 6 (Jan. 1862): 2.

42. "Liberty to the Captive," *Monthly Record of the Free Church of Scotland,* Sept. 1863, 317–18. I am grateful to David Bebbington and Terrance Mann for photocopies of British materials.

43. Daniel, "English Presbyterians, Slavery, and the American Crisis," 50–62.

44. On Henry Van Dyke's veneration of Thornwell, see James Moorhead, *American Apocalypse: Yankee Protestants and the Civil War, 1860–1869* (New Haven, 1978), 128n122. The lack of foreign sympathy for this biblical reasoning speaks against the notion that Thornwell was "arguably, second to none [among theologians] in the United States"; Elizabeth Fox-Genovese and Eugene D. Genovese, "The Divine Sanction of Social Order: Religious Foundations of the Southern Slaveholders' World View," *Journal of the American Academy of Religion* 55 (Summer 1987): 217. By comparison, Charles Hodge, though conservative on slavery, enjoyed much broader repute. No African American ever said of Thornwell what Bishop Daniel Payne said of Hodge, that he was "the greatest theologian which America has yet produced" (Payne, *Recollections of Seventy Years* [New York, 1969 (orig. ca. 1890)], 248). Few if any foreigners came to South Carolina to study with Thornwell, but by the 1860s scores had arrived at Princeton from Ireland, Scotland, and Canada to study with Hodge; see Peter Wallace and Mark Noll, "The Students of Princeton Seminary: A Research Note," *American Presbyterians* 72 (Fall 1994): 203–15.

Chapter 20

1. Theophilus Armenius, "An Account of the Rise and Progress of the Work of God in the Western County," *Methodist Magazine* 2 (1819): 350, as quoted in Nathan O. Hatch, *The Democratization of American Christianity* (New Haven, 1989), 289n5.

2. J. W. Nevin, "The Sect System," *Mercersburg Review* 2–3 (1849–50), as excerpted in *The Mercersburg Theology,* ed. James Hastings Nichols, A Library of Protestant Thought (New York, 1966), 95–119 (quotations 95–100).

3. Horace Bushnell, *God in Christ. Three Discourses . . . with a Preliminary Dissertation on Language* (Hartford, 1849), 92.

4. Orestes Brownson, "'The Church and Its Mission' [18 Feb. 1843]: Sufficiency of the Scriptures," in *American Catholic Religious Thought,* ed. Patrick W. Carey (New York, 1987), 115.

5. Hodge, "The General Assembly," *Princeton Review* 37 (July 1865): 506.

6. William G. T. Shedd, *Calvinism: Pure and Mixed, a Defence of the Westminster Standards* (New York, 1893), 152. I thank Darryl Hart for this reference.

7. Daniel A. Payne, *Recollections of Seventy Years* (New York, 1969 [orig. ca. 1890]), 234.

8. Daniel Alexander Payne, "Welcome to the Ransomed," in *Afro-American Religious History: A Documentary Witness,* ed. Milton C. Sernett (Durham, 1985), 219.

9. A good account of such biblicism is found in Curtis D. Johnson, *Redeeming America: Evangelicals and the Road to Civil War* (Chicago, 1993), 176–77, 182.

10. David W. Blight, *Frederick Douglass' Civil War: Keeping Faith in Jubilee* (Baton Rouge, La. 1989), 111–13.

11. "A Reply to Frederick Douglass, by a Colored Man," *Douglass' Monthly*, Apr. 1863, 820–21 (quotations 821).

12. On the importance of Scripture for African-American Christians in the antebellum period, I have found the following most useful: James Weldon Johnson, ed., *The Book of American Negro Spirituals* (New York, 1925), 20–21; Eugene D. Genovese, *Roll, Jordan, Roll: The World the Slaves Made* (New York, 1976 [orig. 1972]), 159–284; Charles V. Hamilton, *The Black Preacher in America* (New York, 1972), 38–39; Timothy L. Smith, "Slavery and Theology: The Emergence of Black Christian Consciousness in Nineteenth-Century America," *Church History* 46 (Dec. 1972): 497–512; Monroe Fordham, *Major Themes in Northern Black Religious Thought, 1800–1860* (Hicksville, N.Y., 1975), 111–37; Dena J. Epstein, *Sinful Tunes and Spirituals: Black Folk Music to the Civil War* (Urbana, Ill., 1977), 217–37; Lawrence W. Levine, *Black Culture and Black Consciousness: Afro-American Folk Thought from Slavery to Freedom* (New York, 1977), 3–189; Donald G. Mathews, *Religion in the Old South* (Chicago, 1977), 185–236; Albert J. Raboteau, *Slave Religion: The "Invisible Institution" in the Antebellum South* (New York, 1978), 239–43; Vincent L. Wimbush, "The Bible and African Americans: An Outline of an Interpretive History," in *Stony the Road We Trod: African American Biblical Interpretation*, ed. Cain Hope Felder (Minneapolis, 1991); and Janet Duitsman Cornelius, *When I Can Read My Title Clear: Literacy, Slavery, and Religion in the Antebellum South* (Columbia, S.C., 1992).

13. Theophus S. Smith, *Conjuring Culture: Biblical Formations of Black Americans* (New York, 1994).

14. Payne, *Recollections*, 16, 34, 85.

15. Douglass, "Slaveholding Religion," *Douglass' Monthly*, Oct. 1860, 340.

16. Payne, "Welcome to the Ransomed," 224.

17. Albert Raboteau, quoted in Timothy E. Fulop, "'The Future Golden Day of the Race': Millennialism and Black Americans in the Nadir, 1877–1901," *Harvard Theological Review* 84 (1991): 85.

18. See Smith, "Slavery and Theology," 504. This usage approximates what has been helpfully styled "a hermeneutics of typology" by J. Albert Harrill, "The Use of the New Testament in the American Slave Controversy: A Case History in the Hermeneutical Tension between Biblical Criticism and Christian Moral Debate," *Religion and American Culture* 10 (Summer 2000): 162.

19. Blight, *Frederick Douglass' Civil War*, 8, 101–3, 120–21.

20. Douglass, "Ought American Slavery to Be Perpetuated?" *Douglass' Monthly*, Jan. 1859, 5.

21. Abram Pryne (Williamson, N.Y.), "Does the Bible Sanction American Slavery—Reply to Bishop Hopkins of Vermont," *Douglass' Monthly,* May 1861, 455; June 1861, 470–71.

22. By 1860 there were about 2.5 million Catholic adherents, or roughly 8% of the U.S. population and over 20% of the country's religious adherents. The Methodists made up the only Protestant denominational tradition still more numerous than the Catholics. For solid estimates, see Roger Finke and Rodney Stark, "Turning Pews into People: Estimating Nineteenth Century Church Membership," *Journal for the Scientific Study of Religion* 25 (June 1986): 190; Finke and Stark, "How the Upstart Sects

Won America: 1776–1850," ibid. 28 (Mar. 1989): 31; and Edwin Scott Gaustad and Philip L. Barlow, *New Historical Atlas of Religion in America* (New York, 2001), 157.

23. *The Constitution of the Roman Catholic Churches of North Carolina, South Carolina, and Georgia,* 2d ed. (1839), and *Complete Works of the Most Reverend John Hughes,* 2 vols. (New York, 1865), 1:515; both cited in *American Catholic Religious Thought: The Shaping of a Theological and Social Tradition,* ed. Patrick W. Carey (New York, 1987), 75, 40. For further indications of active Catholic negotiation with the era's dominant forms of American thought, see the early sections of Carey's anthology; also Carey, *People, Priests, and Prelates: Ecclesiastical Democracy and the Tension of Trusteeism* (Notre Dame, Ind., 1987); Carey, "Republicanism and American Catholicism, 1785–1860," *Journal of the Early Republic* 3 (1983): 357–77; Carey, "American Catholic Romanticism, 1830–1888," *Catholic Historical Review* 74 (1988): 590–606; and Dale B. Light, *Rome and the New Republic: Conflict and Community in Philadelphia Catholicism between the Revolution and the Civil War* (Notre Dame, Ind., 1996).

24. On interconfessional complexities in this era, see James Hennesey, S.J., *American Catholics* (New York, 1981), 143–57; Jay Dolan, *The American Catholic Experience* (Garden City, N.Y., 1985), 262–320; Jenny Franchot, *Roads to Rome: The Antebellum Protestant Encounter with Catholicism* (Berkeley, 1994); and Randall M. Miller, "Catholic Religion, Irish Ethnicity, and the Civil War," in *Religion and the American Civil War,* ed. Miller, Harry S. Stout, and Charles Reagan Wilson (New York, 1998), 261–96.

25. For an exposition of Newman's argument and also of how Newman considered it to be a conservative argument, see Owen Chadwick, *From Bossuet to Newman,* 2d ed. (Cambridge, 1987), 139–63.

26. See David Spalding, C.F.X., ed., "Martin John Spalding's 'Dissertation on the American Civil War" (Apr. or May 1863), *Catholic Historical Review* 52 (Apr. 1966): 66–85; Robert Emmett Curran, "Rome, the American Church, and Slavery," in *Building the Church in America: Studies in Honor of Monsignor Robert Trisco on His Seventieth Birthday,* ed. Joseph C. Linck, C.O., and Raymond J. Kupke (Washington, D.C., 1999), 30–49; and especially Kenneth J. Zanca, ed., *American Catholics and Slavery: 1789–1866: An Anthology of Primary Documents* (Lanham, Md., 1994).

27. For helpful treatments, see Anthony B. Lalli, S.X., and Thomas H. O'Connor, "Roman Views on the American Civil War," *Catholic Historical Review* 40 (Apr. 1971): 21–41 (to which I owe a reference to the essay from *Civiltà Cattolica* quoted below); Walter G. Sharrow, "John Hughes and a Catholic Response to Slavery in Antebellum America," *Journal of Negro History* 57 (July 1972): 254–69; Sharrow, "Northern Catholic Intellectuals and the Coming of the Civil War," *New York History Society Quarterly* 58 (1974): 35–56; and Judith Conrad Wimmer, "American Catholic Interpretations of the Civil War" (Ph.D. diss., Drew University, 1980).

28. On 11 May 1861, as quoted in Wimmer, "American Catholic Interpretations," 257.

29. For the extraordinary range of Brownson's religious, civil, and civil-religious writings during the war, with annotations, see Patrick W. Carey, *Orestes Brownson: A Bibliography, 1826–1876* (Milwaukee, 1996), 96–108.

30. On 1 Apr. 1865, as quoted in Wimmer, "American Catholic Interpretations," 285n15.

31. "La disunione negli Stati Uniti," *Civiltà Cattolica* 4 (23 Jan. 1861): 317–18. I am grateful to Maria Walford for the translation of this passage.

32. For numbers of German Reformed churches, see table 9.3 in chapter 9 above. The number of Lutheran churches grew from something less than 300 in 1790 to 1,217 in 1850 and then to 2,128 in 1860. See Edmund S. Gaustad, *Historical Atlas of Religion in America*, rev. ed. (New York, 1976), 15, 28, 72, 102; and Gaustad and Barlow, *New Historical Atlas*, 390.

33. Quentin Skinner, *The Foundations of Modern Political Thought*, vol. 2, *The Age of Reformation* (New York, 1978), 65–73.

34. J. H. C. Helmuth, *Betrachtung der Evangelischen Lehre von der Heiligen Schrift und Taufe; samt einigen Gedanken von den gegenwärtigen Zeiten* (Germantown, Pa., 1793), 67: "Höchstschädlich ist es, wenn ein Mensch seine Grillen und Träumereyen in dis heilige Buch hineinträgt. . . . das heißt, aus der Schrift einen Wetterhan machen, der sich in alle Gegenden des Einbildungs-himmels drehet. . . . Das heißt mit der Bibel, wie die Kinder mit einer Puppe spielen und tändeln; das heißt, die Schrift so erklären, als ob sich der hilige Geist nach der Einbildungskraft eines jeden Menschen richten müßte, er mag denn auch so verworren denken, als er immer will. Das heißt, die Bibel zu einem finstern Chaos machen. . . . Die reine Religion Jesu ein Gegenstand des Spotts und der Verachtung wird" (original spelling retained). I thank A. G. Roeber for pointing me to this important work by Helmuth.

35. This period has long been a crux of American Lutheran history; for a positive assessment of Americanization, see Paul P. Kuenning, *The Rise and Fall of American Lutheran Pietism* (Macon, Ga., 1988); and for a more negative assessment, see David A. Gustafson, *Lutherans in Crisis: The Question of Identity in the American Republic* (Minneapolis, 1993).

36. Frederick Henry Quitman, *Evangelical Catechism; or, A Short Exposition of the Principal Doctrines and Precepts of the Christian Religion; for the Use of the Churches Belonging to the Evangelical Lutheran Synod of New York* (Hudson, N.Y., 1814), 6, 7.

37. Compare Mühlenberg, *Erbauliche Lieder-Sammlung zum Gottesdienstlichen Gebrauch in den Vereinigten Evangelisch-Lutherischen Gemeinen in Pennsylvanien*, 2d ed. (Germantown, Pa., 1785), first hymn ("Ach Herr Gott! gib uns deine Geist von oben, / der uns beystand leist, im ohren und im lehren: / vergib die Sund', andacht verlieh, / das herz bereite, daß es sey munter zu deinen ehren" [O Lord God! Give us your Spirit from above, who brings us aid for hearing and learning; forgive our sin, bring us to worship, prepare our heart to be joyful in your glory]); with Quitman, *A Collection of Hymns and Liturgy, for the Use of Evangelical Lutheran Churches* (Philadelphia, 1814), first hymn ("Before Jehovah's awful throne, / Ye nations bow with sacred joy: / Know that the Lord is God alone; / He can create, and he destroy").

38. For expert discussion, see Steven M. Nolt, "Becoming Ethnic Americans in the Early Republic: Pennsylvania German Reaction to Evangelical Protestant Reformism," *Journal of the Early Republic* 20 (Fall 2000): 423–46.

39. *Das Evangelische Magazin der Evangelisch-Lutherischen Kirche* 2 (Feb. 1831): 146, as quoted in Paul A. Baglyos, "In This Land of Liberty: American Lutherans and the Young Republic, 1787–1837" (Ph.D. diss., University of Chicago, 1997), 78–79.

40. S. S. Schmucker, *Elements of Popular Theology, with Special Reference to the Doctrines of the Reformation, as Avowed before the Diet of Augsburg*, MDXXX, 2d ed. (New York, 1834), 2, 42, 98, with opinions of republican government, 272–74. In this same work (275) Schmucker also declared that the Augsburg Confession contained principles to justify the American Revolution, which was a reversal from the more quietistic interpretation of Augsburg that had become standard in Europe.

41. Samuel S. Schmucker, *The American Lutheran Church, Historically, Doctrinally, and Practically Delineated* (Springfield, Ohio, 1851), 121, 123.

42. For a recent assessment of these proposals, see L. DeAne Lagerquist, *The Lutherans* (Westport, Conn., 1999), 74–77.

43. A good account of that criticism is E. Brooks Holifield, "Mercersburg, Princeton, and the South: The Sacramental Controversy in the Nineteenth Century," *Journal of Presbyterian History* 54 (Summer 1976): 238–57.

44. On Schaff's contributions at Mercersburg, and then later from Union Seminary in New York City, see Stephen R. Graham, *Cosmos in the Chaos: Philip Schaff's Interpretation of Nineteenth-Century American Religion* (Grand Rapids, 1995); and Gary K. Pranger, *Philip Schaff (1819–1893): Portrait of an Immigrant Theologian* (New York, 1997).

45. Nevin, "Sect System," 113, 116, 119.

46. Henry Harbaugh, "Synodical Church Authority," *Mercersburg Review* 12 (Jan. 1860) 130, 129.

47. See the discussions in chap. 21 below of Philip Schaff, "Slavery and the Bible," *Mercersburg Review* 13 (Apr. 1861): 288–317; Schaff, *Der Bürgerkrieg und das christliche Leben in Nord-Amerika* (Berlin, 1866); and J. W. Nevin, "The Nation's Second Birth" (Fourth of July address), *German Reformed Messenger* 30, no. 47 (26 July 1865): 1.

48. On Bachman's stance, see Robert M. Calhoon, "Lutheranism and Early Southern Culture," in *"A Truly Efficient School of Theology": The Lutheran Theological Southern Seminary in Historical Context, 1830–1980,* ed. H. George Anderson and Calhoon (Columbia, S.C., 1981), 17–18; and E. Brooks Holifield, *The Gentlemen Theologians: American Theology in Southern Culture, 1795–1860* (Durham, 1978), 163, 165. For an overview of Lutheran accommodations to the views of their various regions, see Robert Fortenbaugh, "American Lutheran Synods and Slavery, 1830–60," *Journal of Religion* 13 (Jan. 1933): 72–92.

49. E. Clifford Nelson and Eugene L. Fevold, *The Lutheran Church among Norwegian Americans,* vol. 1, *1825–1890* (Minneapolis, 1960), 180. I thank Louise Burton for this reference.

50. A representative sample of that conservative work is found in Theodore G. Tappert, *Lutheran Confessional Theology in America, 1840–1880* (New York, 1972). For an assessment of the surprisingly scant Lutheran impact on American public life, see Mark A. Noll, "Ethnic, American, or Lutheran? Dilemmas for a Historic Confession in the New World," *Lutheran Theological Seminary Review* 71 (Winter 1991): 17–38.

51. For persuasive discussions, see T. C. Smout, *A Century of the Scottish People, 1830–1950* (New Haven, 1986), 187–89; and Callum G. Brown, *The Social History of Religion in Scotland since 1730* (London, 1987), 89–168.

52. "Narrative of Kuyper's Conversion," in *Abraham Kuyper: A Centennial Reader*, ed. James D. Bratt (Grand Rapids, 1998), 45–61.

53. Henry Boynton Smith, "The Presbyterian General Assemblies," *American Theological Review* 4 (July 1862): 553; Smith, "The Moral Aspects of the Present Struggle," ibid. 3 (Oct. 1861): 729; see also Smith, "British Sympathy with America," ibid. 4 (July 1862): 487–544.

54. See Vivien Sandlund, "Robert Breckinridge, Presbyterian Antislavery Conservative," *Journal of Presbyterian History* 78 (Summer 2000): 145–54; William S. Barker, "The Social Views of Charles Hodge (1797–1878): A Study in Nineteenth-Century Calvinism and Conservatism," *Presbyterion* 1 (Spring 1975): 1–22; and Allen

C. Guelzo, "Charles Hodge's Antislavery Moment," in *Charles Hodge Revisited,* eds. James Moorhead and John Stewart (Grand Rapids, forthcoming). Of these essays, Sandlund's interpretation comes closest to my own, while Guelzo sees Hodge acting less imaginatively than I picture him here.

55. Robert Breckinridge, "Hints on Colonization and Abolition, with Reference to the Black Race," *Biblical Repertory and Princeton Review* 5 (July 1833): 293.

56. Charles Hodge, "Slavery," *Princeton Review* 7 (1835), reprinted in Hodge's *Essays and Reviews* (New York, 1857), 473–511; "West India Emancipation," Princeton Review 10 (Oct. 1838): 602–44; "Abolitionism," ibid. 16 (Oct. 1844): 545–81; "Emancipation," ibid. 21 (Oct. 1849): 582–607.

57. Hodge, "The Fugitive Slave Law" (from "Civil Government," *Princeton Review* 23 [1851]) and "The Bible Argument on Slavery" (from "Slavery," *Princeton Review* 7 [1835]), in *Cotton Is King, and Pro-Slavery Arguments,* ed. E. N. Elliott (Augusta, Ga., 1860), 810–40, 841–77.

58. Hodge, "Slavery," in *Essays and Reviews,* 510.

59. For an outstanding discussion of the *malum in se* problem, see Robert Bruce Mullin, "Biblical Critics and the Battle over Slavery," *Journal of Presbyterian History* 61 (Summer 1983): 210–26.

60. Breckinridge's sermon on the national fast day, 4 January 1861, was all rhetoric with no exegesis ("The Union to Be Preserved," in *Fast Day Sermons* [New York, 1861]). On Breckinridge's difficulties in maintaining his early position—against intense Kentucky opposition and his own deep fear of racial "amalgamation"—see James C. Klotter, *The Breckinridges of Kentucky, 1760–1981* (Lexington, Ky., 1986), 51–81 (Breckinridge's fear of "amalgamation," 71).

61. David Brion Davis, "Reconsidering the Colonization Movement: Leonard Bacon and the Problem of Evil," *Intellectual History Newsletter* 14 (1992): 4.

62. Frederick Douglass, "The Pro-Slavery Mob and the Pro-Slavery Ministry," *Douglass' Monthly,* March 1861, 417–18.

63. Philip Schaff, "Slavery and the Bible," *Mercersburg Review* 13 (Apr. 1861): 289–91. For another prominent Southern minister who kept alive the Noahic curse, see Stephen Haynes, "Race, National Destiny, and the Sons of Noah in the Thought of Benjamin M. Palmer," *Journal of Presbyterian History* 78 (Summer 2000): 125–44. For a sharp statement of the problem as I am construing it here, see Winthrop Jordan, *White over Black: American Attitudes toward the Negro, 1550–1812* (Chapel Hill, 1968), 18: "the question becomes why a tale which logically implied slavery but absolutely nothing about skin color should have become an autonomous and popular explanation of the Negro's blackness."

64. On the fate of the curse-of-Canaan arguments, see David Brion Davis, *Slavery and Human Progress* (New York, 1984), 21–22, 36, 39, 42–43, 83, 86–87; and specifically for the theologians, Eugene D. Genovese, *A Consuming Fire: The Fall of the Confederacy in the Mind of the White Christian South* (Athens, Ga., 1998), 4, 81, 160n7.

65. Schaff, "Slavery and the Bible," 292.

66. Eugene Genovese, reporting on the work of T. R. R. Cobb, in *"Slavery Ordained of God": The Southern Slaveholders' View of Biblical History and Modern Politics,* Fortenbaugh Memorial Lecture (Gettysburg, Pa., 1985), 13.

67. Schaff, "Slavery and the Bible," 316–17 (italics in original).

68. In November 1862 Frederick Douglass reprinted a letter that a former slave, Sarah Wilson of New Haven, Connecticut, had written to President Millard Filmore ten years before, which shows that at least some African Americans knew about tra-

ditional Reformed teaching on "means": "I have no fear for the deliverance of the slave. Yet I think God works by means, and that it is your and my duty to exert our influence to aid the cause." *Douglass' Monthly*, Nov. 1862, 750.

69. Hodge, "President Lincoln," *Princeton Review* 37 (July 1865): 435–36.

70. Hodge, "Slavery," 479, 480, 500, 502–3, 503, 511 (emphasis added).

71. Historians' aversion to Dabney's postwar racism, as well as his cultural and intellectual conservatism, have obscured the relatively supple character of his prewar opinions; for a hint, see David H. Overy, "When the Wicked Beareth Rule: A Southern Critique of Industrial America," *Journal of Presbyterian History* 48 (Summer 1970): 130–42.

72. Thomas Cary Johnson, *The Life and Letters of Robert Lewis Dabney* (Edinburgh, 1977; orig [1903]), 319–21.

73. R. L. Dabney, "Ecclesiastical Equality of Negroes," in *Discussions: Evangelical and Theological,* 4 vols. (London, 1967 [orig. 1890]), 2:199–217 (quotation 207).

74. Thornwell, "A Southern Address to Christendom," in *American Christianity: An Historical Interpretation with Representative Documents*, 2 vols., ed. H. Shelton Smith, Robert T. Handy, and Lefferts A. Loetscher (New York, 1963), 2:205–10.

Chapter 21

1. *Army and Navy Messenger* (Shreveport, La.), 16 Mar. 1865, 2, as quoted in Kurt Berends, "Proclaiming God's Cause: *The Army and Navy Messenger* in the Civil War" (Wheaton College seminar paper, 1992).

2. Henry Ward Beecher, "Abraham Lincoln," in *Patriotic Addresses* (New York, 1887), 711.

3. Horace Bushnell, "Our Obligations to the Dead," in *Building Eras in Religion* (New York, 1881), 328–29.

4. Unnamed correspondent in the *Occident* 23, no. 4 (July 1865): 172–74; as quoted in Bertram W. Korn, *American Jewry and the Civil War*, 2d ed. (Philadelphia, 1961), 214.

5. G. I. Wood, "A Divine Actor on the Stage," *New Englander* 24 (Oct. 1865): 691–92.

6. John Adger, "Northern and Southern Views of the Province of the Church," *Southern Presbyterian Review* 16 (Mar. 1866): 409, 411. Adger's essay was probably written in October or November; lack of printing supplies was retarding publication of this and most other Southern periodicals.

7. The following paragraphs present material from the very useful survey in August Wenzel, "Theological Implications of the Civil War" (mimeograph, Garrett Theological Seminary Library, Evanston, Ill., 1971).

8. For example, W. C. Wilson, "Darwin on the Origin of Species," *Methodist Quarterly Review* 13 (Oct. 1861); and Daniel Goodwin, "The Antiquity of Man" (on Lyell), *American Presbyterian and Theological Review,* 2d ser., 2 (Apr. 1864).

9. For example, G. Day, "Renan's Life of Jesus," *Freewill Baptist Quarterly* 13 (Jan. 1865).

10. For example, "God and Revelation," *Biblical Repertory and Princeton Review* 34 (Jan. 1862); and E. V. Gerhart, "Mansel's Limits of Religious Thought," *Mercersburg Review* 12 (Apr. 1860).

11. For example, "Herbert Spencer's *First Principles*," *American Quarterly Church Review* 16 (Oct. 1864); and J. E. Barnes, "Herbert Spencer on Ultimate Religious Ideas," *New Englander* 22 (Oct. 1863).

12. For example, W. B. Brown, "Christ Dying for the Sins of Men the Foundation of the Christian Superstructure," *New Englander* 21 (July 1862); and six articles entitled "Imputation and Original Sin" in the *Danville Quarterly Review* 1–2 (Sept. 1861–Dec. 1862).

13. For example, "The Peril and Duty of the American People," *Danville Quarterly Review* 3 (June 1863); and R. S. Gladney, "The Downfall of the Union," *Southern Presbyterian Review* 16 (July 1863).

14. On Lincoln's religion, the most satisfactory account is now Allen C. Guelzo, *Abraham Lincoln: Redeemer President* (Grand Rapids, 1999). Also useful is Ronald C. White, *Lincoln's Greatest Speech: The Second Inaugural* (New York, 2002).

15. The literature on the Second Inaugural is enormous but not particularly helpful for setting it within the contexts of its times. A noteworthy exception is Benjamin Barondess, *Three Lincoln Masterpieces* (Charleston, W.V., 1954), 51–109, which contains transcripts of contemporary newspaper reports. The judgment of Reinhold Niebuhr at the centennial celebration of Lincoln's Gettysburg Address is more to the point: to study "the religion of Abraham Lincoln in the context of the traditional religion of his time and place . . . must lead to the conclusion that Lincoln's religious convictions were superior in depth and purity to those, not only of the political leaders of his day, but of the religious leaders of the era." Niebuhr, "The Religion of Abraham Lincoln," in *Lincoln and the Gettysburg Address*, ed. Allan Nevins (Urbana, Ill, 1964), 72–73.

16. "The Second Inaugural Address," in *The Collected Works of Abraham Lincoln*, 9 vols., ed. Roy P. Basler (New Brunswick, N.J., 1953), 8:333.

17. *New Haven Register* 30, no. 189 (1865), as quoted in David B. Chesebrough, *God Ordained This War: Sermons on the Sectional Crisis, 1830–1865* (Columbia, S.C., 1992), 328.

18. Henry Ward Beecher, "Address at the Raising of the Union Flag over Fort Sumter," in *Patriotic Addresses* (New York, 1887), 688–89.

19. Bushnell, "Our Obligations to the Dead," 332–33.

20. William A. Clebsch, "Christian Interpretations of the Civil War," *Church History* 31 (1961): 215–18. For a similar judgment, see Barbara M. Cross, *Horace Bushnell: Minister to a Changing America* (Chicago, 1958), 136–37.

21. Dabney, "To Major General Howard" (written 12 Sept. 1865), in *Discussions by Robert L. Dabney*, vol. 4, *Secular*, ed. C.R. Vaughan (Mexico, Mo., 1897), 27–31.

22. Adger, "Northern and Southern Views," 397–98.

23. Private people may have been more like him in retaining trust in a mysterious sovereign providence; see Lewis O. Saum, *The Popular Mood of Pre–Civil War America* (Westport, Conn., 1980).

24. *Works of Lincoln*, 4:270–71.

25. Ibid., 5:403–4.

26. Bushnell, "Our Obligations to the Dead," 328–29, 341, 352.

27. John W. Nevin, "The Nation's Second Birth," *German Reformed Messenger*, July 26, 1865, 1, col. 4. Reasoning like Nevin's was common in the North. If natural causes (i.e., God's mediated control over events) seemed to point in one direction and yet something different happened, commentors leaped to the conclusion that God's unmediated actions must be the explanation, rather than a previously over-

looked set of mediated causes. For a particularly clear example of this reasoning, see Wood, "Divine Actor on the Stage," 690–704.

28. Schaff, *Der Bürgerkrieg und das christliche Leben in Nord-Amerika* (Berlin, 1866), 16–17: "Ein Land, wo so viele Ströme edlen Blutes gestossen, wo so viele Opfer von der Regierung und dem Volke gebracht wurden, und wo die Hand Gottes so sichtbar und wunderbar die Ereignisse zu einem glücklichen Ende gelenkt hat, muß nach aller menschlichen Berechnung eine große Zukunft vor sich haben. Es hat die Feuerprobe durchgemacht und ist erst jetzt in das Alter männlicher Kraft und Selbstständigkeit eingetreten."

29. Ralph Waldo Emerson, "Abraham Lincoln: Remarks at the Funeral Services Held in Concord, April 19, 1865," in *The Complete Works of Ralph Waldo Emerson*, 12 vols. bound in 6 (New York, 1926), 11:337–38.

30. Charles Hodge, "President Lincoln," *Biblical Repertory and Princeton Review* 37 (July 1865): 439–40.

31. Adger, "Northern and Southern Views," 398, 399, 410.

32. Nevin, "Nation's Second Birth," 1, col. 3.

33. Nevin, "Commencement Address," in Theodore Appel, *The Life and Work of John Williamson Nevin* (Philadelphia, 1889), 647–48; as quoted in James D. Bratt, "Nevin and the Antebellum Culture Wars," in *Reformed Confessionalism in Nineteenth-Century America: Essays on the Thought of John Williamson Nevin*, ed. Sam Hamstra Jr. and Arie J. Griffioen (Lanham, Md., 1995), 16.

34. Hodge, "President Lincoln," 435–36.

35. Adger, "Northern and Southern Views," 401–3.

36. These reservations about the character of Lincoln's religion are developed in Melvin B. Endy Jr., "Abraham Lincoln and American Civil Religion: A Reinterpretation," *Church History* 44 (June 1975): 229–41.

37. See especially the Northern, secular-leaning subjects of George M. Fredrickson, *The Inner Civil War: Northern Intellectuals and the Crisis of the Union* (New York, 1965); and Anne C. Rose, *Victorian America and the Civil War* (New York, 1992).

38. In general, Shira Wolosky, *Emily Dickinson: A Voice of War* (New Haven, 1984); and more specifically, Richard B. Sewall, *The Life of Emily Dickinson* (New York, 1974), 535–37, 631–32; and Roger Lundin, *Emily Dickinson and the Art of Belief* (Grand Rapids, 1998), 123–25.

39. No. 1021, *The Poems of Emily Dickinson*, 3 vols., ed. Thomas H. Johnson, (Cambridge, Mass., 1963), 2:729.

40. Hawthorne, from *English Notebooks*, 20 Nov. 1856, as quoted in Rowland A. Sherrill, *The Prophetic Melville* (Athens, Ga., 1979), 91.

41. *The Battle-Pieces of Herman Melville*, ed. Hennig Cohen (New York, 1963), 198.

42. The most effective, in my judgment, have been Benjamin P. Thomas, *Abraham Lincoln* (New York, 1952); Guelzo, *Redeemer President*; and recent works based on fresh reconsiderations of traditional Lincolniana, like Douglas L. Wilson, *Lincoln before Washington: New Perspectives on the Illinois Years* (Urbana, Ill., 1997); and Douglas L. Wilson, Rodney O. Davis, and Terry Wilson, eds., *Herndon's Informants: Letters, Interviews, and Statements about Abraham Lincoln* (Urbana, Ill., 1998).

43. For further reflections on this theme, see Mark A. Noll, "The Struggle for Lincoln's Soul," *Books and Culture*, Sept.–Oct. 1995, 3–7.

44. For a summary, see Robert Swierenga, "Ethnoreligious Political Behavior in the Mid-Nineteenth Century: Voting, Values, Cultures," in *Religion and American*

Politics from the Colonial Period to the 1980s, ed. Mark A. Noll (New York, 1989), 146–71.

45. Alexis de Tocqueville, *Democracy in America*, ed. and trans. Harvey Claflin Mansfield and Delba Winthrop (Chicago, 2000), 278.

46. Quotations from Richard J. Carwardine, *Evangelicals and Politics in Ante-bellum America* (New Haven, 1993), 49; and Sydney E. Ahlstrom, *A Religious History of the American People* (New Haven, 1972), 385.

Chapter 22

1. Edwards, "The Justice of God in the Damnation of Sinners" (preached 1734, published 1738), in *Jonathan Edwards: Selections*, ed. Clarence H. Faust and Thomas H. Johnson, rev. ed., (New York, 1962), 113.

2. Taylor, *Lectures on the Moral Government of God*, 2 vols. (New York, 1859), 1:265.

3. Finney, *Lectures on Systematic Theology* (Oberlin, Ohio, 1846), 240.

4. Kramnick, "The 'Great National Discussion': The Discourse of Politics in 1787," *William and Mary Quarterly* 45 (Jan. 1988): 7.

5. John M. Murrin, "Self-Interest Conquers Patriotism: Republicanism, Liberals, and Indians Reshape the Nation," in *The American Revolution: Its Character and Limits*, ed. Jack P. Greene (New York, 1987), 227.

6. Edwards, *The Nature of True Virtue*, in *The Works of Jonathan Edwards*, vol. 8, *Ethical Writings*, ed. Paul Ramsey (New Haven, 1989), 550.

7. Taylor, *Lectures on Moral Government*, 1:253.

8. Finney, *Lectures on Systematic Theology*, 176.

9. Gordon S. Wood, *The Creation of the American Republic, 1776–1787* (Chapel Hill, 1969), 609; Isaac Kramnick, "Religion and Radicalism: English Political Thought in the Age of Revolution," *Political Theory* 5 (Nov. 1977): 514.

10. *The Works of Jonathan Edwards*, vol. 1, *Freedom of the Will*, ed. Paul Ramsey (New Haven, 1957), 163.

11. Taylor, "Man, a Free Agent without the Aids of Divine Grace," in *Tracts Designed to Illustrate and Enforce the Most Important Doctrines of the Gospel* (New Haven, 1818), 6n.

12. Finney, *Lectures on Systematic Theology*, vol. 2 (Oberlin, Ohio, 1847), 17.

13. Robert Baird, *Religion in the United States of America* (Glasgow, 1844).

14. Ibid., 660–63.

15. Ibid., 662–63. The conservative Presbyterian James Waddell Alexander was not pleased with Baird's account of "American theology," for to Alexander, Baird's exposition of the atonement looked like the view of only a few advanced Congregationalists from New England; see "Baird's Religion in America," *Biblical Repertory and Princeton Review* 17 (June 1845): 18–43, esp. 41–42. When Baird brought out a revised version of his work in 1856, Alexander repeated his criticism; see "Baird's Religion in America," ibid. 28 (Oct. 1856): 642–54.

16. For this metaphor and its great fruitfulness, I am indebted to Lamin Sanneh, *Translating the Message: The Missionary Impact on Culture* (Maryknoll, N.Y., 1989).

17. Bonhoeffer, "Protestantism without Reformation," in *No Rusty Swords: Letters, Lectures, and Notes . . . from the Collected Works of Dietrich Bonhoeffer*, vol. 1, ed. E. H. Robertson, trans. Robertson and J. Bowden (New York, 1965), 108.

18. I have expressed opinions on the later consequences of these developments

in "The Rise and Long Life of the Protestant Enlightenment in America," in *Knowledge and Belief in America: Enlightenment Traditions and Modern Religious Thought*, ed. William M. Shea and Peter A. Huff (New York, 1995), 88–124; and *The Scandal of the Evangelical Mind* (Grand Rapids, 1994).

19. Israel Holly, *A Letter to the Reverend Mr. Bartholomew . . . upon Some of His Arguments and Divinity* (Hartford, 1770), 3–4. At the same time, it also seems to me that the Scottish theologian and activist Thomas Chalmers mingled a proper reservation into one of his many encomiums for Edwards when he once said about the experience of reading Edwards's *Freedom of the Will*, "I spent nearly a twelve-month in a sort of mental elysium, and the one idea which ministered to my soul all its raptures was the magnificence of the Godhead, and the universal subordination of all things to the one great purpose for which He evolved and was supporting creation. I should like to be so inspired over again, but with such a view of the Deity as coalesced and was in harmony with the doctrine of the New Testament." William Hanna, *Memoirs of the Life and Writings of Thomas Chalmers*, 2 vols. (Edinburgh, 1851), 1:17.

20. For different versions of this judgment, see Nathan O. Hatch, *The Democratization of American Christianity* (New Haven, 1989), 210–19; and David Martin, *A General Theory of Secularization* (New York, 1978).

Appendix

1. Louis Hartz, *The Liberal Tradition in America* (New York, 1955), 60, 62. Hartz and like-minded thinkers promoted this Lockean vision as a self-conscious alternative to a picture of the founders as motivated primarily by material self-interest. For Hartz's criticism of Charles A. Beard, the leading proponent of such a "progressive" interpretation, see 28–29.

2. The best accounts of the American historiography that I have read are the forum on Gordon Wood's *Creation of the American Republic, 1776–1787* (Chapel Hill, 1969) in *William and Mary Quarterly* 44 (July 1987): 549–640; Daniel T. Rodgers, "Republicanism: The Career of a Concept," *Journal of American History* 79 (June 1992): 11–38; Joyce Appleby's essays collected in *Liberalism and Republicanism in the Historical Imagination* (Cambridge, Mass., 1992); Paul A. Rahe, *Republics Ancient and Modern: Classical Republicanism and the American Revolution* (Chapel Hill, 1992); and several of the essays in *The Republican Synthesis Revisited*, ed. Milton M. Klein, Richard D. Brown, and John B. Hench (Worcester, Mass., 1992), esp. the afterword by Gordon Wood. For clear reports in media res, see Robert Shalhope, "Toward a Republican Synthesis: The Emergence of an Understanding of Republicanism in American Historiography," *William and Mary Quarterly* 29 (1972): 49–80; and Shalhope, "Republicanism and Early American Historiography," ibid. 39 (1982): 334–56.

3. Bernard Bailyn, *The Ideological Origins of the American Revolution* (Cambridge, Mass., 1967), 34.

4. Wood, *Creation of the American Republic*, 53.

5. J. G. A. Pocock, "States, Republics, and Empires: The American Founding in Early Modern Perspective," in *Conceptual Change and the Constitution*, ed., Terence Ball and Pocock (Lawrence, Kans., 1988), 64, 65.

6. An important work that sided with Appleby and Kramnick in reasserting the dominance of liberalism in the founding, but which did so in order to attack the self-

destructive immorality of that liberalism, was John Patrick Diggins, *The Lost Soul of American Politics: Virtue, Self-Interest, and the Foundations of Liberalism* (New York, 1984). A different kind of reassertion of Lockeanism in the founding era was presented by political theorists, sometimes influenced by Leo Strauss, who have attacked the way in which historians relativize political principles in specific historical contexts—e.g., Thomas Pangle, *The Spirit of Modern Republicanism: The Moral Vision of the American Founders and the Philosophy of Locke* (Chicago, 1988). The importance of the republican interpretation of the founding era is indicated by the different kinds of criticism it has received. Besides those mentioned already, others have attacked the republican vision by attempting to recover the strength of Progressive interpretations or by faulting the present-minded consensus-mongering of the neo-Whig historians; both criticisms are found in Colin Gordon, "Crafting a Usable Past: Consensus, Ideology, and Historians of the American Revolution," *William and Mary Quarterly* 46 (Oct. 1989): 671–95.

7. Isaac Kramnick, "Republican Revisionism Revisited," in *Republicanism and Bourgeois Radicalism: Political Ideology in Late Eighteenth-Century England and America* (Ithaca, 1990), 170.

8. Joyce Appleby, "Republicanism in Old and New Contexts," in *Liberalism and Republicanism*, 337.

9. Appleby, "Liberalism and the American Revolution," in *Liberalism and Republicanism*, . 144.

10. Wood, afterword in *Republican Synthesis Revisited*, 145. Other statements of roughly the same conclusion include Pocock, communication to the editor, *William and Mary Quarterly* 45 (Oct. 1988): 815; Pocock, "States, Republics, and Empires," 65; Pocock, *Virtue, Commerce, and History* (Cambridge, 1985), 266–72. An unusually hephful account of the"more textured and pluralistic map of the ideological sources of American republicanism" is presented by Colin Kidd, "Civil Theology and Church Establishments in Revolutionary America," *The Historical Journal* 42 (1999): 1007–26 (quotation, 1010). For an early statement about this ideological complexity for the 1780s and 1790s, see Bernard Bailyn, "The Central Themes of the American Revolution: An Interpretation," in *Essays on the American Revolution*, ed. Stephen G. Kurtz and James H. Hutson (Chapel Hill, 1973), 19. For the same judgment from a perspective outside the United States, see Denis Lacorne, "Les infortunes de la vertu," in *L'Amérique et la France: Deux révolutions*, ed. Élise Marienstras (Paris, 1990), 115. The necessity of making historical accounts of Revolutionary-era ideology conform to the complexity of the documentable past, instead of either historians' convenience or modern ideologies, has become a regular theme in an important subgenre of historical reflection, the essay review: for signal examples of illuminating discussion, see Wood, on *Lost Soul of American Politics*, by John Patrick Diggins, *New York Review*, 28 Feb. 1985, 29–34; Keith Thomas, on *Virtue, Commerce, and History*, by Pocock, ibid., 27 Feb. 1986, 36–39; Charles L. Cohen, on *King and People in Provincial Massachusetts*, by Richard Bushman, *Reviews in American History* 14 (Mar. 1986): 61–67; Pocock, with attention especially to the works of Diggins, Appleby, and Kramnick, in "Between Gog and Magog: The Republican Thesis and the *Ideologia Americana*," *Journal of the History of Ideas* 48 (Apr.–June 1987): 325–46; Lance Banning, on *New Order of the Ages: Time, the Constitution, and the Making of Modern American Political Thought*, by Michael Lienesch, *Reviews in American History* 17 (June 1989): 199–204; Wood, on *Republicanism and Bourgeois Radicalism*, by Kramnic, *New Republic*, 11 Feb. 1991, 32–35; Sean Willentz, on *The Radicalism of the American Revolution* by Wood, and five other books, ibid.,

23 and 30, Dec. 1991, 32–40; Wood, on five books concerning early American capitalism, *New York Review*, 9 June 1994, 44–49; Wood, on *A Struggle for Power: The American Revolution*, by Theodore Draper, *New Republic*, 19 Feb. 1996, 33–37; Wood, on *William Cooper's Town*, by Alan Taylor, *New York Review*, 8 Aug. 1996, 36–39; and P. N. Furbank, on several books by de Tocqueville, ibid., 8 Apr. 1999, 48–52.

11. Respectively, Alan Craig Houston, *Algernon Sidney and the Republican Heritage in England and America* (Princeton, 1991); Michael P. Zuckert, *Natural Rights and the New Republicanism* (Princeton, 1994); and John Dunn, "The Politics of Locke in England and America in the Eighteenth Century," in *John Locke: Problems and Perspectives*, ed. John W. Yolton (Cambridge, 1969), 45–80, esp. 78–80.

12. The 1760s—Kramnick, "Republican Revisionism Revised," in *Republicanism and Bourgeois Radicalism*, 171. During the war—Drew R. McCoy, *The Elusive Republic: Political Economy in Jeffersonian America* (Chapel Hill, 1980), 66–72. Immediately after the war—Gordon S. Wood, *The Radicalism of the American Revolution* (New York, 1992); and Eve Kornfeld, "From Republicanism to Liberalism: The Intellectual Journey of David Ramsay," *Journal of the Early Republic* 9 (Fall 1989): 289–313. Late eighteenth century—Richard R. Beeman, "Deference, Republicanism, and the Emergence of Popular Politics in Eighteenth-Century America," *William and Mary Quarterly* 49 (July 1992): 401–30; and Michael Lienesch, *New Order of the Ages: Time, the Constitution, and the Making of Modern Political Thought* (Princeton, 1988). Early nineteenth century—Robert H. Wiebe, *The Opening of American Society: From the Adoption of the Constitution to the Eve of Disunion* (New York, 1984), 146; and Steven J. Ross, "The Transformation of Republican Ideology," *Journal of the Early Republic* 10 (Fall 1990): 323–30. In and because of the War of 1812—Steven Watts, *The Republic Reborn: War and the Making of Liberal America, 1790–1820* (Baltimore, 1987). Over the whole period—Reginald Horsman, "The Dimensions of an 'Empire for Liberty': Expansion and Republicanism, 1775–1825," *Journal of the Early Republic* 9 (Spring 1989): 1–20.

13. John M. Murrin, "Self-Interest Conquers Patriotism: Republicans, Liberals, and Indians Reshape the Nation," in *The American Revolution: Its Character and Limits*, ed. Jack P. Greene (New York, 1987), 226.

14. Richard B. Morris, "The Judeo-Christian Foundation of the American Political System," in *James Madison on Religious Liberty*, ed. Robert S. Alley (Buffalo, 1985), 112.

15. Kramnick, "The 'Great National Discussion,'" in *Republicanism and Bourgeois Radicalism*, 261.

16. John M. Murrin, "Religion and Ideological Change in the American Revolution," in *Religion and American Politics from the Colonial Period to the 1980s*, ed. Mark A. Noll (New York, 1990), 27.

17. For example, Forrest McDonald, *Novus Ordo Seclorum: The Intellectual Origins of the Constitution* (Lawrence, Kans., 1985).

18. See, as examples, Ruth Bloch, *Visionary Republic: Millennial Themes in American Thought, 1756–1800* (New York, 1985), 3–4; James T. Kloppenberg, "The Virtues of Liberalism: Christianity, Republicanism, and Ethics in Early American Political Discourse," *Journal of American History* 74 (June 1987), 12–14; Rodgers, "Republicanism," 17–27; J. C. D. Clark, *The Language of Liberty, 1660–1832: Political Discourse and Social Dynamics in the Anglo-American World* (Cambridge, 1994), 21–22; Barry Shain, *The Myth of American Individualism: The Protestant Origins of American Political Thought* (Princeton, 1994), xv–xvi; and several of the

essays in the *William and Mary Quarterly* forum (vol. 44 [July 1987]) on Gordon Wood's *Creation of the American Republic*, including Ruth Bloch, "The Constitution and Culture," 554; John Howe, "Gordon S. Wood and the Analysis of Political Culture in the American Revolutionary Era," 571–72; J. T. Main, "An Agenda for Research on the Origins and Nature of the Constitution of 1787–1788," 594, 595; and Wood, "Ideology and the Origins of Liberal America," 637.

19. For example, Bloch, *Visionary Republic*; Patricia U. Bonomi, *Under the Cope of Heaven: Religion, Society, and Politics in Colonial America* (New York, 1986); Shain, *Myth of American Individualism*; Clark, *Language of Liberty*; John G. West Jr., *The Politics of Revelation and Reason: Religion and Civic Life in the New Nation* (Lawrence, Kans., 1996); James H. Hutson, *Religion and the Founding of the American Republic* (Washington, D.C., 1998); Christopher Grasso, *A Speaking Aristocracy: Transforming Public Discourse in Eighteenth-Century Connecticut* (Chapel Hill, 1999); Derek H. Davis, *Religion and the Continental Congress, 1774–1789: Contributions to Original Intent* (New York, 2000); and Jonathan D. Sassi, *A Republic of Righteousness: The Public Christianity of the Post-Revolutionary New England Clergy* (New York, 2001).

Glossary

affectional ethics   Reasoning about conduct based on the moral sense, a sense of the heart, or intuition (in contrast to intellectualist ethics).

antiformalism   Religious beliefs and practices that arise from individuals and their own choices rather than from historical precedents, tradition, or the dictates of superior religious authorities.

antinomianism   Practices that do not heed normal precepts of the law (i.e., anti as against, nomos as the law). In early America this word was never applied by any person or group to themselves.

Arianism   The belief, considered heretical by mainstream Christian tradition, that since God was unified, eternal, and unchanging, Jesus Christ could not be considered fully divine. It was the teaching of Arius, a presbyter of Alexandria, in the early fourth century.

Arminianism   For this book, the doctrines of Methodists who held with John Wesley that God gave prevenient grace (a grace coming before full salvation) to all people so that original sin could be overcome and all could make a free choice for God. Wesleyan Arminianism also included a belief in Christian perfection, or that it was possible for believers to be liberated from all known sin.

Augustinian theology   Historic Christian doctrines linked with Augustine (354–430), including the original sin of humanity that makes it necessary for God to take responsibility for rescuing sinners, the initiative of God in bringing about that salvation, and the human inability (because of unwillingness) to act against the selfish nature of one's own sinful character.

Baconianism   The belief that the empirical, inductive procedures promoted by Francis Bacon (1561–1626) for use in physical sciences provided also the best methods for organizing ethics, epistemology, theology, and study of the Scriptures.

Calvinism   Teachings linked to John Calvin and other sixteenth-century non-Lutheran Protestants that updated Augustinian theology for a more modern Europe. In American history, Puritan Calvinism left the most important legacy because of how the Puritans combined traditional Calvinist theology with dedicated Calvinist concern to make all of life glorify God.

Christian republicanism   The patterns of thought—anticipated during King George's War (1744–1748), strengthened during the French and Indian War (1754–1763), and solidified in the War for Independence—that joined Real Whig political thought to Protestant theology, especially the theology of evangelical revivalists.

civic humanism   The political philosophy originating with Machiavelli and in Renaissance city-states of northern Italy that looked to human reason as protection against tyranny and as the proper basis for promoting the *virtù* without which a commonwealth could not flourish.

classical republicanism   This older strand of republicanism usually favored checks and balances on power, worried about "the democratic mob," and defined virtue as disinterested middle and upper class men acting disinterestedly in public for the good of the whole society.

common sense   As a technical term, derived from Scottish philosophers who sought a source for ethics in human consciousness (Francis Hutcheson) or who wanted to protect human thinking from the skepticism of David Hume (Thomas Reid). In ordinary parlance, this phrase was often used to define a basis for political or religious opinions that was not infected by the corruptions of traditional European practice.

commonwealth thought   The views of those who supported the English Parliamentarian revolution in the 1640s and defended the rights of local communities and reasonable men acting for the common good (i.e., the commonweal or commonwealth) against the oppressive actions of the arbitrary monarch and the corrupt established church.

country thought   Political suspicion of machinations at the court under the English monarchs George I (1714–1727) and George II (1727–1760). The term came to be used more generally for those who suspected centralized authorities of conspiring to take away the property, privileges, or freedom of citizens at large.

Democratic-Republicans   The political party of Thomas Jefferson and James Madison that emerged during the administration of George Washington (1789–1797) in opposition to the Federalist Party. This party opposed the national bank, the expansion of central government, and close ties with Britain, while looking with favor on local government, small-scale farming and industry, and Revolutionary France. It eventually evolved into the Democratic Party of the Jacksonian era (1824–1840) and beyond.

evangelicalism   The form of modern Protestantism characterized by a stress on conversion, the Bible as supreme religious authority, activism manifest especially in efforts to spread the Christian message, and a focus on Christ's death on the cross as the defining reality of Christian faith.

faculty psychology   Reasoning about human nature that defined people as possessing the three separate faculties of reason, passion, and will.

Federalists   The political party of Alexander Hamilton, John Adams, and (reluctantly) George Washington that in the late eighteenth and early nineteenth centuries favored national government over local prerogatives, the creation of a strong national bank, the development of American manufacturing, and closer ties with Britain. It collapsed during the War of 1812, but some Federalist concerns later re-emerged in the Whig and Republican Parties.

formalism   Religious beliefs and practices featuring educated ministers, some respect for tradition, the use of wealth to construct impressive church buildings, and comfortable relations with the middle and upper classes.

Great Awakening   Revivals of the late 1730s and early 1740s that marked the emergence of a more evangelical Calvinism out of the Puritan, Congregational, Baptist, and Presbyterian traditions that had been exported to the colonies from the old world.

imputation   The Christian idea that God counts (or reckons) the results of Adam's original sin to all humanity and the results of Christ's life-giving work to all who are redeemed.

intellectualist ethics   Reasoning about conduct based on the sovereignty of reason over passion, whether defined with Aristotelian or scholastic Christian categories (in contrast to affectional ethics).

Jeffersonianism   The form of American liberal republicanism that stressed the virtues of independent yeoman farmers and worried about the corrupting influences of standing armies, permanent government debt, and governmental initiatives not specified in the U.S. Constitution. Jeffersonianism was sometimes, but not always, practiced by Thomas Jefferson.

liberal republicanism   This newer strand of republicanism, which emerged most strongly after the American Revolution, linked traditional republican principles with a much more democratic trust in the people at large, much more attention to the protection of individual rights, much more concern for enhancing the economic opportunities of all white men, and even occasionally with some concern for the participation of women in public life.

liberalism   A loose term to designate systems of political organization that stress the liberty of individuals in a state of nature, their rights in society, and their freedoms over against coercive authority.

liberty   In all republican visions, the natural concomitant of virtue and the natural opponent of both vice and corruption.

Lockeanism   Principles from John Locke (1632–1704) who stressed individual reason as the key to well-grounded knowledge, personal rights as the most basic ingredients of a well-ordered state, and religious toleration as a prerequisite for a well-regulated social order.

millennialism   The belief that Jesus would return to establish a thousand-year reign of peace on earth. In the eighteenth and nineteenth centuries many Americans of several religious persuasions held that the expansion of American values might lead to a "civil millennialism" on earth.

Moderates (Scotland)   The faction in the established Presbyterian church that made its peace with patronage and some aspects of the Enlightenment in order to preserve the place of the Kirk among the rising classes of urban Scotland. Representatives of the popular, and later evangelical, factions often opposed Moderate plans and positions.

moral philosophy   The formal instruction, standard at American colleges from the mid-eighteenth century, that merged variations of moral-sense ethics with varieties of traditional Christian belief.

moral sense   In the affectional ethics of the Earl of Shaftesbury, Francis Hutcheson, and then many American thinkers, the innate, naturally given intuition of beauty, and of right and wrong, from which it was possible to construct entire systems of ethics, political economy, and even theology.

New Divinity   The followers of Jonathan Edwards (especially Joseph Bellamy and Samuel Hopkins) who tried to extrapolate Edwards's insights into a full theological system.

New Haven theology   The moderate Calvinism of N. W. Taylor and colleagues who left behind Jonathan Edwards's Augustinian principles in order to save Edwards's concern for evangelism and his style of careful philosophical reasoning.

New Lights   The New England Congregationalists, Baptists, and Separates who favored the revivals of the 1740s and who usually adopted some form of Jonathan Edwards's theology. Confusingly, New Lights in Ireland were theological liberals who opposed subscription to the Westminster Confession and moved toward Unitarianism.

New School   The American Presbyterians of the period roughly 1825 to 1870 who favored modifications of traditional Calvinist belief and practice, and also cooperation with New England Congregationalists, in order to be more effective agents of evangelism and civilization in the American setting. A separate New School Presbyterian denomination existed from 1838 to 1869.

New Side   Colonial Presbyterians of the 1740s and 50s who combined the newer revivalistic evangelicalism with a reasonable degree of fidelity to traditional Calvinism. This faction was the predecessor of New School and Old School Presbyterians in the next century.

Old Calvinists   Traditional New England Congregationalists who maintained doctrinal orthodoxy and could sometimes accept moderate forms of revivalism, but who worried that revival would destroy the stable Puritan society and who also opposed the efforts of New Divinity theologians to re-state doctrine in modern categories.

Old Lights   The New England Congregationalists (led by Charles Chauncy) who opposed the New Lights.

Old School   The American Presbyterians who thought the New School was moving too fast in changing traditional beliefs and too recklessly in forming alliances with New England Congregationalists.

Old Side   Colonial Presbyterians who distrusted the newer revivalism as a threat to traditional theology and, even more, to solid social order.

Pelagianism   The belief, maintained first by the Irish monk Pelagius (flourished ca. 400) that humans were capable by nature of initiating their own salvation. Augustine produced much of the theology for which he was later renowned in response to Pelagius.

Real Whigs   In the eighteenth century those who (in their own eyes) upheld the true precepts that had ousted the tyrant James II (1688) and who maintained vigilance for freedom against the corruptions of centralized power. In the complex environment of the War for Independence, Real Whig principles provided the American founding fathers with their most important intellectual guidance.

Reformed   See Calvinism.

Republican Party   The political party that emerged in 1856 as a narrowed expression of positions that had been promoted by the Whig Party, especially preventing the spread of slavery into Western states and expanding the national government's support for farming, commerce, and manufacturing.

republicanism   A flexible term that linked the practice of virtue (however defined) with the presence of freedom and the flourishing of society; republicans invariably held that vice (usually defined as luxury, indolence, and deceit in high places) promoted the corruption of government, led to tyranny, and ruined the social fabric. Within colonial America and the early United States it was possible to discern contrasting strands of liberal and classical republicanism.

Sandemanians   A small sect in late-colonial New England founded by the Scottish immigrant Robert Sandeman (1718–71) who stressed predestination, a rational approach to religion, and the independence of local congregations.

Scottish commonsense philosophy   A term used to describe the affectional ethics of Francis Hutcheson, the sophisticated epistemology of Thomas Reid, the moral philosophy of Adam Smith and Dugald Stewart, and combinations of these teachings. In America some form of Scottish commonsense thinking, though often in popular or diluted forms, was promoted by almost all of the country's public thinkers from the 1790s to the 1840s, and by a large number thereafter.

Second Great Awakening   An imprecise term that is usually taken to refer to a series of revivals managed by Presbyterians and Congregationalists (from the 1790s? from the early 1800s? into the 1830s?) that brought great numbers into the American churches. If used it all, it should feature the less publicized efforts of Methodists and Baptists who did most of the work in churching and civilizing the American populace between the War for Independence and the Civil War.

Separates   New Englanders who during and after the Great Awakening broke with the traditional Congregational churches in order to establish gathered churches where all the members made personal profession of saving faith.

Socinianism   The belief, considered heretical by almost all Christians, that Jesus revealed God but was not divine himself. The name comes from the teachings of the itinerant scholar-preacher Faustus Socinus (1539–1604).

spirituality of the church   The notion particularly strong in the South (until the Civil War began) that the church had no business as an institution meddling with political or social questions.

Tories   A term used for defenders of royal prerogative in the 1680s and then in the eighteenth century for opponents of the Whig supporters of the Hanover monarchs. In America it was applied to those who remained loyal to Britain during the War for Independence and then employed as a term of general abuse during political conflicts of the early nineteenth century.

Unitarians   In America the party within Congregationalism, strongest in Boston and environs, that by the early nineteenth century denied the traditional Christian doctrine of the Trinity while wanting to retain many of the moral, ethical, and social emphases (and also the property) of the traditional New England churches.

vice   In the republican vision a designation for self-serving, corrupt, conspiratorial, luxurious, or venial practices that undercut freedom and destroyed social wellbeing.

virtù, virtue   Originally (for Machiavelli) manly valor displayed in defending the commonwealth, the term later migrated to a more general meaning of disinterested public service by well-positioned men acting for the common good. By the early nineteenth century the term had taken on a stronger female, private, and domestic sense that featured concern for sexual purity. The fact that one term could carry so many overlapping meanings was critical for the development of both political ideology and public theology in the century and a half before the Civil War.

Whig Party   The political party that arose in opposition to Jacksonian Democrats and that in the 1830s and '40s maintained a considerable measure of traditional republicanism while also embracing the market, beginning to oppose slavery, and seeking to link the discipline of self with the discipline of society.

Whigs   A new term in the 1680s for those who worked to oust the Catholic James II from the English throne and who supported his replacement, William III (and Mary); it was later applied to those who stood with the new monarch from Hanover (George I, from 1714). As power flowed into the hands of the Hanovers' favorites, "Real Whigs" began to complain that the nominal Whigs were deserting the principles they had earlier professed.

Select Bibliography

Key Works

Method

Primary Sources and Reference Works
 Modern Collections or Editions of Sources
 Reference Works

American Theological History
 Theology (Including the Bible)—General
 Theology in New England
 Theology in the South, Including African Americans, and the Bible and Slavery
 Other Theological Traditions (Anglican/Episcopal, Baptist, Jewish, Lutheran,
   Methodist, Mormon, Presbyterian, Reformed, Restorationist, Roman Catholic),
   Theologians, and Religious Thinkers beyond New England and the South

Comparative, Transatlantic, Canadian
 General, Comparative, Continental Europe
 England
 Scotland, Ireland
 Canada

Contexts: Religious, Political, Social, Economic, Intellectual

The bibliography highlights the works that I relied on most directly for this book. By the nature of the case, it must be selective. Secondary scholarship on the themes touched here stretches far in every direction, and so I have focused on works that illuminate theology in its American contexts. In a few instances I include titles for topics, individuals, or traditions that I was simply not able to treat but that would belong in a comprehensive, contextual theological history. I have tried to provide logical categories for the works touching theology most directly, but since the distinction between directly theological works and works providing context for theology is shadowy, there can be no hard-and-fast lines between the sections that follow. My own accounting of general scholarly resources may be pursued in literature surveys prepared for other books, including "Bibliography," in *The Old Religion in a New World: The History of North American Christianity* (Grand Rapids, 2001), 301–28; "Guide to Further Reading," in *American Evangelical Christianity: An Introduction* (Oxford, 2001), 289–308; "Select Bibliography," in *The Princeton Theology, 1812–1921*, 2d ed. (Grand Rapids, 2001), 321–41; and "The Evangelical Surge and the Significance of Religion in the Early United States," in *The State of U.S. History*, ed. Melvyn Stokes (Oxford, 2001), 93–114.

Key Works

Before recording general scholarly indebtedness, I would like to mention several works that materially affected my vision of the book's subjects. It has been some years now since I first read George M. Marsden, *The Evangelical Mind and the New School Presbyterian Experience* (New Haven, 1970); D. H. Meyer, *The Instructed Conscience: The Shaping of the American National Ethic* (Philadelphia, 1972); Henry F. May, *The Enlightenment in America* (New York, 1976); and Norman Fiering, *Jonathan Edwards's Moral Thought and Its British Context* (Chapel Hill, 1981), but these works still remain models, both for serious engagement with important subjects and as stimulating examples of how to treat religious thought in broad historical context. Subsequently I received the same benefit from Bruce Kuklick, *Churchmen and Philosophers from Jonathan Edwards to John Dewey* (New Haven, 1985); James Turner, *Without God, without Creed: The Origins of Unbelief in America* (Baltimore, 1985); Harry Stout, *The New England Soul: Preaching and Religious Culture in Colonial New England* (New York, 1986); Boyd Hilton, *The Age of Atonement: The Influence of Evangelicalism on Social and Economic Thought, 1785–1865* (Oxford, 1988); and several works of Eugene Genovese, including *The Slaveholders' Dilemma: Freedom and Progress in Southern Conservative Thought, 1820–1860* (Columbia, S.C., 1992), and *A Consuming Fire: The Fall of the Confederacy in the Mind of the White Christian South* (Athens, Ga., 1999).

I have also been greatly helped by a slightly different class of books, where ideas are present no less prominently, but where those ideas are observed more directly at work in the rough-and-tumble of social and political history. Among such volumes, it is a privilege to acknowledge an enduring intellectual debt to Robert Wiebe, *The Opening of American Society: From the Adoption of the Constitution to the Era of Disunion* (New York, 1984); Adrian Desmond and James Moore, *Darwin: The Life of a Tormented Evolutionist* (New York, 1991); Gordon S. Wood, *The Radicalism of the American Revolution* (New York, 1992); Richard Carwardine, *Evangelicals and Politics in Antebellum America* (New Haven, 1993); Catherine A. Brekus, *Strangers and Pilgrims, 1740–1845: Female Preaching in America* (Chapel Hill, 1998); and Allen C. Guelzo, *Abraham Lincoln: Redeemer President* (Grand Rapids, 1999).

Not until preparing this bibliography did it become clear how much this book amounts to a footnote, filling in gaps and making very gentle revisions, to two delimited collections that themselves constitute compelling interpretations of American religious and cultural life. The first is the work of Daniel Walker Howe, especially as found in "The Decline of Calvinism: An Approach to Its Study," *Comparative Studies in Society and History* 14 (June 1972): 306–27; *The Unitarian*

Conscience: Harvard Moral Philosophy, 1805–1861 (Cambridge, Mass., 1970); *The Political Culture of the American Whigs* (Chicago, 1979); "The Evangelical Movement and Political Culture in the North during the Second Party System," *Journal of American History* 77 (Mar. 1991): 1216–39; and *Making the American Self: Jonathan Edwards to Abraham Lincoln* (Cambridge, Mass., 1997). The second is a quartet of books by Nathan Hatch and George Marsden, into which my story fits perhaps more neatly than I had intended: Hatch, *The Sacred Cause of Liberty: Republican Thought and the Millennium in Revolutionary New England* (New Haven, 1977); Hatch, *The Democratization of American Christianity* (New Haven, 1989); Marsden, *The Evangelical Mind*; and Marsden, *Fundamentalism and American Culture: The Shaping of Twentieth Century Evangelicalism, 1870–1925* (New York, 1980).

Method

Examples from other historians have provided the most important guidance for how I have tried to write this book, especially where close attention to the moral freight of individual words is combined with careful observation of the social constraints working upon language. Notable examples that have served as models include Mark Pattison, "Tendencies of Religious Thought in England, 1688–1750," in *Essays and Reviews* (London, 1860); Edmund Morgan, introduction to *Puritan Political Ideas, 1558–1794* (Indianapolis, 1965); Bernard Bailyn's discussion "The Contagion of Liberty," in *The Ideological Origins of the American Revolution* (Cambridge, Mass., 1967); and John M. Murrin, "Religion and Politics in America from the First Settlements to the Civil War," in *Religion and American Politics*, ed. Mark A. Noll (New York, 1990).

From historians of political thought, especially Quentin Skinner and J. G. A. Pocock, I have been helped by notions of language, especially their insights concerning the way that patterns of speech reveal competing value systems within a society, the intermingling of concepts between spheres, and the tailoring of languages from one sphere to accomplish tasks in another sphere—for example, J. G. A. Pocock, "The Concept of a Language and the *métier d'historien*," in *The Languages of Political Theory in Early-Modern Europe*, ed. Anthony Pagden (Cambridge, 1987); Pocock, *Politics, Language, and Time* (New York, 1971); and Quentin Skinner, introduction to *The Foundations of Modern Political Thought*, vol. 1, *The Renaissance* (Cambridge, 1978). In much the same way, I have benefited also from sociologist Robert Wuthnow's definition of ideology as not merely objectified language projected from more basic social or economic conditions but a feature of social ordering itself (Wuthnow, *Meaning and Moral Order* [Berkeley, 1987]). Personal conversation with Grant Wacker on how languages from different spheres "bleed" into each other provided a decisive stimulus at an early stage of the project.

Finally, from arguments by missiologists about the nature of Christ's incarnation as genuinely temporal (i.e., human) as well as genuinely eternal (i.e., divine), I have been encouraged to study the cultural history of Christian movements as, at least potentially, both fully contextualized into their settings and yet also resistant to a simple identification with the particularities of one time and place. For such guidance, I am particularly grateful to Andrew Walls, *The Missionary Movement in Christian History: Studies in Transmission of Faith* (Maryknoll, N.Y., 1996); and Lamin Sanneh, *Translating the Message: The Missionary Impact on Culture* (Maryknoll, N.Y., 1989).

Primary Sources and Reference Works

Originally I had hoped to write this book after reading American theological literature comprehensively for the period 1730 to 1865 and also mastering relevant secondary materials for the intellectual, cultural, and political history of the same period. Life proved too much beholden to other responsibilities to fulfill these hopes
with any thoroughness. It has been possible, however, to read extensively in the works
of many of the era's most important religious thinkers, including Isaac Backus, Joseph
Bellamy (and those who took part with Bellamy in disputes over the Half-Way Covenant from 1769 to 1778), Charles Chauncy, Samuel Davies, Jonathan Edwards,
Charles Finney, Charles Hodge (along with Archibald Alexander, Samuel Miller, and
others who published with Hodge in the *Biblical Repertory and Princeton Review*),
Israel Holly, Jonathan Mayhew, Samuel Miller, Edwards Amasa Park (historical
writings), Henry Boynton Smith, Samuel Stanhope Smith, N.W. Taylor, George
Whitefield, and John Witherspoon. Much of the reading in these figures was done
earlier in connection with other projects, especially "Church Membership and the
American Revolution: An Aspect of Religion and Society in New England from the
Revival to the War for Independence" (Ph.D. diss., Vanderbilt University, 1975);
"Jonathan Edwards and Nineteenth-Century Theology," in *Jonathan Edwards and
the American Experience*, ed. Nathan O. Hatch and Harry S. Stout (New York, 1988),
260–87; *Princeton and the Republic, 1768–1822: The Search for Christian Enlightenment in the Era of Samuel Stanhope Smith* (Princeton, 1989); "The Bible and Slav-
ery," in *Religion and the Civil War*, ed. Randall M. Miller, Harry S. Stout, and Charles
Reagan Wilson (New York, 1998), 43–73; and *The Princeton Theology, 1812–1921:
Scripture, Science, and Theological Method from Archibald Alexander to Benjamin
Warfield*, 2d ed. (Grand Rapids, 2001). Yet in almost every case, research for this
book also pushed me further into the publications of these authors. For a few of them,
I have also been able to do the sort of archival research that a truly comprehensive
book would require for all the major theologians.

Disappointment about work undone is sharpest for another group of figures
whose writings I have been able to sample in some detail but not digest with anything
like the attention they deserve: Richard Allen, Francis Asbury, Robert Baird, Nathan
Bangs, Catharine Beecher, Henry Ward Beecher, William G. Brownlow, Orestes
Brownson, Horace Bushnell, Alexander Campbell, John Carroll, William Ellery
Channing, Robert Dabney, James Dana, Jonathan Dickinson, Timothy Dwight,
Jonathan Edwards Jr., Nathanael Emmons, Wilbur Fisk, David George, J. R. Graves,
Lemuel Haynes, J. H. C. Helmuth, John Henry Hobart, Samuel Hopkins, John
Ireland, Samuel Johnson, John Leland, James Marsh, Cotton Mather, John
Williamson Nevin, Tom Paine, Phoebe Palmer, Daniel Alexander Payne, Frederick
Henry Quitman, Philip Schaff, Samuel Schmucker, Harriet Beecher Stowe, Moses
Stuart, Gilbert Tennent, J. H. Thornwell, Francis Wayland, Daniel Whedon, and
John Woolman. These two sets of authors contributed the main primary sources on
which this book rests. I am very pleased to note that a forthcoming book by E. Brooks
Holifield will provide a comprehensive treatment of theology in early America,
including many of the figures mentioned here.

Many modern editions of printed primary sources have been especially helpful,
but I must draw attention to two sets of documents that are in a supernal class of their
own for students of early American theology. They are *The Works of Jonathan
Edwards* (New Haven, 1957–), a project superbly guided, in succession, by Perry

Miller, John E. Smith, and Harry S. Stout; and the thirty-two-volume reprint series edited by Bruce Kuklick, American Religious Thought of the Eighteenth and Nineteenth Centuries (New York, 1987). The gray- and blue-clad books of these editions have stood watch as sentinels (when they were not being recruited for more active combat) over the desk at which I wrote almost all of this volume. Without them the book would never have been completed.

For a scholar working from the Midwest on American history before the Civil War, reference works and modern editions are essential. Listed below are modern editions of primary sources and reference works that have been of great usefulness. Sometimes the introductions and notes to the documentary collections, as well as articles in the reference works, constitute the most perceptive scholarship available on their subjects.

Modern Collections or Editions of Sources

Adams, Dickinson W., ed. *Jefferson's Extracts from the Gospels*. The Papers of Thomas Jefferson, 2d ser. Princeton, 1983.

Ahlstrom, Sydney E., ed. *Theology in America: The Major Protestant Voices from Puritanism to Neo-Orthodoxy*. Indianapolis, 1967.

Ahlstrom, Sydney E., and Jonathan S. Carey, eds. *An American Reformation: A Documentary History of Unitarian Christianity*. Middletown, Conn., 1985.

Appleby, Joyce., ed. *Recollections of the Early Republic: Selected Autobiographies*. Boston, 1997.

Armstrong, Maurice W., Lefferts A. Loetscher, and Charles A. Anderson, eds. *The Presbyterian Enterprise: Sources of American Presbyterian History*. Philadelphia, 1956.

Bailyn, Bernard, ed. *The Debate on the Constitution*. 2 vols. New York, 1993.

Bontemps, Arna, ed. *Five Black Lives*. Middletown, Conn., 1971.

Boudinot, J. J., ed. *The Life, Public Services, Addresses, and Letters of Elias Boudinot*. 2 vols. New York, 1971 (orig. 1896).

Bratt, James D., ed. *Abraham Kuyper: A Centennial Reader*. Grand Rapids, 1998.

Bushman, Richard L., ed. *The Great Awakening: Documents on the Revival of Religion, 1740–1745*. New York, 1969.

Butterfield, L. H. , ed. *Letters of Benjamin Rush*. 2 vols. Princeton, 1951.

Carey, Patrick W., ed. *American Catholic Religious Thought*. New York, 1987.

Cherry, Conrad, ed. *God's New Israel: Religious Interpretations of American Culture*. 2d ed. Chapel Hill, 1998.

Chesebrough, David B., ed. *God Ordained This War: Sermons on the Sectional Crisis, 1830–1865*. Columbia, S.C., 1991.

Clark, Elmer T., ed. *The Journals and Letters of Francis Asbury*. 3 vols. Nashville, 1958.

Cross, Barbara M., ed. *The Autobiography of Lyman Beecher*. 2 vols. Cambridge, Mass., 1961.

Dillenberger, John, et al., eds. A Library of Protestant Thought. New York, 1964–. Including:

- *Horace Bushnell*. Ed. H. Shelton Smith. 1965.
- *Lutheran Confessional Theology*. Ed. Theodore G. Tappert. 1972.
- *The Mercersburg Theology* [Nevin, Schaff]. Ed. James H. Nichols. 1966.
- *John Woolman*. Ed. Phillips P. Moulton. 1971.

Farina, John, ed. Sources of American Spirituality. Mahwah, N.J., 1984–. Including:

- *American Jesuits*. Ed. Robert Emmett Curran, S.J. 1988.
- *Orestes Brownson*. Ed. Patrick W. Carey. 1991.
- *Horace Bushnell*. Ed. Conrad Cherry. 1985.
- *William Ellery Channing*. Ed. David Robinson. 1985.
- *Charles Hodge*. Ed. Mark A. Noll. 1987.
- *Phoebe Palmer*. Ed. Thomas Oden. 1988.

George, Timothy, and Denise George, eds. *Baptist Confessions, Covenants, and Catechisms*. Nashville, 1996.

Heimert, Alan, and Andrew Delbanco, eds. *The Puritans in America: A Narrative Anthology*. Cambridge, Mass., 1985.

Heimert, Alan, and Perry Miller, eds. *The Great Awakening: Documents Illustrating the Crisis and Its Consequences*. Indianapolis, 1967.

Houchins, Sue E., ed. *Spiritual Narratives* [Maria Stewart, 1835; Jarena Lee, 1849; Julia Foote, 1886; Virginia Broughton, 1907]. The Schomburg Library of Nineteenth-Century Black Women Writers. New York, 1988.

Jacobson, David L., ed. *The English Libertarian Heritage: From the Writings of John Trenchard and Thomas Gordon in The Independent Whig and Cato's Letters*. Indianapolis, 1965.

Kimnach, Wilson H., Kenneth P. Minkema, and Douglas A. Sweeney, eds. *The Sermons of Jonathan Edwards: A Reader*. New Haven, 1999.

Klein, Milton M., ed. *The Independent Reflector . . . By William Livingston and Others*. Cambridge, Mass., 1963.

Kuklick, Bruce, ed. American Religious Thought of the Eighteenth and Nineteenth Centuries. 32 vols. New York, 1987.

———. *Paine: Political Writings*. New York, 1989.

Kurland, Philip B., and Ralph Lerner, eds. *The Founders' Constitution*. 5 vols. Chicago, 1987.

Langford, Thomas, ed. *Wesleyan Theology: A Sourcebook*. Durham, 1984.

McLoughlin, William G., ed. *Isaac Backus on Church, State, and Calvinism: Pamphlets, 1754–1789*. Cambridge, Mass., 1968.

———, ed. *Lectures on Revivals of Religion by Charles G. Finney*. Cambridge, Mass., 1960.

MacMaster, Richard K., ed. *Conscience in Crisis: Mennonites and Other Peace Churches in America, 1739–1789*. Scottdale, Pa., 1979.

Meyers, Marvin, ed. *The Mind of the Founder: Sources of the Political Thought of James Madison*. Hanover, N.H., 1981.

Miller, Perry, and Thomas H. Johnson, eds. *The Puritans: A Sourcebook of Their Writings*. 2 vols. 2d ed. New York, 1963.

Miller, Perry E., John E. Smith, and Harry S. Stout, general eds. *The Works of Jonathan Edwards*. New Haven, 1957–.

Morgan, Edmund S., ed. *Puritan Political Ideas, 1558–1794*. Indianapolis, 1965.

Newman, Richard, ed. *Black Preacher to White America: The Collected Writings of Lemuel Haynes, 1774–1833*. Brooklyn, 1990.

Noll, Mark A., and David N. Livingstone, eds. *Charles Hodge's What Is Darwinism?* Grand Rapids, 1994.

Powell, Milton B., ed. *The Voluntary Church: American Religious Life, 1740–1860, Seen through the Eyes of European Visitors*. New York, 1967.

Rawlyk, George A., ed. *New Light Letters and Songs*. Hantsport, Nova Scotia, 1983.

————. *The Sermons of Henry Alline*. Hantsport, Nova Scotia, 1986.

Rosell, Garth M., and Richard A. G. Dupuis, eds. *The Memoirs of Charles G. Finney: The Complete Restored Text*. Grand Rapids, 1989.

Sandoz, Ellis, ed. *Political Sermons of the American Founding Era, 1730–1805*. 2d ed. Indianapolis, 1998.

Sarna, Jonathan D., and David G. Dalin, eds. *Religion and State in the American Jewish Experience*. Notre Dame, Ind., 1997.

Schneider, Wallace, and Carol Schneider, eds. *Samuel Johnson: His Career and Writings*. 4 vols. New York, 1929.

Scott, Jack, ed. *An Annotated Edition of Lectures on Moral Philosophy by John Witherspoon*. Newark, Del., 1982.

Sernett, Milton C., ed. *Afro-American Religious History: A Documentary Witness*. Durham, 1985.

Simpson, Robert Drew, ed. *American Methodist Pioneer: The Life and Journals of the Rev. Freeborn Garrettson, 1752–1827*. Rutland, Vt., 1984.

Smith, Hilrie Shelton, Robert T. Handy, and Lefferts A. Loetscher, eds. *American Christianity: An Historical Interpretation with Representative Documents*. 2 vols. New York, 1960.

Smith, John E., Harry S. Stout, and Kenneth P. Minkema, eds. *A Jonathan Edwards Reader*. New Haven, 1995.

Solberg, Winton U., ed. *The Christian Philosopher, by Cotton Mather*. Champaign, Ill., 1994.

Tappert, Theodore G., and John W. Doberstein, eds. *The Journals of Henry Melchior Mühlenberg*. 2 vols. Philadelphia, 1945.

Toulouse, Mark G., and James O. Duke, eds. *Sources of Christian Theology in America*. Nashville, 1999.

Walker, Williston, ed. *The Creeds and Platforms of Congregationalism*. Boston, 1991 (orig. 1893).

Walters, Kerry S., ed. *The American Deists*. Lawrence, Kans., 1992.

Wilson, John F., and Donald L. Drakeman, eds. *Church and State in American History*. 2d ed. Boston, 1987.

Zanca, Kenneth J., ed. *American Catholics and Slavery, 1789–1866: An Anthology of Primary Documents*. Lanham, Md., 1994.

Reference Works

Albaugh, Gaylord P. *History and Annotated Bibliography of American Religious Periodicals and Newspapers Established from 1730 through 1830*. 2 vols. Worcester, Mass., 1994.

Carey, Patrick W. *Orestes A. Brownson: A Bibliography, 1826–1876*. Milwaukee, 1996.

Edwards, Paul, ed. *The Encyclopedia of Philosophy*. 8 vols. New York, 1967.

Fox, Richard Wightman, and James T. Kloppenberg, eds. *A Companion to American Thought*. Cambridge, Mass., 1995.

Garretty, John A., and Mark C. Carnes, eds. *American National Biography*. 24 vols. New York, 1999.

Gaustad, Edwin Scott. *Historical Atlas of Religion in America*. Rev. ed. New York, 1976.

Gaustad, Edwin Scott, and Philip L. Barlow. *New Historical Atlas of Religion in America*. New York, 2001.

Hart, D. G., ed. *Dictionary of the Presbyterian and Reformed Tradition in America*. Downers Grove, Ill., 1999.

Hill, Samuel S., ed. *Encyclopedia of Religion in the South.* Macon, Ga., 1984.

Johnson, Thomas H. *The Printed Writings of Jonathan Edwards, 1703–1758: A Bibliography.* Princeton, 1940.

Lesser, M. X. *Jonathan Edwards: An Annotated Bibliography, 1979–1993.* Westport, Conn., 1994.

———. *Jonathan Edwards: A Reference Guide.* Boston, 1981.

Lewis, Donald M., ed. *Blackwell Encyclopedia of Evangelical Biography.* 2 vols. Oxford, 1995.

Lippy, Charles H., and Peter W. Williams, eds. *Encyclopedia of the American Religious Experience.* 3 vols. New York, 1988.

McLachlan, James, et al., eds. *Princetonians: A Biographical Dictionary.* 5 vols. Princeton, 1976–91.

Reid, Daniel G., et al., eds. *Dictionary of Christianity in America.* Downers Grove, Ill., 1990.

Sprague, William B. *Annals of the American Pulpit.* 9 vols. New York, 1857–69.

Trinterud, Leonard J. *A Bibliography of Colonial American Presbyterianism during the Colonial Period.* Philadelphia, 1968.

Wilson, John F., ed. *Church and State in America: A Bibliographical Guide.* 2 vols. Westport, Conn., 1986–87.

American Theological History

The categories for the works that follow are somewhat arbitrary, but they reflect the fact that for New England and the South there are much richer traditions of scholarship on theology and theologically related subjects than for other American regions.

Theology (Including the Bible)—General

Adamson, Christopher. "Wrath and Redemption: Protestant Theology and Penal Practice in the Early American Republic." *Criminal Justice History* 13 (1992): 75–111.

Ahlstrom, Sydney E. "The Scottish Philosophy and American Theology." *Church History* 24 (1955): 257–72.

———. "Theology in America: A Historical Survey." In *Religious Perspectives in American Culture,* ed. A. Leland Jamison and John E. Smith. Princeton, 1961.

Bozeman, Theodore Dwight. *Protestants in an Age of Science: The Baconian Ideal and Antebellum Religious Thought.* Chapel Hill, 1977.

Brown, Jerry Wayne. *The Rise of Biblical Criticism in America, 1800–1870: The New England Scholars.* Middletown, Conn., 1969.

Cashdollar, Charles D. *The Transformation of Theology, 1830–1890: Positivism and Protestant Thought in Britain and America.* Princeton, 1989.

Chesebrough, David B. *"No Sorrow like Our Sorrow": Northern Protestant Ministers and the Assassination of Lincoln.* Kent, Ohio, 1994.

Grosjean, Paul Eugene. "The Concept of American Nationhood: Theological Interpretation as Reflected by the Northern Mainline Protestant Preachers in the Late Civil War Period." Ph.D. diss., Drew University, 1977.

Gutjahr, Paul C. *An American Bible: A History of the Good Book in the United States, 1777–1880.* Stanford, 1999.

Hart, D. G. "Divided between Heart and Mind: The Critical Period for Protestant Theology in America." *Journal of Ecclesiastical History* 38 (Apr. 1987): 254–70.

———. "Poems, Propositions, and Dogma: The Controversy over Religious Language and the Demise of Theology in American Learning." *Church History* 57 (Sept. 1988): 310–21.

Hatch, Nathan O., and Mark A. Noll, eds. *The Bible in America*. New York, 1982.

Hirrel, Leo P. *Children of Wrath: New School Calvinism and Antebellum Reform.* Lexington, Ky., 1998.

Hood, Fred J. *Reformed America: The Middle and Southern States, 1783–1837.* University, Ala., 1980.

Howe, Daniel Walker. "The Decline of Calvinism: An Approach to Its Study." *Comparative Studies in Society and History* 14 (June 1972): 306–27.

Hughes, Richard T., ed. *The American Quest for the Primitive Church*. Urbana, Ill., 1988.

Jenkins, Thomas E. *The Character of God: Recovering the Lost Literary Power of American Protestantism*. New York, 1997.

Niebuhr, H. Richard. *The Kingdom of God in America*. New York, 1959 (orig. 1937).

Noll, Mark A. "The Bible in Revolutionary America." In *The Bible in American Law, Politics, and Political Rhetoric*, ed. James Turner Johnson. Philadelphia, 1985.

———. "Common Sense Traditions and American Evangelical Thought." *American Quarterly* 37 (1985): 220–25.

———. "The Rise and Long Life of the Protestant Enlightenment in America." In *Knowledge and Belief in America: Enlightenment Traditions and Modern Religious Thought*, ed. William M. Shea and Peter A. Huff. New York, 1995.

Pals, Daniel L. "Several Christologies of the Great Awakening." *Anglican Theological Review* 72 (Fall 1990): 412–27.

Reid-Maroney, Nina. *Philadelphia's Enlightenment, 1740–1800: Kingdom of Christ, Empire of Reason*. Westport, Conn., 2001.

Shea, William M., and Peter A. Huff, eds. *Knowledge and Belief in America: Enlightenment Traditions and Modern Religious Thought*. New York, 1995.

Smith, H. Shelton. *Changing Conceptions of Original Sin: A Study in American Theology since 1750*. New York, 1955.

Toulouse, Mark G., and James O. Duke, eds. *Makers of Christian Theology in America*. Nashville, 1997.

Walters, Kerry S. *Rational Infidels: The American Deists*. Durango, Colo., 1992.

Ward, Patricia A. "Madame Guyon and Experiential Theology in America." *Church History* 67 (Spring 1998): 484–98.

Wells, David F. "Orthodoxy on the Cross: The Debate over the Atonement in Nineteenth-Century American Theology." *Bibliotheca Sacra* 144 (Apr.–June 1987): 123–43; (July–Sept. 1987): 243–53; (Oct.–Dec. 1987): 363–76; 145 (Jan.–Mar. 1988): 3–14.

Wenzel, August. "Theological Implications of the Civil War." Mimeograph, Garrett Theological Seminary Library, Evanston, Ill., 1971.

Theology in New England

Akers, Charles W. *Called unto Liberty: A Life of Jonathan Mayhew, 1720–1766*. Cambridge, Mass., 1964.

Alexis, Gerhard T. "Jonathan Edwards and the Theocratic Ideal." *Church History* 25 (Sept. 1966): 328–43.

Anderson, Glenn Paul. "Joseph Bellamy (1719–1790): The Man and His Work." Ph.D. diss., Boston University, 1971.

Boardman, George Nye. *A History of New England Theology*. New York, 1899.

Bozeman, Theodore Dwight. *To Live Ancient Lives: The Primitivist Dimension in Puritanism*. Chapel Hill, 1988.

Breen, T. H. *The Character of the Good Ruler: Puritan Political Ideas in New England, 1630–1730*. New Haven, 1970.

Breitenbach, William. "Unregenerate Doings: Selflessness and Selfishness in New Divinity Theology." *American Quarterly* 34 (1982): 479–502.

Bushman, Richard L. *From Puritan to Yankee: Character and the Social Order in Connecticut, 1690–1765*. Cambridge, Mass., 1967.

Caskey, Marie. *Chariot of Fire: Religion and the Beecher Family*. New Haven, 1978.

Cherry, Conrad. *Nature and Religious Imagination: From Edwards to Bushnell*. Philadelphia, 1980.

———. *The Theology of Jonathan Edwards: A Reappraisal*. Garden City, N.Y., 1966.

Cohen, Charles L. *God's Caress: The Psychology of Puritan Religious Experience*. New York, 1986.

Conforti, Joseph A. *Jonathan Edwards, Religious Tradition, and American Culture*. Chapel Hill, 1995.

———. *Samuel Hopkins and the New Divinity Movement*. Grand Rapids, 1981.

Corrigan, John. *The Hidden Balance: Religion and the Social Theories of Charles Chauncy and Jonathan Mayhew*. New York, 1987.

———. *The Prism of Piety: Catholick Congregational Clergy at the Beginning of the Eighteenth Century*. New York, 1991.

DeJong, Peter Y. *The Covenant Idea in New England Theology, 1620–1847*. Grand Rapids, 1945.

Fiering, Norman. *Jonathan Edwards's Moral Thought and Its British Context*. Chapel Hill, 1981.

Fitzmier, John R. *New England's Moral Legislator: Timothy Dwight, 1752–1817*. Bloomington, Ind., 1998.

Foster, Charles H. *The Rungless Ladder: Harriet Beecher Stowe and New England Puritanism*. Durham, 1954.

Foster, Frank Hugh. *A Genetic History of the New England Theology*. Chicago, 1907.

Foster, Stephen. *The Long Argument: English Puritanism and the Shaping of New England Culture, 1570–1700*. Chapel Hill, 1991.

Giltner, John H. *Moses Stuart: The Father of Biblical Science in America*. Atlanta, 1988.

Goen, C. C. *Revivalism and Separatism in New England, 1740–1800*. New Haven, 1962.

Granquist, Mark. "The Role of 'Common Sense' in the Hermeneutics of Moses Stuart." *Harvard Theological Review* 83 (1990): 305–19.

Grasso, Christopher. *A Speaking Aristocracy: Transforming Public Discourse in Eighteenth-Century Connecticut*. Chapel Hill, 1999.

Griffin, Edward M. *Old Brick: Charles Chauncy of Boston, 1705–1787*. Minneapolis, 1980.

Guelzo, Allen C. *Edwards on the Will: A Century of American Theological Debate*. Middletown, Conn. 1989.

———. "From Calvinist Metaphysics to Republican Theory: Jonathan Edwards and James Dana on Freedom of the Will." *Journal of the History of Ideas* 56 (July 1995): 413–18.

————. "Oberlin Perfectionism and Its Edwardsian Origins, 1835–1870." In *Jonathan Edwards's Writings: Text, Context, Interpretation*, ed. Stephen J. Stein. Bloomington, Ind., 1996.

Guelzo, Allen C., and Sang Hyun Lee, eds. *Edwards in Our Time: Jonathan Edwards and the Shaping of American Religion*. Grand Rapids, 1999.

Hambrick-Stowe, Charles E. *The Practice of Piety; Puritan Devotional Disciplines in Seventeenth-Century New England*. Chapel Hill, 1982.

————. "The Spirit of the Old Writers: The Great Awakening and the Persistence of Puritan Piety." In *Puritanism: Transatlantic Perspectives on a Seventeenth-Century Anglo-American Faith*, ed. Francis J. Bremer. Boston, 1993.

Haroutunian, Joseph. *Piety versus Moralism: The Passing of the New England Theology*. New York, 1932.

Hatch, Nathan O., and Harry S. Stout, eds. *Jonathan Edwards and the American Experience*. New York, 1988.

Hedrick, Joan D. *Harriet Beecher Stowe: A Life*. New York, 1994.

Hoopes, James. *Consciousness in New England: From Puritanism and Ideas to Psychoanalysis and Semiotic*. Baltimore, 1989.

Howe, Daniel Walker. "The Social Science of Horace Bushnell." *Journal of American History* 70 (Sept. 1983): 305–22.

————. *The Unitarian Conscience: Harvard Moral Philosophy, 1805–1861*. Cambridge, Mass., 1970.

Jenson, Robert. *America's Theologian: A Recommendation of Jonathan Edwards*. New York, 1988.

Johnson, Beth Anne. "The Grand Question of Life: An Analysis of the Relationship between Religion and Education in the Life and Thought of Catharine Beecher." M.A. thesis, Wheaton College Graduate School, 2000.

Kling, David W. *A Field of Divine Wonders: The New Divinity and Village Revivals in Northwestern Connecticut, 1792–1822*. University Park, Pa., 1993.

Lovelace, Richard F. *The American Pietism of Cotton Mather: Origins of American Evangelicalism*. Grand Rapids, 1979.

Lowrie, Ernest Benson. *The Shape of the Puritan Mind: The Thought of Samuel Willard*. New Haven, 1974.

Marini, Stephen A. *Radical Sects in Revolutionary New England*. Cambridge, Mass., 1982.

McDermott, Gerald. *One Holy and Happy Society: The Public Theology of Jonathan Edwards*. University Park, Pa., 1992.

McGiffert, Michael. "From Moses to Adam: The Making of the Covenant of Works, 1585–1615." *Sixteenth Century Journal* 19 (1988): 131–55.

————. "Grace and Works: The Rise and Division of Covenant Divinity in Elizabethan Puritanism." *Harvard Theological Review* 75 (Oct. 1982): 463–502.

————. "The Perkinsian Moment of Federal Theology." *Calvin Theological Journal* 29 (Apr. 1994): 117–48.

McLoughlin, William G. *New England Dissent, 1630–1833: The Baptists and the Separation of Church and State*. 2 vols. Cambridge, Mass., 1971.

May, Henry F., ed. *Harriet Beecher Stowe, Oldtown Folks*. Cambridge, Mass., 1966.

Mead, Sidney. *Nathaniel William Taylor, 1786–1858: A Connecticut Liberal*. Chicago, 1942.

Miller, Perry. *Jonathan Edwards*. New York, 1949.

————. *The New England Mind*. 2 vols. New York, 1939; Cambridge, Mass., 1953.

Morgan, Edmund S. *The Gentle Puritan: A Life of Ezra Stiles, 1727–1795*. Chapel Hill, 1962.

———. *Visible Saints: The History of a Puritan Idea*. New York, 1963.

Moss, Richard J. *The Life of Jedidiah Morse: A Station of Peculiar Exposure*. Knoxville, 1995.

Murray, Iain. *Jonathan Edwards*. Edinburgh, 1987.

Noll, Mark A. "Moses Mather (Old Calvinist) and the Evolution of Edwardseanism." *Church History* 49 (1980): 273–86.

Pope, Earl A. "The Rise of the New Haven Theology." *Journal of Presbyterian History* 44 (Mar. 1966): 24–44; (June 1966): 106–21.

Pope, Robert G. *The Half-Way Covenant: Church Membership in Puritan New England*. Princeton, 1969.

Rohrer, James R. *Keepers of the Covenant: Frontier Missions and the Decline of Congregationalism, 1774–1818*. New York, 1995.

Saillant, John. "A Doctrinal Controversy between the Hopkintonian [Lemuel Haynes] and the Universalist [Hosea Ballou]." *Vermont Historical Review* 61 (Fall 1993): 177–216.

———. "Slavery and Divine Providence in New England Calvinism: The New Divinity and a Black Protest, 1775–1805." *New England Quarterly* 68 (1994): 584–608.

Sklar, Kathryn Kish. *Catharine Beecher: A Study in American Domesticity*. New Haven, 1973.

Snyder, K. Alan. "Foundations of Liberty: The Christian Republicanism of Timothy Dwight and Jedidiah Morse." *New England Quarterly* 56 (1983): 382–97.

Stauffer, Vernon. *New England and the Bavarian Illuminati*. New York, 1918.

Stein, Stephen J., ed. *Jonathan Edwards: Texts and Contexts*. Bloomington, Ind., 1996.

Stoever, William K. B. *"A Faire and Easie Way to Heaven": Covenant Theology and Antinomianism in Early Massachusetts*. Middletown, Conn., 1978.

Stout, Harry S. *The New England Soul: Preaching and Religious Culture in Colonial New England*. New York, 1986.

Stowe, Harriet Beecher. *The Minister's Wooing*. New York, 1859.

———. *Oldtown Folks*. New York, 1869.

Sutton, William R. "Benevolent Calvinism and the Moral Government of God: The Influence of Nathaniel W. Taylor on Revivalism in the Second Great Awakening." *Religion and American Culture* 2 (Winter 1992): 23–48.

Sweeney, Douglas A. "Edwards and His Mantle: The Historiography of the New England Theology." *New England Quarterly* 71 (1998): 97–119.

———. "Nathaniel William Taylor and the Edwardsian Tradition: Evolution and Continuity in the Culture of the New England Theology." Ph.D. diss., Vanderbilt University, 1995.

Thomas, John L. *The Liberator: William Lloyd Garrison*. Boston, 1963.

Tracy, Patricia J. *Jonathan Edwards, Pastor: Religion and Society in Eighteenth-Century Northampton*. New York, 1979.

Valeri, Mark. "The Economic Thought of Jonathan Edwards." *Church History* 60 (Mar. 1991): 37–54.

———. *Law and Providence in Joseph Bellamy's New England: The Origins of the New Divinity in Revolutionary America*. New York, 1994.

———. "The New Divinity and the American Revolution." *William and Mary Quarterly* 46 (1989): 741–69.

Van Dyken, Seymour. *Samuel Willard: Preacher of Orthodoxy in an Era of Change*. Grand Rapids, 1972.

Walsh, James P. "Solomon Stoddard's Open Communion: A Reexamination." *New England Quarterly* 43 (1970): 97–114.

Weber, Donald. *Rhetoric and History in Revolutionary New England*. New York, 1988.

Whittemore, Robert C. *The Transformation of the New England Theology*. New York, 1987.

Wilson, Robert J. *The Benevolent Deity: Ebenezer Gay and the Rise of Rational Religion in New England, 1696–1787*. Philadelphia, 1984.

Woods, Leonard. *History of the Andover Theological Seminary*. Boston, 1885.

Wright, Conrad. *The Beginnings of Unitarianism in America*. Boston, 1955.

Youngs, J. William T., Jr. *The Congregationalists*. Westport, Conn., 1998.

———. *God's Messengers: Religious Leadership in Colonial New England, 1700–1750*. Baltimore, 1976.

Theology in the South, Including African Americans, and the Bible and Slavery

Berends, Kurt O. "'Thus Saith the Lord': The Use of the Bible by Southern Evangelicals in the Era of the American Civil War." D.Phil. diss., Oxford University, 1997.

Blight, David W. *Frederick Douglass' Civil War: Keeping Faith in Jubilee*. Baton Rouge, La. 1989.

Boles, John S. *The Great Revival: Beginnings of the Bible Belt*. 2d ed. Lexington, Ky., 1996.

Calhoon, Robert M. *Evangelicals and Conservatives in the Early South, 1740–1861*. Columbia, S.C., 1988.

Cornelius, Janet Duitsman. *When I Can Read My Title Clear: Literacy, Slavery, and Religion in the Antebellum South*. Columbia. S.C., 1992.

Davis, David Brion. *The Problem of Slavery in the Age of Revolution, 1770–1823*. 2d ed. New York, 1999.

———. *Slavery and Human Progress*. New York, 1984.

Douglass, Frederick. *Narrative of the Life of Frederick Douglass*. Many editions, including New York, 1997.

Epstein, Dena J. *Sinful Tunes and Spirituals: Black Folk Music to the Civil War*. Urbana, Ill., 1977.

Essig, James. *The Bonds of Wickedness: American Evangelicals against Slavery, 1770–1808*. Philadelphia, 1982.

Farmer, James Oscar, Jr. *The Metaphysical Confederacy: James Henley Thornwell and the Synthesis of Southern Values*. Macon, Ga., 1986.

Faust, Drew Gilpin. *The Creation of Confederate Nationalism: Ideology and Identity in the Civil War South*. Baton Rouge, La., 1988.

———. "Evangelicalism and the Meaning of the Proslavery Argument: The Reverend Thornton Stringfellow of Virginia." *Virginia Magazine of History and Biography* 85 (Jan. 1977): 3–17.

———. *A Sacred Circle: The Dilemma of the Intellectual in the Old South, 1840–1860*. Baltimore, 1977.

Felder, Cain Hope, ed. *Stony the Road We Trod: African American Biblical Interpretation*. Philadelphia, 1991.

Foster, Gaines M. *Ghosts of the Confederacy: Defeat, the Lost Cause, and the Emergence of the New South, 1865–1913*. New York, 1987.

———. "Guilt over Slavery: A Historiographical Analysis." *Journal of Southern History* 56 (1989): 665–94.

Fox-Genovese, Elizabeth. *To Be Worthy of God's Favor: Southern Women's Defense and Critique of Slavery.* Fortenbaugh Memorial Lecture. Gettysburg, Pa., 1993.

Fox-Genovese, Elizabeth, and Eugene D. Genovese. "The Divine Sanction of Social Order: Religious Foundations of the Southern Slaveholders' World View." *Journal of the American Academy of Religion* 55 (Summer 1987): 211–33.

Freehling, William W. "James Henley Thornwell's Mysterious Antislavery Moment." *Journal of Southern History* 57 (Aug. 1991): 383–406.

Frey, Sylvia R. *Water from the Rock: Black Resistance in a Revolutionary Age.* Princeton, 1991.

Frey, Sylvia R., and Betty Wood. *Come Shouting to Zion: African American Protestantism in the American South and British Caribbean to 1830.* Chapel Hill, 1998.

Genovese, Eugene D. *A Consuming Fire: The Fall of the Confederacy in the Mind of the White Christian South.* Athens, Ga., 1999.

———. *Roll, Jordan, Roll: The World the Slaves Made.* New York, 1972.

———. *The Slaveholders' Dilemma: Freedom and Progress in Southern Conservative Thought, 1820–1860.* Columbia, S.C., 1992.

———. *"Slavery Ordained of God": The Southern Slaveholders' View of Biblical History and Modern Politics.* Fortenbaugh Memorial Lecture. Gettysburg, Pa., 1985.

Genovese, Eugene D., and Elizabeth Fox-Genovese, "The Religious Ideals of Southern Slave Society." *Georgia Historical Quarterly* 70 (Spring 1986): 1–14.

Goen, C. C. *Broken Churches, Broken Nation: Denominational Schisms and the Coming of the Civil War.* Macon, Ga., 1985.

Gordon, Grant. *The Life of David George: Pioneer Black Baptist Minister.* Hantsport, Nova Scotia, 1992.

Harrill, Albert. "The Use of the New Testament in the American Slave Controversy: A Case History in the Hermeneutical Tension between Biblical Criticism and Christian Moral Debate." *Religion and American Culture* 10 (Summer 2000): 149–86.

Haynes, Stephen R. *Noah's Curse: The Biblical Justification of American Slavery.* New York, 2002.

Holifield, E. Brooks. *The Gentlemen Theologians: American Theology in Southern Culture, 1795–1860.* Durham, 1978.

Leith, John H. "James Henley Thornwell and the Shaping of the Reformed Tradition in the South." In *Probing the Reformed Tradition*, ed. Elsie Anne McKee and Brian G. Armstrong. Louisville, 1989.

Loveland, Anne C. *Southern Evangelicals and the Social Order, 1800–1860.* Baton Rouge, La., 1980.

McKivigan, John R. *The War against Proslavery Religion: Abolitionism and the Northern Churches, 1830–1865.* Ithaca, 1984.

McKivigan, John R., and Mitchell Snay, eds. *Religion and the Antebellum Debate over Slavery.* Athens, Ga., 1998.

Maddex, Jack P., Jr. "'The Southern Apostasy' Revisited: The Significance of Proslavery Christianity." *Marxist Perspectives* 7 (1979): 132–41.

Mathews, Donald G. *Religion in the Old South.* Chicago, 1977.

———. *Slavery and Methodism: A Chapter in American Morality, 1780–1845.* Princeton, 1965.

Mullin, Robert Bruce. "Biblical Critics and the Battle over Slavery." *Journal of Presbyterian History* 61 (Summer 1983): 210–26.

O'Brien, Michael. "Calvinism and Intellectual Modernity: James Henley Thornwell's Theology." Unpublished paper, Southern Historical Society, Bloomington, Ind., Spring 2001.

Peterson, Thomas Virgil. *Ham and Japheth: The Mythic World of Whites in the Antebellum South.* Metuchen, N.J., 1978.

Raboteau, Albert J. *Slave Religion: The "Invisible Institution" in the Antebellum South.* New York, 1978.

Scherer, Lester B. *Slavery and the Churches in Early America, 1619–1819.* Grand Rapids, 1975.

Shattuck, Gardiner H., Jr. *A Shield and Hiding Place: The Religious Life of the Civil War Armies.* Macon, Ga., 1987.

Silver, James W. *Confederate Morale and Church Propaganda.* Tuscaloosa, Ala., 1957.

Smith, Morton. *Studies in Southern Presbyterian Theology.* Phillipsburg, N.J., 1962.

Smith, Timothy L. "Slavery and Theology: The Emergence of Black Christian Consciousness in Nineteenth-Century America." *Church History* 46 (Dec. 1972): 497–512.

Snay, Mitchell. *Gospel of Disunion: Religion and Separatism in the Antebellum South.* New York, 1993.

Sobel, Mechal. *Trabelin' On: The Slave Journey to an Afro-Baptist Faith.* Westport, Conn., 1979.

———. *The World They Made Together: Black and White Values in Eighteenth-Century Virginia.* Princeton, 1987.

Startup, Kenneth. *The Root of All Evil: The Protestant Clergy and the Economic Mind of the South.* Athens, Ga., 1997.

Tise, Larry E. *Proslavery: A History of the Defense of Slavery in America, 1701–1840.* Athens, Ga., 1987.

Whitlock, Luder G., Jr. "James Henley Thornwell." In *Southern Reformed Theology,* ed. David F. Wells. Grand Rapids, 1989.

Wilson, Charles Reagan. *Baptized in Blood: The Religion of the Lost Cause, 1865–1920.* Athens, Ga., 1980.

Wimbush, Vincent L. "The Bible and African Americans: An Outline of an Interpretive History." In *Stony the Road We Trod: African American Biblical Interpretation,* ed. Cain Hope Felder. Minneapolis, 1991.

Wyatt-Brown, Bertram. *Southern Honor: Ethics and Behavior in the Old South.* New York, 1982.

Other Theological Traditions (Anglican/Episcopal, Baptist, Jewish, Lutheran, Methodist, Mormon, Presbyterian, Reformed, Restorationist, Roman Catholic), Theologians, and Religious Thinkers beyond New England and the South

Abzug, Robert H. *Passionate Liberator: Theodore Dwight Weld and the Dilemma of Reform.* New York, 1980.

Allen, C. Leonard. "Baconianism and the Bible in the Disciples of Christ: James S. Lamar and 'The Organon of Scripture.'" *Church History* 55 (1986): 65–80.

Andrews, Dee E. *The Methodists and Revolutionary America, 1760–1800: The Shaping of an Evangelical Culture.* Princeton, 2000.

Baglyos, Paul A. "In This Land of Liberty: American Lutherans and the Young Republic, 1787–1837." Ph.D. diss., University of Chicago, 1997.

Baker, Frank. "The Doctrines in the Discipline." In *From Wesley to Asbury: Studies in Early American Methodism.* Durham, 1976.

Balmer, Randall H. *A Perfect Babel of Confusion: Dutch Religion and English Culture in the Middle Colonies*. New York, 1989.

Barker, William S. "The Social Views of Charles Hodge (1797–1878): A Study in Nineteenth-Century Calvinism and Conservatism." *Presbyterion* 1 (Spring 1975): 1–22.

Barlow, Philip L. *Mormons and the Bible*. New York, 1991.

Beardslee, John W., III. "The Dutch Reformed Church and the American Revolution." *Journal of Presbyterian History* 54 (Spring 1976): 165–81.

Bratt, James D. "From Revivalism to Anti-Revivalism to Whig Politics: The Strange Career of Calvin Colton." *Journal of Ecclesiastical History* 52 (Jan. 2001): 63–82.

———. "Nevin and the Antebellum Culture Wars." In *Reformed Confessionalism in Nineteenth-Century America: Essays on the Thought of John Williamson Nevin*, ed. Sam Hamstra Jr. and Arie J. Griffioen. Lanham, Md., 1995.

Bucke, Emory Stevens, ed. *The History of American Methodism*. Vol. 1. New York, 1964.

Bundy, David. "Thomas Cogswell Upham and the Establishment of a Tradition of Ethical Reflection." *Encounter* 58 (1998): 23–40.

Bushman, Richard L. *Joseph Smith and the Beginnings of Mormonism*. Urbana, Ill., 1984.

Butler, Diana Hochstedt. *Standing against the Whirlwind: Evangelical Episcopalians in Nineteenth-Century America*. New York, 1995.

Calhoon, Robert M. "Lutheranism and Early Southern Culture." In *"A Truly Efficient School of Theology": The Lutheran Theological Southern Seminary in Historical Context, 1830–1980*, ed. H. George Anderson and Calhoon. Columbia, S.C., 1981.

Carey, Patrick W. "American Catholic Romanticism, 1830–1888." *Catholic Historical Review* 74 (1988): 590–606.

———. *People, Priests, and Prelates: Democracy and the Tensions of Trusteeism*. Notre Dame, Ind., 1987.

———. "Republicanism and American Catholicism, 1785–1860." *Journal of the Early Republic* 3 (1983): 413–37.

Carwardine, Richard J. "Methodists, Politics, and the Coming of the American Civil War." *Church History* 69 (Sept. 2000): 578–609.

Casey, Michael W. *The Battle over Hermeneutics in the Stone-Campbell Movement, 1800–1870*. Lewiston, N.Y., 1998.

Coalter, Milton J. *Gilbert Tennent, Son of Thunder*. New York, 1986.

Cohen, Naomi. *Jews in Christian America*. New York, 1992.

Collins, Varnum Lansing. *President Witherspoon*. 2 vols. Princeton, 1925.

Cornman, Thomas. "Securing a Faithful Ministry: Struggles of Ethnicity and Religious Epistemology in Colonial American Presbyterianism." Ph.D. diss., University of Illinois at Chicago, 1998.

Davidson, Edward H., and William J. Scheick. *Paine, Scripture, and Authority: The Age of Reason as Religious and Political Idea*. Bethlehem, Pa., 1994.

Dieter, Melvin Easterday. *The Holiness Revival of the Nineteenth Century*. Metuchen, N.J., 1980.

DiPuccio, William. *The Interior Sense of Scripture: The Sacred Hermeneutics of John W. Nevin*. Macon, Ga., 1998.

Dolan, Jay P. *The American Catholic Experience*. Garden City, N.Y., 1985.

Ellis, Joseph J. *The New England Mind in Transition: Samuel Johnson of Connecticut, 1696–1772*. New Haven, 1973.

Fiering, Norman S. "President Samuel Johnson and the Circle of Knowledge." *William and Mary Quarterly* 28 (1971): 191–236.

Fortenbaugh, Robert. "American Lutheran Synods and Slavery, 1830–60." *Journal of Religion* 13 (Jan. 1933): 72–92.

Franchot, Jenny. *Roads to Rome: The Antebellum Protestant Encounter with Catholicism*. Berkeley, 1994.

George, Timothy, and David S. Dockery, eds. *Theologians of the Baptist Tradition*. 2d ed. Nashville, 2001.

Graham, Stephen R. *Cosmos in the Chaos: Philip Schaff's Interpretation of Nineteenth-Century American Religion*. Grand Rapids, 1995.

Guelzo, Allen C. *For the Union of Evangelical Christendom: The Irony of the Reformed Episcopalians*. University Park, Pa., 1994.

Gustafson, David A. *Lutherans in Crisis: The Question of Identity in the American Republic*. Philadelphia, 1993.

Hambrick-Stowe, Charles E. *Charles G. Finney and the Spirit of American Evangelicalism*. Grand Rapids, 1996.

Hanson, Charles B. *Necessary Virtue: The Pragmatic Origins of Religious Liberty in New England* [on Roman Catholics]. Charlottesville, 1998.

Harrell, David Edwin. *Quest for a Christian America: The Disciples of Christ and American Society to 1866*. Nashville, 1966.

Hatch, Nathan O. "The Puzzle of American Methodism." *Church History* 63 (June 1994): 175–89.

Hatch, Nathan O., and John H. Wigger, eds. *Methodism and the Shaping of American Culture*. Nasvhille, 2001.

Haynes, Stephen. "Race, National Destiny, and the Sons of Noah in the Thought of Benjamin M. Palmer." *Journal of Presbyterian History* 78 (Summer 2000): 125–44.

Heitzenrater, Richard P. "At Full Liberty: Doctrinal Standards in Early American Methodism." *Quarterly Review* 5 (Fall 1985): 6–27.

Hennesey, James, S.J. *American Catholics: A History of the Roman Catholic Community in the United States*. New York, 1981.

Heyrman, Christine Leigh. *Southern Cross: The Beginnings of the Bible Belt*. New York, 1997.

Holifield, E. Brooks. "Mercersburg, Princeton, and the South: The Sacramental Controversy in the Nineteenth Century." *Journal of Presbyterian History* 54 (Summer 1976): 238–57.

Hornberger, Theodore. "Samuel Johnson of Yale and King's College: A Note on the Relation of Science and Religion in Provincial America." *New England Quarterly* 8 (1935): 378–97.

Hughes, Richard T. *Reviving the Ancient Faith: The Story of Churches of Christ in America*. Grand Rapids, 1996.

Kenny, Michael G. *The Perfect Law of Liberty: Elias Smith and the Providential History of America*. Washington, D.C., 1994.

Kuenning, Paul P. *The Rise and Fall of American Lutheran Pietism*. Macon, Ga., 1988.

Lalli, Anthony B., S.X., and Thomas H. O'Connor. "Roman Views on the American Civil War." *Catholic Historical Review* 40 (Apr. 1971): 21–41.

Langford, Thomas. *Practical Divinity: Theology in the Wesleyan Tradition*. Nashville, 1983.

Le Beau, Bruce F. *Jonathan Dickinson and the Formative Years of American Presbyterianism*. Lexington, Ky., 1997.

Lewis, Steven W. "Nathan Bangs and the Impact of Theological Controversy on the Development of Early Nineteenth Century American Thought." Ph.D. diss., St. Louis University, 1998.

Light, Dale B. *Rome and the New Republic: Conflict and Community in Philadelphia Catholicism between the Revolution and the Civil War*. Notre Dame, Ind., 1996.

Loetscher, Lefferts A. *Facing the Enlightenment and Pietism: Archibald Alexander and the Founding of Princeton Theological Seminary*. Westport, Conn., 1983.

Long, Kathryn T. "Consecrated Respectability: Phoebe Palmer and the Refinement of American Methodism." In *Methodism and the Shaping of American Culture*, ed. Nathan O. Hatch and John H. Wigger. Nashville, 2001.

———. "The New England Connection: Thomas Upham and the Nineteenth-Century Holiness Movement." Unpublished paper.

Lyerly, Cynthia Lynn. *Methodism and the Southern Mind, 1770–1810*. New York, 1998.

McLoughlin, William G. *Isaac Backus and the American Pietistic Tradition*. Boston, 1967.

Madden, Edward H., and James E. Hamilton. *Freedom and Grace: The Life of Asa Mahan*. Metuchen, N.J., 1982.

Marsden, George M. *The Evangelical Mind and the New School Presbyterian Experience*. New Haven, 1970.

Mills, Frederick V., Sr. *Bishops by Ballot: An Eighteenth-Century Ecclesiastical Revolution*. New York, 1978.

Moorhead, James H., and John W. Stewart, eds. *Charles Hodge Revisited*. Grand Rapids, forthcoming.

Mulder, John M. "William Livingston: Propagandist against Episcopacy." *Journal of Presbyterian History* 54 (Spring 1976): 83–105.

Muller, Richard A. "Henry Boynton Smith: Christocentric Theologian." *Journal of Presbyterian History* 61 (1983): 429–44.

Mullin, Robert Bruce. *Episcopal Vision/American Reality: High Church Theology and Social Thought in Evangelical America*. New Haven, 1986.

Nelson, E. Clifford, ed. *The Lutherans in North America*. Philadelphia, 1975.

Noll, Mark A. "Ethnic, American, or Lutheran? Dilemmas for a Historic Confession in the New World." *Lutheran Theological Seminary Review* 71 (Winter 1991): 17–38.

———. "The Irony of the Enlightenment for Presbyterians in the Early Republic." *Journal of the Early Republic* 5 (Summer 1985): 149–76.

Nolt, Steven M. "Becoming Ethnic Americans in the Early Republic: Pennsylvania German Reaction to Evangelical Protestant Reformism." *Journal of the Early Republic* 20 (Fall 2000): 423–46.

Numbers, Ronald L. *Prophetess of Health: Ellen G. White and the Origins of Seventh-day Adventist Health Reform*. 2d ed. Nashville, 1992.

Oden, Thomas C. *Doctrinal Standards in the Wesleyan Tradition*. Grand Rapids, 1988.

Pilcher, William George. *Samuel Davies: Apostle of Dissent in Colonial Virginia*. Knoxville, 1971.

Pope, Earl A. "Albert Barnes, 'The Way of Salvation,' and Theological Controversy." *Journal of Presbyterian History* 57 (1979): 27–32.

Potts, David B. *Wesleyan University, 1831–1910: Collegiate Enterprise in New England*. New Haven, 1992.

Pranger, Gary K. *Philip Schaff (1819–1893): Portrait of an Immigrant Theologian*. New York, 1997.

Raser, Harold E. *Phoebe Palmer*. Lewiston, N.Y., 1987.

Ray, Mary Augustina, B.V.M. *American Opinion of Roman Catholicism in the Eighteenth Century*. New York, 1936.

Rhoden, Nancy L. *Revolutionary Anglicanism: The Colonial Church of England Clergy during the American Revolution*. New York, 1999.

Richards, Phillip. "Phillis Wheatley and Literary Americanization." *American Quarterly* 44 (1992): 163–91.

Richey, Russell E. *Early American Methodism*. Bloomington, Ind., 1991.

———. "Methodism and Providence: A Study in Secularization." In *Protestant Evangelicalism: Britain, Ireland, Germany, and America, c. 1750–c. 1950*, ed. Keith Robbins. Oxford, 1990.

———. *The Methodist Conference in America*. Nashville, 1996.

Richey, Russell E., and Kenneth E. Rowe, eds. *Rethinking Methodist History*. Nashville, 1985.

Richey, Russell E., Kenneth E. Rowe, and Jean Miller Schmidt, eds. *Perspectives on American Methodism: Interpretive Essays*. Nashville, 1993.

Riforgiato, Leonard R. *Missionary of Moderation: Henry Melchior Mühlenberg and the Lutheran Church in English America*. Lewisburg, Pa., 1980.

Roeber, A. G. "J. H. C. Helmuth, Evangelical Charity, and the Public Sphere in Pennsylvania, 1793–1800." *Pennsylvania Magazine of History and Biography* 121 (Jan./Apr. 1997): 77–100.

———. *Palatines, Liberty, and Property: German Lutherans in Colonial British America*. Baltimore, 1993.

Salter, Darius L. *Spirit and Intellect: Thomas Upham's Holiness Theology*. Metuchen, N.J., 1986.

Sandlund, Vivien. "Robert Breckinridge, Presbyterian Antislavery Conservative." *Journal of Presbyterian History* 78 (Summer 2000): 145–54.

Sarna, Jonathan D., ed. *The American Jewish Experience*. 2d ed. New York, 1997.

Sawyer, Christian. "Tyrant or Servant? Religious Authority and Character among the Methodists in America, 1767–1792." M.A. thesis, Wheaton College Graduate School, 2000.

Schneider, A. Gregory. *The Way of the Cross Leads Home: The Domestication of American Methodism*. Bloomington, Ind., 1993.

Scott, Leland Howard. "Methodist Theology in America in the Nineteenth Century." Ph.D. diss., Yale University, 1954.

Sharrow, Walter G. "John Hughes and a Catholic Response to Slavery in Antebellum America." *Journal of Negro History* 57 (July 1972): 254–69.

———. "Northern Catholic Intellectuals and the Coming of the Civil War." *New York History Society Quarterly* 58 (1974): 35–56.

Shipps, Jan. *Mormonism: The Story of a New Religious Tradition*. Urbana, Ill., 1985.

Steiner, Bruce E. *Samuel Seabury: A Study in the High Church Tradition*. Columbus, Ohio, 1971.

Tappert, Theodore G. "Henry Melchior Mühlenberg and the American Revolution." *Church History* 11 (Sept. 1942): 284–301.

Taylor, Thomas F. "Samuel E. McCorkle and a Christian Republic, 1792–1802." *American Presbyterians* 63 (Winter 1985): 375–85.

Thompson, Ernest Trice. *Presbyterians in the South*. Vol. 1, *1607–1861*. Richmond, 1963.

Trinterud, Leonard J. *The Forming of an American Tradition: A Re-examination of Colonial Presbyterianism*. Philadelphia, 1949.

Troxel, Craig A. "Charles Hodge on Church Boards." *Westminster Theological Journal* 58 (Fall 1996): 183–207.

Vanderpool, Mark A. "Citizens of Zion: Republican Thought and Early American Methodism, 1770–1800." M.Div. thesis, Asbury Theological Seminary, 1996.

Vander Velde, Lewis G. *The Presbyterian Churches and the Federal Union, 1861–1869*. Cambridge, Mass., 1932.

Van Hoeven, James W., ed. *Piety and Patriotism: Bicentennial Studies of the Reformed Church in America, 1776–1976*. Grand Rapids, 1976.

White, Charles E. *The Beauty of Holiness: Phoebe Palmer as Theologian, Revivalist, Feminist, and Humanitarian*. Grand Rapids, 1986.

Wigger, John. *Taking Heaven by Storm: Methodism and the Rise of Popular Christianity in America*. New York, 1998.

Williamson, Douglas James. "The Ecclesiastical Career of Wilbur Fisk: Methodist Educator, Theologian, Reformer, Controversialist." Ph.D. diss., Boston University, 1988.

Wills, Gregory A. *Democratic Religion: Freedom, Authority, and Church Discipline in the Baptist South, 1785–1900*. New York, 1997.

Wimmer, Judith Conrad. "American Catholic Interpretations of the Civil War." Ph.D. diss., Drew University, 1980.

Comparative, Transatlantic, Canadian

The works that follow suggest some of the excellent resources that are already in place for carrying out the great desideratum of a fully comparative understanding of religious thought in the eighteenth and nineteenth centuries.

General, Comparative, Continental Europe

Adamson, Christopher. "God's Continent Divided: Politics and Religion in Upper Canada and the Northern and Western United States, 1775 to 1841." *Comparative Studies in Society and History* 36 (July 1994): 417–46.

Brecht, Martin, and Klaus Deppermann, eds. *Geschichte des Pietismus*. Vol. 2, *Der Pietismus im achtzehnten Jahrhundert*. Göttingen, 1995.

Campbell, Ted A. *The Religion of the Heart: A Study of European Religious Life in the Seventeenth and Eighteenth Centuries*. Columbia, S.C., 1991.

Carwardine, Richard. *Transatlantic Revivalism: Popular Evangelicalism in Britain and America, 1790–1865*. Westport, Conn., 1978.

Clark, J. C. D. *The Language of Liberty, 1660–1832: Political Discourse and Social Dynamics in the Anglo-American World*. Cambridge, 1994.

Conser, Walter H., Jr. *Church and Confession: Conservative Theologians in Germany, England, and America, 1815–1866*. Macon, Ga., 1984.

Crawford, Michael. *Seasons of Grace: Colonial New England's Revival Tradition in Its British Context*. New York, 1991.

Diamond, Peter J. "Witherspoon, William Smith, and the Scottish Philosophy in

Revolutionary America." In *Scotland and America in the Age of the Enlightenment*, ed. Richard B. Sher and Jeffrey R. Smitten. Princeton, 1990.

Durden, Susan. "A Study of the First Evangelical Magazines, 1740–1748." *Journal of Ecclesiastical History* 27 (1976): 255–75.

———. "Transatlantic Communications and Influence during the Great Awakening: A Comparative Study of British and American Revivalism, 1730–1760." Ph.D. diss., University of Hull, 1978.

Frei, Hans W. *The Eclipse of Biblical Narrative: A Study in Eighteenth and Nineteenth Century Hermeneutics*. New Haven, 1974.

Gäbler, Ulrich. *Auferstehungszeit: Erweckungsprediger des 19. Jahrhunderts*. Munich, 1991.

———, ed. *Geschichte des Pietismus*. Vol. 3, *19. und 20. Jahrhundert*. Göttingen, 2000.

Gilley, Sheridan. "Christianity and Enlightenment: An Historical Survey." *History of European Ideas* 1 (1981): 103–21.

Hempton, David. *Religion and Political Culture in Britain and Ireland: From the Glorious Revolution to the Decline of Empire*. Cambridge, 1996.

———. *The Religion of the People: Methodism and Popular Religion, c. 1750–1900*. London, 1996.

Lacorne, Denis. "Les infortunes de la vertu." In *L'Amérique et la France: Deux révolutions*, ed. Élise Marienstras. Paris, 1990.

Landsman, Ned C. *Scotland and Its First American Colony, 1683–1765*. Princeton, 1985.

Noll, Mark A. "Revival, Enlightenment, Civic Humanism, and the Evolution of Calvinism in Scotland and America, 1735–1843." In *Amazing Grace: Evangelicalism in Australia, Britain, Canada, and the United States*, ed. George A. Rawlyk and Noll. Kingston and Montreal, 1994.

Noll, Mark A., David W. Bebbington, and George A. Rawlyk, eds. *Evangelicalism: Comparative Studies of Popular Protestantism in North America, the British Isles, and Beyond, 1700–1990*. New York, 1994.

O'Brien, Susan Durden. "A Transatlantic Community of Saints: The Great Awakening and the First Evangelical Networks, 1735–1755." *American Historical Review* 91 (Oct. 1986): 311–32.

Ozouf, Jacques, and Mona Ozouf. *La république des instituteurs*. Paris, 1992.

Phillips, Kevin. *The Cousins' Wars: Religion, Politics, Civil Warfare, and the Triumph of Anglo-America*. New York, 1999.

Rawlyk, George A., and Mark A. Noll, eds. *Amazing Grace: Evangelicalism in Australia, Britain, Canada, and the United States*. Kingston and Montreal, 1994.

Robbins, Keith, ed. *Protestant Evangelicalism: Britain, Ireland, Germany, and America, c. 1750–c. 1950*. Oxford, 1990.

Savart, Claude, ed. *Bible de tous les temps*. Vol. 8, *Le monde contemporain et la Bible*. Paris, 1985.

Schmidt, Leigh Eric. *Holy Fairs: Scottish Communions and American Revivals in the Early Modern Period*. Princeton, 1989.

Sher, Richard B., and Jeffrey R. Smitten, eds. *Scotland and America in the Age of Enlightenment*. Princeton, 1990.

Siegfried, André. *America Comes of Age: A French Analysis*. New York, 1927.

Sullivan, Robert. "Rethinking Christianity in Enlightened Europe." *Eighteenth-Century Studies* 34 (2001): 298–309.

Tocqueville, Alexis de. *Democracy in America*. Ed. and trans. Harvey Claflin Mansfield and Delba Winthrop. Chicago, 2000.

Ward, W. R. *Christianity under the Ancien Regime, 1648–1789*. New York, 1999.

———. *The Protestant Evangelical Awakening*. New York, 1992.

Welch, Claude. *Protestant Thought in the Nineteenth Century*. Vol. 1, *1799–1870*. New Haven, 1972.

Westerkamp, Marilyn J. *Triumph of the Laity: Scots-Irish Piety and the Great Awakening, 1625–1760*. New York, 1988.

England

Bebbington, D. W. *Evangelicalism in Modern Britain: A History from the 1730s to the 1980s*. London, 1989.

Bolam, C. Gordon, Jeremy Goring, H. L. Short, and Roger Thomas. *The English Presbyterians: From Elizabethan Puritanism to Modern Unitarianism*. Boston, 1968.

Bradley, James E. *Popular Politics and the American Revolution in England: Petitions, the Crown, and Public Opinion*. Macon, Ga., 1986.

———. *Religion, Revolution, and English Radicalism: Non-conformity in Eighteenth-Century Politics and Society*. Cambridge, 1990.

Clark, J. C. D. *English Society, 1660–1832*. 2d ed. Cambridge, 2000.

Colley, Margaret. *Britons: Forging the Nation, 1707–1837*. New Haven, 1992.

Daniel, W. Harrison. "English Presbyterians, Slavery, and the American Crisis of the 1860s." *Journal of Presbyterian History* 58 (1980): 50–62.

———. "The Reaction of British Methodism to the Civil War and Reconstruction in America." *Methodist History* 16 (1977): 3–20.

———. "The Response of the Church of England to the Civil War and Reconstruction in America." *Historical Magazine of the Protestant Episcopal Church* 47 (1978): 57–72.

Gilley, Sheridan, and W. J. Shiels, eds. *A History of Religion in Britain*. Oxford, 1994.

Hempton, David. *Methodism and Politics in British Society, 1750–1850*. London, 1987.

Hilton, Boyd. *The Age of Atonement: The Influence of Evangelicalism on Social and Economic Thought, 1785–1865*. New York, 1988.

Hole, Robert. "English Sermons and Tracts as Media of Debate on the French Revolution, 1789–99." In *The French Revolution and British Popular Politics*, ed. Mark Philp. Cambridge, 1991.

———. *Pulpits, Politics, and Public Order in England, 1760–1832*. Cambridge, 1989.

Jacob, Margaret. *The Newtonians and the English Revolution, 1689–1720*. Ithaca, 1976.

Larsen, Timothy. *Friends of Religious Equality: Nonconformist Politics in Mid-Victorian England*. Woodbridge, Eng., 1999.

Lovegrove, Deryck W. *Established Church, Sectarian People: Itinerancy and the Transformation of English Dissent, 1780–1830*. Cambridge, 1988.

Morgan, John. *Godly Learning: Puritan Attitudes towards Reason, Learning, and Education, 1560–1640*. New York, 1986.

Pattison, Mark. "Tendencies of Religious Thought in England, 1688–1750." In *Essays and Reviews*. London, 1860.

Rack, Henry D. *Reasonable Enthusiast: John Wesley and the Rise of Methodism*. Philadelphia, 1989.

Reedy, Gerard, S.J. *The Bible and Reason: Anglicans and Scripture in Late Seventeenth-Century England*. Philadelphia, 1985.

Rivers, Isabel. *Reason, Grace, and Sentiment: A Study of the Language of Religion and Ethics in England, 1660–1780*. Vol. 1, *Whichcote to Wesley*. Cambridge, 1991.

———. "Shaftesburian Enthusiasm and the Evangelical Revival." In *Revival and Religion since 1700: Essays for John Walsh*, ed. Jane Garnett and Colin Matthew. London, 1993.

Sullivan, Robert E. *John Toland and the Deist Controversy*. Cambridge, Mass., 1982.

Walsh, John. "Religious Societies: Methodist and Evangelical, 1738–1800." In *Voluntary Religion*, ed. W. J. Shiels and Diana Wood. Oxford, 1986.

Waterman, A. M. C. *Revolution, Economics, and Religion: Christian Political Economy, 1798–1833*. Cambridge, 1991.

Watts, Michael R. *The Dissenters*. Vol. 1, *From the Reformation to the French Revolution*; vol. 2, *The Expansion of Evangelical Nonconformity, 1791–1859*. Oxford, 1978–95.

Scotland, Ireland

Brooke, Peter. *Ulster Presbyterianism, 1610–1970*. New York, 1987.

Brown, Stewart J. *Thomas Chalmers and the Godly Commonwealth in Scotland*. Oxford, 1982.

Brown, Stewart J., and Michael Fry, eds. *Scotland in the Age of the Disruption*. Edinburgh, 1993.

Camerson, James K. "Theological Controversy: A Factor in the Origins of the Scottish Enlightenment." In *The Origin and Nature of the Scottish Enlightenment*, ed. R. H. Campbell and A. S. Skinner. Edinburgh, 1982.

Clark, Ian D. L. "From Protest to Reaction: The Moderate Regime in the Church of Scotland, 1752–1805." In *Scotland in the Age of Improvement*, ed. N. T. Phillipson and Rosalind Mitchison. Edinburgh, 1970.

Currie, David Alan. "The Growth of Evangelicalism in the Church of Scotland, 1793–1843." Ph.D. diss., University of St. Andrews, 1990.

Diamond, Peter J. "Witherspoon, William Smith, and the Scottish Philosophy in Revolutionary America." In *Scotland and America in the Age of the Enlightenment*, ed. Richard B. Sher and Jeffrey R. Smitten. Princeton, 1990.

Drummond, Andrew, and James Bulloch. *The Scottish Church, 1688–1843: The Age of the Moderates*. Edinburgh, 1973.

Dwyer, John. *Virtuous Discourse: Sensibility and Community in Late Eighteenth-Century Scotland*. Edinburgh, 1987.

Elliott, Marianne. *Partners in Revolution: The United Irishmen and France*. New Haven, 1982.

Hempton, David, and Myrtle Hill. *Evangelical Protestantism in Ulster Society, 1740–1890*. London, 1992.

Holmes, R. Finlay. *Henry Cooke*. Belfast, 1981.

———. *Our Irish Presbyterian Heritage*. Belfast, 1985.

Hont, Istavan, and Michael Ignatieff, eds. *Wealth and Virtue: The Shaping of Political Economy in the Scottish Enlightenment*. New York, 1983.

McBride, I. R. *Scripture Politics: Ulster Presbyterians and Irish Radicalism in the Late Eighteenth Century*. Oxford, 1998.

McFarland, E. W. *Ireland and Scotland in the Age of Revolution*. Edinburgh, 1994.

McIntosh, John R. *Church and Theology in Enlightenment Scotland: The Popular Party, 1740–1800*. East Linton, Scotland, 1998.

Mechie, Stewart. "The Theological Climate in Early Eighteenth Century Scotland." In *Reformation and Revolution*, ed. Duncan Shaw. Edinburgh, 1967.

Rendall, Jane, ed. *The Origins of the Scottish Enlightenment*. New York, 1978.

Sefton, Henry. "'New Lights and Preachers Legall': Some Observations on the Beginnings of Moderatism in the Church of Scotland." In *Church, Politics, and Society: Scotland, 1408–1929*, ed. Norman MacDouglas. Edinburgh, 1983.

Skoczylas, Anne. *Mr. Simson's Knotty Case: Divinity, Politics, and Due Process in Early Eighteenth-Century Scotland*. Montreal and Kingston, 2001.

Smout, T. C. *A History of the Scottish People, 1560–1830*. London, 1969.

Stewart, A. T. Q. *A Deeper Silence: The Hidden Origins of the United Irishmen*. London, 1993.

———. "The Transformation of Presbyterian Radicalism in the North of Ireland, 1792–1825." M.A. thesis, Queen's University of Belfast, 1956.

Canada

Armstrong, Maurice W. "Neutrality and Religion in Revolutionary Nova Scotia." *New England Quarterly* 9 (March 1946): 50–62.

Cuthbertson, Brian. *The First Bishop: A Biography of Charles Inglis*. Halifax, Nova Scotia, 1987.

Errington, Jane, and G. A. Rawlyk. "Creating a British-American Community in Upper Canada." In *Loyalists and Community in North America*, ed. Robert M. Calhoon, Timothy M. Barnes, and Rawlyk. Westport, Conn., 1994.

Gauvreau, Michael. *The Evangelical Century: College and Creed in English Canada from the Great Revival to the Great Depression*. Kingston and Montreal, 1991.

Grant, John Webster. *The Church in the Canadian Era*. 2d ed. Burlington, Ont., 1988.

———. *A Profusion of Spires: Religion in Nineteenth-Century Ontario*. Toronto, 1988.

Lipset, Seymour Martin. *Continental Divide: The Values and Institutions of the United States and Canada*. New York, 1990.

Lydekker, John Wolfe. *The Life and Letters of Charles Inglis*. London, 1936.

McKillop, A. B. *A Disciplined Intelligence: Critical Inquiry and Canadian Thought in the Victorian Era*. Kingston and Montreal, 1979.

Mills, David. *The Idea of Loyalty in Upper Canada, 1784–1850*. Kingston and Montreal, 1988.

Morgan, Cecilia. *Public Men and Virtuous Women: The Gendered Language of Religion and Politics in Upper Canada, 1791–1850*. Toronto, 1996.

Murphy, Terrence, and Roberto Perin, eds. *A Concise History of Christianity in Canada*. Toronto, 1996.

Rawlyk, George A. *The Canada Fire: Radical Evangelicalism in British North America, 1775–1812*. Kingston and Montreal, 1994.

———. *Nova Scotia's Massachusetts, 1680–1784*. Kingston and Montreal, 1973.

———. *Ravished by the Spirit: Religious Revivals, Baptists, and Henry Alline*. Kingston and Montreal, 1984.

———., ed. *Aspects of the Canadian Evangelical Experience*. Kingston and Montreal, 1997.

———., ed. *The Canadian Protestant Experience, 1760–1990*. Burlington, Ont., 1990.

Semple, Neil. *The Lord's Dominion: The History of Canadian Methodism*. Kingston and Montreal, 1996.

Van Die, Marguerite. *An Evangelical Mind: Nathanael Burwash and the Methodist Tradition in Canada, 1839–1918*. Kingston and Montreal, 1989.

Vaudry, Richard W. *The Free Church in Victorian Canada, 1844–1861*. Waterloo, Ont., 1989.

Westfall, William. *Two Worlds: The Protestant Culture of Nineteenth-Century Ontario*. Kingston and Montreal, 1989.

Contexts: Religious, Political, Social, Economic, Intellectual

Ahlstrom, Sydney E. *A Religious History of the American People*. New Haven, 1972.

Akers, Charles W. "Calvinism and the American Revolution." In *The Heritage of John Calvin*, ed. John H. Bratt. Grand Rapids, 1973.

Appleby, Joyce. *Inheriting the Revolution: The First Generation of Americans*. Cambridge, Mass., 2000.

———. *Liberalism and Republicanism in the Historical Imagination*. Cambridge, Mass., 1992.

Ashworth, John. "The Jeffersonians: Classical Republicans or Liberal Capitalists?" *Journal of American Studies* 18 (Dec. 1984): 425–35.

Bailyn, Bernard. *The Ideological Origins of the American Revolution*. Cambridge, Mass., 1967.

———. "Religion and Revolution: Three Biographical Studies." *Perspectives in American History* 4 (1970): 83–169.

Baird, Robert. *Religion in the United States of America*. Glasgow, 1844.

Baldwin, Alice M. *The New England Clergy and the American Revolution*. Durham, 1928.

Ball, Terence, and J. G. A. Pocock, eds. *Conceptual Change and the Constitution*. Lawrence, Kans., 1988.

Banning, Lance. *The Jeffersonian Persuasion: Evolution of a Party Ideology*. Ithaca, 1978.

Berens, John F. *Providence and Patriotism in Early America, 1640–1815*. Charlottesville, 1978.

Bilhartz, Terry D. *Urban Religion and the Second Great Awakening: Church and Society in Early National Baltimore*. Rutherford, N.J., 1986.

Billington, Ray Allen. *The Protestant Crusade, 1800–1860*. New York, 1938.

Bloch, Ruth H. "The Gendered Meanings of Virtue in Revolutionary America." *Signs: Journal of Women in Culture and Society* 13 (1987): 37–58.

———. *Visionary Republic: Millennial Themes in American Thought, 1756–1800*. New York, 1988.

Bonomi, Patricia. *Under the Cope of Heaven: Religion, Society, and Politics in Colonial America*. New York, 1986.

Bonomi, Patricia U., and Peter R. Eisenstadt. "Church Adherence in the Eighteenth-Century British American Colonies." *William and Mary Quarterly* 39 (Apr. 1982): 245–86.

Bratt, James D. "The Reorientation of American Protestantism, 1835–1845." *Church History* 67 (Mar. 1998): 52–82.

Breen, T. H. "'Baubles of Britain': The American and Consumer Revolutions of the Eighteenth Century." *Past and Present* 119 (May 1980): 73–104.

————. "An Empire of Goods: The Anglicization of Colonial America, 1690–1776." *Journal of British Studies* 25 (1986): 467–99.

Brekus, Catherine. *Strangers and Pilgrims: Female Preaching in America, 1740–1845.* Chapel Hill, 1998.

Bridenbaugh, Carl. *Mitre and Sceptre: Transatlantic Faiths, Ideas, Personalities, and Politics, 1689–1775.* New York, 1962.

Bumsted, J. M., and John E. Van de Wetering. *What Must I Do to Be Saved? The Great Awakening in Colonial America.* Hinsdale, Ill., 1976.

Bushman, Richard L. *King and People in Provincial Massachusetts.* Chapel Hill, 1985.

Butler, Jon. *Awash in a Sea of Faith: Christianizing the American People.* Cambridge, Mass., 1990.

————. "Enthusiasm Described and Decried: The Great Awakening as Interpretive Fiction." *Journal of American History* 69 (1982–83): 305–25.

Carwardine, Richard J. *Evangelicals and Politics in Antebellum America.* New Haven, 1993.

————. "Unity, Pluralism, and the Spiritual Market-Place: Interdenominational Competition in the Early American Republic." In *Unity and Diversity in the Church*, ed. Robert Swanson. Oxford, 1996.

Clebsch, William A. "Christian Interpretations of the Civil War." *Church History* 31 (1961): 215–18.

Cmiel, Kenneth. *Democratic Eloquence: The Fight over Popular Speech in Nineteenth-Century America.* Berkeley, 1990.

Conser, Walter H., Jr. *God and the Natural World: Religion and Science in Antebellum America.* Columbia, S.C., 1993.

The Creation of the American Republic, 1776–1787 [by Gordon S. Wood]: *A Symposium of Views and Reviews.* Special issue of *William and Mary Quarterly* 44 (July 1987): 549–640.

Curry, Thomas J. *The First Freedoms: Church and State in America to the Passage of the First Amendment.* New York, 1986.

Dallimore, Arnold A. *George Whitefield.* 2 vols. Edinburgh, 1989–90.

Davis, Derek H. *Religion and the Continental Congress, 1774–1789: Contributions to Original Intent.* New York, 2000.

D'Elia, Donald J. *Benjamin Rush: Philosopher of the American Revolution.* Transactions of the American Philosophical Society, vol. 64, part 5. Philadelphia, 1974.

Diggins, John Patrick. *The Lost Soul of American Politics: Virtue, Self-Interest, and the Foundations of Liberalism.* New York, 1984.

Dunn, John. "The Politics of Locke in England and America in the Eighteenth Century." In *John Locke: Problems and Perspectives*, ed. John W. Yolton. Cambridge, 1969.

Elkins, Stanley M., and Eric L. McKitrick. *The Age of Federalism.* New York, 1993.

Endy, Melvin B., Jr. "Abraham Lincoln and American Civil Religion: A Reinterpretation." *Church History* 44 (June 1975): 229–41.

————. "Just War, Holy War, and Millennialism in Revolutionary America." *William and Mary Quarterly* 42 (1985): 3–25.

Ferguson, Robert A. *The American Enlightenment, 1750–1820.* New York, 1997.

Fiering, Norman. *Moral Philosophy at Seventeenth-Century Harvard.* Chapel Hill, 1981.

Finke, Roger, and Rodney Stark. "How the Upstart Sects Won America: 1776–1850." *Journal for the Scientific Study of Religion* 28 (Mar. 1989): 27–44.

Flower, Elizabeth, and Murray G. Murphey. *A History of Philosophy in America.* Vol. 1. New York, 1977.

Foster, Charles I. *An Errand of Mercy: The Evangelical United Front, 1790–1837.* Chapel Hill, 1960.

Fox, Richard Wightman. *Trials of Intimacy: Love and Loss in the Beecher-Tilton Scandal.* Chicago, 1999.

Fredrickson, George M. *The Inner Civil War: Northern Intellectuals and the Crisis of the Union.* New York, 1965.

From, Joel L. "The Moral Economy of Nineteenth-Century Evangelical Activism." *Christian Scholar's Review* 30 (Fall 2000): 37–56.

Gaustad, Edwin S. *The Great Awakening in New England.* New York, 1957.

Gienapp, William E. *The Origins of the Republican Party, 1852–1856.* New York, 1987.

Goff, Philip. "Revivals and Revolution: Historiographic Turns since Alan Heimert's *Religion and the American Mind.*" *Church History* 67 (1998): 695–721.

Greene, John C. *American Science in the Age of Jefferson.* Ames, Iowa, 1984.

Gribbin, William. *The Churches Militant: The War of 1812 and American Religion.* New Haven, 1973.

———. "The Covenant Transformed: The Jeremiad Tradition and the War of 1812." *Church History* 40 (Sept. 1971): 297–305.

Griffin, Keith L. *Revolution and Religion: The American Revolutionary War and the Reformed Clergy.* New York, 1994.

Guelzo, Allen C. *Abraham Lincoln: Redeemer President.* Grand Rapids, 1999.

———. "God's Designs: The Literature of the Colonial Revivals of Religion, 1735–1760." In *New Directions in American Religious History*, ed. Harry S. Stout and D. G. Hart. New York, 1997.

———. "'The Science of Duty': Moral Philosophy and the Epistemology of Science in Nineteenth-Century America." In *Evangelicals and Science in Historical Perspective*, ed. D. N. Livingstone, D. G. Hart, and M. A. Noll. New York, 1999.

Haakonssen, Knud. "Scottish Common Sense Realism." In *A Companion to American Thought*, ed. Richard Wightman Fox and James T. Kloppenberg. Cambridge, Mass., 1995.

Hall, Timothy D. *Contested Boundaries: Itinerancy and the Reshaping of the Colonial American Religious World.* Durham, 1994.

Handy, Robert. *A Christian America: Protestant Hope and Historical Realities.* 2d ed. New York, 1984.

Hanley, Mark Y. *Beyond a Christian Commonwealth: The Protestant Quarrel with the American Republic, 1830–1860.* Chapel Hill, 1994.

Hardesty, Nancy A. *Your Daughters Shall Prophesy: Revivalism and Feminism in the Age of Finney.* Brooklyn, 1991.

Hatch, Nathan O. *The Democratization of American Christianity.* New Haven, 1989.

———. *The Sacred Cause of Liberty: Republican Thought and the Millennium in Revolutionary New England.* New Haven, 1977.

Heimert, Alan. *Religion and the American Mind, from the Great Awakening to the Revolution.* Cambridge, Mass., 1966.

Hein, David. "Lincoln's Theology and Political Ethics." In *Essays on Lincoln's Faith and Practice*, ed. Kenneth W. Thompson. Lanham, Md., 1983.

———. "Research on Lincoln's Religious Beliefs and Practices: A Bibliographical Essay." *Lincoln Herald* 86 (1984): 2–5.

Helmstadter, Richard, ed. *Freedom and Religion in the Nineteenth Century.* Stanford, 1997.

Heyrman, Christine Leigh. *Southern Cross: The Beginning of the Bible Belt.* New York, 1997.

Hoffman, Ronald, and Peter J. Albert, eds. *Religion in a Revolutionary Age.* Charlottesville, 1994.

Holifield, E. Brooks. *Era of Persuasion: American Thought and Culture, 1521–1680.* Boston, 1989.

Holt, Michael F. *The Rise and Fall of the American Whig Party: Jacksonian Politics and the Onset of the Civil War.* New York, 1999.

Houston, Alan Craig. *Algernon Sidney and the Republican Heritage in England and America.* Princeton, 1991.

Hovenkamp, Herbert. *Science and Religion in America, 1800–1860.* Philadelphia, 1978.

Howe, Daniel Walker. "European Sources of Political Ideas in Jeffersonian America." In *The Promise of American History,* ed. Stanley I. Kutler and Stanley N. Katz. Baltimore, 1982.

———. "The Evangelical Movement and Political Culture in the North during the Second Party System." *Journal of American History* 77 (Mar. 1991): 1216–39.

———. *Making the American Self: Jonathan Edwards to Abraham Lincoln.* Cambridge, Mass., 1997.

———. *The Political Culture of the American Whigs.* Chicago, 1979.

———. "Why the Scottish Enlightenment Was Useful to the Framers of the American Constitution." *Comparative Studies in Society and History* 31 (July 1989): 572–87.

Hughes, Richard T., and C. Leonard Allen. *Illusions of Innocence: Protestant Primitivism in America, 1630–1875.* Chicago, 1985.

Hutson, James H. *Religion and the Founding of the American Republic.* Washington, D.C., 1998.

———, ed. *Religion and the New Republic: Faith in the Founding of America.* New York, 2000.

Isaac, Rhys. "Preachers and Patriots: Popular Culture and the Revolution in Virginia." In *The American Revolution: Explorations in the History of American Radicalism,* ed. Alfred F. Young. DeKalb, Ill., 1976.

———. "Radicalised Religion and Changing Lifestyles: Virginia in the Period of the American Revolution." In *The Origins of Anglo-American Radicalism,* ed. Margaret Jacob and James Jacob. London, 1984.

———. *The Transformation of Virginia, 1740–1790.* Chapel Hill, 1982.

John, Richard R. *Spreading the News: The American Postal System from Franklin to Morse.* Cambridge, Mass., 1995.

———. "Taking Sabbatarianism Seriously: The Postal System, the Sabbath, and the Transformation of American Political Culture." *Journal of the Early Republic* 10 (Winter 1990): 517–67.

Johnson, Curtis. *Islands of Holiness: Rural Religion in Upstate New York, 1790–1860.* Ithaca, 1989.

———. *Redeeming America: Evangelicals and the Road to the Civil War.* Chicago, 1993.

Johnson, Paul E. *A Shopkeeper's Millennium: Society and Revivals in Rochester, New York, 1815–1837.* New York, 1978.

Jordan, Winthrop. *White over Black: American Attitudes toward the Negro, 1550–1812.* Chapel Hill, 1968.

Juster, Susan. *Disorderly Women: Sexual Politics and Evangelicalism in Revolutionary New England.* Ithaca, 1994.

Kammen, Michael. *A Machine That Would Go of Itself: The Constitution in American Culture.* New York, 1986.

Keillor, Steven J. *This Rebellious House: American History and the Truth of Christianity*. Downers Grove, Ill., 1996.

Kidd, Colin. "Civil Theology and Church Establishments in Revolutionary America." *The Historical Journal* 42 (1999): 1007–26.

Klein, Milton M., Richard D. Brown, and John B. Hench, eds. *The Republican Synthesis Revisited*. Worcester, Mass., 1992.

Kloppenberg, James T. "The Virtues of Liberalism: Christianity, Republicanism, and Ethics in Early American Political Discourse." *Journal of American History* 74 (June 1987): 9–37.

Konig, David Thomas, ed. *Devising Liberty: Preserving and Creating Freedom in the New American Republic*. Stanford, 1995.

Korn, Bertram W. *American Jewry and the Civil War*. 2d ed. Philadelphia, 1961.

Kramnick, Isaac. *Republicanism and Bourgeois Radicalism: Political Ideology in Late Eighteenth-Century England and America*. Ithaca, 1990.

Kuehne, Dale S. *The Design of Heaven; Massachusetts Congregationalist Political Thought, 1760–1790*. Columbia, Mo., 1996.

Kuklick, Bruce. *Churchmen and Philosophers: From Jonathan Edwards to John Dewey*. New Haven, 1985.

———. "The Two Cultures in Eighteenth-Century America." In *Benjamin Franklin, Jonathan Edwards, and the Representation of American Culture*, ed. Barbara B. Oberg and Harry S. Stout. New York, 1993.

Lambert, Frank. *Inventing the "Great Awakening."* Princeton, 1999.

———. *Pedlar in Divinity: George Whitefield and the Transatlantic Revivals, 1737–1770*. Princeton, 1994.

Landsman, Ned C. *From Colonials to Provincials: American Thought and Culture, 1680–1760*. Boston, 1997.

Lazerow, Jama. *Religion and the Working Class in Antebellum America*. Washington, D.C., 1995.

Leach, Douglas Edward. *Roots of Conflict: British Armed Forces and Colonial Americans, 1677–1763*. Chapel Hill, 1986.

Lewis, Jan. "The Republican Wife: Virtue and Seduction in the Early Republic." *William and Mary Quarterly* 44 (1987): 689–721.

Livingstone, David N., D. G. Hart, and Mark A. Noll, eds. *Evangelicals and Science in Historical Perspective*. New York, 1999.

Long, Kathryn Teresa. *The Revival of 1857–58: Interpreting an American Religious Awakening*. New York, 1998.

Lundin, Roger. *Emily Dickinson and the Art of Belief*. Grand Rapids, 1998.

Lutz, Donald. *The Origins of American Constitutionalism*. Baton Rouge, La., 1988.

———. "The Relative Influence of European Writers on Late Eighteenth-Century American Political Thought." *American Political Science Review* 78 (Mar. 1984): 189–97.

McCoy, Drew R. *The Elusive Republic: Political Economy in Jeffersonian America*. Chapel Hill, 1980.

McCurry, Stephanie. "The Two Faces of Republicanism: Gender and Proslavery Politics in Antebellum South Carolina." *Journal of American History* 78 (1992): 1245–64.

McDermott, Gerald R. "Civil Religion in the American Revolutionary Period." *Christian Scholar's Review* 18 (June 1989): 346–62.

McLoughlin, William G. *Cherokees and Missionaries, 1789–1839*. New Haven, 1984.

MacMaster, Richard K., with Samuel L. Horst and Robert F. Ulle. *Conscience in*

Crisis: Mennonites and Other Peace Churches in America, 1739–1789. Scottdale, Pa., 1979.

McPherson, James M. *Battle Cry of Freedom: The Civil War Era.* New York, 1988.

———. *For Cause and Comrades: Why Men Fought in the Civil War.* New York, 1997.

Marini, Stephen A. "The Government of God: Religion in Revolutionary America, 1764–1792." Unpublished manuscript.

———. "Religion, Politics, and Ratification." In *Religion in a Revolutionary Age*, ed. Ronald Hoffman and Peter J. Albert. Charlottesville, 1994.

Marsden, George M. *Fundamentalism and American Culture: The Shaping of Twentieth-Century Evangelicalism, 1870–1925.* New York, 1980.

Mathews, Donald G. "The Second Great Awakening as an Organizing Process." *American Quarterly*, 21 (1969), 23–43.

Matthews, Jean V. *Toward a New Society: American Thought and Culture, 1800–1830.* Boston, 1991.

Matthews, Richard K., ed. *Virtue, Corruption, and Self-Interest: Political Values in the Eighteenth Century.* Bethlehem, Pa., 1994.

May, Henry F. *The Enlightenment in America.* New York, 1976.

Meinig, D. W. *The Shaping of America: A Geographical Perspective on Five Hundred Years of History.* Vol. 1, *Atlantic America, 1492–1800*, vol. 2, *Continental America, 1800–1867.* New Haven, 1986–93.

Meyer, D. H. *The Instructed Conscience: The Shaping of the American National Ethic.* Philadelphia, 1972.

Middlekauf, Robert. *The Glorious Cause: The American Revolution, 1763–1789.* New York, 1982.

Miller, Glenn T. *Piety and Intellect: The Aims and Purposes of Ante-bellum Theological Education.* Atlanta, 1990.

Miller, Perry. "From the Covenant to the Revival." In *The Shaping of American Religion*, ed. James Ward Smith and A. Leland Jamison. Princeton, 1961.

———. *The Life of the Mind in America from the Revolution to the Civil War.* New York, 1965.

———. *Nature's Nation.* Cambridge, Mass., 1967.

Miller, Randall M., Harry S. Stout, and Charles Reagan Wilson, eds. *Religion and the American Civil War.* New York, 1998.

Moorhead, James. H. *American Apocalypse: Yankee Protestants and the Civil War, 1860–1869.* New Haven, 1978.

Morgan, Edmund S. "The American Revolution Considered as an Intellectual Movement." In *Paths of American Thought*, ed. Arthur M. Schlesinger Jr. and Morton White. Boston, 1963.

———. *American Slavery, American Freedom: The Ordeal of Colonial Virginia.* New York, 1975.

———. *Inventing the People: The Rise of Popular Sovereignty in England and America.* New York, 1988.

———. "The Puritan Ethic and the Coming of the Revolution." *William and Mary Quarterly* 24 (Jan. 1967): 3–18.

Mott, Frank Luther. *A History of American Magazines, 1741–1850.* New York, 1930.

Murrin, John M. "Escaping Perfidious Albion: Federalism, Fear of Aristocracy, and the Democratization of Corruption in Postrevolutionary America." In *Virtue, Corruption, and Self-Interest: Political Values in the Eighteenth Century*, ed. Richard K. Mathews. Bethlehem, Pa., 1994.

———. "The Great Inversion, Court versus Country: A Comparison of the Revolution Settlements in England (1688–1721) and America (1776–1816)." In *Three British Revolutions: 1641, 1688, 1776*, ed. J. G. A. Pocock. Princeton, 1980.

———. "Religion and Politics in America from the First Settlements to the Civil War." In *Religion and American Politics*, ed. Mark A. Noll. New York, 1990.

———. "A Roof without Walls: The Dilemma of American National Identity." In *Beyond Confederation: Origins of the Constitution and American National Identity*, ed., Richard Beeman et al. Chapel Hill, 1987.

———. "Self-Interest Conquers Patriotism: Republicans, Liberals, and Indians Reshape the Nation." In *The American Revolution: Its Character and Limits*, ed. Jack P. Greene. New York, 1987.

Niebuhr, Reinhold. "The Religion of Abraham Lincoln." In *Lincoln and the Gettysburg Address*, ed. Allan Nevins. Urbana, Ill., 1964.

Noll, Mark A. *Christians in the American Revolution*. Grand Rapids, 1977.

———. *One Nation under God? Christian Faith and Political Action in America*. San Francisco, 1988.

———. *Princeton and the Republic, 1768–1822: The Search for a Christian Enlightenment in the Era of Samuel Stanhope Smith*. Princeton, 1989.

———, ed. *God and Mammon: Protestants, Money, and the Market, 1790–1860*. New York, 2001.

———, ed. *Religion and American Politics from the Colonial Period to the 1980s*. New York, 1990.

Noll, Mark A., Nathan O. Hatch, and George M. Marsden. *The Search for Christian America*. 2d ed. Colorado Springs, 1989.

Nord, David Paul. "Benevolent Capital: Financing Evangelical Book Publishing in Early-Nineteenth-Century America." In *God and Mammon: Protestants, Money, and the Market, 1790–1860*, ed. Mark A. Noll. New York, 2001.

———. "Free Grace, Free Books, Free Riders: The Economics of Religious Publishing in Early Nineteenth-Century America." *Proceedings of the American Antiquarian Society* 106 (1996): 241–72.

Norton, David Fate. "Francis Hutcheson in America." *Studies on Voltaire and the Eighteenth Century* 154 (1976): 1547–68.

Oakes, James. "From Republicanism to Liberalism: Ideological Change and the Crisis of the Old South." *American Quarterly* 37 (Fall 1985): 551–71.

Pangle, Thomas. *The Spirit of Modern Republicanism: The Moral Vision of the American Founders and the Philosophy of Locke*. Chicago, 1988.

Pocock, J. G. A. *The Machiavellian Moment: Florentine Political Thought and the Atlantic Republic Tradition*. Princeton, 1975.

———. "Political Thought in the English-Speaking Atlantic, 1760–1790: Part 1: The Imperial Crisis." In *The Varieties of British Political Thought, 1500–1800*, ed. Pocock. New York, 1993.

———. "States, Republics, and Empires: The American Founding in Early Modern Perspective." In *Conceptual Change and the Constitution*, ed. Terence Ball and Pocock. Lawrence, Kans., 1988.

Pointer, Richard W. *Protestant Pluralism and the New York Experience*. Bloomington, Ind., 1988.

Rable, George C. *The Confederate Republic: A Revolution against Politics*. Chapel Hill, 1994.

Rahe, Paul. *Republics Ancient and Modern: Classical Republicanism and the American Revolution*. Chapel Hill, 1992.

Religion in Early America. Special issue of *William and Mary Quarterly* 54 (Oct. 1997): 693–848.

Riley, I. Woodbridge. *American Philosophy: The Early Schools*. New York, 1907.

Robbins, Caroline. *The Eighteenth-Century Commonwealthman: Studies in the Transmission, Development, and Circumstance of English Liberal Thought from the Restoration of Charles II until the War with the Thirteen Colonies*. Cambridge, Mass., 1959.

———. "'When It Is That Colonies May Turn Independent': An Analysis of the Environment and Politics of Francis Hutcheson." *William and Mary Quarterly* 11 (1954): 214–51.

Rodgers, Daniel T. "Republicanism: The Career of a Concept." *Journal of American History* 79 (June 1992): 11–38.

Rorabaugh, W. J. *The Alcoholic Republic: An American Tradition*. New York, 1979.

Rose, Anne C. *Victorian America and the Civil War*. New York, 1992.

Rosenfeld, Richard N. *American Aurora: A Democratic-Republican Returns*. New York, 1997.

Ross, Dorothy. "Liberalism." In *Encyclopedia of American Political History*, vol. 2, ed. Jack P. Greene. New York, 1984.

Roth, Randolph. *The Democratic Dilemma: Religion, Reform, and the Social Order in the Connecticut River Valley of Vermont, 1791–1850*. New York, 1987.

Ryan, Mary. *Cradle of the Middle Class: The Family in Oneida County, New York, 1790–1865*. New York, 1981.

Sandoz, Ellis. *A Government of Laws: Political Theory, Religion, and the American Founding*. Baton Rouge, La., 1990.

Sassi, Jonathan D. *A Republic of Righteousness: The Public Christianity of the Post-Revolutionary New England Clergy*. New York, 2001.

Saum, Lewis O. *The Popular Mood of Pre–Civil War America*. Westport, Conn., 1980.

Schmidt, Leigh Eric. *Hearing Things: Religion, Illusion, and the American Enlightenment*. Cambridge, Mass., 2000.

Schneewind, J. B. *The Invention of Autonomy: A History of Modern Moral Philosophy*. New York, 1998.

Sellers, Charles. *The Market Revolution: Jacksonian America, 1815–1846*. New York, 1991.

Shain, Barry Alan. *The Myth of American Individualism: The Protestant Origins of American Political Thought*. Princeton, 1994.

Shalhope, Robert. "Republicanism and Early American Historiography." *William and Mary Quarterly* 39 (1982): 334–56.

———. "Toward a Republican Synthesis: The Emergence of an Understanding of Republicanism in American Historiography." *William and Mary Quarterly* 29 (1972): 49–80.

Sharp, James Roger. *American Politics in the Early Republic: The New Nation in Crisis*. New Haven, 1993.

Sloan, Douglas. *The Scottish Enlightenment and the American College Ideal*. New York, 1971.

Smith, James Ward. "Religion and Science in American Philosophy." In *The Shaping of American Religion*, ed. Smith and A. Leland Jamison. Princeton, 1961.

Smith, Timothy L. *Revivalism and Social Reform: American Protestantism on the Eve of the Civil War*. Nashville, 1957.

Smylie, James H. "The President as Republican Prophet and King: Clerical Reflections on the Death of Washington." *Journal of Church and State* 18 (Spring 1976): 233–52.

Stark, Rodney, and Roger Finke. "American Religion in 1776: A Statistical Portrait." *Sociological Analysis* 49 (Spring 1988): 39–51.

Stevenson, Louise L. *Scholarly Means to Evangelical Ends: The New Haven Scholars and the Transformation of Higher Learning in America, 1830–1890.* Baltimore, 1986.

Stokes, Melvyn, and Stephen Conway, eds. *The Market Revolution in America: Social, Political, and Religious Expressions, 1800–1880.* Charlottesville, 1996.

Stout, Harry S. *The Divine Dramatist: George Whitefield and the Rise of Modern Evangelicalism.* Grand Rapids, 1991.

———. "Religion, Communications, and the Ideological Origins of the American Revolution." *William and Mary Quarterly* 34 (1977): 519–41.

———. "Rhetoric and Reality in the Early Republic: The Case of the Federalist Clergy." In *Religion and American Politics from the Colonial Period to the 1980s,* ed. Mark A. Noll. New York, 1990.

Sutton, William R. *Journeymen for Jesus: Evangelical Artisans Confront Capitalism in Jacksonian Baltimore.* University Park, Pa., 1998.

Sweet, Leonard I. "Nineteenth-Century Evangelicalism." In *Encyclopedia of the American Religious Experience.* Vol. 2, ed., Charles H. Lippy and Peter W. Williams. New York, 1988.

Swierenga, Robert. "Ethnoreligious Political Behavior in the Mid-Nineteenth Century: Voting, Values, Cultures." In *Religion and American Politics from the Colonial Period to the 1980s,* ed. Mark A. Noll. New York, 1989.

Taves, Ann. *Fits, Trances, and Visions: Experiencing Religion and Explaining Experience from Wesley to James.* Princeton, 1999.

Taylor, Alan. *William Cooper's Town: Power and Persuasion on the Frontier of the Early American Republic.* New York, 1995.

Taylor, Charles. *Sources of the Self: The Making of the Modern Identity.* Cambridge, Mass., 1989.

Thomas, George. *Revivalism and Cultural Change: Christianity, Nation Building, and the Market in the Nineteenth-Century United States.* Chicago, 1989.

Tracy, Joseph. *The Great Awakening: A History of the Revival of Religion in the Time of Edwards and Whitefield.* Boston, 1845.

Turner, James. "Secularization and Sacralization: Speculations on Some Religious Origins of the Secular Humanities Curriculum, 1850–1900." In *The Secularization of the Academy,* ed. George M. Marsden and Bradley J. Longfield. New York, 1992.

———. *Without God, without Creed: The Origins of Unbelief in America.* Baltimore, 1985.

Valeri, Mark. "Francis Hutcheson." In *American Colonial Writers, 1735–1781,* ed. Emory Elliott. Detroit, 1984.

West, John G. *The Politics of Revelation and Reason: Religion and Civic Life in the New Nation.* Lawrence, Kans., 1996.

Wiebe, Robert. *The Opening of American Society: From the Adoption of the Constitution to the Era of Disunion.* New York, 1984.

Wilson, Major. "Republicanism and the Idea of Party in the Jacksonian Period." *Journal of the Early Republic* 8 (Winter 1988): 419–42.

Witte, John, Jr. *Religion and the American Constitutional Experiment: Essential Rights and Liberties.* Colorado Springs, 2000.

Woloch, Isser, ed. *Revolution and the Meanings of Freedom in the Nineteenth Century.* Stanford, 1996.

Wolterstorff, Nicholas. *Thomas Reid and the Story of Epistemology*. New York, 2001.
Wood, Gordon S. "Conspiracy and the Paranoid Style: Causality and Deceit in the Eighteenth Century." *William and Mary Quarterly* 39 (1982): 401–41.
———. *The Creation of the American Republic, 1776–1787*. Chapel Hill, 1969.
———. "Evangelical America and Early Mormonism." *New York History* 61 (1980): 359–86.
———. "Ideology and the Origins of Liberal America." *William and Mary Quarterly* 44 (July 1987): 628–40.
———. *The Radicalism of the American Revolution*. New York, 1991.
Wootton, David, ed. *Divine Right and Democracy: An Anthology of Political Writing in Stuart England*. London, 1986.
———, ed. *Republicanism, Liberty, and Commercial Society, 1649–1776*. Stanford, 1994.
Worden, Blair. "Classical Republicanism and the Puritan Revolution." In *History and Imagination: Essays in Honour of H. R. Trevor-Roper*, ed. H. Lloyd-Jones, V. Pearl, and Worden. London, 1981.
———. "Milton's Republicanism and the Tyranny of Heaven." In *Machiavelli and Republicanism*, ed. G. Bock, Q. Skinner, and M. Viroli. New York, 1990.
———. "Part 1" [on English republicanism, 1649–83]. In *Republicanism, Liberty, and Commercial Society, 1649–1776*, ed. David Wootton. Stanford, 1994.
———. "Providence and Politics in Cromwellian England." *Past and Present* 109 (Nov. 1985): 55–99.
———. "The Revolution of 1688–89 and the English Republican Tradition." In *The Anglo-Dutch Moment: Essays on the Glorious Revolution and Its World Impact*, ed. Jonathan I. Israel. Cambridge, 1991.
Wosh, Peter J. *Spreading the Word: The Bible Business in Nineteenth-Century America*. Ithaca, 1994.
Wyatt-Brown, Bertram. *Lewis Tappan and the Evangelical War against Slavery*. Cleveland, 1969.
Zuckert, Michael P. *Natural Rights and the New Republicanism*. Princeton, 1994.

Index

comparisons between America and
Europe, 7–8
comparisons with Puritanism, 173–
74
convictions of, 170–74
defined, 5, 503n3, 564–65
linked with Enlightenment, 94–95,
103, 110
and nation-building, 187–208
organization of, 195–202
periodization for, 179–86
polarities within, 175–79
its rise in early national America,
165–86
its weakness in Revolutionary
period, 161–65
exercise scheme, 282–84, 298

faculty psychology, 279, 283–84, 289–
90, 353, 355–56, 565 (defined)
fall (of Adam), 4, 24, 38, 125, 132, 266,
273, 327, 333
Farmer, Oscar, 547n35
Faust, Drew, 384
Federalist Party, 176, 211, 220, 253,
257, 261, 565
Ferguson, Adam, 65
Fiering, Norman, 94, 103, 482n25,
428n29, 570
Filmer, Robert, 110
Finke, Roger, 166, 497n1, 506n35,
549n22
Finley, Samuel, 25–26, 126–27,
460n18
Finney, Charles, 170, 176, 184, 264,
354, 382–83, 440, 528n49,
529n70, 531n101
as anti-Calvinist, 307, 314
as anti-traditionalist, 380
and Baconian method, 236, 265
on common sense, 307
at New Lebanon convention,
295–96
and republican thought, 219, 308,
313
as revivalist, 183, 191, 236, 247, 263,
293, 306–8
on slavery, 308, 444
as Whig theologian, 313–14
on the will, 314, 441, 529n71

Fisk, Wilbur, 356, 358, 362, 537n3
as transitional Methodist theologian,
352–54
Fitch, Eleazer, 264
Fitzhugh, George, 369
Fitzmier, John, 514n22
Fletcher, John, 69, 219, 333–34, 336,
349, 356, 359, 361
Fletcher, Mary, 359
Floding, Matthew, 460n18
Foote, Julia, 501n56
Forbes, Robert, 544n1
formalism, 5, 175–76, 513n4, 565
(defined)
Foster, Charles, 182, 532n10
Foster, Frank Hugh, 131, 283, 490n50,
525n56
Foster, Stephen, 33, 37
Fox, Richard Wightman, 546n20
Fox-Genovese, Elizabeth, 479n69,
544n1, 548n44
Franklin, Benjamin, 27, 63, 75, 143–44,
164, 203, 507n52
Franklin, James, 75
Fredrickson, George, 546n29
freedom. See liberty
freedom of the will, 266–67 (options).
See also moral ability, natural
ability
analyzed by Henry Boynton Smith,
287–89
and Beecher, Catharine, 328
and Bledsoe, A. T., 539n37
and Bushnell, Horace, 237
and Edwards, Jonathan, 24, 237,
272–73, 280, 356–57, 558n19
and Emmons, Nathanael, 283
and Finney, Charles, 237, 313–14
and Fisk, Wilbur, 353
and Hopkins, Samuel, 272–73
and Johnson, Samuel, 27
and Madison, James, 128
and Methodists, 335
and Taylor, N. W., 237, 380,
299
and Whedon, Daniel, 356–57,
539n37
Freehling, William, 547n35
Freewill Baptists, 153–55, 168
Frei, Hans, 371

Wallace, Peter, 519n7, 548n44
Walls, Andrew, 1, 182, 499n16, 571
Walpole, Robert, 82
Walter, Nathaniel, 78–79
Walters, Kerry, 143, 493n35
War for Independence. *See* American
Revolution
Ward, Patricia, 539n54
Ward, W. R., 455n13, 533n5
Ware, Henry, 264, 284–86
Ware, Thomas, 340
Washington, George, 53, 63, 72, 137,
164, 205, 206
on republican calculus of virtue and
freedom, 203–4
Waterman, A. M. C., 456n20, 470n33,
505n21, 513n56
Watson, Richard, 354–55
Watters, William, 339
Watts, Michael, 471n53
Wayland, Francis 94, 222, 250–52
Weed, Michael, 516n31
Weeks, William, 247, 296
Weld, Theodore Dwight, 176, 391
Wells, David, 439
Wenzel, August, 554n7
Wesley, Charles, 12, 69, 219, 332–33,
337
Wesley, John, 12, 180, 246, 336, 349,
351, 356–57, 359, 362–64
and American Methodist church,
337–39
as critic of Francis Hutcheson, 99
on entire sanctification, 335, 361
on imputation, 534n15
on republicanism, 51, 69, 219, 245,
338
on sin and grace, 348–50
his theology in outline, 332–33, 343
Wesley, Susanna, 359
Wesleyan University, 343, 354
West, John, 203, 507n46
Westminster Confession and
Catechisms, 20–21, 26, 32, 28, 98,
127, 258, 295, 300, 313, 324
Wharton, Charles Henry, 122
Wheatley, Phillis, 147
Whedon, Daniel, 360, 361, 362, 363–64
on Edwards, Jonathan, 355–57,
539n37

and faculty psychology, 355
on free will, 355–57
on moral sense, 355, 357–58, 365
on sinfulness only in the sinning,
358
Whig Party, 176, 189, 208, 212, 253,
257, 312, 410, 565. *See also* whig
thought
whig thought, 79, 91, 107, 116–17, 140,
312–19, 410, 565. *See also* Whig
Party
Whitaker, Nathaniel, 77, 476n21
Whitby, Daniel, 140
White, Bp. William, 120–21
White, Ronald, 555n14
Whitefield, George, 13, 22, 29, 44, 128,
145, 147, 153, 156, 163, 221, 229,
336
as Calvinist, 232, 444
and Real Whig thought, 76–78,
475n15
Whitlock, Luder, 547n35
Wiebe, Robert, 207, 504n6, 541n17,
570
on the rise of evangelicalism, 189–91
Wigger, John, 500n37
Wilberforce, William, 164, 175
Wilkes, John, 65
will. *See* freedom of the will; Edwards,
Jonathan; Finney, Charles; Taylor,
Nathaniel W.; Whedon, Daniel
Willard, Samuel, 21, 43, 269
Williams, Roger, 40
Williams, Solomon, 46–48, 466n67
Wilson, Douglas, 556n42
Wilson, James, 203
Wilson, John, 164
Wilson, Major, 509n11
Wilson, Sarah, 553n68
Winchester, Elhanan, 65, 153
Winthrop, John, 39, 45, 464n34
Wise, John, 75
Wishart, William, 98
Wisner, William, 391
Witherspoon, John, 124–25, 127, 164,
203, 264
as leader of Populist party in
Scotland, 98
as proponent of Scottish moral
philosophy, 105–6, 111, 113, 234